Transformative
Social Work
Practice

We dedicate this book to social workers who have chosen this noble profession with a commitment to promoting the greater good and to the resilient clients and diverse communities that we serve. We are honored by each of you every day as you encourage us to expand our knowledge.

Transformative
Social Work
Practice

Editors

Erik M. P. Schott
University of Southern California

Eugenia L. Weiss
University of Southern California

Los Angeles | London | New Delhi
Singapore | Washington DC

Los Angeles | London | New Delhi
Singapore | Washington DC

FOR INFORMATION:

SAGE Publications, Inc.
2455 Teller Road
Thousand Oaks, California 91320
E-mail: order@sagepub.com

SAGE Publications Ltd.
1 Oliver's Yard
55 City Road
London, EC1Y 1SP
United Kingdom

SAGE Publications India Pvt. Ltd.
B 1/I 1 Mohan Cooperative Industrial Area
Mathura Road, New Delhi 110 044
India

SAGE Publications Asia-Pacific Pte. Ltd.
3 Church Street
#10-04 Samsung Hub
Singapore 049483

Printed in the United States of America

Library of Congress Cataloging-in-Publication Data

Transformative social work practice/[edited by] Erik Schott, Eugenia L. Weiss.

pages cm

Includes bibliographical references and index.

ISBN 978-1-4833-5963-2 (pbk. : alk. paper) 1. Social workers—United States. 2. Social service—Practice—United States. I. Schott, Erik. II. Weiss, Eugenia L.

HV40.8.U6T735 2016
361.3'20973—dc23   2015015637

Acquisitions Editor: Kassie Graves
Editorial Assistant: Carrie Montoya
Production Editor: Kelly DeRosa
Copy Editor: Diana Breti
Typesetter: Hurix Systems Pvt. Ltd.
Proofreader: Laura Webb
Indexer: Maria Sosnowski
Cover Designer: Anupama Krishnan
Marketing Manager: Shari Countryman

SUSTAINABLE FORESTRY INITIATIVE
Certified Chain of Custody
Promoting Sustainable Forestry
www.sfiprogram.org
SFI-01268
SFI label applies to text stock

15 16 17 18 19 10 9 8 7 6 5 4 3 2 1

Brief Contents

Detailed Contents

SAGE was founded in 1965 by Sara Miller McCune to support the dissemination of usable knowledge by publishing innovative and high-quality research and teaching content. Today, we publish more than 850 journals, including those of more than 300 learned societies, more than 800 new books per year, and a growing range of library products including archives, data, case studies, reports, conference highlights, and video. SAGE remains majority-owned by our founder, and after Sara's lifetime will become owned by a charitable trust that secures our continued independence.

Los Angeles | London | New Delhi | Singapore | Washington DC

More than ever, social workers face increasingly complex and rapidly changing contexts that need to be addressed when preparing the future workforce. Among others, these include increasing racial and ethnic population diversity, scientific advances that outpace translation to practice, globalization, and policy and technological developments. As the social work profession works to identify grand challenges, a central question is how best to prepare its future workforce to understand and respond to the prevalent issues of current times. In *Transformative Social Work Practice,* the editors and contributing authors provide an outstanding textbook that will prepare students to analyze and respond to such challenges using conceptually, empirically, and ethically grounded principles.

I was intrigued when editors Erik M. P. Schott and Eugenia L. Weiss offered me the privilege of introducing readers to this book on contemporary advanced social work practice. After all, I am not trained as a social worker. Having received my training in psychology and being a faculty member for more than 30 years in schools of medicine, public health, and health sciences certainly did not qualify me. However, I discovered that their choice was based on the nexus of my work during the last three-plus decades, which has been largely focused on the intersection of research and practice to inform the development and adaptation of evidence-based behavioral health interventions with diverse populations, and my interest in equity and social justice, which are hallmarks of social work as a field. Still unsure, I decided to plunge into the book's contents.

I was impressed with the scholarly and conceptually sound approach to the series of complex issues presented. Readers will be delighted to find deep yet practical discussions on a wide variety of highly relevant topics not only for social workers but also anyone working in the health and human services professions. Perhaps even individuals in the legal profession and law enforcement would benefit from the content related to various populations, such as people experiencing mental illness, disability, family violence, sexual minority status, and socioeconomic factors that shape behaviors and social conditions encountered in their work. In the true tradition of social work, *Transformative Social Work Practice* examines individual, family, community, and policy factors that need to be considered in the broad practice of social work. Using a scaffolding pedagogical approach, each chapter follows a similar structure, presenting new information in challenging but manageable increments. The incredible scope of this book renders it the perfect textbook for undergraduate and graduate social work practice courses. Its focus on multilevel analysis of issues provides a consistent and sound framework for training students to understand clinical and contextual factors and better prepare them for the call to social action against social injustice, which is central to the tradition and ethical standards of the field of social work.

Schott and Weiss are experienced clinicians and teachers with deep understanding of evidence-based practice in social work, psychology, and education. The diverse background and significant clinical and programmatic experience of the contributing authors provide the practice gravitas necessary for this comprehensive textbook on contemporary social work topics and challenges.

I began this foreword by noting the significant challenges facing contemporary social work practice. *Transformative Social Work Practice* sets a new standard for social work practice. The book's unique comprehensive discussion of issues within a meta-analytic framework makes it an excellent textbook choice for social work training. As a psychologist and public health researcher and practitioner, I can say without exaggeration that despite the rich clinical and social work relevance of the book, it is also accessible and likely to be of value and interest for courses in other health and human services disciplines. Indeed, the book achieves Schott's and Weiss's aspiration of contributing "to the discussion of cultivating a new generation of social workers who are prepared to translate and implement social work research into practice and policy."

Hortensia Amaro, PhD
Associate Vice Provost for Community Research Initiatives and
Dean's Professor, School of Social Work and Department of Preventive Medicine
University of Southern California

Acknowledgments

SAGE Publications would like to thank the following reviewers:

Carolyn S. Gentle-Genitty, Indiana University School of Social Work

Carolyn F. Hester, Grambling State University

Laura Quiros, Adelphi University School of Social Work

About the Editors

Erik M. P. Schott, MSW, LCSW, EdD, is a clinical associate professor at the University of Southern California (USC) School of Social Work in Los Angeles, California. His areas of research interests include ADHD and LGBT+ studies. Throughout his years as an educator, practicing licensed clinical social worker, and educational psychologist, Dr. Schott has counseled hundreds of clients from diverse backgrounds and taught and advised thousands of social work graduate students. Before joining the USC faculty in 2005, Erik was program director at the Serra Project. He maintains a small clinical practice in the Silver Lake neighborhood of Los Angeles. A portion of the profits generated from this book will be donated annually to various nonprofit service organizations.

Eugenia L. Weiss, MSW, LCSW, PsyD, is an educator and a California-licensed clinical social worker and licensed psychologist. She is a clinical associate professor at the University of Southern California (USC) School of Social Work and currently serving as the director of the Orange County Academic Center at USC. She maintained a private practice for 18 years, working with military personnel and their families. She is the author and co-author of multiple peer-reviewed journal publications and is co-author of the book *A Civilian Counselor's Primer to Counseling Veterans* (2nd ed., Linus Books, 2011), co-editor of the *Handbook of Military Social Work* (Wiley & Sons, 2013), and co-editor of *Supporting Veterans in Higher Education: A Primer for Administrators, Faculty, and Academic Advisors* (Lyceum, 2015). Her research interests include military/veteran behavioral health, diversity in social work practice, and higher education.

List of Contributors

Gary Adler, PhD, is president and CEO of Pegasus Rising.

Hortensia Amaro, PhD, is associate vice provost for community research initiatives and dean's professor in the School of Social Work and Department of Preventive Medicine at the University of Southern California, Los Angeles.

Catherine K. Arnold, MS, is the director of community education in the Institute on Disability and Human Development at the University of Illinois at Chicago.

Glenda Bawden, MSW, MAASW, is senior manager of social work and aboriginal services at Monash Health, Victoria, Australia.

Brandon Burton, MFA, MSW, is a social worker with the California Ventura County Department of Children and Family Services.

Julie A. Cederbaum, MSW, MPH, PhD, is assistant professor in the School of Social Work at the University of Southern California, Los Angeles.

Wilhelmina De Castro, MSW, LCSW, is adjunct faculty in the School of Social Work at the University of Southern California, Los Angeles.

Amber Denbleyker, MSW, LCSW, is a social worker with Children's Hospital Los Angeles and guest lecturer in the School of Social Work at the University of Southern California, Los Angeles.

Shannon L. Dunlap, MSW, is a doctoral student in the Department of Social Welfare in the Luskin School of Public Affairs at the University of California, Los Angeles.

Elizabeth Eastlund, MSW, LCSW, is the director of programs at Rainbow Services and guest lecturer in the School of Social Work at the University of Southern California, Los Angeles.

Annalisa Enrile, PhD, is clinical associate professor in the School of Social Work at the University of Southern California, Los Angeles.

Moshe Farchi, PhD, is head of the Stress, Trauma and Resilience Studies in the School of Social Work at Tel-Hai College, Israel.

William Feuerborn, MSW, LCSW, is adjunct assistant professor in the School of Social Work at the University of Southern California, Los Angeles.

Kimberly Finney, PsyD, ABPP, ABMP, is clinical associate professor in the School of Social Work at the University of Southern California, Los Angeles.

Cynthia Franklin, PhD, is assistant dean for doctoral education and Stiernberg/Spencer family professor in mental health in the School of Social Work at the University of Texas at Austin.

Colleen Friend, LCSW, PhD, is associate professor and director of the Child Abuse and Family Violence Institute in the Department of Communication Disorders at the California State University at Los Angeles.

Timothy Fong, MD, is associate clinical professor of psychiatry at the Semel Institute for Neuroscience and Human Behavior at the University of California Los Angeles and is the co-director of the UCLA Gambling Studies Program.

Jeremy T. Goldbach, LMSW, PhD, is assistant professor in the School of Social Work at the University of Southern California, Los Angeles.

Juan Guo, PhD, is an instructor of social work practice in the School of Social Development at East China Normal University, Shanghai, China.

Wen-Jui Han, PhD, is professor in the Silver School of Social Work at the New York University and co-director of NYU-ECNU.

Xiaoyan Han, PhD, is associate professor of social work and associate director of the School of Social Development at East China Normal University, Shanghai, China.

Shira Hantman, PhD, is professor and vice-president for academic affairs in the School of Social Work at Tel-Hai College, Israel.

Mary Beth Harris, LCSW, PhD, is clinical associate professor in the School of Social Work at the University of Southern California, Los Angeles.

Krystal Hays, MSW, LCSW, is a doctoral student in the School of Social Work at the University of Southern California, Los Angeles.

Robert Hernandez, MSW, is adjunct assistant professor in the School of Social Work at the University of Southern California, Los Angeles.

Susan Hess, MSW, LCSW, is visiting clinical assistant professor, field education, in the School of Social Work at the University of Southern California, Los Angeles.

Jim Hjort, MSW, LCSW, operates a private psychotherapy practice, is the founder of the Right Life Project and is a guest lecturer in the School of Social Work at the University of Southern California, Los Angeles.

Laura Hopson, MSSW, PhD, is associate professor in the School of Social Work at the University of Alabama, Tuscaloosa.

Eddie Hu, MSW, MSG, is a social worker with the Department of Preventative Medicine in the Keck School of Medicine at the University of Southern California, Los Angeles.

Karen Kay Imagawa, MD, is assistant professor of pediatrics in the Keck School of Medicine at the University of Southern California and is director of the USC University Center for Excellence in Developmental Disabilities at Children's Hospital, Los Angeles.

Nadia Islam, LCSW, PhD, is the clinical director of USC Telehealth in the School of Social Work at the University of Southern California, Los Angeles.

Dawn Joosten, LCSW, PhD, is clinical associate professor in the School of Social Work at the University of Southern California, Los Angeles.

Shawnmari Kaiser, MSW, LCSW, is adjunct faculty in the School of Social Work at the University of Southern California, Los Angeles.

Min Ah Kim, PhD, is assistant professor in the Department of Social Welfare at Myongji University, Seoul, Korea.

Heather A. Klusaritz, MSW, PhD, is an instructor and health services researcher with the Department of Family Medicine and Community Health and School of Social Policy and Practice at the University of Pennsylvania, Philadelphia.

Helen Land, LCSW, PhD, is associate professor in the School of Social Work at the University of Southern California, Los Angeles.

Karen D. Lincoln, MSW, MA, PhD, is associate professor and director of the Hartford Center of Excellence in Geriatric Social Work in the School of Social Work at the University of Southern California, Los Angeles.

Amy D. Lyle, MSSW, CAPSW, is a social worker with the Waisman Center at the University of Wisconsin, Madison.

Nadia Mishael, LCSW, PsyD, is adjunct faculty in the School of Social Work at the University of Southern California, Los Angeles.

Jacquelene F. Moghaddam, PhD, is a postdoctoral fellow in psychiatry and biobehavioral sciences at the David Geffen School of Medicine, University of California, Los Angeles.

Saeed Momtazi, MD, is professor at the Zanjan University of Medical Sciences, Iran and is with the Integrated Substance Abuse Programs in the David Geffen School of Medicine at the University of California, Los Angeles.

Murali D. Nair, PhD, is clinical professor in the School of Social Work at the University of Southern California, Los Angeles.

Eric Awich Ochen, PhD, is a lecturer and coordinator of fieldwork and special projects with the Department of Social Work and Social Administration in the School of Social Sciences at Makerere University, Kampala, Uganda.

Diana Pineda, MHA, MSW, LCSW, is adjunct faculty and project manager of building capacity and welcoming practices in the School of Social Work at the University of Southern California, San Diego Academic Center.

Rory C. Reid, LCSW, PhD, is assistant professor and research psychologist at the University of

California, Los Angeles in the Semel Institute for Neuroscience and Human Behavior in the Department of Psychiatry.

Alberto Reynoso, MS, MSW, LCSW, is adjunct faculty in the School of Social Work at the University of Southern California, Los Angeles.

Gilbert Richards, MSW, is a social worker with the Los Angeles Unified School District.

Samih Samaha, MSW, is adjunct faculty in the School of Social Work at the University of Southern California, Los Angeles and a social worker with the Los Angeles County Department of Children and Family Services.

Fred P. Stone, LCSW, PhD, is clinical associate professor in the School of Social Work at the University of Southern California, Los Angeles.

Hilary N. Weaver, DSW, is professor and associate dean for academic affairs in the School of Social Work at the State University of New York, Buffalo.

Barbara Yoshioka Wheeler, RN, PhD, is associate professor of clinical pediatrics in the Keck School of Medicine at the University of Southern California and is associate director for the USC University Center for Excellence in Developmental Disabilities at Children's Hospital, Los Angeles.

Marian E. Williams, PhD, is assistant professor of clinical pediatrics in the Keck School of Medicine at the University of Southern California, Los Angeles.

Leslie H. Wind, LCSW, PhD, is associate dean of academic programs and is clinical associate professor in the School of Social Work at the University of Southern California, Los Angeles.

Edmund W. Young, MSG, LCSW, EdD, is adjunct faculty in the School of Social Work at the University of Southern California, Los Angeles and a social worker with the U.S. Department of Veteran Affairs.

Kristen Zaleski, LCSW, PhD, is clinical assistant professor in the School of Social Work at the University of Southern California, Los Angeles.

CHAPTER 1

Introduction

Eugenia L. Weiss & Erik M. P. Schott

Our aim in editing this book was to address an evolving health care landscape with the Patient Protection and Affordable Care Act (ACA) of 2010 and all of its iterations and to explore the myriad ways that we can redefine or retool ourselves as social workers in an era of unprecedented technological growth, globalization, and change. Our profession is being propelled into uncharted territories that have the potential for transformative processes and outcomes—for instance, developing interdisciplinary partnerships that we may not have imagined as bedfellows, such as social workers collaborating with engineers. The book adheres to the conventional ecological (Bronfenbrenner, 1989) and systemic roots (von Bertalanffy, 1969) applied in social work practice plus the infusion of current scientific research and innovative practice models that encompass the multidimensionality of the human experience both in terms of understanding hardship and of fostering resilience through evidence-based practice (EBP) process and empirically supported treatments (EST). Social work practice knowledge and skills with diverse populations in the areas of health, mental wellness, recovery, addictions, schools, family, and community are necessary ingredients to meet the complexity of contextual demands along with fulfilling our professional responsibility to ethical, evidence-informed practices and the promotion of client- or system-level advocacy and social justice (the pillars of our profession, as delineated by the National Association of Social Workers, 2008). Thus a combination of tradition with innovation within a matrix of multiple realities (and complexities) is what we hope to render the reader, whether a beginning social worker or a seasoned one, and whether practicing in the United States or abroad. Through the crossing of technological boundaries, global access, and mobility, social workers need to not only be versed in what impacts and helps to empower local communities, but also take into account national and international influences (both strengths and crises) and apply this knowledge in realistic, resourceful, and culturally responsive ways in their immediate practice domains. Borrowing from the field of public health, we consider multiple determinants of health (e.g., social, cultural, economic, occupational, and environmental), the impact of those factors on health care outcomes (Institute of Medicine [IOM], 2002), and the reciprocal effects of health on those social determinants. This allows us to take a person-in-environment perspective (Germain, 1981; Perlman, 1957), which is seminal to social work practice. The book provides many examples of health inequities within racial and ethnic minority populations and how to intervene in addressing these disparities. As we know, racial and ethnic minority populations in the United States have disproportionately higher rates of preventable chronic illnesses and shorter life spans than whites (Thomas, Quinn, Butler, Fyer, & Garza, 2011). We are also incorporating integrative practices to represent not only integrated delivery systems (IOM, 2001), where we work in interdisciplinary teams that serve to treat the "whole" person (e.g., integration of mental health and health), but also a broader conceptualization of combining elements and systems in terms of a gestalt, or holistic approach, as in the biopsychosocial-spiritual orientation that we espouse in our profession (Woods & Hollis, 2000).

We have several main goals in this text. First, in the true social work tradition, we offer an ecological or systemic perspective to understanding and intervening with clients and/or systems within a contextual frame of reference (Guadalupe & Lum, 2014). We also adhere to assessment and intervention through the current lens of EBP and provide real-world case scenarios from a multilevel contextual and integrative approach to practice. Rubin and Bellamy (2012) remind us that EBP is a cyclical process involving several steps as we approach client care:

(1) Question formulation, (2) Searching for the best evidence to answer the question, (3) Critically appraising the evidence, (4) Selecting an intervention based on critical appraisal of the evidence and integrating that appraisal with practitioner expertise and awareness of the client's preferences and clinical state and circumstances, and (5) monitoring client progress. Depending on the outcome observed in the fifth step, the cycle may need to go back to an earlier step to seek an intervention that might work better for the particular client, perhaps one that has less evidence to support it but which might nevertheless prove to be more effective for the particular client in light of the client's needs, strengths, values and circumstances. (p. 14)

Additionally, we consider EBP from the perspective of our colleagues Soydan and Palinkas (2014), as professional competence in an "imperfect world in which real life conditions change in terms of time and space and our methods of capturing reality of that social and behavioral world have shortcomings. EBP prescribes use of the best available evidence, recognizing that this evidence is not the ultimate truth but only a temporary estimate of causal relations in real-life situations" (p. 1).

We also adhere to a meta-framework theoretical approach from Breunlin, Schwartz, and Kunne-Karrer (1992), who proposed a systemic therapy orientation based on interactional patterns, a blueprint for an explanatory theory based on a distillation of multiple theories. Thus, the book is an amalgamation of practice issues along with varied theoretical and evidence-based approaches within contextual frameworks that account for complex systems and practice orientations. (Due to space limitations here, please see Sanger and Giddings (2012) for a more complete explanation of complexity theory as applied to social work practice.)

Our second goal with the book to is to further support collegial and interdisciplinary connections and transactions. The Council on Social Work Education (CSWE, 2008) has set guidelines for educational programs based on competencies, the Educational Policy and Accreditation Standards (EPAS). The EPAS are currently undergoing revisions and adaptations, which have not been released at the time of this writing. It is our hope that this book will contribute to the discussion of cultivating a new generation of social workers who are prepared to translate and implement social work research into practice and policy and who can communicate theory-driven evidence-based interventions in the language of the re-engineering of our profession as the present and future demands and needs of humankind continue to evolve and our methods of providing social work interventions are being revolutionized through innovations and unprecedented cross-collaborative efforts in order to meet the profession's Grand Challenges as proposed by the American Academy of Social Work and Social Welfare (see Chapter 25).

Last, the term *transformative* in the title of the book not only alludes to change but also borrows from Witkin's (2014) approach to social work education and his argument that transformation "enables and requires learners (including teachers) to maintain an ongoing critical stance towards their own and others' ideologies, theories, beliefs, assumptions, and practices" (p. 569). Thus, it is a method of learning that then informs how social workers practice. In our interpretation of Witkin's work, based on Mezirow's (2003, p. 58) "critical-dialectical discourse" that allows for "democratic citizenship," therefore, a questioning of dominant social discourses must occur in order to examine oppression and privilege, as a philosophical and applied approach to "transform" realities given the complex world that we live in, utilizing "imagination, creativity and innovation" (Witkin, 2014, p. 594). While even if we seemingly contradict ourselves in taking a positivistic stance where we apply an EBP process to intervention, we believe, like others in the field, that it is possible to examine existing empirical knowledge and be able to imagine future possibilities and alternatives to practice and to incorporate both into the practice decision-making process with the clients that we serve without furthering oppressive practices. Thyer and Pignotti (2011) eloquently noted, as others have as well, that "EBP asks the practitioner to locate the best *available* evidence, to evaluate its findings and potential applicability" (p. 330) along with considering the practitioner's clinical expertise and the client's values as well as preferences—which is different from merely applying empirically supported treatments. While Zayas, Drake, and Jonson-Reid (2011) inform us that the roots of EBP, as defined by Sackett and colleagues (1996), are founded on evidence along with the use of clinical judgement and consideration of client values, we need to be careful to not become too narrow in our focus, only emphasizing the evidentiary aspect and not the other two components of practice. Brekke (2014) summarizes that professional social work today is "an integrative science that allows for the blending of values and scientific rigor that are crucial to maintaining the identity of social work and for increasing its relevance and capacity for solving critical problems in living" (p. 522). Thus, at the risk of oversimplification, it is not an "either/or" proposition (i.e., science or social work values)

nor is it micro (clinical practice) versus macro, but instead it is about embracing an integrative perspective, with all of its complexity, without having to make binary choices between opposites, as Robins (2015) and others suggest.

OVERVIEW OF CONTENTS

This transformative social work practice text consists of 36 chapters organized into three sections (with the caveat that the sections are, in a sense, arbitrary and artificial because there are no true divisions in real life or in social work practice, except for the demarcations that we create for the convenience of organizing our world and ultimately our curricula). Additionally, we were inspired by the efforts of our School of Social Work at the University of Southern California in re-envisioning our curricula with the hopes of developing a generation of social workers who would be better equipped and versatile in their helping roles to meet the needs of their respective agencies, organizations, and communities regardless of which emphasis they choose to study in professional social work education. Thus, we are taking the perspective of the *advanced generalist* as proposed by Dran (2014), as a professional social worker who "works patiently in multiple dimensions at once, alert to new patterns that emerge. In a complex situation that may overwhelm the generalist, the advanced generalist creatively responds by discovering new interventions to apply in new ways" (p. 569).

The first two sections of the book are separated by population; that is, issues and interventions as applied to adults and aging are covered in Part I, followed by a Part II on children, youth, and families. Part III covers diverse communities and provides a global survey of social work practices outside the United States. Keep in mind that most of the chapters throughout the book contain diversity considerations, and the case vignettes that are housed in most chapters represent a variety of ethnic groups, diverse individuals and communities reflecting true social work practice and the intersectionality of various forms of difference (i.e., age, gender identity, sexual identity (orientation), ethnicity, culture, disability, socioeconomic status, etc.). The intent here is to develop practitioner *sensitivity* to difference, which we are borrowing and adapting from Stafford and associates (1997), as an awareness of differences and their effects on client values, worldviews, and behaviors. We are expanding the definition of diversity according to Ortiz and Jani's (2010) proposition that it must be understood and approached

> within a broader social context, one that recognizes social location as a function of institutional arrangements, considers the intersection of multiple subordinating identities and acknowledges that theories based on broad generalizations do not adequately address the rapidly changing nature of diversity in the United States. (p. 176)

Most of the chapters in the book are structured in a similar fashion, except for global social work chapters, which are written within the realm of the authors' own cultural perspectives and realities—as it would be unfitting for us to impose our own worldviews of how social work should look in other parts of the world outside of the American perspective. Thus we allowed the authors greater room to deviate from the formal outline that we provided authors to help organize their chapters, in order to learn from each nation's approach to how they conceptualize, formulate, and practice social work.

The majority of the chapters in the book commence with learning objectives and a case vignette that serves to illustrate the issues that are salient in that chapter. The case scenarios provide the reader an opportunity to think about how the material is applied and make the necessary connections between the content and real-world practice as recognized by adult learning theorists (Knowles, Holton, & Swanson, 2005). After an introduction, the chapters then provide a micro perspective with key theoretical principles and constructs important to social work assessment and intervention. Once again, particular attention is paid to unique considerations of client diversity or multiple forms of difference. Authors summarize basic treatment approaches and, where appropriate, empirically

supported interventions are utilized. Many of the chapters highlight potential transference and countertransference reactions that provide a space for clinician self-reflection and considerations regarding the therapeutic encounter. Legal and ethical concerns are also addressed as part of a comprehensive approach to social work practice. In addition, each chapter enables the reader to gain an appreciation of the interaction between micro (individual or family level), mezzo (group, community, or organizational level), and macro (society, government, or policy level) perspectives, thereby providing an integrative and ecosystemic approach while engaging in a critical analysis of each section. In fact, the chapters are organized around the micro, mezzo, and macro levels of practice. Furthermore, most chapters contain a list of Internet resources and conclude with discussion questions for the reader to contemplate as part of critical analysis and to promulgate further professional dialogue.

Part I starts off the book with 11 chapters and delves into areas of practice concerning adults and aging populations with health and/or mental health–related conditions. For instance, Chapter 2 explores health-related issues of palliative and hospice care within the context of social work practice; here, the intervention of advanced care planning is examined. A biopsychosocial-spiritual assessment is conducted on a Vietnamese immigrant woman, and the treatment planning incorporates her beliefs about illness, pain, and suffering that impacts end-of-life care decision making.

Chapter 3 explores the practice of social work with diverse groups of people affected by HIV/AIDS and their caregivers. In this chapter, the EBP of psychoeducation and the intervention of group therapy in coping with HIV/AIDS is discussed as well as the historical stigma and disenfranchisement associated with this condition and the role of the social worker in supporting and advocating for these clients. Chapter 4 delves into serving adult clients with chronic illnesses, utilizing a case study of a Latina client who is suffering from diabetes and associated complications, and explains how the social worker can best assess and intervene.

Chapter 5 presents the dynamics of social work practice with those suffering from a Major Depressive Disorder and how the use of psychopharmacology along with psychoeducation can work in tandem. Here social workers are key players as part of interdisciplinary teams to support medically driven interventions. Chapter 6 provides a discussion of the implementation of mindfulness-based practices in individuals suffering from mental illness. A case example is provided that demonstrates how to utilize this approach with an individual who has been diagnosed with Borderline Personality Disorder and is exhibiting symptoms of depression. Advances in the interventions of Mindfulness-Based Stress Reduction (MBSR) and Mindfulness-Based Cognitive Therapy (MBCT) are highlighted.

Substance abuse and other addictions are important topics addressed by this social work practice book. For example, Chapter 7 provides an overview of substance abuse, namely the abuse of drugs and alcohol in adults and emphasizes the use of motivational interviewing, harm reduction, and cognitive behavioral approaches in helping clients within a health care community setting. Chapter 8 gives the reader insight into hypersexual behaviors through a case scenario of a heterosexual couple and the challenges encountered in an intimate relationship when a partner engages in excessive viewing of pornography. The chapter examines the tools to assess and to treat clients who are struggling with sex addiction. Chapter 9 addresses problem gambling behaviors as a new DSM-5 diagnosis (American Psychiatric Association [APA], 2013). The chapter addresses the continuum of associated gambling behaviors, the actual disorder as defined by the DSM-5, and the application of behavioral interventions.

Chapter 10 delves into technologically innovative web-based social work services. In this chapter, USC Telehealth, a social work–driven virtual counseling center, is illustrated as part of the case study. The authors describe the building of the therapeutic alliance through a virtual platform with a client afflicted with an Adjustment Disorder. The chapter provides the reader with an understanding of the intersectionality of client identities (e.g., gender and sexual identity, ethnicity, race, and prior military service) and the social worker being able to build rapport with the client through the Internet.

Chapter 11 presents equine assisted counseling as a method of complementing an empirically supported intervention such as prolonged exposure therapy and/or as an alternative treatment for trauma. A case study of a Latino military veteran suffering from Posttraumatic Stress Disorder is utilized and a proposed treatment protocol when working with the horse and the client is provided. The value of an animal-assisted therapy is discussed when helping traumatized populations.

Social work in skilled nursing facilities is described in Chapter 12, where a client vignette demonstrates how a social worker can intervene in cases where both mental health and health related conditions co-occur, while understanding the laws and regulations that govern nursing home settings and the role of the social worker. This is the final chapter in the adult and healthy aging section of the book.

Part II of the book focuses on children, youth, and families and commences with Chapter 13, which addresses the role of social workers in school settings. Solution-focused brief therapy (SFBT) interventions in schools are described along with emerging trends in school social work practice. For instance, a Response to Intervention (RTI) framework is used that requires school personnel including social workers to continuously monitor and evaluate treatment goals and interventions in order to improve student outcomes, and school climate needs to be considered as well as the use of culturally responsive assessments and interventions.

Child maltreatment and child welfare are topics covered in Chapter 14. This chapter delineates the importance of building a trauma-focused child welfare system and the use of Parent Child Interaction Therapy (PCIT) as well as Trauma-Focused Cognitive Behavioral Therapy (TF–CBT) . This is one of a series of chapters involving traumatized children and youth. The organizational or systems-level aspects, including constraints within the child welfare system, are examined and social workers having an awareness of the risk factors associated with racial disproportionality are all brought to bear in this comprehensive chapter.

Developmental disabilities and associated interventions are presented in Chapters 15 and 18; the former includes a lifespan perspective and the latter is specific to Autism Spectrum Disorder (ASD). The long-term care needs of individuals with disabilities are described in Chapter 15 along with the need for community inclusion, least restrictive environment, family-centered care, and person-centered planning. Applied Behavior Analysis (ABA) is a behaviorally based therapy explained in Chapter 18 on ASD, and the authors discuss the various approaches and systems that need to be in place when assessing and intervening with this population. The use of assistive technologies and the coordination between agencies and services demonstrates that this is not a one-size-fits-all approach, but rather must be tailored to the individual and family needs of the client.

Chapter 16 is on youth coping and resilience after exposure to disaster. Psychological First Aid (PFA) is implemented with a young African American male and his mother as survivors of Hurricane Katrina. Interorganizational networks and the promotion of community resilience and recovery efforts are discussed in relation to how social workers intervene in helping children and families overcome stress and trauma in the aftermath of disasters. Chapter 22, on crisis intervention for the treatment of adolescent victims of sexual assault, also utilizes PFA and describes the challenges for sexual minority youth victims in dispelling shame and self-blame. Intervening with protective agencies and law enforcement to reduce retraumatization for young survivors of sexual assault is another important aspect of social worker involvement.

Chapter 17 offers a view of pediatric oncology and the role of the social worker in health settings and in assisting children and their families cope. Pediatric oncology survivors face unique challenges in their transitional care from childhood to adulthood, and social workers play a significant role in supporting the client through a smooth transition process to ensure continued health care.

Chapter 19 covers intimate partner violence, utilizing a trauma-informed care (TIC) framework to help the survivor and a nonviolent parenting approach to parenting young children who witness intimate partner violence. The chapter enables the reader to understand the impact of adverse childhood experiences and the contribution of those experiences to adult relationships. Chapter 21 also looks at trauma from an adolescent victim of bullying perspective. The author utilizes TF–CBT approach for children and youth to help overcome the negative effects of traumatic life events, including bullying and cyberbullying. A school-based intervention, the Cognitive Behavioral Intervention for Trauma in Schools (CBITS), is illustrated along with case of a young Latina female. Current antibullying legislation is discussed in the policy or macro component of the chapter as well as implications for social workers.

Chapter 20 delves into social work with gang-involved youth. This chapter is the first of two that explores the use of Multisystemic Therapy (MST). Street socializing youth and the violence-related trauma that they experience is addressed in this chapter along with an understanding of the ecological risk factors that are at play for youth becoming gang affiliated. The MST intervention encompasses the family, peer, school, and community or a multiple systemic method of intervening with these at-risk youths. A novel Community Based Gang Intervention Model that provides integrative services that also addresses institutional barriers is introduced. While Chapter 23 also demonstrates the use of MST, this chapter deals with adolescents in juvenile detention and the overrepresentation of minority youth in the U.S. juvenile justice system. The author makes the argument that our nation is overcriminalizing youth and explains the importance of youth receiving appropriate evidence-based interventions that are also gender specific for improved rehabilitation services. The Fair Sentencing for Youth Senate Bill is also mentioned as a way of providing the opportunity to petition for resentencing to those who are serving time in prison without the option of parole.

Finally, the first section of Part III concentrates on diverse communities within the U.S. and the second section encompasses global social work outside of the U.S. Chapter 24 begins with an overview of 21st-century health needs and the anticipated social work skills required in the present and future field of social work practice integrated with public health. The authors introduce the commonalities between public health and social work and how social justice is the driving force for both professions, particularly to enhance the lives and well-being of marginalized populations; both disciplines utilize similar tools to effect change and reduce health disparities.

Chapter 25 looks into collaborative partnerships with the field of engineering and the infusion of technology in social work practice with vulnerable communities. The use of electronic mobile devices/applications (apps) to assist children and families with school transitions is offered as an innovative program initiated by researchers at the University of Southern California, School of Social Work in conjunction with the University's School of Engineering and partnered with school districts in the San Diego region of Southern California.

As previously mentioned, diversity is covered throughout the book; however, there are designated chapters that highlight specific groups that have been historically underrepresented. For instance, Chapters 26 and 27 involve social work practice and mental health promotion among African Americans and social work assessment and interventions with sexual minorities, respectively. Cultural adaptations for mental health interventions in working with an older African American is recommended in Chapter 26, which takes into consideration historical and cultural elements as well as religious preferences, utilizing strengths and resources to move beyond mental illness and emphasize health and well-being. Collaborations between treating mental health professionals and trusted community resources are noted as significant components of successful treatment outcomes. Experiences related to race and engagement with mental health services for African Americans in this country are brought to the forefront.

Chapter 27 provides a historical account of sexual minorities (lesbian, gay, bisexual, and transgender [LGBT]) and civil rights in this country as the background to understanding how to assess and intervene in culturally appropriate ways given the stress these individuals face of not always fitting into dominant societal expectations. The authors discuss how to conduct a biopsychosocial assessment that is inclusive with regard to sexual identity (orientation) and gender identity, and a case vignette of a young Latino Native American male having suicide ideation is introduced. In this case, the client identifies as bisexual and assigned gender at birth was female, but the internal gender is male. The importance of identity, labels, and the correct use of language (i.e., terminology) in the therapeutic environment are emphasized as tools of engagement.

Chapter 28 delves into understanding the impact of intergenerational trauma in indigenous peoples from North America, and Chapter 36 probes into Australia's indigenous population. In Chapter 28, the author provides a Cheyenne woman's perspective and a historical trauma explanatory framework for understanding the high prevalence of substance abuse, violence, and suicide in Native American communities. The use of TIC is once again explored, as well as an empowerment perspective that incorporates cultural adaptations to intervention that involve native and traditional practices. Social workers are tasked to advocate for social justice and confront contemporary racism and injustice at all levels of practice.

A chapter dedicated to military populations is included in the book as Chapter 29, and it explores combating suicide in military clients utilizing crisis intervention and Brief Cognitive Behavioral Therapy (BCBT). Particular attention is paid to risk and protective factors in suicide and the rising trends in this population. Department of Defense programs to address this crisis are also part of the discussion, as well as ethical dilemmas faced by social workers in military settings.

Global or international social work is a major theme in this book. According to Gabel and Healy (2012), "globalization is evident in numerous spheres of life, including economic, demographic, environmental, cultural and social welfare…. That one in five households in the United States is an international family makes global learning essential for every social worker" (p. 627). Thus, the book offers six chapters delineating social work practices in countries outside of the U.S. that can inform both international and local approaches to social problems. Gambel (2012) eloquently stated, "globalization, the increasingly rapid exchange of ideas, finances, resources and people with all corners of the globe, requires us to think globally even when working locally" (p. 681).

Thus, Chapter 30 opens this section by defining the roles of Community-Based Organizations (CBOs) and Nongovernmental Organizations (NGOs) in social work with volunteer and employment opportunities abroad. This chapter sets the stage for the remaining global chapters.

Chapter 31 focuses on human trafficking and modern-day slavery and explores the Philippines as a case study for this global epidemic. Intensive case management derived from Assertive Community Treatment (ACT) is employed, and an example of a community agency is provided: the People's Recovery, Empowerment, and Development Assistance Foundation and their application of primal therapy to help the young victims of sexual exploitation as a culturally responsive approach. Additionally, the Anti-Trafficking in Persons Act is an example of grassroots and community efforts turned legislation to end trafficking in the Philippines.

Chapter 32 provides a model of psychosocial support for youth affected by armed conflict in northern Uganda. Abducted youth held in captivity by rebel forces either escape their captors or are rescued to then have to resettle in their communities and make significant adjustments to their lives as a result of captivity and the effects of civil war. The author delineates the suffering and the struggles experienced by these young people and the intersections between the social, political, cultural, and economic structures to support these survivors that enhance or constrain their reintegration opportunities. The author provides a social work model that was created to respond to the resettlement challenges at every level of practice, which includes the use of Narrative Exposure Therapy (NET) to help youth cope with the trauma

of captivity and the transition into their respective communities; a community regeneration plan with reception centers and volunteers to support the youth; and the governmental response of a Peace Recovery and Development Plan.

Chapter 33 provides an adapted PFA model and the use of a Psychological First Aid Center by social work first responders as part of an interdisciplinary team working with traumatized youth and communities in Israel. The authors delineate neurobiological principles and psychosocial aspects of functioning that inform the intervention in helping individuals cope with disaster or trauma resulting from terrorist attacks. The authors also provide a protocol for helping the helper, in order to prevent traumatization in first responders.

Chapter 34 provides an example of a positive Chinese youth development program as well as the current status of the social work profession in China, including social and national resources as well as limitations. The authors describe a school-based youth development program, the Positive Adolescent Training Through Holistic Social Programmes (PATHS), as a strengths-based and prevention approach to address rising rates of juvenile delinquency and idleness in China. The country's burgeoning need for trained and educated social workers is articulated and emphasized.

Chapter 35 provides a cultural view of drug abuse and intervention in the Middle East, with an outline of Iran's drug policies given the country's proximity to Afghanistan as the leading opium producers in the world and the challenges afforded with border drug smuggling. Iranian interventions include harm reduction programs as well as the required presence of social work professionals in substance abuse drug treatment facilities.

Part III concludes with Chapter 36, on social work with Australia's indigenous population. The chapter opens with a case vignette of a young Aboriginal couple expecting a child with unexpected consequences and complications in terms of labor/delivery and health care. A cultural care plan is devised by a social worker that includes strengths- and rights-based practices for effectively helping the couple and the health care staff transact in a hospital setting that does not fit with the couple's cultural worldviews.

CONCLUSION

Our intent is that this book will be useful to a variety of readers, including social work educators, students, and practitioners. The book will be of service to those providing social work care or aspiring to be practitioners and policy makers or advocates in an era of constant change and new frontiers, and the readings will spur professional conversations about our identity as social workers in an evolving and expanding world climate and inform us how to promote health, peace, and well-being in our backyards as well as in communities around the globe. It is our hope that the book will provide the necessary backdrop to engage in evidence-based practice as a process and to lay the foundation for responsive services that uphold our values of social justice as a driving force. Through case scenarios and applications, the practitioner will gain added appreciation of the interrelationships between micro, mezzo, and macro social work practice and solidify the profession's call to ethical and multi-level competencies. The ability to traverse various domains and levels of practice simultaneously is what makes the social work profession unique among the helping professions, and it is how we can make a sustained impact in society and the world around us.

REFERENCES

American Psychiatric Association. (2013). *Diagnostic and statistical manual of mental disorders* (5th ed.). Arlington, VA: Author.

Brekke, J. S. (2014). A science of social work and social work as an integrative scientific discipline: Have we gone too far, not far enough? *Research on Social Work Practice, 24*(5), 517–523.

Breunlin, D. C., Schwartz, R. C., & Kunne-Karrer, B. M. (1992). *Metaframeworks: Transcending the models of family therapy.* San Francisco, CA: Jossey-Bass.

Bronfenbrenner, U. (1989). Ecological systems theory. In R. Vasta (Ed.), *Annals of child development: Six theories of child development: Revised formulations and current issues* (pp. 187–247). Greenwich, CT: JAI Press.

Council on Social Work Education. (2008). *Educational policy and accreditation standards.* Retrieved from http://www.cswe.org/Accreditation/Reaffirmation.aspx

Dran, D. S. (2014). Teaching note-beyond bricoleur: A guiding portrait of the advanced generalist. *Journal of Social Work Education, 50*(3), 568–578.

Gable, S. G., & Healy, L. (2012). Introduction to special issue: Globalization and social work education. *Journal of Social Work Education, 48*(4), 627–633.

Gamble, D. N. (2012). Well-being in a globalized world: Does social work know how to make it happen? *Journal of Social Work Education, 48*(4), 669–689.

Germain, C. B. (1981). The ecological approach to people-environment transactions. *Social Casework, 62*(6), 323–331.

Guadalupe, K. L., & Lum, D. (2014). *Multidimensional contextual practice: Diversity and transcendence.* Belmont, CA: Brooks/Cole.

Institute of Medicine. (2001). *Crossing the quality chasm: A new health system for the 21st century.* Washington, DC: National Academy Press.

Institute of Medicine. (2002). *The future of the public's health in the 21st century.* Washington DC: National Academy Press.

Knowles, M. S., Holton, E. F. I., & Swanson, R. A. (2005). *The adult learner: The definitive classic in adult education and human resource development* (6th ed.). San Diego, CA: Elsevier.

Mezirow, J. (2003). Transformative learning as discourse. *Journal of Transformative Education, 1*(1), 58–63.

National Association of Social Workers. (2008). *Code of ethics.* Retrieved from http://socialworkers.org/pubs/code/default.asp

Ortiz, L., & Jani, J. (2010). Critical race theory: A transformational model for teaching diversity. *Journal of Social Work Education, 46*(2), 175–193.

Perlman, H. H. (1957). *Social casework: A problem-solving process.* Chicago, IL: University of Chicago Press.

Robbins, S. P. (2015). From the editor: The red pill or the blue pill? Transcending binary thinking. *Journal of Social Work Education, 51*(1), 1–4.

Rubin, A., & Bellamy, J. (2012). *Practitioner's guide to using research for evidence-based practice* (2nd ed.). Hoboken, NJ: John Wiley & Sons.

Sackett, D. L., Rosenberg, W. M. C., Gray, J. A. M., Haynes, R. B., & Richardson, W. S. (1996). Evidence-based medicine: What it is and what it isn't. *British Medical Journal, 312,* 71–72.

Sanger, M., & Giddings, M. C. (2012). A simple approach to complexity theory. *Journal of Social Work Education, 48*(2), 369–376.

Soydan, H., & Palinkas, L. A. (2014). *Evidence-based practice in social work: Development of a new professional culture.* New York, NY: Routledge.

Stafford, J. R., Bowman, R., Eking, T., Hanna, J., & Lopez-DeFede, A. (1997). *Building cultural bridges.* Bloomington, IN: National Education Service.

Thomas, S. B., Quinn, S. C., Butler, J., Fryer, C. S., & Garza, M. A. (2011). Toward a fourth generation of disparities research to achieve health equity. *Annual Review of Public Health, 32,* 399–416.

Thyer, B. A., & Pignotti, M. (2011). Evidence-based practices do not exist. *Clinical Social Work Journal, 39*(4), 328–333.

von Bertalanffy, L. (1969). *General systems theory.* New York: George Brazziller.

Witkin, S. L. (2014). Change and deeper change: Transforming social work education. *Journal of Social Work Education, 50*(4), 587–598.

Woods, M. E., & Hollis, M. (2000). *Casework: A psychosocial therapy.* New York, NY: McGraw-Hill.

Zayas, L. H., Drake, B., & Jonson-Reid, M. (2011). Overrating or dismissing the value of evidence-based practice: Consequences for clinical practice. *Clinical Social Work Journal, 39*(4), 400–405.

PART I

Social Work Practice

Interventions With Adults and Healthy Aging

CHAPTER 2

Palliative and Hospice Care Settings

Dawn Joosten

CHAPTER OBJECTIVES

- Learn how to conduct a biopsychosocial-spiritual assessment in settings where hospice and palliative care can be beneficial;
- Develop an awareness of how to engage in advance care planning with patients and families when providing end-of-life care;
- Describe the importance of recognizing legal and ethical concerns when working with patients with chronic and life-threatening illnesses and their families;
- Understand the role of the social worker as an advocate at micro, mezzo, and macro levels.

CASE VIGNETTE

Lien was a 65-year-old female who emigrated from Vietnam in 1977 with her spouse and four children to the United States. She had nine grandchildren and several siblings and extended family members living within a three-mile radius of her home. She and her spouse owned a small business and were active members at the Buddhist temple in their community. Lien had a history of diabetes, hypertension, and moderate alcohol use. When Lien was 55, she was diagnosed with kidney disease; shortly after her diagnosis she was informed that her kidney function was below 15% and she started hemodialysis. Over a period of two years, Lien's functional health began to rapidly deteriorate and she became increasingly homebound. She started receiving home health services that included a nurse, physical therapist, occupational therapist, and a social worker. Lien preferred that her spouse and eldest son be involved in all meetings and decisions surrounding her care. Lien's physician advised her that without a kidney transplant, her condition would continue to get worse. She and her spouse and son collectively decided to forgo her being placed on the transplant list, stating that an organ transplantation was against their family/cultural beliefs and practices. When Lien was 62, she started experiencing excessive fluid retention requiring monthly hospitalizations and paracentesis (a procedure using a needle to drain excess fluid from the abdomen). Lien maintained a hope for life despite her increasing frailty and rapidly deteriorating health. She was alert and oriented to person, place, time, and situation up until the last weeks of her life.

INTRODUCTION

Clinical social workers in health settings are key members of the interdisciplinary team that works collaboratively with patients living with chronic and life-threatening illnesses and their families. When working with myriad populations in health, community, and institutional settings, it is essential for clinical social workers to engage in professional practice informed by theory, research, and policy. A core role of the clinical social worker when working with patients with chronic and life-threatening illnesses is that of advocate. Advocacy occurs at individual (micro); family, organizational, community (mezzo); and legislative (macro) levels. Social workers bring a biopsychosocial-spiritual perspective that informs the development of an interdisciplinary team's plan of treatment. Although each team member possesses an equally important disciplinary perspective related to the assessment of patient needs and how to treat/intervene, often the emphasis is placed on the physical needs of the patient to the exclusion of other aspects of functioning. Unique to the social work profession is the understanding of the patient's unique situation informed by the ecological, systems, and lifespan perspectives. This perspective allows the interdisciplinary team to gain an understanding of the multiple factors outside the medical setting that impact care and inform the holistic assessment and treatment plan development of the interdisciplinary team. In health care settings, clinical social workers must be familiar with service options for patients with chronic and life-threatening illnesses, such as home health, palliative, and hospice care services.

To ensure that patients with chronic or life-threatening illnesses and their families are aware of options as the trajectory of illness and/or psychosocial needs change over time, social workers must be proficient in providing interventions such as advance care planning, long-term care planning, resource coordination, grief and bereavement counseling and therapy, participating in interdisciplinary team meetings, and case and/or policy advocacy.

HOSPICE

The hospice concept was first introduced in the United States in 1965 during a lecture at Yale University by Dame Cicely Saunders, a social worker, physician, and nurse who sparked a grassroots hospice movement that led to the establishment of the first U.S. hospice in 1974, through the efforts of the dean of the School of Nursing at Yale (Raymer & Reese, 2004). The Medicare hospice benefit was established by Congress in 1982. The number of Medicare-participating hospice agencies in the United States has grown from 31 in 1984 to 3,407 in 2010 (Hospice Association of America, 2010).

Hospice care focuses on both pain and symptom management for dying patients and maximizing the quality of life for patients and their families through medical, psychosocial, and spiritual care that is family centered. Raymer and Reese (2004) emphasize that a key feature of hospice care is patient self-determination, which is intended to ensure that the end-of-life preferences of the patient are carried out; thus, interdisciplinary care focuses on "helping people live as fully as possible until they die in the manner in which they choose to live" (p. 150). Under Medicare guidelines and most health insurance plans, patients who are expected to die within six months can be enrolled in hospice. The services are available in home, community, institutional, and/or hospital settings. A condition of enrollment is that the patient no longer receives aggressive treatments for a life-threatening illness, such as chemotherapy or radiation treatment for a metastatic cancer. In some states, patients are required to have a Do Not Resuscitate (DNR) order signed by their physician as a condition of service. The interdisciplinary hospice team is composed of nurses available on call 24 hours, physicians, social workers, chaplains, home health aides, respite care workers/volunteers, and bereavement care. Durable medical equipment, such as hospital beds and wheelchairs, are provided and medications are often delivered to the home. Hospice is appropriate when the outcome or goal of treatment shifts from cure to managing disease-related symptoms and facilitating end-of-life care.

To date, a large body of evidence demonstrates positive outcomes of hospice services in improvements in quality of life of patients and families as well as symptom management. Hospice care services are, however, underutilized for a variety of reasons, such as the training of physicians to save lives rather than support those who are dying; patients' lack of access; and/or perceptions of health care providers, patients, or family members that signing up for service means giving up and not fighting. Often patients are signed onto service in the last day(s) of life and thus do not have the opportunity to receive the full benefits of the care. Lynn, Teno, Phillips, Wu, and Desbiens (1997) conducted a prospective cohort study of 9,105 seriously ill patients who did not receive hospice care in five teaching hospitals and 3,357 of their descendants. They found that 63% of patients had difficulty managing physical and emotional symptoms, severe pain was reported for 40% of patients, and 25% of patients displayed moderate to high levels of depression or anxiety.

PALLIATIVE CARE

Palliative care, like hospice care, is often underutilized for a variety of reasons. Unnecessary pain and suffering can be prevented when patients with chronic and life-threatening illnesses gain access to hospice and palliative care services. The social worker in health settings plays a key role as advocate to ensure access to these services. Like hospice, palliative care focuses on pain and symptom management and quality of life, and it is family centered, with

an interdisciplinary team that provides a holistic approach to care. Hospice care occurs at the end stages of disease, whereas palliative care "should be initiated concurrently with a diagnosis of a serious illness and at the same time as curative or disease-modifying treatments, given the near universal occurrence of patient and family distress" and the need for both support and information to develop appropriate goals for treatment and care (Meier, 2011, p. 345). The interdisciplinary team is primarily composed of a physician, social worker, nurse practitioner, and chaplain; additionally, pharmacists and dieticians may also be involved in care (National Cancer Institute, 2010). Unlike hospice, patients with chronic and life-threatening illnesses can continue to receive treatments such as chemotherapy or radiation while receiving palliative care services. Like hospice, palliative care is often underutilized in health settings and results in improvements in quality of life and symptom management. Although a national trend for inpatient, hospital-based palliative care programs is growing in the United States, research suggests that there is a variation nationally among states in terms of access to palliative care services; for example, Goldsmith, Dietrich, Du, and Morrison (2008) discovered a "total of 52.8% of hospitals with 50 or more total facility beds reported hospital palliative care [with considerable variation by state]; 40.9% (144/352) of public hospitals, 20.3% (84/413) of for-profit hospitals, and 28.8% (160/554) of Medicare sole community providers" (p. 1094).

This chapter will explore micro, mezzo, and macro perspectives to inform social work practice with patients and families in settings where hospice and palliative care services could be beneficial. The case study that opened the chapter will be utilized to illustrate micro, mezzo, and macro practice implications.

MICRO PERSPECTIVE
Assessment

In health settings, all social work interventions begin with a comprehensive assessment of the patient and family situation and circumstances using a biopsychosocial-spiritual perspective to identify needs, set goals and target outcomes, and develop a treatment plan. The National Association of Social Workers (NASW, 2004) defined the biopsychosocial-spiritual perspective as one that

> Recognizes that health care services must take into account the physical or medical aspects of ourselves (bio); the emotional or psychological aspects (psycho); the sociocultural, sociopolitical, and socioeconomic issues in our lives (social); and how people find meaning in their lives (spiritual). This approach draws from the strengths perspective of social work practice. The strengths perspective recognizes an individual's strengths and abilities to cope with problems; and awareness and use of the client's strengths...[it] is seen in social work practice through our role of enhancing personal strengths and resources, helping clients solve both interpersonal and environmental problems, and helping clients mobilize for change. (pp. 9–10)

According to NASW (2004), comprehensive biopsychosocial-spiritual assessment is informed by stage- and task-based grief and loss theories, systems and ecological perspectives, lifespan theory, developmental theory, and the strengths perspective. The key domains in a biopsychosocial-spiritual assessment include (1) health related factors— history and present physical and mental health, functional health (past level of functioning and current performance of activities of daily living [ADLs] and instrumental activities of daily living [IADLs]) and the effects of pain on quality of life; (2) family factors—the roles of family members, interpersonal dynamics, structure of the family, the degree to which family member(s) participate in decision making and care, as well as patient's designation of family of origin versus family of choice; (3) developmental stage—of the patient and family members participating in the plan of care; (4) diversity—the patient's cultural and spiritual preferences, values, rituals, and practices, including sexual identity (orientation); (5) support system—formal and informal support; availability of and current or past use of home- and community-based services; support from faith, diversity, or cultural groups in community; (6) social, environmental, or financial barriers—to accessing support system and health care–related programs and services; (7) grief and loss history—prior deaths and losses; perceptions of the meaning of illness, loss, and pain; prior coping responses; (8) current psychological functioning—mental status to determine capacity for and competence in decision making; mood or behavior indicators of anxiety, depression, or other mental illness; suicidal or homicidal ideations; (9) special circumstances of the patient—minor children and adolescents, incarcerated adults or youth, and homeless populations; and (10) interdisciplinary team communication—the social worker conveys to the interdisciplinary team the specific biopsychosocial-spiritual needs of the patient and family.

Application of the Biopsychosocial-Spiritual Assessment to Lien

The social worker's assessment was completed with Lien six months prior to her death, when she was receiving home health care services.

1. Health-related factors: Lien has a history of diabetes, hypertension, and moderate alcohol use. She has been living with kidney disease for a decade and up until the past two years was independent with ADLs/IADLs. Prior to this time she continued operating the family business and reported pain was under control and did not impact her quality of life. Lien reported that the changes in her functional health and moderate to high levels of pain had negatively impacted her quality of life over the past two years.

2. Family factors: Lien's family was patrilineal, with her spouse and eldest son assuming the roles of the key decision makers of the family regarding the business and Lien's health care. Lien's reported family consisted of her spouse, children, grandchildren, and extended family members, all of whom were actively involved in providing physical and emotional support to Lien. Lien reported that the family had openly communicated emotions characteristic of an affective family communication style (which conflicts with the literature

that suggests nonexpressive communication styles among Asian populations).

3. Developmental stage: At age 65, Lien was in Erikson's (1959) developmental stage of Integrity vs. Despair, and her rapidly deteriorating health may have interfered with the resolution of this developmental crisis (Hutchinson, 2013).

4. Diversity: Lien self-identified as a heterosexual married female. She is a first-generation immigrant from Vietnam. She reported that she and her family had maintained Vietnamese cultural practices, customs, and traditions; continued attending a Buddhist temple in their community; and actively practiced the values and principles of their Buddhist faith.

5. Support system: Lien received psychosocial support from her large family and extended family as well as from several members of the Buddhist temple. Lien had a preference for receiving informal support from family and friends rather than formal support or care from agencies.

6. Social, environmental, or financial barriers: There were no identified barriers to accessing Lien's social support system. Due to Lien's changes in her functional health, disability access in the home became an environmental barrier in the provision of dialysis and leaving the home safely. Lien had Medicare as her primary insurance and a PPO for her secondary insurance; the income from the family business had covered costs related to her care and copayments for inpatient, outpatient, and home care.

7. Grief and loss history: Lien experienced the loss of her family members during the Vietnam War and as a result of emigration to the United States. Lien lost a sibling two years ago. Lien reported that her Buddhist faith and family support helped her to cope adaptively with previous losses. She reported no unresolved traumatic, complicated grief from her prior losses. Lien's beliefs about pain and suffering were consistent with her Buddhist faith, that "through faith in a higher being [Buddha] one might be saved from" suffering in the world and "Amida Buddha helps suffering beings perfect themselves" (Truitner & Truitner, 1993, p.127).

8. Current psychological functioning: Lien was alert and oriented to person, place, time, and situation. Lien presented with no mood or behavioral indicators of anxiety, depression, or other psychological symptoms; she was coping adaptively to changes in her health status.

9. Special circumstances of the patient: No special circumstances were indicated for Lien.

10. Interdisciplinary team communication: Lien, her spouse, and her son were receptive to the social worker communicating the psychosocial needs to the interdisciplinary team.

Diversity Considerations

When working with diverse populations, it is recognized within the social work profession that best practices reflect culturally competent social workers who become knowledgeable about the groups they work with. When conducting a cultural assessment, it is extremely important for social workers to put aside assumptions based on what they have learned or experienced with other patients; instead, they should meet the patient where he or she is, and allow the patient to be the expert in his or her experience as it relates to diversity (i.e., culture, spirituality, or subculture group experiences). When working with sexual minority (LGBT+) patients, for example, Walter and McCoyd (2009) suggest that the role of the social worker is to "bear witness" to; create a safe space for the patient, family, or couple to talk; and provide support and validation of their experience. Variations exist among individual/familial expression of cultural and/or spiritual beliefs, values, and practices; therefore, allowing the patient to educate the social worker builds rapport in the therapeutic relationship and allows the social worker to tailor the plan of treatment to the unique values, preferences, and beliefs of the client/family about end-of-life care.

An assessment of the cultural or spiritual values and beliefs held by the patient and his or her family that influence preferences for end-of-life treatment and decision-making processes is an extremely important component of cultural assessment. Variations among cultural groups exist when it comes to end-of-life care. For example, African Americans request "more life-sustaining treatment at the end of life. Religious beliefs, a strong sense of family, or a notion that quality of life is linked with survival" are explanatory factors for requesting such treatment despite a health care provider's recommendation for other treatment (Csikai & Chaitin, 2006, p. 60). Hispanic or Latino Americans often will not withdraw life-sustaining medical treatment and are more likely to "choose full ICU care including intubation, CPR, and dialysis, and believe that limiting therapy is a choice for a doctor to make and the timing of death is a decision for God" (p. 62). Among Asian Americans, generally, the family is involved in planning care and there is a belief that diagnoses or the delivery of bad news should be discussed with the family, not the patient, as it is believed that the information can cause harm to the patient, especially if it refers to death (Csikai & Chaitin, 2006). However, note that Lien was involved in planning her care, which will be discussed in the next section.

It is important to identify language barriers that may affect decision-making processes of the patient/family system throughout the disease trajectory as this may impact the access to high-quality care that a patient with limited English proficiency may receive. Approximately 20% of all Americans aged 5 and older speak a language other than English at home (U.S. Census Bureau, 2013). According to the 2011 National Health Disparities Report, although health care quality is improving in the United States overall, "access and disparities are not improving" and for minority groups, "health care quality and access are suboptimal" (Agency for Healthcare Research Quality, 2012, p. 2). Cultural competence is a standard for professional practice in palliative and end-of-life care and applies to social workers as follows:

> Social workers shall have, and shall continue to develop, specialized knowledge and understanding about history, traditions, values, and family systems as they relate to palliative and end-of-life care within different groups. Social workers shall be knowledgeable about, and act in accordance with, the NASW Standards for Cultural Competence in Social Work Practice. (NASW, 2004, p. 4)

Another factor to consider is the preference for and use of complementary and alternative medicine (CAM) by the patient. The physician, nurse, and social worker should be aware of the type of CAM the patient utilizes in order to ensure that it does not interact with any of the prescribed medications the patient is taking. In a study that examined the use of CAM among 4,410 Vietnamese and Chinese Americans with limited English proficiency in West, South, Midwest and Eastern regions of the United States, 74% reported use of CAM; only 7.4% reported discussing their use of CAM with their attending physician, and higher quality of care was associated with such discussions with their care provider (Ahn et al., 2006).

Application of Diversity to Lien

When conducting a cultural assessment, the social worker asked the patient, spouse, and eldest son to educate her about their particular values, preferences, and beliefs about illness, pain, and suffering and how these may influence the decisions they make for end-of-life care. Consistent with the research on Asian American families in the United States, Lien's preference for decision making was a family decision-making model with her spouse and eldest son participating; however, she expressed a preference to be involved in and aware of all information pertaining to her end-of-life care and took the role of a joint decision maker with her spouse and son. Lien was proficient in speaking English and college educated, as was her spouse and son; therefore, the use of professional translation services was not indicated in Lien's case. Lien used the following traditional CAMs of Vietnamese culture, which did not present risk for interactions or complications with her treatment: coining, a "Southeast Asian therapy of rubbing a coin and menthol oil on a patient's spine and ribs"; cupping, which involves "the use of cups to apply suction to the skin by means of heat"; and massage (Ahn et al., 2006, p. 648).

Intervention

Social workers should incorporate a biopsychosocial-spiritual assessment into the construction of and carrying out of treatment plans that maximize autonomy and self-determination in patient/family decision making for end-of-life care (NASW, 2004). A key intervention that social workers introduce to patients with chronic and life-threatening illnesses is advance care planning. Advance care planning (ACP) involves discussions tailored to allow an individual to articulate his or her end-of-life preferences and wishes (Csikai & Chatin, 2006). Quality of life is a central focus of the discussion, which occurs with the patient, designated family members, and health care providers. The discussion reduces stress and improves a sense of well-being and control for the patient, and it also reduces the stress that family members may be faced with if their loved one is in a critical stage when decisions need to be made about use of or withdrawal of life-sustaining measures such as cardiopulmonary resuscitation, ventilators, respirators, and feeding tubes. ACP involves interventions surrounding the discussion and documentation of end-of-life preferences through advance directives, living wills, and/or physician orders documented on forms such as the DNR order used in most states or the Physician Order for Life-Sustaining Treatment (POLST) used in California.

Long-term care planning is an intervention commonly used to facilitate discussions about care options and preferences over the continuum of illness. With long-term care planning, the social worker facilitates discussions with a patient and designated family members about the appropriate recommended residential or custodial level of care in the community, based on the current physical and psychosocial needs of the patient (e.g., home, with family, assisted living, board and care, custodial or skilled nursing care, or long-term acute care); the apprehensions and preferences of the patient and family for residential versus custodial care; financial resources and options available to finance the care; available home- and community-based services to supplement care; support services available; and the availability of health programs and services such as home health, palliative care, and hospice care across the continuum of the illness.

Resource coordination is an important aspect of all social work intervention treatment plans. Social workers tailor resources to the biopsychosocial-spiritual needs of the patient and family. Resource coordination may involve referral and coordination of a range of services, including housing; county, state, and/or federal benefits; specific home- and community-based services to meet ADL and IADL needs; legal services for living wills or advocacy when systemic barriers to treatment are experienced; as well as referrals for insurance services, support groups, health care associations, and patient assistance programs through pharmaceutical companies.

In addition to the provision of resources, social workers also provide their patients and families grief and bereavement counseling, and these interventions should draw upon patient and family strengths and promote adaptive coping for grief reactions as they adapt to loss and adjust to changes in roles; relationships; micro, mezzo, and macro systems they interface with; and world views that result from living with a chronic or life-threatening illness, preparing for end-of-life, or surviving a loved one. Worden (2009) defined grief counseling as "helping people facilitate uncomplicated, or normal, grief to a healthy adaptation to the tasks of mourning within a reasonable time frame" (p. 83). Grief counseling is appropriate to assist the bereaved who experience uncomplicated or normal grief. In contrast, grief therapy is appropriate for the bereaved who experience complicated grief (Worden, 2009). For example, in grief therapy, the goal is to "identify and resolve the conflicts of separation that preclude the completion of mourning tasks in individuals whose grief is chronic, delayed, excessive, or masked as physical symptoms" (p. 153). Patients living with chronic and life-threatening illnesses and their families may experience a variety of normal psychological, physical, emotional, and cognitive grief reactions. Although each individual's journey of grief looks different, as does the time trajectory to move through grief, it may involve an initial period of disorganization during which the griever protests and experiences shock; a period of searching spiritually or existentially through the mind or body and despair; a period of reorganization; and a period of reinvestment in self, others, and community that ultimately leads to resolution of grief and a sense of meaning and purpose (Worden, 2009).

Another important facet to intervention involves the social worker engaging in the presentation of patient and family preferences and professional recommendations for the treatment plan during interdisciplinary team meetings. Case and family conferences can assist with key decision-making options for treatments as well as developing the goals of care. All members of the interdisciplinary team should be present for the former and latter interventions.

Application of Intervention to Lien

Lien identified her spouse and eldest son as key members to be involved in her ACP. In discussions with her family about what she wanted in terms of life-sustaining treatment, she stated she did want all life-sustaining measures to be taken because in her culture, any form of withholding of care or withdrawal of care is perceived as euthanasia, which conflicted with her Buddhist faith. Decisions regarding "passive euthanasia" (i.e., withdrawal of life support) in Vietnamese culture are influenced by the Buddhist faith; euthanasia is generally perceived as "not acceptable because people have their own karmas to fulfill" (Braun & Nichols, 1997, p. 343). Passive euthanasia is generally perceived as "wrong, and the family would not allow the life to be shortened, even if suffering was great" (Braun & Nichols, 1997, p. 344). She spoke with her physician about her preferences, and a POLST was completed and signed to document her preferences for cardiopulmonary resuscitation (CPR) and mechanical life support with no organ donation. Lien also made it clear that her

preference was to remain in the home; she did not want to go to hospice and preferred to die in the hospital. She was referred to an attorney to draw up a living will and trust, which designated power of attorney for estate, health, finances, and person (which gives the authority to place someone in an institution) if she became cognitively incapacitated. The social worker worked with the physical and occupational therapists to ensure home modification for accessibility in the home and out to the community and dialysis. Resource coordination included a city home improvement program that installed wheelchair ramps and grab bars in the home. Wheelchair accessible transportation services were also accessed. Interdisciplinary team meetings focused on disease and symptom management to maximize quality of life and overall functioning; the team referred her to palliative care for consultation for further pain and symptom management. Lien was receptive to grief counseling throughout the length of stay on home health; her spouse and son both declined counseling services. The social worker provided weekly counseling sessions with Lien over a period of eight weeks when she first signed onto home health services. She initially experienced emotional numbness and avoided talking about her new wheelchair-bound and homebound status (in accordance with Kübler-Ross's Stage 1). By the third session, Lien began to process her thoughts and feelings about the loss; she expressed some guilt over the care "burden" she placed on the family (in accordance with Kübler-Ross's Stage 2). A family session was held to facilitate discussions surrounding this upon Lien's request. By the fifth session, Lien shifted into the third stage and task of grief described by Kübler-Ross (2009), that of reintegration. Lien's acceptance of her functional health status, deteriorating health, and role changes allowed her to reorganize her life, adjust to the new ways she could move through her home, and access her support networks in her community and reconnect with her Buddhist faith, which brought a renewed sense of hope to Lien about her rebirth. She began receiving spiritual care from the Buddhist minister in her home.

Transference and Countertransference Issues

To gain awareness about the emotional connections between social workers and the patients and families they work with, supervision, consultation with peers, and therapy are recommended (Renzenbrink, 2004). Managing transference and countertransference issues when working with patients living with chronic and life-threatening conditions and their families is important for self-care and professional practice. Transference, or the "reliving of past interpersonal relations in current situations," may occur when the patient transfers thoughts and feelings he or she has about someone else onto the social worker (Renzebrink, 2004, p. 854). On the other hand, countertransference may occur when the therapist begins "to have strong feelings toward the patient" and may "manifest itself in end-of-life care when social workers attempt to rescue the patient while reliving their own experiences" (Renzenbrink, 2004, p. 854).

Legal and Ethical Concerns

Living wills, advance health care directives, competency to provide consent to medical treatment, informed consent, and culturally competent care are important legal and ethical concerns social workers frequently encounter when working with patients with chronic and life-threatening illnesses appropriate for palliative and hospice care services. Equally important is knowledge of the ethical principles in professional care relationships, as outlined by NASW (www.socialworkers.org), such as beneficence, non-maleficence, justice, and autonomy. Beneficence, to further the welfare of patient, is also known as benefits vs. burdens of medical indications. Non-maleficence, the duty to do no harm, is also known as benefits vs. burdens vs. autonomy or quality of life. Justice concerns equality, provider, family, patient, legal, organizational, and financial factors that may affect treatment decision making or allocation of end-of-life resources. Autonomy, the patient's right to refuse

and/or determine the course of treatment, concerns patient preferences and the use of health care agents who will make appropriate decisions that honor a patient's wishes if he or she becomes cognitively incapacitated. In palliative and hospice care settings, it is important for social workers to be able to recognize when ethical dilemmas exist and how to initiate a bioethics consultation for a case. This may occur, for example, when health care providers or family members provide care that directly conflicts with the patient's wishes, or there are conflicts between health care agents of a cognitively incapacitated patient regarding provision or withdrawal of care. Social workers recognize when it is appropriate to refer a patient for a legal consultation to address problems with service access, autonomy, unresolved ethical dilemmas, and/or problems with access to end-of-life care. In working within the scope of practice and competence, social workers who work with this population follow the NASW code of ethics (www.socialworkers.org), the NASW standards for social work practice in hospital settings (2005), and the NASW (2004) standards for social work practice in palliative and end-of-life care.

MEZZO PERSPECTIVE

There may be procedures and protocols within organizations and agencies that limit patient autonomy and violate ethical rights; for example, when an organization or agency limits information about or does not provide access to the range of palliative or end-of-life interventions and care. An agency may disregard the culturally preferred processes for decision making that a patient or family has for palliative or end-of-life care; for example, it may fail to make arrangements through case conferences or meetings to facilitate the patient's and family's preference to make decisions about end-of-life care collectively throughout the disease trajectory. Another issue pertains to the lack of coordinated care between health care providers and community-based agencies to ensure patient safety or a patient's wish to remain in the community.

A hospital or other transitional setting may inadequately prepare a patient or her family on how to manage the disease or the symptoms of a chronic or life-threatening illness once discharged into a community setting.

Application of Mezzo Issues to Lien's Case

The social worker was initially referred to Lien's case due to concerns by the primary care physician that Lien's treatments may be adversely affecting her quality of life. Lien began having frequent trips to the emergency room and hospitalizations monthly; her health was rapidly declining and her prognosis was poor. As such, a consultation for hospice and advance directives was requested. The interdisciplinary team and inpatient palliative care providers recommended Lien consider discontinuing dialysis and going onto hospice care services. The social worker provided advocacy for Lien to ensure that her preferences to continue treatment were communicated to the interdisciplinary team. Lien's interdisciplinary team explained the benefits vs. burdens of continuing treatment. Lien continued to receive dialysis and home health services. Lien's condition continued to deteriorate, and her family was called into the hospital during Lien's last hospitalization, where she died. Permission was received from the hospital to allow a large number of Lien's family to come to her room to perform the death ritual customary to their culture and Buddhist faith, which involved chanting and holding hands around her in a circle.

MACRO PERSPECTIVE

The Patient Self-Determination Act (PSDA) of 1990 requires all Medicare and Medicaid acute care hospitals, home health agencies and nursing homes to ask at the time of admission whether a patient has an advance directive and ensures that patients have access to and assistance with completing one. A precedent for the passage of the PSDA and patient's rights was set in *Cruzan vs. Director, Missouri Department of Health*. The case involved the parents of Nancy Cruzan (a patient who was in a vegetative state for seven years due to an automobile accident) suing for withdrawal of life support, which resulted in the ruling that states could allow for the withdrawal of life support from a cognitively incapacitated patient. The ruling also upheld the right of a competent patient to refuse life-sustaining treatment (Csikai & Chaitin, 2006). The Uniform Determination of Death Act of 1980 established death criteria for patients with neurological impairment: It states that a patient who has "irreversible cessation of circulatory and respiratory functions" or "irreversible cessation of functions of the entire brain, including the brain stem, is dead" (Devettere, 2000, as cited in Csikai & Chatin, 2006, p. 27).

Policy Advocacy

Social workers, in accordance with the NASW Code of Ethics, are called to provide policy advocacy to ensure that patients' ethical rights are not violated and to ensure that patients receive culturally competent end-of-life care. Provisions in the original drafts of the Patient Protection and Affordable Care Act included the introduction of ACP (Fleming, 2011) and the establishment of International Classification of Diseases (ICD) coding to promote ACP with physicians. This provision was publicly debated when opponents equated this provision with "death talks," and some argued that it would lead to legalized euthanasia. Social workers can provide policy advocacy in this area to advocate for ICD codes for billing for ACP by physicians and social workers, to ensure patients with chronic and life-threatening illnesses that are appropriate for palliative and hospice care services have access to health care providers to engage in discussions about their end-of-life preferences, options, and benefits vs. burdens of treatment as well as the quality of life they desire.

CONCLUSION

This chapter explored micro, mezzo, and macro perspectives that clinical social workers can use to inform social work practice with patients and families when hospice and palliative care services could be beneficial. A comprehensive biopsychosocial-spiritual assessment that incorporates diversity and grief are essential when formulating culturally appropriate and preferred interventions with patients and family. Throughout the process from initial referral to discharge, clinical social workers recognize and address transference and countertransference issues, legal and ethical issues, organizational issues that may involve flaws in procedures, or protocols that impact patient care or violate ethical rights. Last, social workers have an ethical obligation to the profession to provide policy advocacy that leads to improved access to health care providers by patients and their families to discuss end-of-life preferences.

INTERNET RESOURCES

- Palliative care: http://innovations.ahrq.gov
- End-of-life care: http://innovations.ahrq.gov
- American Cancer Society: http://www.cancer.org
- Center for the Study of Ethics for Professions: http://ethics.iit.edu/
- Compassion and Choices: http://www.compassionandchoices.org/
- Hospice Association of America: http://www.nahc.org/HAA/home.html
- Hospice Education Institute: http://www.hospiceworld.org
- Hospice Net: http://www.hospicenet.org
- National Association for Home Care & Hospices: http://www.nahc.org/haa/
- NASW Standards for Social Work Practice in Palliative and End-of-Life Care: http://www.socialworkers.org/practice/bereavement/standards/default.asp
- National Hospice and Palliative Care Organization: http://www.caringinfo.org
- National Kidney and Urologic Disease Information Clearinghouse: http://kidney.niddk.nih.gov/KUDiseases/pubs/vascularaccess/index.aspx
- Culinary Kidney Cooks: http://www.culinarykidneycooks.com/
- American Kidney Fund: http://www.akfinc.org/
- Affordable Care Act: http://www.healthcare.gov
- Centers for Medicare and Medicaid Services: https://www.cms.gov

- ChampVA (Veterans): http://www.va.gov/hac/forbeneficiaries/champva/champva.asp
- Family Caregiver Alliance: http://www.caregiver.org/caregiver/jsp/home.jsp
- National Family Caregivers Association: http://www.nfcacares.org/

DISCUSSION QUESTIONS

1. Why is it important to begin with a comprehensive biopsychosocial-spiritual assessment when working with patients with chronic and life-threatening conditions in need of end-of-life care?

2. What do you know about how hospice and palliative care services are offered to patients in your organization/agency? What are the procedures and protocols for referring a patient to hospice or palliative care services at the organization/agency where you work?

3. Are there any barriers to obtaining referrals from providers at the organization/agency where you work? How might a social worker provide advocacy at the organizational level to improve the procedures/protocols surrounding referrals for hospice or palliative care?

4. To what extent are hospice and palliative care services available in the community or county where you work? How might a social worker advocate for improving access to hospice or palliative care services in the community?

5. How might a social worker provide policy advocacy for legislative changes at the county, state, or federal level to improve access to hospice and/or palliative care services?

REFERENCES

Agency for Healthcare Research Quality. (2012, March). *National healthcare disparities report 2011.* Pub. No. 12-0006. Washington, DC: U.S. Department of Health and Human Services.

Ahn, A. C., Ngo-Metzger, Q., Legedza, A. T. R., Massagli, M. P., Clarridge, B. R., & Phillips, R. S. (2006). Complementary and alternative medical therapy use among Chinese and Vietnamese Americans: Prevalence, associated factors, and effects of patient–clinician communication. *American Journal of Public Health, 96*(2), 647–653.

Braun, K. L., & Nichols, R. (1997). Death and dying in four Asian American cultures: A descriptive study. *Death Studies, 21*(4), 327–359.

Cruzan v. Director, Missouri Department of Health, 497 U.S. 261 (1990).

Csikai, E., & Chaitin, E. (2006). *Ethics in end of life decisions in social work practice.* Chicago, IL: Lyceum Books.

Erikson, E. (1959). *Identity and the life cycle.* New York, NY: W. W. Norton.

Fleming, C. (2011, January 6). Fact vs. fiction in advance care planning, take two. *Health Affairs Blog.* Retrieved from http://healthaffairs.org/blog/2011/01/06/fact-vs-fiction-in-advance-care-planning-take-two/

Goldsmith, B., Dietrich, J., Du, Q., & Morrison, S. (2008). Variability in access to hospital palliative care in the United States. *Journal of Palliative Medicine, 11*(8), 1094–1102.

Hospice Association of America. (2010). *Hospice facts and statistics.* Retrieved from http://www.nahc.org/assets/1/7/HospiceStats10.pdf

Hutchinson, E. D. (2013). *Essentials of human behavior: Integrating person, environment, and the life course.* Thousand Oaks, CA: Sage.

Kübler-Ross, E. (2009). *On death and dying: What the dying have to teach doctors, nurses, clergy and their own families.* London: Taylor & Francis.

Lynn, J., Teno, J., Phillips, R., Wu, A., & Desbiens, N. (1997). Perceptions by family members of the dying experience of older and seriously ill patients. *Annals of Internal Medicine, 126*(2), 97–106.

Meier, D. E. (2011). Increased access to palliative care and hospice services: Opportunities to improve value in health care. *Milbank Quarterly, 89*(3), 343–380.

National Association of Social Workers. (2004). *NASW standards for palliative & end-of-life care.* Washington, DC: Author.

National Association of Social Workers. (2005). *NASW standards for social work practice in health care settings.* Washington, DC: Author.

National Cancer Institute. (2010). *Palliative care in cancer.* Retrieved from http://www.cancer.gov/cancertopics/factsheet/Support/palliative-care

Raymer, M., & Reese, D. (2004). The history of social work in hospice. In J. Berzoff & P. R. Silverman (Eds.), *Living with dying: A handbook for end-of-life healthcare practitioners* (pp. 226–241). New York, NY: Columbia University Press.

Renzenbrink, I. (2004). Relentless self-care. In J. Berzoff & P. R. Silverman (Eds.), *Living with dying: A handbook for end-of-life healthcare practitioners* (pp. 226–241). New York, NY: Columbia University Press.

Truitner, K., & Truitner, N. (1993). Death and dying in Buddhism. In D. Irish, K. Lundquist, & V. Nelsen, (Eds.), *Ethnic variations in dying, death, and grief: Diversity in universality* (pp. 125–136). Philadelphia, PA: Taylor & Francis.

U.S. Census Bureau. (2013). *State and county quick facts.* Retrieved from http://quickfacts.census.gov/qfd/states/00000.html

Walter, C., & McCoyd, J. (2009). *Grief and loss across the lifespan: A biopsychosocial perspective.* New York, NY: Springer.

Worden, J. W. (2008). *Grief counseling and grief therapy: A handbook for the mental health practitioner.* New York, NY: Springer.

CHAPTER 3

Diverse People Affected by HIV/AIDS

Helen Land

CHAPTER OBJECTIVES

- Learn how to conduct a biopsychosocial assessment and design a treatment plan for people affected by HIV/AIDS using evidence-based practices;
- Understand how historical issues of stigma and disenfranchisement have affected service organizations and those living with HIV/AIDS;
- Compare how cultural issues and background factors influence intervention on micro, mezzo, and macro levels with diverse people affected by HIV/AIDS;
- Identify the role of the social worker in helping people affected by HIV/AIDS.

CASE VIGNETTE

Rose is a single 45-year-old African American woman living with HIV/AIDS in a high density, older section of a Northeastern United States city with high crimes rates, little police protection, and few services. One evening she was rushed to the county hospital due to vomiting and was seen in the emergency room after a wait of several hours. Tests revealed that she suffered from one of the many opportunistic infections associated with Human Immunodeficiency Virus (HIV), which causes Acquired Immune Deficiency Syndrome (AIDS). The following day, Rose was discharged with medication and was picked up by a friend, Delores, who has become her caregiver. The young physician who treated Rose was reluctant to prescribe new medication for the infection and HIV as Rose had admitted to poly drug use (including marijuana and Oxy-Contin) to control nausea and the joint pain. The physician's concern was that Rose could become immune to medications if she did not take them consistently as prescribed. Rose had been taking medication for

HIV for some time, yet drugs and alcohol could both affect her immune system negatively and cloud her memory. Delores had advocated for Rose once she was informed that no other treatment would be given specifically for HIV unless Rose stopped her drug and alcohol use. Rose has five children who seldom visit, are not available for direct support, nor do they provide Rose with emotional support. Delores, a 65-year-old single African American woman, lives across the hall from Rose. The two women have been friends for many years. Delores assumed immediate care initially until Rose was stabilized, but she continues to provide Rose with rudimentary housekeeping (e.g., grocery shopping, cleaning, and laundry) and reminds Rose to take her medications. Delores is clearly Rose's best friend and caregiver. Delores communicated to the physician that she would assist with the medication regimen, help Rose stay off drugs, and provide general caregiving. Delores also looks after two of her grandchildren during the week and visits with her three children. She is retired from the Unified School District where she worked as a secretary for 25 years. Delores receives social security and a pension. Rose is on Public Assistance, Medicaid, and is living on the margin, below the poverty line. Even with the very little money she has, Rose is inclined to give her adult children money when they make a very occasional visit to see their mother. Often they bring alcohol in return. Delores has registered Rose for services with the AIDS Service Organization (ASO) across town so that Rose is eligible for the food bank. In addition, she helps Rose in and out of the Medivan, which transports Rose to and from doctor appointments. This information was in Rose's chart. Further information indicates that Rose most probably contracted the virus from an occasional boyfriend who was an injection drug user and local drug supplier. During first home visits, charting notes indicated that Rose appeared to be weak, quite thin, depressed, and may have been drinking alcohol, did not talk readily, and lay listless on the couch during most of the interview. In addition, despite Delores's undeniable fatigue as a caregiver, she was very vocal, stating that she would always be there for Rose as Rose has no one else to care for her, that African American women with AIDS were very stigmatized in their neighborhood, that to her knowledge no others in the building knew Rose had HIV/AIDS, and that she could not tolerate Sunday Christians at her church who were "so holy on one day and wouldn't lift a finger to help anyone in need the other six days of the week." She also added, "Even my own kids say I shouldn't wear myself out on Rose. She's my friend and would do the same for me. Women got to stick together 'cause no one's going to care for us but one another." Since then, Rose has been in and out of the hospital as a result of opportunistic infections. You are the social worker assigned to Rose. The case has had several workers since it was opened and was transferred to you when a previous worker left the agency. It is your responsibility to develop an updated service plan.

INTRODUCTION

Meta-Framework Perspective

Being a social worker for someone with HIV/AIDS is a demanding, challenging experience. HIV/AIDS affects biological, psychological, and social aspects of the individual carrying the virus, as well as his or her caregiver, the medical and service organization involved in care, and even political forces associated with funding for HIV/AIDS. This chapter addresses how these forces impact Rose, Delores, their environment, and the systems of care. To understand this broad perspective, it is important to comprehend how the history and background of various groups continues to impact those living with HIV/AIDS. This chapter focuses on how AIDS affects both the carrier of the virus and the caregiver. Hence, social workers must assess varying conditions of both the person with HIV and the caregiver and respond with differential treatment plans. In addition, attention is given to mezzo and macro factors that impact the course of the illness for both the people with AIDS and their significant others.

Background and Today's Challenge

Since the early 1980s, when an unknown, perplexing, virulent, and terminal virus appeared in gay men in New York and California, HIV caregivers have assumed roles of support giver, nurse, psychotherapist, spiritual provider, breadwinner, housekeeper, and advocate. Often carrying the virus themselves, the majority of caregivers were partners and friends of young gay men requiring care (Pearlin, Mullan, Aneshensel, Wardlaw, & Harrington, 1994). Mothers, sisters, and other family members who were less visible to the public eye also were caregivers during the relatively short and steep decline of the care recipient. Because AIDS first manifested in gay men who had contracted the virus through unprotected anal sex and through illicit intravenous drug use, people living with HIV/AIDS (PLWAs) have been heavily stigmatized, as have their caregivers. At the dawn of this new disease in the United States, AIDS caregivers, many of whom were not related to the patient, faced striking challenges as they were denied access to hospital rooms, doctor visits, and other support services required for ongoing HIV care. Despite the circumstances, caregivers stood as a protective bulwark, giving direct and indirect support and advocating for access to dental care, nurse visits, health insurance, job security, and medical clinical trials for those with this fatal disease. Providing hope, humor, distraction, and information, HIV caregivers traveled an emotional rollercoaster across days and weeks, administering medication, diapering and bathing the care recipient, changing soiled sheets, wiping raging fevers, keeping house, and feeding their loved ones (Land, Hudson, & Steifel, 2003). Many caregivers confronted anger, sadness, fear, and anticipatory grieving as the focus of their care changed from long-range planning to day-to-day realities of declining health and disease manifestation (Le Blanc & Wight, 2000). Many of these young men experienced role overload, with too much to do and too little time to do it and the strain and loss altering their roles from partner to caregiver (Land et al., 2003; Pearlin et al., 1994). Moreover, because countless caregivers were and often are at an earlier stage of disease manifestation, they saw what they were likely to endure themselves: extreme fatigue, previously unknown opportunistic infections, wasting syndrome, purple blotches covering the body (Kaposi's Sarcoma), nausea, vomiting, and ultimately death. The illness was named the 20th-Century Plague. Over time, multiple losses left a kind of posttraumatic stress reaction in the bereaved and in their communities. Yet fortitude remained. Caregivers mourned their losses, formed support groups, organized AIDS service organizations out of their living rooms, and lobbied for funding for AIDS research. In fact, the Names Project was born as caregivers sewed quilt patches together so in the days ahead others would remember their loved ones. Many times, these caregivers garnered their strength and went on to provide care for another friend or family member suffering with AIDS, until they themselves needed care.

Over a period of time the face of HIV/AIDS has changed. Today, not only are gay men affected but also their disenfranchised and disempowered cohorts. HIV/AIDS affects men and women, gay and straight, Latinos, African American, Asians, children, homeless youth, adults in the prime of life, and even seniors. The diversity of those with HIV/AIDS is astounding, yet common to many are poverty, stigmatization, and often shame.

For many, life improved dramatically with advent of highly active antiretroviral therapy (HAART). Called the resurrection drug, HAART has resulted in prolonged life and a move from hospital to home for many. Today, HIV/AIDS in industrialized countries has become more of a chronic illness and death is more likely to occur because of opportunistic infections. Although newer forms of combination therapies continue to evolve, their long-term use has deficits. Many who have taken HAART over years exhibit accelerated aging, including arrhythmia and breathing problems, liver damage, bone death, mineral loss and osteoporosis, diarrhea, elevated blood sugar (hyperglycemia), excessive acidity of the blood detrimental to cells, disfiguring fat deposits (lipodystrophy), nausea, and skin eruptions (Pritchard, 2010). Thus, for some, informal caregivers continue to be needed. The stress proliferation process is likely to occur when there are many losses due to HIV/AIDS and a change in roles for both caregiver and care recipient culminating in a powerful equation for depression, particularly when HIV-related discrimination has occurred (Fredriksen-Goldsen, Kim, Muraco & Mincer, 2009). Buffers to depression include health optimism and positive self-esteem.

MICRO PERSPECTIVE
Completing a Biopsychosocial Assessment

Because HIV/AIDS strikes such a diversity of groups, it is important to understand the particular issues involved with HIV-affected individuals and their caregivers. As always, the social worker who provides services to those affected by HIV/AIDS must build a strong and empathic therapeutic alliance across culture, age, ethnicity, race, and socioeconomic levels. Moreover, rather than stating that clients appear guarded, as was the case with a previous worker for Rose, it is better to ask yourself whether there is a reason for the care recipient to trust someone new on the service scene. It is incumbent on workers to educate themselves ahead of time about the culture of both the care receiver *and* the caregiver, if there is one. Moreover, understand that many people have lost significant numbers of friends and family due to HIV/AIDS. Starting with a new service provider may be burdensome.

Beginning with the biological assessment, examine the general health level for both care recipient and caregiver, in addition to HIV-specific complaints. Diabetes, hypertension, and other chronic illnesses may be sustained and left without care. Rose had not had a physical assessment in a period of time; thus, she was seen on emergency due to an opportunistic infection. Next, move to the psychological issues. Assess for the impact of stress on the system, consider how such stress is experienced across diverse cultural groups, and evaluate the psychological outcome.

Diversity Considerations
African Americans

In the African American community, young women may be providing care for HIV-infected children and male partners, while older women may be caring for daughters with HIV or providing care for their orphaned grandchildren. As one woman stated of providing care to another with HIV, "I feel I have lost my identity to what I was, . . . I just always give . . . my son, my grandson, my husband, my aunt who is sick, it's a constant" (Mitchell & Knowlton, 2012, p. 280). Role overload and stress is a common feature and must be assessed. In addition, a sizeable minority of women within non-kin ties are providing care for another woman or man with HIV, as is the case of Rose and Delores. These may be caregivers who are disproportionately HIV-infected themselves. Concomitantly, as in the case example above, the HIV-infected may experience great stigma within their communities. Alcoholism and drug abuse may be a result of stigmatization and shame rather than a reason for contracting HIV, or they may have been involved in both (Mitchell & Knowlton, 2012). If intravenous drugs are being used, harm reduction programs may be available for the exchange of clean needles. Hence, it is important to assess for such issues. The service provider must assess psychological issues in both caregiver and care receiver, including depression, self-esteem, exposure to stigma, level of stress, anxiety, and health optimism. Of note, as in other populations, many have a history of being sexually or physically abused, and they may have become homeless at a young age to escape abuse (Wyatt, Carmona, Loeb, & Williams, 2005). If established instruments are used, such as depression inventories, make sure they are culturally sensitive and normed on the population you are serving. I include this material because depression and other mental health issues are differentially experienced across cultures. Assess also for exit events such as number of losses incurred due to HIV/AIDS. The African American community has taken an enormous loss to HIV. As late as 2005, the death rate of African American women with AIDS was 23 times that of Caucasian women (Land, 2012). Next, move to an assessment of coping. What are common methods of coping used by the care recipient and caregiver? Is there a reliance on spiritual and religious coping? For many years the black church provided little direction for high rates of HIV/AIDS. This situation may be one reason why Delores feels the way she does about "Sunday Christians." What types of positive coping are used? Some methods may include reaching out to a confidant, information seeking, cognitive restructuring, and distraction. Negative coping may include drinking, using illicit drugs, oversleeping, and overeating. When common psychological issues have been assessed, move to social/structural issues. Does the system have adequate social support for both caregiver and care receiver? Is respite care needed? The presence of a strong female social network in the African American community is associated with less role overload (Mitchell & Knowlton, 2012). Would either party benefit from an HIV/AIDS support group? Is transportation to and from doctor appointments needed? Then move to structural issues. Investigations suggest that caregivers report their ability to provide care is reduced due to structural issues including financial deprivation (Latkin, Sherman, & Knowleton, 2003). Is the care recipient adequately covered by medical and financial services? Does the person living with HIV/AIDS have an adequate relationship with a physician? If finances are an issue, there may be emergency financial services available, such as the programs funded by the Ryan White HIV/AIDS Treatment Modernization Act. Thus, the social worker completes a full biopsychosocial assessment and begins to design a service plan for the needs of both the caregiver and care recipient. If loss has been experienced, bereavement recovery groups may be available. If no groups exist, workers may be able to deliver services themselves. Much of what we do in HIV/AIDS service provision is linking people with services. Where none exist, we provide psychosocial intervention ourselves, including counseling and support. The tradition of caregiving is long and strong in this group; thus, services should be gender sensitive and focus on the needs of the African American female experience. Programs must be designed to be relevant to these women who have cared for others across generations.

Latinos/Latinas

In the Latino community, many of the assessment issues remain the same; however, the context is quite different. With the rise in immigration to the United States over the last 30 years, HIV/AIDS has occurred in both Caribbean immigrants residing in large east coast cities and Central and South Americans moving north to California's urban settings. Female caregivers constitute the great majority of HIV/AIDS caregivers in Latino communities (Oliveros, 2008). As a service provider, as with other groups affected by HIV it is essential to learn about cultural values if you are not Latina/o. Moreover, it is paramount to spend time building the therapeutic relationship between yourself and your clients. If you are not bilingual, it is very helpful to take a translator with you for the assessment process. Personalism (*personalismo*) is a cultural value that is expected and valued. Introduce yourself, remember to address both women and men by their surnames out of respect *(respeto)*, and spend a few minutes in conversation on a casual topic (Land & Hudson, 2004). To establish the relationship, share something about yourself of a personal nature and something you and your clients have in common; for example, you might ask about the children's names and their likes and dislikes and, if you have children, you might share their names and interests. Even the weather is an acceptable topic. If you do not speak Spanish, make sure your translator offers strong respect for the client as well. Often women from the great variety of Latino subcultures share cultural values, such as closely knit extended families *(familismo)*, yet many continue to keep the AIDS diagnosis of husbands, children, and themselves secret because strong stigma prevails. Unfortunately, loneliness results; thus, the buffering effects of familism are absent for many (Land & Hudson, 2004). Caregiving is allocated to women because of strong cultural role expectations. In fact, female caregivers in the Latino/a community dedicate an enormous portion of their life to family caregiving, not only for their nuclear family but also for sick relatives, the orphaned, elderly parents, and grandparents, in addition to HIV/AIDS caregiving.

For a variety of reasons, caregiving may be quite stressful for this group of caregivers and especially for those who are poorer and newer to the United States. Frequently, these are women coping with the stress of acculturation and accompanying isolation. Many have completed only through the eighth grade of education as that is where compulsory education ends for those living in poverty in most Latin American countries. Moreover, although some have lived in the United States for generations, there is a sizeable majority who come from rural villages; thus, adjusting to complex urban environments with multilevel bureaucratic systems of care is foreign and stressful. The complexities of HIV treatment for both adults and children may involve multiple services to manage the disease. To meet the needs of children or adults with HIV, the caregiver must first comprehend the nature of the illness, facilitate required services, and become involved in multilevel service systems instituting care plans. Moreover, some rely on local individuals who inject vitamins, and thus, some may not be aware of issues related to clean needle exchange and HIV/AIDS. Assessing for these conditions is a must in this group affected by HIV/AIDS. For the undocumented, fear of being deported further delays treatment. Likewise, psychoeducation is indicated. Most women with HIV/AIDS and their caregivers who have emigrated from Central America reside in poverty where few resources exist, and the family may view outside resources as unnecessary, insensitive to family needs, intrusive, or these caregivers may be unaware of their existence altogether. Studies reveal that about half of all HIV family caregivers are seropositive themselves,

with the HIV transmission route coming through heterosexual contact with a partner who has had unsafe sex with another man, an injection drug user, or through unclean injecting equipment (Land, 2010). Being seropositive while providing care to partners and children can leave the caregiver depleted and vulnerable to a variety of other chronic illnesses. It is common for Latina HIV/AIDS caregivers to put the needs of others ahead of themselves due to the cultural value of *sympatia* coupled with the value of *Marianisma*; that is, being long suffering and strong in imitation of the Virgin Mary (Neff, Amodei, Valescue, & Pomeroy, 2003). Thus, the biopsychosocial assessment must take these factors into consideration.

As in other groups, biological issues must be assessed for both the person with HIV/AIDS and his or her caregiver. For example, women report greater frequency of non–HIV-related chronic illnesses, including heart disease, hypertension, asthma, and diabetes. One study documents that a full 89% experienced one or more chronic illnesses (Land & Hudson, 2004). Linking these individuals affected by HIV/AIDS with care providers who are sensitive to their cultural values, are Spanish speaking, and can provide adequate medical care is the job of the service provider. When assessing stressful life events, and particularly exit events, be aware that major life events such as being forced to move the place of residence occur in greater frequency in this group.

Role stress may be less burdensome due to caregiving expectations for Latina caregivers. As one woman put it when asked if she wanted respite care, "Why? It's my job." Others may not be aware of services such as food banks for those living with HIV/AIDS. When assessing social support, social workers should know that in one investigation, nearly all caregivers had refrained from disclosure to other family members that they were caring for someone with HIV/AIDS (Land & Hudson, 2004). Thus, social constriction is common and social support is reduced. Be aware of disclosure issues when assessing social support. Further, as compared to other cohorts, Latina HIV caregivers are more likely to experience anxiety over medication adherence. Study results suggest that these care-givers may be more aware of lack of medication adherence and hence become more anxious (Beals, Wight, Aneshensel, Murphy, & Miller-Martinez, 2006). Findings suggest that poorer health, exit events, managing cognitive and behavioral dif-ficulties in the care recipient, role captivity and isolation, and poor self-esteem predict poorer mental well-being, such as anxiety and depression, for HIV/AIDS caregivers (Land & Hudson, 2002). On the other hand, religious coping is quite high, as is turning adversity to strength and distraction. In many ways, Latinas who have HIV/AIDS and their caregivers have every reason to be stressed out, have poorer health, and have feelings of isolation and captivity, yet given their situations, they are long enduring and dedicated people who cope very positively with what could be termed enormous obstacles.

Fathers Caring for Children With HIV/AIDS

Heterosexual male caregivers are a little-known and understudied group. As mothers died due to HIV, fathers, uncles, and grandfathers took on caregiving of the children when grandmothers and other female relatives were not present. The major-ity (about 75%) are birth and adoptive fathers; approximately 10% are providing care for more than one child with HIV. About half have other children in the home for whom they provide care. A large percentage of these caregivers are African American (58%) and Latino (23%) men providing care for children between the ages of 5 and 12 years (Land, 2010). Roughly a quarter of this population are estimated to be HIV infected themselves. These male caregivers of color experience problems that are absent from other caregiver groups. The service provider should be aware that most prominent is the stigma associated with the prototype of the absent father (McAdoo, 1993). Its influence negatively impacts the mentalities of medical and other service providers; thus, advocacy is elemental for this population. Too frequently, formal service providers suffer from the erroneous belief that male caregivers lack role models to set limits with

children or that they are limited in caring for or communicating with a sick child. These are care-givers whose custodial rights have been challenged, thus adding stress to an already difficult situation. For others, placement of children has been dis-cussed without adequate assessment of family life. Interrogation by school and medical providers is common and may be experienced as shaming and emotionally exhausting in this group.

For these many reasons, it is crucial that the service provider demonstrate sensitivity to the male caregiver and give extra consideration to building a relationship and showing respect for an often challenging situation. Remember to address the adult by the surname when introduc-ing yourself. Show admiration for coping with a sometimes very stressful set of circumstances. Caring for HIV-infected children is not a simple task for heterosexual male caregivers who may have little experience being a single parent or primary caregiver. Although some are children who have been orphaned by HIV, others continue to see their mothers, who are debilitated by HIV and in a state of decline. Orphaned children often grow up with significant emotional, developmental, and physical limitations; hence, parenting these children poses a significant challenge (Land, 2010). Moreover, most of these caregivers live alone and have little instrumental and emotional support from rela-tives or friends. Thus it is very important for the service provider to assess the level of support and design a service plan to assist with support of child care where needed. Within this context, both child and parent may be actively grieving the loss of the female relationship presence and thus may feel quite depleted and depressed. Hence, in the begin-ning it is important to review the circumstances of the loss and determine whether or not a bereave-ment support group or a phone buddy is needed to work through loss. If none is desired, the social worker may offer to set up individual or family sessions for purposes of bereavement recovery and support. In addition, men and children may grieve quite differently; thus, the adult must be able to provide variable emotional responses to bereaved children while suffering from his own grief: often a formidable challenge without the complicating factor of HIV/AIDS. If the caregiver feels overwhelmed, it is possible to offer services for the children, such as after school programs or counseling, either at the school site, if available, or at a counseling center.

Men with jobs outside the home face particular challenges. With potentially conflicting roles of breadwinner and caregiver, secondary stress proliferation will likely mount. Reduced employment predictably results in anxiety about meeting financial concerns during economically depressed times. Under such circumstances, it is little wonder that these male primary caregivers are hesitant to approach social services for assistance or are resistant to services when needed. These conditions often result in a cycle of growing need and little support (Land, 2010).

Within this context, service providers must take the time to build a strong working alliance and be cognizant of caregiver issues. Be aware of the culture of which the caregiver is a part and the cultural values held by both adult and children. African American male caregivers may have more experience with role fluidity in parenting prior to loss of the female figure in the home than do Latino caregivers. Such may be the case due to historic racism: African American females were hired for work before African American men; thus, men may have had experience with many aspects of parenting, from cooking to taking care of children. Comprehensive care plans should include special attention to an assessment of the developmental needs of all children living in the household as well as the idiosyncratic needs of each child. Additionally, providers should access the family dynamics in the home, the coping style of the adult caregiver, along with an alcohol and drug history, as with other groups. In addition, it may be helpful to include an assessment of available supports to the family system and how the male caregiver runs the household. Thus, working within the system, the provider completes a comprehensive assessment of needs and coaches from a stance of trust. As one man said, "Children can be very demanding and repetitive in their needs for care. I love my children but I have to say that at times they drive me crazy. This is about children, and AIDS, and being the parents of these kids" (Strug, Rabb, & Nanton, 2002, p. 310). Other aspects of the biopsychosocial assessment include the overall physical health of the caregiver and children; the manifestations of HIV/AIDS in the life of the family; the relationship with the medical care provider; and psychological issues of anxiety, depression, bereavement, and coping. Make sure you understand how the adult copes with the family stress process as well as how the children are coping. Make sure to evaluate also the level of support obtained by the family and the relationship between the adult caregiver and the school system. In the social aspect of the biopsychosocial assessment, be sure to examine the social and structural needs of the family, including living quarters, social network availability, and economic need.

Gay Men

This group is often represented by partners and friends providing care to a loved one. Gay males are the oldest surviving group affected by HIV/AIDS, and often they have served others affected by HIV/AIDS because they have fought for everything from rudimentary services, to anti-stigma campaigns, to Federal legislation such as the Ryan White HIV/AIDS Treatment Modernization Act (Kull, 2010). When HIV/AIDS first appeared, dentists refused to treat the infected, hospitals demanded gowns and masks for visiting, and often, partners and friends were not given visitation rights because they were not first-order relatives. At the same time, employers often fired the HIV infected, and families of the deceased banished partners from funerals and memorial services, preferring to announce death due to cancer or other wasting syndrome. Similarly, very few partners and friends received death benefits such as days off work or financial remuneration. Many middle-aged gay men can recall the high numbers of losses of friends and partners, at times reaching triple figures. Gay men have known AIDS stigma like no other group.

Gay men have long endured the effects of HIV. Those in their middle years are more likely to remember a disease that was almost always fatal. Often heard from this population are remarks indicating that they never expected to live as long as they have. The effects of stigma and multiple loss have left some men in a traumatized state with PTSD symptoms. Most have been remarkably resilient, probably due to strong social support among friends and neighbors. These are men who have built ASOs from scratch, advocated for funding for HIV/AIDS research, and were in the vanguard of change in our thinking about HIV/AIDS.

Gay men continue to be at risk for HIV/AIDS. Young gay men may contract the virus due to drug use, especially when using methamphetamines and alcohol, which may impair judgment and increase likelihood of engaging in unsafe sex. In addition, runaway adolescents from other parts of the country may soon become homeless and turn to survival sex work and drug use, thus increasing the likelihood of having unsafe sex and contracting STDs, including HIV/AIDS. Because older gay men have taken HAART for longer periods than other groups, leaving them with possible negative side effects, some may need the help of a caregiver as they age. Studies report that gay male caregivers who are seropositive consistently report more and different kinds of stressors than their female counterparts (Land et al., 2003). Reported in the literature over time is role overload; that is, feeling overwhelmed and overloaded by specific acts of caregiving like changing linen or cleaning up toilet accidents. Perhaps this is because men are less likely to be socialized to perform such caregiving acts, and thus, lack of familiarity becomes a stressor. The service provider is urged to complete a thorough biopsychosocial assessment. Assessment of biological issues should cover general health as well as the particular side effects of HIV/AIDS medications. Other assessment questions should address the relationship between the medical doctor and the care recipient. This is important because rates of HIV/AIDS may differ across race and ethnicity. Relationships between patient and doctor are crucial for good HIV/AIDS care. The rate of HIV/AIDS for Latino gay men is twice the rate of their Caucasian peers (Campsmith, Rhodes, Hall, &

Green, 2008). And HIV prevalence rates are highest for black men (Hall et al., 2009). The social worker should note particularly whether the Affordable Care Act has resulted in poorer health coverage. Specifically in this group is the greater frequency of both caregiver and care recipient being seropositive for HIV/AIDS.

Regarding psychological issues, the worker should also note whether gay men of color are experiencing more severe mental health symptoms, such as depression and anxiety due to family of origin conflict. African American families may be less likely to emotionally support a gay son if their religion sanctions a literal interpretation of the Bible. Likewise, Latino families who are Roman Catholic may be less supportive due to the church hierarchy's stance on gay relationships. In fact, some men who have sex with men (MSMs) come from countries where homosexuality is criminalized (see www.amfar.org). Likewise, Caucasian families may react similarly if they are conservative Christians. Other psychological issues for assessment include the enduring stressors such as managing problematic behavior and cognitive impairment in the care recipient, which can often result in more severe depressive episodes for gay male caregivers, especially those who are seropositive and aging rapidly (Wight, 2000). Vulnerability to depression increases as ecological background risk factors increase. Younger age, coupled with background and structural factors such as lower educational level, lower income, and unemployment, result in greater probabilities of experiencing depression in gay male caregivers. For older gay caregivers, internalized homophobia, perceptions of HIV alienation, stigma, and conflict in the social network are associated with higher rates of depression. In fact, both discrimination and poor relationship quality are associated with greater depression in both care recipient and caregiver. Further, when one partner experiences the role transition to caregiver, the bunching of developmentally unexpected life transitions interacting with the stress proliferation process is a recipe for poorer mental health outcome (Land & Hudson, 2004). Moreover, findings suggest that relationship quality moderates the impact of discrimination as a risk factor for gay and bisexual adults (Fredriksen-Goldsen et al., 2009). Other issues to mark for assessment include traumatic bereavement and PTSD-like symptoms due to high rates of relationship loss and the potential for negative coping through alcohol and illicit drug use. Conditions that buffer the relationship between stress and depression include higher self-esteem, dispositional optimism, and feelings of mastery and efficacy over life (Land & Hudson, 2004). Social issues include the degree of social support and social networking and strength of the support system. Economic issues can also take a toll on mental health; thus, assessment of economic security should be addressed as a social issue.

Designing an Evidence-Based Treatment Plan for Micro-Level Interventions

Designing an evidence-based treatment plan with interventions based on the differential biopsychosocial assessment assures comprehensive coverage. Next, I offer interventions designed and tested with HIV-related issues and diverse populations. Keep in mind that any intervention is only as good as its provider and that cultural matching between client and treatment method are a must.

Support Groups

Support groups come in a variety of types. Some have open membership while others are closed. Some are run as drop-in groups with different membership each week, so the facilitator treats each session as a full cycle of group dynamics in a single session. Others run for a predetermined period of time. Homogeneous groups are often offered, such as only caregivers, only for gay males, or only care recipients and their caregivers. Outcome studies have successfully demonstrated a decrease in depression and increased coping for both caregiver and care recipient (Pakenham, Dadds, & Lennon, 2002). Some groups designed for adolescent caregivers have been very efficacious

(Esu-Williams et al., 2006). Support groups may be based on culture and ethnicity, such as groups for Latinas who are monolingual Spanish speaking, or groups for African American women who are seropositive. This kind of group may have been helpful for Rose and Delores because it may have helped Rose conquer her sense of stigma and shame while creating a connection with other African American women living with HIV/AIDS. Social networks can be very healing for those who feel isolated. In addition, if Rose were able to emotionally support another woman, she may feel a sense of empowerment and efficacy. Strength in numbers is the operative edict.

Some support groups are designed for bereavement recovery while others are for general support. Another was formed for parents and children who had HIV/AIDS and was found to increase coping in both (Kmita, Baranska, & Niemiec, 2002). Others are strictly for adolescents or for children living with HIV/AIDS. With Rose from the initial case vignette, a support group might be beneficial to increase social networks and decrease isolation.

Support groups decrease feelings of isolation and depression as they build universality and altruism. The elemental factor here is to provide emotional support and even advice giving, rather than psychotherapy and confrontation. When running a support group, it is crucial that facilitators talk with one another both before and after group time for the sake of common interpretation and coherence in facilitating the group. Planning the type of support group is a must, and interviewing potential group members ahead of the first session is vital. Support groups are very efficacious and have helped countless numbers of people through the crisis of living with HIV/AIDS (Boon et al., 2009).

Telephone Support

Built on a support model, telephone support has been documented as being effective. Telephone support includes emergency hotlines to answer questions about HIV contagion, medication effects, HIV testing, depression and anxiety management, and suicide prevention and ongoing support services. Phone buddies talk with one another and brainstorm for solutions to problems. Phone buddies are usually a pair of one experienced person and one neophyte to the process. Another typology pairs a therapist who provides support with a client. The positive experience is based on the notion that it is easier to reach someone over the phone than have them come to a central locale. Those who are depleted physically have a much easier time connecting over the phone or Skyping. Telephone interventions have been associated with greater medication adherence, higher T-cell counts, and lower stigma levels (Herman et al., 2006). Some telephone interventions take the form of a group conference call. One study reported greater confidence in caregiving, less loneliness and isolation, and greater feelings of support (Stewart et al., 2001). Telephone support has much documented efficacy behind it, with some respondents indicating that it is easier to reveal information when not face-to-face (Meier, Galinsky, & Rounds, 1995).

Stress-Reduction Training

Stress-reduction training is important for people living with HIV/AIDS because the future is uncertain and anxiety may be present in the care recipient and the caregiver. Some guided imagery has been effective in increasing T-cell counts (Eremin et al., 2009). In one study, alterations in the brain and immune function were produced by Mindfulness Meditation (Davidson et al., 2003). Stress-reduction training may take place in either a group or an individual setting. Much research has been conducted on guided imagery, which is designed to increase relaxation while decreasing anxiety and stress. Coming from a behavioral background, Wolpe and Wolpe (1981) theorized and then tested successfully the premise that it is impossible to hold two contradictory thoughts at the same time. There are several different kinds of stress-reduction formats. The safe place exercise helps individuals to imagine a safe place and then work through the senses, picturing how it looks, smells, feels, tastes, and sounds. Another relaxation exercise asks participants to tense then relax various muscle groups until the whole body is relaxed.

Psychoeducation

Psychoeducation is an important intervention that derives from a teaching standpoint. Often using a group treatment format, psychoeducation makes use of both group content and group process. For example, one investigation for medication management was found to be very effective in increasing knowledge and decreasing anxiety (Boone et al., 2009). Often the teaching aspect is presenting initially in a group session followed by a reflection time in group. For Rose, the application of psychoeducational techniques might prove extremely effective in improving her medication compliance and reducing her polysubstance abuse.

Individual and Group Psychotherapy

Although individual and group psychotherapy may not always be necessary for people living with HIV/AIDS, there are circumstances in which it is extremely useful. One issue involves refusal of HAART, which can result in a full-blown case of AIDS. This situation then becomes a public health issue. Additionally, when depression becomes disabling for people with HIV/AIDS or their caregivers, psychotherapy is often useful. Similarly, when an individual has experienced multiple losses and is experiencing PTSD or debilitating anxiety, individual treatment is called for. Often gay-affirmative treatment is helpful for gay men who have come out due to HIV/AIDS. In other instances, cognitive behavioral therapy (Beck, 1996), interpersonal psychotherapy (Weisman, 2006), and emotion-focused treatment (Johnson, 2008) all provide excellent depression treatment outcomes within a relatively short period of time. Relatedly, bereavement recovery is often helped by either individual sessions or group settings. Expressive treatments such as letter writing, art therapy, or holding memorials for the deceased facilitate the resolution of bereavement. Many permit an integrated approach, which makes use of spiritually sensitive psychotherapy (Land, 2014). Facilitating memories of the individuals who have died provides comfort and succor to those in need.

Transference and Countertransference Issues

With individual and group psychotherapy, transference and countertransference are issues the facilitator will likely encounter. Out of their own needs for support, group members may be protective of facilitators because they provide a safe place free of stigma and negative judgement. Thus although Delores may benefit from group psychotherapy that attunes specifically to her issues and needs, such as the inevitable psychological burden of providing care and guilt at not doing enough for Rose, she may struggle with allowing herself to be cared for or need to act as the protector of the facilitator. Thus, group members may act in ways that shelter the clinician from psychologically demanding sessions. Likewise, in both individual and group psychotherapy, workers may experience countertransference in their need to rescue the caregiver or the care recipient or provide a completely stress-free experience, which is improbable for anyone receiving therapy. Other issues in countertransference include failure to recognize the trauma from multiple bereavements and compassion fatigue. Relatedly, some workers do struggle with the need for perfect performance in sessions, much like a parent who must be perfect in providing care for her child. Sometimes we cannot solve all the problems of people living with HIV/AIDS, and the best psychotherapy we can give is providing a safe holding environment and supportively witnessing the struggle of people living with HIV/AIDS. All of the issues should be examined in peer supervision.

Legal and Ethical Concerns

As in other care settings, legal and ethical concerns include the need for consent to treatment, obtaining written informed consent, and being up-to-date in training for workplace harassment.

Moreover, social workers are mandated reporters, and under law they must report those who are a danger to themselves or others. In addition, workers must observe the privacy rights of individuals under their care (HIPPA), and for those in a palliative care setting, advance directives are often useful.

Thirty-five states in the U.S. have criminal laws that punish HIV-positive people for infecting others with the HIV virus. These laws punish individuals even if they take precautions or do not realize their HIV status. There is much debate over the effectiveness of these laws. Some argue these laws deter people from spreading the virus. Others argue they stigmatize the disease and fail to accurately address the most current advances in the medical field related to HIV/AIDS transmission (see www.lambdalegal.org/publications/fs_hiv-criminalization).

Currently, social workers do not have a legal right to violate the confidentiality of an HIV-positive client and disclose his or her status to another individual or organization (see www.socialworker.com/feature-articles/ethics-articles/Duty_to_Warn,_Duty_to_Protect/). Each state in the U.S. and various countries across the world have very different laws pertaining to this legal issue. For example, in the United Kingdom, 24 citizens have been prosecuted for infecting a partner with the virus in the past two decades (see www.aidsmap.com/HIV-transmission-and-the-criminal-law/page/1255092/). In 2014, the U.S. Department of Justice release a best practices guide to assist states in updating their biased and discriminatory laws that criminalize HIV transmission.

MEZZO PERSPECTIVE

Mezzo factors center on organizations and community. Older organizations that began in an emergency situation at the onset of the AIDS crisis have come a long way from needing to provide dental and medical services to men living with AIDS who were refused treatment. Some continue to be comprehensive in providing low-cost care while others have used a referral service where there is a need. Some have developed branch settings so that services can be provided within various communities affected heavily by HIV/AIDS. This situation is ideal in that it is often difficult for people living with HIV/AIDS (including caregivers) to travel across town to a central office. Neighborhood-based facilities, which may go unmarked for sake of confidentiality, are growing. Some have connections with teaching hospitals for adult and child health care. Some service exclusively monolingual Spanish-speaking populations, while others serve a more diverse clientele.

Because people affected by HIV/AIDS present a distinctive set of cultural and gender circumstances, it is imperative for those who design programs to be knowledgeable about the wide range of populations served in their area. Moreover, important factors to remember include the degree to which the facility welcomes communities of a diverse nature. Gone are the days when HIV care was designed solely around the needs of young gay men. For these reasons, ASOs should provide a welcoming atmosphere for everyone, women and men, gay, transsexual, and straight, seniors and adults, teens, and children. Facilities that have not made the switch to welcoming diverse groups will be struggling to keep adequate funding as female clients will go elsewhere or complain that there are no pictures of women and families on the walls and that bathrooms have no sanitary protection for women and no changing tables for diapering infants and toddlers. Additionally, a waiting room for children and young families should include crayons and pictures to color along with age-appropriate toys to keep children occupied while waiting to see the service provider. People of diverse races should feel comfortable walking into the lobby. Likewise, personnel employed, from volunteers up to the executive director at the ASO, should reflect the population that is served in its broadest sense. Board members should reflect the diversity of care recipients. Without the power to set direction and raise funds for the future of the ASO, a commitment to diversity is short lived. For Rose, being registered with an ASO has reduced the gap in services and resources for her. She now has better access to transportation and food.

Working at an ASO can be a rewarding, if challenging, job. Burnout may be a problem for some, as was suggested in the turnover rate for workers who had met with Rose and Delores. To fight burnout, ASOs should engage in a self-study schedule once every five years. Exit interviews with staff should be undertaken by the Human Resources coordinator, not the director. Other mechanisms could include an anonymous electronic drop box for suggestions, the encouragement to take time off for vacations, and the availability of flex scheduling. In ASOs there is no room for workers to feel an atmosphere of threat and punishment.

MACRO PERSPECTIVE

Macro factors in HIV/AIDS fall into several categories: (1) prevention, education, and science; (2) racial and ethnic disparities in health care; and (3) funding (Bailey, 2010). With the Affordable Care Act, the day may dawn when HIV education and paying for science and services will become part of the structure of the health care system at the federal level. HIV/AIDS is a disease of health care disparities targeting historically disenfranchised populations: gay and bisexual MSMs and particularly those of color, women of color, children of color, and the homeless. Access to health care, access to medicine, and continuity of care have direct effects on people living with HIV/AIDS. Securing Ryan White HIV/AIDS Treatment Modernization Act reauthorization is a must, as only then will HIV prevention, education, and services for the HIV/AIDS-affected be secured. Without reauthorization, new medical advances or changes in the population wouldn't be covered, leaving huge gaps in services. Other issues abound. Inadequate housing has become a national disgrace, given the wealth in our country. Its relationship to HIV/AIDS is a public health issue. Within the last decade, HIV/AIDS has become a global pandemic. HIV/AIDS is spread in prison settings and locales where crowding exists and freedom is curtailed. Social workers are particularly suited to working with vulnerable populations through a patchwork of programs. The need is great in our profession. Returning to

Rose for one final consideration, social workers must take into account the macro perspective when planning treatment. Rose's wraparound services include medical and mental health treatment, substance abuse treatment, housing services, food and transportation, as well as ongoing home care. Each of these services cannot be considered without understanding how the organizations that deliver them are affected by funding and policies.

CONCLUSION

The storied lives of people affected by HIV/AIDS are at once similar and different. They are united in their steadfast struggle against HIV/AIDS. In a sense, they may have HIV but HIV does not own them. Many care recipients feel a sense of isolation and are likely stigmatized. Most are strapped by financial insecurity. Often the degree of social support they receive is spotty, and many caregivers also bear substantial burdens of looking after other family members in their household in addition to the care recipient. Some live in neighborhoods ravaged by drugs and are themselves drug addicted. Most have been strong resources for HIV/AIDS care, whether the care recipient is a family member or a friend. Many have lost someone to the disease: a partner, child, or grandchild. In developing countries, and even at times in the United States, some caregivers are children and adolescents pressed into an adult role out of necessity. Teens may have had to leave school to look after a mother or an uncle. There are many uncertainties in the lives of these people, yet findings from intervention studies point to how they are bound together by their committed fight against HIV/AIDS. They are often bending but not often bowed; rather, they are brave and resilient figures who have taught us much about living life.

INTERNET RESOURCES

- HIV/AIDS treatment information: http://www .thebody.com
- *Journal of HIV/AIDS and Social Services*: http:// www.tandfonline.com
- Psychology and AIDS Exchange Newsletter: http://www.apa.org/pi/aids/resources/exchange/ index.aspx
- AIDS Project Los Angeles: http://www.apla.org
- Gay Men's Health Crisis: http://www.gmhc.org
- Professional Association of Social Workers in HIV and AIDS (PASWHA): http://www.paswha .org

DISCUSSION QUESTIONS

1. How can knowledge of historical factors in the HIV/AIDS crisis inform practice?

2. Why is knowledge of cultural issues crucial to designing a treatment plan?

3. How can research findings contribute to choice of clinical interventions?

4. Discuss treatment modalities that make use of mind, brain, and body and why they are useful for people affected by HIV/AIDS.

5. What are a social worker's ethical and/or legal obligations when a client discloses she is having unprotected sex with a partner to whom she has not disclosed her HIV status?

REFERENCES

Bailey, G. (2010). HIV-related political and legislative intervention. In C. Poindexter (Ed.), *Handbook of HIV and social work: Practice, principles, and populations* (pp. 173–182). New York, NY: John Wiley & Sons.

Beals, K. P., Wight, R. G., Aneshensel, C. S., Murphy, D., & Miller-Martinez, D. (2006). The role of family caregivers in HIV medication adherence. *AIDS Care, 18*(6), 589–596.

Beck, D. M. (1996). Listening with open ears. *Journal of the Association for Music and Imagery, 5,* 25–35.

Boon, H., Ruiter, R. A. C., James, S., Van Den Borne, B., Williams, E., & Reddy, P. (2009). The impact of a community-based pilot health education intervention for older people as caregivers of orphaned and sick children as a result of HIV and AIDS in South Africa. *Journal of Cross Cultural Gerontology, 24,* 373–389.

Campsmith, M. L., Rhodes, P., Hall, H. I., & Green, T. (2008). HIV prevalence estimates: United States, 2006. *Morbidity and Mortality Weekly Reports, 57*(39), 1073–1076.

Davidson, R. D., Kabat-Zinn, J., Schumacher, J., Rosenkranz, M., Muller, D., Santorelli, S. F., . . . Sheridan, J. F. (2003). Alterations in brain and immune function produced by mindfulness meditation. *Psychosomatic Medicine, 65,* 564–570.

Eremin, O., Walker, M. B., Simpson, E., Heys, S. D., Ah-See, A. K., Hutcheon, A. W., . . . Walker, L. G. (2009). Immuno-modulatory effects of relaxation training and guided imagery in women with locally advanced breast cancer undergoing multimodality therapy: A randomized controlled trial. *Breast, 18*(1), 17–25.

Esu-Williams, E., Schenk, K. D., Geibel, S., Motsepe, J., Zulu, A., Bweupe, P., & Weiss, E. (2006). We are no longer called club members but caregivers: Involving youth in HIV and AIDS caregiving in rural Zambia. *AIDS Care: Psychological and Social-Medical Aspects of AIDS/HIV, 18*(8), 888–894.

Fredriksen-Goldsen, K., Kim, H. J., Muraco, A., & Mincer, S. (2009) Chronically ill midlife and older lesbians, gay men, and bisexuals and their informal caregivers: The impact of the social context. *Journal of Sexuality, Research, and Social Policy, 6*(4),1–53.

Hall, H. I., Geduld, J., Boulos, D., Rhodes, P., An, Q., Mastro, T. D., ... & Archibald, C. P. (2009). Epidemiology of HIV in the United States and Canada: current status and ongoing challenges. *Journal of AIDS and Journal of Acquired Immune Deficiency Syndromes, 51,* S13-S20.

Herman, D. S., Bishop, D., Anthony, J. L., Chase, W., Trisvan, E., Lopez, R., & Stein, M. D. (2006). Feasibility of a telephone intervention for HIV patients and their informal caregivers. *Journal of Clinical Psychology in Medical Settings, 13*(1), 81–91.

Johnson, S. (2008). Emotionally focused couple therapy. In A. Gurman (Ed.), *Clinical handbook of couples therapy* (pp. 107–137). New York, NY: Guilford Press.

Kmita, G., Baranska, M., & Niemiec, T. (2002). Psychosocial intervention in the process of empowering families with children living with HIV/AIDS: A descriptive study. *AIDS Care: Psychological and Social-Medical Aspects of AIDS/HIV, 14*(2), 279–284.

Kull, R. M. (2010). HIV history, illness, transmission, and treatment. In C. Poindexter (Ed), *Handbook of HIV and social work: Practice, principles, and populations* (pp. 3–30). New York, NY: John Wiley & Sons.

Land, H. (2010). HIV-affected caregivers. In C. C. Poindexter (Ed), *Handbook of HIV and social work: Practice, principles, and populations* (pp. 311–326). New York, NY: John Wiley & Sons.

Land, H. (2014). *Spirituality, religion, and faith in psychotherapy: Evidence-based expressive methods for mind, brain, and body.* Chicago, IL: Lyceum Press.

Land, H., & Hudson, S. (2002). HIV serostatus and factors related to physical and mental well-being in Latina family AIDS caregivers. *Social Science and Medicine, 54*(1), 147–159.

Land, H., & Hudson, S. (2004). Stress, coping, and depressive symptomatology in Latina and Anglo AIDS caregivers. *Psychology and Health, 19*(5), 643–666.

Land, H., Hudson, S., & Stiefel, B. (2003). Stress and depression among HIV-positive and HIV-negative gay and bisexual AIDS caregivers. *AIDS and Behavior, 7*(1), 41–53.

Latkin, C. A., Sherman, S., & Knowlton, A. (2003). HIV prevention among drug users: Outcome of a network-oriented peer outreach intervention. *Health Psychology, 22*(4), 332.

Le Blanc, A. J., & Wight, R. G. (2000). Reciprocity and depression in AIDS care giving. *Sociological Perspectives, 43*(4), 631–649.

McAdoo, J. L. (1993). The roles of African American fathers: An ecological perspective. *Families in Society, 74,* 1.

Meier, A., Galinsky, M. J., & Rounds, K. A. (1995). Telephone support groups for caregivers of persons with AIDS. *Social Work and Groups, 18*(1), 99–108.

Mitchell, M., & Knowlton, A. (2012). Caregiver role overload and network support in a sample of predominantly low-income, African-American caregivers of persons living with HIV/AIDS: A structural equation modeling analysis. *AIDS and Behavior, 16*(2), 278–287.

Neff, J. A., Amodei, N., Valescu, S., & Pomeroy, E. C. (2003). Psychological adaptation and distress among HIV+ Latina women: Adaptation to HIV in a

Mexican American cultural context. *Social Work in Health Care, 37*, 55–74.

Oliveros, C. (2008). The Latino caregiver experience among dementia and non-dementia caregivers: Can community-based care management improve caregiver health? *Dissertation Abstracts, 69*(4B), 2275.

Pakenham, K. I., Dadds, M. R., & Lennon, H. V. (2002). The efficacy of a psychosocial intervention for HIV/AIDS caregiving dyads and individual caregivers: A controlled treatment outcome study. *AIDS Care: Psychological and Social-Medical Aspects of AIDS/HIV, 14*(6), 731–750.

Pearlin, L. I., Mullan, J. T., Aneshensel, C. S., Wardlaw, L., & Harrington, C. (1994). The structure and function of AIDS care giving relationships. *Psychosocial Rehabilitation Journal, 17*, 51–67.

Pritchard, J. (2010). *The side effects of HAART.* Retrieved from http://www.livestrong.com/article/249257-the-side-effects-of-haart/

Ryan White HIV/AIDS Treatment Extension Act of 2009, Pub. L. 111-87, October 30, 2009, 123 Stat. 2885, codified as amended at 42 U.S. Code § 201.

Stewart, M. J., Hart, G., Mann, K., Jackson, S., Langille, L., & Reidy, M. (2001). Telephone support group intervention for persons with hemophilia and HIV/AIDS and family caregivers. *International Journal of Nursing Studies, 38*, 209–225.

Strug, D., Rabb, L., & Nanton, R. (2002). Provider views of the support service needs of male primary caretakers of HIV/AIDS-infected and affected children: A needs assessment. *Families in Society, 83*(3), 303–313.

Weisman, M. M. (2006). A brief history of interpersonal psychotherapy. *Psychiatric Annals, 36*(8), 553.

Wight, R. G. (2000). Precursive depression among HIV-infected AIDS caregivers over time. *Social Science and Medicine, 51*, 759–770.

Wolpe, J., & Wolpe, D. (1981). *Our useless fears.* Boston, MA: Houghton Mifflin.

Wyatt, G., Carmona, J., Loeb, T., & Williams, J. (2005). HIV-positive black women with histories of childhood sexual abuse: Patterns of substance use and barriers to health care. *Journal of Health Care for the Poor and Underserved, 16*, 9–23.

CHAPTER 4

Chronic Illness

A Case Study Application With a Latina Client

Dawn Joosten

CHAPTER OBJECTIVES

- Learn how to conduct a biopsychosocial-spiritual assessment with individuals with chronic illnesses and from diverse backgrounds;
- Be able to incorporate evidence-based interventions into practice when working with individuals with chronic illnesses;
- Recognize the important legal and ethical concerns when working with patients with chronic illnesses and their families;
- Understand the role of the social worker as an advocate at micro, mezzo, and macro levels.

CASE VIGNETTE

Maria is a 51-year-old Mexican American female referred by her primary care physician to the social worker for a consultation due to dietary and medication noncompliance with diabetes. According to the physician's report, her blood sugar was 750 over the weekend and she went to the ER. Maria also presented with a necrotic big toe, which became infected, requiring partial amputation. Maria has hypertension, high LDL cholesterol, is overweight, and smokes one pack of cigarettes per day. She lives in an inner city community with few grocery stores and multiple liquor stores and fast food restaurants. She works in a fast food restaurant earning minimum wage, with no employer-provided health coverage. She has three children, and her spouse also works at a fast food restaurant. She and her family are members of the local Catholic parish in their community; she has siblings and extended family nearby. Her primary language is Spanish; she speaks minimal English, and the highest grade level she completed was eighth grade. She does not drive; she uses the public transit system for transportation. Maria was admitted to Home Health after her hospitalization; she has a health nurse providing wound care and education on medication management/compliance. Physical therapy and occupational therapy are working with Maria on ambulation, ADLs, and home safety.

INTRODUCTION

The recent growth of Integrated Health Care/ Behavioral Health models in the United States present a unique opportunity for social workers to have an increasing role in health care settings when working with individuals living with chronic illnesses. In 2005, the Center for Disease Control and Prevention (CDC) reported that nearly 50% of all Americans live with at least one chronic illness (National Center for Chronic Disease Prevention and Health Promotion, 2012). Heart disease, lower respiratory diseases, cerebrovascular diseases, neurocognitive disorder due to Alzheimer's disease, and diabetes were among the top seven leading causes of death in the United States in 2011 (Hoyert & Xu, 2012). Heart disease is the leading cause of death in the United States, accounting for one in four deaths for men and women, and it is the number one cause of hospitalizations among adults 65 and older (National Center for Chronic Disease Prevention and Health Promotion, 2013). Diabetes, obesity, hypertension, a sedentary lifestyle, inadequate diet, and excessive alcohol consumption are chronic illness and lifestyle factors that increase an individual's risk for heart disease (National Center for Chronic Disease Prevention and Health Promotion, 2012).

Health disparities exist for health outcomes among minority populations in the United States for chronic illnesses such as obesity and hypertension (CDC, 2011a). Both African Americans and Mexican Americans have higher obesity prevalence rates than Non-Hispanic whites (CDC, 2011a). Between 2005 and 2008, a lower prevalence of control for hypertension was reported for foreign-born, males, Mexican Americans, individuals with diabetes, and individuals without health insurance (CDC, 2011a). There is an increasing trend for children to be diagnosed with a chronic illness at a younger age. Approximately 20% of children between the ages of 6 and 19 are obese in the United States (National Center for Chronic Disease Prevention and Health Promotion, 2012). In 2010, there were 215,000 individuals aged 20 and under diagnosed with diabetes (CDC, 2011b). In 2010, the risk for being diagnosed with diabetes in comparison to non-Hispanic whites was 77% higher for African Americans, 66% higher for Hispanic Americans, and 18% higher for Asian Americans (CDC, 2011b).

Social workers can improve chronic disease management for individuals with chronic illnesses such as heart disease, stroke, diabetes, and obesity through evidence-based interventions tailored to clients that emphasize motivational interviewing (MI), problem-solving therapy (PST; Nezu & Nezu, 2001) and cognitive behavioral therapy (CBT; Beck & Tompkins, 2007). Evidence-based interventions provided by social workers can improve the overall plan of treatment and desired patient goals and outcomes for chronic disease management identified by the health care team, such as interventions targeted to change patient behaviors. Integrated care models that approach patient care with a team consisting of social workers, physicians, nurses, and physical and occupational therapists, and that emphasize chronic disease management can prevent disease-related complications such as depression, disability, and premature death.

Using an ecological perspective, social workers recognize the myriad systems that a patient interacts with that affect his or her ability to manage chronic disease. Collaboration with health care providers and linkage to agencies in the client's community are also essential in chronic disease management. Adjustment issues related to an underlying chronic illness can often cause a patient to present for treatment. Some patients who may be newly diagnosed with a chronic health condition, such as heart disease or diabetes, may initially experience difficulty with accepting the lifestyle changes. They may also experience subsequent change behaviors that need to occur to manage disease symptoms and prevent progression, as well as complications from chronic disease over the life course. Collaboration with primary care physicians and other health care providers, such as nurses, social workers, and physical and occupational therapists, are key to improving desired outcomes for treatment with patients.

Among Hispanics in 2009, Puerto Ricans and Mexican Americans had the highest prevalence rate for diabetes, 13.8% and 13.3% respectively (Center for Disease Control and Prevention, 2011b). In 2011, Hispanics represented 16.7% of the total population in the United States, and they are expected to grow to 30% of the total population by 2050 (Office of Minority Health & Health Equity, 2012). Given the prevalence of diabetes among Hispanic populations, the high risk for being diagnosed with diabetes, and the projected growth of the Hispanic population in the United States, social workers can be key interdisciplinary providers in chronic disease management interventions geared toward diabetes. This chapter will explore micro, mezzo, and macro perspectives to inform social work practice with patients with chronic illnesses and their families. The utilization of a Latina female case study will illustrate the micro, mezzo, and macro practice implications.

MICRO PERSPECTIVE: THE CLIENT/CONSUMER, FAMILY, OR GROUP

Assessment

Selection of the appropriate evidence-based intervention is informed by a thorough biopsychosocial-spiritual assessment; prioritizing the patient's presenting problem; incorporating the patient's values, preferences, attitudes, and actions pertaining to a desired intervention to change behavior; a thorough literature search for the evidence-based intervention that provides the best fit for the patient and presenting problem; and the expertise of the clinical social worker in considering all of the former factors and making a recommendation for treatment (Yeager, 2006).

All evidence-based interventions begin with a thorough biopsychosocial-spiritual assessment informed by the strengths perspective, ecological meta-framework, lifespan, and developmental theories (National Association of Social Workers [NASW], 2005). There are several factors that comprise a biopsychosocial-spiritual assessment: (1) health: current and past functional, physical, and psychological health; (2) family: family dynamics, roles, structure, and degree of participation in chronic disease management; (3) developmental stage of the patient; (4) diversity: the patient's cultural and spiritual preferences, health beliefs, values, and sexual identity; (5) support system: availability and use of support networks (e.g., formal, informal, community, faith-based, or diverse group); (6) social, environmental, or financial barriers that may impact the patient's ability to access health care and maintain treatment compliance; (7) grief and loss history: how the patient perceives loss as it relates to adjustment to living with a chronic disease, coping responses used to adjust; (8) current psychological functioning: mental status, mood, behavior, affect, psychotropic medication use, current or past suicidal ideations; (9) special circumstances of the patient: incarceration or homelessness; and (10) interdisciplinary team communication: regarding the needs of the patient and desired goals of treatment (NASW, 2005).

Application of the Biopsychosocial-Spiritual Assessment

Maria's *health-related factors* are as follows: Maria has Type I diabetes, diabetes that is typically diagnosed in children and requires insulin (U.S. Department of Health & Human Services [DHHS], 2010); she was diagnosed at age 6 with diabetes and has been insulin dependent since that time. Currently, Maria has complications from her chronic disease manifested by amputation of a partial big toe and blood sugars out of control. She reports having had no functional health limitations prior to hospitalization; however, she has limitations in ambulation and the ability to perform activities of daily living (ADLs) due to partial amputation of her big toe. She reports no history of depression or anxiety. With respect to *family factors*, Maria reports no strain in family dynamics between her spouse, children, and extended family who live nearby. She reports that she sees her extended family, siblings, and nieces/nephews several times per week. Maria works full time at a fast food restaurant as does her spouse, and her extended family assist with getting her three children to and from school. Maria does most of the household tasks, such as laundry, cooking, and cleaning, and she does the shopping. Her spouse manages the family finances and pays the bills. Maria has been independent in administering her insulin in the past, not requiring assistance from her spouse or other family members. Maria states a preference for her spouse to be involved in her health care decision making. At the age of 51, Maria's *developmental stage* is that of generativity vs. stagnation, according to Erik Erikson's (1959) theory of the stages of life cycle development; she is meeting the developmental milestones characteristic of her developmental stage as she has been working and guiding the next generation (raising her own children; Hutchison, 2013). Considering *diversity factors*, Maria was born in Mexico and immigrated to the United States at age 13; she practices Catholicism and is actively involved in her parish. Maria believes that God can heal her diabetes and complications she is experiencing; she reports no use of complimentary or alternative medicine. Maria married her spouse at the age of 18. Her primary language is Spanish; she speaks minimal English and prefers communication and documents in Spanish. Maria's *support system* consists of her spouse, children, extended family, and friends (i.e., informal support); physician and home health professionals (i.e., formal support); her friends and priest from her parish (faith-based support). Maria reports she has not accessed community support such as diabetes education or *promotores* programs, which train community members to provide health education in community settings (WestRasmus, Pineda-Reyes, Tamez, & Westfall, 2012). Regarding the *social, environmental, or financial barriers,* Maria reports that she has had difficulty with obtaining diabetes supplies to maintain compliance with diabetes management. Maria reports that she has difficulty accessing fresh fruits and vegetables. Specifically, she reports that they cost too much at the local store. She reports she does not get regular exercise due to fears of crime in her neighborhood. With respect to her *grief and loss history*, Maria reports that she has been living with diabetes her entire life; she reports that the best way for her to cope is to seek support from and talk with her family and friends. She also reports her faith and parish provide her with strength and support. Her parents are still living. Immigration-related losses she reports pertain to the adjustment to living in a new country as an adolescent; she reports that family and her faith helped her adjust to the loss. The *current psychological functioning* of Maria is that she is alert and oriented to person, place, time, and situation. She presents with a pleasant mood, bright affect, and appropriate behavior. Maria is currently not prescribed psychotropic medications nor does she have a history of use of psychotropic medications; she has no current or past suicidal ideation. There are no *special circumstances* affecting Maria. The *interdisciplinary team* developed the goals of treatment to assist Maria with diabetes management and home safety, which includes accessibility to the home, fall prevention, and the use of appropriate durable medical equipment to improve ambulation throughout the home.

Diversity Considerations

One of the standards established by the NASW (2005) for social work practice in health care settings is that of "cultural competence," which requires social workers to gain and seek knowledge regarding the beliefs, values, customs, and history of diverse client and family groups as they pertain to decision-making preferences, attitudes, and preferences for health care. An understanding, recognition, respect for, and appreciation of patient and family preferences from diverse groups is essential to establishing a therapeutic relationship (NASW, 2005) and informs interventions, advocacy efforts, and interdisciplinary treatment plans. Culturally competent social workers in health settings assist patients and their families to ensure that meaningful health practices are incorporated and recognize that aspects of culture and diversity influence patient treatment adherence and choices (NASW, 2005). They also recognize the role of diversity and cultural preferences in health care decision making. Along with medication adherence and exercise, dietary compliance is an important aspect of diabetes management. In fact, according to Flores et al. (2010), dietary changes play a role in the epidemic of chronic diseases among Mexican Americans in the United States that are related to nutrition. Flores et al. (2010) examined the dietary patterns of 15,890 Mexican Americans and identified three distinct patterns: (T) traditional Mexican American diet (e.g., corn, beans, rice, and meat), (RS) refined foods and sweets (e.g., fast food, soda, sweets, snacks, and white bread), and (D) a diverse diet that has a low proportion of corn and high proportions of dairy, saturated fat, pasta, rice, and meat. Among Mexican American households there has been a shift in the dietary patterns from traditional diets to diets with low vegetable and fruit consumption and high consumption of refined foods and sweets (Flores et al., 2010). There is an association between being obese (increased risk of 20%) or overweight (increased risk of 17%) among those with diverse (D) dietary patterns in comparison to (T) traditional dietary patterns among Mexican Americans (Flores et al., 2010).

Application of Diversity Assessment to Maria

Maria expressed a preference to have her spouse involved in her health care decision making; therefore, he attended all visits with the physician, diabetes nurse practitioner, and social worker. Maria reports no use of complementary and alternative medicine. Her Catholic faith influences her perceptions of health and she believes that God can heal her, and respect for this belief was demonstrated by health care providers and recognized as a strength. Maria follows a diverse dietary pattern. She reports that she consumes a traditional Mexican American diet of maize foods (e.g., corn), rice, beans, and meat; very little fruits and vegetables (due to the cost); and a high amount of refined foods and sweets (due to easy access and low cost). Discussions between Maria, her spouse, the physician, and nurse educator surrounding dietary preferences and the relationship between diet and chronic disease occurred; the social worker provided reinforcement of this association and explored barriers to accessing fruits and vegetables. She speaks Spanish primarily; therefore, the social worker ensured that translation services were in place for encounters with health care providers and that all materials were provided to her in her preferred language, Spanish.

Intervention

Prior to selecting an evidence-based intervention social workers must (1) conduct a comprehensive biopsychosocial-spiritual assessment; (2) identify presenting biopsychosocial-spiritual issues; (3) prioritize issues and discuss these with the patient in the plan of care and assess the patient's readiness to engage in change behaviors; (4) meet with the interdisciplinary team and develop an interdisciplinary treatment plan that includes the presenting problems or issues and goals of treatment as well as desired outcomes. A review of the literature informs the selection of an appropriate evidence-based intervention that will provide the best fit for the patient and the presenting issue the intervention will address. Identifying efficacious evidence-based studies with patient samples that match those of the practitioner's patient or patient population can present challenges (Egan, 2010), especially when working with diverse populations. The fidelity of the evidence-based treatment should be considered before modifying evidence-based interventions as it may alter the treatment effect. Evidence-based interventions can, however, be modified successfully to the population of interest. For example, Vincent, Pasvogel, and Barrera (2007) modified a chronic disease management skills program with Mexican American adults by using *promotoras* to recruit and retain participants; they found statistically significant improvements in client self-efficacy and diabetes knowledge. A second evidence-based intervention frequently used with patients with chronic illnesses is motivational interviewing (MI), a client-centered, practitioner-directed approach to changing behavior and improving self-efficacy based on cognitive behavioral and problem-solving approaches (Egan, 2010). MI involves the following principles that guide implementation of the evidence-based intervention with the client: develop discrepancy, express empathy, avoid argumentation, roll with resistance, and support self-efficacy (Miller & Rollnick, 1991). MI has specific skills the practitioner uses: affirmations, reflective listening, open-ended questions, summarization, and eliciting change talk (Miller & Rollnick, 1991). MI effectively changes behaviors favorably with adolescent and adult populations with diabetes. For example, MI interventions improve self-efficacy among adolescents (Channon et al., 2007) and weight loss as well as physical activity among adults (Greaves et al., 2008; Smith, Heckemeyer, Kratt, & Mason, 1997; Smith-West, DiLillo, Bursac, Gore, & Greene, 2007). Along with evidence-based interventions, resource coordination is an important intervention that social workers provide within the plan of care that can improve a patient and family's access to organizational, community, physical, psychological, legal, insurance, and financial resources that a patient may need in order to address any psychosocial issues that may create barriers to chronic disease management (NASW, 2005). The need for and referral to and or coordination of relevant resources should be assessed during the initial biopsychosocial-spiritual assessment and throughout the treatment plan.

Application of the Intervention to Maria

The social worker described the MI perspective to Maria as well as the evidence on the use of MI with Mexican Americans with diabetes. Maria consented to six weekly sessions with the social worker; phone interpretation services were utilized for the sessions. Using the principles and skills of MI, the social worker delivered the intervention consistently and monitored the effects of the intervention each session on Maria's ambivalence about change as well as her motivation and readiness to engage in change behaviors that would promote diabetes management. By the third session, Maria's ambivalence about medication compliance and dietary and physical exercise patterns was reduced, and Maria's self-efficacy increased as she expressed a desire to work with the interdisciplinary team to effectively take actions that would lead to diabetes management. Self-efficacy was assessed using the Self Efficacy Assessment Tool, an eight-item Likert-scale tool used to assess chronic illness self-management skills in Hispanic populations (La Clinica de La Raza, 2005). The interdisciplinary team developed a treatment plan to include a nurse educator emphasizing psychoeducation, medication, and dietary compliance. The physical therapist emphasized a physical exercise regime that Maria could access and maintain. The social worker assisted with ongoing counseling throughout the treatment plan. The social worker provided referrals to the American Diabetes Association for ongoing literature and support, assistance with applying for state disability compensation, and identified community resources to improve her access to fresh fruits and vegetables through community gardens, farmer's markets, food banks, and transportation services.

Transference and Countertransference Issues

When working with patients and families with chronic illnesses, social workers must manage any potential transference and countertransference issues. Transference has to do with bringing past relationships into current relationships; for instance, in the therapeutic relationship, transference may occur when the patient "transfers to the therapist some of the thoughts and feelings they have about" an individual with whom the patient has an interpersonal relationship (Renzenbrink, 2004, p. 854). In a countertransference reaction, "the therapist may begin to have strong feelings toward the patient" (Renzenbrink, 2004, p. 854). A social worker who suffers from a chronic disease or who has family members or friends who have a chronic illness should be aware of the potential for countertransference issues that may arise in the therapeutic relationship. The social worker may, for example, over-identify with the patient and feel a strong commitment to save the patient from complication because of personal experience, which in turn may affect the way that interventions are selected and implemented with the patient. Steps should be taken to manage countertransference when these issues do arise in the therapeutic relationship.

Legal and Ethical Concerns

Consistent with the NASW code of ethics, there are four ethical principles that are important in professional relationships between health care providers and patients: beneficence, nonmaleficence, autonomy, and justice (NASW, 2005). In health care settings, the principle of beneficence requires health care providers to consider whether interventions are furthering the welfare of the patient; it concerns the issue of the benefits and burdens of treatment options, which should ethically be reviewed with each patient as a process of obtaining informed consent for the intervention. Nonmaleficence is a principle that charges health care providers with the duty to do no harm. This principle requires health care professionals to engage in discussions about quality of life and how treatment interventions may or may not impact or change the quality of life desired by the patient. The principle of justice requires health care providers to consider factors that influence treatment decision making. It specifically pertains to ensuring justice and equal treatment when it comes to decision making about treatment interventions; it requires health care providers consider cultural, legal, family, provider, financial, spiritual, or any other

factors, such as organizational factors, that may create conflicts of interest that influence treatment decision making. Autonomy is the principle that requires providers to respect a patient's right to self-determination; it concerns informed consent, mental capacity to provide consent, and whether surrogate or proxy health care agents are following the wishes of the patient if he or she is cognitively incapacitated to provide consent for treatment.

Of equal concern is the ethical requirement for social workers as health care providers to be competent and work within the scope of practice. Social workers and members of the interdisciplinary team should be trained in all evidence-based interventions they provide to the patient; if they are not, then they could potentially harm clients.

MEZZO PERSPECTIVE: ORGANIZATION AND COMMUNITY ISSUES

Flawed procedures and protocols within health care organizations/agencies that do not provide culturally relevant or preferred care may be a potential issue at the organizational or mezzo level that social workers may encounter when working with patients who suffer from chronic illnesses. There may be variations among health care agencies in terms of the implementation of the 15 standards set forth by the Office of Minority Health and Health Equity (2011), referred to as Culturally and Linguistically Appropriate Services (CLAS) standards. The standards are divided into three categories: mandates, guidelines, and recommendations. The mandated CLAS standards that social workers should keep in mind when working with patients like Maria require health care organizations that receive federal funding to provide ongoing staff education for culturally and linguistically competent services (language assistance and interpreter services at no charge, verbal and written notification of interpreter service availability in the language of the patient, and competent interpreter services; Office of Minority Health & Health Equity, 2011). Social workers should be aware of these mandated standards and provide advocacy to help improve flawed procedures and protocols that may result in improper implementation of these standards in health care organizations.

Additional issues that social workers should be aware of include a lack of attention to environmental and social factors that interfere with chronic disease management. Social workers should provide leadership in cultural competence training within health care organizations to ensure that patients are not stigmatized or labeled as noncompliant when environmental, financial, or social/cultural factors may affect the patient's ability to access desired resources and services to maintain compliance. Another issue social workers should recognize when working with patients with chronic diseases is the general lack of coordinated care between health care providers and community-based agencies to ensure barriers to chronic disease management are addressed. Last, social workers should ensure that preparation of a patient/family to adequately manage disease/symptoms for a chronic illness occurs at discharge to prevent acute care readmissions and increase patient self-efficacy to ensure compliance with the treatment regimen for the chronic illness.

MACRO PERSPECTIVE: POLICY AND GOVERNMENT

The passage of the Affordable Care Act (ACA; Hayes et al., 2013) represents a shift toward prevention of chronic illness in the United States. Early screening and detection is key to preventing and delaying the onset of chronic diseases. This shift toward prevention is extremely important not only for the quality of life, prevention of disability, and chronic disease complications for individuals who develop and live with chronic illness. It also represents a step toward reducing health care costs in general in the United States. In 2011, according to the DHHS Secretary, Kathleen Sebelius, nearly 75% of the $2.5 trillion spent on medical care in the United States was spent on chronic diseases. Within the ACA are initiatives and provisions that promote chronic illness prevention in states and within workplaces. In 2011, the DHHS announced a $40 million request for proposals for territorial and state health departments that coordinate their health promotion and chronic disease prevention activities specifically for the following chronic diseases: arthritis, diabetes, heart disease, stroke, and cancer. The award fund coincided with President Obama's campaign for a new Prevention and Wellness Month "highlighting announcements, activities, and tips that will help Americans get healthy and stay healthy" (DHHS, 2011, para. 3). The initiative also supported the implementation of "public health programs, surveillance of chronic disease, translation of research into public health practice, and development of tools and resources for health workers and other leaders" at community, state, and national levels (para. 3).

Within the ACA, the Prevention and Public Health Fund (PPHF) was established, which has provisions designed to "improve public health and wellness...in four key prevention areas: (1) community prevention, (2) clinical prevention, (3) public health infrastructure and training, and (4) research and surveillance focused on workforce wellness" (Anderko et al., 2012, p. 1). The three key provisions for chronic disease prevention of the PPHF are "community prevention service funding, programs for workplace wellness, and preventive service waivers for cost shares" (p. 1). Worksite wellness programs are part of the national strategy to address chronic disease increases in the United States under the ACA. In 2011, $10 million were made available for workplace wellness programs. Growing concern by public health advocates of future reductions to the PPHF was sparked in February, 2012, by the passage by Congress of the Middle Class Tax Relief and Job Creation Act (HR 3630), which reduced the initial $15 billion set to the PPHF by $10 billion for 2013–2023 (Anderko et al., 2012).

There are also several key provisions for chronic disease management established under the ACA. For example, one key provision, "reimbursement for chronic disease management services," established a set of essential benefits for new insurance plans to cover chronic disease management as well as prevention and wellness services (Cartwright-Smith, 2011, para. 5). A second key provision is a "chronic disease management component of health plan reporting," which establishes an online, public reporting of health plans in terms of health outcomes from activities such as case management, chronic disease management, and care coordination (para. 5). Additional provisions under the ACA that social workers should be aware of when working with patients with chronic illnesses are those provisions that target chronic disease management: medication management grants; patient navigation programs; early retiree "cost reduction for chronic and high-cost conditions" through a reinsurance program; Medicare wellness and community-based prevention programs; Medicare models that test innovations to improve the care of chronic diseases; and education funding for chronic care management health care providers, with courses in long-term care, geriatrics, and chronic disease/care management (para. 7). Social workers who are aware of the former provisions can provide advocacy at micro, mezzo, and macro levels when working with patients with chronic illnesses by ensuring that patients have access to such services.

Policy Advocacy

Social workers can engage in policy advocacy at organizational, community, and legislative levels (county, state, federal) to ensure that patients receive culturally competent care. Social workers can advocate for and be a part of providing cultural competence training in health organizations. Another key area for social workers to be engaged in is improving coordinated care between health care systems and the community. Again, this advocacy can occur at organization and legislative levels. Provisions within the ACA support coordinated care models. At a community level, social workers can advocate for safer communities and for physical fitness in low socioeconomic neighborhoods. They can also be involved in bringing salience of the issue of chronic disease to community members and

leaders and collaborate with community members and leaders to develop community-based fitness programs that are accessible and affordable to residents. Social workers can advocate at county, state, and federal levels for improved access to fresh fruits and vegetables through the Supplemental Nutrition Assistance Program (SNAP). They can also advocate for improved access to education and enrollment in the new health insurance exchanges established under the ACA.

CONCLUSION

This chapter provides an overview of the important micro factors to consider when working with patients with chronic diseases, including assessment, diversity (particularly when working with a Latina client), ethics, and evidence-based practice (as well as adaptations), along with potential countertransference issues. The mezzo implications for organizational levels can inform practice by increasing social workers' awareness of how ethical principles operate in professional and patient relationships in health settings and the important role that social workers play as advocates to ensure patients' ethical rights are not violated when treatment decision making occurs. This chapter also summarizes macro implication areas for social workers, specifically providing policy advocacy to ensure equality and social justice in areas of access to preventive care, insurance, and chronic disease management resources at community, county, state, and federal levels.

INTERNET RESOURCES

- Agency for Healthcare Research and Quality (AHRQ) innovations and tools to improve quality: http://innovations.ahrq.gov/
- Health Information Technology: Patient-Provider Electronic Messenger in Chronic Illness: http://healthit.ahrq.gov/ahrq-funded-projects/patient-provider-electronic-messenger-chronic-illness
- American Diabetes Association: http://www.diabetes.org/

- American Heart Association: http://www.heart.org/HEARTORG/
- CDC Mobile Apps: http://www.cdc.gov/mobile/mobileapp.html
- United States Department of Agriculture-Supplemental Nutrition Assistance Program: http://www.fns.usda.gov/snap

DISCUSSION QUESTIONS

1. Why is it important for social workers to demonstrate cultural competence when assessing the biopsychosocial-spiritual needs, developing care plans, and planning subsequent interventions with clients who have chronic illnesses?

2. What are some characteristics of a culturally competent social worker? What does cultural competence look like in social work practice? Think of a client case in which you demonstrated cultural competence and one in which you recognized a need to have greater cultural competence. What was the difference between the two cases? How can social workers improve their cultural competence skills? What efforts or actions can social workers engage in to increase their knowledge of diverse populations with chronic illnesses?

3. What is evidence-based practice? What are the benefits of evidence-based interventions on client outcomes? What are some of the barriers and opportunities for implementing evidence-based interventions with diverse clients in your practice setting?

4. What is the role of social workers in ensuring that the ethical principles beneficence, nonmaleficence, autonomy, and justice are adhered to between health care providers and patients? What is the role of social workers when conflicts or violations surrounding these ethical principles arise between health care providers and patients?

5. How can social workers provide policy advocacy at the organizational level to improve flawed procedures and protocols surrounding culturally competent health care delivery? How might social workers engage in policy advocacy for legislative changes at the county, state, or federal level to improve access to culturally competent preventive care and evidence-based chronic disease management programs?

REFERENCES

Anderko, L., Roffenbender, J., Goetzel, R., Millard, F., Wildenhaus, K., & DeSantis, C. (2012). *Promoting prevention through the Affordable Care Act, Vol 9.* Atlanta, GA: Centers for Disease Control and Prevention.

Beck, J. S., & Tompkins, M. A. (2007). Cognitive therapy. In N. Kazantzis & L. L'Abate (Eds.), *Handbook of homework assignments in psychotherapy* (pp. 51–64). New York, NY: Springer.

Cartwright-Smith, L. (2011). *Chronic disease management.* HealthReformGPS. Retrieved from http://www.healthreformgps.org

Centers for Disease Control and Prevention. (2011a). *Fact sheet. CDC health disparities and inequalities report: U.S. 2011.* Atlanta, GA: Author. Retrieved from http://www.cdc.gov/minorityhealth/CHDIReport.html

Centers for Disease Control and Prevention. (2011b). *The facts about diabetes: A leading cause of death in the U.S.* Atlanta, GA: Author.

Channon, S., Huws-Thomas, M., Rollnick, S., Cannings-John, R., Rogers, C., & Gregory, J. (2007). A multicenter randomized controlled trial of motivational interviewing in teenagers with diabetes. *Diabetes Care, 30*(6), 1390–1395.

Egan, M. (2010). *Evidence-based interventions for social work in health care.* New York, NY: Taylor & Francis.

Erikson, E. (1959). *Identity and the life cycle.* New York, NY: W. W. Norton.

Flores, M., Macias, N., Rivera, M., Lozada, A., Barquera, S., & Rivera-Dommarco, J. (2010). Dietary patterns in Mexican adults are associated with risk of being overweight or obese. *The Journal of Nutrition, 140*(10) 1869–1873.

Greaves, C., Middlebrok, A., O'Laughlin, L., Holland, S., Piper, J., & Steele, A. (2008). Motivational interviewing for modifying diabetes risk: A randomized controlled trial. *British Journal of General Practice, 58,* 535–540.

Hayes, K., Lopez, N., Teitelbaum, J., Burke, T., Dorley, M., Hyatt Thorpe, J., . . . Rosenbaum, S. (2013). ACA policy implementation: A snapshot of key developments and what lies ahead. *HealthReformGPS*. Retrieved from http://www.healthreformgps.org

Hoyert, D. L., & Xu, J. Q. (2012). Deaths: Preliminary data for 2011. *National Vital Statistics, (61)*6, 1–52.

Hutchison, E. D. (2013). *Essentials of human behavior: Integrating person, environment, and the life course.* Thousand Oaks, CA: Sage.

La Clinica de La Raza. (2005). *Self-efficacy assessment tool.* Oakland, CA: Robert Wood Foundation.

Miller, R. W., & Rollnick, S. (1991). *Motivational interviewing: Preparing people to change addictive behavior.* New York, NY: Guilford Press.

National Association of Social Workers. (2005). *NASW standards for palliative & end-of-life care.* Washington, DC: Author.

National Center for Chronic Disease Prevention and Health Promotion. (2012). *Chronic diseases and health promotion.* Atlanta, GA: Centers for Disease Control and Prevention.

National Center for Chronic Disease Prevention and Health Promotion. (2013). *Heart disease facts.* Atlanta, GA: Centers for Disease Control and Prevention.

Nezu, A. M., & Nezu, C. M. (2001). Problem-solving therapy. *Journal of Psychotherapy Integration, 11*(2), 187–205.

Office of Minority Health & Health Equity. (2011). *National standards for culturally and linguistically appropriate services (CLAS) in health and health care.* Atlanta, GA: Centers for Disease Control and Prevention.

Office of Minority Health & Health Equity. (2012). *Hispanic or Latino populations.* Atlanta, GA: Centers for Disease Control and Prevention.

Renzenbrink, I. (2004). Relentless self-care. In J. Berzoff & P. Silverman (Eds.), *Living with dying: A handbook for end-of-life healthcare practitioners* (pp. 848–868). New York, NY: Columbia University Press.

Smith, D., Heckemeyer, C., Kratt, P., & Mason, D. (1997). Motivational interviewing to improve adherence to a behavioral weight-control program for older women with NIDDM: A pilot study. *Diabetes Care, 20,* 52–58.

Smith-West, D., DiLillo, V., Bursac, Z., Gore, S., & Greene, P. (2007). Motivational interviewing improves weight loss in women with Type 2 diabetes. *Diabetes Care, 30*(5), 1081–1087.

U.S. Department of Health & Human Services. (2010). *Diabetes: Frequently asked questions.* Washington, DC: Author.

U.S. Department of Health & Human Services. (2011). *Approximately $40 million in Affordable Care Act funds for statewide chronic disease prevention programs.* Washington, DC: Author.

Vincent, D., Pasvogel, A., & Barrera, L. (2007). A feasibility study of culturally tailored diabetes intervention for Mexican Americans. *Biological Research Nursing, 9*(2), 130–141.

WestRasmus, E. K., Pineda-Reyes, F., Tamez, M., & Westfall, J. M. (2012). Promotores de salud and community health workers: An annotated bibliography. *Family & Community Health, 35*(2), 172–182.

Yeager, K. (2006). A practical approach to formulating evidence-based questions in social work. In A. Roberts & K. Yeager (Eds.), *Foundations of evidence-based social work practice* (pp. 47–58). New York, NY: Oxford University Press.

CHAPTER 5

Psychopharmacology and Psychoeducation for the Treatment of Major Depressive Disorder

Kimberly Finney & Erik M. P. Schott

CHAPTER OBJECTIVES

- Define criteria for depression and improve the understanding of the use of psychotropic medications and psychoeducation as a treatment modality;
- Understand how to design a treatment plan for and conduct clinical case management with a client being treated with psychotropic medication;
- Identify selective serotonin reuptake inhibitors (SSRI), their mechanism of action, and three side effects associated with their use;
- Clarify the role of the social worker in a multidisciplinary team.

CASE VIGNETTE

Carlos, a 53-year-old Mexican American male, presented to the emergency room with complaints of depression. He reports that he has been in good health until five months ago, when he was fired from his job due to downsizing. Carlos was not psychologically or financially prepared to be out of work; in fact, he had planned to work another 20 years. He is worried about his ability to take care of his wife and family. After five months of not working and sitting around the house, he has no appetite and decreased energy and concentration. He also has difficulty remembering things. He is not sleeping at night and has no desire to get out of bed to clean himself or eat. He describes his mood as "sad" but does not endorse suicidal ideation. On the mental status exam, the client is calm and demonstrates no behaviors of distress, but he is poorly groomed and malodorous. Carlos exhibits blunt affect and slow, monotone speech.

When asked about his medical history, the client denies past surgeries or current medical conditions but says that he was in the hospital when he was 35 years old for pneumonia. He is not taking any medications and denies food and drug allergies. Carlos denies illegal drug use and reports drinking an average of two beers each weekend. He says that he had a drinking problem when he was in his 20s and he sought psychotherapy, which he says was "successful." Carlos is a smoker and states that he smokes one pack every two days. He has been married for 32 years and has three children, who are now grown and out of the house. He describes his marriage as "okay." He says that he is very proud of his children and that he and his wife see them several times each month.

Carlos is a first-generation Mexican American and identifies strongly with his Latino culture. He grew up bilingual and often served as a language "broker" and negotiator for his mother in his early developmental years when he would interface with the medical community on behalf of his mother. In his early adulthood before joining the military, Carlos was an active volunteer at the Museum of Latin American Art. Much of Carlos's connection to his heritage disappeared once he enrolled in the military, as Carlos had a strong desire to assimilate into the military culture. His identity during his 10 years of active service became consumed by the military. He is a veteran of the Iraq war.

Carlos says "I have never felt like this before" and that he is "somewhat" worried. He notes some gastric pains, a mild nonproductive cough, and occasional night sweats. After a comprehensive medical examination by a physician, other medical conditions have been ruled out at this time.

INTRODUCTION

Modern social work practice is informed by the scientist-practitioner model, which calls for social workers as well as other mental health care providers to use research to guide their practice, including the use of evidence-based interventions when treating a client with a given diagnosis. Social workers are also trained to conduct assessment, diagnosis, and treatment within a biopsychosocial framework. However, often novice practitioners' attempts to use the biopsychosocial framework are ineffective due to a lack of understanding of neurobiology. As a result, novice practitioners analyze the psychosocial portion of a client's behavior but direct very little attention to the biological explanation of behaviors. In turn, their ability to be well-rounded and effective scientist-practitioners is also compromised. Therefore, it can be helpful for social workers to broaden their scope of knowledge regarding neurobiology and psychopharmacology for a number of reasons, which are delineated below.

First, doing so can help them become better consumers of research regarding mental illness and behaviors. Second, experts in the field believe that mental illness is characterized by a transaction between biological and psychological processes and, hence, that using both psychopharmacology and psychoeducation in treatment is an efficient and effective approach in the treatment of depression (Substance Abuse and Mental Health Services Administration [SAMHSA], 2011). Third, social workers usually see their clients more frequently than the prescribing provider does—weekly or biweekly, on average. As a result, according to Davidson (2010), well-trained and knowledgeable social workers can play key roles in client education, compliance, and monitoring adverse side effects and adverse reactions to psychotropic medications.

Etiology of Depression

Are Carlos's symptoms related to biological factors or are they best explained by a psychosocial theory? This has been the great debate with regard to etiology and treatment of major mental disorders (Delgado, 2000). One biological explanation is the monoamine depression theory, which suggests that the primary symptoms of clinical depression are caused by a dysregulation of certain neurotransmitters: norepinephrine, dopamine, and serotonin (Stahl, 2009). Neurotransmitters have also been shown to increase the production of neuroprotective proteins (brain-derived neurotrophic factor, or BDNF) and reduce levels of stress hormones (e.g., cortisol; Stahl, 2009). Antidepressant medications are able to restore normal neurochemical functioning in key structures of the brain (Davidson, 2010).

Psychologically oriented mental health providers view symptoms as resulting from emotional stressors, early childhood trauma, chronic environmental stressors, and other nonbiological factors (Becker & Kleinman, 2013). Some instances of depression are purely psychological or psychosocial (e.g., loss of job, death of loved one, low self-esteem). Other instances of depression are purely biological in nature (i.e., endogenous neurochemical malfunction or as reactions to medications or medical conditions that will be mentioned later in the chapter). Some instances of depression are an interplay of environment/psychological and biochemical dysfunction (Preston & Johnson, 2012).

Prevalence of Depression

Depression has been compared to the common cold in that it can affect anyone at any time (Bender, 2012). A National Institute of Mental Health (NIMH, 2012) report found that depression affects approximately 14.8 million American adults annually. However, there is a marked difference by age group: Eighteen to 29-year-old individuals experience depression at a rate three times greater than that of individuals age 60 years or older. Although the average age of onset of depression is 32 years old in the general population, 3.3% of 13- to 18-year-olds have experienced a seriously debilitating depressive disorder. Statistics also show that females experience 1.5 to 3 times higher rates of depression than males, beginning in early

adolescence, and that blacks are 40% less likely than non-Hispanic whites to experience depression during their lifetime (NIMH, 2001). For Latinos, like Carlos, depression and anxiety may be undertreated (Wassertheil-Smoller et al., 2014). Twenty-seven percent of Hispanics/Latinos report high levels of depressive symptoms, with a low of 22.3% among Mexican Americans and a high of 38% among Puerto Ricans. There is a relatively low use of antidepressant and anti-anxiety medications among Hispanics/Latinos; only 5% of the study sample used antidepressants (Wassertheil-Smoller et al., 2014).

Criteria for Depression

Signs and symptoms of Major Depressive Disorder (MDD) include depressed mood (e.g., feelings of sadness, emptiness, or hopelessness) and a marked diminishment in interest or pleasure in activities for all, or almost all, of the day, as outlined in the criteria for MDD in the *Diagnostic and Statistical Manual of Mental Disorders* (DSM-5; American Psychiatric Association [APA], 2013). People with depression may experience significant weight loss (when not dieting) or weight gain (i.e., a change of more than 5% of body weight in a month) or decrease or increase in appetite nearly every day. Other markers of depression include insomnia or hypersomnia, psychomotor agitation or retardation, fatigue or loss of energy, feeling worthless or excessively guilty, diminished ability to think or concentrate, indecisiveness, recurrent thoughts of death, and recurrent suicidal ideation (with or without a plan; APA, 2013).

The publication of the DSM-5 included some slight changes from the previous version (DSM-IV-TR) in terms of the clinical features and differential diagnoses associated with depression (APA, 2013). For instance, the condition, which was called Dysthymic Disorder in the DSM-IV-TR is now called Persistent Depressive Disorder; some of the salient symptoms of Persistent Depressive Disorder are depressed mood, poor appetite or overeating, insomnia or hypersomnia, and low self-esteem (APA, 2013).

The DSM-5 also established a new diagnostic category for further study: Persistent Complex Bereavement (PCB).

> Individuals with persistent complex bereavement disorder, or complex or prolonged grief disorder, are incapacitated by grief and focused on the loss to the exclusion of other interests and concerns. These are present every day, cause distress or functional impairment and persist for more than 6 months after bereavement. (Drake, 2015, para. 3)

Rumination about the death, longing, feelings for reunion with the deceased, denial of the loss, loss of pleasure in life, and anger are symptoms of PCB. Twenty-five percent of the population diagnosed with Persistent Complex Bereavement Disorder will develop Major Depression and 10% will develop a trauma syndrome due to personal loss. The DSM reports that 2.4% to 4.8% of the population experiencing loss after one year will develop Persistent Complex Bereavement Disorder (APA, 2013). Medical illnesses and medications can also cause depressive symptoms. Research and clinical case studies have also shown that hypothyroidism, minor tranquilizer and alcohol use, and chronic pain, to name a few, may also cause depressive symptoms (APA, 2013).

Psychopharmacology and Depression

There are several classes of antidepressants to treat depression: monoamine oxidase inhibitors (MAOI), tricyclic antidepressants (TCA), serotonin norepinephrine reuptake inhibitors (SNRI), and selective serotonin reuptake inhibitors (SSRI). Serotonin (which is also called 5-HT or 5-hydroxytryptamine) is thought to play a role in the regulation of mood, pain, eating, sleep, dreaming, arousal, and sexual functioning (der Does & Willem, 2001). The amino acid tryptophan, an essential amino acid, is the precursor of serotonin. Foods high in tryptophan include turkey, milk, yogurt, eggs, meat, nuts, beans, fish, and cheese. Cheddar, Gruyere, and Swiss cheese are particularly rich in tryptophan (der Does & Willem, 2001). It is important to assess a client's diet to rule out any potential side effects that may be dietary in etiology.

In the frontal cortex of the brain, serotonin plays a role in concentration, interest, pleasure, fatigue, psychomotor agitation, suicidal ideation, guilt, and mood. In the basal ganglia, serotonin dysregulation can produce psychomotor agitation and negatively impact energy (Hensler, 2006). The limbic system mediates serotonin's regulatory function upon emotions, panic, memory, and anxiety. The limbic system is the area of the brain that regulates activities such as emotions, physical and sexual drives, and the stress response. There are various structures of the limbic system that are of particular importance. The hypothalamus is a small structure located at the base of the brain. It is responsible for many basic functions such as body temperature, sleep, appetite, sexual drive, stress reaction, and the regulation of other activities. The hypothalamus plays a role in the body's fight, flight, or freeze response; eating behaviors; libido; sleep; and temperature. The hypothalamus also controls the function of the pituitary gland. The pituitary gland regulates key hormones. The amygdala and hippocampus are other structures within the limbic system that are associated with emotional reaction. The activities of the limbic system are so important and complex that disturbances in any part of it, including how neurotransmitters function, could affect one's mood and behavior (Hensler, 2006).

Serotonin (a neurotransmitter) is released from neurons located in the central nervous system as needed, into the synaptic cleft, where it binds to receptors on the post-synaptic neurons (see Figure 5.1). This binding can then potentiate that neuron to release serotonin. Excess serotonin in the cleft, or serotonin that is not bound, is then taken up by a reuptake pump and returned to the releasing (pre-synaptic) neuron. SSRIs block the reuptake pump inhibiting the return of excess serotonin and, as a result, more serotonin is available for binding to postsynaptic neuron receptors (Hensler, 2006).

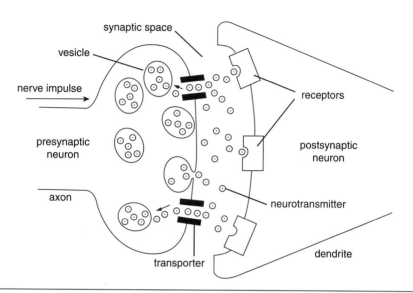

Figure 5.1 The synapse is the site where chemical signals pass between neurons. Neurotransmitters (such as serotonin) are released from the presynaptic neuron terminals into the extracellular space, the synaptic cleft or synaptic space. The released neurotransmitter molecules can then bind to specific receptors on the postsynaptic neuron to elicit a response. Excess neurotransmitter can then be reabsorbed into the presynaptic neuron through the action of specific reuptake molecules called transporters. This process ensures that the signal is terminated when appropriate (Biological Sciences Curriculum Study, 2010, p. 47).

SOURCE: National Institute of Health. (n.d.) Curriculum Supplement Series: The Brain: Understanding Neurobiology Through the Study of Addiction. Lesson 2: Neurons, Brain Chemistry, and Neurotransmission.

Indications for Selective Serotonin Reuptake Inhibitors

Symptoms of serotonin dysregulation include significant changes in functioning with unstable neurovegetative symptoms such as sleep disturbances (e.g., early morning awakening, decreased sleep efficiency, frequent awakenings throughout the night, or hypersomnia). Appetite disturbance, fatigue, decreased sex drive, restlessness, agitation, or psychomotor agitation may be evident. Clients may also report diurnal (day time or morning) variations in mood (worse in morning), impaired concentration, forgetfulness, significant anhedonia, guilt, and decreased energy (Ferguson, 2001). The mnemonic "Depressed Patients Seem Anxious, So Claim Psychiatrists" may be useful for understanding neurovegetative symptoms, as follows:

1. **D**epression and other mood disorders (Major Depression Disorder, Bipolar Disorder, Persistent Depressive Disorder);

2. **P**ersonality disorders (primarily Borderline Personality Disorder);

3. **S**ubstance abuse disorders;

4. **A**nxiety disorders (Panic Disorder with Agoraphobia, Obsessive-Compulsive Disorder);

5. **S**omatization disorder, eating disorders (these two disorders are combined because both involve disorders of bodily perception);

6. **C**ognitive disorders (Neurocognitive Disorder, Delirium);

7. **P**sychotic disorders (Schizophrenia, Delusional Disorder and psychosis accompanying depression, substance abuse or Neurocognitive Disorder. (Carlant, 1998, p. 1617)

SSRIs are the most widely prescribed class of antidepressants. They have been shown to be effective in the treatment of Major Depressive Disorder (MDD), Persistent Depressive Disorder (Dysthymia), Obsessive-Compulsive Disorder

(OCD), Panic Disorder, Bulimia Nervosa, Post-Traumatic Stress Disorder (PTSD), Generalized Anxiety Disorder (GAD), and social phobia (www.fda.gov). SSRIs are also effective in the treatment of Bipolar Disorder and Premenstrual Dysphoric Disorder (Ferguson, 2001). They may also be effective in the treatment of pain syndromes (such as migraine headaches and chronic pain), impulse control disorders, and Borderline Personality Disorder (Ferguson, 2001).

The starting dose varies depending on the SSRI: 5–10 mg for paroxetine (e.g., Paxil), 10–20 mg for citalopram (e.g., Celexa), 5–10 mg for escitalopram (e.g., Lexapro), 10–20 mg for fluoxetine (e.g., Prozac), and 50 mg for sertraline (e.g., Zoloft). However, after 1–2 weeks, the dosage may be increased gradually to standard dosages. A client's culture and age must be taken into account due to variations in the metabolic rate (Cooper et al., 2003). For example, as a first-generation Mexican American, Carlos is more trusting of the medical community than his mother was as a new immigrant. His trust is also influenced by his experiences within the military system. Having established trust with his mental health providers has allowed Carlos to overcome the stigma of accessing mental health services he received from his heritage and military cultural experiences.

The side effects (i.e., effects other than the intended therapeutic ones) of SSRIs are primarily mediated by their interaction with serotonergic transmission. Gastrointestinal effects such as nausea and diarrhea are the most common adverse reactions, although reported nausea usually improves after the first few days. Syncope (fainting or passing out), confusion, tremors, sexual dysfunction, and weight gain are other possible side effects (Ferguson, 2001).

Adverse drug reactions are harmful and undesired effects resulting from a medication. A therapist should be especially aware of the following four types of adverse reactions because intervention can be lifesaving: Serotonin Syndrome, SSRI Discontinuation Syndrome, teratogenic effects, and mania (Ferguson, 2001).

Serotonin Syndrome can occur when SSRI are combined with MAOI or in combination with other medications, and possible reactions include nausea, confusion, hyperthermia, autonomic instability, tremor, myoclonus (sudden, involuntary jerking of a muscle or group of muscles), seizures, coma, and death. SSRIs should not be used for two weeks before or after the use of MAOI; for fluoxetine (e.g., Prozac), five to six weeks should elapse after discontinuation because of its long half-life (Boyer & Shannon, 2005). Serotonin toxicity involves excessive levels of serotonin in the central nervous system (Boyer & Shannon, 2005).

SSRI Discontinuation Syndrome symptoms are usually transient and are more likely to occur with short-acting agents such as paroxetine (e.g., Paxil) and fluvoxamine (e.g., Luvox). The syndrome can induce influenza-like symptoms, such as fatigue, chills, sweating, sleep disturbances, and gastrointestinal disturbances, among others (Boyer & Shannon, 2005).

Teratogenic effects (the combined consequences of consuming a harmful substance, such as alcohol, on a developing fetus) are associated with the use of SSRIs in pregnant mothers and can include a range of mild to severe abnormalities of physiological development for the child (Alwan, Reefhuis, Rasmussen, Olney, & Friedman, 2007). It is important to note that all SSRIs are pregnancy Category C, which means that there are no definitive human studies regarding the risk of major birth defects in humans from the use of SSRI during pregnancy (Alwan et al., 2007). The risks and benefits should be discussed with the prescribing clinician and with the medical providers overseeing the woman's pregnancy.

However, there are other known risks. For one, SSRIs can be found in breast milk, so breast-feeding while taking an SSRI is contraindicated (Alwan et al., 2007). Oberlander, Warburton, Misir, Aghajanian, and Hertzman (2006) found that when taken toward the end of pregnancy, SSRIs may cause the following adverse effects on the newborn: agitation, abnormal muscle tone, abnormal suction, respiratory difficulties, seizure, low Apgar score (determines how well the baby tolerated the birthing process), hypernatremia (an elevated sodium level in the blood), and bleeding disorder including intracranial hemorrhage.

Thus, SSRIs should be used with utmost caution during pregnancy. However, the impact of untreated depression on the mother and fetus must also be considered when weighing the risks and benefits of taking an SSRI. Finally, like all types of antidepressants, SSRIs have been known to induce mania or rapid cycling in bipolar clients (Alwan et al., 2007).

MICRO PERSPECTIVE

Assessment

In clinical settings, all social work interventions begin with a comprehensive biopsychosocial assessment (Roberts & Greene, 2002). This assessment assists the social worker in becoming aware of any diversity or other considerations that may affect the therapeutic relationship or the client. Prior to intervention, the social worker collaborates with the client to identify what he or she desires from treatment. They set mutually agreed-upon goals, with specific objectives to be targeted for each. Following goal setting, a treatment plan is developed. Ultimately, progress toward the goals will be measured.

Biopsychosocial assessments typically include (1) the study, which is the inference-free fact gathering by the social worker; and (2) the assessment, which presents the worker's inferences, impressions, and hypotheses about etiology of behavior (Roberts & Greene, 2002). The assessment also includes the problems within and relationships between systems. The key domains that are covered in the fact gathering and assessment are identifying information; setting; reason for referral or presenting problem; client's description and functioning; physical and economic environment; social functioning (per client's self-report or secondary input); personal and family history relevant to current focus; psychological functioning (note strengths and limitations); emotional functioning; behavioral functioning; environmental issues and constraints affecting the situation; motivation for change and commitment to services; and social worker's understanding of the presenting

problem. The social worker can also administer the Beck Depression Inventory or other reliable and valid client self-report assessment scales as part of the comprehensive evaluation (Aalto, Elovainio, Kivimäki, Uutela, & Pirkola, 2012).

The social worker completed Carlos's assessment prior to his receiving psychopharmacology as indicated by his prescribing provider and psychoeducation services provided by his social worker, who in this context is acting as a case manager and not as a psychotherapist, as follows. Identifying information: Carlos is a 53-year-old Mexican American heterosexual male who is married with three adult children. Setting: Carlos is receiving services from the prescribing provider and case management from a social worker at a county mental health agency in Panorama City, California. Reason for referral or presenting problem: Carlos was referred to mental health services by a primary care physician who treated him for his physical symptoms. Carlos is aware he is depressed and that he has coped poorly in the past. Historically, the stigma of mental illness from his Mexican American cultural viewpoint added barriers to him seeking services (Cooper et al., 2003), as did his military history (Hoge et al., 2004). However, due to the current severity of his symptoms, Carlos is eager to begin treatment and has set aside any reservations he may have once had about mental health interventions. The fact he had sought services in the past for his alcohol use made facilitating access to service this second time around a more efficient process due, in part, to the exposure to psychoeducation intervention. Client's description and functioning: Carlos is a shorter than average, stocky, well-groomed, but at times malodorous, man who makes good eye contact with his care providers. He is polite and smiles during the first meeting with the mental health team. His affect is blunted and his speech is often slow. He appears to struggle at times with effective communication and interpersonal skills. He reports being able to discuss things with his wife and adult children—for example, the struggles he has with depression and his need to seek services at the clinic—although doing so is difficult for him. Carlos is of average intelligence and endorses forgetfulness at times. Physical and economic environment: Carlos was recently fired from his place of employment, where he worked as a supervisor in a media distribution warehouse. He currently lives with his wife, who earns minimal income. He is currently uninsured due to the loss of employment, but he is eligible for services at the local county mental health agency and through the local Department of Veterans Affairs (VA); however, the client is not choosing to participate in VA services at this time. He and his wife own their home in a neighborhood in Los Angeles County that has a large Latino population. Carlos reports that there are stores, restaurants, and services that reflect his culture in the immediate vicinity of his home. Social functioning (per client's self-report or secondary input): Carlos's family describes him as being withdrawn. He reports no history of abuse (child or domestic) and is very clear that he is never physically violent. He states that he grew up in a household where he witnessed his uncle being violent against his grandmother, and that Carlos could never lift a finger against anyone. Carlos has not been attending Catholic mass lately; in the past he had found comfort and a sense of community there. He currently struggles with maintaining social relationships due to his depression. He has lost virtually all his co-worker friendships since being laid off from his employment. Personal and family history relevant to current focus: Carlos currently smokes daily and consumes a small amount of alcohol weekly. There is a family history of alcohol abuse with his father and paternal uncles, as well as his own history of alcohol abuse and witnessing domestic violence. He does report his own history of alcohol abuse quite readily during the assessment phase of treatment. He has been married for 32 years and appears to have successfully met all of his biopsychosocial developmental milestones. Psychological functioning and mental status (note strengths and limitations): Carlos is alert and oriented to person, place, time, and situation. He presented with mood and behavioral indicators of major depression. Emotional functioning: His speech is slow and affect is blunted at times. His insight, impulse control, and judgment are fair. Behavioral

functioning in relation to past alcohol use: Carlos is not abusing alcohol currently, but the service providers must consider his past abuse of alcohol. Environmental issues and constraints affecting the situation: Carlos has the means to transport himself to appointments, but due to his current cognitive state his wife has been driving him. Some cultural barriers affecting treatment have been overcome, as his insight into the severity of his symptoms has propelled Carlos into action. Motivation for change and commitment to services: Carlos appears highly motivated to get better, and he is supported by the commitment of his immediate family as well. Carlos arrived for the initial appointment with his providers ahead of time and with all of the required paperwork already filled out. Social worker's understanding of the presenting problem: The social worker and the multidisciplinary treatment team (including the treating psychologist and psychiatrist) have diagnosed Carlos with 296.32 Major Depressive Disorder, Moderate, Recurrent Episode (APA, 2013).

Diversity Considerations

As discussed earlier, culture should always be considered when gathering a client's history, making an assessment, setting goals, and planning for intervention. In mental health and health systems, the treatment team often views the social worker as the cultural competency expert (Canda & Furman, 2009). Cultural competence is also a standard for professional social work practice (National Association of Social Workers [NASW], 2008).

Social workers consider diversity to include "sociocultural experiences of people of different genders, social classes, religious and spiritual beliefs, sexual orientations, ages, and physical and mental abilities" (NASW, 2008, p. 8). Culture, age, ethnicity, and other diversity issues often dictate how a client conceptualizes his or her mental illness and physical health and inform how a client will proceed with treatment (SAMHSA, 2011). For example, some individuals' cultures do not favor medications as a treatment option (SAMHSA, 2011).

Living with mental illness is an extremely important diversity consideration in that there may be cultural explanations for mental illness and interventions that do not necessarily align with Western medicine. Additionally, how an individual may be marginalized and experience microaggressions (MAs) in multiple systems, such as in the workplace or in school, is often not considered during assessment at a mental health services agency. MAs include unintended discrimination against marginalized groups (Suárez-Orozco et al., 2015). MAs are commonplace, occurring in a blink of an eye, and can include verbal, behavioral, or environmental indignities (whether intentional or unintentional). MAs "communicate hostile, derogatory, or negative . . . slights and insults" to members of minority groups (Sue et al., 2007, p. 271). Research is beginning to indicate that MAs have negative emotional, cognitive, and behavioral implications for their victims (Suárez-Orozco et al., 2015). Carlos is both a veteran and suffers from mental illness—both considered vulnerable groups that are often the target of microaggressions. Consideration of a client's spiritual community and culture is also essential when considering diversity because cultural bias on the part of the provider affects the quality of client care (Boyle & Springer, 2001). Having an understanding of a client's culture and spirituality strengthens the support between client and provider, which improves treatment outcomes (Boyle & Springer, 2001). In Carlos's case, the social worker must be aware of his Christian faith—specifically, Catholicism—and consider whether he holds any spiritual beliefs that may influence his treatment (Canda & Furman, 2009). Finally, it is extremely important for the social worker to understand the military culture and the history of Carlos's prior military service as this may impact his worldview (Coll, Weiss, & Metal, 2013).

Intervention: Psychopharmacology, Case Management, and Psychoeducation

Psychopharmacology, case management, and psychoeducation are proven effective interventions when working with clients with MDD (Preston & Johnson, 2012). Social workers are also encouraged to implement treatment plans that maximize autonomy and self-determination in clients with MDD (NASW, 2008). Together, these elements comprise part of the evidence-based practice: the integration of the best research evidence with clinical expertise and client values (Institute of Medicine, 2001).

Psychoeducation

When antidepressant medications are used to treat the symptoms of depression, this psychopharmacological intervention is provided by a licensed professional trained in prescribing medications (SAMHSA, 2011). Social workers then become a critical component on the treatment team when they provide psychoeducation in conjunction with psychopharmacological case management from a qualified prescribing provider.

It is noteworthy to state that one of the most effective combinations of interventions is psychopharmacology in conjunction with psychotherapy, which is supported by the literature on the treatment of MDD (Casacalenda, Perry, & Looper, 2002). Psychotherapy could include Cognitive Behavioral Therapy (CBT). CBT is one of the most effective interventions for treating MDD. Studies show that antidepressant medication and psychotherapy are almost twice as efficacious as control conditions in producing full remission in outpatients with MDD (Casacalenda et al., 2002). However, this chapter will highlight the role of the social worker providing case management services rather than rendering a full description of the application of CBT, as CBT is discussed in greater depth in other chapters of this book. In this particular scenario, it is understood that Carlos would receive CBT from the psychologist who is part of the treatment team.

Psychoeducation combines education and other activities, such as counseling and supportive interventions (Preston & Johnson, 2012). Psychoeducational interventions are typically delivered in a therapeutic setting or during a home visit conducted by the social worker, but they can also be delivered online; telephonically; or via pamphlets, videos, or podcasts. Psychiatry.org is an excellent example of an online interactive resource a social worker might refer a client to for more information on depression. The intervention may be tailored or standardized. It may also be delivered in the format of group or family intervention, such as a psychoeducation group for newly diagnosed individuals. Psychiatry.org could be an effective educational resource for Carlos as the site has information specific to the Latino community dealing with depression (www.psychiatry.org/mental-health/people/hispanics-latinos).

Psychoeducation generally includes providing clients with information pertaining to treatments, symptoms, resources, and services. It can also include training to provide care and respond to disease-related problems, such as HIV/AIDS or diabetes, and problem-solving strategies for coping with diseases like cancer. Research on psychoeducational interventions tends to vary substantially in specific content, format, frequency, and timing of the interventions (Preston & Johnson, 2012). This is due, in part, to the wide application of the intervention in treating so many clinical issues in health and mental health. Although a strength of the intervention, this becomes a challenging limitation with the research surrounding psychoeducation. Psychoeducation is generally considered one of the most prominent evidence-based practices (EBP) in the field of social work (Bellamy, Bledsoe, & Traube, 2006).

The social worker intervening with Carlos would utilize the intervention of psychoeducation within a clinical case management framework. Carlos would also benefit from either short-term or long-term cognitive behavioral therapy (CBT). As previously mentioned, in the context of this vignette, the social worker is referring out for CBT and is currently only providing Carlos with clinical case management and psychoeducation. It is important to note that the social worker would be working as part of a multidisciplinary team to treat Carlos. The nature of case management is different depending on the provider's scope of practice. Treatment goals include decreasing Carlos's depressive symptoms. Because prescribing psychopharmacology as an intervention is outside the scope of a social worker's practice, he or she would collaborate to provide ancillary interventions alongside a competent medical provider. Medical providers able to prescribe Carlos an antidepressant and provide psychopharmacological case management or medication management include a psychiatrist (MD), primary medical doctor (MD), nurse practitioner (NP), psychiatric mental health nurse practitioner (PMHNP), physician's assistant (PA), or a licensed prescribing psychologist (PsyD/PhD). "Psychologists are able to prescribe medications in the military and the Indian Health Service as well as in Louisiana and New Mexico. Professional psychologists gained prescribing privileges in New Mexico in 2002 and in Louisiana in 2004" (Cherry, 2015, para. 2). If a client were not already connected to one of these types of providers, then a goal of treatment would be for the social worker to provide a referral. These actions are based on the social worker's assessment of the client's depression. In the case of Carlos, his depressive symptoms were severe enough to warrant psychopharmacological intervention as deemed appropriate by his prescribing provider. Psychoeducation is an intervention not only applicable to the interventions provided by the treating social worker, but it is also an intervention employed by the other treating members of the multidisciplinary team.

Psychoeducation incorporates both illness-specific information and tools for managing related circumstances, such as MDD, making the model extremely flexible. Psychoeducation has broad potential for many forms of illnesses and varied life challenges (Lukens & McFarlane, 2004).

Psychoeducation assimilates a dynamic combination of psychotherapeutic and educational interventions. It is a professionally delivered treatment modality. According to Lukens and McFarlane (2004):

Forms of psychosocial intervention are based on traditional medical models designed to treat pathology, illness, liability, and dysfunction. In contrast, psychoeducation reflects a paradigm shift to a more holistic and competence-based approach, stressing health, collaboration, coping, and empowerment. It is based on strengths and focused on the present. The client and/or family are considered partners with the provider in treatment, on the premise that the more knowledgeable the care recipients and informal caregivers are, the more positive health-related outcomes will be for all. To prepare participants for this partnership, psychoeducational techniques are used to help remove barriers to comprehending and digesting complex and emotionally loaded information and to develop strategies to use the information in a proactive fashion. The assumption is that when people confront major life challenges or illnesses, their functioning and focus is naturally disrupted. (p. 206)

Ecological systems theory, cognitive behavioral theory, learning theory, group practice models, stress and coping models, social support models, and narrative approaches are all complementary theories and models of clinical practice that can be integrated with psychoeducation (McFarlane, Dixon, Lukens, & Lucksted, 2003). Bronfenbrenner's (1979) ecological systems theory provides the framework for assessing and helping people understand their mental health diagnosis of MDD. Other systems in a client's life, for example significant others, family, school, health care organizations, and policy makers, are more thoroughly understood from this theory's framework. Individuals, families, groups, or communities are all systems for which psychoeducation can be adapted (Lukens & McFarlane, 2004). "There is significant evidence that psychoeducational interventions are associated with improved functioning and quality of life, decreased symptomatology, and positive outcomes for both the person with illness and family members as well" (p. 208).

Psychopharmacology

Psychopharmacological intervention in this case involves antidepressant medications that are prescribed by a health care practitioner who regularly monitors the client and adjusts the medication dosage accordingly. Although the role of social workers is not to provide the medication, it is their role to monitor the effects and effectiveness of the medication on the client and to follow the client for medication compliance. A variety of types of antidepressant medications can reduce symptoms of depression for clients. As discussed earlier, SSRIs are often effective in treating depression. TCAs are an older and sometimes less expensive type of medicine for depression. MAOIs are another group of older antidepressant medications that are rarely prescribed due to dietary restrictions and complications, and only in situations when other antidepressants have failed. Other non-SSRI antidepressants include duloxetine (e.g., Cymbalta), trazadone (e.g., Desyrel), venlafaxine (e.g., Effexor), nefazodone (e.g., Serzone), mirtazapine (e.g., Remeron), and bupropion (e.g., Wellbutrin; SAMHSA, 2011). In this case, Carlos was prescribed 20 mg of fluoxetine (Prozac).

Transference and Countertransference Issues

The management of transference and countertransference issues while working with individuals with MDD taking psychotropic medications is essential. Certain issues are more salient when engaging with this population. Transference is the client's unconscious tendency to assign to others in one's present environment feelings and attitudes associated with people in one's early life. Transference is associated with the client's reaction to the treating provider. Alternatively, countertransference is the conscious or unconscious, positive or negative emotional response of a social worker to a client (Jung, 1946/2013).

Potential transference issues for Carlos could involve his experience with medical and mental health providers. The age, gender identity and expression, and race/ethnicity/culture of the social worker providing services to Carlos could also be themes for potential transference issues. For example, if there was a large gap in age between the provider and Carlos, a transference around age could occur. With a younger provider, Carlos might feel a transference around the provider reminding him of one of his children. On the other hand, being a heterosexual male and his Mexican American identity could all give rise to a countertransference reaction by the social worker, depending on the social worker's ethnic and sexual identities (if these differ from the client's). Additionally, if there is a gap in knowledge related to a client's ethnic history and culture, then it is the responsibility of the social worker to gain education and attain cultural competency. The social worker could also experience countertransference around the issue of depression. For example, if Carlos's social worker had someone in his or her family with a history of depression or someone who has taken an antidepressant medication, he or she may potentially over-identify with Carlos.

Legal and Ethical Concerns

Social workers should look to the NASW Code of Ethics for information about working with clients diagnosed with MDD and who are taking psychotropic medications (NASW, 2008). Social workers must consider the ethical principle of autonomy. Autonomy is the client's right to refuse and/or determine treatment. Often clients taking medication may decide to discontinue it without medical consent or against medical advice. It is the social worker's goal to continue to assist the client in maintaining his or her autonomy, despite potentially contradictory directives from attending professionals (Britten, Riley, & Morgan, 2010). In these situations, discussing the risks and benefits of the decision with the client can help him or her reach an informed and well-thought-out decision.

The collaboration with other professionals in the treatment of clients with MDD leads to another legal concern for social workers. Social workers have a strict legal obligation to maintain client confidentiality. When working as part of a multidisciplinary team, social workers must obtain written legal consent to exchange information with other providers. This ensures compliance with the Health Insurance Portability and Accountability Act (HIPAA) regulations concerning the exchange of confidential and protected patient records. In the case of Carlos, a social worker should obtain a legal consent for each provider working on his team, particularly if the providers are from outside agencies. This release to exchange information typically expires one year from the date it was signed by the client. A release must be obtained specific to each professional or agency/organization with whom the social worker wishes to discuss Carlos's case information (Dolgoff, Harrington, & Loewenberg, 2011). Typically, if both the social worker and prescribing mental health professional operate under the same treatment facility umbrella, informed consent is obtained for all treating professionals at the time of intake. Obtaining releases to exchange medical and mental health information is most necessary when members of the multidisciplinary team are interfacing from different systems (e.g., a social worker in private practice coordinating care for Carlos with a psychiatrist based in another county mental health clinic). The ethical practices just highlighted are considered to be essential components of the ethical social work practice of maintaining client confidentiality, as outlined in the NASW Code of Ethics (NASW, 2008).

With a client who uses psychotropic medications, social workers should monitor the potential for suicidal ideation or the abuse of medications. When a client presents as actively suicidal, with a plan and the means with which to complete the action, social workers are legally mandated to take action to ensure the safety of their client, including breaking the client's confidentiality, if necessary (Dolgoff et al., 2011). Typically, having a client voluntarily commit himself or herself to the hospital or inpatient setting is the best course of action. Often, though, clients are resistant to voluntary commitment, and when this occurs a social worker must take the steps to have a client involuntarily committed. This action typically involves notifying a Psychiatric Emergency Team (PET), if such a service exists, or contacting the local police department (Walsh, 2012).

MEZZO PERSPECTIVE

Depression impacts the client and the client's family as well (Schulz & Martire, 2004). This makes sense when you view treatment from a systems theory perspective (Rintala, Jaatinen, Paavilainen, & Astedt-Kurki, 2013). A central tenet of systems theory is that systems self-regulate; that is, they self-correct through the use of feedback (Rintala et al., 2013). Families can benefit from assistance with this self-regulation and adjustment process. For example, Carlos's family is already supportive and fully invested in a positive treatment outcome for him. After Carlos's assessment and development of a treatment plan, the social worker could facilitate change and adjustment within the family by initiating a discussion with the family (with Carlos's agreement and written consent) regarding its limitations, barriers, stressors, support, and understanding of Carlos's condition (Rintala et al., 2013).

Families are complex in that they are diverse and composed of multiple, interconnected elements (e.g., children, parents, grandparents, aunts, extended family members, and kinship systems) that may play a role in the success of a client's recovery. According to Schulz and Martire (2004), families are also adaptable in that they have the capacity to change and learn from experiences and, in this way, aid in the prevention of relapse. Social workers' case management should include the consideration of the impact of the mental illness on the family and the provision of psychoeducation for the family on the disorder and the treatment. The family should know what to expect and how to best support the client. Carlos is also part of a Christian faith community. Helping Carlos to access support from his religious community is another example of a mezzo-level intervention that could increase his resiliency.

MACRO PERSPECTIVE

The Equal Employment Opportunity Commission was established by Title VII of the Civil Rights Act of 1964 to assist in the protection of U.S. employees from discrimination. It was the first federal law designed to protect most U.S. employees from employment discrimination based upon that employee's (or applicant's) race, color, religion, sex, or national origin. Along with those five protected classes, more recent statutes have protected other classes, including employees aged 40 and older (via the Age Discrimination Act of 1967; U.S. Equal Employment Opportunity Commission, 2012). Carlos is worried that he will be discriminated against in the workplace based on the mental illness he suffers from. The Americans With Disabilities Act (ADA) of 1990 outlaws discrimination based on disability, such as Carlo's MDD. The ADA affords similar protections against discrimination as the Civil Rights Act of 1964 (Fitzpatrick, 2013).

Carlos is 53 years old and is attempting to re-enter the work force. He is recovering from a major depressive episode. He has had three job interviews but no offers, and everyone he interviewed with was half his age and with more education. Carlos continues to feel hopeless, but his symptoms are gradually improving. Symptom improvements are concrete evidence of the effectiveness of a combination of psychoeducational, psychopharmacological, and psychotherapeutic interventions. As improvement continues, the prescribing provider will continue psychopharmacological case management with Carlos, to be reassessed for ongoing need. Interactions with the social worker may move into the maintenance phase, requiring Carlos to check in with the social worker as needed or even terminate services if this is a mutually agreed-upon goal between the client and social worker.

CONCLUSION

When working with clients taking psychotropic medications for MDD, a social worker should complete a comprehensive biopsychosocial assessment that incorporates diversity and devise culturally appropriate interventions, like psychoeducation, with clients as well as EBPs such as psychotropic medication and psychotherapy because these have been shown to be essential in comprehensive care (Boyle & Springer, 2001). A social worker should also have a solid grasp of the signs and symptoms of depressive disorders. By expanding their knowledge of neurobiology and the action of psychotropic medication, social workers can better take biological factors into consideration in their assessment and provide more competent psychoeducation and case management services and be able to effectively work within an interdisciplinary team. Throughout the treatment process, social workers should recognize and address transference and countertransference issues, as well as any legal and ethical concerns.

INTERNET RESOURCES

- American Psychological Association: http://www.apa.org/helpcenter/understanding-depression.aspx
- National Institute of Mental Health: http://www.nimh.nih.gov/health/topics/depression/index.shtml; http://www.nimh.nih.gov/health/publications/mental-health-medications/index.shtml
- The Mayo Clinic: http://www.mayoclinic.org/diseases-conditions/depression/basics/symptoms/con-20032977
- American Psychiatric Association Online Assessment Measurements: http://www.psychiatry.org
- Web MD Depression Help Center: http://www.webmd.com
- National Association of Social Workers: http://www.naswdc.org

DISCUSSION QUESTIONS

1. Describe the general effect an antidepressant medication has on the biopsychosocial functioning of a client with Major Depressive Disorder, and name five commonly prescribed antidepressant medications.

2. Name three points you would consider covering when providing Carlos with psychoeducation.

3. What are the legal and ethical considerations a social worker must be aware of when treating a depressed client who is taking psychotropic medications?

4. Acknowledge two potential countertransference issues when working with a client who identifies as a heterosexual Mexican American male.

5. Conduct an Internet search and identify the closest county or state mental health counseling and treatment facility to your residence.

REFERENCES

Aalto, A. M., Elovainio, M., Kivimäki, M., Uutela, A., & Pirkola, S. (2012). The Beck Depression Inventory and General Health Questionnaire as measures of depression in the general population: a validation study using the Composite International Diagnostic Interview as the gold standard. *Psychiatry Research*, *197*(1), 163–171.

Alwan, S., Reefhuis, J., Rasmussen, S. A., Olney, R. S., & Friedman, J. M. (2007). Use of selective serotonin-reuptake inhibitors in pregnancy and the risk of birth defects. *New England Journal of Medicine*, *356*(26), 2684–2692.

American Psychiatric Association. (2013). *Diagnostic and statistical manual of mental disorders, fifth edition.* Washington, DC: Author.

Becker, J., & Kleinman, A. (Eds.). (2013). *Psychosocial aspects of depression.* New York, NY: Routledge.

Bellamy, J. L., Bledsoe, S. E., & Traube, D. E. (2006). The current state of evidence-based practice in social work: A review of the literature and qualitative analysis of expert interviews. *Journal of Evidence-Based Social Work*, *3*(1), 23–48.

Bender, J. (2012). *Frontline psych with Doc Bender: The reality of depression.* Retrieved from http://www.dcoe.mil/blog/12-10-25/Frontline_Psych_with_Doc_Bender_The_Reality_of_Depression.aspx

Biological Sciences Curriculum Study. (2010). Neurons, brain chemistry, and neurotransmission. In *The brain: Understanding neurobiology through the study of addiction.* Retrieved from http://science.education.nih.gov/supplements/nih2/addiction/guide/pdfs/lesson2.pdf

Boyer, E. W., & Shannon, M. (2005). The serotonin syndrome. *New England Journal of Medicine*, *352*(11), 1112–1120.

Boyle, D. P., & Springer, A. (2001). Toward a cultural competence measure for social work with specific populations. *Journal of Ethnic and Cultural Diversity in Social Work, 9*(3/4), 53–71.

Britten, N., Riley, R., & Morgan, M. (2010). Resisting psychotropic medicines: A synthesis of qualitative studies of medicine-taking. *Advances in Psychiatric Treatment, 16*(3), 207–218.

Bronfenbrenner, U. (1979). *The ecology of human development: Experiments by nature and design.* Cambridge, MA: Harvard University Press.

Canda, E. R., & Furman, L. D. (2009). *Spiritual diversity in social work practice: The heart of helping.* Oxford, UK: Oxford University Press.

Carlant, D. J. (1998). The psychiatric review of symptoms: A screening tool for family physicians. *American Family Physician, 58*(7), 1617–1624.

Casacalenda, N., Perry, J. C., & Looper, K. (2002). Remission in major depressive disorder: A comparison of pharmacotherapy, psychotherapy, and control conditions. *American Journal of Psychiatry, 159*(8), 1354–1360.

Cherry, K. (2015). Can psychologists prescribe medications? *About.com.* Retrieved from http://www.psychology.about.com/od/psychotherapy/f/can-psychologists-prescribe-medications.htm

Coll, J. E., Weiss, E. L., & Metal, M. (2013). Military culture and diversity. In A. Rubin, E. L. Weiss, & J. E. Coll (Eds.), *Handbook of military social work* (pp. 21–36). Hoboken, NJ: Wiley & Sons.

Cooper, L. A., Gonzales, J. J., Gallo, J. J., Rost, K. M., Meredith, L. S., Rubenstein, L. V., . . . & Ford, D. E. (2003). The acceptability of treatment for depression among African-American, Hispanic, and white primary care patients. *Medical Care, 41*(4), 479–489.

Davidson, J. R. (2010). Major depressive disorder treatment guidelines in America and Europe. *Journal of Clinical Psychiatry, 71*(E1), 4.

Delgado, P. L. (2000). Depression: The case for a monoamine deficiency. *Journal of Clinical Psychiatry, 61*(6), 7–11.

der Does, V., & Willem, A. J. (2001). The effects of tryptophan depletion on mood and psychiatric symptoms. *Journal of Affective Disorders, 64*(2), 107–119.

Dolgoff, R., Harrington, D., & Loewenberg, F. (2011). *Brooks/Cole empowerment series: Ethical decisions for social work practice.* Boston, MA: Cengage Learning.

Drake, M. (2015). Persistent complex bereavement disorder DSM-5. *Therapedia.* Retrieved from http://www.theravive.com/therapedia/Persistent-Complex-Bereavement-Disorder-DSM--5

Ferguson, J. M. (2001). SSRI antidepressant medications: Adverse effects and tolerability. *Primary Care Companion to the Journal of Clinical Psychiatry, 3*(1), 22.

Fitzpatrick, R. B. (2013). Americans with Disabilities Act of 1990. *Journal of the National Association of Administrative Law Judiciary, 11*(1), 2.

Hensler, J. G. (2006). Serotonergic modulation of the limbic system. *Neuroscience Biobehavioral Review, 30*(2), 203–214.

Hoge, C. W., Castro, C. A., Messer, S. C., McGurk, D., Cotting, D. I., & Koffman, R. L. (2004). Combat duty in Iraq and Afghanistan: Mental health problems and barriers to care. *New England Journal of Medicine, 351*(1), 13–22.

Institute of Medicine, Committee on Quality of Health Care in America. (2001). *Crossing the quality chasm: A new health system for the 21st century.* Washington, DC: National Academies Press.

Jung, C. G. (2013). An account of the transference phenomena based on the illustrations to the "rosarium philosophorum." *The Psychology of the Transference.* Abingdon, UK: Routledge. (Original work published 1946)

Lukens, E. P., & McFarlane, W. R. (2004). Psychoeducation as evidence-based practice: Considerations for practice, research, and policy. *Brief Treatment and Crisis Intervention, 4*(3), 205.

McFarlane, W. R., Dixon, L., Lukens, E., & Lucksted, A. (2003). Family psychoeducation and schizophrenia: A review of the literature. *Journal of Marital and Family Therapy, 29*(2), 223–245.

National Association of Social Workers. (2008). *Code of ethics of the National Association of Social Workers.* Washington, DC: Author.

National Institute of Mental Health. (2001). *Mental health: Culture, race, and ethnicity.* Retrieved from http://www.ncbi.nlm.nih.gov/books/NBK44251/

National Institute of Mental Health. (2012). *Major depression among adults.* Retrieved from http://

www.nimh.nih.gov/health/statistics/prevalence/major-depression-among-adults.shtml

Oberlander, T. F., Warburton, W., Misir, S., Aghajanian, J., & Hertzman, C. (2006). Neonatal outcomes after prenatal exposure to selective serotonin reuptake inhibitor antidepressants and maternal depression using population-based linked health data. *Archives of General Psychiatry, 63*(8), 898–906.

Preston, J. D., & Johnson, J. (2012). *Clinical psychopharmacology made ridiculously simple.* Miami, FL: MedMaster.

Rintala, T. M., Jaatinen, P., Paavilainen, E., & Astedt-Kurki, P. (2013). Interrelation between adult persons with diabetes and their family: A systematic review of the literature. *Journal of Family Nursing, 19,* 3–21.

Roberts, A. R., & Greene, G. J. (Eds.). (2002). *Social workers' desk reference.* New York, NY: Oxford University Press.

Schulz, R., & Martire, L. M. (2004). Family caregiving of persons with dementia: Prevalence, health effects, and support strategies. *The American Journal of Geriatric Psychiatry, 12*(3), 240–249.

Stahl, S. M. (2009). *Stahl's illustrated antidepressants.* Cambridge, MA: Cambridge University Press.

Suárez-Orozco, C., Casanova, S., Martin, M., Katsiaficas, D., Cuellar, V., Smith, N. A., & Dias, S. I. (2015). Toxic rain in class: Classroom interpersonal microaggressions. *Educational Researcher, 44*(3), 151–160. doi: 10.3102/0013189X15580314

Substance Abuse and Mental Health Services Administration, U.S. Department of Health and Human Services. (2011). *The treatment of depression in older adults: Selecting evidence-based practices for treatment of depression in older adults.* HHS Pub. No. SMA-11-4631. Rockville, MD: Center for Mental Health Services.

Sue, D. W., Capodilupo, C. M., Torino, G. C., Bucceri, J. M., Holder, A. M. B., Nadal, K. L., & Esquilin, M. (2007). Racial microaggressions in everyday life: Implications for clinical practice. *American Psychologist, 62*(4), 271–286. doi: 10.1037/0003-066X.62.4.271

U.S. Equal Employment Opportunity Commission. (2012). The Age Discrimination in Employment Act 1967 (ADEA). http://www.eeoc.gov/laws/types/age.cfm

Walsh, B. W. (2012). *Treating self-injury: A practical guide.* New York, NY: Guilford Press.

Wassertheil-Smoller, S., Arredondo, E. M., Cai, J., Castaneda, S. F., Choca, J. P., Gallo, L. C., . . . Zee, P. C. (2014). Depression, anxiety, antidepressant use, and cardiovascular disease among Hispanic men and women of different national backgrounds: Results from the Hispanic Community Health Study/Study of Latinos. *Annals of Epidemiology, 24*(11), 822–830.

CHAPTER 6

Mindfulness in Mental Health Care Settings

Jim Hjort

CHAPTER OBJECTIVES

- Understand the origin of mindfulness meditation practice and its key concepts;
- Learn clinical best practices concerning the implementation of mindfulness-based practices in populations of people with mental illness;
- Review mindfulness-based practices and two well-known mindfulness-based therapies and their evidence base;
- Identify resources for further research, education, and training for clinicians interested in using mindfulness-based practices in their work;
- Explore some of the economic and sociocultural factors influencing the availability of mindfulness-based practices to clients.

CASE VIGNETTE

Robert is a 52-year-old Caucasian man who had a troubled childhood, including long-term sexual abuse by two uncles and an emotionally distant mother. As an adult, he has had several long-term but volatile romantic relationships with women that were characterized by reciprocal emotional abuse. He often displays poor judgment and inappropriate anger.

He was fired three years ago after he threw a picture frame at his supervisor during a dispute regarding his work schedule. He stopped looking for new employment after a few months and began spending his days alone at home. He was hospitalized for suicidality two years ago and began treatment at a public mental health agency shortly thereafter, on the advice of his physician. He was hospitalized again for suicidality nine months ago.

INTRODUCTION

Mindfulness-based practices (MBPs) are based upon meditation techniques that derive from Buddhist meditation practices (Kabat-Zinn, 2003). The practice of mindfulness meditation involves cultivating concentration and awareness of internal and external experiences in a particular way (Baer, 2003). As Kabat-Zinn (2003) stated, "Mindfulness is the awareness that emerges through paying attention on purpose, in the present moment, and nonjudgmentally to the unfolding of experience moment by moment" (p. 145). While initially using a fixed object of concentration such as the breath, meditators are gradually advised to expand their field of awareness and observation to include all physical, emotional, and cognitive events (including thinking, daydreaming, remembering, and the like) as they occur (or not) in each moment (Kabat-Zinn, 1982). The practice is deceptively simple because the meditator's mind tends to become caught up by thoughts and emotions and drift away from present-moment observation. Once a meditator becomes aware that this has occurred, he or she is encouraged to reacquire awareness of the present moment.

A meditator's close observation of his or her present-moment experience can reveal important lessons firsthand. These include the innate transience of negative thoughts and experiences, the tendency to identify with thoughts despite their inherent insubstantiality, and how, in the long run, facing them can reduce the impact of their unpleasantness on one's mood and ability to experience satisfaction with life. It is knowledge that must be gained experientially. However, a person does not exist in a vacuum. The cultivation of mindfulness in the individual is affected by sociocultural factors and mezzo and macro systems and, inasmuch as those systems are composed of individuals, mindfulness practice has the potential to influence them in return.

Blending mindfulness with psychoeducation and psychotherapeutic techniques as mindfulness-based therapies (MBTs), which are typically manualized, can produce benefits that are helpful to people with certain mental health problems, including depression, substance abuse, anxiety, and Borderline Personality Disorder (BPD; Baer, 2003). However, it is important to note that the value of mindfulness is by no means restricted to clinical populations, just as the benefits of a healthy diet and exercise are not limited to people with heart disease or obesity.

Indeed, regardless of whether clinical goals exist, mindfulness meditation itself is, rather paradoxically, practiced without the intention of achieving a different state or experience (Baer, 2003). It is the emphasis on acceptance of one's experience and adopting a neutral stance toward physical and mental functions, and the corresponding deemphasis on making change, that produces positive change in meditation practitioners. Mindfulness-based practices can provide significant benefits to nearly anyone who undertakes them, including reduced feelings of anxiety and depression (Shapiro, Schwartz, & Bonner, 1998), more positive emotional states in general (Brown & Ryan, 2003), and more robust immune system function (Davidson et al., 2003).

Theoretical Underpinnings

The researchers and developers of MBTs have put forth numerous hypotheses for the mechanisms by which the benefits of mindfulness meditation practice are realized. For instance, in meditators with chronic pain, the benefit may arise from being exposed to the painful sensations and then observing that nothing dire follows (Baer, 2003). This mechanism can be extrapolated to include any physical or emotional discomfort. That is, by reducing the anticipation of, and adversarial stance toward, unpleasant experiences, the subjective experience of these can improve. Others note that an individual's attitude toward his or her thoughts may change with sustained meditation practice. As a result, thoughts, feelings, impulses, and urges are increasingly seen as transitory phenomena, and an individual begins to stop taking thought content as the unassailable truth about an individual's self or situation (Frewen, Elspeth, Maraj, Dozois, & Partridge, 2008), thus alleviating the psychological suffering that may arise from repetitive negative thought patterns.

As a corollary, other researchers have pointed out that a person's de-identification with his or her thoughts expands the range of potential responses to them, which can yield increased feelings of control (Kabat-Zinn et al., 1992) and self-efficacy (Kabat-Zinn, 1990). By learning to observe the cognitive and emotional activity of his or her mind, a meditator learns to tolerate negative feelings rather than reacting to them in a reflexive and maladaptive way, and he or she gains the ability and opportunity to consider and employ more effective ways of coping with them (Baer, 2003).

Literature Review

As the first MBT to be introduced, Mindfulness-Based Stress Reduction (MBSR) is among the most extensively studied interventions. In his original 1982 research, Kabat-Zinn found that participants enjoyed significant pain reduction (50% reported 33% or greater reduction in pain, and between 35% and 50% of participants reported 50% or greater improvement) and similarly significant improvement in total medical symptoms. Their symptoms of depression, anxiety, obsessive-compulsive behavior, and somatization also improved (Kabat-Zinn, 1982). Later studies focused specifically on mental health disorders and found similar results (Kabat-Zinn et al., 1992), which were sustained at three years (Miller, Fletcher, & Kabat-Zinn, 1995). Later studies have produced similar findings with respect to MBSR's benefits in reducing stress, anxiety, and rumination (Khoury et al., 2013; Zainal, Booth, & Huppert, 2012) and even increasing empathy and self-compassion (Chiesa & Serretti, 2009).

In studies of another widely studied intervention, Dialectical Behavior Therapy (DBT), (which will be discussed in greater detail later) participants tend to experience lower rates of suicidal and parasuicidal behavior (Linehan et al., 2006; Verheul et al., 2003)

and improvements in anger, depressive symptoms, interpersonal functioning, and overall quality of life (McMain, Guimond, Streiner, Cardish, & Links, 2012; McMain et al., 2009). Evidence also suggests that DBT is effective in treating substance dependence among those with co-occurring BPD (Dimeff, Rizvi, Brown, & Linehan, 2000; Linehan et al., 2002; Linehan et al., 1999).

The preceding interventions are two of the better-known MBTs, and they have been the focus of much of the research interest in the past 30 years. However, it is important to highlight that the therapeutic benefits of MBTs are not necessarily restricted to the disorders for which they were developed. For example, recent research has continued to support the effectiveness of both MBSR and Mindfulness-Based Cognitive Therapy (MBCT) in reducing anxiety disorder symptoms (Arch et al., 2013; Craigie, Rees, & Marsh, 2008; Evans et al., 2008), possibly because they address maladaptive processes that negatively impact well-being in general and are salient in a variety of disorders (Hofmann, Sawyer, Witt, & Oh, 2010).

Furthermore, evidence suggests that the practice of mindfulness meditation itself, without any particular therapeutic goal, provides psychological benefits (Brown & Ryan, 2003; Friese, Messner, & Schaffner, 2012). Using functional magnetic resonance imaging (fMRI), researchers have observed changes in brain activity patterns consistent with some of the observed differences in more mindful people. These include an improved subjective experience of pain (Zeidan et al., 2011), more positive mood (Davidson et al., 2003), the ability to recognize others' emotional states faster, and an improved ability to regulate their own emotional states (Creswell, Way, Eisenberger, & Lieberman, 2007). In findings that particularly energized the field of mindfulness research in recent years, neuroscientists have observed that mindfulness meditation is associated with physical growth of the prefrontal cortex, right anterior insula, and other areas involved in sensory processing, awareness of internal bodily sensations, and attention (Holzel et al., 2007; Lazar et al., 2005).

MICRO CONSIDERATIONS

Assessment

With the exception of MBSR, MBTs were developed with certain mental health diagnoses in mind. For instance, DBT was developed to help people with BPD develop adaptive coping skills for the strong emotional responses that they experience (Linehan, Armstrong, Suarez, Allmon, & Heard, 1991). MBCT was developed to support people recovering from Major Depressive Disorder (MDD; Frewen et al., 2008; Ma & Teasdale, 2004; Segal, Williams, & Teasdale, 2002), while Mindfulness-Based Relapse Prevention is often used with people in recovery from substance dependence or other compulsive or addictive behaviors (Baer, 2003). Mindfulness-Based Stress Reduction is the most generalized MBT because it was developed to help relieve people's suffering, both mental and physical, and develop a greater sense of well-being overall (Kabat-Zinn, 2003).

There is some debate regarding the wisdom of employing MBPs with people actively experiencing positive psychotic symptoms or with a history of them or mania. Some research has revealed worsening manic or psychotic symptoms with meditation (mostly Zen or transcendental meditation, which are not mindfulness meditation; Lustyk, Chowla, Nolan, & Marlatt, 2009; Melbourne Academic Mindfulness Interest Group [MAMIG], 2006). On the other hand, some researchers have found no adverse consequences and have even observed MBPs to help people with psychosis cope better with hallucinations (Davis, Strasburger, & Brown, 2007). In fact, research suggests that some MBTs, such as Acceptance and Commitment Therapy, may be effective adjunctive therapies for use with those individuals suffering from psychoses (Bach, Gaudino, Pankey, Herbert, & Hayes, 2006; Lustyk et al., 2009).

These potential risks and benefits should be considered when deciding whether to use MBPs with a person who is experiencing active psychosis. The policies of a clinician's mental health agency may also influence that decision.

Diversity Considerations

The clinician providing MBPs must face the potential complication of mindfulness meditation being based in the Buddhist tradition. This fact gives some clients pause because they fear that MBPs will be incongruous with their own religious beliefs, if any (MAMIG, 2006). In the interest of making MBPs attractive to as many clients as possible, it is important for a clinician to present MBPs in a secular way, emphasizing the empirical support for them and that people can benefit from them regardless of their spiritual beliefs, if any. Mindfulness-based practices are simply a way for individuals to use and cultivate their inborn capacity for present-moment awareness to help them cope better with the difficulties that may arise in their lives. A closer and more accepting relationship with his or her moment-to-moment experience of life allows a meditation practitioner to disengage from conditioned ways of thinking and *reacting* and be more open to new ways of thinking and *responding* that are less likely to cause future distress.

Application of the Assessment to Robert's Case

Robert's clinician met with him to gather information about his life history and symptoms of mental illness. Based on Robert's interpersonal difficulties, chronic suicidality, mood lability, impulsivity, and explosive outbursts of anger, the clinician gave Robert a diagnosis of BPD. Robert also endorsed symptoms of depression that began around 2 1/2 years ago, which indicated that MDD is a possible secondary diagnosis.

Robert's clinician felt that Robert would be a good candidate for the clinic's DBT program, in which he would learn, among other things, how better to tolerate strong emotions and resolve conflicts in his relationships in a more adaptive fashion than he was used to. There was a waiting list for the DBT program, so his clinician suggested that he attend the clinic's eight-week MBSR course in the meantime. There, he would learn mindfulness meditation skills that would be useful in DBT and also ways to use his awareness to ease his distress when he felt anxious, overly emotional, and depressed.

Despite identifying as a Christian, Robert was not put off by the origins of mindfulness in Buddhist thought. In fact, he was open to trying new things, having already tried several kinds of contemplative practices, including prayer and listening to tapes of visualization meditation exercises, and physical practices such as yoga and tai chi in an attempt "to be more settled," as he put it.

Robert and his clinician met with Robert's psychiatrist to discuss the treatment plan. The psychiatrist agreed with the diagnoses and treatment goals and prescribed Robert an antidepressant medication to treat Robert's depressive symptoms.

Intervention

Competent Deployment of Mindfulness-Based Practices

The ways that thoughts and emotions may cause or exacerbate mental illness, and how mindful awareness might help one cope with them, are relatively straightforward. However, an intellectual, theoretical understanding of mindfulness is not the same as having the experiential understanding of it. It must be practiced to be truly learned.

It is widely held among MBP researchers and advanced practitioners that clinicians providing MBPs should have established mindfulness meditation practices themselves in order to be effective providers (Irving, Dobkin, & Park, 2009; Kabat-Zinn, 2003; MAMIG, 2006; Thompson & Gauntlett-Gilbert, 2008). The clinician employing MBPs who relies upon a manual and lacks a firsthand understanding and experience of mindful awareness is poorly equipped to provide instruction when experiential questions and observations inevitably arise during a client's practice. As stated by Kabat-Zinn (2003), "Without the foundation of personal practice and the embodying . . . of what one is teaching, attempts at mindfulness-based intervention run the risk of becoming caricatures of mindfulness, missing the radical, transformational essence" (p. 150).

Furthermore, the benefits of mindfulness practice (both outside of the therapy room and during sessions), such as improved presence and empathy, can be useful in clinicians' therapeutic relationships with clients (Bien, 2008; Hick, 2008). Using MBPs in clinical settings is a parallel process of growth and insight for client and clinician alike.

The Use of Metaphor

Many clients respond well to the use of metaphor in conveying mindfulness principles. For instance, clients who are frustrated by their mind's seemingly uncontrollable activity during a meditation session can find comfort in the metaphor of the busy mind as a glass of water clouded with silt. There is no way to force the sediment to settle. Rather, the settling is accomplished by simply setting the glass down (e.g., by returning one's attention to the breath) and allowing nature to take its course.

Another example is the metaphor of the "Chinese handcuffs" (Hayes, Strosahl, & Wilson, 1999, p. 104). (For the uninitiated, Chinese handcuffs are toys: woven tubes into which one inserts the fingers. Pulling the fingers apart tightens the grip of the tube; freedom is possible only by relaxing and moving the fingers together.) This metaphor can be helpful in conveying the utility of turning toward and accepting difficulty and the ultimately counterproductive nature of resisting it. Clinicians can be creative in developing metaphors from their own experience, although care should be taken that they can be comprehended readily by the population being served.

Mindfulness-Based Stress Reduction (MBSR)

In 1982, Kabat-Zinn developed and published the first study of MBSR with patients with chronic pain; he also evaluated changes in a number of medical symptoms, mood, and other psychological symptoms. MBSR is formulated as an eight-week program that participants attend for two and one-half to three hours weekly (Davidson et al., 2003). Participants are guided in meditation practices including mindfulness of the breath and body sensations, as well as mindfulness while engaging in other activities, such as walking, eating, and yoga. The program also includes a daylong meditation intensive, psychoeducational material regarding stress and coping skills, and participants are required to meditate daily at home (Kabat-Zinn et al., 1992).

Application of Mindfulness-Based Stress Reduction to Robert's Case

Because of Robert's previous experience with practicing yoga, he especially enjoyed the yoga component of his MBSR class. He was also happy to learn new methods of meditative practice that he could do anywhere. Robert also gained a solid understanding of mindfulness principles and received encouragement to practice mindfulness meditation at home. After completing the class, he chose to begin attending weekly drop-in mindfulness meditation groups at his clinic. In that group, he receives guided instruction in a variety of meditation practices that he can practice at home, and he enjoys having a group of fellow meditators with whom he can exchange ideas.

Robert found a new part-time job one month ago, and he is using techniques that he learned in MBSR to help him keep it. He practices seated meditation at home three or four times per week and tries, at least once daily, to bring present-moment awareness to his activities of daily life. At work he practices using crossing through a doorway as a reminder to be aware of his present-moment experience. As a result, when he enters a different area of his workplace, including his supervisor's office, he does so with a greater sense of acceptance, open-mindedness, and equanimity than he used to.

Dialectical Behavior Therapy (DBT)

Dialectical behavior therapy is a type of cognitive behavioral therapy, combined with principles of mindfulness and acceptance from Zen Buddhism, which was originally conceived by Linehan for use with chronically suicidal clients and was subsequently adapted for use with people with substance abuse problems (Linehan et al., 2002). Currently, although there exist other psychotherapeutic approaches to the treatment of BPD, DBT is currently among the most widely used and studied interventions for individuals diagnosed with BPD. The "dialectics" referred to in DBT relate to both a fundamental worldview that the whole is the sum of interrelated, opposing parts, as well as the approach of the DBT clinician who, through a validating approach with the client, helps clients to accept themselves as they are currently, while encouraging the development of the ability to tolerate change (Linehan, 1993). The intervention is meant to address emotional dysregulation, which Linehan viewed as the underlying cause of BPD, by strengthening clients emotionally and equipping them with adaptive strategies for emotion regulation (Linehan, 1993).

DBT mindfulness exercises are shorter and less formal than in other MBPs. Rather than emphasizing lengthy formal meditation sessions, DBT focuses on practicing ways for clients to bring awareness and distress tolerance to their activities of daily life (Baer & Krietemeyer, 2006). It includes several treatment modalities, including individual psychotherapy, individual skills coaching, and group therapy/psychoeducation, and lasts for one year (Linehan et al., 1991).

Application of Dialectical Behavior Therapy to Robert's Case

Because Robert had been practicing the skills he'd learned in his MBSR while he waited to begin his clinic's DBT program, when he began DBT he already had some experience exploring the physical manifestations of strong emotions when they arose, but sometimes they were too much for him. So, in his DBT group, he was happy to learn that when he felt that he might be overwhelmed by emotions, he could "ground" himself by directing his attention to the sensations of his hands resting on the arms of his chair, his feet pressing against the floor, or his breath. He learned that he wasn't avoiding his emotions by doing this but putting them into context along with the many other aspects of his present-moment experience. He also found that he could be aware of angry thoughts and urges to act on them, gauge their alignment with his ultimate recovery goals, and respond more wisely to them. He has found that having less knee-jerk reactivity to people's words and actions has enabled him to cultivate more social support.

Recently his supervisor criticized him for his performance, and Robert felt the sensations of anger quickly arising within him. Unlike in previous situations like this, he observed the feelings of anger as they arose, saw them for what they were, and de-identified with them. That helped him not to be swept away by them and react in a way that might have cost him his job. It was difficult, but Robert was able to accept his supervisor's input and actually improve his performance as a result. Afterward, he was happy with himself for handling the situation in the way he did.

Mindfulness in Other Types of Therapy

Mindfulness-based practices are readily adaptable to individual psychotherapy. During a session, a client may touch upon a distressing topic, for instance, and reflexively change the subject in order to avoid further experience of anxiety. Such avoidant reactions to distressing present-moment experiences can have the unintended consequence of making the experiences more frequent, exacerbating the distress they cause, and limiting the potential responses to them (Hayes, 2004; Hayes, Luoma, Bond, Masuda, & Lillis, 2006). In such a case, clients may be directed to imagine that their thoughts are like leaves floating by on a stream (Hayes, 2004) or simply to bring mindful awareness to the difficult emotions that arise in session (Orsillo, Roemer, Lerner, & Tull, 2004). Learning to accept the experience of the emotion and observe its transitory nature should gradually reduce the desire to control or avoid it (Orsillo et al., 2004; Roemer, Salters-Pedneault, & Orsillo, 2006). When clients begin to be overwhelmed by an emotion, a clinician may direct the client to describe an element of their present-moment experience that is pleasant or neutral. A client can use practices

like these (which are also taught in DBT) to self-regulate outside the therapy room when faced with distressing situations or emotions (Swales, Heard, & Williams, 2000).

It is important to highlight that MBPs must be used judiciously in this area because each client and situation is, of course, unique. A client with Post-Traumatic Stress Disorder, for instance, may not be prepared at first to face the extreme distress that may result from facing the anxiety that he or she ordinarily avoids and could be retraumatized (Lustyk et al., 2009; Walsh, 1999, as cited in Lysack, 2008). Therefore, it may not be clinically indicated for the client to do so without being adequately prepared by the clinician first and the clinician being sufficiently competent to handle potential adverse reactions (Lustyk et al., 2009; Walsh, 1999, as cited in Lysack, 2008).

Mindfulness meditation can also be practiced during interactions with others, whether in groups or conjoint or individual therapy. This can involve an individual monitoring his or her emotional and somatic responses to others' words and actions (using the same observational stance practiced in other MBPs) and conveying a sense of presence with, and validating, another person verbally and/or nonverbally (Fruzzetti & Iverson, 2004). During dyadic exercises, clients may be instructed to try to convey presence with the other through the use of eye contact and posture and to make the effort to be openly receptive to the person's words and reflect them to convey understanding (Fruzzetti & Iverson, 2004). At the same time, clients might be directed to retain some awareness of their own somatic and mental experience as the other person speaks (Fruzzetti & Iverson, 2004; Kramer, Meleo-Meyer, & Turner, 2008). These experiences could include somatic responses to emotion-laden discourse or the listener's mental activity in planning a response to the speaker, instead of just listening (Fruzzetti & Iverson, 2004). Over time, an individual's paying attention to his or her involuntary reactions and urges in response to another's words can reveal automatic, maladaptive communication patterns and the consequences of them for both parties (Carson, Carson, Gil, & Baucom, 2006).

The DBT group lasted for a year, and there were times when Robert felt like dropping out, but at those times he would consider how much better he was interacting with people these days and decide to see it through. He graduated from the formal DBT program two months ago, and he now attends the weekly DBT "skills" and drop-in mindfulness meditation groups at his clinic. Robert has remained compliant with his antidepressant medication and maintains a personal meditation practice at home (about five days per week, on average). He found the individual therapy component of DBT very useful and has now begun psychotherapy with a clinician who is a practitioner of mindfulness meditation herself. She helps him to be attuned to his present-moment experiences and their interpersonal process as they work together.

Termination

Termination in MBPs and MBTs tends to be handled differently than in other psychotherapeutic interventions. Clients are usually encouraged to continue their practice of mindfulness meditation techniques at home after the conclusion of formal instruction or an MBT, so that benefits can be maintained and continue to accrue. Clinicians may also institute regular mindfulness meditation classes and groups to provide both basic instruction and an opportunity for ongoing practice under the same roof (in addition to encouraging clients to practice frequently outside the clinic, at home, and/or in nonclinical MBP practice settings). Whether or not they have mental illness, many people find that a daily, lifelong, mindfulness meditation practice promotes a greater sense of well-being in many areas of life.

Application of Termination Issues to Robert's Case

Today, Robert says, "I still have a long way to go before I'm calm all the time. I doubt I'll ever have that, but I realize now that I don't have to. Little by little, I'm learning to accept what's going on right now and not be so fixated on all the thoughts of my past and future and changing everything and everyone else. And now when I feel disappointed or sad, I can identify those feelings and stay there with them, rather than just getting angry right away and making dumb decisions. It's a lot easier living that way, and I'm not as sad or worried as often, either. All the effort I'm making seems to be paying off for me."

MEZZO CONSIDERATIONS

Mindfulness meditation practitioners can sometimes become bored with it or face doubts that their investment of time and energy is worthwhile. So, it can be very helpful for the client to be part of a community of like-minded others who meet regularly to practice as a group and share their experiences of both formal meditation sessions and their implementation of mindfulness in daily life. Ideally, these groups would be facilitated by an experienced mindfulness practitioner, to clarify mindfulness principles and answer questions. They could also take the form of simple groups for people who have previously received meditation instruction to meditate collectively and discuss among themselves.

For their part, clinicians can help maintain clients' interest in attending groups by offering a variety of meditation exercises, such as mindfulness of external and internal bodily sensations, taste and other senses, walking or other types of movement. Here again, the clinician's personal familiarity with a variety of techniques, and the ability to provide feedback to clients practicing them, is very important.

In addition to helping clients remain interested in practicing mindfulness meditation, offering groups helps to bolster clients' social support networks. Clients suffering from disorders such as MDD, for instance, often isolate at home. Having a group of others to meet with regularly, united by at least one common interest, can help people satisfy their basic social needs, which itself is known to have a significant impact on one's mental and physical health (Berkman, 1995; House, Landis, & Umberson, 1988).

The mental health practitioner may have logistical hurdles to negotiate in providing practice opportunities for clients. Clinic-based practitioners must, of course, contend with any space, staffing, or funding limitations and any resistance that arises from administrators who question the need for mindfulness offerings. In these cases, it is helpful for the clinician to be armed with the research evidence of the benefits of mindfulness practice, in order to lobby effectively for any needed resources.

MACRO CONSIDERATIONS

Insurance Coverage

Insurance coverage for MBPs varies widely, just as it does for psychotherapy in general. Some insurance plans are openly more inclusive and progressive, offering online meditation instruction to policyholders (Aetna, 2013), while others are silent on the issue and review claims on a case-by-case basis. Some insurers exclude treatment for people with a primary diagnosis of a personality disorder altogether (University of Pittsburg Medical Center Health Plan, n.d.), which would presumably preclude coverage for DBT. The American Psychological Association notes that many clinicians deal with insufficient coverage of personality disorders by billing only for the treatment of the features of disordered mood or anxiety that are usually comorbid with a personality disorder (Kersting, 2004).

Ironically, given the significant cost of DBT, which is a long-term treatment, indigent clients who have access to DBT through a public mental health agency may be better off than insured individuals in this regard.

Societal Trends

Mindfulness-based practices are becoming more mainstream. Major corporations, including Fortune 500 companies, have begun integrating mindfulness meditation training programs in the workplace as a benefit to their employees, a means of improving the workplace environment through stress reduction, and a means of improving overall workplace efficiency (Essig, 2012; Gelles, 2012) by virtue of reduced reactivity and improved decision making.

Other organizations are actively working to promote the widespread adoption of mindfulness practice in an effort to achieve positive social change. Mindful Schools is one such organization, which believes that exposing children to mindfulness will help them maintain a mindfulness program into later life. They claim to have taught 18,000 children directly and, through their trained facilitators, approximately 10,000 children annually (Mindful Schools, n.d.).

Such initiatives will benefit greatly from legislative support, and there has been recent progress in this area. In 2012, Congressman Tim Ryan announced publicly that he began a mindfulness meditation practice in response to a fear of burnout and had achieved a greater sense of calm and well-being as a result. Going further, he stated that mindfulness practice "could prevent a lot of war, suffering in the healthcare system, these kids who don't even graduate from schools, mental health, depression, addiction, [and] burnout" (Miles, 2012). His book, *A Mindful Nation: How a Simple Practice Can Help Us Reduce Stress, Improve Performance, and Recapture the American Spirit*, expresses a broader vision of hope that widespread mindfulness practice could shift American culture for the better.

CONCLUSION

Mindfulness meditation has its origins in ancient meditative techniques, but its application in mental health settings is the subject of much interest among modern researchers and clinicians. One major reason for this is the broad range of mental health (and physical health) benefits that its practice can afford, regardless of whether it is directed toward a therapeutic goal (Brown & Ryan, 2003; Friese et al., 2012). Indeed, even the clinicians providing MBPs can benefit from practicing them, in ways that can help them be more effective in their work (Bien, 2008; Hick, 2008). Unlike many interventions, mindfulness meditation practice also readily lends itself to practice at home, without the involvement of a clinician, which is another benefit for increasingly cost-conscious healthcare providers and their clients. As its evidence base and popularity grow, modern clinicians would be well served by at least acquainting themselves with MBPs and then seeking training in their delivery if they wish to help their clients enjoy the benefits.

INTERNET RESOURCES

- UCLA's Mindful Awareness Research Center: http://marc.ucla.edu/
- The UCSD Center for Mindfulness: http://health.ucsd.edu/specialties/mindfulness/Pages/default.aspx
- Mindful: http://www.mindful.org/
- Mindful Schools: http://www.mindfulschoools.org

DISCUSSION QUESTIONS

1. What are some ways a person could use mindfulness-based practices when experiencing urges to use a drug from which he or she wishes to remain abstinent?

2. What are some potential problems that could arise for a person beginning to practice mindfulness meditation without the guidance of a clinician or instructor?

3. What problems could arise for a clinician attempting to guide a client in mindfulness meditation without having training and his or her own experience with mindfulness practice?

4. Is there a paradox involved in practicing mindfulness meditation in hopes of clinical improvement (i.e., changing something) when mindfulness practice stresses the acceptance of one's present-moment experience? If not, then why not? And if so, how might it be resolved?

5. Imagine (or role-play) two people having an argument, with each person remaining aware of the sensations in their bodies and the thoughts that arise as the interaction proceeds. What might they notice, and what insights might those observations reveal?

REFERENCES

Aetna. (2013, April 15). *Aetna launches new programs designed to help reduce metabolic syndrome risk factors.* Retrieved from https://news.aetna.com/news-releases/aetna-launches-new-programs-designed-to-help-reduce-metabolic-syndrome-risk-factors

Arch, J. A., Ayers, C. R., Baker, A., Almklov, E., Dean, D. J., & Craske, M. G. (2013). Randomized clinical trial of adapted mindfulness-based stress reduction versus group cognitive behavioral therapy for heterogeneous anxiety disorders. *Behaviour Research and Therapy, 51*(4–5), 185–196. doi: 10.1016/j.brat.2013.01.003

Bach, P. A., Gaudino, B., Pankey, J., Herbert, J. D., & Hayes, S. C. (2006). Acceptance, mindfulness, values, and psychosis: Applying acceptance and commitment therapy (ACT) to the chronically mentally ill. In R. A. Baer (Ed.), *Mindfulness-based treatment approaches* (pp. 285–306). Burlington, MA: Elsevier.

Baer, R. A. (2003). Mindfulness training as a clinical intervention: A conceptual and empirical review. *Clinical Psychology: Science and Practice, 10*(2), 125–143. doi: 10.1093/clipsy/bpg015

Baer, R. A., & Krietemeyer, J. (2006). Overview of mindfulness- and acceptance-based treatment approaches. In R. A. Baer (Ed.), *Mindfulness-based treatment approaches* (pp. 3–27). Burlington, MA: Elsevier.

Berkman, L. F. (1995). The role of social relations in health promotion. *Psychosomatic Medicine, 57,* 245–154. doi: 10.1093/clipsy/bpg015

Bien, T. (2008). The four immeasurable minds: Preparing to be present in psychotherapy. In S. F. Hick & T. Bien (Eds.), *Mindfulness and the therapeutic relationship* (pp. 37–54). New York, NY: Guilford Press.

Brown, K. W., & Ryan, R. M. (2003). The benefits of being present: Mindfulness and its role in psychological well-being. *Journal of Personality* and Social Psychology, 84(4), 822–848. doi: 10.1037/0022-3514.84.4.822

Carson, J. W., Carson, K. M., Gil, K. M., & Baucom, D. H. (2006). Mindfulness-based relationship enhancement (MBRE) in couples. In R. A. Baer (Ed.), *Mindfulness-based treatment approaches* (pp. 309–331). Burlington, MA: Elsevier.

Chiesa, A., & Serretti, A. (2009). Mindfulness-based stress reduction for stress management in healthy people: A review and meta-analysis. *The Journal of Alternative and Complementary Medicine, 15*(5), 593–600. doi: 10.1089/acm.2008.0495

Craigie, M. A., Rees, C. S., & Marsh, A. (2008). Mindfulness-based cognitive therapy for generalized anxiety disorder: A preliminary evaluation. *Behavioural and Cognitive Psychotherapy, 36,* 553-568. doi: 10.1017/S135246580800458X

Creswell, J. D., Way, B. M., Eisenberger, N. I., Lieberman, M. D. (2007). Neural correlates of dispositional mindfulness during affect labeling. *Psychosomatic Medicine, 69,* 560–569. doi: 10.1097/PSY.0b013e3180f6171f

Davidson, R. J., Kabat-Zinn, J., Schumacher, J., Rosenkranz, M., Muller, D., Santorelli, S., . . . Sheridan, J. (2003). Alterations in brain and immune function produced by mindfulness meditation. *Psychosomatic Medicine, 65,* 564–570. doi: 10.1097/01.PSY.0000077505.67574.E3

Davis, L. W., Strasburger, A. M., & Brown, L. F. (2007). Mindfulness: An intervention for anxiety in schizophrenia. *Journal of Psychosocial Nursing, 45*(11), 23–29. doi: 10.1016/j.janxdis.2007.07.005

Dimeff, L., Rizvi, S. L., Brown, M., & Linehan, M. M. (2000). Dialectical behavior therapy for substance abuse: A pilot application to methamphetamine-dependent women with borderline personality disorder. *Cognitive and Behavioral Practice, 7,* 457–468. doi: 10.1097/01.PSY.0000077505.67574.E3

Essig, T. (2012, April 30). Google teaches employees to "search inside yourself." *Forbes.* Retrieved from http://www.forbes.com/sites/toddessig/2012/04/30/google-teaches-employees-to-search-inside-yourself/

Evans, S., Ferrando, S, Findler, M., Stowell, C., Smart, C., & Haglin, D. (2008). Mindfulness-based cognitive therapy for generalized anxiety disorder. *Journal*

of Anxiety Disorders, 22, 716–721. doi: 10.1016/j.janxdis.2007.07.005

Frewen, P. A., Elspeth, M. E., Maraj, N., Dozois, D. J. A., & Partridge, K. (2008). Letting go: Mindfulness and automatic negative thinking. *Cognitive Therapy Research, 32,* 758–774. doi: 10.1007/s10608-007-9142-1

Friese, M., Messner, C., & Schaffner, Y. (2012). Mindfulness meditation counteracts self-control depletion. *Consciousness and Cognition, 21*(2), 1016–1022. doi: 10.1016/j.concog.2012.01.008

Fruzzetti, A. E., & Iverson, K. M. (2004). Mindfulness, acceptance, validation, and "individual" psychopathology in couples. In S. C. Hayes, V. M. Follette, & M. M. Linehan (Eds.), *Mindfulness and acceptance: Expanding the cognitive-behavioral tradition* (pp. 168–191). New York, NY: Guilford Press.

Gelles, D. (2012, August 24). The mind business. *The Financial Times.* Retrieved from http://www.ft.com/cms/s/2/d9cb7940-ebea-11e1-985a-00144feab49a.html#axzz2ApW2UUXh

Hayes, S. C. (2004). Acceptance and commitment therapy and the new behavior therapies: Mindfulness, acceptance, and relationship. In S. C. Hayes, V. M. Follette, & M. M. Linehan (Eds.), *Mindfulness and acceptance: Expanding the cognitive-behavioral tradition* (pp. 1–29). New York, NY: Guilford Press.

Hayes, S. C., Luoma, J. B., Bond, F. W., Masuda, A., & Lillis, J. (2006). *Acceptance and commitment therapy: Model, processes, and outcomes.* Psychology Faculty Publications, Georgia State University, Paper 101.

Hayes, S. C., Strosahl, K., & Wilson, K. G. (1999). *Acceptance and commitment therapy: An experiential approach to behavior change.* New York, NY: Guilford Press.

Hick, S. F. (2008). Cultivating therapeutic relationships: The role of mindfulness. In S. F. Hick & T. Bien (Eds.), *Mindfulness and the therapeutic relationship* (pp. 3–18). New York, NY: Guilford Press.

Hofmann, S. G., Sawyer, A. T., Witt, A. A., & Oh, D. (2010). The effect of mindfulness-based therapy on anxiety and depression: A meta-analytic review. *Journal of Consulting and Clinical Psychology, 78*(2), 169–183. doi: 10.1037/a0018555

Holzel, B. K., Ott, U., Gard, T., Hempel, H., Weygandt, M., Morgen, K., & Vaitl, D. (2007). Investigation of mindfulness meditation practitioners with voxel-based morphometry. *Social Cognitive and Affective Neuroscience, 3*(1), 55–61. doi: 10.1093/scan/nsm038

House, J. S., Landis, K. R., & Umberson, D. (1988). Social relationships and health. *Science, 241*(4865), 540–545.

Irving, J. A., Dobkin, P. L., & Park, J. (2009). Cultivating mindfulness in health care professionals: A review of empirical studies of mindfulness-based stress reduction (MBSR). *Complementary Therapies in Clinical Practice, 15*, 61–66. doi: 10.1016/j.ctcp.2009.01.002

Kabat-Zinn, J. (1982). An outpatient program in behavioral medicine for chronic pain patients based on the practice of mindfulness meditation: Theoretical considerations and preliminary results. *General Hospital Psychiatry, 4*, 33–47. doi: 10.1016/0163-8343(82)90026-3

Kabat-Zinn, J. (1990). *Full catastrophe living* (15th anniversary ed.). New York, NY: Bantam Dell.

Kabat-Zinn, J. (2003). Mindfulness-based interventions in context: Past, present, and future. *Clinical Psychology: Science and Practice, 10*(2), 144–156. doi: 10.1093/clipsy/bpg016

Kabat-Zinn, J., Massion, A. O., Kristeller, J., Peterson, L. G., Fletcher, K. E., Pbert, L., . . . Santorelli, S. F. (1992). Effectiveness of a meditation-based stress reduction program in the treatment of anxiety disorders. *American Journal of Psychiatry, 149*(7), 936–943.

Kersting, K. (2004). *Axis II gets short shrift.* Retrieved from http://www.apa.org/monitor/mar04/axis.aspx

Khoury, B., Lecomte, T., Fortin, G., Masse, M., Therien, P., Bouchard, V., . . . Hofmann, S. (2013). Mindfulness-based therapy: A comprehensive meta-analysis. *Clinical Psychology Review, 33*(6), 763–771. doi: 10.1016/j.cpr.2013.05.005

Kramer, G., Meleo-Meyer, F., & Turner, M. L. (2008). Cultivating mindfulness in relationship: Insight Dialogue and the Interpersonal Mindfulness Program. In S. F. Hick & T. Bien (Eds.), *Mindfulness and the therapeutic relationship* (pp. 195–214). New York, NY: Guilford Press.

Lazar, S. W., Kerr, C. E., Wasserman, R. H., Gray, J. R., Greve, D. N., Treadway, M. T., . . . Fischl, B. (2005). Meditation experience is associated with increased cortical thickness. *Neuroreport, 16*(17), 1893–1897. doi: 10.1891/0889.8391.22.1.15

Linehan, M. M. (1993). *Skills training manual for treating borderline personality disorder.* New York, NY: Guilford Press.

Linehan, M. M., Armstrong, H. E., Suarez, A., Allmon, D., & Heard, H. L. (1991). Cognitive-behavioral treatment of chronically parasuicidal borderline patients. *Archives of General Psychiatry, 48*, 1060–1064.

Linehan, M. M., Comtois, K. A., Murray, A. M., Brown, M. Z., Gallop, R. J., Heard, H. L., . . . Lindenboim, N. (2006). Two-year randomized controlled trial and follow-up of dialectical behavior therapy vs. therapy by experts for suicidal behaviors and borderline personality disorder. *Archives of General Psychiatry, 63*, 757–766. doi: 10.1001/archpsyc.63.7.757

Linehan, M. M., Dimeff, L., Reynolds, S. K., Comtois, K. A., Welch, S. S., Heagerty, P., & Kivlahan, D. R. (2002). Dialectical behavior therapy versus comprehensive validation therapy plus 12-step for the treatment of opioid dependent women meeting criteria for borderline personality disorder. *Drug and Alcohol Dependence, 67*, 13–26. doi: 10.1016/S0376-8716(02)00011-X

Linehan, M. M., Schmidt III, H., Dimeff, L., Craft, J. C., Kanter, J., & Comtois, K. A. (1999). Dialectical behavior therapy for patients with borderline personality disorder and drug-dependence. *The American Journal on Addictions, 8*, 272–292. doi: 10.1080/105504999305686

Lustyk, M. K. B., Chowla, N., Nolan, R. S., & Marlatt, G. A. (2009). Mindfulness meditation research: Issues of participant screening, safety procedures, and researcher training. *Advances in Mind-Body Medicine, 24*(1), 20–30.

Lysack, M. (2008). Relational mindfulness and dialogic space in family therapy. In S. F. Hick & T. Bien (Eds.), *Mindfulness and the therapeutic relationship* (pp. 141–158). New York, NY: Guilford Press.

Ma, S. H., & Teasdale, J. D. (2004). Mindfulness-based cognitive therapy for depression: Replication and exploration of differential relapse prevention effects. *Journal of Consulting and Clinical Psychology, 72*(1), 31–40. doi: 10.1037/0022-006X.72.1.31

McMain, S. F., Guimond, T., Streiner, D. L., Cardish, R. J., & Links, P. S. (2012). Dialectical behavior therapy compared with general psychiatric management for borderline personality disorder: Clinical outcomes and functioning over a 2-year follow-up. *American Journal of Psychiatry, 169*, 650–661. doi: 10.1176/appi.ajp.2012.11091416

McMain, S. F., Links, P. S., Gnam, W. H., Guimond, T., Cardish, R. J., Korman, L., & Streiner, D. L. (2009). A randomized trial of dialectical behavior therapy versus general psychiatric management for borderline personality disorder. *American Journal of Psychiatry, 166*(12), 1365–1374. doi: 10.1176/appi.ajp.2009.09010039

Melbourne Academic Mindfulness Interest Group (MAMIG). (2006). Mindfulness-based psycho-therapies: A review of conceptual foundations, empirical evidence and practical considerations. *Australian and New Zealand Journal of Psychiatry, 40*, 285–294. doi: 10.1080/j.1440-1614.2006.01794.x

Miles, K. (2012, June 5). Tim Ryan, Ohio congressman, shares his mindfulness vision for the country. *The Huffington Post.* Retrieved from http://www.huffingtonpost.com/2012/06/05/tim-ryan-ohio-congressman_n_1571489.html

Miller, J. J., Fletcher, K., & Kabat-Zinn, J. (1995). Three-year follow-up and clinical implications of a mindfulness meditation-based stress reduction intervention in the treatment of anxiety disorders. *General Hospital Psychiatry, 17*(3), 192–200. doi: 10.1016/0163-8343(95)00025-M

Mindful Schools (n.d.). *Our story.* Retrieved from http://www.mindfulschools.org/about/our-story/

Orsillo, S. M., Roemer, L., Lerner, J. B., & Tull, M. T. (2004). Acceptance, mindfulness, and cognitive-behavioral therapy. In S. C. Hayes, V. M. Follette, & M. M. Linehan (Eds.), *Mindfulness and acceptance: Expanding the cognitive-behavioral tradition* (pp. 66–95). New York, NY: Guilford Press.

Roemer, L., Salters-Pedneault, K., & Orsillo, S. M. (2006). Incorporating mindfulness-and acceptance-based strategies in the treatment of generalized anxiety disorder. In R. A. Baer (Ed.), *Mindfulness-based treatment approaches* (pp. 51–74). Burlington, MA: Elsevier.

Segal, Z. V., Williams, J. M. G., & Teasdale, J. D. (2002). *Mindfulness-based cognitive therapy for depression: A new approach to preventing relapse.* New York, NY: Guilford Press.

Shapiro, S. L., Schwartz, G. E., & Bonner, G. (1998). Effects of mindfulness-based stress reduction on medical and premedical students. *Journal of Behavioral Medicine, 21*(6), 581–599. doi: 10.1023/A:1018700829825

Swales, M., Heard, H. L., & Williams, J. M. G. (2000). Linehan's dialectical behavior therapy (DBT) for borderline personality disorder: Overview and adaptation. *Journal of Mental Health, 9*(1), 7–23. doi: 10.1080/09638230016921

Thompson, M., & Gauntlett-Gilbert, J. (2008). Mindfulness with children and adolescents: Effective clinical application. *Clinical Child Psychology and Psychiatry, 13*(3), 395–407. doi: 10.1177/1359104508090603

University of Pittsburg Medical Center Health Plan. (n.d.). *Exclusions.* Retrieved from http://www.upmchealthplan.com/pdf/Exclusions.pdf

Verheul, R., van den Bosch, L. M. C., Koeter, M. W. J., de Ridder, M. A. J., Stinjen, T., & van den Brink, W. (2003). Dialectical behavior therapy for women with borderline personality disorder. *British Journal of Psychiatry, 182*, 135–140. doi: 10.1192/bjp.02.184

Zainal, N. Z., Booth, S., & Huppert, F. A. (2012). The efficacy of mindfulness-based stress reduction on mental health of breast cancer patients: A meta-analysis. *Psycho-Oncology, 22*(7), 1457–1465. doi: 10.1002/pon.3171

Zeidan, F., Martucci, K. T., Kraft, R. A., Gordon, N. S., McHaffie, J. G., & Coghill, R. C. (2011). Brain mechanisms supporting the modulation of pain by mindfulness meditation. *The Journal of Neuroscience, 31*(14), 5540–5548. doi: 10.1111/j.1750-8606.2012.00241.x

CHAPTER 7

Substance Abuse

A Harm Reduction Approach

Elizabeth Eastlund & Eugenia L. Weiss

CHAPTER OBJECTIVES

- Explore the application of harm reduction principles and practical strategies to working with persons who are using (abusing) drugs and alcohol;
- Describe the process of behavior change and exploring a client's motivation to change;
- Identify the similarities between harm reduction and the ethics and values of social work practice;
- Understand the integration of a cognitive behavioral approach with harm reduction.

CASE VIGNETTE

Jerry is a 43-year-old male of mixed Caucasian and African American heritage. He identifies as heterosexual. Jerry was born addicted to heroin. His parents were both addicted to heroin and not capable of caring for him. At the age of 3, he was found wandering the streets of Hollywood, CA, in a dirty diaper. He was immediately placed in foster care with a family who eventually adopted him. His foster parents were emotionally and physically abusive most of his childhood. Jerry struggled with behavioral and emotional issues from an early age. He was sexually abused as a young boy by a foster family member. In his teenage years he began drinking alcohol and smoking marijuana. Jerry was admitted to his first chemical dependency treatment facility at the age of 15. He dropped out of high school and eventually ran away from home and remained homeless on the streets of Hollywood for more than a decade. He spent 27 years using drugs and alcohol to deal with the overwhelming effects of his adverse childhood experiences, and he was in and out of substance abuse recovery programs and prison. Jerry was successful with sobriety for periods of time and held odd jobs in construction. He has been married three times (no children) and is currently divorced and single. He was diagnosed with the Human Immunodeficiency Virus (HIV) at age 26 and Hepatitis C (Hep C) at the age of 33. Both diseases are easily transmitted through sharing needles for intravenous drug use, and this is likely how Jerry contracted both HIV and Hep C. After years of using, he realized that the drugs would likely kill him before either HIV or Hep C would. The social worker has been seeing Jerry at a community health care facility to provide case management and supportive psychotherapy (including motivational interviewing and a harm reduction approach). The social worker also provides assistance with food and housing as part of an interdisciplinary team of providers. Jerry is currently on methadone treatment for heroin dependence and medications for HIV and Hep C, which are overseen by a physician at the health clinic.

INTRODUCTION

The use of licit and illicit drugs in the United States is a serious public health issue. The chronic use of drugs and alcohol can have serious effects on a person's physical, emotional, and spiritual health as well as on their relationships ("Impact of Drug Use on Your Life," 2013). The 2012 National Survey on Drug Use and Health found that 9.2% of Americans over the age of 12 had used illicit drugs in the previous month, with marijuana being the most commonly used (United States Substance Abuse and Mental Health Services Administration [SAMHSA], 2012). Denning, Little and Glickman (2004) describe a continuum of alcohol and drug use: no use, experimentation, occasional, regular, heavy, abuse, dependence, and chaos. Chaos in drug use is most closely related to addiction.

The United States currently operates within the moral and disease model approaches to drug and alcohol treatment. Zinberg (1984) describes the "moralistic" view of drug use as all illicit drug use is bad, inevitably harmful, psychologically addictive, or physically addictive (p. 3). The disease model asserts that a person's use will get worse over time and does not take into account environmental factors that may contribute to addiction (Denning et al., 2004). The moral and disease models can be described as rigid, punitive, and limiting in treating and providing knowledge as to why people use drugs and alcohol in maladaptive ways. Substance use treatment programs focus on the complete abstinence from drug use rather than exploring the underlying issue of why a person begins to use

drugs, including addressing traumatic experiences and harm reduction versus abstinence. The moral and disease models often fail to explore why some clients accelerate to chaotic addiction while others have the ability to continue to use socially and responsibly.

Harm reduction philosophy was first developed in response to the HIV/AIDS crisis in the 1980s in an attempt to reduce the incidence of HIV infection among injecting drug users (IDUs) by utilizing a public health philosophy and a variety of interventions aimed at reducing the harms caused by drug use. Since its origins, harm reduction principles have been applied to a wide variety of alcohol and drug treatment approaches in an effort to reduce the negative consequences of alcohol and drug use. Rather than focusing solely on the use of drugs, harm reduction principles view the user as the expert in his or her own life and assists individuals to identify the harm that is being caused by their use and their ability to make informed decisions about their use. Providing users with education about their options and assisting them to increase their understanding of the consequences of their use allows them to make their own decisions about their use. "Harm reduction values the uniqueness of each individual and helps each person define her own particular problems related to drug use" (Denning et al., 2004, p. 9). Harm reduction aligns with the basic social work practice of meeting clients where they are at and the concept of self-determination according to the ethics of the National Association of Social Workers (NASW, 2008). Harm reduction does not minimize the harm caused by drug use; instead, it recognizes drug use as part of our society and works to educate users about the continuum of behaviors and how some ways of using are safer than others.

Additionally, co-occurring disorders are common among persons struggling with addiction. Drugs and alcohol are often used for self-medicating purposes and can complicate the social worker's ability to properly diagnose an individual. "Dual diagnosis is common yet difficult to treat. Addiction of all types—to nicotine, alcohol, drugs—is often found in people with a wide variety of mental illnesses including anxiety disorder, unipolar and bipolar depression, schizophrenia, and borderline and other personality disorders" (American Psychological Association [APA], 2001, para. 2). Identifying ways to properly assess individuals from a nonjudgmental stance is critical in providing services that are effective for individuals seeking treatment as it builds a sense of connection with the client (Herman, 1997). Although Jerry from the opening case scenario has not been formally diagnosed with any mental health conditions, the social worker is continuously assessing for comorbidity or co-occurring disorders.

MICRO PERSPECTIVE

Assessment

Properly assessing persons actively using substances will include exploring the impact of their behavioral choices on psychological functioning. Harm reduction focuses on the strengths of the client and assessment includes assisting the client in the identification of their strengths. The assessment explores harm and risks associated with drug use. Zinberg (1984) described the importance of examining drug, set, and setting to take into account the context in which the drug is being used. Zinberg (1984) described the *drug* as pharmacology; the *set* as the individual drug user and what the person brings to the drug experience; and the *setting* as the contexts of the drug use itself. Examining the

risk people are taking while obtaining and using drugs is essential in assisting the client in exploring options for how they may be able to reduce risks associated with their use.

The assessment is more than exploring the client's use of drugs, including type of drugs, quantity and frequency, individual's alcohol- and drug-related problems, including family history of alcohol and drug use, but also attempting to determine why clients are using, including asking them about the benefits of using and why the individual is seeking help at the current time. Reliable and valid self-report drug and alcohol screening instruments that are typically easy and fast to administer, such as the Michigan Alcoholism Screening Test (MAST), Drug Abuse Screening Test (DAST), and Substance Abuse Subtle Screening Inventory (SASSI), among others, can be utilized as part of the comprehensive assessment and can be administered and scored by social workers and others (see McNeece & DiNitto, 2012 for a review of these instruments). According to McNeece and DiNitto, a thorough assessment includes social and psychological/psychiatric history; current social and family relationships; employment; education; military history; legal history; current medical conditions and history including medications. Religious affiliation and spiritual/faith-based beliefs are also important as potential avenues of support. The primary goal of the assessment period is to establish safety in an effort to assist clients in increasing awareness of the risks and/or harm they may be engaging in as a result of their use. Additionally, it is important to assess for early childhood trauma or adverse experiences with persons actively using drugs as their use may be their attempt to deal with painful memories (Felitti et al., 1998). According to Mate (2010), "addictions always originate in pain whether held openly or hidden in the unconscious. They are emotional anesthetics. Heroin and cocaine, both powerful physical painkillers, also ease psychological discomfort" (p. 36). Mate goes on to say that "not all addictions are rooted in abuse or trauma, but I do believe they can be traced to painful experiences…the effects of early stress or adverse experiences directly shape both the psychology and the neurobiology of addiction in the brain" (p. 38). The author notes that addiction is a complex condition that needs to be examined and treated from a multidimensional perspective that includes neurobiology and the interaction with the environment and has "biological, chemical, neurological, psychological, medical, emotional, social, political, economic and spiritual underpinnings" (p. 138). This discussion is beyond the scope of this chapter and the reader is recommended to see Mate (2010) for an in-depth analysis.

In the context of harm reduction, assessment includes starting where the client is at in an effort to build rapport. Hepworth, Rooney, Rooney, and Strom-Gottfried (2013) suggested that building rapport is essential for supporting clients in the interview process. Goals of treatment are set with the client and the assessment process examines the client's readiness for change or motivation for recovery (which will be discussed in the next section of the chapter). The Harm Reduction Coalition (www.harmreduction.org) describes that harm reduction encourages the client to define what success looks like to them while providing education and increased awareness of their options, and it "affirms drug users as the primary agents of reducing the harms of their drug use, and seeks to empower users to share information as they support each other in strategies which meet their actual conditions of use" (Harm Reduction Coalition, 2013, para. 8).

The *Diagnostic and Statistical Manual of Mental Disorders, 5th edition* (DSM-5) includes Substance Related and Addictive Disorders, which includes 10 different classes of drugs and the behavioral addiction of gambling (American Psychiatric Association, 2013). The disorders are divided into two groups: substance-related disorder and substance-induced disorders. The DSM-5 does not use the term *addiction,* yet it describes substance use disorder as covering a wide range of use "from a mild form to a severe state of chronically relapsing, compulsive drug taking" (pp. 65–66). The World Health Organization (WHO, 1992) 10th edition of the *International Classification of Diseases* (ICD-10) also contains diagnostic criteria for alcohol and drug disorders.

Diversity Considerations

According to the Harm Reduction Coalition (2013), harm reduction principles include "Recognizing that the realities of poverty, class, racism, social isolation, past trauma, sex-based discrimination and other social inequalities affects people's vulnerabilities to and capacity for effectively dealing with drug related harms" (para. 9). Studies show that persons of different ethnicities use illicit drugs at about the same rate. Among persons struggling with addictions, for instance, persons of color are more likely to have had a history of incarceration related to their drug use than others because African American and Latino populations are disproportionally overrepresented in the criminal justice system (Drug Policy Alliance, 2014). Additionally, cultural pain and anger among African American men and distrust of majority-group counselors has been found in a study by Williams (2008; as cited in McNeece & DiNitto, 2012); thus, the client's experience with discrimination and the ensuing psychological pain should be addressed by psychotherapists. Culturally competent strengths perspective and empowerment approaches have been recommended for use with African American clients as well as considering the potential importance of religious affiliation as sources of spiritual strength and hope (Kogan, 2005).

Additionally, in February 2012, a U.S. Centers for Disease Control report stated that African Americans are disproportionally represented among those infected with Hep C and have a substantially higher rate of chronic infection (CDC, 2014). Within the African American community, the leading cause of death among persons aged 45–64 is chronic liver disease, often Hep C–related.

Interventions

For many years, behavioral health practitioners would refuse to see users who were active in their addiction (National Alliance on Mental Illness [NAMI], 2013). Yet in a health care setting, building rapport while an addict is being treated for medical issues is essential in providing options for addictions related treatment. Needle exchange programs provide a wide range of services for the injection drug user (IDU) including health assessments, education about safe injecting, and information and referral to substance abuse treatment programs. Needle exchange programs are an example of attempting to assist persons in reducing the potential risks of drug use (i.e., disease transmission) without requiring abstinence. Needle exchange programs create relationships with IDUs in an attempt to establish and maintain a connection. When the IDU makes the decision to attempt abstinence, he or she has knowledge of the support systems that exist.

SAMHSA (2011, para. 3) provides a working definition of recovery: "Recovery is a process of change through which individuals improve their health and wellness, live a self-directed life, and strive to reach their full potential." Additionally, SAMHSA's most recent working definition of recovery included addressing trauma:

> Recovery is supported by addressing trauma: the experience of trauma (such as physical or sexual abuse, domestic violence, war, disasters, and others) is often a precursor to or associated with alcohol and drug use, mental health problems, and related issues. Services and supports should be trauma-informed to foster safety (physical and emotional) and trust, as well as promote choice, empowerment, and collaboration. (para. 14)

See the Internet Resources section for more information on SAMHSA's Guiding Principles of Recovery. Exploring Jerry's traumatic experiences as a child is an important step in his recovery once he is in a safe place to do so.

Major behavioral change models utilized in harm reduction interventions include the Stages of Change Theory and Motivational Interviewing. The Stages of Change Theory was developed by Prochaska and DiClemente in the 1980s and provides a framework for a number of interventions aimed at improving health through lifestyle changes. The stages of change model can be applied to working with those individuals who are using or abusing substances in identifying their readiness for change. The stages of change are precontemplation, contemplation, preparation, action, and maintenance. Prochaska and DiClemente (1982) describe relapse as part of the stages of behavioral change as the progress is not necessarily orderly. Each stage offers the practitioner an opportunity to connect with the client and to provide education aimed at increasing the client's awareness of their options and assisting them with focusing on their strengths.

Prochaska and DiClemente (1982) describe the precontemplative phase as one in which clients may appear to be resistant and defensive when discussing their use of drugs. During this phase, it is important for the practitioner to be engaging and build trust with the client. Being where the client is means understanding that he or she may not be prepared to discuss behavior change. During the contemplative phase, clients' awareness of the negative consequences of using is increasing. They may be more open to information and to exploring their ambivalence about using versus changing. The preparation phase includes discussing the various options for behavior change and experimenting with some of those options. It is important for the practitioner to emphasize the client's options during all phases. The action phase includes implementation of the activities that support the behavior change. During the action phase, the practitioner continues to follow up and provide encouragement regarding the behavior change. The maintenance phase is a period in which the client is sustaining the behavior change. The practitioner's main intervention during the maintenance phase is to reinforce the positive aspects of behavior change and to continue highlighting the strengths of the client. A client may move back and forth between the contemplative, preparation, action, and maintenance phases. For instance, when Jerry was active in his addiction, he would keep some of his medical appointments to address his HIV and Hep C conditions. During the visits, the social worker continued to build rapport with Jerry and offered education and information about needle exchange programs from a nonjudgmental stance and also offered free condoms.

The social worker was not condoning Jerry's IV heroin use; however, by providing information, educating him about the needle exchange program, and building rapport, the social worker aimed to increase the likelihood that Jerry would return for his medical appointments and also use clean needles if he continued to inject drugs (Jerry was concerned about infecting his spouse at the time as she was also an IV drug user). After a relapse, Jerry would begin his change cycle again by contemplating his options, preparing for change by either contacting his social worker or taking action by entering a treatment program. He was able to maintain sobriety, sometimes for several months, prior to relapsing again. Additionally, providing education about the stages of change can be beneficial for the client in understanding the process of behavioral change. It is important to focus on the strengths of the client and review what has supported his efforts toward sobriety in the past while exploring his options for trying new approaches. Providing validation of his ability to engage in behavior change and identifying ways in which he has already begun the process is paramount in continuing to build trust with the client. Assessing a person's value of changing harmful behaviors as well as his confidence in mastering the coping skills necessary to make the change will include exploring the importance of change while encouraging his strengths.

Motivational Interviewing (MI) is a client-centered counseling style that assists in exploring and resolving ambivalence about changing harmful behaviors (Miller & Rollnick, 1991). The philosophy behind MI includes an understanding that change cannot be imposed and change depends on the benefits (pros) of change outweighing the costs (cons). Similar to the harm reduction principle that affirms the drug user as the primary agent of reducing the harms of their drug use, MI sees the client as being competent to make her own choices and changes in her life. MI utilizes techniques to assess a person's readiness for behavioral change. Using open-ended questions, the practitioner can assist a person in identifying the discrepancies in her motivation toward change and her current

behavior. Skills that are fundamental to MI include reflective listening, responding to change talk, and responding to resistance. According to Miller and Rollnick, the principles associated with MI include expressing empathy, which communicates respect and stresses freedom of choice and determination; developing discrepancy between where the client is and where he or she would like to be; always avoiding argument, as it tends to evoke resistance in the client; rolling with resistance by understanding that ambivalence is normal and not pathological; and supporting self-efficacy by assisting the client to see that change is possible.

Kurtz (1990) described "change talk" as being the movement toward change and as being opposite of "resistance," which is the movement away from change (p. 47). The practitioner can assist the client by encouraging change talk and increasing awareness of the discrepancies between change and resistance. Change talk examines the disadvantages of remaining the same; the advantages of change; optimism for change; and the intention to change (Kurtz, 1990). Motivational Interviewing examines the client's motivation to change by increasing awareness of how the benefits of change outweigh the negative consequences of drug use and how the costs of current maladaptive behaviors outweigh the benefits. Once Jerry had achieved some time of sobriety, he was able to articulate the pros and cons of sobriety versus drug use in an effort to reinforce the maintenance phase of his behavior change (see Figure 7.1).

Identifying the pros and cons of drug use provides an opportunity to increase the client's awareness and respects his autonomy to make his own choices. Discussing other less harmful activities in which the client can work toward obtaining the pros of drug use is emphasized. Jerry identified "feeling more courageous" (see Figure 7.1) as a pro of using drugs. In session, the social worker can explore the self-esteem and self-efficacy issues that are likely the root of this statement. This is where the social worker can combine elements of Cognitive Behavioral Coping Skills Training (CBST) based on the cognitive behavioral model (Parrish, 2009). Assisting Jerry in defining courageous

	PROS	CONS
Drug Use	• Elixir–in social settings • Anesthetize • Felt more courageous	• Physical illness/disease • Possible death more likely • Homelessness • Institutionalization • Negative effects on family • Violence • Selfishness • Relapse–inability to stay clean
Sobriety	• Improved memory • Improved physical health • Housed • Free • Peaceful • Healthy relationships • Supportive family • Emotionally present • Increased awareness of what I am saying	• Fear of people • Hypersensitive • High expectations of others • More inhibited • Isolation • Second-guessing myself

Figure 7.1   An Overview of Jerry's Benefits and Deficits of Drug Use and Sobriety

actions and ways he may engage in experiences that improve his self-esteem are key in increasing his awareness of harmful versus supportive behaviors. The CBST approach as espoused by Monti, Kadden, Rohsenow, Cooney, and Abrams (2002) is an empirically supported treatment approach that utilizes coping skills training from an interpersonal and intrapersonal perspective. For instance, in the interpersonal realm, the social worker helps the client to develop increasingly adaptive ways of dealing with high-risk relapse situations and maintaining positive social support networks that promote healthy choices. The intrapersonal skills training has a more cognitive focus; the social worker can help the client with anger management strategies, tackle negative thinking patterns, help with problem solving and assist the client to prepare for emergencies. (See the Internet Resources section of this chapter for the link to the CBST manual). Mate (2010) offers the following quote:

Another powerful dynamic perpetuates addiction despite the abundance of disastrous consequences: the addict sees no other possible existence for himself. His outlook on the future is restricted by his entrenched self-image as an addict. No matter how much he may acknowledge the costs of his addiction, he fears a loss of self if it were absent from his life. In his own mind, he would cease to exist as he knows himself. (p. 45)

This is part of what the social worker needs to tackle in his or her CBST approach to successfully treat a client such as Jerry. Issues of identity, self-image and self-perceptions are topics that can be worked through in CBST.

Transference and Countertransference Issues

It is important for social workers to have an understanding of their own thoughts, beliefs, and attitudes about drug use and working with those who use drugs. Social workers may have their own histories of addiction or have known someone who has struggled with addiction. It is important to understand our own biases and judgments regarding substance abuse when working with persons struggling with addictions. Working in the addictions field can be frustrating when attempting to support a person who may be chronically relapsing. Understanding the role of a social worker and being able to detach from the decisions being made by the person struggling with substance use is essential. Our role as social workers is to provide support and education regarding a person's options toward recovery and to assist in facilitating the healing process when the person is ready. The client may want to know whether the social worker has ever engaged in or had problems with substance use. The therapist does not need to be a recovering addict to be able to assist his or her client. However, the client may insist that the provider be in recovery in order to understand the mindset of a substance user. The therapist needs to consider boundaries very carefully in this instance and discuss with a supervisor or consult with other professionals in terms of what to share or not to share. In some settings, it is common for the therapist to be in recovery and to share with his clients, and in other settings it is less common. Also, if the social worker has not had a personal experience with drug or alcohol use, he can work with the client to build that trust and relationship because most of the time, the client is really asking, "Can you help me?" rather than holding the notion that the therapist has to be an addict to be able relate to another addict. The harm reduction approach emphasizes self-care for those working in the field of addictions, as well as obtaining supervision and peer support to process the often tragic realities of addiction for the clients and learning about the adverse childhood experiences that often come with the territory.

Legal and Ethical Concerns

The main legal concern in working with clients who are active in their addiction is the potential for the client to be arrested for possession, driving under the influence, or engaging in other criminal behavior related to the use of drugs or alcohol. Disclosure of criminal activity may present ethical concerns for the social worker. The social worker has a duty to protect when clients disclose their intent and specific plan to harm another individual as well as themselves (Granich, 2011). Practitioners may ethically struggle with a client's disclosure of unsafe sexual behaviors or sharing needles with others when possessing the knowledge that the client has an HIV-positive diagnosis and Hep C. Currently there is no mandate to disclose the HIV or Hep C status of an individual who may be participating in unsafe behaviors, and it is good practice to verify state laws in the state in which the social worker practices. Additionally, substance use at chaotic levels can be seen as self-destructive behavior. The main dilemma becomes how to support a client knowing that his continuation of drug use may ultimately cause his death. Additionally, if an individual is using or exposing his or her minor children to drug use, the social worker may need to involve child protective services.

MEZZO PERSPECTIVE

Needle exchange programs are the classic example of the application of harm reduction principles. Needle exchange sites allow for injection drug users to dispose of dirty needles and obtain clean needles. Rather than promoting drug use, harm reduction approaches drug use from a nonjudgmental, public health view. Needle exchanges offer more than just clean needles. Basic medical care, including wound checks, education on overdose, HIV testing, and advocacy services are also provided. This is where Jerry was identified as being HIV positive. Through attending a needle exchange program, IDUs were more likely to eventually enter a treatment program compared to IDUs who did not participate in needle exchange programs. In 2000, U.S. Surgeon General Satcher stated,

> After reviewing all of the research to date, the senior scientists of the Department and I have unanimously agreed that there is conclusive scientific evidence that syringe exchange programs, as part of a comprehensive HIV prevention strategy, are an effective public health intervention that reduces the transmission of HIV and does not encourage the use of illegal drugs. (p. 11)

There are numerous types of facilities and organizations addressing substance use issues. During the past few decades, it has become apparent that there is a need to integrate treatment to address substance abuse and mental health issues simultaneously. Services available to persons struggling with substance use issues include individual counseling, group support, 12-step meetings (self-help groups), inpatient settings, day programs, and sober living facilities. Rather than continuing to address drug use from a judicial systems approach, harm reduction promotes the need for a public health approach in which education, health care, and substance abuse treatment are readily available.

MACRO PERSPECTIVE

Organizations such as the Harm Reduction Coalition and the Drug Policy Alliance work to effect change with the ineffective drug policies created by the so-called War on Drugs. They provide education and policy advocacy to promote a public health rather than a criminal justice approach to addressing addictions. The Fair Sentencing Act of 2010 was the Obama administration's attempt at decreasing the disparity in drug sentencing laws (Papa, 2013). The law reduces the disparity between sentencing for crack versus powder from 100-to-1 to an 18-to-1 weight ratio. The law also eliminated the mandatory minimum five-year sentencing for possession of crack cocaine. There are still about 5,000 persons in prison because the Fair Sentencing Act did not include language that would make the law retroactive and provide judicial relief for those still serving time under the unjust laws (Papa, 2013).

In August 2013, U.S. Attorney General Eric Holder announced his intention to address the mandatory minimum sentencing for simple possession of controlled substances, as long as the defendant is a nonviolent, low-level offender with no connection to a drug cartel or gang (Papa, 2013). California Proposition 36, the Substance Abuse and Crime Prevention Act of 2000, provides drug treatment as an alternative to jail for first- and second-time drug offenders. Funding was provided for the first five years of the program. Although the Proposition continues to be law under California Penal Code and the California Health and Safety Codes, State funding was discontinued in 2009. According to the statistics from the Drug Policy Alliance (2009),

> Over a four-year period, California entirely eliminated treatment funding for Proposition 36—from a high of $145 million in 2007–08 to nothing in 2010–11. Since 2000, Prop 36 has provided treatment to 36,000 people a year, sharply reduced the number of drug offenders in prison, and reduced state costs by $2 billion. Over 280,000 people have entered community-based treatment under Prop 36, half of whom had never received treatment before. The number of people in state prison for drug possession has decreased 40% since Prop 36 took effect. According to University of California at Los Angeles (UCLA), for every $1 invested in Prop 36, the state saves a net $2.50 to $4.00. Average per-person treatment costs are about $3,300, while incarceration in state prison costs $49,000 per year. (para. 2–3)

CONCLUSION

In conclusion, there are no easy solutions to the complexity of substance abuse, however, there are ways to attempt to mitigate some of the risks and encourage people like Jerry to continue to seek medical care for addiction and for health-related conditions. Sending addicts to prison does not necessarily rehabilitate them, and many will likely relapse after being released and thus recidivate (McNeece & DiNitto, 2012). This is what Mate (2010) and others have called the revolving door for addicts, namely, in and out of the correctional system. Working with this population can be challenging; however, social workers can make inroads through a nonjudgmental stance paired with a harm reduction approach. Future success in terms of long-term solutions for those who have difficulty with recovery will need to take into account the multidimensional aspects of this disorder both in terms of prevention and intervention efforts.

INTERNET RESOURCES

- Harm Reduction Coalition: http://www.harmreduction.org
- The Drug Policy Alliance: http://www.drugpolicy.org
- United States Substance Abuse and Mental Health Services Administration (SAMHSA): http://www.samhsa.gov
- SAMHSA's Guiding Principles of Recovery: http://blog.samhsa.gov/2012/03/23/defintion-of-recovery-updated/#.VbqBOrNVhBc
- The House I Live In: http://www.thehouseilivein.org
- Cognitive-Behavioral Coping Skills Therapy Manual: http://pubs.niaaa.nih.gov/publications/MATCHSeries3/index.htm

DISCUSSION QUESTIONS

1. Why is it important to explore the benefits of drug use with clients?

2. How can the stages of change be beneficial to working with persons using drugs?

3. What are the similarities between harm reduction principles and social work practice?

4. How can social workers address unsafe sexual or drug using practices with clients who are living with HIV?

5. How can a social worker integrate a cognitive behavioral therapy such as CBST into harm reduction methods?

REFERENCES

American Psychiatric Association. (2013). *Desk reference to the diagnostic criteria from DSM-5.* Arlington, VA: Author.

American Psychological Association. (2001, December 3). Mental illness and drug addiction may co-occur due to disturbances in part of the brain. *Science Daily.* Retrieved from http://www.sciencedaily.com/releases/2007/12/071203090143.htm

Denning, P., Little, J., & Glickman, A. (2004). *Over the influence: The harm reduction guide for managing drugs and alcohol.* New York, NY: Guilford Press.

Drug Policy Alliance. (2009). *Legislature eliminates funding for Prop 36 voter-mandated drug treatment: Ends incarceration of nonviolent drug offenses.* Retrieved from http://www.drugpolicy.org/departments-and-state-offices/california/proposition-36- victory

Drug Policy Alliance. (2014). *California fair sentencing act to eliminate the disparities between crack and powder cocaine sentencing passes its first committee today.* Retrieved from http://www.drugpolicy.org/news/2014/04/california-fair-sentencing-act-eliminate-disparities-between-crack-and-powder-cocaine

Felitti, V. J., Anda, R. F., Nordenberg, D., Williamson, D. F., Spitz, A. M., Edwards, V., Koss, M. P., & Marks, J. S. (1998). Relationship of childhood abuse and household dysfunction to many of the leading causes of death in adults: The Adverse Childhood Experiences (ACE) Study. *American Journal of Preventive Medicine, 14,* 245–258.

Granich, S. (2011). Duty to warn, duty to protect. *The New Social Worker.* Retrieved from http://www.socialworker.com/feature-articles/ethics-articles/Duty_to_Warn,_Duty_to_Protect/

Harm Reduction Coalition. (2013). *Principles of harm reduction.* Retrieved from http://harmreduction.org/about-us/principles-of-harm-reduction/

Hepworth, D. H., Rooney, R. H., Rooney, G. D., & Strom-Gottfried, K. S. (2013). *Direct social work practice theory and skills.* Belmont, CA: Brooks/Cole.

Herman, J. (1997). *Trauma and recovery: The aftermath of violence—from domestic abuse to political terror.* New York, NY: Basic Books.

Impact of drug use on your life. (2013). *ReachOut.com.* Retrieved from http://us.reachout.com/facts/factsheet/impact-of-drug-use-on-your-life

Kogan, S. (2005). Risk and protective factors for substance abuse among African-American high school dropouts. *Psychology of Addictive Behaviors, 19*(4), 382–381.

Kurtz, R. (1990). *Body centered psychotherapy: The Hakomi Method.* Mendocino, CA: LifeRythm.

Mate, G. (2010). *In the realm of hungry ghosts: Close encounters with addiction.* Berkeley, CA: North Atlantic Books.

McNeece, C. A., & DiNitto, D. M. (Eds.). (2012). *Chemical dependency: A systems approach* (4th ed.). New York, NY: Pearson.

Miller, R., & Rollnick, S. (1991). *Motivational interviewing: Preparing people to change addictive behavior.* New York, NY: Guilford Press.

Monti, P. M., Kadden, R. M., Rohsenow, D. J., Cooney, N. L., & Abrams, D. B. (2002). *Treating alcohol dependence: A coping skills training guide* (2nd ed.). New York, NY: Guilford Press.

National Alliance on Mental Illness. (2013). *Dual diagnosis: Substance abuse and mental illness.* Retrieved from http://www.nami.org/Content/NavigationMenu/ Inform_Yourself/About_Mental_Illness/By_Illness/ Dual_Diagnosis_Substance_Abuse_and_Mental_ Illness.htm

National Association of Social Workers. (2008). *Code of Ethics of the National Association of Social Workers.* Retrieved from http://www.socialworkers.org/ pubs/code/code.asp

Papa, A. (2013). Mandatory minimum sentencing and potential pardons by President Obama. *Huffington Post.* Retrieved from http://www .huffingtonpost.com/anthony-papa/serving-15-life-under-_b_3806933.html

Parrish, D. E. (2009). Cognitive behavioral coping skills therapy for adults. In D. W. Springer & A. Rubin (Eds.), *Substance abuse treatment for youth and adults: A clinician's guide to evidence-based practice* (pp. 259–310). Hoboken, NJ: John Wiley & Sons.

Prochaska, J., & DiClemente, C. (1982). Transtheoretical therapy: Toward a more integrative model of change. *Psychotherapy: Theory, Research, and Practice, 19*(3), 276–288.

Satcher, D. (2000). *Evidence-based findings on the efficacy of syringe exchange programs: An analysis from the Assistant Secretary for Health and Surgeon General of the scientific research completed since April 1998.* Washington, DC: Department of Health and Human Services.

United States Centers for Disease Control and Prevention. (2014). *Hepatitis C in the African American community.* Retrieved from http:// www.cdc.gov/hepatitis/populations/

United States Substance Abuse and Mental Health Services Administration. (2011). *SAMHSA announces a working definition of "recovery" from mental disorders and substance use disorders.* Retrieved from: http://www.samhsa.gov/ newsroom/press-announcements/201112220300

United States Substance Abuse and Mental Health Services Administration. (2012). *Results from the 2012 National Survey on Drug Use and Health: Summary of national findings.* NSDUH Series H-46, HHS Publication No. (SMA) 13-4795. Rockville, MD: Author.

World Health Organization. (1992). *ICD-10 classification of mental and behavioural disorders: Clinical descriptions and diagnostic guidelines.* Geneva: Author.

Zinberg, N. (1984). *Drug, set and setting: The basis for controlled intoxicant use.* New Haven, CT: Yale University Press.

CHAPTER 8

Hypersexual Behavior

Helping Clients Through Diagnosis and Treatment

William Feuerborn

CHAPTER OBJECTIVES

- Identify hypersexual behavior and diagnose sexual addiction in clients;
- Learn how to plan and execute appropriate interventions;
- Assess how sex addiction affects the family system;
- Evaluate what experiences and situations can cause sex addiction to develop.

CASE VIGNETTE

Jason is a 42-year-old heterosexual male who has been married to Janelle for six years. They have twins, a son and a daughter, age 5. Janelle discovered that Jason has been viewing pornography regularly for several years, spending hours per day looking for "just the right images and videos." Janelle is devastated, believing that Jason is not attracted to her anymore. She compares herself to the women in the pornography and believes she is getting too old and that her body is not attractive. Janelle is unaware that Jason has also been looking for escorts online and has visited massage parlors on several occasions seeking out sexual experiences. She also doesn't know that Jason has been viewing pornography at work and that his first marriage broke up because he was having sexual encounters with women when he would go out of town on business. Jason has tried on many occasions to curb or stop his behavior. However, he is never able to go longer than two weeks without returning to the old behaviors.

> Jason and Janelle saw a psychotherapist a year ago. This therapist (who is not specifically trained to assess or treat sexual addiction) told them that Jason's behavior was caused by the fact that Janelle didn't want sex often enough and that the root of his sexual behaviors was related to his problems within the marital relationship. Janelle felt invalidated and responsible; Jason felt like his behavior had been excused and justified.

INTRODUCTION

It is a common misperception—even in the mental health field—that when one partner acts out sexually, it is a clear result of problems within a relationship. Although this can be the situation, it is vital for social workers to be aware of the significant possibility that the behavior could be symptomatic of a pattern that has little—or nothing—to do with the relationship, but is instead caused by another process. Awareness of what is really going on with a client is vital in order for social workers to intervene appropriately.

MICRO PERSPECTIVE: SEX ADDICTION

Assessment

A pattern of sexual behaviors that disregards boundaries, violates a person's own values or morals, or causes some form of harm to the self or others, is indicative of sexual addiction. There are multiple terms referring to the same manifestation of symptoms and behavior associated with sex addiction. *Sexual addiction* is the most commonly used term and has gained popularity over the years both from treatment professionals who recognize the similarities between sex addiction and substance addiction, and from members of the media, who often sensationalize the topic. Carnes (2001) wrote the first widely available book on sex addiction, *Out of the Shadows*, first published in 1983. Carnes continues to be a significant author, clinician, and researcher

on the phenomenon. The term *hypersexual disorder* is gaining in popularity as some researchers do not agree that there is enough data to classify hypersexual behavior as an addictive process (Kafka, 2010).

Client behaviors that can alert a social worker to consider the possibility of sex addiction include masturbation that is excessive in frequency or duration, affairs outside a committed relationship, use of prostitutes, long periods of pornography use, cybersex, voyeurism, exhibitionism, sexual harassment, and sexual offending (Carnes & Wilson, 2002). Additional behaviors to consider are arrest for sex in public, checking escort or massage rating websites, nude webcamming, engaging in chatting or dating sites when in a committed relationship, and so on. Social workers should be aware to the possibility of sex addiction when a client presents for therapy after a partner has discovered his or her betraying sexual behaviors, or when a client reports a sex-related arrest, such as soliciting a prostitute or having sex in public. Additionally, if a client presents with a sexually transmitted infection, such as syphilis, HPV, or HIV, or with a pregnancy that has occurred outside of their primary relationship, sex addiction should be considered as a possibility. A good guideline when considering sex addiction is to note when sexual behavior continues despite the result of negative life consequences (Carnes, 2001). When determining the presence of sex addiction, social workers should consider the following questions in order to diagnose sex addiction (Giugliano, 2009):

1. Does the client have a sense that she or he has lost control over whether or not she or he engages in the specific out-of-control sexual behavior?

2. Is she or he experiencing significant consequences because of the specific out-of-control sexual behavior?

3. Is she or he constantly thinking about any specific out-of-control sexual behavior, even when 'she or he doesn't want to? (p. 289)

The client Jason from the opening vignette has experienced a loss of control over his behavior as he has escalated to viewing pornography at work, not just at home. Also he has been seeking in-person sexual encounters with prostitutes and women at massage parlors. The main consequence of his out-of-control sexual behavior is hurting his wife Janelle, causing her to experience many painful emotions while blaming herself. In interviewing Jason, he will likely disclose that he frequently thinks about acting out, even at inappropriate times, like when he is home watching his children or even during sex with Janelle.

Differential diagnosis is vital to ensure clients receive proper treatment. For example, if a client has a diagnosis of bipolar disorder, hypersexual behavior could manifest during a manic episode (American Psychiatric Association [APA], 2013). This would not indicate sex addiction unless the behavior occurred in the absence of a manic or mixed episode. Consider the presence of paraphilic disorders, which are well documented in the *Diagnostic and Statistical Manual of Mental Disorders* (APA, 2013). Sex addiction can be present with or without a paraphilic disorder, such as exhibitionistic disorder, voyeuristic disorder, or frotteuristic disorder. The diagnostic guidelines for sex addiction—loss of control, consequences, and frequent thoughts of the behavior (Giugliano, 2009)—must be considered when assigning a diagnosis.

Other data that can help with diagnosis are looking for what Carnes refers to as collateral indicators. These are not symptoms or diagnostic criteria, but rather client qualities and experiences that are common for many other people with sexual addiction. Examples of these collateral indictors include having grown up in a family with sex addiction or even other addictions; experiencing emotional, physical, or sexual abuse as a child; growing up in a rigid family; or growing up in a disengaged family (Carnes & Wilson, 2002).

Exploring the Causes

There are many theories about what causes the development of sex addiction. Many clinicians and researchers believe that childhood trauma, such as abuse or neglect, plays a role. Schwartz and Southern (2002) wrote that most individuals who show symptoms of either hyposexuality or hypersexuality experienced child abuse or neglect.

Carnes (2013) noted that most people with sexual addiction had experienced emotional, physical, or sexual abuse as children, and most were from rigid and disengaged family systems.

When people have been abused or neglected as children, they struggle to regulate their emotions. Sex addiction can develop in response to uncomfortable affective experiences as a way to self-regulate (Schwartz & Southern, 2002). People with sexual addiction frequently show an inability to successfully practice self-regulation or co-regulation, turning to sexual behavior to soothe and regulate themselves (Katehakis, 2009). For secure attachment, the limbic systems of infants need the psychobiological regulation of the primary caregiver. In families with abuse or neglect, the caregiver regulation of the infant does not occur (Schore, 2001). Without such co-regulation, children do not learn how to self-regulate and attachment is impaired.

Another childhood situation that can lead to sex addiction is when a child becomes sexualized early, without adequate processing from caregivers. For example, many sex addicts will describe viewing pornography as early as 6 years old. Some children are sexualized early through being sexually abused. Others have also witnessed poor sexual boundaries in their families of origin. When children are exposed to pornography, the results include increased sexual activity and even increased sexual violence. Additionally, exposure to pornography in childhood affects the individual's sexual attitudes and developing moral values (Greenfield, 2004).

There are some clients who seek treatment for sexual addiction who have not experienced child trauma nor early sexualization. In these cases, it is important for the social worker to be open-minded to other possible causes, including cultural issues. At times, there seems to be no apparent cause, but treatment is still necessary.

Sex Addiction Versus Sex Offending

Often, people confuse sexual addiction with sex offending. Sex offending involves the crossing of another person's boundary or the breaking of a law.

Examples of sex offending include molesting a child, rape, frotteurism, voyeurism, exhibitionism, and so on. Sexual addiction can include these behaviors, but very often it does not. It is important to be aware that when sexual offending behavior is present, treatment protocols differ in order to comply with the requirements of the criminal justice system. Sex offender treatment is mainly cognitive behavioral therapy and relapse prevention (Stinson & Becker, 2013).

Ecological Systems Meta-Framework

Sexual addiction, especially as it progresses in volume and scope, affects the lives of those involved at multiple levels. Bronfenbrenner's (1989) ecological systems perspective provides a helpful lens through which to look at the problems caused by the behavior. The ecological systems framework provides a structure focused on the micro, mezzo, and macro system perspectives.

Beginning with the microsystem, the individual who engages in sexually addictive behavior experiences a range of potential issues. For some, the behavior may be minimal and have a limited effect on their lives. But for others, the effects are far greater (Carnes, 2001). People whose sexual behavior is compulsive report a loss of control, anxiety, obsessional thinking, mood instability, and significant impairment in their daily lives (Chaudhri & Karim, 2012). Often, these behaviors are counter to the person's value system and agreements made in his or her primary relationship, causing the person to feel shame, guilt, and despair after the conclusion of the behavior. Sexually compulsive behavior can elevate the risk of sexually transmitted infections.

The effect on family members is also included in the micro-level analysis. When spouses and partners discover the sexual acting out, they experience betrayal and loss of trust (Pollard, Hook, Corley, & Schneider, 2014). Schneider (2000) wrote that more than 22% of couples where cybersex was identified as a problem proceeded to separate or divorce. *Cybersex* is the term used when people access the Internet for sexual purposes (Goldberg, Peterson, Rosen, & Sara, 2008).

Partners of sex addicts typically experience their own shame, often blaming themselves for not being attractive enough. Research shows that partners have high levels of distress regarding their partner's hypersexual behavior and about the relationship itself, but they do not usually exhibit signs of ongoing psychopathology (Reid, Carpenter, & Draper, 2011). Many social workers as well as other clinicians use a trauma-informed approach in working with partners of sexually addicted clients. A significant number of partners show evidence of symptoms consistent with Post-Traumatic Stress Disorder (PTSD), such as flashbacks, sleep disturbance, intrusive thoughts, emotional numbing, and impaired concentration (Steffens & Rennie, 2006).

Children are frequently aware of a parent's sexual acting out behavior. A study by Black, Dillon, and Carnes (2003) showed that 60 of 89 children of sex addicts surveyed were aware of the parent's sexual acting out behavior. Minor children in a family with sex addiction frequently experience exposure to pornography, parental verbal altercations, and "lack of attention because of one parent's involvement with the computer and the other parent's preoccupation with the cybersex addict" (Schneider, 2000, p. 32).

An analysis of sex addiction on the mezzo level refers to the effects on a community. The behavior affects more than just the family. For example, politicians whose exploits make the news, cause constituents to feel betrayed. Sexual harassment in employment settings causes the victim of the harassment to experience stress, particularly causing negative outcomes in job attitudes and work behaviors (Schneider, Swan, & Fitzgerald, 1997). Church pastors and teachers regularly make the television news for sexual boundary violations that, in some cases, result in criminal acts.

Employers can experience losses from sexually compulsive behavior as well. People struggling with sex addiction report distraction, time loss, unmanageability, and poor decision-making abilities (Carnes, 2001). Medium to large companies are now monitoring employee Internet use because they are aware of the costs associated with compulsive pornography or cybersex use.

Finally, in looking at the macro system, are the effects of sexually compulsive behavior on a society and culture. For example, many young people get their ideas about love and romance from the media (Eadie, 1997). Early exposure to pornography predicts less progressive gender role attitudes for both males and females. In males, early exposure to pornography can also lead to greater levels of sexual harassment perpetration (Brown & L'Engle, 2009). "Pornography is likely to contribute to sexually objectifying understandings of and behaviors toward girls and women" (Flood, 2009, p. 392).

Treatment Considerations

When individuals seek sex addiction treatment, it is frequently after discovery by a partner, when the behavior has been discovered at work, or when there are legal consequences, such as arrest. In some instances, a person could be facing all three consequences.

Discovery by partners is often in the form of discovering chats on a mobile phone, viewing history in the web browser, finding photos, and many more scenarios. For partners who are blindsided by the addict's behavior, the results are devastating. Some partners may choose to leave the relationship, whether temporarily or permanently. Many partners want to stay in the relationship because of love, children, financial support, and for many other reasons. Whether they stay in the relationship or not, a common response for partners is to question themselves, their attractiveness, and the meaning of the many years of the relationship.

Work consequences are frequently just as devastating. Many employers now monitor Internet behavior, tracking websites and downloads. This can end poorly for employees found to have viewed material against the policy of their employer. Frequently, the result is immediate termination, followed by a period of unemployment and difficulty in finding new work.

Legal consequences can occur from arrest for having sex in public, solicitation of a prostitute, or downloading of illegal images, such as pornography depicting minors. In some communities, these individuals may be required to register as sex offenders. Additionally, jail time, community service, and fines are common.

According to Carnes (2001), many people with sex addiction have a fear of stopping. They will identify sex as their most important need, experiencing fear at the thought of giving up the behavior. Remember that in many cases, the behavior developed as an adaptive response to a family of origin dynamic. Many have tried repeatedly to stop, only to return to the behavior time and time again.

Treatment Planning

As with other types of mental health and addiction treatment, treatment planning is vital to working successfully with sex addicts desiring recovery. Treatment planning serves multiple functions. First, as the social worker collaborates with the client (and family) to gather information and plan services, an alliance is built. Secondly, appropriate treatment planning helps ensure the assessment was completed in a culturally competent way. Treatment planning also helps the social worker identify client strengths, as well as needs and preferences, in order to empower the client as much as possible. Finally, treatment planning serves multiple functions in justifying the need for treatment, documenting progress, and also for evaluating the efficacy of a program or intervention strategy (Adams & Grieder, 2004).

Before designing a treatment plan, the social worker must first complete a thorough assessment. This is best done when there is plenty of time to facilitate the engagement and trust-building process, as is necessary with most types of social work assessment.

Several components are helpful in completing a thorough assessment of the client's behavior. The first step is the clinical interview. Due to stigma, some information may be difficult for social workers to elicit from a client, especially in a first session. Social workers should be proficient in interview techniques designed to sensitively raise shameful topics. Normalization is an interview technique that lets a client know that many people experience what he or she might be experiencing. Shame attenuation is another interview technique that enables the interviewer to connect with the client's pain, thereby reducing shame and enabling a more honest response (Shea, 2009).

There are a variety of treatment intensity levels for sexual addiction, from inpatient programs that are at least 30 days in length, intensive outpatient programs that are anywhere from 2 weeks to 18 weeks, as well as more traditional outpatient therapy treatment. The best scenario is when clients can attend the highest level of care indicated for their behaviors and recovery process. Whatever level of care is chosen, individual and group therapy are necessary for recovery (Carnes, 2013).

In the early stages of treatment, individual therapy helps clients stop—or achieve sobriety from—their behaviors and learn to tolerate uncomfortable emotions. At this time, the social worker works with the client to decrease the denial of the problem through taking a sexual history, as well as an inventory of consequences and secrets. It also helps to teach the client about strategies he or she uses to maintain acting-out behaviors, such as global thinking (e.g., All men look at porn), rationalization (e.g., I have a higher sex drive than others), minimizing (e.g., It doesn't hurt anyone if no one knows), comparison (e.g., At least I have never paid money for sex like Joe has), uniqueness (e.g., I have lots of stress and sex helps me relax), avoiding (e.g., I'm not going to talk about that), blaming (e.g., If you weren't so heavy, I would want to have sex with you more), intellectualizing (e.g., What is sex really? It's not the same as love or intimacy), hopelessness/helplessness (e.g., I have nothing else in my life that I enjoy), manipulation (e.g., It's your fault that I do this; you're away every evening so I surf for porn), compartmentalizing (e.g., I'm going to put this in a box in my mind and not think about it when I am with family), crazy-making (e.g., You're imagining things again), or seduction (e.g., You know you are the only one I want, baby; Carnes, 2010). Acknowledging the thinking that perpetuates the behavior begins the process of being more honest with the self.

During this time in early treatment, the recovering addict needs to learn to accept the reality of the problem (Carnes, 2010) and learn problem-solving skills, social skills, and self-care so he or she has alternative coping strategies when the craving to act out is present. This will also help the sex addict become more comfortable to reach out to a support network of others who can provide recovery support (Turner, 2009).

As treatment continues, social workers help clients understand how and why they become preoccupied with sex and how they then move into a ritualized pattern of behavior, which can quickly move into the problematic sexual behavior. Social workers should also help their clients identify what triggers their desire to act out sexually, frequently self-hostility or shame. Many researchers and clinicians believe that sexual acting-out behavior serves as way to distract or minimize the experience of painful emotional states, such as pain, shame, fear, or anger (Reid, 2010).

Mindfulness is a strategy that can be quite helpful to clients as they begin their recovery process. Mindfulness helps recovering sex addicts to self-regulate, to moderate their stress levels, and to tolerate the thoughts and desires to act out sexually (Reid, Bramen, Anderson, & Cohen, 2014). Mindfulness is a central strategy in Dialectical Behavior Therapy (DBT), which is helpful as a therapeutic strategy for sex addiction clients in early recovery (Linehan, 1993). Using DBT, social workers can help their clients tolerate the emotions they experience, then engage in new behaviors that are in line with their recovery goals. DBT's concept of distress tolerance is also helpful to recovering sex addicts, as they must become accustomed to experiencing distressing emotions, rather than escaping them.

As therapy progresses, deeper issues are addressed using a variety of therapy models. Cognitive behavioral therapy is useful in helping identify and correct self-defeating beliefs; humanistic therapy helps reduce internalized shame that, if left unaddressed, can cause a sense of hopelessness for change; and psychodynamic and ego-based therapy help clients learn how their family of origin impacted them and can help them process through the remaining emotions stored in their bodies. According to Turner (2009), Eye Movement

Desensitization and Reprocessing (EMDR) is helpful in this middle phase. Turner adds that the middle phase of treatment is an important time to resolve family-of-origin wounds, usually through trauma work.

During the final phase of therapy for sex addiction recovery, the focus is on building and strengthening relationships. Couples therapy is usually indicated at this stage, as well as continued individual work to assist in building and strengthening attachment to the partner, improving communication, and tolerating emotional intimacy. Building healthy sexuality is also emphasized in this stage (Turner, 2009). Carnes (2013) writes that the recovery process takes from three to five years.

Group therapy is necessary for sex addiction recovery. In fact it is a staple treatment modality in inpatient treatment centers for sex addiction (Nerenberg, 2000). Group therapy provides a variety of benefits to the recovering person. Irvin Yalom's 11 therapeutic factors offer the best descriptions of the benefits of group therapy. According to Yalom, these therapeutic factors are necessary to help a client improve (Yalom & Leszcz, 2005). Of the 11 therapeutic factors, instillation of hope, universality, and imparting information are extremely important early in the treatment process. Instillation of hope refers to the client believing that therapy can be helpful and effective. Universality enables the client to realize that he or she is not alone in the struggle. Imparting information describes the process of psychoeducation that occurs in group therapy (Nerenberg, 2000).

The partner or spouse should also engage in treatment. Individual therapy and group therapy are both necessary to help him or her recover from the multiple traumas of the partner's sex addiction. Often partners view the need for their own therapy as blaming them, that they are somehow part of the problem. It is important that social workers avoid giving the impression that the partner is at all to blame—this would further the trauma and create treatment-induced trauma (Minwalla, 2012). In fact, partners of sex addicts have been significantly affected by years of the partner's lies, suspecting something is wrong, only to have it vehemently denied. This interferes with their need to trust their senses, leading to confusion about what is real in their lives. Partners also have experienced many betrayals that create a sense of fear and need for safety, not unlike what is experienced by people who suffer from PTSD (Minwalla, 2012).

In the vignette at the beginning of this chapter, Janelle blames herself for her husband's behavior. This is common and must be worked on therapeutically to empower Janelle to set limits and begin to care properly for herself. Also, the social worker must enable Janelle to explore her grief about the loss of the relationship she thought she had. This can be thought of as traumatic and as a betrayal. Processing grief and trauma, and working on self-empowerment will strengthen Janelle's role in the family system, so she will not identify as a victim, but as an important part of the process of recovering the relationship, if the couple decide to remain together.

Couples or conjoint therapy is not indicated until the addicted client has achieved some recovery time. The individuals are usually not skilled at self-care, social skills, or problem solving, so individual work helps build these skills as the addict gains some recovery time and both partners improve their recovery support systems (Turner, 2009). In the long run, many couples eventually realize that the chaos they have gone through has actually enabled them to be more intimate, communicating their vulnerabilities in a way that they never knew how to do.

Epidemiology and Diversity Considerations

Fong (2006) states that approximately 6% of the U.S. population engages in sexually compulsive behavior. Men make up the majority of individuals who are addicted to sex (Goodman, 1998). Many women are affected by this addiction as well.

Gay men are also affected by sexual addiction. Although the treatment methods are, for the most part, the same, it is important for the social worker to be aware of some of the possible developmental and relational trauma gay men may have experienced, which differs from their heterosexual counterparts. Gay men have often experienced repression of their homosexual feelings in childhood (Weiss, 2002), may have trauma related to grief over losses due to HIV/AIDS (Weiss, 2002), and may have experienced childhood bullying because of their sexual identity (orientation). It is important for the social worker to be aware of these and other possibilities as sources of trauma. It is also important for social workers working with gay clients to be aware of differing cultural norms regarding sex and monogamy, while maintaining a nonjudgmental presence with the client (Weiss, 2002). Little research has been completed in relation to possible racial and cultural differences in the prevalence of sex addiction (Robinson, 1999).

Transference and Countertransference Issues

Client transference is likely when working with sexual issues. Clients will frequently react defensively when facing their behavior, feel accountable to another person like the social worker, or feel entitled (Tays, Garrett, & Earle, 2002). This will often present as anger in the client. The responsibility of the social worker is to work with the client to understand what is occurring.

It is helpful to clients for the social worker to use the transference to provide a corrective or healing attachment experience for the client. For example, when a client shares their deepest shame-filled secrets, and the social worker responds in a validating, containing way, the client experiences a reduction of shame, promoting a healing experience, and empowering behavior change.

When working with the client Jason from the vignette, the social worker will need to take plenty of time to build rapport and trust, using supportive eye contact, reflective listening, and validation. After several sessions, Jason should begin to think of his time with his social worker as a safe and supportive place where he can tell the truth about who he is, without fear of judgment. In addition to enabling effective treatment, transparency and honesty—with the social worker's acceptance—will reduce shame, enabling empowerment for change.

Countertransference is also extremely likely for the social worker working with sex addicts or their partners. Therapists can find themselves reacting to a client's behaviors—at times with repulsion or on the other hand with their own sexual arousal. Appropriate boundaries are vital when working with this population, as they often present in early phases of treatment with a high level of sexual energy. The best scenario for social workers is to have clinical supervision and psychotherapy regularly because a social worker's own sexual issues and family of origin history are frequently triggered.

Legal and Ethical Concerns

Social workers should be aware of potential legal issues that can occur. For example, clients could disclose that they have abused a child. For this reason, it is vital to inform clients of your mandated reporting status for child abuse and elder abuse as a social worker.

In the case of Jason and Janelle in the vignette, all the social workers and clinicians involved in the case should inform the clients of reporting requirements, explaining their mandated reporting status. If Jason were to disclose that he had sexually abused a child during his acting-out behavior, it would be necessary for the social worker to break confidentiality and file a report with child protective services. It is vital that the client is aware of this in advance of a disclosure like this.

It is also possible that social workers will find out that a client who has HIV, for example, has had unprotected sex with unknowing people. In most states, this is not reportable to the authorities and would be breaking confidentiality if reported. Likely this will be more of an ethical dilemma, and the social worker will choose to work with the client therapeutically regarding this issue and obtain supervision or consult with a colleague.

Since sexual issues are sensitive, social workers should use care when writing their clinical documentation, keeping in mind the audience, and the possible use of records in court cases, including divorce proceedings. Charting should be thorough and ethical, without so much detail that could jeopardize the client. Social workers should obtain legal consultation for clarity here.

Neither sex addiction, hypersexual disorder, nor Internet addiction is included in the DSM-5. Therefore, if the client is pursuing insurance reimbursement, a diagnosis of 312.30 Impulse Control Disorder NOS might be appropriate. Clinicians also use 302.9 Sexual Disorder NOS (APA, 2013). Ethically, the social worker must ensure the client meets the diagnostic criteria for whatever diagnosis is chosen.

Barriers to Treatment

Both the stigma of hypersexual behavior and the lack of treatment options are barriers to treatment. Stigma and taboo related to topics of sexuality are still strong in most cultures. Specific and in-depth training in the treatment of sex addiction, both for the hypersexual individual and his or her partner, is still relatively rare. The most comprehensive training offered is by the International Institute of Trauma and Addiction Professionals (IITAP, n.d.). Not much information is provided in a Master of Social Work program, except for some information given in a human sexuality elective course.

Another barrier to treatment is cost. Inpatient and intensive outpatient facilities are expensive and insurance companies will not typically pay to treat hypersexual behavior. Often, clients can be accurately dually diagnosed with depression, anxiety, or substance abuse; so some of the cost can be covered by insurance companies in this way (Hagedorn, 2009).

Often when clients use cost as the reason they do not engage in treatment, it can help to reflect on the cost of their addiction. Many clients have spent thousands of dollars on escorts, massage parlors, websites, legal fees, and so on. Social workers can become skilled in gently reminding clients of the costs associated with their hypersexual behavior, and the need to invest in their treatment.

MEZZO PERSPECTIVE: EFFECTS ON THE COMMUNITY

Sex addiction affects not only the individual and the family but also the community. The media regularly reports on celebrities, politicians, and sports figures discovered to be having a sexual relationship with someone other than their spouse or partner. Frequently these individuals enter sex addiction treatment (Reay, Attwood, & Gooder, 2012). Social workers must be aware of how revelations of inappropriate sexual behavior can affect clients and the larger culture. Although people frequently joke about celebrities and sex addiction, their disclosure of sex addiction and treatment serves to destigmatize the problem, enabling more sufferers to seek help (Ryan, 2010).

Sexual harassment of work colleagues or subordinates is another behavior frequently exhibited by sexual addicts. Sexual harassment negatively affects job attitudes and behavior at work for those who have been harassed (Schneider et al., 1997).

Excessive pornography use is shown to cause problems at the community level as well. In fact, pornography use is how most male sexual addicts began their addictive behavior (Sussman, 2007). Increased exposure to pornography is correlated with higher levels of behavioral aggression. Also, higher levels of pornography exposure lead to a lower level of empathy for victims of sexual assault (Foubert, Brosi, & Bannon, 2011). For many sex addicts, pornography consumption is their main source of acting out (Sussman, 2007), so social workers must be aware of the potential for problems resulting from excessive pornography use, including greater adherence to sexist or harmful ideas about sex and sexuality and increased likelihood of engaging in sexual assault (Flood, 2009).

MACRO PERSPECTIVE: SOCIAL POLICY ISSUES

A significant issue related to macro-level policy exists. Nothing related to hypersexual behavior or sex addiction is present in the DSM-5 (APA, 2013), so third-party reimbursement (i.e., health insurance companies) does not directly cover treatment. This means clients without another reimbursable diagnosis will have to pay for their treatment completely out of pocket, preventing many individuals from getting the help that they and their families need.

There are opportunities for social workers to advocate for policy changes. First, social workers can educate people about the devastation this addiction brings to people's lives. Education of community leaders, healthcare providers, politicians, and so on, will help decrease the stigma associated with this disorder and increase the public's awareness of the problem and appropriate services.

Education of community members is also helpful at decreasing stigma and making people aware of services. Over time, this will serve to change the public's view of sex addiction, so it is no longer viewed with scorn as something celebrities claim when they have gotten caught but as a real problem that causes heartache and pain to all involved.

Advocacy for government and insurance companies to view sex addiction as a real problem would be immensely helpful as well. This problem is as devastating as substance addictions and mental disorders, so it would enable more people to access services if third-party payers, including Medicare and Medicaid, would cover a portion of treatment costs.

CONCLUSION

The field of sex addiction treatment continues to develop and grow as researchers and clinicians try to keep up with ever-changing technology and its effects on people and their sexual behavior. When people are struggling with sex addiction and its consequences, the eventual goal is for them to reach a place of integrating healthy sex into their lives. Social workers, as experts in human relationships, are uniquely suited to providing helpful interventions to this pain-filled group of people. Even if the terminology changes to hypersexual disorder, or another term entirely, the devastation caused to individuals and families is real and deserves the attention of the social work profession.

INTERNET RESOURCES

- Sex Addicts Anonymous: http://www.saa-recovery.org
- Sexual Compulsives Anonymous: http://www.sca-recovery.org
- Sex and Love Addicts Anonymous: http://www.slaafws.org/
- Novus Mindful Life Institute: http://www.novusmindfullife.com
- The Sexual Addiction Screening Test (SAST; available through the International Institute for Trauma and Addiction Professionals): http://www.sexhelp.com
- Hypersexual Behavior Inventory (HBI; available at the website of Rory Reid, PhD): http://www.rory.net

DISCUSSION QUESTIONS

1. Sex and sexual practices are difficult for most people to discuss, due to cultural taboos, religious beliefs, family traditions, and internalized sexual shame. How comfortable would you feel asking your clients about specific sexual practices?

2. Clients can sense a social worker's discomfort in a session. How might your discomfort show up in session?

3. How could you increase your comfort level in advance of client work with sex addicts or their partners?

4. Think of when you have heard about celebrities or politicians who disclose sex addiction or are arrested for illegal behavior. What was your reaction at the time? Has your opinion changed?

5. Imagine you have a client whom you believe to be sex addicted. Discuss how you would confront his or her likely denial, attempting to move the client toward acceptance and motivation to change.

REFERENCES

Adams, N., & Grieder, D. M. (2004). *Treatment planning for person-centered care: The road to mental health and addiction recovery*. Burlington, MA: Elsevier Academic Press.

American Psychiatric Association. (2013). *Diagnostic and statistical manual of mental disorders* (5th ed.). Arlington, VA: Author.

Black, C., Dillon, D., & Carnes, S. (2003). Disclosure to children: Hearing the child's experience.

Sexual Addiction and Compulsivity: The Journal of Treatment & Prevention, 10(1), 67–78.

Bronfenbrenner, U. (1989). Ecological systems theory. In R. Vasta (Ed.), *Annals of child development: Six theories of child development: Revised formulations and current issues* (pp. 187–247). Greenwich, CT: JAI Press.

Brown, J., & L'Engle, K. (2009). X-rated: Sexual attitudes and behaviors associated with U.S. early adolescents' exposure to sexually explicit media. *Communication Research, 36*(1), 129–151.

Carnes, P. (2001). *Out of the shadows* (3rd ed.). Center City, MN: Hazelden.

Carnes, P. (2010). *Facing the shadow: Starting sexual and relationship recovery.* Carefree, AZ: Gentle Path Press.

Carnes, P. (2013). *Don't call it love: Recovery from sexual addiction.* New York, NY: Bantam.

Carnes, P., & Wilson, M. (2002). The sexual addiction assessment process. In P. Carnes & K. Adams (Eds.), *Clinical management of sex addiction* (pp. 3–20). New York, NY: Brunner-Routledge.

Chaudhri, P., & Karim, R. (2012). Behavioral addictions: An overview. *Journal of Psychoactive Drugs, 44*(1), 5–17.

Eadie, B. (1997, March). Men, women, and pornography. *Spectra, 6*–10.

Flood, M. (2009). The harms of pornography exposure among children and young people. *Child Abuse Review, 18*(6), 384–400.

Fong, T. W. (2006). Understanding and managing compulsive sexual behaviors. *Psychiatry (Edgmont), 3*(11), 51–58.

Foubert, J., Brosi, M., & Bannon, R. (2011). Pornography viewing among fraternity men: Effects on bystander intervention, rape myth acceptance and behavioral intent to commit sexual assault. *Sexual Addiction & Compulsivity: Journal of Treatment and Prevention, 18*(4), 212–231.

Giugliano, J. R. (2009). Sexual addiction: Diagnostic problems. *International Journal of Mental Health and Addiction, 7*(2), 283–294.

Goldberg, P. D., Peterson, B. D., Rosen, K. H., & Sara, M. L. (2008). Cybersex: The impact of a contemporary problem on the practices of marriage and family therapists. *Journal of Marital and Family Therapy, 34,* 469–480.

Goodman, A. (1998). *Sexual addiction.* Madison, WI: International Universities Press.

Greenfield, P. M. (2004). Inadvertent exposure to pornography on the Internet: Implications of peer-to-peer file-sharing networks for child development and families. *Journal of Applied Developmental Psychology, 25*(6), 741–750.

Hagedorn, W. B. (2009). The call for a new *Diagnostic and Statistical Manual of Mental Disorders* diagnosis: Addictive disorders. *Journal of Addictions & Offender Counseling, 29,* 110–127.

International Institute for Trauma and Addiction Professionals (IITAP). (n.d.). Retrieved from http://www.iitap.com

Kafka, M. P. (2010), Hypersexual disorder: A proposed diagnosis for DSM-V. *Archives of Sexual Behavior, 39,* 377–400.

Katehakis, A. (2009). Affective neuroscience and the treatment of sexual addiction. *Sexual Addiction and Compulsivity: The Journal of Treatment & Prevention, 16*(1), 1–31.

Linehan, M. (1993). *Cognitive behavioral treatment of borderline personality disorder.* New York, NY: Guilford Press.

Minwalla, O. (2012). *Thirteen dimensions of sex addiction-induced trauma (SAIT) among partners and spouses affected by sex addiction.* Retrieved from http://theinstituteforsexualhealth.com/thirteen-dimensions-of-sex-addiction-induced-trauma-sait-among-partners-and-spouses-impacted-by-sex-addiction

Nerenberg, A. (2000). The value of group psychotherapy for sexual addicts in a residential setting. *Sexual Addiction and Compulsivity: The Journal of Treatment & Prevention, 7*(3), 197–209.

Pollard, S. E., Hook, J. N., Corley, M. D., & Schneider, J. P. (2014). Support utilization by partners of self-identified sex addicts. *Journal of Sex and Marital Therapy, 40*(4), 339–348.

Reay, B., Attwood, N., & Gooder, C. (2012). Inventing sex: The short history of sex addiction. *Sexuality & Culture, 17*(1), 1–19.

Reid, R. C. (2010). Differentiating emotions in a sample of men in treatment for hypersexual behavior. *Journal of Social Work Practice in the Addictions, 10*(2), 197–213.

Reid, R. C., Bramen, J. E., Anderson, A., & Cohen, M. S. (2014). Mindfulness, emotional dysregulation, impulsivity, and stress proneness among hypersexual patients. *Journal of Clinical Psychology, 70*(4), 313–321.

Reid, R. C., Carpenter, B. N., & Draper, E. D. (2011). Disputing the notion of psychopathology among women married to hypersexual men using the MMPI-2-RF. *Journal of Sex and Marital Therapy, 37*(1), 45–55.

Robinson, D. (1999). Sexual addiction as an adaptive response to posttraumatic stress disorder in the African American community. *Sexual Addiction and Compulsivity: The Journal of Treatment & Prevention, 6*(1), 11–22,

Ryan, H. (2010). Celebrities add credence to sex addiction therapy. *Chicago Tribune.* Retrieved from http://libproxy.usc.edu

Schneider, J. (2000). Effects of cybersex addiction on the family: Results of a survey. *Sexual Addiction and Compulsivity: The Journal of Treatment & Prevention, 7,* 31–58.

Schneider, K. T., Swan, S., & Fitzgerald, L. F. (1997). Job-related and psychological effects of sexual harassment in the workplace: Empirical evidence from two organizations. *Journal of Applied Psychology, 82*(3), 401.

Schore, A. (2001). Effects of a secure attachment relationship on right brain development, affect regulation, and infant mental health. *Infant Mental Health Journal, 22*(1–2), 7–66.

Schwartz, M., & Southern, S. (2002). The sexual addiction assessment process. In P. Carnes & K. Adams (Eds.), *Clinical management of sex addiction.* New York, NY: Brunner-Routledge.

Shea, S. (2009). Suicide assessment. *Psychiatric Times, 26*(12), 1–26.

Steffens, B. A., & Rennie, R. L. (2006). The traumatic nature of disclosure for wives of sexual addicts. *Sexual Addiction & Compulsivity: Journal of Treatment and Prevention, 13*(2–3), 247–267.

Stinson, J., & Becker, J. (2013). *Treating sex offenders: An evidence-based manual.* New York, NY: Guilford Press.

Sussman, S. (2007). Sexual addiction among teens: A review. *Sexual Addiction & Compulsivity: Journal of Treatment and Prevention, 14*(4), 257–278.

Tays, T., Garrett, B., & Earle, R. (2002). Clinical boundary issues with sexually addicted clients. In P. Carnes & K. Adams (Eds.), *Clinical management of sex addiction.* New York, NY: Brunner-Routledge.

Turner, M. (2009). Uncovering and treating sex addiction in couples therapy. *Journal of Family Psychotherapy, 20*(2–3), 283–302.

Weiss, R. (2002). Treatment concerns for gay male sex addicts. In P. Carnes & K. Adams (Eds.), *Clinical management of sex addiction.* New York, NY: Brunner-Routledge.

Yalom, I., & Leszcz, M. (2005). *Theory and practice of group psychotherapy* (5th ed.). New York, NY: Basic Books.

CHAPTER 9

Gambling Disorders

Rory C. Reid, Jacquelene F. Moghaddam, & Timothy Fong

CHAPTER OBJECTIVES

- Explain the epidemiology, risk factors, and associated clinical characteristics of gambling disorders;
- Learn about the diagnostic and assessment issues for clients seeking help for a gambling problem;
- Discuss pharmacological and psychotherapeutic approaches used in the treatment of gambling disorders;
- Describe a social worker's role in understanding the diversity, legal, advocacy, and policy considerations for gambling disorders.

CASE VIGNETTE 1

John is a 27-year-old Caucasian man living in Southern California. John owns a carpet cleaning company, which allows some flexibility in his work schedule. John was an only child and grew up observing his father playing poker in a weekly game night with neighbors and friends. John's mother had a disability that limited her capacity to adequately care for John and often required John to help with various tasks such as cooking, cleaning, and running errands. These additional responsibilities often required John to forego activities with his friends, causing some resentment toward his mother and his family circumstances. John's father struggled with the situation and felt guilty his son had to help out so much. To compensate, whenever John's father had a big win from poker night, he would reward John with some type of gift. Over time, gambling became both a source of escape but also comfort when winnings translated to rewards. Naturally, John learned how to play poker and established a weekly gambling night with friends during his college years in Southern California. Additionally, John would travel to Las Vegas during spring break and long weekends to gamble with friends, using fake identification cards to meet the legal age requirement of 21. On one of his first trips to Vegas, John won big at a poker table, making him the envy of his buddies and their girlfriends. He spent the winnings paying for their dinners, night shows, and other entertainment in Vegas. The popularity was intoxicating for John and filled a void he had felt for years growing up without a "normal mom" like the rest of his friends. John began spending more and more time preoccupied with gambling activities, organizing poker games, or planning his next trip to Vegas. He began to use gambling to escape the stress of college life and the emotional pain of having lost his childhood opportunities in order to care for his mother. He applied for, and received, several credit cards that he used to finance gambling activities and cover losses he incurred. Because of the money spent gambling in Vegas, John would receive mailers offering free rooms and meals at hotels where he had played poker. On one occasion, after a few losses at the poker table, John's friends decided to go dancing. John told them he would catch up later and returned to the poker table determined to win back the money he had lost. Unfortunately, John lost more money, racking up $5,000 of credit card debt. When asked by his friends later that night, John lied, telling them, "I scored a big win," and he offered to buy them all drinks, which he paid for with a credit card. This pattern continued until John had to take a semester off college to work and pay off some of his debt. This diminished some of his gambling behaviors, but only for a time. John would return to gambling despite multiple attempts to curtail his gambling and in spite of negative consequences it was having in his life. When asked by others about his winnings, John kept secret the fact that he was losing money, which only contributed to his desire to continue to gamble in pursuit of a big win. After college, John started his carpet cleaning business and secured a number of contracts with several local hotel chains and hired employees to do the work, which freed up some of his time to gamble. He also found creative ways to rationalize using gambling-related expenditures for tax deductions. However, this led to more and more time at the casinos and less time paying attention to work-related matters, and his business revenues and contracts began to decline. This added further to John's stress that would lead him to gamble more to escape the personal financial difficulties he was having. John's relationships also suffered, as he would isolate from others into the world of gambling. This diminished his relationships with close friends and potential romantic interests. Although John realized he had a problem with gambling, he felt a sense of powerless over his cravings and urges to escape to the intoxicating world of poker.

INTRODUCTION

Approximately 70% to 90% of adults in North America report having participated in some type of gambling (Petry, Stinson, & Grant, 2005). For some, however, gambling activities can lead to significant consequences, such as financial problems, recurrent fixation with gambling, relationship discord, emotional distress, and legal challenges. Such individuals often report feeling unable to control their gambling activities and experience multiple unsuccessful attempts to reduce or discontinue harmful gambling behaviors. The American Psychiatric Association (2013) asserts individuals experiencing such symptoms may suffer from a gambling

disorder, with lifetime prevalence rates of approximately 1%–3% in the general population.

Gambling is defined as wagering money or something of material value on an event whose outcome is uncertain, in anticipation of winning additional money or goods. Several forms of gambling exist and include the use of slot machines, playing casino games, bingo, keno, purchasing lottery tickets, playing cards for money, online gambling, and betting on sports events. As previously noted, although 70% to 90% of adults have partaken in some variation of gambling, only 1%–3% are considered pathological in regards to their gambling activities (Petry et al., 2005; Raylu & Oei, 2002).

Gambling researchers have conceptualized gambling behaviors on a continuum, operationalized by gambling-related problems and gambling involvement (Oei & Gordon, 2008). This paradigm suggests three groups of gamblers:

1. *Social or recreational gamblers* are readily able to control the time and money they spend gambling. Social and recreational gamblers do not have reported consequences related to their gambling. They comprise the largest group of gamblers.

2. *Problem gamblers* indicate some consequences associated with their gambling, including gambling-related debt, spending more time or money gambling than anticipated, and neglecting aspects of their lives in order to gamble. These individuals may also feel guilty about their gambling.

3. *Compulsive, addicted, or pathological gamblers* have significant gambling-related consequences, which often inhibit their daily functioning. These individuals frequently report extreme thoughts about gambling activities and irresistible urges and cravings to gamble. A key characteristic of this group is repetitive unsuccessful attempts to reduce or stop gambling. These individuals put their jobs or relationships at risk or involve themselves in criminal activities in order to gamble. These gamblers also report gambling in order to divert negative emotions or manage difficult situations. These individuals usually meet *Diagnostic and Statistical Manual of Mental Disorders* (DSM-5) diagnostic criteria for a gambling disorder (American Psychiatric Association, 2013).

This chapter provides an overview of gambling disorders, including diagnostic issues, identified groups at risk for problem gambling, legal and ethical concerns, and clinical interventions for individuals who may seek treatment for gambling disorders. Approaches to working with individuals from diverse communities as well as issues arising in work with clients presenting with problem gambling behaviors will also be addressed. Finally, a brief policy analysis as it relates to problem gambling–relevant legislation and/or legal issues will be highlighted for social workers interested in advocacy.

MICRO PERSPECTIVE

Assessment

Individuals who appear to meet criteria for a gambling disorder are among those often referred to social workers and other mental health professionals for an assessment. Typically such assessments combine a personal history from the gambler, collateral information from someone familiar with the gambler's activities such as a significant other or family member (with permission from the client), and self-report questionnaires. Common questionnaires used in assessment include the National Opinion Research Center (NORC) Diagnostic Screen for Gambling Problems–Self Administered (NODS-SA), South Oaks Gambling Screen (SOGS), and Problem Gambling Severity Index (PGSI). These questionnaires typically go beyond the DSM criteria and gather additional information that provides more specificity about gambling history and can be easily administered and scored. Although diagnosis of gambling disorders is within the scope of social work practice, consultations or referrals to psychologists or psychiatrists should be considered if the presenting case is more complex. For example, if a patient who has been diagnosed with Parkinson's disease develops a gambling problem, it may be related to medications used to treat the disease and a medical evaluation would be appropriate.

In the case illustration of John, he would appear to meet the DSM-5 criteria for a gambling disorder. His gambling activities escalated over time, with greater amounts of money being spent that required him to acquire credit card debt in order to gamble. John appears to sense that his gambling behavior is problematic, yet despite attempts to cut down on his gambling, he continues to pursue gambling in ways that cause problems. Moreover, he used gambling activities to cope with the stress of college life and later to deal with the stress related to his business. He is lying to others in order to conceal the extent to which he has a gambling problem, and his gambling is actually exacerbating his declining business revenues. It also appears John may be crossing the line in how he's doing his tax accounting, which could put him at risk for legal consequences. As noted in the DSM-5, when individuals manifest 4 of the 9 symptom criteria in a 12-month period, the diagnostic threshold is met, provided such symptoms are not explained by other conditions, such as occurring exclusively within the context of a manic episode.

Risk Factors and Clinical Characteristics

Several clinical and epidemiological studies have identified groups at increased risk for developing a gambling disorder; they include male gender, younger-aged individuals or the elderly, those from lower socioeconomic status, physical disability status, non-white ethnic/racial background, and divorced or separated marital status (Petry, 2005b; Toneatto & Nguyen, 2007). Certain psychiatric risk factors have also been associated with a vulnerability for developing a gambling disorder across an individual's lifetime, including those with co-occurring psychiatric disorders, particularly substance abuse, attention-deficit hyperactivity disorder, mood disorders, anxiety disorders, and antisocial personality disorder (Dickson-Gillespie, Rugle, Rosenthal, & Fong, 2008; Johansson, Grant, Kim, Odlaug, & Götestam, 2009). Evidence demonstrates pathological gambling is a heritable disease (Slutske, Meier et al., 2009). Although the specific genetic processes are still unclear, it has been speculated they may be related to common underlying traits of risk taking, sensitivity to immediate rewards, or diminished perspectives related to loss aversion.

Some have suggested differences in the neurobiology in the brain may be associated with gambling problems. Research has linked reduced judgment, impulsivity, emotional reactivity, and diminished decision making, all commonly found among pathological gamblers, to executive dysfunctioning (Ledgerwood et al., 2012; Reid, McKittrick, Davtian, & Fong, 2012). Moreover,

mounting evidence indicates that numerous neurotransmitter systems (e.g., dopaminergic, serotonergic, noradrenergic, opioidergic) may also play a role in the pathophysiology of disordered gambling (Potenza, 2008).

Current research has focused on the relationship between Parkinson's disease, namely dopamine agonists, and pathological gambling. Although a causal link between the two disorders has not been ascertained, there has been striking evidence of Parkinson's patients medicated with dopamine agonists who have developed problematic gambling behaviors (O'Sullivan, Evans, & Lees, 2009; Steeves et al., 2009; Weintraub et al., 2009). This relationship has reinforced the dopamine reward pathway in the onset or progression of gambling disorders.

Different aspects of personality have also been examined in the study of gambling disorders, particularly impulsivity, which is routinely linked to problem gambling. Using a personality index, the NEO Personality Inventory-Revised (Costa & McCrae, 1992), researchers have identified interpersonal sensitivity, distress intolerance, distrust of others, and feelings of frustration as commonly observed traits among pathological gamblers. Compared to individuals without gambling problems, pathological gamblers are also known to endorse lower levels of self-control and competence and make decisions in a rash or impetuous manner (Reid et al., 2011). It has been suggested that pathological gamblers are narcissistic; however, research has indicated that rates of narcissistic personality disorder among pathological gamblers do not differ from those of the general population (Sacco, Cunningham-Williams, Ostmann, & Spitznagel, 2008).

Diversity Considerations

As individuals from low-SES backgrounds, ethnic/racial minorities, and those with physical disabilities have been found to be at increased risk for developing a gambling disorder (Petry, 2005b; Toneatto & Nguyen, 2007), social workers helping members of these groups should be aware of diversity considerations. Clients from ethnic/racial minority backgrounds may prefer to work with therapists from their own cultural background. Likewise, clients for whom English is a second language may desire to work with clinicians who speak their native language and prefer

---

CASE VIGNETTE 2

Flor is a 55-year-old woman who emigrated from Mexico when she was a teenager. She currently resides in New Jersey with her husband of 25 years, Rodolfo. She is fluent in both English and Spanish; however, Spanish is her preferred language. The couple has two adult children, both of whom reside in Texas. Flor has a large extended family, most of whom reside still in Mexico. Flor has worked as a legal secretary in a boutique law firm for the last 25 years. Until recently, Rodolfo was a supervisor in an office supplies warehouse. Eight months ago, Rodolfo was laid off from his position due to downsizing. Flor has recently taken on a second job as a clerk in a pharmacy to help with expenses. The past couple of months have become increasingly frustrating and stressful for Flor as money is increasingly tight in her household due to a mortgage and car payments. The couple also send money every month to Flor's family in Mexico. Recently, Rodolfo, who feels it is a "man's duty" to support his family, has become increasingly depressed and irritable about his unemployment. Although Flor has asked that Rodolfo help with the housework while she is away at work, he often spends the day drinking and watching TV. One day, Flor purchased a few scratchers while filling up her car at the gas station; she won $200. Flor was thrilled at the idea of being able to pay some of her monthly bills with these winnings. She continued to buy scratchers at the gas station, as well as the supermarket and convenience store, in hopes she might "win big." A few weeks later while driving home from work, Flor saw a billboard for the casino in her town. She thought about how much money she could win to help her family. Flor parked, walked inside, and stopped by a row of slot machines, where she decided she would play $50. Within a few minutes, Flor had doubled her money. The experience was intoxicating. The stress of working two jobs, Rodolfo's unemployment and his drinking, and having to care for her extended family in Mexico was numbed. Before she knew it, though, three hours had passed and Flor had lost her winnings, as well as an additional $475. Flor returned home, guilty and ashamed. She didn't tell Rodolfo where she had been. The next day, she went to work, thinking about how much overtime she would have to put in to "work off" her losses at the casino. The idea was overwhelming. On her way home from work the next evening, Flor told Rodolfo she would be staying late at work. Instead, Flor pulled into the casino parking lot and budgeted exactly how much she needed to win back her losses. Within five minutes, her money was gone. Flor remembered her "emergency" credit card and promised herself she wouldn't play more than $50. Flor's $50 was quickly lost and she returned home, thinking of ways to get back to the casino as soon as possible, with as much money as she could. Within six months, Flor was spending several hours at the casino every day, progressing to higher stakes slots with time. She would go days with just a few hours of sleep, often forgetting to take her diabetes medication. She was frequently leaving for the casino during her lunchtime, telling her co-workers she was going to run errands. Flor's visits to the casino were impacting her work; she rarely arrived on time anymore. Instead, she was exhausted and unable to concentrate and meet her deadlines. She had also cut down on hours at her second job in order to free up time for gambling. She had racked up more than $7,000 in credit card debt. When Rodolfo asked why she wasn't bringing home as much money anymore, Flor told him her company was cutting down on her overtime. In the last couple of months, with her credit cards maxed out and low on cash, it was impossible for Flor to help out her family in Mexico. Fraught with guilt and shame, Flor began to think she may have a gambling problem.

learning materials, including workbooks and other literature, in their native languages. When therapists in a clients' native language are unavailable, interpreters may be necessary. Therapists working with clients with limited incomes may work with their respective state-funded gambling treatment programs to obtain affordable gambling treatment services for their clients. Case Vignette 2 highlights some of the pertinent issues, such as shame and economic status, that may be relevant in working with diverse clients who present with gambling disorders. Research indicates that Latinos are more likely to develop pathological gambling than their Caucasian counterparts (Barry, Stefanovics, Desai, & Potenza, 2011).

Models Explaining the Cause of Gambling Disorders

Family members of pathological gamblers, and the gambler themselves, often want insight into the development of a gambling problem. Given the complexity of human behavior, however, this can be a difficult task to address. Researchers in the field have developed two predominant integrative models as possible explanations for how gambling disorders develop: the biopsychosocial model (Sharpe, 2002; Sharpe & Tarrier, 1993) and the pathways model (Blaszczynski & Nower, 2002). In a recent overview of gambling disorders (Hodgins, Stea, & Grant, 2011), Hodgins and colleagues comment on these models:

> The biopsychosocial model is essentially predicated on a cognitive-behavioural and diathesis-stress framework, whereby predisposing factors (e.g., poor problem-solving and coping skills and genetic vulnerabilities) interact with early gambling experiences (e.g., receiving large wins early, receiving a high proportion of small wins early) and adverse psychosocial experiences (e.g., stressful life problems, boredom) to give rise to gambling disorders. Both the biopsychosocial and pathways models describe similar factors and processes involved in the development and maintenance of gambling problems. The major difference is that

the biopsychosocial model assumes homogeneity of gambling disorders and the pathways model postulates heterogeneity of gambling disorders manifested as three main pathways leading to three subtypes of problem gamblers: behaviourally conditioned, emotionally vulnerable, and antisocial impulsivist. The behaviourally conditioned subtype is characterised by an absence of premorbid psychopathological changes and impaired control over gambling results from the effects of conditioning, distorted cognitions, and poor decision making associated with frequent exposure to gambling. These same environmental principles are involved in the cause of the other two subtypes, although premorbid pathological changes are a complicating factor in terms of motives for gambling and course of the disorder. The emotionally vulnerable subtype has pre-existing depression, anxiety, and poor coping and problem-solving skills, and a history of trauma and gambling helps to modulate affective states. The third subtype has preexisting impulsivity, attentional difficulties, and antisocial features, and gambling serves as a risky and exciting activity. (p. 1878)

At the present time, many problem gamblers have been identified as a heterogeneous population, leading to a wider adoption of the pathways model as an explanation for gambling disorders. In the case of John, he had a difficult childhood involving emotional neglect that constituted a predisposing risk factor for seeking escape from his unpleasant mood states through gambling. He had an early big win that further served to maintain gambling behaviors. He also encountered "adverse psychosocial experiences," given the stressors of college life and demands of his education. Under the pathways model, he would likely be classified as an emotionally vulnerable gambler, similar to the case of Flor discussed earlier.

Consequences of Problem Gambling

The consequences of pathological gambling can include illegal activity, substance abuse, financial losses, domestic abuse, and compromised productivity. All consequences are specific to the individual case. Suicidal behavior affects nearly 25% of pathological gamblers (Wong, Chan, Conwell, Conner, & Yip, 2010). Physical and medical consequences are also varied and can include sleep deprivation, insomnia, stress-related illness, and decreased attention to self-care. Consequences of problem gambling can also affect partners and significant others of the gambler, including personal distress, which may manifest itself in clinical levels of anxiety and/or depression. Partners of gamblers may also face increasing burdens as a result of the consequences triggered by their gambling partner. These burdens may be financial in nature and require increasing amounts of responsibilities and stress (e.g., a mother who takes on a second job to provide for her family). This process may be stressful and exhausting, and in some cases, it may lead to physical illness. In some instances, partners may feel the consequences they suffer far exceed those encountered by the problem gambler.

Treatment Interventions

To date, no one treatment approach for gambling disorders has emerged as the most beneficial. In fact, most gambling treatment programs advocate for a combined biopsychosocial approach. Currently, research suggests that psychotherapy is more beneficial for problem gamblers than pharmacological treatments. According to prevalence surveys, fewer than 10% of individuals with a gambling disorder will ever receive treatment for their symptoms (Cunningham, 2005; Slutske, Blaszczynski, & Martin, 2009). Identified responses as to why individuals with gambling problems choose not to seek treatment include a desire to address the gambling problem on their own, shame or stigma, and/or denial about the problem. In fact, most individuals who are recovered from problem gambling have done so without undergoing any type of formal treatment (Slutske, 2006). These recovered gamblers ascribe their success to behavior modification approaches, including engagement in activities discordant with gambling as well as avoiding locations that might trigger relapse

(e.g., not going to a gambling venue; Hodgins & el-Guebaly, 2000).

Brief treatment interventions for pathological gambling have been developed, including the use of a self-help workbook based on cognitive behavioral therapy (CBT) and motivational enhancement approaches; such interventions have been associated with positive results. Involvement in a 12-step support group or some psychological treatment has been shown to be more effective than no treatment at all. Pathological gamblers may also seek out social support through Gambler's Anonymous (GA), which has been in operation for more than 50 years. GA holds regular meetings throughout the United States and is a network for peer support in recovery and fellowship. For GA members, abstinence has been associated with attendance, participation, and higher social capital (Oei & Gordon, 2008; Petry, 2005a). Recent studies have underscored the significance of focusing on both the irrational beliefs and cognitive distortions associated with continued gambling in the treatment process. Individual therapy has been shown to be helpful in several domains, including developing the gambler's sense of self-control over gambling, reduction in gambling frequency, and building skills for relapse prevention. Practical approaches to implement with pathological gamblers include discussions of limiting access to gambling venues such as casinos, as well as limiting factors that enable gambling, such as credit and transportation to gambling venues. There are several published manuals and therapist guides that have been employed in clinical testing for clinicians interested in utilizing CBT for pathological gamblers. A recent meta-analysis of CBT for pathological gambling indicated a hopeful therapeutic effect size as well as reductions in pathological gambling behavior that remained intact for at least 12 months (Gooding & Tarrier, 2009). CBT approaches typically involve cognitive restructuring of irrational beliefs that perpetuate gambling problems or the underlying issues that influence choices to gamble, for example, tendencies to escape uncomfortable mood states such as depression.

Pharmacological Treatments

Currently, there are no FDA-approved medications for pathological gambling. Although it is outside the scope of social work practice to give clients advice about medications, social workers helping problem gamblers may want to ensure that clients are aware that any medications used to address gambling problems are being conducted off-label and are founded on limited research. Although clinical trials for pathological gambling medications exist, they are encumbered by high placebo response rates, limited knowledge of pathophysiology, the varied use of outcome mechanisms, and the heterogeneous course of problem gambling. Currently, clinical trials, which have tested several types of medications, have produced varying results. Opioid receptor antagonists (naltrexone and nalmefene), which moderate the dopaminergic transmission in the mesolimbic pathway, have shown promising results in clinician trials; they have been proven to decrease the fixation with gambling thoughts, intensity of gambling urges, and gambling behaviors (Grant, Kim, & Hartman, 2008; Grant et al., 2006; Grant, Odlaug, Potenza, Hollander, & Kim, 2010). Other groups of medications, including antidepressants and mood stabilizers, are associated with differing degrees of efficacy for pathological gambling specifically.

Recently, clinical trials investigating specific agents including N-Acetyl Cysteine and modafinil have produced interesting preliminary data but require replication and additional analysis (Grant, Kim, & Odlaug, 2007; Zack & Poulos, 2008). N-acetyl cysteine is a glutamatergic regulator thought to be implicated in the reward pathway. Modafinil's role is less understood, but it is speculated to involve dopamine modulation and therefore impacts attention and executive functioning capabilities. Current, ongoing trials of memantine, acamprosate, and topiramate in pathological gamblers are being conducted and soon will provide new insights into the specific targets of medications for pathological gambling.

Mindfulness Meditation Interventions

Mindfulness is typically defined as the process of bringing awareness and nonjudgmental acceptance to one's present moment experience of thoughts, emotions, and bodily sensations. Essentially, mindfulness consists of two components that have been operationalized in the literature (Bishop et al., 2004). First, it involves the *self-regulation of attention* so it is directed and maintained on the immediate experience (including unpleasant emotions, addictive cravings, or whatever else may arise at a given moment). Many mindfulness exercises are dedicated to simple practices, such as sustaining attention on the breath. The second component of mindfulness entails adopting an *orientation toward one's present experience,* characterized by openness, curiosity, and acceptance. Collectively, these principles are incorporated into mindfulness-based approaches with problem gamblers who exhibit significantly lower levels of mindfulness compared to healthy controls (Reid, Di Tirro, & Fong, 2014). Moreover, evidence is emerging that suggests mindfulness can be helpful in reducing problem gambling behaviors (Toneatto, Pillai, & Courtice, 2014). In the case of John, he could be referred to a local Mindfulness-Based Stress Reduction class where he might learn ways to increase his tolerance for the difficult emotions he experiences or develop new ways to interact with his gambling cravings or the stress he encounters in various domains of his life.

Practical Techniques and Overcoming Treatment Barriers

A vital aspect to working with pathological gamblers is financial counseling, an area that many therapists find challenging because many lack formal training in this area. In addition, engaging family members and significant others in the beginning stages of treatment is essential for encouraging treatment compliance, promoting retention, and reducing enabling behaviors.

Difficulties that treatment providers may encounter in working with pathological gamblers include ambivalence about treatment, noncompliance, and low levels of motivation. Pathological gamblers may often feel intense shame and guilt. A nonjudgmental stance is encouraged when confronting the impairment and consequences caused by the gambling. Social workers may consider additional training in approaches such as Motivational Interviewing, which has been used with addictive populations (Miller & Rollnick, 2012).

Transference and Countertransference Issues

Awareness of transference and countertransference issues when working with problem gamblers is essential for professional practice and maintaining appropriate boundaries. Many gamblers report difficult childhood traumatic experiences that can be triggering for some clinicians who may have had similar experiences. Gamblers who experience big wins only to lose the money through chasing losses can also raise issues for providers who may have histories involving financial deprivation. These several experiences represent examples of transference. Transference by clients often takes the form of resistance to treatment. Some clinicians report countertransference such as strong feelings that arise toward the plight of the romantic partners of gamblers who suffer abuse, betrayal, or feelings of powerlessness over the gamblers' behavior. Such issues can usually be addressed adequately through supervision, consultation with peers, or personal therapy, if needed.

Legal and Ethical Concerns

As with any clinical population, social workers should maintain confidentiality at all times, except in cases of risk of suicide, homicide ideation, or knowledge of child or elder abuse. During the course of treatment, gamblers may disclose their involvement in illegal acts. Social workers should defer to the ethical code of their respective professional organizations and laws of the state they practice in, but in most cases, such disclosures are not reportable. As noted previously, pathological gamblers have a high rate of lifetime suicidal behaviors. Individuals who work with pathological gamblers should take proper precautions to ensure the safety of their gambling clients, including regular suicide assessments.

Some problem gamblers steal or embezzle money to finance their gambling activities. This can lead to criminal charges. Given the lack of understanding about gambling disorders common among court personnel (judges, juries, attorneys, etc.), mental health professionals may be called upon to testify in trials or criminal proceedings about issues related to gambling disorders. Moreover, providers may be asked to provide progress notes or other documentation related to gambling treatment for clients being adjudicated.

MEZZO PERSPECTIVE

Social workers have the ability to positively influence local organizations and agencies devoted to helping problem gamblers. Social workers can become aware of local resources to assist problem gamblers, such as state-funded treatment programs or agencies with clinicians who specialize in working with gambling disorders. Social workers can be aware of gambling laws in the community and advocate for social change when gambling entities violate laws in their advertising or marketing campaigns. Social workers can also work with local community officials to promote events that bring attention to problem gambling or provide education on problem gambling for youth groups or schools. Many university campuses have clubs that might sponsor agendas that educate college-aged young adults about the potential consequences associated with gambling addictions and how to promote responsible gambling. Social workers can work with cities that have drug courts to explore opportunities to extend their services to create gambling courts to address crimes related to gambling disorders. Many communities have suicide hotlines, and the volunteer workers who take calls for suicide risk can greatly benefit from training about the unique issues associated with gambling disorders and suicide. Collectively, social workers can make significant contributions on the mezzo level to create change regarding problem gambling.

MACRO PERSPECTIVE

In many states, regulating bodies such as government agencies oversee and monitor the gaming industry. These state-run organizations may offer treatment services for problem gambling as a part of their responsible gaming program. As of 2013, 39 states operated publicly funded problem gambling treatment programs (Marotta, Bahan, Reynolds, Vander Linden, & Whyte, 2014). These treatment programs may include intensive residential, outpatient, and telephone counseling options for problem gamblers and affected individuals, including the significant other of a disordered gambler.

Furthermore, for individuals who have committed illegal acts related to their gambling, problem gambling diversion programs may be offered in lieu of incarceration. Gambling diversion programs were born out of the advocacy and policies that asserted that pathological gamblers who committed crimes related to their disorder could properly be rehabilitated outside of the jail or prison systems. Problem gambling diversion programs use individualized problem gambling treatment, as mandated by a judge, when an individual has committed a crime related to gambling and the case is suitable for a diversion program. Problem gambling treatment per diversion programs can include financial restitution, mandatory individual or group therapy, and GA attendance. Problem gambling diversion programs operate on a state-by-state basis and currently operate in a limited number of locations.

Policy and laws often lag behind the rapidly changing technology in the gaming industry. This technology creates challenges, obstacles, and opportunities. A prominent issue currently facing the field is how each state will address online gambling via the Internet and various digital device applications. Policy and laws address whether online gambling will be legal, how it will be regulated, and how proceeds from such business operations will be taxed. As with other platforms utilizing technology, online gambling sites require monitoring and compliance with laws to ensure public safety and in order to prevent fraud.

CONCLUSION

Gambling disorders can be devastating, affecting 1%–3% of the U.S. population at some point during their lifetime. Pathological gambling can cause social, financial, and health consequences to gamblers, their families, and significant others. Research concerned with pathological gambling is growing, particularly in terms of treatment. Treatment for pathological gambling is varied; it includes self-help workbooks, group and individual therapy, and 12-step programming. Currently, there is no FDA-approved medication for pathological gambling, although this field continues to develop. To date, no single type of treatment has been identified as the most beneficial for pathological gamblers; a biopsychosocial approach is encouraged. Clinicians who work with pathological gamblers should be aware of common therapeutic issues that may arise during treatment.

INTERNET RESOURCES

- National Council on Problem Gambling: http://www.ncpgambling.org
- National Center for Responsible Gaming: http://www.ncrg.org

Many states, with the exception of those without legalized gambling (e.g., Utah), have a state agency or council that is committed to helping with problem gambling, for example,

- Massachusetts Council on Compulsive Gambling: http://www.masscompulsivegambling.org
- California Department of Public Health Office of Problem Gambling: http://www.problemgambling.ca.gov
- Florida Council on Compulsive Gambling: http://www.gamblinghelp.org

- Gamblers Anonymous: http://www.gamblersanonymous.org
- Gam-Anon, for partners and family members: http://www.gam-anon.org

DISCUSSION QUESTIONS

1. What type of client might be at risk for developing a gambling disorder? What are some questions you could ask to screen for a gambling problem?

2. What legal and ethical issues should be considered in working with gambling-disordered populations?

3. Is gambling legal where you live? If so, what resources are available to clients with gambling disorders in your community?

4. What are some ways social workers can advocate for gambling issues in communities and what organizations might be approached as allies in advocacy work?

REFERENCES

American Psychiatric Association. (2013). *Diagnostic and statistical manual of mental disorders* (5th ed.). Arlington, VA: Author.

Barry, D. T., Stefanovics, E. A., Desai, R. A., & Potenza, M. N. (2011). Gambling problem severity and psychiatric disorders among Hispanic and white adults: Findings from a nationally representative sample. *Journal of Psychiatric Research, 45*(3), 404–411.

Bishop, S. R., Lau, M., Shapiro, S., Carlson, L., Anderson, N. D., Carmody, J., . . . Devins, G. (2004). Mindfulness: A proposed operational definition. *Clinical Psychology: Science and Practice, 11*(3), 230–241.

Blaszczynski, A., & Nower, L. (2002). A pathways model of problem and pathological gambling. *Addiction, 97,* 487–499.

Costa, P. T., & McCrae, R. R. (1992). *Neo-personality inventory-revised (NEO PI-R).* Odessa, FL: Psychological Assessment Resources.

Cunningham, J. A. (2005). Little use of treatment among problem gamblers. *Psychiatric Services, 56,* 1024–1025.

Dickson-Gillespie, L., Rugle, L., Rosenthal, R., & Fong, T. (2008). Preventing the incidence and harm of gambling problems. *Journal of Primary Prevention, 29*(1), 37–55.

Gooding, P., & Tarrier, N. (2009). A systematic review and meta-analysis of cognitive-behavioral interventions to reduce problem gambling: Hedging our bets? *Behavior Research and Therapy, 47*(7), 592–607.

Grant, J. E, Kim, S. W., & Hartman, B. K. (2008). A double-blind, placebo-controlled study of the opiate antagonist naltrexone in the treatment of pathological gambling urges. *Journal of Clinical Psychiatry, 69,* 783–789.

Grant, J. E., Kim, S. W., & Odlaug, B. L. (2007). N-acetyl cysteine, a glutamate-modulating agent, in the treatment of pathological gambling: A pilot study. *Biological Psychiatry, 62*(6), 652–657.

Grant, J. E., Odlaug, B. L., Potenza, M. N., Hollander, E., & Kim, S. W. (2010). Nalmefene in the treatment of pathological gambling: Multicentre, double-blind, placebo-controlled study. *British Journal of Psychiatry, 197,* 330–331.

Grant, J. E., Potenza, M. N., Hollander, E., Cunningham-Williams, R., Nurminen, T., Smits, G., & Kallio, A. (2006). Multicenter investigation of the opioid antagonist nalmefene in the treatment of pathological gambling. *American Journal of Psychiatry, 163*(2), 303–312.

Hodgins, D., & el-Guebaly, N. (2000). Natural and treatment-assisted recovery from gambling problems: A comparison of resolved and active gamblers. *Addiction, 95,* 777–789.

Hodgins, D. C., Stea, J. N., & Grant, J. E. (2011). Gambling disorders. *The Lancet, 378*(9806), 1874–1884.

Johansson, A., Grant, J. E., Kim, S. W., Odlaug, B. L., & Götestam, K. G. (2009). Risk factors for problematic gambling: A critical literature review. *Journal of Gambling Studies, 25*(1), 67–92.

Ledgerwood, D. M., Orr, E. S., Kaploun, K. A., Milosevic, A., Frisch, G. R., Rupcich, N., & Lundahl, L. H. (2012). Executive function in pathological gamblers and healthy controls. *Journal of Gambling Studies, 28*(1), 89–103.

Marotta, J., Bahan, M., Reynolds, A., Vander Linden, M., & Whyte, K. (2014). *2013 national survey of problem gambling services*. Washington, DC: National Council on Problem Gambling.

Miller, W. R., & Rollnick, S. (2012). *Motivational interviewing: Helping people change* (3rd ed.). New York, NY: Guilford Press.

Oei, T. P., & Gordon, L. M. (2008). Psychosocial factors related to gambling abstinence and relapse in members of gamblers anonymous. *Journal of Gambling Studies, 24*(1), 91–105.

O'Sullivan, S. S., Evans, A. H., & Lees, A. J. (2009). Dopamine dysregulation syndrome: An overview of its epidemiology, mechanisms and management. *CNS Drugs, 23*(2), 157–170.

Petry, N. M. (2005a). Gamblers anonymous and cognitive-behavioral therapies for pathological gamblers. *Journal of Gambling Studies, 21*(1), 27–33.

Petry, N. M. (2005b). *Pathological gambling: Etiology, comorbidity, and treatment*. Washington, DC: American Psychological Association.

Petry, N. M., Stinson, F. S., & Grant, B. F. (2005). Comorbidity of DSM–IV pathological gambling and other psychiatric disorders: Results from the national epidemiologic survey on alcohol and related conditions. *Journal of Clinical Psychiatry, 66*, 564–574.

Potenza, M. N. (2008). The neurobiology of pathological gambling and drug addiction: An overview and new findings. *Philosophical Transactions of the Royal Society Biological Sciences, 363*(1507), 3181–3189.

Raylu, N., & Oei, T. P. S. (2002). Pathological gambling: A comprehensive review. *Clinical Psychological Review, 22*, 1009–1061.

Reid, R. C., Di Tirro, C., & Fong, T. W. (2014). Mindfulness in patients with gambling disorders. *Journal of Social Work Practice in the Addictions, 14*(4), 327–337.

Reid, R. C., Li, D. S., Lopez, J., Collard, M., Parhami, I., Karim, R., & Fong, T. (2011). Exploring facets of personality and escapism in pathological gamblers. *Journal of Social Work Practice in the Addictions, 11*, 60–74.

Reid, R. C., McKittrick, H. L., Davtian, M., & Fong, T. (2012). Self-reported differences on measures of executive function in a patient sample of problem

gamblers. *International Journal of Neuroscience, 122*(9), 500–505.

Sacco, P., Cunningham-Williams, R. M., Ostmann, E., & Spitznagel, E. L. (2008). The association between gambling pathology and personality disorders. *Journal of Psychiatric Research, 42*(13), 1122–1130.

Sharpe, L. (2002). A reformulated cognitive-behavioral model of problem gambling: A biopsychosocial perspective. *Clinical Psychology Review, 22*(1), 1–25.

Sharpe, L., & Tarrier, N. (1993). Towards a cognitive-behavioural theory of problem gambling. *British Journal of Psychiatry, 162*, 407–412.

Slutske, W. S. (2006). Natural recovery and treatment-seeking in pathological gambling: Results of two U.S. national surveys. *American Journal of Psychiatry, 163*, 297–302.

Slutske, W. S., Blaszczynski, A., & Martin, N. G. (2009). Sex differences in the rates of recovery, treatment-seeking, and natural recovery in pathological gambling: Results from an Australian community-based twin survey. *Twin Research and Human Genetics, 12*, 425–432.

Slutske, W. S., Meier, M. H., Zhu, G., Statham, D. J., Blaszczynski, A., & Martin, N. G. (2009). The Australian Twin Study of Gambling (OZ-GAM): Rationale, sample description, predictors of participation, and a first look at sources of individual differences in gambling involvement. *Twin Research and Human Genetics: The Official Journal of the International Society for Twin Studies, 12*(1), 63–78.

Steeves, T. D. L., Miyasaki, J., Zurowski, M., Lang, A. E., Pellecchia, G., Eimeren, T. V., . . . Strafella, A. P. (2009). Increased striatal dopamine release in Parkinsonian patients with pathological gambling: A [11C]raclopride PET study. *Brain: A Journal of Neurology, 132*(5), 1276–1385.

Toneatto, T., & Nguyen, L. (2007). Individual characteristics and problem gambling behavior. In G. Smith, D. D. Hodgins, & R. J. Williams (Eds.), *Research and Measurement Issues in Gambling Studies* (pp. 279–393). San Diego, CA: Academic Press.

Toneatto, T., Pillai, S., & Courtice, E. L. (2014). Mindfulness-enhanced cognitive behavior therapy for problem gambling: a controlled pilot study. *International Journal of Mental Health and Addiction, 12*(2), 197–205.

Weintraub, D., Hoops, S., Shea, J. A., Lyons, K. E., Pahwa, R., Driver-Dunckley, E. D., . . . Potenza, M. N. (2009). Validation of the questionnaire for impulsive-compulsive disorder in Parkinson's disease. *Movement Disorders, 24*(10), 1461–1467.

Wong, P. W., Chan, W. S. C., Conwell, Y., Conner, K. R., & Yip, P. S. F. (2010). A psychological autopsy study of pathological gamblers who died by suicide. *Journal of Affective Disorders, 120*(1–3), 213–216.

Zack, M., & Poulos, C. X. (2008). Effects of the atypical stimulant modafinil on a brief gambling episode in pathological gamblers with high vs. low impulsivity. *Journal of Psychopharmacology, 23*(6), 660–671.

CHAPTER 10

Web-Based Practice

Nadia Islam & Gilbert Richards

CHAPTER OBJECTIVES

- Highlight biopsychosocial assessment and interventions in a virtual and web-based treatment context (i.e., telehealth);
- Discover the development of rapport/therapeutic alliance in a virtual therapeutic environment;
- Explore web-based social work practice's capacity to help underserved communities access mental health care;
- Understand the relevance of research in the utilization of web-based social work practice intervention.

CASE VIGNETTE

"After a while, I forgot that we weren't in the same room," said Cory, a tele-mental health client.

Cory is a 45-year-old African American man who is a divorced father of two adult daughters. Motivated to search the Internet for information about childhood sexual abuse after an abrupt termination of his intimate relationship, Cory learned about the University of Southern California's (USC) Telehealth services while he was visiting the website of a partner organization. At the initial assessment, Cory reported experiencing intrusive thoughts and flashbacks of sexual abuse and exhibited feelings of confusion, despondency, and anger. He reported recent changes in his sleeping and eating patterns, experiencing interrupted sleep at night and diminished appetite, and decreases in his level of energy, concentration, and interest in activities he once enjoyed. He disclosed that at least twice in the week prior to this first interview, he was unable to leave bed in order to attend work as scheduled. He reported experiencing angry feelings almost constantly and feared that his struggles with managing these emotions would impact his performance at his place of employment.

Despite an extensive abuse history starting from early childhood, Cory never had participated in therapy prior to his appointment at USC Telehealth. From age 4 until his early teens, he and his siblings shared a residence with their mother and her partner, who abused alcohol and other substances. Children in the household witnessed physical violence perpetrated against their mother. At age 5, both he and his younger brother were sexually abused by three adolescent males, one of whom was the son of their mother's friend. At age 7, he was molested by the adolescent daughter of the family living in the apartment above theirs in the same building. In a later incident, another boy who lived in the same neighborhood offered him money in exchange for accompanying him into a bathroom where he subsequently attempted to sodomize him. Lastly, as a soldier in the U.S. Army, he was sexually assaulted by a bunkmate. This sexual assault instigated a series of events that culminated in an "other-than-honorable" discharge connected to a conflict with an officer, documented as insubordination.

At the point of initial assessment, Cory had estranged relationships with most surviving members of his immediate family, including his siblings, ex-wife, daughters, and most recent intimate partner. His mother had died about 18 months prior to his first appointment. His ex-wife had been physically, psychologically, and emotionally abusive; however, he attributed her behavior to his acknowledgment that he did not love her and had been motivated to enter their relationship by self-interest. He interpreted his children's negative attitudes toward him as an outgrowth of their mother's feelings and actions after their divorce. At the same time, he lamented his sense of failure, explaining, "Having kids is supposed to validate you as a father, and being a good father should validate you as man." His ex-girlfriend ended their relationship after she became pregnant and Cory declined to marry but agreed to move in with her in order to support their new family. His ex-girlfriend responded to his disinterest in marriage by ending their relationship and terminating her pregnancy. Current feelings of guilt, shame, grief, and loss complicated his long-standing sense of failure as a father and a man.

INTRODUCTION

This chapter presents USC Telehealth, a virtual outpatient psychotherapy clinic affiliated with the University of Southern California's (USC) School of Social Work, as an example of web-based social work practice within a meta-framework perspective. The chapter introduces virtual "face-to-face" clinical intervention to readers by focusing on short-term psychotherapy with a USC Telehealth client, Cory, who presented in crisis after the unexpected termination of his intimate relationship. Although Cory has been diagnosed as having an adjustment disorder with depressed mood, the case presentation illustrates his intrapsychic and interpersonal challenges related to his experiences of childhood sexual abuse by multiple older children and adolescent male and female perpetrators

and an unreported sexual assault by a fellow male service member that culminates in Cory's other-than-honorable discharge from military service. The case presentation discusses Cory's intersecting identities, including not only his gender, sexual identity, race/ethnicity, and veteran status but also his identities as a father and survivor of sexual violence.

WEB-BASED SOCIAL WORK PRACTICE

Web-based social work practice encompasses a broad range of Internet-supported therapeutic interventions. Intended to promote physical and mental health, these activities conducted over the Internet have been called many names: telemedicine, telehealth, tele-mental health, web-based therapy, e-therapy, cybertherapy, eHealth, e-interventions, computer-mediated interventions, and online therapy. Even these terms might not reflect other uses of the Internet for mental health prevention, treatment, and maintenance, including psychoeducational web sites; interactive, self-guided interventions; online support groups and blogs; smart phone applications; and therapeutic software that uses artificial intelligence for simulation, gaming, and virtual realities (Barak & Grohol, 2011; Barak, Klein, & Proudfoot, 2009). Casting a wide net to define Internet-supported interventions, online counseling and therapy is distinct from web-based interventions, Internet-operated therapeutic software, and other online activities.

Web-based social work practice has been facilitated by not only the increasing acceptance of the Internet for communication but also computer hardware and software improvements that have made the Internet more easily navigable and assured consumers of their privacy; the adoption of ethical guidelines and training opportunities by various professional organizations, signaling their acceptance of web-based practice; and expanding research supporting its efficacy (Barak et al., 2009). Web-based interventions may be primarily educational, self-guided, and/or supported by human interaction; however, they typically consist of a self-guided, prescribed sequence of activities designed to increase knowledge, awareness, and understanding of health and mental health topics through information and interactive features. Relatively static, a web-based educational intervention provides information about a specific problem, including criteria to fulfill its diagnosis, symptoms, causes, effects, and treatment. In contrast, a self-guided web-based therapeutic intervention intends to change its participant's thoughts, feelings, and behaviors. Informed by cognitive behavioral or another practice theory and often extrapolated from empirically supported treatments, this second category of web-based intervention usually comes in highly structured modules, incorporating various multimedia formats and activities that offer automated feedback via text, graphics, or e-mails. Finally, human-supported web-based therapeutic interventions, like Cory's online psychotherapy, replace or augment automated feedback with a medical or mental health professional or peer. Whereas peer support often is offered as an adjunctive component via online support groups or forum postings, a professional's participation in a web-based intervention typically assumes central importance through exchange of personalized e-mails, instant messaging/chat, or videoconferencing sessions (Barak et al., 2009).

In the mid-1990s, advances in computer hardware and software, Internet communication technology, and web design converged to make online counseling or therapy both efficient and convenient (Barak et al., 2009; Grohol, 1998, 2004). While some consumers connect with a virtual therapist via a web search, web link, or recommendation, others encounter "virtual clinics" that list competing online practitioners along with their credentials and fees (Barak et al., 2009; Barak & Grohol, 2011). Although the American Telemedicine Association identifies "two-way, interactive videoconferencing" as the best practice in tele-mental health care (Grady et al., 2011, p. 135), the term *online counseling* typically has referred to a therapeutic relationship forged by text through e-mail (Finn & Barak, 2010) or instant messaging/chat communication (Barak et al., 2009). Adapting Richards and Vigano's (2012) definition of online counseling, the chapter limits its discussion of web-based social work intervention to the virtual delivery of clinical intervention by a professional social worker to one or more clients using computer-mediated communication technologies, either as a client's primary form of treatment or as a supplement to other services.

USC TELEHEALTH

USC Telehealth is a virtual, online psychotherapy and counseling clinic that uses secure, HIPAA-compliant video technologies to provide empirically supported psychotherapy services to clients in the convenience of their homes or other private locations. Service delivery occurs exclusively by videoconference rather than phone, e-mail or instant messaging/chat communication. Affiliated with the School of Social Work at USC Los Angeles, USC Telehealth also functions as an academic center and teaching clinic that conducts scholarly research while training graduate students of social work through its field practicum programs. Led by a multidisciplinary team of professionals representing social work, psychiatry, and business, the clinic's staff consists of both licensed clinical social workers (LCSW) and graduate social work interns.

Rapport and Therapeutic Alliance

The development of rapport in tele-mental health services starts prior to the client's first contact with his or her social worker. In most outpatient clinical settings, a receptionist greets clients in a waiting area prior to their appointment and offers instructions to complete required tasks prior to starting treatment. In a virtual environment, this staff person, sometimes called a "navigator," has the additional charge of helping the client learn how to effectively use videoconferencing technology. In a virtual clinic context, a navigator explains the technology requirements and procedures to obtain electronic signatures on mandatory informed consent documents. Preceding the initial introduction to a social worker, the navigator greets the client in the virtual session. During a brief period prior to meeting his or her social worker, the client tests his or her audio and video quality to ensure that they are adequate to proceed with the scheduled assessment interview. During this preliminary conversation, clients are informed that some troubleshooting at the start of the session might be necessary and that such problems usually can be resolved. Often, partnering with the social worker to overcome the technology glitch serves to facilitate a connection between the client and practitioner.

As in the delivery of face-to-face clinical social work intervention, privacy must be ensured by preventing observation of any auditory or visual interactions by anyone other than the social worker and client. The room(s) where each party sits during a virtual psychotherapy session must be safe, sufficiently lit, provide comfortable seating,

and minimize interruptions by humans or electronic devices (Grady et al., 2011). Interruptions in audio or video streaming can derail rapport and development of the therapeutic alliance. In addition to preparing clients for interruptions, practitioners can take steps to minimize their likelihood.

At USC Telehealth, practitioners maintain high-speed cable Internet access that plugs into their computers, rather than wireless Internet connectivity, to minimize disruptions. In preference over fluorescent overhead lights, practitioners arrange their desks to face an uncovered window or surround their web cameras with soft lighting from lamps. Daylight or evenly dispersed lamp light minimizes shadows or reflective spots that interfere with visibility and both parties' capacity to read each other's facial expressions and other nonverbal communication. Finally, practitioners are advised to wear pale, solid colors rather than patterned or striped clothing because the latter demands more bandwidth to update. Any delays to update the dynamic picture, in addition to the image itself, may become a distraction or disturb the client.

Existing research suggests that tele-mental health consumers successfully establish rapport with their providers (Ghosh, McLaren, & Watson, 1997; Richards & Vigano, 2013; Simpson, 2001) and disclose historical content, cognitions, emotions, and symptoms as they would in a proximate face-to-face environment (Jerome & Zaylor, 2000; Reynolds, Stiles, & Grohol, 2006; Urness, Wass, Gordon, Tian, & Bulger, 2006). Similar to other clients who have accessed USC Telehealth's services, Cory expressed that during the initial session, he had become so engaged in sharing his narrative with the social worker that he forgot that they were not in the same physical space. His disclosure supports findings by Day and Schneider (2002) that there are no significant differences in working alliance or outcomes between clients participating in face-to-face, telephone, or video psychotherapy. The same investigators found that clients in virtual (phone or video) psychotherapy participated more actively than participants in face-to-face sessions. Although their study included a sample of only

80 clients presenting with a broad range of issues, Liebert, Archer, Munson, and York (2006) found that individuals seeking treatment for certain problems or disorders, including posttraumatic stress disorder (PTSD), agoraphobia, and eating disorders, reported heighted feelings of safety and control as a benefit the virtual medium confers. Cory emphasized that the ability to participate in sessions from his own home increased his comfort with participating in therapy and discussing traumatic experiences he previously never had disclosed.

Biopsychosocial Assessment

Similar to best practice in a textual therapeutic relationship, using e-mail or instant messaging/chat, virtual social work practitioners demonstrate a greater reliance on words and verbal expressions. At the same time, when therapeutic contact occurs by videoconference, both parties' torsos typically are visible to one another, and the practitioner relies on facial expressions and hand gestures in order to complete observations relevant for assessment and convey empathy, genuineness, and warmth. Web-based social work practice may demand a higher level of awareness and creativity to maximize the utility of perceptible nonverbal communication (Grady et al., 2011).

In Cory's case, the first session consisted of a 90-minute initial assessment interview using a structured interview guide. The structured interview guide features open-ended questions framed in language intended to be the least stigmatizing possible. Applying a strengths-based, empowerment-oriented approach, the 90-minute interview fulfilled a standard biopsychosocial assessment, including a current mental status exam, safety assessment, and questions to elicit Cory's symptoms; history of present problems; medical conditions; current medications; substance use; and past psychiatric, family psychiatric, trauma, family, social, developmental, educational/occupational, and legal history.

Consistent with USC Telehealth's mission to expand access to empirically supported psychotherapy services, the assessment process reflected techniques used in motivational interviewing (MI; Miller & Rollnick, 2002), problem solving therapy (PST; Nezu & D'Zurilla, 2007; Nezu & Nezu, 2007), and cognitive behavioral therapy (CBT; Beck, 2011; Cully & Teten, 2008). For example, early in the interview, Cory was asked to describe any challenges that he confronted with sleep, interest, guilt, energy, concentration, appetite, and mood over the past week. The social worker demonstrated active listening with the liberal application of reflective statements, including simple reflection (e.g., "You're unmotivated to get up out of bed in the morning to get to work on time"), reflections of feeling (e.g., "You feel guilty about your girlfriend getting an abortion after you told her you didn't want to marry"), and double-sided reflections to normalize and clarify when two seemingly contradictory thoughts or feelings existed concurrently in Cory's experience (e.g., "You were willing to move in together and financially support your new family; at the same time, you didn't think it was the right time to make a decision about marriage"). Through open-ended questions, the social worker generated a list of about five problems that were most pressing to Cory at present and documented how frequently they occurred, their intensity, and their impact on daily functioning.

The client confirmed that he had developed his emotional and behavioral symptoms immediately after his girlfriend informed him that she had terminated her pregnancy and no longer wanted to continue their intimate relationship. Since the stressor occurred, Cory reported observable changes in mood, interest, sleep, appetite, energy, concentration, and feelings of guilt. His symptoms did not represent bereavement, had occurred for a duration of less than two weeks, and did not meet the threshold for significance on the PTSD Checklist–Specific (PCL-S) (Freedy et al., 2010). In summary, the disturbance did not fulfill the necessary criteria for another specific disorder such as major depressive disorder or PTSD. Based on the client's self-reported assessment data and consultation with his clinical supervisor, the social worker concluded that Cory's condition fulfilled criteria for an adjustment disorder with depressed mood.

Cognitive Behavioral Therapy Intervention

Practitioners have experimented with videoconferencing for various psychotherapy interventions, including supportive (Bose, McLaren, Riley, & Mohammedali, 2001), exposure (Oakes, Battersby, Pols, & Cromarty, 2008), CBT (Bouchard et al., 2004; Day & Schneider, 2002; Griffiths, Blignault, & Yellowlees, 2006; Manchanda & McLaren, 1998), eye movement desensitization and reprocessing (EMDR; Todder & Kaplan, 2007), and hypnosis (Simpson, Morrow, Jones, Ferguson, & Brebner, 2002); however, the preponderance of available evidence shows that CBT has been the most common application within tele-mental health services (Grady et al., 2011). Presenting problems and diagnoses represented in these studies have been diverse, ranging from bulimia nervosa, panic disorder, agoraphobia, obsessive compulsive disorder, depression, to PTSD (Cluver, Schuyler, Frueh, Brescia, & Arana, 2005; Cowain, 2001; Himle et al., 2006; Mitchell et al., 2008; Shepherd et al., 2006). Social workers' experience at USC Telehealth suggests that CBT (and interventions developed from a cognitive behavioral theoretical framework) may lend itself to virtual psychotherapy due to its structured session format, emphasis on written assignments between contacts, and reliance on words/text for skills acquisition.

Acknowledging evidence that supports the use of CBT to treat adjustment, anxiety, and mood disorders (Chambless & Ollendick, 2001; DeRubeis & Crits-Christoph, 1998), the social worker integrated CBT into Cory's treatment plan. After 12 sessions, Cory's symptoms markedly had improved. His course of treatment consisted of 17 sessions, after which he and the social worker executed a planned termination.

Their collaborative goals were consistent with those of CBT: to increase awareness of thoughts and emotions; identify how situations, thoughts, and behaviors influence emotions; and alter emotions by assessing and revising maladaptive thoughts and behaviors (Cully & Teten, 2008). First, the social worker oriented Cory to CBT by explaining the purpose of the session's structure, incorporating weekly mood checks, agenda-setting, and a period at the end of each session to elicit Cory's feedback about his experience during the session. The social worker provided psychoeducation about psychological trauma and how a recent stressor like the unanticipated end of his four-year intimate relationship could trigger depressive and trauma-related symptoms that he had not experienced in the recent past. After helping Cory learn how to utilize deep breathing, progressive muscle relaxation, and guided imagery to manage his feelings of anger, fear, and sadness, the social worker introduced cognitive restructuring, using an Antecedents, Behavior, Consequences (ABC) model and seven-column thought record to support Cory in recognizing when he experienced a shift in mood and identifying automatic thoughts and emotions (Cully & Teten, 2008). USC Telehealth's virtual platform permitted the social worker and Cory to open a document on their respective computers and "share their screens" with one another. This allowed for multiple variations of written exercises, including those in which Cory completed a thought record verbally while the social worker transcribed his words or Cory showed the social worker a completed thought record and discussed his experience while the social worker read alongside him.

Transference and Countertransference Issues

Transference reactions occur when the client unrealistically perceives or attributes desires or feelings that emanate from past experiences with significant others to his or her social worker (Hepworth, Rooney, Rooney, Strom-Gottfried, & Larsen, 2013). Often, these thoughts impact the therapeutic relationship and sometimes become an obstacle to desired change. For example, Cory disclosed that he had no emotionally intimate relationships with men. He actively avoided associations with them, declining invitations to socialize after work with his male colleagues. His psychotherapy with the social worker involved the first relationship he had with another man since adulthood. During their work together, Cory became encouraged to accept the invitation to socialize with one male coworker for whom he had positive regard. Despite his initial discomfort, behavioral rehearsal in session along with his positive experience with a male social worker motivated him to persist.

Analogously, social workers may experience distorted perceptions due to their client's characteristics or their own conscious or unconscious thoughts and feelings that are grounded in past relationships (Hepworth et al., 2013). Countertransference reactions can lead to lapses in professional judgment and detrimental emotional responses that impede therapeutic progress (Kahn, 1997). The social worker utilized individual supervision and consultation to manage countertransference reactions as soon as they reached his own awareness or his field instructor's observation. For example, the social worker initially was challenged to differentiate the therapist's active role demanded by CBT from offering advice. Second, after the second instance, he recognized that he had unintentionally extended his appointment with Cory considerably past the allotted time. The social worker and his clinical supervisor acknowledged and jointly monitored his feelings of concern and protectiveness. Through introspection and a commitment to appropriate professional boundaries, the social worker maintained a realistic perspective on his relationship with Cory that maximized the likelihood of its success.

Diversity Considerations

Cory openly discussed how his childhood in a major urban area during the U.S. civil rights movement afforded him many positive representations of African American culture; however, he reported that it offered next to no examples of African Americans in roles of authority and multiple examples of African Americans representing social dysfunction. Although his social worker immigrated to the United States from a Caribbean nation and personally identifies as black,

Cory did not indicate that his identification with the social worker overtly influenced the strength and efficacy of the therapeutic relationship. For example, he disclosed, "I just feel like I can say anything to you. I can't really explain it." Multiple variables contribute to the strength and development of the therapeutic alliance. Both intrapersonal factors, such as personality and mood, and interpersonal factors including communication, empathy, and nonjudgmental attitudes may exert a stronger influence than a similar racial or ethnic identity shared by the practitioner and client (Murphy, Faulkner, & Behrens, 2004; Gelso & Mohr, 2001).

With regard to his sexual identity, Cory disclosed that he identified as heterosexual. At the same time, his multiple experiences of sexual abuse and assault inspired doubts in his mind about any characteristics that could have increased his susceptibility to these attacks or caused others to believe him to be homosexual. Finally, Cory's experience as a military veteran also may have influenced not only his adult perceptions of his childhood sexual trauma and assault by a fellow serviceman but also his willingness to seek help for mental health–related problems due to widespread stigma against mental illness (Hoge, Auchterloine, & Milliken, 2006).

Cory explained that after his assault by a fellow serviceman, he slowly overcame the fear of reprisal informing his reluctance to report the crime. In the context of "Don't Ask, Don't Tell," an exclusionary military policy that prohibited openly gay, lesbian, bisexual, or transgender (GLBT) individuals from serving in the military until its repeal in 2010 (Repeal Act of 2010, P.L. 111-321), Cory believes that his other-than-honorable discharge was a direct consequence of his disclosure. Existing research shows that military veterans underreport mental health symptoms, are hesitant to access services, and when they overcome their reluctance, often prematurely end participation in treatment (Hoge et al., 2006; Weiss & Coll, 2011). Cory expressed intermediate beliefs that aligned with military cultural values, which Weiss and Coll (2011) identified as part of many veterans' worldviews, including subordination of his individual needs in preference for those of his loved ones, devotion to duty, and emotional restraint. Despite the decades since his discharge, Cory's attitudes about seeking help and values related to duty and stoicism continue to be influenced by not only his socialization into and acceptance of military cultural values but also his experience of military sexual assault and its aftermath.

Legal and Ethical Concerns

General ethical concerns within the context of web-based clinical practice relate to possible misrepresentation of clients' or practitioners' identities; fulfillment of mandated reporting responsibilities; crisis intervention and management; overreliance on technology and barriers to access required technology, including reliable Internet connectivity; and obstacles to demonstrating empathy and culturally competent communication. Related legal concerns are licensing, adherence to professional standards, negligence, and privacy (Barak et al., 2009).

In alignment with clinical guidelines published by the American Telemedicine Association (2013), for example, clients at USC Telehealth must disclose their first and last name during registration with the clinic's navigator. During the client's first virtual "face-to-face" encounter with the navigator prior to the initial assessment, the client shows a government-issued photo identification in order for the navigator to verify his or her identify. The navigator captures the image in a screen shot that becomes part of the client's electronic record.

The clinic's policies and procedures require practitioners to consult with their supervisors whenever a client discloses content triggering a mandated report, including disclosure of suspected abuse or neglect of a child, elder, or dependent adult or the client's intent to harm self (suicide ideation) or another (homicide ideation). Graduate interns meet with their assigned LCSW field instructor on a weekly basis via the same virtual platform on which clients meet with practitioners. Graduate interns must submit documentation of any clinical interaction on the same day the service is delivered, and LCSW field instructors review and co-sign this documentation within 24 hours, ensuring appropriate oversight and execution of mandated reporting responsibilities.

Prior to launching services, the clinic's navigator verifies the location where the client will connect to sessions and the name and telephone number of an emergency contact person. During the first telephone contact, the navigator explains that a client participating from a professionally unsupervised location must ensure that she or he is in a private space where no discussion may be witnessed by anyone outside of the clinical interaction. This requirement excludes participants who seek to join sessions at public computing labs, libraries, or using their own devices at a wireless-enabled commercial location (e.g., cybercafé).

When a client logs into sessions from home or any other professionally unsupervised setting, the practitioner must assess the client's ability to maintain a private environment in which to participate in virtual psychotherapy and manage safety concerns. Practitioners evaluate a client's appropriateness for virtual psychotherapy on an ongoing basis by considering the following factors: the client's competence with technology, cognitive capacity, current support system, medical status, history of treatment compliance and relationships with professionals, current and past substance abuse, history of self-harm or violence toward others, and geographic distance to nearest emergency medical facility (American Telemedicine Association, 2013). The consent process includes informing the client that services may be discontinued if they are no longer appropriate.

IMPLICATIONS FOR MEZZO PRACTICE

As mezzo intervention is designed to influence systems that directly impact clients (Hepworth et al., 2013), web-based social work intervention has the most potential to change how members of underserved communities access mental health care. Web-based social work intervention has the strongest implications for individuals and families who lack access to quality mental health care due to multiple barriers, including geographical isolation, inadequate transportation, limitations on mobility due to chronic or acute health conditions, inconsistent employment schedules, and for caregivers, inadequate child or respite care. Tele-mental health services provide options for potential consumers who forego opportunities to access care in traditional settings, including those not only struggling with personal prejudice or social stigma surrounding mental health but also confronting specific disorders like PTSD, panic disorder with or without agoraphobia, and obesity or body image issues such as bulimia nervosa (Liebert et al., 2006).

Aggravating barriers to mental health care notwithstanding environmental obstacles and factors that decrease intrinsic motivation, existing providers including both public agencies and private nonprofit organizations are unable to meet current demand for intervention services, especially face-to-face psychotherapy. Contracting with tele-mental health providers or a virtual clinic may offer a lower-cost alternative to fulfill unmet needs in communities, as agencies displace traditional overhead costs for employee office space and transportation (for field-based work) with "tele-suites" where clients who lack personal equipment (e.g., computer, web camera, microphone, and speakers) may travel to meet with an off-site social worker. For example, USC Telehealth has launched a partnership with a public/private entity that operates over a dozen family resource centers in Southern California. The majority of their constituents are indigent and lack the required equipment, Internet connectivity, and privacy to participate in tele-mental health services from their locations. At the same time, the organization acknowledged that many of their office spaces, all of which are already equipped with desks, computers, and high-speed cable Internet, are occupied intermittently during the workday. Staff at each family resource center has made these spaces available during specific days and hours each week in order for their consumers to log in with a social worker at USC Telehealth.

Because each center has only a single part-time therapist at best, this partnership has afforded high-quality, evidence-based care to individuals who would have languished on a waiting list or foregone treatment altogether.

IMPLICATIONS FOR MACRO PRACTICE

Tele-mental health services have been adopted by providers ranging from large public health and mental health systems, to moderately sized community-based organizations, to private individual practitioners seeking to expand access to appropriate care for their constituents. As there currently exists no national license for clinical social workers, tele-mental health providers who also are professional social workers must restrict their practice to consumers residing in their state of licensure. Although the lack of a national license artificially restricts the power of tele-mental health to remove existing barriers to care, the most significant hurdles relate to payment and coverage of services delivered via tele-health (Thomas & Capistrant, 2015). While nearly half of all states have tele-medicine parity laws for private insurance, a comparable number either have no parity law or place multiple limitations on it, including geography, provider and/or patient setting, and type of technology. Twenty-three states and the District of Columbia have enacted full parity laws, defined as coverage and reimbursement of services provided via tele-health comparable to those provided in person. While 48 state Medicaid programs provide some coverage for tele-mental health services provided via videoconferencing, only 20 states cover services provided by a licensed social worker (Thomas & Capistrant, 2015). Social work professionals and aspiring practitioners can increase their knowledge about the policy environment in their states and engage in advocacy efforts to improve policies for tele-mental health service provision by consulting the American Telemedicine Association and the National Association of Social Workers (see Internet Resources on p. 130).

CONCLUSION

Considering USC Telehealth as a case example of web-based social work practice, virtual face-to-face psychotherapy has specific implications for clinical practice with social work clients. Led by faculty at the USC School of Social Work, USC Telehealth seeks to conduct research that will supply stronger empirical evidence to examine which clients and/or presenting problems may experience the most benefit from participation in web-based social work intervention. Future research will address multiple unanswered questions, including the efficacy and effectiveness of empirically supported clinical interventions delivered via face-to-face videoconferencing technologies; unique mediating and facilitative variables impacting efficacy and effectiveness; development of rapport/therapeutic alliance utilizing videoconferencing technologies; suitability for participation in virtual treatment (e.g., differences in treatment adherence/acceptance and symptom improvement/recurrence based on presenting problem/diagnosis, client population, and provider type, i.e., LCSW or MSW intern); and multidisciplinary collaboration to improve patient care. Presently, there exist no clinical trials or research focused on videoconferencing applications specifically by social workers (Grady et al., 2011). In collaboration with organizational partners, clients, students, and faculty, USC Telehealth intends to remedy this gap.

In addition to demonstrating how transference and countertransference issues and legal/ethical concerns carefully are addressed within the agency's context, the social worker's short-term psychotherapy with Cory illustrates how rapport building, biopsychosocial assessment, and CBT intervention can be adapted to fit the development of a therapeutic relationship in a virtual treatment context. As a means to increase access to empirically supported mental health care, web-based social work intervention inevitably will change not only how social work clients seek assistance to address their problems but also how future social workers learn how to partner with their clients to achieve goals they value.

INTERNET RESOURCES

- USC Telehealth: http://usctelehealth.com/
- The National Association of Social Workers (NASW) and the Association of Social Work Boards (ASWB): http://www.socialworkers.org/practice/standards/naswtechnologystandards.pdf
- American Telemedicine Association (ATA): http://www.americantelemed.org/home
- The International Society for Mental Health Online: http://ismho.org/
- The National Center for Telehealth & Technology (T2): http://t2health.org/
- US Department of Health and Human Services: http://www.hrsa.gov/ruralhealth/about/telehealth/
- The California Telehealth Network: http://www.caltelehealth.org/
- National Telehealth Technology Assessment Resource Center: http://www.telehealthtechnology.org/

DISCUSSION QUESTIONS

1. To what extent could web-based social work practice build rapport with clients if it excludes videoconferencing, relying instead on text-based instant messaging/chat or e-mail?

2. Compare and contrast the engagement phase in a face-to-face therapeutic relationship with the engagement phase in a virtual therapeutic relationship.

3. Cognitive behavioral therapy has been the most common application within tele-mental health services (Grady et al., 2011). What other empirically supported interventions might be appropriate for implementation on a virtual platform involving videoconferencing?

4. How would a social worker practicing in a virtual context complete safety planning with a client who expressed suicidal ideation?

5. Identify at least three underserved communities or populations that might benefit from expanded access to mental health care via web-based social work practice.

REFERENCES

American Telemedicine Association. (2013, May). *Practice guidelines for video-based online mental health services.* Retrieved from http://www .americantelemed.org/practice/standards/ata-standards-guidelines/practice-guidelines-for-video-based-online-mental-health-services

Barak, A., & Grohol, J. M. (2011). Current and future trends in internet-supported mental health interventions. *Journal of Technology in Human Services, 29*, 155–196.

Barak, A., Klein, B., & Proudfoot, J. G. (2009). Defining internet-supported therapeutic intervention. *Annals of Behavioral Medicine, 38*, 4–17.

Beck, J. (2011). *Cognitive behavior therapy: Basics and beyond* (2nd ed.). New York, NY: Guilford Press.

Bose, U., McLaren, P., Riley, A., & Mohammedali, A. (2001). The use of telepsychiatry in the brief counseling of non-psychotic patients from an inner-London general practice. *Journal of Telemedicine and Telecare, 7*(1), 8–10.

Bouchard, S., Paquin, B., Payeur, R., Allard, M., Rivard, V., Fournier, T., . . . Lapierre, J. (2004). Delivering cognitive behavior therapy for panic disorder with agoraphobia in videoconference. *Telemedicine and e-Health, 10*, 13–25.

Chambless, D. L., & Ollendick, T. H. (2001). Empirically supported psychological interventions: Controversies and evidence. *Annual Review of Psychology, 52*, 685–716.

Cluver, J. S., Schuyler, D., Frueh, B. C., Brescia, F., & Arana, G. W. (2005). Remote psychotherapy for terminally ill cancer patients. *Journal of Telemedicine and Telecare, 11*, 157–159.

Cowain, T. (2001). Cognitive-behavioural therapy via videoconferencing to a rural area. *Australian and New Zealand Journal of Psychiatry, 35*, 62–64.

Cully, J. A., & Teten, A. L. (2008). *A therapist's guide to brief cognitive behavioral therapy.* Houston, TX: Department of Veterans Affairs.

Day, S. X., & Schneider, P. L. (2002). Psychotherapy using distance technology: A comparison of face-to-face, video and audio treatment. *Journal of Counselling Psychology, 49*(4), 499–503.

DeRubeis, R. J., & Crits-Christoph, P. (1998). Empirically supported individual and group psychological treatments for adult mental disorders. *Journal of Consulting and Clinical Psychology, 66*(1), 37–52.

Finn, J., & Barak, A. (2010). A descriptive study of e-counsellor attitudes, ethics, and practice. *Counselling and Psychotherapy Research, 10*, 268–277.

Freedy, J. R., Steenkamp, M. M., Magruder, K. M., Yeager, D. E., Zoller, J. S., Hueston, W. J., & Carek, P. J. (2010). Post-traumatic stress disorder screening test performance in civilian primary care. *Family Practice, 27*(6), 615–24.

Gelso, C. J., & Mohr, J. J. (2001). The working alliance and the transference/countertransference relationship: Their manifestation with racial/ethnic and sexual orientation minority clients and therapists. *Applied & Preventive Psychology, 10*, 51–68.

Ghosh, G. J., McLaren, P. M., & Watson, J. P. (1997). Evaluating the alliance in videolink teletherapy. *Journal of Telemedicine and Telecare, 3*(1), 33–35.

Grady, B., Myers, K. M., Nelson, E., Belz, N., Bennett, L., Carnahan, L., . . . Voyles, D. (2011). Evidence-based practice for telemental health. *Telemedicine and e-health, 17*, 131–148.

Griffiths, L., Blignault, I., & Yellowlees, P. (2006). Telemedicine as a means of delivering cognitive-behavioural therapy to rural and remote mental health clients. *Journal of Telemedicine and Telecare, 12*, 136–140.

Grohol, J. M. (1998). Future clinical directions: Professional development, pathology, and psychotherapy online. In J. Gackenback (Ed.), *Psychology and the internet: Intrapersonal, interpersonal, and transpersonal implications* (pp. 111–140). San Diego, CA: Academic Press.

Grohol, J. M. (2004). Online counseling: A historical perspective. In R. Kraus, J. Zack, & G. Stricker (Eds.), *Online counseling: A handbook for mental health professionals* (pp. 51–68). San Diego, CA: Academic Press.

Hepworth, D. H., Rooney, R. H., Rooney, G. D., Strom-Gottfried, K., & Larsen, J. (2013). *Direct social work practice: Theory and skills* (9th ed.). Belmont, CA: Brooks/Cole.

Himle, J. A., Fischer, D. J., Muroff, J. R., Van Etten, M. L., Lokers, L. M., Abelson, J. L., & Hanna, G. L. (2006). Videoconferencing-based cognitive-behavioral therapy for obsessive-compulsive disorder. *Behaviour Research & Therapy, 44*, 1821–1829.

Hoge, C. W., Auchterloine, J. L., & Milliken, C. S. (2006). Mental health problems, use of mental health services, and attrition from military service after returning from deployment to Iraq or Afghanistan. *Journal of the American Medical Association, 295*(9), 1023–1032.

Jerome, L. W., & Zaylor, C. (2000). Cyberspace: Creating a therapeutic environment for telehealth applications. *Professional Psychology: Research & Practice, 31*, 478–483.

Kahn, M. (1997). *Between therapist and client: The new relationship.* New York, NY: W. H. Freeman & Company.

Leibert, T., Archer, J., Jr., Munson, J., & York, G. (2006). An exploratory study of client perceptions of internet counseling and the therapeutic alliance. *Journal of Mental Health Counseling, 28*, 69–83.

Manchanda, M., & McLaren, P. (1998). Cognitive behavior therapy via interactive video. *Journal of Telemedicine and Telecare, 4*(1), 53–55.

Miller, W. R., & Rollnick, S. (2002). *Motivational interviewing: Preparing people for change* (2nd ed.). New York, NY: Guilford Press.

Mitchell, J. E., Crosby, R. D., Wonderlich, S. A., Crow, S., Lancaster, K., Simonich, H., . . . Myers, T. C. (2008). A randomized trial comparing the efficacy of cognitive-behavioral therapy for bulimia nervosa delivered via telemedicine versus face-to-face. *Behaviour Research & Therapy, 46*, 581–592.

Murphy, M. J., Faulkner, R. A., & Behrens, C. (2004). The effect of therapist–client racial similarity on client satisfaction and therapist evaluation of treatment. *Contemporary Family Therapy, 26*(3), 279–292.

Nezu, A. M., & D'Zurilla, T. J. (2007). *Problem-solving therapy: A positive approach to clinical intervention.* New York, NY: Springer.

Nezu, A. M., & Nezu, C. M. (2007). *Solving life's problems: A five-step guide to enhanced well-being.* New York, NY: Springer.

Oakes, J., Battersby, M. W., Pols, R. G., & Cromarty, P. (2008). Exposure therapy for problem gambling via videoconferencing: A case report. *Journal of Gambling Studies, 24*, 107–118.

Reynolds, D. J., Stiles, W. B., & Grohol, J. M. (2006). An investigation of session impact and alliance in internet based psychotherapy: Preliminary results. *Counseling & Psychotherapy Research, 6*, 164–168.

Richards, D., & Vigano, N. (2012). Online counseling. In Y. Zheng (Ed.), *Encyclopedia of Cyber Behavior* (Vol. 1, pp. 699–713). New York, NY: IGI Global.

Richards, D., & Vigano, N. (2013). Online counseling: A narrative and critical review of the literature. *Journal of Clinical Psychology, 69*(9), 994–1011.

Shepherd, L., Goldstein, D. Whitford, H., Thewes, B., Brummell, V., & Hicks, M. (2006). The utility of videoconferencing to provide innovative delivery of psychological treatment for rural cancer patients: Results of a pilot study. *Journal of Pain Symptom Management, 32*, 453–461.

Simpson, S. (2001). The provision of telepsychology service to Shetland: Client and therapist satisfaction and the ability to develop a therapeutic alliance. *Journal of Telemedicine and Telecare, 7*(1), 34–36.

Simpson, S., Morrow, E., Jones, M., Ferguson, J., & Brebner, E. (2002). Video-hypnosis: The provision of specialized therapy via videoconferencing. *Journal of Telemedicine and Telecare, 8*(2), 78–79.

Thomas, L., & Capistrant, G. (2015, May). *State telemedicine gaps analysis coverage and reimbursement.* Retrieved from http://www.americantelemed.org/docs/default-source/policy/50-state-telemedicine-gaps-analysis---coverage-and-reimbursement.pdf?sfvrsn=10

Todder, D., & Kaplan, Z. (2007). Rapid eye movements for acute stress disorder using video conference communication. *Telemedicine and e-Health, 13*, 461–464.

Urness, D., Wass, M., Gordon, A., Tian, E., & Bulger, T. (2006). Client acceptability and quality of life: Telepsychiatry compared to in-person consultation. *Journal of Telemedicine and Telecare, 12*, 251–254.

Weiss, E., & Coll, J. E. (2011). The influence of military culture and veteran worldviews on mental health treatment: Practice implications for combat veteran help-seeking and wellness. *International Journal of Health, Wellness, and Society, 1*(2), 75–86.

CHAPTER 11

Equine Assisted Counseling
An Alternative Approach for Trauma

Eugenia L. Weiss, Shawnmari Kaiser, & Gary Adler

CHAPTER OBJECTIVES

- Explain trauma with regard to the value of using animal-assisted therapy or counseling;
- Define equine assisted counseling;
- Describe the theoretical frameworks embedded in equine assisted counseling;
- Identify intervention techniques associated with an equine assisted counseling program.

CASE VIGNETTE

Juan is a 29-year-old single Latino male who received an honorable discharge from the United States Marine Corps. Juan had joined the service following in the footsteps of his stepfather and step-grandfather. In 2004, he was deployed in Iraq where he served as a machine gunner. During that deployment, he suffered injuries that caused him to be airlifted to the military hospital in Landstuhl, Germany and eventually back to the continental U.S. for treatment related to a compound fracture of his left arm. Sadly, during that deployment he also experienced the loss of several battle buddies.

Thank you to Deborah Salazar Shapiro and Allison Santoyo Alcala for their initial contributions to this chapter.

Juan was deployed again in 2005 to Iraq as a lead gunner and vehicle commander. Although he had feelings of anger regarding the loss of his friends in the first deployment, he reported being trained to "not feel anything" and to detach emotionally from situations, family, and peers. Juan had been advised, by his unit leader, that he would need to grieve the loss of his friends later. But, later never came. Juan experienced "survivor guilt" in the form of feelings of remorse and excessive guilt due to being unable to save the lives of his comrades and friends.

When he returned from his second deployment, he began to have symptoms of Posttraumatic Stress Disorder (PTSD), including nightmares of his fallen comrades and flashbacks of the war. For the next four years, Juan self-medicated with heavy drinking. To compound the situation, three of his U.S. Marine Corps friends committed suicide. Upon the death of his third friend, he had an "emotional breakdown" and began to have suicidal thoughts of his own. Juan sought professional help and was able to maintain sobriety for nine months until a battalion reunion in 2009 brought back too many painful memories and he relapsed. Juan stated that he used sleeping pills and alcohol as a "crutch" and he continued drinking to "block" everything out. This behavior continued until the suicide of a fourth friend (see Chapter 29 on suicide and the military) and his own accidental overdose of sleeping pills mixed with alcohol, which almost killed him. This life event led Juan to a veteran's residential program sponsored by the Veterans Healthcare Administration (VHA). In this program, Juan received individual and group therapies and was able to participate in equine assisted counseling through Pegasus Rising, a nonprofit organization located in San Diego County, CA (www.pegasusrising.org).

This chapter will utilize Pegasus Rising to illustrate a sample of techniques used in equine assisted counseling programs. Although the client has agreed to have his story related here, the details have been altered to protect the client's privacy and to highlight the application of the intervention methods.

A NOTE ABOUT TRAUMA

Juan is not unlike many persons who have experienced traumatic events either personally or vicariously, only to find themselves haunted by the remnants of the events. Trauma can affect an individual on many levels, including physical, cognitive/emotional, spiritual, and relational. Though not all trauma experiences lead to a clinical diagnosis of PTSD (nor do all veterans suffer from PTSD; estimates vary; see the review by Yarvis, 2013), many who experience traumatic events will experience features of the disorder, specifically symptoms such as irritability and angry outbursts, exaggerated startle responses, increased anxiety, depersonalization, dissociation, sleep disturbances, flashbacks, and obsessive thoughts of the traumatic event (American Psychiatric Association [APA], 2013). These symptoms tend to impact daily living and functioning and can create a sense of anguish and helplessness in the individual.

INTRODUCTION

Standard and traditional treatment practices for traumatized clients address emotional regulation, cognitive disturbances and disruptive behavioral patterns. Although evidence-based treatments such as prolonged exposure (PE; Foa, Hembree, & Rothbaum, 2007) and cognitive processing therapy (CPT; Resick & Schnicke, 1992; Resick, Monson, Price & Chard, 2007) have had documented success with clients experiencing PTSD, some clients, particularly military personnel and veterans, withdraw prematurely from treatment or reject traditional therapeutic services within office settings, often due to stigma and other barriers (Hoge et al., 2004). In addition to stigma, there could be difficulties in establishing trust in the therapeutic relationship. This trust factor may be rooted in the trauma experience (Benamer & White, 2008) or have its etiology in the development of one's personality (Bretherton, 1992; Lyons-Ruth, Dutra, Shuder, & Bianchi, 2006), causing clients to reject the standard modalities due to an inability to relate the trauma experience to the outside world (Wilson, D'Ardenne, & Scott, 2012) or due to an insecure attachment style resulting from trauma (Bretherton, 1992). It has been speculated that any of these factors may impede development of a therapeutic bond with the mental health clinician. Thus, it is recommended that a shared decision-making process be utilized wherein the client's preferences along with the therapist's expertise and recommendations founded on evidence-based practices determine the selection of treatment interventions (The Management of Post-Traumatic Stress Working Group, 2010). As part of the evidence-based practice process, the decision of which modality or combination of treatment approaches to utilize would include those that best suit the client, thus opening the door to utilizing a creative or alternative approach to trauma counseling.

Equine assisted counseling (EAC) is a growing field that offers therapeutic interventions in an experiential format to meet the client where he or she is at using the horse as a medium that can facilitate building a bond of trust with the psychotherapist. This model of intervention may be beneficial in conjunction with traditional therapeutic modalities. Alternatively, for clients who have not found the standard 50-minute office session to be advantageous to therapeutic progress, EAC may provide therapeutic success. EAC brings together aspects of multiple therapeutic frameworks, including cognitive behavior therapy (Sudekum Trotter, Chandler, Goodwin-Bond, & Casey, 2008) and mindfulness (Frewin & Gardiner, 2005), all within the context of experiential learning, with the horse acting as both metaphor and companion throughout the therapeutic process (Schultz, Remick-Barlow, & Robbins, 2007).

BACKGROUND OF EQUINE ASSISTED COUNSELING

Equine therapy dates back to ancient Greece, where Hippocrates identified a therapeutic value, through to the early 1900s, when horses were used with wounded soldiers of World War I (Nelson, 2014). It has provided multiple therapeutic uses for persons of all ages with various physical handicaps as well as traumatic brain injuries, autism, emotional and behavioral disorders in children, at-risk children and adolescents, as well as children who have witnessed domestic violence (MacLean, 2011; Nelson, 2014; Sudekum Trotter et al., 2008). A key therapeutic value lies in the similarity between horses and humans. Horses are considered "pack animals," traveling together in herds, desiring connection and socialization with other horses (Hill, 2006). Human beings have an intrinsic need for contact and relationship, as historical studies by Lorenz and Hess on animal "imprinting" reveal, as well as Harlow's work with rhesus monkeys and studies by Bowlby and Ainsworth on childhood attachment; all inform the innate human need for connection (Ainsworth, 1969; Hess, 1958; Van der Horst, LeRoy, & Van der Veer, 2008). This need for connectivity plays an integral part in human social and physical survival and continues to be significant throughout an individual's life (Bowlby, 1979). Due to a trauma experience (or multiple experiences), often persons will struggle with connecting to and trusting others. However, research reveals that persons who struggle with human relationships can find connection with animals (Ewing, MacDonald, Taylor, & Bowers, 2007; Klontz, Bivens, Leinart, & Klontz, 2007). These people are more able to relate to animals because they tend to be more accepting and nonjudgmental than other humans (MacLean, 2011). Horses present a dual experience. Being large and powerful, they can elicit fear and command respect; at the same time, they are a prey animal, so they are hypervigilant of the environment until they determine they are not in danger (Hill, 2006; Schultz et al., 2007). This, too, is similar to persons experiencing features of PTSD. Sudekum Trotter et al. (2008) noted the ability to interact and control such powerful animals can empower a client and facilitate self-confidence. It has been argued that these components can forge a bond between the horse and the client that often cannot occur within a traditional talk therapy session (MacLean, 2011; Sudekum Trotter et al., 2008).

EAC is rooted in experiential learning and humanistic philosophy (Klontz et al., 2007) and utilizes a cognitive behavioral framework for clinical processing (Sudekum Trotter et al., 2008). Typically provided by a licensed psychotherapist such as a clinical social worker, it offers a holistic approach to treatment. The psychotherapist integrates EAC activities into a multitheoretical framework, which includes clinical processing to increase cognitive behavioral insight in a client and facilitate reframing and/or restructuring negative and distorted thinking patterns as well as modify problematic behaviors (Sudekum Trotter et al., 2008). EAC also utilizes gestalt-style techniques and metaphors within an experiential modality (Schultz et al., 2007); in fact, key to EAC is the experiential component of the therapeutic process. Kolb, Boyatzis, and Mainemelis (2000) defined experiential learning as a process of procuring knowledge as a result of the combination of acquisition and transformation of experience. Active participation of the whole person with emphasis on behavior, affect, and cognitive dimensions will allow for the full benefits of experiential learning (Gentry, 1990). Therapeutic work with horses is a metaphor-based intervention (Sudekum Trotter et al., 2008) that allows the client to be immersed in the experiential process. Gentry (1990) noted that contact with the environment, in this case horses, and the variability and uncertainty of interacting with them can be analogous to real-life situations that clients have had or will experience. Experiential exposure provides an opportunity to develop abstract conceptualization of concrete experiences, as it allows for active experimentation and reflective observation (Kolb et al., 2000). Bandura (1971) found that exploratory activities encouraged the development of new patterns of behavior. These new patterns of behavior can, therefore, enhance the client's relationship to self and others. Bandura (1994) noted successful experiential exercises have adaptive benefits and lead to increased self-efficacy. Though EAC has been used to treat a multitude of psychosocial concerns, currently there is limited research on its effectiveness (Klontz et al., 2007). However, previous exploratory studies of EAC with both male and female juvenile offenders revealed improved communication and increased relationship-building skills (Sudekum Trotter et al., 2008). Improved Global Assessment of Functioning (GAF) Scale scores in children exposed to domestic violence have also been found (Schultz et al., 2007). Additionally, positive results of EAC have been elucidated through self-reports of military veterans diagnosed with PTSD in regulation of emotions and improved communication skills (MacLean, 2011).

EQUINE ASSISTED COUNSELING AND TRAUMA SYMPTOMS

Traumatized persons often have lost the sense of psychological and physical boundaries and need to develop a safe space that allows them to remain grounded when they experience a trigger response (Williams & Poijula, 2002). Additionally, as dissociation and emotional numbness are common symptoms of PTSD (APA, 2013), an individual may lose awareness of personal sensations and perceptions as well as the ability to accurately identify emotional and para-verbal cues of others (MacLean, 2011; Sudekum Trotter, 2012). Because body language is the primary language of horses, the human-horse relationship can facilitate development of stronger awareness of mannerisms in the person experiencing trauma symptoms (MacLean, 2011). Nussen and Becker (2012) described how therapeutic work with horses allows clients to create and experience safe boundaries with expression of thoughts and feelings through verbal and nonverbal communication. Additionally, horses are motivated by their basic needs and utilize similar social structures as humans (e.g., hierarchies and need for attachment relationships with other horses), which can provide a healthy role model for individuals who, through the experience of trauma, may have lost the ability to care for themselves and others (Hill, 2006; Nussen & Becker, 2012). Furthermore, due to being prey animals, horses are mindful of their surroundings and can mirror human emotional responses (e.g., if an individual is fearful, tense, or irritable, the horse will sense it and will respond in a variety of ways such as ignoring commands, pulling away, spooking, or becoming aggressive; Hill, 2006; Schultz et al., 2007). The ability to lead a horse through a command can facilitate an individual's development of self-confidence as well as improve communication and boundary setting. Post–horse activity, the clinician processes with the client, through talk therapy, the impact of the exercise. According Nussen and Becker (2012), clients gain a stronger sense of empowerment as they are able to command their space and feel more secure with the aid of the powerful friend (i.e., horse).

MICRO PERSPECTIVE

Recommended Screening Process and Assessment

Though the literature does not reveal any studies that indicate harmful risks associated with EAC, there remain inherent risks due to the nature of the modality and, therefore, a screening process of clients and horses is important for safety concerns. Horses can spook, kick, bite, or buck in response to an environmental stimulus. A horse could cause harm to an individual by accidentally stepping on a client's foot or pressing the client against a fence, wall, or gate. Persons selected for EAC need to be able to interact with the horse; however, a horse handler (or equine behaviorist) must always be in close proximity for the safety of the client and horse. In addition to safety screenings, baseline assessments of client symptoms and functioning are recommended before determination of treatment goals and should be followed by evaluation post-treatment (as is true with any evidence-based practice).

The clinician needs to be well versed in the symptoms of trauma in order to make the appropriate determination for this method of therapeutic intervention. It is strongly recommended that a client with any history of engaging in animal abuse be more closely supervised or not permitted to engage in this modality of therapy. If being in the presence of the horse causes the client to feel retraumatized, the clinician may choose another method of treatment or another animal-based practice (e.g., canine therapy; see Urichuk & Anderson, 2003). Additionally, if during any session a client identifies an acute occurrence of or increase in distress symptoms of any type that may render the client or horse unsafe, the session should be terminated immediately.

Diversity Considerations

Although, as noted earlier, EAC is utilized with various ages, genders, and problem-focused backgrounds, the literature reveals limited data on its utility with diverse client groups. However, one study used horses with First Nations and Inuit youth as part of recovery from solvent inhalant abuse (Dell et al., 2011). Whitely (2009) cited historical use of animals in Italy, England, and Germany as therapeutic agents and provided current utilization in numerous agencies worldwide that provide equine therapeutic services. Lujan (2012) discussed the vital need for multicultural competence in counselors using equine counseling in North America's southwest region, where it is vitally important for the clinician to be aware of his or her own cultural identity as well as the client's, so as to avoid negative missteps in preparation of experiential activities or discussions. Additionally, several agencies that provide EAC are licensed as charitable organizations and have scholarship provisions for clients with limited financial resources (see the Equine Assisted Growth and Learning Association [EAGALA] website in the resource section of this chapter to locate agencies worldwide that provide equine therapeutic services).

With regard to diversity considerations in the opening case scenario of a military veteran, there are distinctive differences between military and civilian cultures as well as hypothesized worldviews (Weiss, Coll, & Metal, 2011) that may present challenges to traditional treatment approaches; thus, EAC may be a good alternative or complementary therapeutic option.

Interventions

Both broke and unbroke (i.e., a horse that has never been trained with a saddle) horses can be utilized in the therapeutic format of EAC. At Pegasus Rising, unbroke horses are used in this treatment modality with military veterans and other clients suffering from trauma. Pegasus Rising horses are a herd of rescued Polish Arabians, all within the same family, that have been gentled down to the level of approachability and grooming, allowing for a special relationship between the client and the horses. They live in outdoor corrals rather than in barn stalls. This provides a more natural environment and allows for "pack" mentality and behavior because, being prey animals, they are more secure when they live as part of a herd (Hill, 2006).

Interventions and Training Prior to Working With the Horse

Before a client enters into the arena with the horses, due to the potential manifestation of distress symptoms, it is imperative that clients are taught personal safety and anxiety reduction exercises first. For example, there are several techniques that can be utilized with clients prior to approaching or working with a horse that can facilitate reduction of potential anxious reactions. Williams and Poijula (2002) addressed the need for persons working through trauma symptoms to feel safe and provided several exercises to address safety. One such exercise encouraged the creation of a *safe place* wherein they feel protected and secure. This is a visual image that clients are coached to practice and can access when they are feeling distressed and anxious. Additionally, due to the physiological responses to stress hormones, it is vital that the client is taught deep breathing techniques to reduce escalation of stress reactions and return breathing to a normal flow. Deep breathing exercises also facilitate reduction of a rapid heartbeat and

increased blood pressure brought on by the surging of adrenaline in the system (Benson & Proctor, 2010). Several authors have also advocated for providing the client with relaxation techniques in order to help calm the mind and body (Benson & Proctor, 2010; Williams & Poijula, 2002). One simple technique is progressive relaxation, which follows a sequence of tightening and relaxing muscle groups from the head to the toes (Davis, Robbins Eshelman, & McKay, 2008; Williams & Poijula, 2002). This technique can be taught to clients, allowing them to practice it on their own. Along with breathing and other relaxation exercises, Davis et al. (2008) advocated for the use of a stress-awareness diary wherein the client identifies daily stressful events along with manifesting symptoms. This information can be employed before, during, and after EAC exercises and processed with the social worker. Additionally, because dissociation is a common symptom for persons experiencing trauma, often they are left without clear understanding of their emotions at any given time or the ability to identify emotions. Providing a simple list of common emotions and asking clients to identify when they experience a particular sentiment ("I feel _____ when _____") will help them begin to ascertain and articulate their feelings. In addition to the above preparatory exercises, clients need to be empowered to articulate their need to terminate a session at any time they feel unsafe or exhausted, either emotionally or physically.

Pegasus Rising is a brief therapeutic program that utilizes four sequential exercises, with the overall goal being to enable the client to increase his or her self-awareness, improve emotional regulation, and utilize critical thinking processes in the abatement of trauma symptomology. A client may participate in an exercise more than once before moving on to the next exercise. They are sequential; one exercise must be sufficiently mastered in order to move forward to the next activity.

At Pegasus Rising, Juan reported learning techniques that increased his self-awareness and facilitated management of his trauma symptoms. At the time that Juan was seen at Pegasus Rising, formal assessment and treatment evaluation measures were not employed (neither at baseline nor following the intervention). An example of a self-report instrument that could have been used is the 17-item PTSD checklist, military version (PCL-M; Blanchard, Jones-Alexander, Buckley, & Forneris, 1996). However, according to Juan's report, the EAC experience enabled him to manage community outings with fewer PTSD-related symptoms. He stated that "in order to be with the horses, you need to be relaxed." He reported that during one particular evening out at a crowded park, he experienced flashbacks and symptoms of hypervigilance. During that night, although his flashbacks transported him into a market place in Iraq, he was able to "stop" the images and anxiety with the steps he used before going to the corral to be with the horses. He closed his eyes, took a few deep breaths, and consciously thought to himself, "Let it go." Juan stated that it was not easy at first to apply the teachings from interacting with the horses to life in the outside world, but with practice, "it worked." A note to the reader: Although Juan reports experiencing benefits as a result of EAC, this is not meant to imply that his individual and group therapies obtained through the VHA were ineffective, as it is impossible to make such determinations when the client is receiving multiple interventions at once. However, the client seemed to be impressed by the powerful nature of this intervention and the human-horse connection.

Transference and Countertransference Issues

Although not particular to EAC, working with clients who have experienced trauma can result in secondary traumatic stress for the clinician (see Rubin & Weiss, 2013), and as Shay (2014) poignantly stated, "A diet of horrific trauma survivor narratives can damage the mental health of clinicians that work with them" (p. 189). According to Shay, another aspect of clinician countertransference that needs to be self-monitored is passing judgment on the acts of war committed by a combat veteran, particularly in light of the ambiguous or lack of a clear enemy in the theatres of Iraq and Afghanistan (where children and other civilians are used as human shields by the enemy). What the combat veteran may have experienced has been theorized by experts as *moral injury*. Litz et al. (2009) conceptualized moral injury as occurring when "service members are confronted with numerous moral and ethical challenges in war. They may act in ways that transgress deeply held moral beliefs or they may experience conflict about the unethical behaviors of others. Warriors may also bear witness to intense human suffering and cruelty that shakes their core beliefs about humanity" (p. 696).

Shay (2014) described moral injury experienced by a service member:

> When there has been (a) a betrayal of "what's right"; (b) either by a person in legitimate authority (my definition), or by one's self—"I did it"; (c) in a high stakes situation. Both forms of moral injury impair the capacity for trust and elevate despair, suicidality, and interpersonal violence. (p. 182)

Once again, the clinician may experience his or her own reaction to the client's narrative associated with moral injury and needs to closely monitor his or her countertransference responses toward the client.

In terms of transference reactions, Shay (2014) offered the following from the client's perspective, where the client who has been traumatized is asking himself or herself or even the therapist directly or indirectly, "Why should I trust you [clinician]? Are you another perpetrator? Are you a rescuer? Are you a self-serving bystander? Are you a victim like me? (If so, what the hell good are you?)" (p. 188). The hope of EAC is that by incorporating the horse as a neutral and mediating third party, the potentially damaging and negative transference and countertransference reactions that could potentially arise in the therapeutic relationship may be minimized.

Legal and Ethical Concerns

As with any for-profit or nonprofit organization, there are logistical matters that must be taken into consideration when contemplating the provision of EAC services. The practical matter of zoning ordinances for the purpose of conducting business on the property must be investigated to ensure compliance with the law. Adequate liability insurance to cover any bodily injury, in addition to the normal malpractice insurance a licensed therapist must carry, needs also to be evaluated and obtained. Payment for services through a third party provider (i.e., insurance company) must be investigated via state/federal guidelines and regulations.

Although there is a movement toward establishment of a certification/credentialing process, currently there is a lack of clarity on the theoretical and practice frameworks an individual or organization would be mandated to follow. However, the very nature of EAC interventions would require they be provided by a licensed mental health provider who should meet the legal obligations of the state in which he or she is providing the therapeutic services. Furthermore, if the licensed mental health provider is not adept at working with horses, then an equine behavior specialist should be employed along with the clinician to assure the safety and wellness of both the client and horse.

Lastly, legal and ethical issues with regard to client care: The client should be informed that this type of therapy is experimental and considered an alternative approach, as it has not been widely evaluated by research, whereas other types of trauma therapies have evidence supporting their effectiveness and should be offered first.

Please see Appendix A on p. 144 for the EAC program exercises and processes protocol that includes the description of the four sessions.

Case Vignette Conclusion

Juan reported that equine counseling has assisted him in reducing feelings of anxiety. It has allowed him to be able to "trust more," as he is more open to talking with people and even feels more comfortable at the veteran facility in which he resides. This newfound openness has also helped him to reconnect with his family. Juan describes that he feels at ease around horses because they are "structural" (i.e., hierarchical) like his chain of command in the Marine Corps (for more information on military culture, see Coll, Weiss, & Metal, 2013; Exum, Coll, & Weiss, 2011). He said it was all about the "instinct, the emotion, because horses defend their family," and he feels "understood" by the animals, but most important, he "does not feel judged."

Juan described that after completing the program at Pegasus Rising, he was eager to continue working with the horses and help others. Thus, he decided to volunteer at Pegasus Rising and began learning new skills of horse care. He was able to apply what he learned from the program to his volunteer work, building on skills to advance his volunteer efforts to working with fellow military veterans. Currently, Juan volunteers at the Pegasus Rising on the weekends while he is working toward an Associate's Degree from the local community college with his Post-9/11 GI Bill benefits, and he would like to transfer to a State University to study psychology. He would also like to become certified by the Equine Assisted Growth and Learning Association (EAGALA) to work in horse-human interaction to help others. His ultimate goal is to open an EAC center of his own to help combat veterans.

MEZZO PERSPECTIVE

The variety of techniques in the delivery of EAC services is dependent on the organization and mission of the business. An EAC agency or organization may be owned as a sole proprietorship where delivery of services is through the licensed mental health practitioner who owns the horse(s) and space in which treatment is provided. It may be organized similarly to Pegasus Rising, a charitable 501(c)(3) organization that contracts its services to other agencies, such as The San Marcos Vet Center, Veterans Village of San Diego, and Interfaith Services Recuperative Care, to provide treatment to their clients. The organization providing the services has the freedom to determine the mode of delivery of services to clients based on their business/organizational structure.

Treatment services can be delivered to individuals, families, or groups. As noted earlier, it can provide services to certain populations that have been studied, such as juvenile offenders, at-risk youth, trauma survivors, veterans, and others. The business model may be organized to administer services in a stationary locale or have the flexibility for staff to travel to an alternative location to provide treatment.

Juan was a client of a veteran's residential rehabilitation center. The center contracted with Pegasus Rising to provide EAC to their clients. The center provided transportation to and from the ranch. Without this collaborative agreement between the center and Pegasus Rising, Juan would not have had the opportunity for treatment.

MACRO PERSPECTIVE

Although this form of alternative therapeutic intervention is becoming increasingly utilized, current research is limited and there are no national or state requirements for credentialing EAC therapists (Kachelmeier, 2009). Although more empirical research is needed to develop these techniques into evidence-based practices, there are several organizations that are committed to providing guidelines and education to ensure quality services and safety for the horse and the participating client. It is recommended that the clinician obtain education and/or mentoring prior to engaging in this form of therapeutic intervention. Names and contact information of these organizations are provided in the Internet Resources section of this chapter. Additionally, appropriate selection of the horse(s) for EAC as well as evaluation of the facility in terms of adequate room to provide services is paramount to the well-being of the horse(s) and the needs of the client (Sudekum Trotter, 2012).

CONCLUSION

Although many may benefit from conventional and traditional therapeutic mental health interventions, many others would find EAC an advantageous modality, providing them with the nurturing qualities of nature coupled with experiential learning under the guidance of a trained mental health clinician. EAC appears to have advantages for both Juan and perhaps the horse as well when partnered together under the umbrella of security, therapeutic bonding, and wellness. However, additional research is needed in this field to further validate the effectiveness and soundness of this intervention. It is hoped that as this method of treatment continues to be pursued, so too will the research.

INTERNET RESOURCES

- Pegasus Rising: http://pegasusrising.org/
- Equine Assisted Growth and Learning Association (EAGLA): http://www.eagala.org/
- Professional Association of Therapeutic Horsemanship (PATH): http://www.pathintl.org/
- Certification Board for Equine Interaction Professionals (CBEIP): http://www.cbeip.com/
- National Institute of Mental Health (NIMH): http://www.nimh.nih.gov/health/index.shtml
- Department of Veterans Affairs Health Benefits: http://www.va.gov/healthbenefits/online/

DISCUSSION QUESTIONS

1. What value does experiential learning have in the development of EAC therapeutic interventions?

2. How can EAC decrease distressing trauma or PTSD symptoms?

3. What legal/ethical concerns need to be taken into consideration when applying EAC?

4. Name the safety and anxiety reduction exercises identified in the chapter and their purpose.

5. Describe a therapeutic session and the rationale.

REFERENCES

Ainsworth, M. D. S. (1969). Object relations, dependency, and attachment: A theoretical review of the infant-mother relationship. *Child Development, 40*, 969–1025.

American Psychiatric Association. (2013). *Diagnostic and statistical manual of mental disorders* (5th ed.). Washington, DC: Author.

Bandura, A. (1971). *Social learning theory*. New York, NY: General Learning Press.

Bandura, A. (1994). Self-efficacy. In V. S. Ramachaudran (Ed.), *Encyclopedia of human behavior* (Vol. 4, pp. 71–81). New York, NY: Academic Press.

Benamer, S., & White, K. (2008). *Trauma and attachment: The John Bowlby Memorial Conference monograph 2006*. London, UK: Karnac.

Benson, H., & Proctor, W. (2010). *Relaxation revolution*. New York, NY: Scribner.

Blanchard, E. B., Jones-Alexander, J., Buckley, T. C., & Forneris, C. A. (1996). Psychometric properties of the PTSD checklist (PCL). *Behavioral Research & Therapy, 34*, 669–673.

Bowlby, J. (1979). *The making and breaking of affectional bonds*. London, UK: Tavistock.

Bretherton, I. (1992). The origins of attachment theory: John Bowlby and Mary Ainsworth. *Developmental Psychology, 28*, 759–775.

Coll, J. E., Weiss, E. L., & Metal, M. (2013). Military culture and diversity. In A. Rubin, E. L. Weiss, & J. E. Coll (Eds.), *Handbook of military social work* (pp. 21–36). Hoboken, NJ: John Wiley & Sons.

Davis, M., Robbins Eshelman, E., & McKay, M. (2008). *The relaxation & stress reduction workbook* (6th ed.). Oakland, CA: New Harbinger.

Dell, C. A., Chalmers, D., Bresette, N., Swain, S., Rankin, D., & Hopkins, C. (2011). A healing space: The experiences of First Nations and Inuit youth with equine assisted learning (EAL). *Child Youth Care Forum, 40,* 319–336. doi:10.1007/s10566-011-9140-z

Erikson, E. (1980). *Identity and the life cycle*. New York, NY: Norton.

Ewing, C. A., MacDonald, P. M., Taylor, M., & Bowers, M. J. (2007). Equine-facilitated learning for youths with severe emotional disorders: A quantitative and qualitative study. *Child Youth Care Forum, 36,* 59–72. doi: 10.1007/s 10566-006-9031-x

Exum, H., Coll, J. E., & Weiss, E. L. (2011). *A civilian counselor's primer for counseling veterans* (2nd ed.). Deerpark, NY: Linus.

Foa, E. B., Hembree, E. A., & Rothbaum, B. O. (2007). *Prolonged exposure therapy for PTSD: Emotional processing of traumatic experiences, therapist guide*. New York, NY: Oxford University Press.

Frewin, K., & Gardiner, B. (2005). New age or old sage? A review of equine assisted psychotherapy. *The Australian Journal of Counseling Psychology, 6*, 13–17.

Gentry, J. W. (1990). *Guide to business gaming and experiential learning: Association for business simulation and experiential learning*. London, UK: Nichols/GP.

Hess, E. H. (1958). Imprinting in animals. *Scientific American, 198*(3), 81–90.

Hill, C. (2006). *How to think like a horse: The essential handbook for understanding why horses do what they do*. North Adams, MA: Storey.

Hoge, C. W., Castro, C. A., Messer, S. C., McGurk, D., Cotting, D. I., & Koffman, R. L. (2004). Combat duty in Iraq and Afghanistan, mental health problems, and barriers to care. *New England Journal of Medicine, 351*(1), 13–22.

Kachelmeier, P. A. (2009). *Starting an equine-assisted program: An investigative study into the creation of an equine-assisted psychotherapy or learning business*. Retrieved from ProQuest Dissertations and Theses. Order No. UMI 1462067.

Klontz, B. T., Bivens, A., Leinart, D., & Klontz, T. (2007). The effectiveness of equine-assisted experiential therapy: Results of an open clinical trial. *Society and Animals, 15*(3), 257.

Kolb, D. A., Boyatzis, R. E., & Mainemelis, C. (2000). Experiential learning theory: Previous research and new directions. In R. J. Sternberg & L. F. Zhang (Eds.), *Perspectives on cognitive, learning, and thinking styles* (pp. 227–248). Hillsdale, NJ: Lawrence Erlbaum.

Litz, B. T., Stein, N., Delaney, E., Lebowitz, L., Nash, W. P., Silva, C., & Maguen, S. (2009). Moral injury and moral repair in war veterans: A preliminary model and intervention strategy. *Clinical Psychology Review, 29*, 695–706.

Lujan, K. M. (2012). *The challenges and discoveries in using equine assisted psychotherapy approaches by* counseling practitioners in the southwest. Retrieved from ProQuest Dissertations and Theses. Order No. UMI 3527225.

Lyons-Ruth, K., Dutra, L., Shuder, M., & Bianchi, I. (2006). From infant attachment disorganization to adult dissociation: Relational adaptations or traumatic experience? *Psychiatric Clinics of North America, 29*(1), 63–86. doi:10.1016/j.psc.2005.10.011

MacLean, B. (2011). Equine-assisted therapy. *Journal of Rehabilitation Research and Development, 48*(7), ix–xii.

The Management of Post-Traumatic Stress Working Group. (2010). *VA/DoD clinical practice guideline for management of post-traumatic stress. Version 2.0.* Washington, DC: Department of Veterans Affairs.

Nelson, L. (2014). *Group Intervention: Equine assisted therapy in children with emotional and behavioral disorders.* University of Minnesota, Duluth. Retrieved from http://www.d.umn.edu/~lbye/SW%208111%20Generalist%20Practice%20Micro/GroupInterventionEquineAssistedTherapyin Children with.htm

Nussen, J., & Becker, L. (2012). *Soul recovery.* Norco, CA: Equine Works.

Resick, P. A., Monson, C. M., Price, J. L., & Chard, K. M. (2007). *Cognitive processing therapy: Veteran/military version: Trainer's manual.* Washington, DC: Department of Veterans Affairs.

Resick, P. A., & Schnicke, M. K. (1992). Cognitive processing therapy for sexual assault survivors. *Journal of Consulting & Clinical Psychology, 60,* 748–756.

Rubin, A., & Weiss, E. L. (2013). Secondary trauma in military social work. In A. Rubin, E. L. Weiss, & J. E. Coll (Eds.), *Handbook of military social work* (pp. 67–78). Hoboken, NJ: Wiley & Sons.

Schultz, P. N., Remick-Barlow, G., & Robbins, L. (2007). Equine-assisted psychotherapy: A mental health promotion/intervention modality for children who have experienced intra-family violence. *Health & Social Care in the Community, 15*(3), 265–271.

Shay, J. (2014). Moral injury. *Psychoanalytic Psychology, 31*(2), 182–191.

Singer, D., & Revenson, T. (1996). *A Piaget primer: How a child thinks.* New York, NY: Penguin Group.

Sudekum Trotter, K. (2012). *Harnessing the power of equine assisted counseling.* New York, NY: Rutledge Taylor & Francis Group.

Sudekum Trotter, K., Chandler, C., Goodwin-Bond, D., & Casey, J. (2008). A comparative study of the efficacy of group equine assisted counseling with at-risk children and adolescents. *Journal of Creativity in Mental Health, 3*(3) 254–284.

Urichuk, L. J., & Anderson, D. L. (2003). *Improving mental health through animal-assisted therapy.* Edmonton, Alberta, Canada: Chimo Project.

Van der Horst, F. C., LeRoy, H. A., & Van der Veer, R. (2008). "When strangers meet": John Bowlby and Harry Harlow on attachment behavior. *Integrative Psychological and Behavioral Science, 42*(4), 370–388.

Walsh, F. (2006). *Strengthening family resilience.* New York, NY: Guilford Press.

Weiss, E. L., Coll, J. E., & Metal, M. (2011). The influence of military culture and veteran worldviews on mental health treatment: Implications for veteran help seeking and wellness. *International Journal of Health, Wellness & Society, 1*(2), 75–86.

Whitely, R. (2009). *Therapeutic benefits of equine assisted psychotherapy for at-risk adolescents.* Retrieved from ProQuest Dissertations and Theses. Order No. UMI 3405795.

Williams, M., & Poijula, S. (2002). *The PTSD workbook: Simple and effective techniques for overcoming traumatic stress symptoms.* Oakland, CA: New Harbinger.

Wilson, N., D'Ardenne, P., & Scott, C. (2012). Survivors of the London bombings with PTSD: A qualitative study of their accounts during CBT. *Traumatology, 18,* 75–84.

Yarvis, J. S. (2013). Posttraumatic stress disorder (PTSD) in veterans. In A. Rubin, E. L. Weiss, & J. E. Coll (Eds.), *Handbook of military social work* (pp. 81–97). Hoboken, NJ: John Wiley & Sons.

APPENDIX A

PEGASUS RISING EQUINE ASSISTED COUNSELING PROGRAM EXERCISES AND PROCESSES

The following are sample sessions derived from actual sessions provided at Pegasus Rising (developed by a Pegasus Rising licensed mental health clinician and reprinted here with permission). Special note: Additional components have been included here to provide theoretical background and descriptive clinical interventions.

Orientation

All clients attend an orientation to the EAC process where they are provided an overview of the value of experiential learning, the history of the horses they will be working with, and most important, horse safety. Prior to the sessions, the therapist provides an introduction and description of the session. Each client has previously determined goals for the outcome of the four sessions.

Exercise 1: Observing the Horses

Introduction: Similar to humans, horses are keenly social animals. This session focuses on both self and other observation skills. The client observes how the horses socialize with other herd members and compares their behavior to the client's own socialization process.

Rationale: Bandura's (1994) social learning theory reflects the importance of attention and self-observation in the process of learning and the development of self-efficacy.

Equipment: Two or more horses present in an outdoor paddock. No equipment necessary.

Description: The participant enters the paddock and begins to observe how the horses interact. This observation exercise can vary depending on the participant. Allow the participant to spend time with the horses. Leave 15 to 30 minutes at the end for processing.

SOURCE: Reprinted with permission from Gary Adler.

Announce the session is ending, have him say good-bye to the horses, and come out of the paddock area.

Equine Behaviorist: Remains in the paddock throughout the session to ensure safety and guide human/equine interaction.

Mental Health Practitioner Observations:

- Watch the participant's reactions.
- What is his or her mood in the beginning of the exercise?
- How comfortable does he or she appear?
- Did he or she ask for help?
- Did he or she approach the exercise with confidence?
- Did he or she manifest an emotional response in the process of the exercise?

Optional Debriefing of the Experience:

Ask the client to

1. Provide objective details of what happened during the session

2. Identify any sensory impressions (e.g., what did he or she hear, see, touch, smell or taste?)

3. Identify thoughts that went through his or her mind during the session

4. What emotions did he or she experience during the session?

5. Did he or she experience any reactionary symptoms?

Therapeutic Processing:

Questions to consider asking at some time after the session is completed:

1. What were the horses doing?

2. Is there anything that the horses were doing that reminds the participant of himself or herself?

3. Is there evidence of the horses taking care of themselves?

4. Which horse is the participant's favorite?

5. Which horse is his or her least favorite?

6. Is there a horse that looks or behaves most like him or her?

7. Is there a horse that looks or behaves least like him or her?

8. Which horse seems like the leader?

9. Encourage expansion of each of the answers.

10. Encourage journal writing of the experience.

Exercise 2: Approaching and Interacting With a Horse

Introduction: Life brings about multiple scenarios that require a willingness to insert oneself into the uncertainty of a situation. The unknown can be uncomfortable and increase levels of anxiety. Just as horses may experience the "fight or flight" response, so do humans, when exposed to levels of uncertainty. Persons diagnosed with PTSD tend to be more prone to the "fight or flight" response. This exercise encourages mindfulness and assertiveness, building on the previous exercise of self and other observation.

Rationale: Bandura's (1971) social learning theory, whereby learning occurs through direct experience and modeling. Participant demonstrates the ability to attend to, retain, and reproduce instructions as well as the ability to regulate emotions and make healthy judgments.

Equipment: No equipment necessary.

Description: The participant picks a horse he or she would like to interact with, proceeds without verbal language, and attempts to approach the horse or get the horse to approach him or her. Participant may touch/pet the horse if successful at getting close enough to do so. Leave 15 to 30 minutes at the end for processing. Announce the session is ending, have them say goodbye to the horse, and come out of the paddock area.

Equine Behaviorist: Guides human/equine interaction. Educates participant in appropriate approach and touch methods. Remains in the paddock throughout the session to ensure safety.

Mental Health Practitioner Observations:

- Watch the participant's reactions.
- What is his or her mood in the beginning of the exercise?

- How comfortable does he or she appear?
- Did he or she ask for help?
- Did he or she approach the exercise with confidence?
- Did he or she manifest an emotional response in the process of the exercise?
- Does the participant "check in" with the horse?
- What approach does the participant have with the horse(s)?
- Is the participant engaging with the horse? How so?
- What type of relationship does the participant seem to have with the horse?
- It is important to allow the participant time to interact without jumping in and talking at the same time. Pay attention to the frustration level. In some cases it is okay to stop and walk over and ask the participant how he or she is doing. Also, encourage the participant to utilize calming self-talk when he or she recognizes a rise in emotional distress.

Optional Debriefing of the Experience:

Ask the client to

1. Provide objective details of what happened during the session

2. Identify any sensory impressions (e.g., what did the participant hear, see, touch, smell, or taste?)

3. Identify thoughts that went through his or her mind during the session

4. What emotions did he or she experience during the session?

5. Did he or she experience any reactionary symptoms?

Therapeutic Processing:

Questions to consider asking at some time after the session is completed:

1. What feelings was he or she experiencing?

2. What was his or her internal dialog?

3. What does he or she think is being communicated to him or her by the horse?

4. Are there any similarities between what is happening with the horse and other people or situations in his or her life?

5. Can the participant remember a time when he or she was asked to do something that he or she was unsure how to do? How did he or she respond? How did others respond?

6. Encourage expansion of each of the answers.

7. Encourage journal writing of the experience.

Exercise 3: Grooming and Paraverbal Communication

Introduction: Goal setting, decision making, task preparation, and implementation of steps with empathic understanding.

Rationale: Ego mastery (Erikson, 1980) requires the ability to set goals and navigate internal and external conflicts that may impede their actualization. Utilization of concrete levels of cognitive development (Singer & Revenson, 1996) is necessary to basic problem solving and empathic understanding. Development of self-efficacy (Bandura, 1994) requires mastery of learning experiences.

Equipment: Halter, lead rope, and basic grooming tools (e.g., rubber curry, stiff-bristled brush, & soft body brush).

Description: The participant is asked to build on the skills that he or she learned in Exercise 2. Without verbal language, restraint, or force, the participant is to encourage/guide the horse with the specific goal in mind to groom the horse. Session will commence with haltering and leading the horse to a grooming area. Participant grooms the horse while learning basic caretaking skills. Leave 15 to 30 minutes at the end for processing. Announce the session is ending, have him or her say goodbye to the horse, and come out of the paddock area.

Equine Behaviorist: Teaches the participant haltering, leading, and appropriate grooming techniques and remains in the paddock throughout the session to ensure safety as well as guide human/equine interaction.

Mental Health Practitioner Observations:

- Limit the amount of directions to the participant and be prepared to see a combination of responses (deliberate lack of clarity allows the horses to do their work).
- Observe the participant's reactions.
- What is his or her mood at the beginning of the exercise?
- How comfortable does he or she appear?
- Did he or she ask for help?
- Did he or she approach the exercise with confidence?
- Did he or she manifest an emotional response during the exercise?
- Does the participant "check in" with the horse?
- Did the participant use the same horse as in Exercise 2?
- Is the participant engaging with the horse? How so?
- What type of relationship does the participant seem to have with the horse?
- What approach does the participant have with the horse(s)?

Optional Debriefing of the Experience:

Ask the client to

1. Provide objective details of what happened during the session

2. Identify any sensory impressions (e.g., what did he or she hear, see, touch, smell, or taste?)

3. Identify thoughts that went through his or her mind during the session

4. What emotions did he or she experience during the session?

5. Did he or she experience any reactionary symptoms?

Therapeutic Processing:

Questions to consider asking at some time after the session is completed:

1. Inquire how the participant chose which horse to groom. Encourage reflection on the process the participant uses.

2. How did the participant communicate with the horse(s)?

3. If the participant used verbal language when engaging with the horse, what did he say? How did he say it?

4. Did the horse seem to have areas that it do not like touched/approached? How did he or she handle it?

5. Have the participant label some of the emotions he or she perceived the horse to have during the session.

6. What emotions did he or she experience?

7. What was his or her internal dialog?

8. What was it like to participate in the exercise?

9. Encourage expansion of each of the answers.

10. Encourage journal writing of the experience.

Exercise 4: Moving Horse Through an Obstacle Course

Introduction: Trauma experiences can rob the individual of the capacity to cognitively process conflict. Due to negative alterations in mood and cognitive abilities (APA, 2013) and the high level of emotional response with "fight or flight" reaction, a person suffering from PTSD struggles with remaining in the present when faced with conflict.

Rationale: Working though obstacles can facilitate the development of resilience (Walsh, 2006) and self-efficacy. It strengthens ego functioning and capacity to manage and control impulses and emotions (Erikson, 1980). Contending with conflict promotes personal empowerment and reduces learned helplessness.

Equipment: One or more horses plus cones, tires, poles, and barrels that can be used to create an obstacle course. Be sure to have the client create a number of obstacles.

Description: Participant is asked to build a series of obstacles in the arena. Have the participant build a pathway from past to present and future. The pathway must include some twists and turns. The therapist asks the participant to identify for herself the metaphor of the obstacle(s) and positive future goal as well as processes that the twists and turns represent. Without verbal language, restraint, or force, the participant is to encourage/guide the horse from behind through the obstacle course. The participant's obstacle course can act as a metaphor that represents the biggest challenge(s) she may see in moving forward.

Another Option: Have the participant set up a large square in the center made out of poles. Let her know she needs to move two horses into the "box" for 3 minutes. Participant is to label the box as the most common area of life that she gets stuck in, for example, drugs, alcohol, relationships. The participant cannot talk, bribe, or touch the horses. Leave 15 to 30 minutes at the end for processing. Announce the session is ending, have her say goodbye to the horses, and come out of the paddock area.

Equine Behaviorist: Remains in the paddock throughout the session to ensure safety of human/equine interaction.

Mental Health Practitioner Observations:

- Watch the participant's reactions.
- What is his or her mood before beginning the exercise?
- How comfortable does he or she appear?
- Did he or she ask for help?
- Did he or she approach the exercise with confidence?
- Did he or she manifest an emotional response?
- Watch as he or she maneuvers with the horse to get through the path.
- Pay attention to how the participant manages the consequences.

Optional Debriefing of the Experience:
Ask the client to

1. Provide objective details of what happened during the session

2. Identify any sensory impressions (e.g., what did he or she hear, see, touch, smell, or taste?)

3. Identify thoughts that went through his or her mind during the session.

4. What emotions did he or she experience during the session?

5. Did he or she experience any reactionary symptoms?

Therapeutic Processing:

Questions to consider asking at some time after the session is completed:

1. Have the participant discuss the obstacle(s) and his or her positive goal.

2. Process how he or she chose the horse. Listen to the process the participant used to make the decision.

3. Have the participant list what tools/coping skills he or she needs for handling both positive and negative challenges.

4. Identify in what area the participant thinks he or she has gotten the most stuck in his or her life.

5. Allow time to discuss cycles (e.g., getting stuck and what it takes to move through it).

6. Add in the concept that in life there are consequences and what happens if the participant violates them.

7. Let him or her come up with the answer. Watch what unfolds.

8. Ask what it was like to participate.

9. What horse was easiest to move in the obstacle course? Hardest?

10. What were the challenges?

11. Who was doing the leading?

12. How did the participant communicate with the horse(s)?

13. Did the participant think it would work successfully?

14. When the horse(s) went out of the lines/boundaries, what happened? When in life has the participant had difficulty like this?

15. Encourage expansion of each of the answers.

16. Encourage journal writing of the experience.

CHAPTER 12

Social Work in Skilled Nursing Homes

Edmund W. Young

CHAPTER OBJECTIVES

- Describe the role of a social worker in a nursing home setting;
- Assess the patient using a biopsychosocial framework;
- Identify the psychosocial interventions necessary to facilitate appropriate patient care;
- Comprehend and discuss how differing laws impact clinical practice.

CASE VIGNETTE

Mr. Anthony Jones is an English-speaking (primary language) 45-year-old single African American male with a prolonged history of homelessness. He is disabled. He currently receives Supplemental Security Income (SSI) and Medi-Cal insurance (or Medicaid). He was recently discharged from the local county general hospital (acute care hospitalization) for continued monitoring and stabilization from the following conditions: Human immunodeficiency virus (HIV), hypertension, muscle weakness, diabetes, Chronic Obstructive Pulmonary Disease, depression, Psychotic Disorder Not Otherwise Specified (NOS) and Polysubstance Dependence. Prior to being in the county hospital, Mr. Jones was living in the streets of Los Angeles because he had nowhere to turn. Mr. Jones has been a long-time resident in the Skid Row area of Los Angeles but refuses to enter a shelter because he was previously physically assaulted by another resident. Living on the streets has been a difficult lifestyle for Mr. Jones to manage, given the multitude of medical conditions he is grappling with.

Upon entering the Northwood Care Center in Los Angeles, Mrs. Adams, the social worker, completed the biopsychosocial evaluation in order to gather more information about the resident. The assessment revealed that Mr. Jones has been living with his medical problems for the last five years or more, since his heavy dependency on heroin, crack cocaine, methamphetamine, and alcohol overtook his life. From that point on, he began to "spiral out of control," and his physical health became impacted by his prolonged drug and alcohol dependency. Mr. Jones has been in and out of treatment facilities for the past couple of years but always seems to return to the hospital for stabilization. Mr. Jones believes the lack of support and housing assistance has caused him to remain in this "ping pong–like" situation where he enters the acute care hospital from the streets, then is discharged to a nursing facility, to be later discharged again back to the streets without a stable and permanent living environment. Because Mrs. Adams is a qualified mental health practitioner (master's prepared), her biopsychosocial evaluation will help her to create a case management treatment plan inclusive of discharge planning, to avoid rehospitalization. Understanding the problem will allow the worker to pair correlative interventions to meet the needs of the resident. Because Mr. Jones will require continued monitoring post-discharge from the nursing facility, he was amenable to a referral to a board and care facility. Mrs. Adams assisted Mr. Jones with the referral paperwork to the Windsor Recovery Home (a licensed board and care facility). Mrs. Adams received written consent for release of information from Mr. Jones so that she could advocate for him with the local Department of Public Social Services regarding his Medi-Cal (Medicaid) and the Social Security Administration regarding increasing his SSI benefits to the Board and Care rate in order to cover his stay at the Windsor Recovery Home. Mrs. Adams was also able to facilitate transportation and a site visit to the Windsor Recovery Home in order to successfully transition Mr. Jones.

INTRODUCTION

Social work practice in nursing home settings is usually seen as an adjunctive service provided to patients and their support systems. Nursing facilities or skilled nursing facilities usually offer the patient skilled nursing services, and rehabilitation services inclusive of physical therapy (PT), occupational therapy (OT), and speech therapy (ST) as ordered by a physician. In California, for example, many nursing facilities employ Social Service Designees (SSD), who are usually paraprofessional staff with little to no specific training in social work who operate also as the Social Services Director of the facility. According to Byrd (2009), a physician must complete the initial history and physical (H&P) that will determine the treatment needs for the individual. Regarding social work practice in this setting, it is not uncommon for a nursing home chain to employ one licensed clinical social worker (LCSW) to supervise a few SSDs located at different facilities. These paraprofessional staff often refer to themselves as social workers despite not having the clinical training or education.

Federal law (42 CFR 483.15) requires that all skilled nursing facilities provide "medically related social services to attain or maintain the highest practicable resident physical, mental, and psychosocial well-being." Nursing homes with more than 120 beds are required to employ a full-time social worker with at least a bachelor's degree in social work or "similar professional qualifications." Facilities with 120 beds or fewer must still provide social services, but they do not need to have a full-time social worker on staff. Although federal nursing home regulations have a general requirement that facilities use licensed personnel, this regulation has not been enforced in the case of social work. (Social Work Policy Institute, 2014)

The lack of geriatric social work competencies has been well documented, which led to the large disparity in knowledge and skills (Naito-Chan, Damron-Rodriguez, & Simmons, 2008). However, the level of care provided by the facility social worker will dictate the level of training and education that is necessary to perform the duties of the position. For example, Institutes of Mental Disease are locked nursing facilities that have professional mental health services in addition to supervised nursing services. In these types of settings, it is common to have master's level practitioners (unlicensed/licensed) as the facilities often provide individual and group psychotherapeutic services. Most government agencies will require social workers to have either a bachelor's or master's degree, dependent upon the job function or "scope of practice" required of the position. According to Simpson, Williams, and Segall (2007), the social work specialization was developed to meet specific population needs (i.e., person-in-situation perspective).

Historically and societally, nursing homes were commonly thought of as places where older adults would live out the remainder of their lives. However, in clinical practice, this is often not a reality. Many nursing home clients are younger people (less than 65 years old) who may require recuperative or skilled nursing care services, usually after acute hospitalization, to further stabilize their medical and/or psychiatric conditions. This is evident in the case of Mr. Jones, who is in need of skilled nursing and rehabilitation services to prevent rehospitalization. Rehabilitation services (e.g. PT, OT and/or ST) may be ordered by medical providers to assist an individual with his or her abilities to perform activities of daily living such as bathing, dressing, grooming, and toileting, or instrumental activities of daily living such as budgeting, transportation, laundry, and cooking, among others. These services are usually ordered for several times per week and scaled down as the individual gains more functional independence. Social workers often work alongside nursing staff and the adjunctive rehabilitation services to provide a holistic approach to recovery.

MICRO PERSPECTIVE

Social workers in care facilities provide a range of services: the coordination of external appointments for the individual, arranging for transportation services, assisting with care planning and discharge planning, case management/linkage to various agencies, providing consultation, facilitating family meetings, performing psychosocial evaluations, and providing supportive counseling (depending upon education and licensure). Although LCSWs are trained and certified to perform psychotherapeutic services, their services are often underutilized, possibly due to the medical team's and/or facility's lack of understanding of the social workers' clinical abilities and scope of practice. Social workers with a master's degree are licensed to either practice at the general practice level or at the advanced/independent practice level, as specified by each state's licensing board. The advanced/independent practice level incorporates the ability to perform clinical work in the form of differing psychotherapeutic modalities (e.g., individual, family, and/or group psychotherapy) and the rendering of psychiatric diagnosis as per DSM-5 criteria. Although social work staff complete a biopsychosocial assessment on each patient who remains in the facility for at least three days (a requirement that may differ by state as well as by facility), assessment is generally utilized as a tool to determine psychosocial supports and augment information obtained from the medical team, rather than for purposes of determining a mental health diagnosis or treatment. Because the social worker usually has greater contact with residents in a given facility, it is customary for the social worker to provide feedback to psychiatrists and psychologists with regard to a resident's mental health functioning, in order to enhance treatment efficacy. It is not uncommon for nursing facilities to contract their mental health service needs to external providers (e.g., psychiatrists and psychologists as noted in the medical record) and, to a lesser degree, LCSWs practicing independently. This is also seen when perusing the physician's orders in the medical record that would explicitly state psychiatry and/or psychology consults to address the individual's mental health needs. Some clinicians speculate the lack of LCSWs providing mental health services in nursing facilities has a direct correlation with the lack of title protection for the clinical social workers (i.e., SSDs referring to themselves as social workers, as referenced earlier). Social workers are also responsible for completing sections of the Minimum Data Set (MDS) that correspond with the discharge planning and psychosocial needs of the resident. However, some facilities may have a MDS coordinator (usually a RN) who is tasked with the completion of this required document. The reader is encouraged to check with the facility regarding internal policies and procedures, as this is not a standard practice across all facilities. The MDS provides a "multidimensional" snapshot of an individual's overall functioning (Centers for Medicare and Medicaid Services, 2014). Performing social service–related duties may periodically require the practitioner to report suspected cases of abuse. Although elder and dependent adult abuse are the more typical forms of abuse that will be reported to authorities, it is not uncommon for social workers in nursing facilities to report suspected cases of child abuse. According to the California Advocates for Nursing Home Reform (2014), elder abuse can take differing forms and can be both civil and criminal offenses.

> Criminal elder abuse occurs where any person who knows that a person is an elder and willfully causes or permits any elder to suffer, or inflicts unjustifiable physical pain or mental suffering on the elder. It also covers situations where a person willfully causes or permits the elder to be placed in a situation in which elder's health is endangered. . . . Civil law defines elder abuse to mean physical abuse, neglect, financial abuse, abandonment, isolation, abduction, or other treatment resulting in physical harm or pain or mental suffering. It also means the deprivation by case custodian of goods or services that are necessary to avoid physical harm or mental suffering. (Welfare & Institutions Code Section 15610.07)

In Los Angeles County, Adult Protective Services is the entity to which reports of alleged cases of abuse of older adults or dependent adults can be made (California Department of Social Services, 2014). Similarly, the Department of Child and Family Services is tasked with handling cases related to child abuse. Of special note, the local Ombudsman can also be contacted for any infractions or suspected abuse issues in long-term care facilities. The contact information for the Ombudsman is required to be posted in designated areas in the care facility. Each region may have these departments listed under different names, so it is important to know your state laws that govern practice as well as the reporting agency in your jurisdiction.

Assessment

Biopsychosocial evaluations, often referred to as psychosocial evaluations, are assessments to view the various domains or systems of an individual that assist the professional to deepen his or her understanding of how a person functions. It is critical for the clinician to have an accurate assessment so that the correlative treatment plan and interventions can be created and implemented. Therefore, a detailed review of a biopsychosocial evaluation will be provided to enhance your understanding. According to the Los Angeles County Department of Mental Health (2013), these biopsychosocial evaluations should include the following data: demographic data, presenting problems, medical problems, current medications, alcohol and drug usage, family constellation/primary supports, secondary supports, educational background, religion/spiritual considerations, and legal involvement, considerations, and issues.

Demographic Data

Demographic data provides a snapshot of a client. This is information that should include the following: name, age, race/ethnicity, gender, preferred language, and marital status. Demographic information advises the treatment team how to address a client and the preferred language in which he or she would like to communicate. For example, if a patient is Spanish-speaking only, the provider would know that the patient only communicates in the Spanish language, so he or she may use a translator if the provider does not speak the same language. This is crucial so that the individual's needs are properly communicated, understood, and supported, and it facilitates culturally sensitive practice.

Presenting Problems

It is crucial to understand the "presenting problem" or the reason the individual is admitted to the nursing facility. This may incorporate both medical and mental health diagnoses. The presenting problem also justifies the need for nursing home placement for insurance reimbursement. Here are some questions to ask: What are his or her current diagnoses? Why is he or she seeking assistance currently? What has he or she done to resolve the problem in the past? What was effective and what was not? What are the current symptoms (looking at frequency, chronicity, severity of all symptoms, and how they impair his or her functional ability; this helps to justify medical necessity). Is there a history of suicidal or homicidal ideation or attempts for this individual or in his or her family? This information can be gathered by reviewing the MD orders, the History and Physical (H&P) in the chart, discharge information from an acute hospitalization, transfer summary, the MDS, nursing notes, and/or through the client's self-report.

Medical Problems

It is important to know the specific medical problems for which the patient is receiving treatment. This domain is important to understand as medical illness often impacts overall mental functioning, which may be reciprocal and/or magnified. The practitioner should list all current physical health problems. You can find this information from the patient's face sheet data, the MD orders, the MDS, or through the H&P. Some of this information can be solicited from the patient directly, but he or she may not be able to provide all the medical diagnoses for which he or she is being treated.

Current Medications

Often patients are prescribed multiple medications to treat both physical conditions and psychiatric illnesses. It is important to list all current medications (i.e., the dose, the frequency, and the response to the medications). Please note any side effects and cost/benefits from the medications. This information may be crucial to relay to the prescribing provider and the treatment team so that they can assist in monitoring the patient's overall health and functioning.

Alcohol and Drugs

It is important to obtain a complete list of all current and/or past alcohol and drugs used. Ascertaining the specific types of drugs used, duration, and any issues related to tolerance, withdrawal, or chronic use will assist you to make provisional diagnoses as appropriate, and it will give the provider a global understanding of an individual's issues and how his or her substance use pattern may or may not be contributing to his or her clinical presentation. This data could also be utilized to understand how the patient attempts to self-medicate his or her symptoms. For example, an anxious client may opt to use alcohol to cope with his or her inability to self-regulate, without fully understanding how this substance may contribute to other physiological and psychological problems, as well as potentially amplify underlying depression.

Family Constellation / Primary Supports

This domain is crucial to understand as it sheds light upon how the individual views his or her family structure, his or her connectedness with family members, and the likelihood he or she will seek assistance from them to aid in coping during difficult times. The practitioner should gather information regarding the family of origin, birth order, feelings toward family members, and how culture may have influenced his or her perception of the family dynamics. It is also important to gather information regarding the individual's partner, spouse, girlfriend/boyfriend, relations, and any children. It is ideal to utilize support systems where and when possible to assist the individual to cope with stressors as well as reinforce therapeutic interventions that are implemented in the treatment process. Likewise, if the clinician identifies the family system to be maladaptive or a source of great tension for the client, this would inform the practitioner to avoid them or gradually desensitize the individual from them, depending upon the mutually agreed upon treatment goals.

Secondary Supports

It is important to gather information regarding the patient's friends and support system. This will aid the therapist in creating interventions to assist the individual with coping, similar to the use of primary supports. Some individuals may not have a primary support system in the form of biological family and/or extended kin, but they may view their support system to be inclusive of "close" friends. Whatever the scenario, it is ideal to have a firm grasp of the patient's support system to assist with pairing appropriate treatment interventions. This will also enable the therapist to understand how his or her client relates socially with others or to identify potential personality disorders.

Educational Background

It is important to ascertain your patent's academic background (highest level of education, grades, IEP, academic probation, field of study). This will not only assist in tailoring individualized interventions to the person's level of cognitive functioning but inform of his or her academic interests as well as enable benchmarking his or her current functioning with previous ability.

Religion/Spiritual Considerations

It is ideal to ascertain from the patient his or her religious and spiritual beliefs. This can be a tremendous source of coping for the infirm. Facilities usually have religious services to meet the spiritual needs of the residents. Social workers can also assist in coordinating religious/spiritual events and visits by religious practitioners or organizations. Having an understanding of the patient's religion, faith, or spiritual beliefs may also assist with potential discharge planning for the client. For example, if

a patient is of the Jewish faith, you may want to explore with the individual the faith-based services and/or placements that may be appropriate for him or her.

Legal Involvement, Considerations, and Issues

Many clients are involved with the legal system in some fashion. This area is important to gather information about, especially regarding the decision-making ability of the individual. Is the client on probation or parole? Is the person conserved? Does he or she have a Durable Power of Attorney for Healthcare? Does he or she have an Advanced Directive on file? Are there any legal issues that need to be addressed to ensure the safety of the individual and/or the public? For example, in California, do any of the presenting issues warrant initiating a writ for a Welfare and Institutions Code (WIC) 5150 involuntary hold/observation, Tarasoff requirements (reasonable attempts at informing an identifiable party regarding threats of violence/death and imminent risk to his or her personal safety; *Tarasoff v. Regents of the University of California,* 1976), and/or mandatory reporting (e.g., child abuse, elder abuse, or dependent adult abuse)? Please check with your state laws governing social work and mental health practice, as this may differ by region. Has the person been involved with the justice system before? If so, in what capacity? Is he or she on probation or parole? If he or she has been arrested, what prompted his or her detention? Does the person exhibit remorse? Are there any behavior patterns to note? This information may assist you in considering a provisional diagnosis. It is common for the biopsychosocial evaluation to utilize diagnoses that are rendered by the medical team. This is especially useful if the worker is not master's-level prepared or independently licensed so that the scope of practice is maintained.

Application of the Biopsychosocial Evaluation to Mr. Jones

In the case of Mr. Jones, it is imperative for the social work practitioner to have a thorough biopsychosocial evaluation completed in order to fully understand how this client presents (functional ability based upon past and current life events, coping skills, and patterns of relating with himself and his external environment), the underlying issues for the client, and how best to intervene on behalf of the client to ameliorate barriers and/or stressors that may prevent him from optimal functioning. After completing the biopsychosocial evaluation, the social worker will be able to assist Mr. Jones with a mutually agreed upon treatment plan, which may include appropriate psychotherapies and/or targeted case management services. Having a well-rounded understanding of Mr. Jones's situation will provide the social worker with an understanding of the issues that placed Mr. Jones in his current predicament, enable her to pair culturally sensitive interventions, and may yield higher treatment adherence. For example, Mr. Jones has co-occurring conditions of depression, Psychotic Disorder NOS and Polysubstance Dependence, homelessness, and a history of assault while being a resident in a local shelter in the Skid Row area. It is important to have a comprehensive biopsychosocial assessment so that a more accurate provisional diagnosis can be rendered that directly correlates with the treatment plan. An accurate evaluation will cue the social worker to coordinate a feasible discharge plan that may address his issues without placing him back in the area where he was assaulted—possibly into a board and care facility in a residential community away from the Skid Row area that can address all his immediate needs regarding his medical and mental health conditions coupled with basic needs of food, clothing, and shelter. Therefore, a social worker must have a thorough understanding of the array of resources in the local area to assist clients as appropriate.

Diversity Considerations

It is important for social work clinicians to consider all federally protected categories with regard to the clients they are serving: religion, sexual orientation, gender, race, ethnicity, religion, age, as well as physical and/or mental disability. Having a comprehensive knowledge of these diversity considerations will afford the practitioner a better mental schema regarding an individual's possible clinical presentation, which may be substantiated via the clinical interview/assessment, collateral information, and medical chart information. It is crucial for the clinician to be flexible, empathic, and open to diversity as each case must be treated on an individual basis, allowing for the individual's history and current presentation to be fully evaluated and understood.

With regard to Mr. Jones, it would be useful for the social work clinician to have a comprehensive awareness of any pertinent diversity considerations as it will validate and respect the client's presentation as well as assist the worker to pair possible interventions that will have a greater applicability for him. As a result, this may yield higher treatment adherence by Mr. Jones as the correlative interventions have been tailored to his individual needs and circumstance. Mrs. Adams was able to validate Mr. Jones's presentation and afforded him the opportunity to share his personal story of how he became addicted to substances that led him down the path of homelessness and declining health. Mrs. Adams operated from a nonjudgmental stance and took care not to assume that she knew what was happening with Mr. Jones because she had dealt with prior patients who were living with HIV, substance abuse, medical problems, mental health issues, and homelessness. Rather, she allowed Mr. Jones to tell his unique story, which validated his experience and assisted in the process of developing therapeutic rapport.

Interventions

It is important for the social work clinician to understand the various evidence-based practices. Evidence-based practices are treatment approaches that have been validated via a body of research data. Because the length of nursing home stays fluctuates based upon the functional ability (medical need and/or safety) of the individual coupled with payment reimbursements from various funding sources such as Medicare, Medicaid, long-term care insurance, and so on, it is crucial for providers to use evidence-based approaches as these are generally time bound, regimented, and efficacious. For example, cognitive behavioral therapy (an evidence-based approach) has been proven to be effective in the treatment of depression. Please ensure that you receive proper education, supervision, and/or consultation when implementing a new treatment approach as it would be unethical to render such services without this training.

During the assessment process, Mrs. Adams was able to uncover concurrent underlying depression that Mr. Jones felt comfortable in divulging. Mr. Jones informed Mrs. Adams that he was unable to share this previously with other providers as he did not feel safe. Because Mrs. Adams took the time to develop rapport and a therapeutic alliance with Mr. Jones, he felt that it was safe space for him to share his life experience. Via cognitive behavioral therapy, Mrs. Adams aided Mr. Jones to decrease his cognitive distortions regarding his situation that resulted in his self-medication with drugs and alcohol (maladaptive coping skills). Mr. Jones was able to decrease his automatic thoughts that he was a "failure," and he realized that his situation was in part due to circumstance and partly due to his untreated mental health condition. With regard to his diagnosis of Psychotic Disorder NOS, she was able to assist him in grounding his pattern of thinking and used their clinical sessions as a "sounding board" where he was able to verbalize his thoughts and perception of issues in order to receive feedback. Mrs. Adams diligently monitored his mental health condition and often consulted with his psychiatrist to assist in stabilizing his symptoms of psychosis. Through the therapeutic process, Mr. Jones was able to develop trust in his relationship with Mrs. Adams to where he felt comfortable in letting her know that his voices (auditory hallucinations) were telling him that others were "out to get him." Mrs. Adams was able to convey in an emphatic fashion that his paranoid delusions were solely internal to his experience. She was also able to provide him with psychoeducation regarding

the deleterious effects of substance abuse and its impact upon mental health functioning. During the treatment process, Mrs. Adams was successful at linking Mr. Jones to support groups in the community and securing a sponsor he can readily access upon discharge.

Transference and Countertransference Issues

Social work practitioners need to understand the various competing transferential and countertransferential dynamics that may impede the therapeutic rapport and process with a client. According to Hughes and Kerr (2000), transference is a phenomenon whereby individuals unconsciously transfer or project feelings and attitudes from a person or situation in their past to a person or situation in the present. Likewise, countertransference is the direct converse of transference whereby the practitioner is undergoing a parallel process of unconscious reenactment and/or projection of thoughts, feelings, and/or attitudes from prior experiences onto the client. Therefore, it is important for the clinician to be as cognizant as possible when these competing issues may be at play so they can be processed and worked through.

Mr. Jones reported to Mrs. Adams that he felt comfortable sharing his issues with her because she reminded him of his mother. This positive transference enabled Mr. Jones to project his issues upon Mrs. Adams during their clinical dialogue. Mrs. Adams was able to use this transference to clinically bond with the client, and it allowed her to subtly intervene without the client feeling threatened. It is important for the social work clinician to understand issues related to transference and countertransference as well as recognize that this can be used either positively or negatively, depending upon the clinical presentation by the client in conjunction with the skill level of the therapist. Mrs. Adams was able to manage her thoughts and feelings regarding the multiple issues faced by Mr. Jones. She often consulted with colleagues both internal and external to her agency, which afforded her greater perspective of the issues

Mr. Jones was grappling with. Unbeknownst to Mr. Jones, Mrs. Adams also had family members and close friends who experienced mental health problems and substance abuse. Because she was cognizant of these issues and readily sought consultation, Mrs. Adams was able to gain greater perspective and not allow potential countertransference reactions to compromise her professional relationship with Mr. Jones.

Legal and Ethical Concerns

The National Association of Social Workers (NASW) *Code of Ethics* provides a guide to professional conduct for social workers. It is crucial for social work practitioners to have a working understanding of these ethical guidelines as it ensures safety for the client, the general public, and the profession. It is important for the social worker to abide by all applicable local, state, and federal laws governing clinical practice. For example, the social work practitioner should be knowledgeable regarding issues of child abuse, elder abuse, dependent adult abuse, and the scope of practice, to list a few.

In the case of Mr. Jones, the social worker clinician, Mrs. Adams, completed a comprehensive biopsychosocial evaluation and determined that the client was not in danger of suicide, homicide, or grave disability. Implicit in the evaluation process, Mrs. Adams also evaluated Mr. Jones for any potential red flags, such as abuse issues, in efforts to maintain the safety of the client and the general public.

MEZZO PERSPECTIVE

Social workers in care facilities often provide training to the clinical team in order to broaden their understanding of psychosocial factors that impact a resident's functioning as well as to keep team members abreast of differing social service programs and resources. Social workers may also be required to facilitate various groups (psychotherapeutic, educational, and/or socialization) depending upon the needs of the particular facility. In California, for example, it is important for the social worker to

understand California Law Title 22, which applies to laws, regulations, and services that are rendered in residential care facilities. Mr. Jones was referred to Windsor Recovery Homes, a board and care facility that is subject to Title 22 requirements. Please check with your regional and/or state jurisdiction for applicable laws governing social work practice to ensure legal and ethical compliance. It is important for the social worker to understand the difference between a licensed and unlicensed residential care facility, in order to provide the most appropriate referral for aftercare placement. Facilities can be licensed or registered on the local or state level as well as via Joint Commission accreditation. Because nursing facilities are considered health care facilities, they must meet local, state, and federal regulatory measures with regard to the types of services offered, who may provide services, and how services may be reimbursed.

> Nursing homes in California are licensed, regulated, inspected, and/or certified by a number of public and private agencies at the state and federal levels, including the California Department of Public Health (CDPH) Licensing and Certification Division (L&C) and the U.S. Department of Health and Human Services' Centers for Medicare and Medicaid Services (CMS). These agencies have separate—yet sometimes overlapping—jurisdictions.
>
> California Department of Public Health (CDPH) is responsible for ensuring nursing homes comply with state laws and regulations. In addition, the CDPH has a cooperative agreement with the U.S. Department of Health and Human Services' Centers for Medicare and Medicaid Services (CMS) to ensure that facilities accepting Medicare and Medi-Cal (in California, Medicaid is referred to as Medi-Cal) payments meet federal requirements. Of California's 126,800 nursing home beds, on any given day approximately 68% are occupied by a Medi-Cal beneficiary. (California Health Facilities Consumer Information System, 2014)

In the case of Mr. Jones, it may be import to provide inservice training to staff on homelessness, mental health diagnoses, and available community resources such as the local Department of Social

Services, vocational rehabilitation, and board and care facilities. Because many nursing facilities do not have mental health providers on staff, the various disciplines may turn to the social worker for this support. Please remember your scope of practice based upon your level of education and correlative licensure status as appropriate, as this may require you to seek external providers to consult. In addition, it is critical for the social work practitioner to have a fundamental knowledge of applicable local, state, and federal laws governing practice. Please check with your licensing boards for more information and to ensure compliance in efforts to maintain safety.

MACRO PERSPECTIVE

As the need arises, social workers may be asked to complete outreach services for the facility as well as perform marketing to the community, network providers, and other hospitals/care facilities. Because social workers are usually familiar with the core services offered by the program, knowledgeable regarding various funding streams, and have an affinity for connecting with people on a personal level, they are often asked by facility administrators to use these skills to market the facility to generate additional residents. The social worker may also be utilized to provide facility tours to potential clients (e.g., family members, potential residents, and other agency care providers). The Nursing Home Reform Act of 1987 assisted to clarify required patient services that culminated in a Residents' Bill of Rights as well as a method for ongoing monitoring/survey of facility compliance with the law.

The 1987 Nursing Home Reform Act requires each nursing home to care for its residents in a manner that promotes and enhances the quality of life of each resident, ensuring dignity, choice, and self-determination. All nursing homes are required "to provide services and activities to attain or maintain the highest practicable physical, mental, and psychosocial well-being of each resident in accordance with a written plan of care that . . . is initially prepared, with participation, to the extent practicable,

of the resident, the resident's family, or legal representative" (Dementia Today, 2015, para. 2). This means a resident should not decline in health or well-being as a result of the way a nursing facility provides care. The following are the central tenets regarding the Residents' Bill of Rights: "(a) the right to freedom from abuse, mistreatment, and neglect; (b) the right to freedom from physical restraints; (c) the right to privacy; (d) the right to accommodation of medical, physical, psychological, and social needs; (e) the right to participate in resident and family groups; (f) the right to be treated with dignity; (g) the right to exercise self-determination; (h) the right to communicate freely; (i) the right to participate in the review of one's care plan and to be fully informed in advance about any changes in care, treatment, or change of status in the facility; and (j) the right to voice grievances without discrimination or reprisal" (Klauber & Wright, 2001, para. 5).

In the case of Mr. Jones, it may be ideal to provide him with a list of all these rights upon admission and have him sign a form acknowledging receipt and/or have them posted in a visible location throughout the facility, such as on bulletin boards where other facility information is provided. Having these issues addressed upon admission may give the resident a greater sense of empowerment and may increase likelihood that he will feel included in the nursing home setting. Should Mr. Jones or other residents have difficulty reading these rights, they should be read to them and noted as part of the informed consent process. Likewise, it may be ideal for the social worker to provide Mr. Jones with a tour of any board and care facilities that the team is considering for discharge planning, as a way to have greater "buy in" from the client as well as strengthen the working relationship between facility entities.

CONCLUSION

Social work in nursing home settings is a challenging but rewarding journey. It is important for practitioners to have a working understanding of the different levels of social work practice and the legal and ethical considerations. Depending upon the size of the nursing facility (in terms of number of residents), often there may be only one social work professional to provide the psychosocial care necessary. It is important for social workers to have a firm understanding of how to complete a psychosocial evaluation; create treatment and/or care plans; have a working understanding of the MDS assessment tool; and provide case management services, crisis intervention, and counseling/psychotherapy (per licensure status of the provider). Many nursing home residents have both medical and mental health conditions that they are trying to manage simultaneously. Therefore, an effective social work clinician would need to understand both the medical and mental health conditions of their patients and the interplay between them. It is important for the social work practitioner to have a fundamental understanding of the different local, state, and federal laws and regulations that govern clinical practice. Social workers in nursing home settings often provide inservice trainings to staff regarding various psychosocial topics as well as community resources. The facilitation of support groups, the provision of outreach services, marketing, and networking with various providers may be a requisite part of the duties of a social worker in this type of setting. It is important for practitioners to familiarize themselves with the various local, regional, and state resources available in their jurisdiction.

INTERNET RESOURCES

- Alzheimer's Association: http://www.alz.org
- California Adult Protective Services (APS): http://www.cdss.ca.gov/agedblinddisabled/PG1298.htm
- Centers for Medicare and Medicaid Services: http://www.cms.gov
- ICD 9 Codes: http://www.icd9data.com/2014/Volume1/default.htm
- Medicare Nursing Home Coverage: http://www.medicare.gov/nursinghomecompare/search.html
- National Association of Social Worker Code of Ethics: http://www.socialworkers.org/pubs/code/default.asp

- National Long-Term Care Ombudsman: http://www.ltcombudsman.org/
- Nursing Home Quality Initiative Minimum Data Set: http://www.cms.gov/Medicare/Quality-Initiatives-Patient-Assessment-Instruments/NursingHomeQualityInits/
- Social Security Administration: http://www.ssa.gov/
- Social Work Policy Institute: http://www.social-workpolicy.org
- Tarasoff Law: http://en.wikipedia.org/wiki/Tarasoff_v._Regents_of_the_University_of_California

DISCUSSION QUESTIONS

1. As a social work clinician, what would your biopsychosocial assessment entail?

2. With regard to Mr. Jones, what is known about the case and what is not known? How would you go about ascertaining this information if you were the assessing social worker?

3. What interventions would you perform to assist Mr. Jones? If you were doing therapy with Mr. Jones, which perspective would be most appropriate? Justify your rationale. How would that look in practice?

4. What case management activities would you perform? Make sure that each problem identified has correlative interventions to offset the stress.

5. What are some of the ethical and legal considerations for this case?

REFERENCES

Byrd, L. (2009). Standard services codes in nursing homes. *Geriatric Nursing, 30*(6), 437–443.

California Advocates for Nursing Home Reform. (2014, March 31). *Long term care justice and advocacy: Recognizing and reporting elder abuse.* Retrieved from http://canhr.org/factsheets/abuse_fs/html/fs_elderabuse.htm

California Department of Social Services. (2014, January 12). *Adult protective services.* Retrieved from http://www.cdss.ca.gov/agedblinddisabled/PG1298.htm

California Health Facilities Consumer Information System. (2014, April 3). Retrieved from https://hfcis.cdph.ca.gov/aboutUs.aspx

Centers for Medicare and Medicaid Services. (2014, January 5). Retrieved from http://www.cms.gov/Research-Statistics-Data-and-Systems/Files-for-Order/IdentifiableDataFiles/LongTermCareMinimumDataSetMDS.html

Dementia Today. (2015, May 14). *Nursing home residents' rights: It's the law.* Retrieved from http://www.dementiatoday.com/nursing-home-residents-rights-its-the-law/

Hughes, P., & Kerr, I. (2000). Transference and countertransference in communication between doctor and patient. *Advances in Psychiatric Treatment, 6.* Retrieved from http://apt.rcpsych.org/content/6/1/57.short?rss=1&ssource=mfr

Klauber, M., & Wright, B. (2001). *The 1987 Nursing Home Reform Act.* Retrieved from http://www.aarp.org/home-garden/livable-communities/info-2001/the_1987_nursing_home_reform_act.html

Los Angeles County Department of Mental Health. (2013, December 26). *Adult assessment form.* Retrieved from http://file.lacounty.gov/dmh/cms1_159897.pdf

Naito-Chan, E., Damron-Rodriguez, J., & Simmons, W. J. (2008). Identifying competencies for geriatric social work practice. *Journal of Gerontological Social Work, 43*(4), 59–78.

Simpson, G. A., Williams, J. C., & Segall, A. B. (2007). Social work education and clinical learning. *Clinical Social Work Journal, 35*(1), 3–14.

Social Work Policy Institute. (2014, January 5). *Social work services in nursing homes: Toward quality psychosocial care.* Retrieved from http://www.socialworkpolicy.org/ research/social-work-services-in-nursing-homes-toward-quality-psychosocial-care.html

Tarasoff v. Regents of the University of California, 131 Cal. Rptr. 14 (1976).

PART II

Social Work Practice

Interventions With Children, Youth, and Families

CHAPTER 13

Social Work Practice in School Settings

Laura Hopson, Cynthia Franklin, & Mary Beth Harris

CHAPTER OBJECTIVES

- Analyze research-based assessment and intervention strategies for school social work practice at the micro, macro, and mezzo levels;
- Explain solution-focused brief therapy interventions in schools;
- Demonstrate various school social work roles;
- Discuss emerging trends in school social work practice.

CASE VIGNETTE

The following vignette is a fictitious case and is not intended to represent any particular school or individuals within a school. Diana Jones is a school social worker at Lakeside school. Lakeside is a public elementary school located in an urban community in the southeastern United States. The school serves both low-income and higher income neighborhoods. As a result, approximately half of the students are from low-income households. In recent years, the school has failed to meet some accountability standards as measured by scores on standardized tests, resulting in funding cuts. In addition, only 55% of the students graduate in four years from the district's high school. School records indicate that students from low-income families are less likely to pass standardized tests and are more likely to be suspended from school than students from higher income families. In addition, since the school implemented zero tolerance disciplinary policies three years ago, the number of students who are suspended in a typical week has increased dramatically. The majority of students who are suspended are students from low-income families and students of color.

The school has many students who have an identified disability. The Individualized Education Plan for these students typically calls for weekly individual or group sessions with Ms. Jones. As a result, she spends much of her time in a typical day conducting individual and group sessions that focus on social and problem-solving skills and behavior management. Although she spends much of her time working with individual students, Ms. Jones has also taken on the role of advocating for changes in the school environment that she feels can reduce suspensions, especially for students from low-income families and students of color.

A second-grade teacher, Ms. Andrews, refers David Johnson to Ms. Jones due to an escalation of behavior problems in the classroom. David is an 8-year-old African American student. His parents are employed but their family income is low, making him eligible for reduced-price lunches at school. His parents are also separated, and his father has recently moved to another apartment. David has struggled with basic academic skills, including learning to read. The behavior problems, including hitting other children and shouting at the teacher, were evident at the beginning of the school year but have escalated during the past three weeks. David has not been identified as having a disability, nor does he have an Individualized Education Plan. When a student begins having difficulty, the social worker will typically gather information about the child and family functioning as well as classroom dynamics that may be influencing the child's behavior. As a result of this assessment process, the social worker may recommend strategies that the parents and teachers implement. If these strategies are not successful, the child may be referred for special education services and the development of an IEP.

INTRODUCTION

The challenges that Diana Jones faces at Lakeside School are not unusual. Nationally, schools that serve large numbers of students of color and economically disadvantaged students struggle to meet accountability standards set by state and federal policies, including No Child Left Behind (NCLB; Berliner, 2006, 2010). These standards tend to focus on grades, test scores, attendance, graduation rates, and suspensions. School social workers face challenges in helping students meet these standards because of complex social processes that contribute to the success or failure of each student. The social and contextual needs of students are largely overlooked in policies at the school and district levels, making it more difficult to muster resources needed to meet the accountability standards for low income students and students of color (Hopson & Lawson, 2011). Reducing the achievement gap calls for interventions that go beyond skill development and student support services to the development of positive environments in students' homes and schools that will foster the health and well-being of all students. This chapter provides an overview of assessment strategies and interventions that are consistent with school social work practice using an ecological perspective (Bronfenbrenner, 1979). The chapter emphasizes the importance of research-supported interventions that aim to affect change at multiple ecological levels, including the individual student, family system, peer group, the classroom and school environment, and policies that shape school social work practice.

THE NEED FOR SCHOOL SOCIAL WORK SERVICES

Approximately 12% to 22% of all children in the U.S. under the age of 18 are likely to need support for mental, emotional, or behavioral problems at some point during their school career (Adelman & Taylor, 2006). These rates are higher in schools serving large numbers of economically disadvantaged students, where up to 50% of students may have identified learning and emotional problems (Adelman & Taylor, 2006). As a result, schools have become the primary provider of social services to many families.

Barriers to meeting the mental health needs of students include insufficient school-based social workers or other mental health professionals, inadequate training for teachers in managing student behavior, insufficient funding, stigma associated with receipt of mental health services, and competing priorities that take precedence over mental health services (e.g., NCLB standardized testing scores; Reinke, Stormont, Herman, Puri, & Goel, 2011).

AN ECOLOGICAL FRAME FOR SCHOOL SOCIAL WORK PRACTICE

School social workers are trained mental health professionals who work on the student services team in schools, becoming a link between schools, families, and communities. School social workers provide a range of services that address the physical, mental, and emotional health of students, and their work may integrate micro, mezzo and macro practice strategies. School social work is grounded in ecological theory, which proposes that students and families are embedded in multiple systems as they grow and develop, and they are influenced and shaped by social processes within three systemic levels, defined by Bronfenbrenner (1979) as the microsystem, the mezzosystem, and the macrosystem. These levels function and impact one another along a continuum defined by the amount of direct interaction between the individual and the systems within each level. Proximal processes and relationships in the immediate microsystem and mezzosystem in which youths participate directly tend to have the most direct effect on behavior and outcomes (Bronfenbrenner, 1979).

Research examining the responsibilities of school social workers indicates a wide range of tasks that school social workers are called on to perform, including case management, agency referrals, advocacy, therapy, crisis intervention, and home visits (Allen-Meares, 1977, 1994; Franklin, Harris, & Lagana-Riordan, 2010; Kelly, Raines, Stone, & Frey, 2010). Recent surveys investigating the tasks of school social workers indicate,

however, that school social workers spend most of their time working within microsystems with individuals and small groups. This research indicates a need for more work with families because family interactions are microsystem processes that fundamentally affect a child's functioning at school. Additional interventions are also indicated within mezzosystems, including interactions between teachers and school support staff, parents, and community groups, as well as larger macro and structural-based interventions that shape educational systems and their policies (Kelly et al., 2010).

Assessment and interventions across ecological systems are also consistent with the mission and values of the social work profession to improve the well-being and enhance the social functioning of individuals and families in society. School social workers are equipped to address micro-, mezzo-, and macro-systems, but the demands on a school social worker's time may be greatly influenced by the school systems in which he or she works. There may also be considerable variability in terms of the demands placed on school social workers from one school district to the next across regions and states. A school social worker's role is often dependent on how his or her position is funded. The role corresponds with education reform movements and their associated educational mandates. This means that school social work must also adapt to the chronosystem (i.e., shifts and transitions in a child's environment over time; Bronfenbrenner, 1979) as educational mandates evolve and various changes in schools are ushered into practice. The profession of school social work, therefore, continues to face challenges in balancing the expectations of the school setting and social work professional values and ethics and social workers' desires to work across ecological systems to make changes.

MICRO PERSPECTIVE

The microsystem is defined by influential others with whom an individual has regular face-to-face contact, such as family and friends (Heffernan, Shuttlesworth, & Ambrosino, 1992). Through microsystem interventions, the social worker intervenes with the individual student directly and may include those with whom the student has direct contact, such as family members or teachers (Hepworth, Rooney, Rooney, & Strom-Gottfried, 2013). As indicated above, microsystem interventions comprise much of the school social worker's responsibilities (Kelly et. al., 2010). The following section describes assessment strategies at the microsystem level. Because the factors that influence student behavior and academic performance are ecological in nature, it is critical that an assessment include information about not only the child's behavior, but also the classroom and family environments.

Assessment

School social workers are in the unique position of having easy access to the classroom environment. Conducting direct behavioral observation in the classroom is a valuable assessment tool that provides rich information on students' behavior and the social context that shapes that behavior (Jordan & Franklin, 2011). In addition to direct behavioral observation, social workers rely on a number of self-report scales to assess children's behavior. Some tools that are reliable and valid for diverse youth include the Child Behavior Checklist (Achenbach, 1991, 1992), the Behavior Problems Checklist (Quay & Peterson, 1987), and the Conners Teacher Rating Scale (Conners, 1997). In assessing for depression, social workers may use the Beck Depression Inventory (Beck, Steer, & Brown, 1996) or the Children's Depression Inventory (Kovacs, 1992).

In the example presented in the introductory vignette, Ms. Jones would conduct an assessment to better understand David's behavior. She could, for example, observe David's behavior in the classroom and record information about the frequency of the behaviors described by his teacher, along with the events that precede and follow the behavior. The social worker would assess how teachers respond to David's behavior and examine whether these responses serve to improve or escalate the behavior. In conducting observations, it is important

to consider carefully whether to alert the child to the fact that he is being observed. For example, David may change his behavior if he knows that he is being observed, making the observations vulnerable to bias. However, secretly observing David might compromise their relationship after he learns that he has been observed.

Ms. Jones could also ask David's teacher and mother to complete the Achenbach Child Behavior Checklist. Finally, she might visit David's home to conduct a family assessment, including asking family members about the structure of the family, family members' roles and responsibilities, and stressors and social supports that affect family functioning. Part of this assessment may include questions related to exposure to trauma. The social worker would want to know whether David had ever experienced any form of abuse or neglect, along with other potential traumas, such as the death of a close family member or witnessing violence.

As with David's teacher, the social worker would need to know how his parents respond to his behavior and what disciplinary strategies they typically use. Since David's behavior has escalated in the past 3 weeks, Ms. Jones would ask about recent changes in his home life that may be contributing to his behavior at school.

In keeping with the ecological frame for school social work practice, Bowen and colleagues developed the School Success Profile (SSP; Bowen, Richman, & Bowen, 2002), a comprehensive tool for assessing youths' strengths and needs in the context of their social environment. Corcoran and Fischer (2013) and Jordan and Franklin (2011) also reviewed several additional assessment measures that can be used with children and families. School social workers can supplement data gathered from these measures with data collected by the school, including information on attendance, grades, and disciplinary referrals.

For children receiving special education services, school social workers are also likely to be members of the Individual Education Program (IEP) team, which also includes the student's parent or guardian, a school administrator, and other relevant school personnel. If ongoing assessment indicates that a child such as David continues to struggle in school despite efforts to improve his behavior at home and at school, the teacher or social worker may refer him for an assessment to determine whether he is eligible for an IEP.

The IEP team is responsible for conducting a Functional Behavioral Assessment of the student (Geltner & Leibforth, 2008; Harris, Powell, & Franklin, 2014; Harrison, 2009). As part of this assessment, the social worker may gather information from individuals in the home, school, and community. This may involve interviewing individuals who are involved in the child's life, such as juvenile justice officers, health care providers, child welfare workers, and mental health providers. The social worker is trained to assess the dynamics in these systems in which the student is embedded and synthesize information from multiple sources within these systems (Ashford, LeCroy, & Lortie, 2006; Cournoyer, 2008). This process allows the social worker to frame the student's behavior within an ecological context and develop a deeper understanding of the behavior (Harris et al., 2014).

Intervention

Most referrals for school social work services are for students exhibiting internalizing or externalizing behavior problems, similar to those described in the introductory vignette, that adversely affect academic performance. Because children often have few mental health resources available to them, school social workers become the primary source of mental health intervention.

Individual, Group, and Family Interventions

Evidence-based interventions are typically grounded in behavioral and cognitive behavioral therapy (Wodarski & Hopson, 2011). Evidence-based brief therapies are especially valuable to school social workers because they are designed to achieve client-centered goals in a relatively short period of time, typically 9 to 12 weeks. This means that social workers can feasibly deliver these interventions during the course of an academic year or even a single semester. These models include cognitive behavioral therapy (Graham, 1998), brief solution-focused therapy (Lipchik, Derks, LaCourt, & Nunnally, 2012), and brief consultation models (Cohen & Kaufmann, 2005). Many of these interventions can be delivered using treatment manuals, which greatly reduces the time and resources needed to learn these interventions (Franklin & Hopson, 2004).

Typical groups offered in a school environment include social skills groups, problem-solving groups, or social support groups. The Good Behavior Game, for example, is a behavior management intervention for youth aged 6–10 that aims to improve disruptive classroom behavior by improving teachers' capacity to set rules, define tasks and discipline students (Hoagwood, Burns, Kiser, Ringeisen, & Schoenwald, 2001). The intervention has been shown to reduce disciplinary referrals and teacher-reported behavior problems (Hoagwood et al., 2001; Kellam et al., 2008).

Many schools also provide group-based interventions designed to prevent risk behavior. These include violence-prevention programs, such as Gang Resistance Education and Training (GREAT); Keepin' it REAL, an evidence-based substance abuse prevention program (Marsiglia & Hecht, 2005); and Taking Charge, a dropout prevention program for pregnant and parenting teens (Harris & Franklin, 2006).

Family interventions may consist of case management services or more therapeutic interventions, which typically employ behavior management strategies, problem-solving, communication and relationship skills, and opportunities to practice newly learned skills in role-plays and homework assignments. In addition, family therapy approaches aim to create positive interaction patterns among family members and establish appropriate roles and boundaries within the family. Family interventions with solid research support include Brief Strategic Therapy (Szapocznik, Hervis, & Schwartz, 2003), Multidimensional Family Therapy (Hogue, Liddle, Becker, & Johnson-Leckrone, 2002), and Strengthening Families (Kumpfer, Pinyuchon,

Teixeira de Melo, & Whiteside, 2008). These interventions aim to improve family relationships, promote resiliency in children, and decrease the risk of substance abuse or behavior problems.

Solution-Focused Brief Therapy (SFBT) is a strengths-based intervention that has been used successfully with individuals, small groups, families, classrooms, and in mental health training with teachers (Lipchik et al., 2012). As discussed later in this chapter, it has been used as a whole school improvement model, as well. SFBT evolved through clinical work in which practitioner/researchers used qualitative research methods to learn what worked best for families with multiple, complex presenting problems (Lipchik et al., 2012). SFBT is grounded in the assumption that clients have the knowledge, strength, skills, and insights to solve their own problems (Berg, 1994). Four underlying assumptions guide SFBT sessions: each client and family is unique; clients already possess the strength and resources to achieve their goals; clients and their families are constantly changing, and a small change in one part of a family system can produce changes in another part of the system; and sessions should focus on the present and future because it is impossible to change the past (Lipchik, 2002).

Throughout the intervention, the therapist helps clients to define the situation and goals using their own perceptions and language. The therapist adopts a collegial stance and uses questions to elicit the clients' ideas about solutions, rather than issuing directives for change. The question that therapists use in this process tend to focus on the following:

- Exploring previous solutions, or times in the past when clients were able to cope with problems similar to those they are currently experiencing;
- Exception questions, which involve discussing times when the problem could have occurred but did not;
- Maintaining a focus on the present and future;
- The miracle question, which involves asking clients to describe how their daily life would be different if the problem were no longer in their lives.

Therapists also use compliments during these discussions to acknowledge what clients are doing well (de Shazer et al., 2006). We apply these techniques to David's case below.

Based on her assessment and an initial meeting with David, Ms. Jones decides that it is important to meet regularly with David's family. She agrees to visit David, his brother, and his mother in their home once each week. David's parents are separated, and his father has recently moved to a separate residence, but David visits him every other weekend. David's escalation in disruptive behavior at school seems to coincide with this move. David's father agrees to join as many of the family sessions as he can.

Ms. Jones begins the first session by asking the family to provide a brief description of the problem. The family describes feeling overwhelmed because David's mother and father each work long hours, leaving David's brother responsible for child care during the afternoons. When his mother tries to address his behavior at school, David becomes angry and threatens to move in with his father. David expresses anger with his father for leaving the family and living outside their home. David's mother and father are frustrated with David's behavior, which has become increasingly oppositional, with David refusing to do homework or chores at home.

During weekly sessions with the family, Ms. Jones uses Exception Questions to ask the family to discuss when the challenges with behavior at school and at home were more manageable. Through these discussions, Ms. Jones learns about strategies that have worked for the family in the past, such as asking David's grandmother for help with childcare after school. Ms. Jones uses the Miracle Question to help the family visualize solutions that will assist them in communicating better and in minimizing oppositional behavior at home and at school. For example, the family explains that if the oppositional behavior were no longer a problem, they would laugh more and would do more fun things together as a family, including going to the park or watching a movie. Through these conversations, Ms. Jones helps the family to articulate specific goals that they can work toward.

There are now 48 experimental outcome studies on the effectiveness of SFBT, two independent meta-analyses, and one systematic review of the effectiveness of SFBT with children in schools (Gingerich, Kim, Stams, & MacDonald, 2012; Kim & Franklin, 2009). The research tends to demonstrate that SFBT results in similar outcomes as longer therapies, but clients receiving SFBT show improvement in a much shorter amount of time (Franklin, Trepper, McCollum, & Gingerich, 2012). For example, a meta-analysis conducted by Kim (2008) demonstrated that most SFBT interventions were completed in no more than eight sessions.

A recent systematic review of SFBT with children and adolescents also showed that this intervention was useful in early intervention with internalizing and externalizing behavioral problems (Bond, Woods, Humphrey, Symes, & Green, 2013). SFBT has demonstrated effectiveness in reducing behavior problems (Corcoran & Stephenson, 2000; Franklin, Biever, Moore, Clemons, & Scamardo, 2001; Franklin, Corcoran, Nowicki, & Streeter, 1997; Newsome, 2005) and improving social skills (Newsome, 2005). Research links SFBT with improved academic performance and motivation (Daki & Savage, 2010; Kim & Franklin, 2009). SFBT has demonstrated efficacy in reducing conduct problems and substance abuse in schools and other institutional settings (Kim & Franklin, 2009; Seagram, 1997, as cited in Gingerich & Eisengart, 2000). Some research has also demonstrated that SFBT results in positive outcomes for improving parenting skills (Zimmerman, Jacobsen, MacIntyre, & Watson, 1996).

Culturally Responsive Assessment and Intervention

Children of color and children living in poverty, such as David presented in the case vignette, are more vulnerable to school failure than white children and those from higher income families (Planty et al., 2008). In addition, students of color are more likely to face school expulsion or stricter disciplinary consequences than their white peers for similar behavior (Skiba et al., 2011). School social workers offer a valuable perspective on these disparities because of their social justice orientation. They are trained to observe aspects of the social environment that create these inequities, rather than viewing these trends in terms of deficits in individual students. For example, a school social worker may offer the perspective that a school in which students of color perform worse than white students indicates that the school environment is designed to better meet the needs of white students than the needs of children of color (Blanchett, Mumford, & Beachum, 2005; Shealey, 2006).

In an organizational environment that has been based traditionally on white, mainstream cultural skills and expectations, the school social worker can model culturally grounded techniques to school staff, students, and families (Hecht & Krieger, 2006). School social workers can advocate for multicultural education that goes beyond the inclusion of curricular content about various cultures. More meaningful approaches to multicultural education include using culturally responsive instructional methods, communication strategies, disciplinary approaches, interactions with students' families, and educational goals (Banks & Banks, 2010). Social workers can suggest adjusting curricula to match observable characteristics (i.e., language) and deeper influences (i.e., values, norms, environment) of a given culture (Hecht & Krieger, 2006). Kumpfer et al. (2008) offer steps for implementing culturally relevant interventions, including assessing the needs of the target population and choosing a program that is a good match for the population in terms of age, ethnicity, language, length, and staff capacity to implement the intervention (Eggert, Seyl, & Nicholas, 1990; Hooven, Herting, & Snedker, 2010; Kumpfer et al., 2008). Before implementing an intervention, a social worker would want to review the research literature to identify interventions, such as SFBT, that have been effective with children and families from ethnic minority backgrounds who have complex problems and limited financial resources (Kim & Franklin, 2009).

Transference and Countertransference Issues

Social work practitioners need to be attentive to issues of transference and countertransference, as they may determine whether an intervention is effective. Transference refers, generally, to the client's reactions to the clinician, and countertransference is the clinician's reactions to the client (Jacobs, 1999). Typically, these reactions are grounded in past experiences in other important relationships, such as relationships with parents. Practicing self-awareness will help social workers to monitor their reactions to clients. For example, social work practice can be influenced by social workers' desire to be liked by their clients or a tendency to over-identify with clients whose problems are similar to those of the social worker (Walsch, 2002). Working closely with supervisors, identifying feelings about clients that are potentially problematic, and establishing clear boundaries with clients can help to prevent issues of transference and countertransference from becoming barriers to effective treatment (Walsch, 2002).

It is likely that David will refuse to follow the social worker's rules or refuse to participate actively in sessions. He may even be verbally or physically aggressive. Until David knows Ms. Jones better, he is likely to assume that she is similar to other adults in his life and will respond to his behavior in similar ways. He might assume that she will send him to the principal's office, the way his teacher often does, or yell at him, as his mother sometimes does.

These behaviors are likely to be emotionally taxing for Ms. Jones. She may become irritated and frustrated with David, which could impede her ability to implement appropriate interventions. Self-awareness is critical under these circumstances. Ms. Jones will need to recognize when her feelings toward David might be related to countertransference, or feelings that are grounded in other relationships (e.g., a relationship with her own child or a sibling). In these cases, it is important for Ms. Jones to have the support of a supervisor or colleague who can debrief with her. This can be more difficult in a school setting, in comparison to a mental health clinic or social services agency, because Ms. Jones may be the only social worker in the school. Some school social workers hire social workers who can serve as their clinical supervisors. Other school social workers may be part of a professional community of school social workers and can draw on this network for support. Ms. Jones meets regularly with a clinical social worker who provides supervision to her bi-weekly. This helps Ms. Jones to understand her reactions to David's behavior and, once understood, she can use these reactions in her work with David and his parents. For example, her reactions can help Ms. Jones understand other adults' reactions to David and help them process their reactions so that they do not get in the way of helping him improve his behavior.

Legal and Ethical Concerns

Philosophical differences between the professional values of social workers and educators present unique challenges to school social workers. Schools relate to children and adolescents as students, whereas social workers view them as client consumers (Gambrill, 2007; Han & Weiss, 2005). In the hierarchy of school organization, student stakeholders have the least power and participation in determining their own outcomes. As social work clients, the same children and adolescents have more input into their own intervention and significant options in decision making and responses.

In educational settings, poor school performance is often perceived in terms of students' personal cognitive and motivational deficits and pathologies in their social environments (Lucio, Hunt, & Bornovalova, 2012). In contrast, the strengths perspective used by social workers posits that the strengths and resources of people and their environment, rather than their problems and pathologies, should be emphasized (Saleebey, 2011). Social workers will need to rely on their skills in interprofessional collaboration and advocacy, in addition to their clinical skills, in order to create a culture that focuses on the strengths and resources that students and their families bring to the table.

A recent survey of school mental health practitioners (Raines & Dibble, 2013) identified five ethical issues that practitioners find most difficult in the school environment. These include maintaining the confidentiality of students and their families, protecting the privacy of student records, and advocating for parents' rights to be involved in their children's education. Social workers also identified that intervening in cases of dangerous or violent student behavior was difficult for them. Finally, it was challenging to balance their role as members of the school community and their role as advocate for children and their families. Navigating these dilemmas will require prioritizing social work professional responsibilities and recognizing that the student is the primary client (Raines & Dibble, 2013). With these priorities in mind, school social workers will then need to collaborate with other stakeholders in the school to find common ground and advocate for the course that is in the best interests of students.

Social workers also have a responsibility to assess for child abuse and neglect and are mandated to report suspected abuse. In discussing issues of confidentiality with clients, social workers have to be clear that they can maintain confidentiality except under certain conditions. These conditions include any disclosure of information that suggests a child is being abused or neglected or an intention to harm oneself or others.

MEZZO PERSPECTIVE

The mezzosystem is defined by relationships between the microsystems that do not include the individual student but affect the individual's behavior. The mezzosystem includes interactions between a child's parents, between parents and teachers, or between a child's peers (Heffernan et al., 1992). It may also include schools, school boards, community organizations, and local government. School social workers often find that the success of their work with individual students, groups of students, and families depends greatly on the school environment. Thus, mezzo-level interventions that create positive classroom and school environments are a prerequisite for the micro-level interventions that consume much of a school social worker's day (Hopson & Lawson, 2011).

In the case presented in the vignette, the school social worker, Ms. Jones, might coordinate a meeting of teachers and staff who know David and could offer the referring teacher some insight into strategies that might be effective in increasing his on-task behavior. During her observations of the classroom, Ms. Jones notes aspects of the social environment of the classroom that encourage David's disruptive behavior. Peers support his behavior by laughing when he disrupts the class or pushes a student's papers onto the floor. She also notes that the school's disciplinary policies may inadvertently reinforce the behavior by consistently pushing David out of the classroom and allowing him to avoid work that is challenging for him. Finally, she notes that David's teacher has few opportunities to discuss strategies for managing challenging behaviors with other teachers and support staff.

In response to these observations, Ms. Jones coordinates a meeting of teachers and staff who know David and could offer some insight into strategies that might be effective in increasing his on-task behavior. She also decides to meet with the principal about planning professional development opportunities that focus on providing incentives for positive behavior with the intent of reducing teachers' reliance on sending children out of the classroom in response to disruptive behavior.

School Climate

School climate interventions have received particular attention due to mounting research evidence linking a positive school climate with academic success (Cohen & Geier, 2010). School climate is defined as the psychological impact of the school's norms, values, and practices on the adults and children within the school. During the past two decades, researchers have examined dimensions of school climate related to relationships, safety, methods of teaching and learning, connectedness to school, and the physical structure of the school. Each of these dimensions of school climate has been connected to academic success and healthy development across a large and growing number of research studies (Cohen & Geier, 2010).

Relationships among individuals within and connected to the school are fundamental to the quality of the school climate. Key relationships include (1) relationships among students, (2) relationships between students and school personnel (i.e., teachers, staff, and administrators), (3) relationships among school personnel, (4) relationships between school personnel and families, and (5) school-community relationships (Richman, Bowen, & Woolley, 2004).

School Climate Assessment

Assessing the quality of a school's climate is a prerequisite for any successful school climate intervention. A number of reliable and valid measurement instruments provide the means of measuring school climate in ways that are easy to administer while gathering input from a range of stakeholders, including students, adults in the school, and parents (Cohen, McCabe, Michelli, & Pickeral, 2009). Among these measures are the School Success Profile, Learning Organization (Bowen, Rose, & Bowen, 2005), the Comprehensive School Climate Inventory (Stamler, Scheer, & Cohen, 2009), the Organizational Health Inventory (Hoy & Feldman, 1987), and the School Climate Scale (Haynes, Emmons, & Comer, 1993).

School social workers are in a good position to advocate for an assessment of school climate because they are trained in an ecological perspective and understand the importance of mezzo-level influences on children's development. School social workers can also assist school administrators in identifying and administering appropriate assessment instruments.

School Climate Intervention

Efforts to improve school climate include interventions that address selected dimensions of school climate (i.e., student-teacher relationships or bullying) and interventions that aim to alter the whole school environment. Whole school improvement interventions engage all school stakeholders in the intervention. When schools do not have the capacity to implement these large-scale interventions, they can employ less labor-intensive interventions that target improving key relationships within the school, such as school-based mentoring programs designed to strengthen relationships between teachers and students.

Whole School Improvement

Many states now require that school-based interventions be implemented within a Response to Intervention (RTI) framework. RTI is a process that aims to match effective interventions to students based on need and requires ongoing monitoring to make decisions about whether goals or interventions need to be changed to improve student outcomes (Hawken, Vincent, & Schumann, 2008). An RTI framework begins with a thorough assessment of students' academic, social, and behavioral needs (Hawken et al., 2008). This assessment is designed to help school personnel identify students who may require intervention in order to succeed academically.

RTI employs interventions at the individual, classroom, and school levels to create the conditions for academic success (National Center on Response to Intervention, 2010). This work requires clear and consistent expectations for students, parents, and teachers and close collaboration between teachers and school support personnel. Teachers and staff also involve students and parents in decision making. Ongoing evaluation is used to monitor the progress of students and determine whether the interventions are appropriate and effective (National Center on Response to Intervention, 2010).

RTI addresses the unique needs of students through a tiered framework consisting of three levels of intervention: universal programs (i.e., teaching general social skills to all students);

selective programs, which call for more intensive services for children who are identified as at risk for future mental health issues; and indicated programs for students with identified mental health issues (Cohen et al., 2009).

Often used in conjunction with RTI, Positive Behavioral Interventions and Supports (PBIS) is perhaps the most widely implemented whole school intervention, as it is being used in over 8,000 schools nationwide. Applying principals from behavioral, social learning, and organizational theories, PBIS provides teachers and school staff with tools for setting clear expectations and using positive reinforcement of positive behavior (Bradshaw, Koth, Thornton, & Leaf, 2009). Students may be recognized for positive behavior and given incentives, such as a field trip (Spaulding, Horner, May, & Vincent, 2008).

As with RTI, PBIS creates systems of support at three levels: primary (school-wide/universal), secondary (targeted/selective), and tertiary (individual/indicated). Students are assessed to determine who could benefit from services at each of the three levels. Each student's progress is monitored through ongoing data collection. School personnel rely on ongoing assessments of student progress to determine whether they need to change or amplify the services a student is receiving. Research on PBIS is effective in fostering friendly, collegial relationships among teachers and staff, egalitarian leadership, and respectful, collaborative relationships among students (Bradshaw et al., 2009).

Another whole-school intervention applies techniques from SFBT, discussed earlier as a micro-level intervention, to create solution-building schools (Franklin, Streeter, Kim, & Tripodi, 2007). All adults and children within the school are trained in solution-focused techniques, which encourage mutual respect, collaboration, relationship building, trust, and high expectations. Research indicates that solution-building schools are likely to have a positive school climate in which students are engaged in school (Franklin et al., 2007). Garza High School in Austin, TX adopted SFBT principles to create a solution-building

school. All teachers and staff within the school are trained in SFBT strategies, which encourage strengths-based, future-focused dialogue with students that helps students to develop their own goals. Because all personnel in the school are trained in the model, the school environment is one in which individuals share the same vision and a consistent approach to working with students. For example, practitioners assisting students use the SFBT strategies to help students articulate the ways in which the solution is already occurring in their lives. They, then, define small, measurable goals toward the solution (Franklin & Streeter, 2003; Martin & Halperin, 2006).

Building Key Relationships Within the School

One important strategy for improving school climate is to organize faculty, staff, and other key personnel into teams that meet regularly and work together to discuss students' needs (Hopson & Lawson, 2011). In this context, the school social worker not only collaborates with other professionals but is also required to understand the viewpoints and main concerns of other professions in negotiating common goals and objectives for the school (Harris et al., 2014). Some schools develop strengths-based impact teams, for example. When a student is having difficulty, a team of teachers and staff members meets to collaborate with the student and generate solutions. This ensures that all personnel connected with the student understand the needs and challenges related to the problem and will respond to the student's needs in consistent ways (Hopson & Lawson, 2011).

In order to foster positive student-teacher relationships, some schools have implemented mentoring programs. These programs are most effective when mentors and mentees maintain the relationship for a year or more and spend time together regularly (DuBois, Holloway, Valentine, & Cooper, 2002; Grossman & Rhodes, 2002). Unfortunately, the structure of the academic year often means that school-based mentoring programs allow for fewer contact hours between mentors and youth than traditional community-based mentoring programs, such as Big Brothers and Big Sisters. Services often last for a shorter period of time (Komosa-Hawkins, 2009; Randolph & Johnson, 2008). It is often helpful to provide incentives for school personnel to serve as mentors and encourage ongoing mentoring for the entire academic year and even during the summer months.

Check and Connect is a dropout prevention program in which students and their families work with a monitor, an adult within the school who helps students track their school performance and intervene when they are not progressing. Research indicates that the program may improve academic success and reduce the likelihood of dropping out (Sinclair, Christenson, & Thurlow, 2005; U.S. Department of Education, 2006). Using similar methods, Check In Check Out (CICO) is a program in which teachers or staff provide students and parents with a daily report card that provides feedback about positive behavior, in addition to any behavior problems. Students may also receive reinforcement for positive behavior, such as points that they can use to receive a reward. Research on the model suggests that it improves student behavior and reduces attention-seeking problem behavior (Hawken & Horner, 2003; Todd, Campbell, Meyer, & Horner, 2008).

Bullying prevention programs have been implemented to build positive peer relationships within the school. The Olweus Bullying Prevention Program is one of the most well researched bullying prevention programs. It aims to inhibit bullying by engaging students in school, setting clear limits on bullying behavior, and applying consistent consequences for bullying. In schools implementing the model, students report significant improvement to the school climate and reduced bullying behavior (Olweus & Limber, 2000).

Interventions That Target Family Involvement in School

Promoting family involvement in school is fundamental to efforts for improving academic performance and behavior. Many interventions, including PBIS, Check and Connect, and the Olweus Bullying Prevention Program, involve families. For example, the Family Check Up (FCU) is an intervention that has been used in conjunction with PBIS to connect families with needed resources and services (Reinke, Splett, Robeson, & Offut, 2009).

Some schools have Family Resource Centers (FRCs), which aim to involve parents in school life while providing information on parenting practices that promote academic success (Reinke et al., 2009). FRCs may also provide services, such as medical care, counseling, and parenting classes, as well as connecting families with childcare and early childhood programs, including Head Start.

Fostering School-Community Partnerships

Partnerships with community organizations can provide students with access to services that are essential for academic success and healthy development. Perhaps the most ambitious approach to integrating community-based services into a school is the full-service or community school model. In these schools, students are provided with physical and mental health services in the school building (Dryfoos, 2005). They serve as one-stop centers in which families can access a range of social services under one roof. Because full-service schools vary widely in terms of the services they provide, there is limited research on the effectiveness of these models. However, the research that exists suggests that the services provided in these schools are particularly helpful for economically disadvantaged youth, who often are coping with poverty-related stressors that affect their academic performance (Hocutt, McKinney, & Montague, 2002). This work could be helpful for David, presented in the case vignette. For example, the school social worker could work to build partnerships with mental health service providers and community organizations that provide after school programs so that these services could be provided at the school for little or no cost to his family.

Developing full-service schools is resource intensive. When this model is not feasible,

Communities in Schools (CIS) provides another mechanism for connecting students with important services. CIS is a community-based social services program that is located within the school and provides services that schools are often unable to provide, including mental health treatment and health education. Students in schools with CIS programs tend to experience higher graduation rates and lower dropout rates (Porowski & Passa, 2011). As with full-service schools, CIS programs appear to be especially helpful for schools that serve impoverished communities (Hocutt et al., 2002; Porowski & Passa, 2011), as students in these schools may have unaddressed health and mental health needs (Berliner, 2010).

MACRO PERSPECTIVE

The macrosystem is defined by societal factors, such as cultural values and social policy. Macro-level interventions relevant to school social work include community organization and advocacy for policies that support healthy youth development and academic success for all students (Heffernan et al., 1992). School social workers tend to spend less of their time on macro-level interventions, in comparison to micro- and mezzo-level interventions. However, political advocacy can be essential for effective social work practice, since federal and state policies may determine whether social work interventions are likely to have any meaningful impact on youth outcomes.

The Individual with Disabilities in Education Act (IDEA) and No Child Left Behind (NCLB) are policies that have shaped schools' capacity to respond to students' needs. IDEA, originally passed in 1994 and reauthorized in 2004, allocates funding for school-based programs including individual counseling with mental health workers, early intervention programs to prevent the progression of behavioral health problems, and small group curriculum-based activities for children with signs of both externalizing and internalizing symptoms (U.S. Department of Education, n.d.; Kataoka, Rowan, & Hoagwood, 2009). IDEA requires that schools provide any

necessary supports that will allow a child with special needs to receive the same educational opportunities as any other child. These services may include psychological services, counseling services, speech-language pathology, therapeutic recreation, psychiatric services for diagnostic and evaluation purposes, parent counseling and training, school health services, and social work services in schools (U.S. Department of Education, n.d.; Kataoka et al., 2009).

The No Child Left Behind Act of 2001 is a complex policy intervention aimed at changing school, district, and state department of education policies and practices in order to improve student outcomes. NCLB is grounded in the assumption that better outcomes for students depend on improved school and district quality and accountability. Thus, NCLB calls for consistent standards for curriculum and instruction across schools, districts and state departments of education, authentic assessments of learning, results-oriented accountability (as driven by standardized achievement tests), and the use of evidence-based teaching and learning strategies.

From an ecological perspective, the main problem with IDEA and NCLB is that they focus solely on processes within the school building in order to improve student outcomes. Although improving student skills and setting high standards are essential for promoting school success, they are insufficient for affecting meaningful improvement, especially for students who are most vulnerable, such as those coping with poverty-related stressors in their homes and neighborhoods. These policies fail to address the ecologies that serve as the foundation for children's development and school success, including the social environments of their homes, neighborhoods, and schools (Hopson & Lawson, 2011).

Thus, school social workers can advocate for policies that convey a more holistic understanding of children and their social environments. Instead of focusing interventions solely on micro-level processes, policies can be designed to encourage schools to measure ecological processes that influence academic performance, including school climate. The social and emotional health of students could be emphasized alongside academic outcomes.

Standards and Accountability

The requirements from current policies, such as NCLB, for schools to demonstrate students' academic success with clear data is likely to remain, as well as the threat of loss of federal funding when schools are unable to show evidence of progress. At the same time, schools must compete for private grants and foundation funds to provide services to students. In this climate, school social workers must demonstrate how their services clearly lead to improved educational achievement (Bowen, 2013). Toward this end, social workers must be able to provide data demonstrating the effectiveness of their services in terms of outcomes that are meaningful to school administrators. This means connecting social work services to educational outcomes, such as attendance, grades, behavior, and retention.

School social workers will need to provide periodic progress reports to stakeholder groups, including principals, teachers and staff, and school district personnel. Bowen (2013, pp. 894–895) suggests the following strategies for presenting evidence related to school social work services:

- Explain the data on outcomes of social work service provision and their importance for academic success.
- Identify the sources of the data.
- Use simple statistics, such as means and percentages.
- Illustrate trends in the data using simple graphics, such as line and bar charts.
- Interpret the tables and charts to the audience.
- Provide handouts summarizing the data.
- Explain how these results will improve problems that are important to them.

CONCLUSION

This chapter has presented school social work practice using an ecological framework. School social workers provide an essential service by addressing students' individual needs and facilitating the development of social and emotional competencies. Although direct, clinical practice with young people will continue to fill a critical need, school social workers are increasingly needed to bring their ecological perspectives to bear on creating school environments that foster healthy youth development. Thus, the school social worker confronts the difficult, but important, challenge of intervening with students (as individuals and in groups), targeting organizational interventions to foster a positive school climate, and advocating for policies that emphasize a holistic understanding of children within their social environments.

INTERNET RESOURCES

- The What Works Clearinghouse (WWC): http://ies.ed.gov/ncee/wwc/
- California School-Based Health Alliance: http://www.schoolhealthcenters.org
- School Social Work Association of America: http://www.sswaa.org
- The School Social Worker Association of America: http://www.sswaa.org

DISCUSSION QUESTIONS

1. Discuss solution-focused questions the school social worker in the vignette might ask David to help him to develop his own goals for his behavior.

2. Discuss solution-focused questions that the school social worker in the vignette could use with Ms. Andrews to develop goals for her work with David.

3. What potential barriers might a school social worker face in working to implement a whole-school intervention? How might the social worker begin to address these barriers?

4. How can a school social worker demonstrate the importance of his or her role in schools to key stakeholders, including students, parents, school administrators, and school board members?

5. What steps could a school social worker take to conduct an assessment of school climate?

REFERENCES

Achenbach, T. (1991). *Manual for the Child Behavior Checklist/4–18 and 1991 profile.* Burlington: University of Vermont Department of Psychiatry.

Achenbach, T. (1992). *Manual for the Child Behavior Checklist/2–3 and 1992 profile.* Burlington: University of Vermont Department of Psychiatry.

Adelman, H. S., & Taylor, L. (2006). Mental health in schools and public health. *Public Health Reports, 121*(3), 294–298.

Allen-Meares, P. (1977). Analysis of tasks in school social work. *Social Work, 22,* 196–201.

Allen-Meares, P. (1994). Social work services in schools: A national study of entry-level tasks. *Social Work, 39*(5), 560–565.

Ashford, J. B., LeCroy, C. W., & Lortie, K. L. (2006). *Human behavior in the social environment: A multidimensional perspective* (3rd ed.). Belmont, CA: Brooks/Cole.

Banks, J. A., & Banks, C. A. M. (2010). *Multicultural education: Issues and perspectives* (7th ed.). Indianapolis, IN: Wiley.

Beck, A. T., Steer, R. A., & Brown, G. K. (1996). *Manual for the Beck Depression Inventory-II.* San Antonio, TX: Psychological Corporation.

Berg, I. K. (1994). *Family-based services: A solution-focused approach.* New York, NY: W. W. Norton.

Berliner, D. C. (2006). Fixing schools isn't everything. *NEA Today,* 38–39.

Berliner, D. C. (2010). Are teachers responsible for low achievement by poor students? *Education Digest, 75*(7), 4–8.

Blanchett, W. J., Mumford, V., & Beachum, F. (2005). Urban school failure and disproportionality in a post-Brown era: Benign neglect of the constitutional rights of students of color. *Remedial and Special Education, 26*(2), 70–81.

Bond, C., Woods, K., Humphrey, N., Symes, W., & Green, L. (2013). Practitioner review: The effectiveness of solution focused brief therapy with children and families: A systematic and critical evaluation of the literature from 1990–2010. *Journal of Child Psychology and Psychiatry, 54*(7),707–23. doi: 10.1111/jcpp.12058

Bowen, N. K. (2013). Using data to communicate with school stakeholders. In C. Franklin, M. B. Harris, & P. Allen-Meares (Eds.), *The school services sourcebook* (2nd ed., pp. 889–902). New York, NY: Oxford University Press.

Bowen, G. L., Richman, J. M., & Bowen, N. K. (2002). The School Success Profile: A results management approach to assessment and intervention planning. In A. R. Roberts & G. J. Greene (Eds.), *Social workers' desk reference* (pp. 787–793). New York, NY: Oxford University Press.

Bowen, G. L., Rose, R. A., & Bowen, N. K. (2005). *The reliability and validity of the School Success Profile.* Philadelphia, PA: Xlibris.

Bradshaw, C. P., Koth, C. W., Thornton, L. A., & Leaf, P. J. (2009). Altering school climate through school-wide positive behavioral interventions and supports: Findings from a group-randomized effectiveness trial. *Prevention Science, 10,* 100–115.

Bronfenbrenner, U. (1979). *The ecology of human development: Experiments by nature and design.* Cambridge, MA: Harvard University Press.

Cohen, E., & Kaufmann, R. (2005). *Early childhood mental health consultation.* Washington, DC: Center for Mental Health Services of the Substance Abuse and Mental Health Services Administration and the Georgetown University Child Development Center.

Cohen, J., & Geier, V. K. (2010). *School climate research summary: January 2010.* New York, NY: National School Climate Center. Retrieved from www.schoolclimate.org/climate/research.php

Cohen, J., McCabe, L., Michelli, N. M., & Pickeral, T. (2009). School climate: Research, policy, practice, and teacher education. *Teachers College Record, 111,* 180–193.

Conners, C. K. (1997). *Conners' rating scales—revised: Long form.* North Tonawanda, NY: Multi-Health Systems.

Corcoran, J., & Stephenson, M. (2000). The effectiveness of solution-focused therapy with child behavior problems: A preliminary report. *Families in Society, 81,* 468—474.

Corcoran, K., & Fischer, J. (2013). *Measures for clinical practice and research.* New York, NY: Oxford University Press.

Cournoyer, B. R. (2008). *The social work skills workbook.* Belmont, CA: Brooks/Cole.

Daki, J., & Savage, R. (2010). Solution-focused brief therapy: Impacts on academic and emotional difficulties. *The Journal of Educational Research, 103,* 309–326.

de Shazer, S., Dolan, Y. M., Korman, H., Trepper, T. S., McCollum, E. E., & Berg, I. K. (2006). *More than miracles: The state of the art of solution focused therapy.* New York, NY: Haworth Press.

Dryfoos, J. (2005). Full-service community schools: A strategy, not a program. *New Directions for Youth Development, 107,* 7–14.

DuBois, D. L., Holloway, B. E., Valentine, J. C., & Cooper, H. (2002). Effectiveness of mentoring programs for youth: A meta-analytic review. *American Journal of Community Psychology, 30*(2), 157–197.

Eggert, L., Seyl, C., & Nicholas, L. (1990). Effects of a school-based prevention program for potential high school dropouts and drug abusers. *International Journal of the Addictions, 25,* 773–801.

Franklin, C., Biever, J., Moore, K., Clemons, D., & Scamardo, M. (2001). The effectiveness of solution-focused therapy with children in a school setting. *Research on Social Work Practice, 11,* 411—434.

Franklin, C., Corcoran, J., Nowicki, J., & Streeter, C. L. (1997). Using client self-anchored scales to measure outcomes in solution-focused therapy. *Journal of Systemic Therapies, 16,* 246–265.

Franklin, C., Harris, M., & Lagana-Riordan, C. (2010). The delivery of social work services. In P. Allen-Meares (Ed.), *Social work services in the schools* (6th ed., pp 278–321). Boston, MA: Allyn & Bacon.

Franklin, C., & Hopson, L. (2004). Into the schools with evidence-based practice. *Children & Schools, 26*(2), 67–70.

Franklin, C., & Streeter, C. L. (2003). *Solution-focused accountability schools for the twenty-first century: A training manual for Gonzalo Garza Independence High School.* Austin, TX: The Hogg Foundation for Mental Health.

Franklin, C., Streeter, C. L., Kim, J. S., & Tripodi, S. J. (2007). The effectiveness of a solution-focused, public alternative school for dropout prevention and retrieval. *Children & Schools, 29*(3), 133–144.

Franklin, C., Trepper, T. S, McCollum, E. E., & Gingerich, W. (2012). *Solution-focused brief therapy: A handbook of evidence based practice.* London: Oxford University Press.

Gambrill, E. (2007). Transparency as the route to evidence-informed professional education. *Research on Social Work Practice, 17*(5), 553–560.

Geltner, J. A., & Leibforth, T. N. (2008). Advocacy in the IEP process: Strengths-based school counseling in action. *Professional School Counseling,* 162–165.

Gingerich, W. J., & Eisengart, S. (2000). Solution-focused brief therapy: A review of the outcome research. *Family Process, 39,* 477–498.

Gingerich, W. J., Kim, J. S., Stams, G. J. J. M., & MacDonald, A. J. (2012). Solution-focused brief therapy outcome research. In C. Franklin, T. S. Trepper, W. J. Gingerich, & E. E. McCollum (Eds.), *Solution-focused brief therapy.* New York, NY: Oxford University Press.

Graham, P. (1998). *Cognitive behaviour therapy for children and families.* Cambridge, MA: Cambridge University Press.

Grossman, J. B., & Rhodes, J. E. (2002). The test of time: Predictors and effects of duration in youth mentoring programs. *American Journal of Community Psychology, 30,* 199–219.

Han, S. S., & Weiss, B. (2005). Sustainability of teacher implementation of school-based mental health programs. *Journal of Abnormal Child Psychology, 33,* 665–679.

Harris, M., & Franklin, C. (2006). The delivery of social work services. In P. Allen-Meares (Ed.), *Social work services in school* (5th ed.). Boston, MA: Allyn & Bacon.

Harris, M. B., Powell, T., & Franklin, C. (2014). The design of social work services: School environment. In P. Allen-Meares (Ed.), *Social work services in schools* (7th ed.). Boston, MA: Pearson.

Harrison, K. (2009). The school social worker's role in the tertiary support of functional assessment. *Children in Schools, 31*(2), 119–127.

Hawken, L. S., & Horner, R. H. (2003). Evaluation of a targeted intervention within a schoolwide system of behavior support. *Journal of Behavioral Education, 12*(3), 225–240.

Hawken, L., Vincent, C., & Schumann, J. (2008). Response to intervention for social behavior: Challenges and opportunities. *Journal of Emotional and Behavioral Disorders, 16,* 213–225.

Haynes, N., Emmons, C., & Comer, J. P. (1993). The Yale School Development Program: Process, outcomes, and policy implications. *Urban Education, 28*(2), 166–199.

Hecht, M. L., & Krieger, J. K. (2006). The principle of cultural grounding in school-based substance use prevention: The Drug Resistance Strategies Project. *Journal of Language and Social Psychology, 25,* 301–319.

Heffernan, J., Shuttlesworth, G., & Ambrosino, R. (1992). *Social work and social welfare: An introduction.* Minneapolis, MN: West.

Hepworth, D. H., Rooney, R. H., Rooney, G. D., & Strom-Gottfried, K. (2013). *Direct social work practice: Theory and skills* (9th ed.). Belmont, CA: Brooks/Cole.

Hoagwood, K., Burns, B., Kiser, L., Ringeisen, H., & Schoenwald, S. (2001). Evidence-based practice in child and adolescent mental health services. *Psychiatric Services, 52*(9), 1179–1189. doi: 10.1176/appi.ps.52.9.1179

Hocutt, A., McKinney, J. D., & Montague, M. (2002). Impact of managed care on efforts to prevent development of serious emotional disturbances in young children. *Journal of Disabilities Policy Studies, 13,* 51–60.

Hogue, A., Liddle, H. A., Becker, D., & Johnson-Leckrone, J. (2002). Family-based prevention counseling for high-risk young adolescents: Immediate outcomes. *Journal of Community Psychology, 30*(1), 1–22.

Hopson, L. M., & Lawson, H. (2011). Social workers' leadership for positive school climates via data-informed planning and decision-making. *Children & Schools, 33*(2), 106–118.

Hooven, C., Herting, J., & Snedker, K. (2010). Long-term outcomes for promoting the CARE suicide prevention program. *American Journal of Health Behavior, 34,* 721–736.

Hoy, W. K., & Feldman, J. A. (1987). Organizational health: The concept and its measure. *Journal of Research and Development in Education, 20*(4), 30–36.

Jacobs, T. J. (1999). Countertransference past and present: A review of the concept. *International Journal of Psychoanalysis, 80,* 575–594.

Jordan, C., & Franklin, C. (2011). *Clinical assessment for social workers. Quantitative and qualitative methods* (3rd ed.). Chicago, IL: Lyceum Books/Nelson Hall Books.

Kataoka, S. H., Rowan, B., & Hoagwood, K. E. (2009). Bridging the divide: In search of common ground in mental health and education research and policy. *Psychiatric Services, 60*(11), 1510–1515.

Kellam, S. G., Brown, C. H., Poduska, J. M., Ialongo, N. S., Wang, W., Tobino, P., . . . Wilcox, H. C. (2008). Effects of a universal classroom behavior management program in first and second grades on young adult behavioral, psychiatric, and social outcomes. *Drug and Alcohol Dependence, 95*(Suppl 1), S5–S28.

Kelly, M. S., Raines, J. C., Stone, S., & Frey, A. (2010). *School social work: An evidence-informed framework for practice.* New York, NY: Oxford University Press.

Kim, J. (2008). Examining the effectiveness of solution-focused brief therapy: A meta-analysis. *Research on Social Work Practice, 32,* 49–64.

Kim, J. S., & Franklin, C. (2009). Solution-focused brief therapy in schools: A review of the outcome literature. *Children and Youth Services Review, 31,* 464–470.

Komosa-Hawkins, K. (2009). Best practices in school-based mentoring programs for adolescents. *Child & Youth Services, 31*(3/4), 121–137.

Kovacs, M. (1992). *Children's Depression Inventory.* North Tonawanda, NY: Multi-Health Systems.

Kumpfer, K. L., Pinyuchon, M., Teixeira de Melo, A., & Whiteside, H. O. (2008). Cultural adaptation process for international dissemination of the strengthening families program. *Evaluation in the Health Professions, 31*(2), 226–239. doi: 10.1177/0163278708315926

Lipchik, E. (2002). *Beyond technique in solution-focused therapy: Working with emotions and the therapeutic relationship.* New York, NY: Guilford Press.

Lipchik, E., Derks, J., LaCourt, M., & Nunnally, E. (2012). The evolution of Solution Focused Brief Therapy. In C. Franklin, T. S. Trepper, W. J. Gingerich, & E. E. McCollum (Eds.), *Solution focused brief therapy: A handbook of evidence based practice* (pp. 3–19). New York, NY: Oxford University Press.

Lucio, R., Hunt, E., & Bornovalova, M. (2012). Identifying the necessary and sufficient number of risk factors for predicting academic failure. *Developmental Psychology, 48*(2), 422–428. doi: 10.1037/a0025939

Marsiglia, F., & Hecht, M. (2005). *Keepin it REAL: Drug resistance strategies: Teacher guide.* Santa Cruz, CA: ETR Associates.

Martin, N., & Halperin, S. (2006). *Whatever it takes: How twelve communities are reconnecting out-of-school youth.* Washington, DC: American Youth Policy Forum.

National Center on Response to Intervention. (2010). *Essential components of RTI—A closer look at response to intervention.* Washington, DC: U.S. Department of Education.

Newsome, W. (2005). The impact of solution-focused brief therapy with at-risk junior high school students. *Children & Schools, 27,* 83–90.

No Child Left Behind (NCLB) Act of 2001, Pub. L. No. 107–110, § 115, Stat. 1425 (2002).

Olweus, D., & Limber, S. (2000). *Bullying prevention program.* Boulder, CO: Center for the Study and Prevention of Violence.

Planty, M., Hussar, W., Snyder, T., Provasnik, S., Kena, G., Dinkes, R., . . . Kemp, J. (2008). *The condition of education 2008* (NCES 2008–031). Washington, DC: U.S. Department of Education.

Porowski, A., & Passa, A. (2011). The effect of communities in schools on high school dropout and graduation rates: Results from a multiyear, school-level quasi-experimental study. *Journal of Education for Students Placed at Risk, 16*(1), 24–37.

Quay, H. C., & Peterson, D. R. (1987). *Interim manual for the Revised Behavior Problems Checklist.* Miami, FL: University of Miami.

Raines, J. C., & Dibble, N. T. (2013). Ethical decision making in school mental health. In C. Franklin, M. Harris, & P. Allen-Meares (Eds.), *The school services sourcebook* (2nd ed., pp. 37–38). New York, NY: Oxford University Press.

Randolph, K. A., & Johnson, J. L. (2008). School-based mentoring programs: A review of the research. *Children & Schools, 30*(3), 177–185.

Reinke, W. M., Splett, J. D., Robeson, E. N., & Offutt, C. A. (2009). Combining school and family interventions for the prevention and early intervention of disruptive behavior problems in children: A public health perspective. *Psychology in the Schools, 46*(1), 33–43.

Reinke, W. M., Stormont, M., Herman, K. C., Puri, R., & Goel, N. (2011). Supporting children's mental health in schools: Teacher perceptions of needs, roles, and barriers. *School Psychology Quarterly, 26,* 1–13.

Richman, J. M., Bowen, G. L., & Woolley, M. E. (2004) School failure: An eco-interactional developmental perspective. In M. W. Fraser (Ed.), *Risk and resilience in childhood* (2nd ed., pp. 133–160). Washington, DC: NASW Press.

Saleebey, D. (2011). Some basic ideas about the strengths perspective. In F. Turner (Ed.), *Social work treatment: Interlocking theoretical approaches* (5th ed., pp. 447–485). New York, NY: Oxford University Press.

Shealey, M. W. (2006). The promise and perils of "scientifically-based" research for urban schools. *Urban Education, 41*(1), 5–19.

Sinclair, M. F., Christenson, S. L., & Thurlow, M. L. (2005). Promoting school completion of urban secondary youth with emotional or behavioral disabilities. *Exceptional Children, 71*(4), 465–482.

Skiba, R. J., Horner, R. H., Chung, C.-G., Rausch, M. K., May, S. L., & Tobin, T. (2011). Race is not neutral: A national investigation of African American and Latino disproportionality in school discipline. *School Psychology Review, 40*(1), 85–107.

Spaulding, S. A., Horner, R. H., May, S. L., & Vincent, C. G. (2008). *Implementation of school-wide PBIS across the United States.* Retrieved from http://www.pbis.org/evaluation/evaluation_briefs/nov_08_(2).aspx

Stamler, J. K., Scheer, D. C., & Cohen, J. (2009). *Assessing school climate for school improvement: Development, validation and implications of the Student School Climate Survey.* Internal report to Center for Social Emotional Education (the National School Climate Center).

Szapocznik, J., Hervis, O. E., & Schwartz, S. (2003). *Brief strategic family therapy for adolescent drug abuse* (NIH Publication No. 03–4751). NIDA Therapy Manuals for Drug Addiction. Rockville, MD: National Institute on Drug Abuse.

Todd, A. W., Campbell, A. L., Meyer, G. G., & Horner, R. H. (2008). The effects of a targeted intervention to reduce behavior problems. *Journal of Positive Behavior Interventions, 10*(1), 46–55.

U.S. Department of Education. (n.d.). *IDEA 2004.* Retrieved September 15, 2011 from http://idea .ed.gov/

U.S. Department of Education. (2006). *What works clearinghouse.* Retrieved December 13, 2012 from http://ies.ed.gov/ncee/wwc/pdf/intervention_ reports/WWC_Check_Connect_092106.pdf

Walsch, J. (2002). Supervising the counter-transference reactions to case managers. *The Clinical Supervisor, 21*(2), 129–144.

Wodarski, J. S., & Hopson, L. M. (2011). *Research methods for evidence-based practice.* Thousand Oaks, CA: Sage.

Zimmerman, T. S., Jacobsen, R. B., MacIntyre, M., & Watson, C. (1996). Solution-focused parenting groups: An empirical study. *Journal of Systemic Therapies, 15,* 12–25.

CHAPTER 14

Child Maltreatment and Child Welfare

Alberto Reynoso & Colleen Friend

CHAPTER OBJECTIVES

- Name one aspect of micro, mezzo, and macro practice in child welfare;
- Utilize the case vignette to highlight the dynamics and realize the intricacies of an abuse situation;
- Identify at least two of each of the following: diversity issues, legal issues, and ethical issues related to child welfare practice;
- Recognize at least two clinical concerns related to child welfare practice with an emphasis on transference and countertransference issues.

CASE VIGNETTE

Mary, age 10, resides with her mother, Josephine, and two younger siblings, Jimmy, age 8, and Timmy, age 2. The family is of Latino background. Her father has had limited contact with the family since her parent's divorce a year earlier and the family's relocation to another state. Josephine's boyfriend, Louis, drops Mary off at school in the morning and accompanies her home in the afternoon before he leaves for work. Louis is an attendant at an all-night convenience store. Louis does not reside with the family. Josephine works long hours as a waitress and is unavailable. She struggles to provide basic necessities for the family. Over the past month, Mary cries as the end of the school day approaches. Mary's teacher reports that she had recently become withdrawn and disinterested in learning and play, and she thinks these behaviors are unusual as Mary had been outgoing and engaged in school. Josephine reports that Mary had seemed fine at home until recently. Josephine noted that Mary's appetite has decreased and that Mary has been asleep when the mother arrives home from work; however, she has difficulty sleeping at night. Mary has also been experiencing nightmares, is afraid to be alone, and she is anxious and worried. Additionally, Mary has taken to showering several times a day because she feels dirty, according to her mother. Josephine noted that until recently, Mary and Louis had a good relationship as he often treated her as special by buying her things and taking her out. The mother had attributed recent changes in Mary's behavior to the divorce. Thus the mother felt disbelief and shock when Mary told her that Louis had been touching her private parts when she was alone with him. When Josephine asked Mary why she had not said anything, Mary stated that she had been told to be careful of strangers, and since Louis is not a stranger, she did not feel compelled to disclose. Josephine is distressed and in crisis about what to do. Josephine holds strong religious beliefs and has sought guidance through prayer. She has asked Mary not to share any information about the abuse with anyone outside of the home. As a result, Mary is ambivalent and confused about having disclosed the abuse to her mother.

INTRODUCTION

Mary's story is revealing of a child who has experienced child maltreatment. Child maltreatment continues to engender personal and social concern and has provoked ongoing efforts to develop and enhance a thoughtful and responsive trauma-focused child welfare (CW) system. This chapter will provide a broad overview of current CW delivery systems and emerging trends in policy and practice. While some texts make a distinction between the broader child welfare system and the government operated child protective service (CPS) system, and the terms are sometimes used synonymously, the term *child welfare* (CW) will be used here.

Most of the early efforts to protect children in the United States were focused on the care and adoption of orphans. More recently, children's rights gained some ascendancy in the 1960s and, for the first time, foster care homes had to be licensed by the state. In the 1970s and 1980s, the once fairly unregulated CW agencies began to face increasing oversight from the federal government and the Juvenile Court (Brittain & Equibel-Hart, 2004). One of the most significant developments in CW in the last 15–20 years is an awareness that, despite their best efforts, child welfare agencies could not alone be responsive to ensuring the welfare of children and that federal mandates to protect children and strengthen families increasingly required the collective response of concerned individuals, institutions, and communities.

Currently, federal legislation known as the Adoptions and Safe Families Act (ASFA), enacted in 1997 (P.L.105–89) directs CW practice. Among its key provisions, ASFA is intended to (1) ensure the promotion of child safety at every step of the child protective services process; (2) place the emphasis on child well-being including physical, mental, emotional, and social health and welfare; and (3) ensure the placement of children with permanent families. Having established ASFA as the federal foundation for CW services, the next step is to examine the scope of child maltreatment.

In the United States, during federal fiscal year 2011, The National Child Abuse and Neglect Data System (NCANDS) estimated 3.4 million reports of child abuse and neglect were received by Child Protective Services (CPS) agencies (U.S. Department of Health and Human Services [HHS], 2012). The national estimate included approximately 6.2 million children. Of these reports, 45 states reported counts of both screened-in and screened-out reports. Based on these data, 60.8% were screened in and 39.2% were screened out (U.S. Department of Health and Human Services, [HHS], 2012). These figures raise concerns in a number of areas. First, some advocates have asserted that the criteria for suspicion and reporting are too vague and cause the system to be overwhelmed with reports, many of which are screened out (Besharov,

1985). Second, these reports are considered by many experts to be an under reflection of the true incidence and prevalence rates of child maltreatment (Sedlak & Broadhurst, 1996). Third, questions arise when some states report data one way and others comply a different way, yet they end up in the same composite figure. For these reasons, the federal government has commissioned four National Incidence Studies (NIS) where information was solicited from a nationally representative sample of cases and community mandated reporters, asking them to identify all cases they had contact with that met The Harm Standard (NIS-1) or both the Harm and Endangered Standards (NIS 2, 3 and 4; Sedlak, McPherson, & Das, 2010). Under NIS-1, children were only identified as maltreated if they had already experienced harm from abuse and neglect. Under the broader Endangerment Standard, they were identified if they were at risk of harm. In sum, NIS 2 and 3 found significantly higher rates of abuse and neglect than had previously been investigated in the child protection system, while the NIS 4 found that these rates were decreasing (Sedlak et al., 2010). A unique contribution of these NIS studies is their ability to differentiate what portion of child maltreatment cases were known to mandated reporters from those that actually received an investigation. As this chapter will point out, this is one of the many complexities in CW practice. Considerable data are collected, but because of state-to-state variance in laws and practices as well as the development of innovative programs such as alternative responses where the report is not recorded as an investigation, it is difficult to know the full scope of child maltreatment and the CW response in this country. The most common form of child maltreatment is child neglect (general and severe forms including medical neglect), followed by physical abuse, sexual abuse and exploitation, emotional/psychological neglect and abuse, and parental absence and/or incapacity (HHS, 2012). Zastrow and Kirst-Ashman (2012) noted that while child abuse involves harming a child through actions, child neglect causes a child harm by not doing what is necessary to ensure the child's needs are being sufficiently met in order to survive and thrive. The Child Abuse Prevention and Treatment Act (CAPTA) of 1980, (42 U.S.C. §5101), as amended by the CAPTA Reauthorization Act of 2010 (P.L.111–320), retained the existing definition of child abuse and neglect as, at a minimum:

> Any recent act or failure to act on the part of a parent or caretaker which results in death, serious physical or emotional harm, sexual abuse or exploitation; or an act or failure to act, which presents an imminent risk of serious harm. (HHS, 2012)

MICRO PERSPECTIVE
Assessment

At the onset, a distinction needs to be made between an assessment and investigation in CW. Upon receiving a report of alleged child maltreatment, typically through a telephonic reporting hotline, CW agencies determine the appropriate response for the alleged maltreatment based on the statute described above, other state laws and the application of actuarial-based safety and risk assessment instruments. Based on the information from all sources, the decision is made to accept or reject a referral. Acceptance of a referral warrants an assessment of the allegations. The assessment of child maltreatment involves information gathering through interviews with the child, parents, and other relevant parties and the review of pertinent documentation. This will lead to a conclusion about what the child and family's social, mental, and physical health needs are, and what might be done to address them. Some assessments may lead directly to an alternative response, which precludes the case from going to an investigation. An investigation, on the other hand, is the gathering of information to determine what actually happened and whether or not child maltreatment can be substantiated. Some assessments lead to investigations and some are initiated simultaneously. Substantiated in a CW context, means there is evidence to support the allegations (Office on Child Abuse and Neglect, 2006a). CW may make the finding that the allegations are inconclusive or unfounded, which means that the allegation lacks credible evidence, but does not necessarily mean the allegation did not occur. Some states have a third classification, "inconclusive" which indicates that there is some evidence but not enough to substantiate the allegations. Once this fundamental decision is made, the worker and supervisor will make the decision to close or open a case. The case opening may or may not warrant Juvenile Court involvement. In this chapter, the term worker will be used interchangeably with child welfare worker and social worker. Not all child welfare workers have a social work degree; however, they all receive the same new worker training including training in the areas of decision making and assessment. An informed decision regarding the disposition of maltreatment allegations is contingent on an accurate assessment and the accumulation of facts and information. At a direct practice level, the quality of the assessment, particularly in the initial stages of an investigation, depends on both the approach or style of the CW professional and the application of actuarial risk assessment instruments. While states may choose different instruments, it is important to understand that the application of this evidence-based practice (EBP) has provided considerable reliability across jurisdictions (Reed & Karpilow, 2009). Typically these instruments facilitate making a determination of low, medium or high risk. This in turn will guide the level of services and type of case opened. Zastrow and Kirst-Ashman (2012) noted that the initial assessment process will guide the child welfare professional's decision regarding the maltreatment allegations, guide interventions, and establish case plan goals to address and remedy identified difficulties in family functioning. It should be noted that while early stage assessment is critical, the assessment process is fluid and thus revisited throughout the life of a child's and family's involvement in the child welfare process. Ongoing assessment is critical in determining child and family functioning in the following seven areas: (1) adaptation and progress toward case plan goals, (2) the child and family's underlying strengths and needs, (3) the child's ongoing safety and well-being,

(4) the child's and family's coping skills and resilience, (5) subsequent decisions about the child's long-term safety, (6) minimization of further risk or harm, and (7) the family's protective capacity in order to recommend exit from the child protective services system (Office on Child Abuse and Neglect, 2006a).

Assessment is an important component to newly integrated models of practice that have been adopted by child welfare professionals. These practice models are grounded in key social work values and beliefs. An effective practice model will consider all of its values, principles and guidance in building and supporting the vital relationship between staff and children, youth and families (American Public Human Services Association, 2011). The purpose of an effective practice model is to define how the public child welfare agency engages families, youth and the community in developing and delivering a services array that meets the unique needs of those served by the agency and leads the agency to achieve desired outcomes (American Public Human Services Association, 2011). An effective practice model attempts to engage individuals and families in the process of identifying problems in biopsychosocial functioning and the interventions necessary to address and overcome their challenges. Practice models emphasize an approach that is congruent with the family's culture and individual preferences.

A key paradigm shift has been the integration of a strength-based family centered orientation to the provision of CW services. Within the spectrum of a strength-based approach to practice is first, a focus on relationship building and collaboration throughout the service delivery system and second, the integration of evidence-informed practices in the assessment and intervention processes. A social worker being attuned to the specific biopsychosocial needs of children and families allows for the identification of individual and family strengths as well as areas of functioning that may be challenging and thus be an antecedent to their involvement in the CW process. Family-centered practice is a way of working with families, both formally and informally, across service systems to enhance their capacity to care for and protect their children. It focuses on children's safety and needs within the context of their families and communities and builds on families' strengths to achieve optimal outcomes (Child Welfare Information Gateway, 2013b). In the case vignette described earlier, let us assume that Mary's mother, Josephine, confided in a friend about Mary's disclosure. The friend in turn made an anonymous report to the CW Hotline and a suspected child abuse report and investigation was initiated. In many jurisdictions, a cross-report to law enforcement would be generated, and CW would likely respond in some collaborative way with them. In the initial assessment and investigation phase, it would be important to skillfully develop trust with Mary and her siblings in an effort to elicit information regarding the allegations of abuse. This phase is driven by child safety concerns and must involve all minors who were exposed to the risk. The development of rapport and engagement would be the foundation to the assessment and information gathering process. In CW cases, this is often complicated by the involuntary nature of the relationship. In addition to skill demonstration, the assessment process requires knowledge of child abuse dynamics. A variety of factors contribute to child maltreatment and family violence (Charlesworth, 2007; Choi & Tittle, 2002; Freisthler, Merritt, & LaScala, 2006 as cited in Hutchison, 2013). According to Charlesworth, Wood, and Viggiani (2013) these factors include parental, child, family, community, and cultural characteristics. Charlesworth et al. (2013) also noted that it is typically the dynamic interplay of these characteristics that contribute to maltreatment. In Mary's case, there exists a single mother of three children who is recently divorced, living in a new community, and without the support system of extended family members. While she may depend on Mary to assist in caring for her younger siblings, she is also depending on her boyfriend to fulfill caregiving responsibilities such as transporting and caring for Mary after school. She is also creating an environment that communicates to her children that she depends on the boyfriend to share in some of the parenting responsibilities and that

he perhaps fulfills her need for companionship. The family dynamic is one in which the boyfriend has unmonitored access to Mary, thus there is the presence of physical isolation and opportunity for the abuse to occur. As an oldest child in a family that recently experienced divorce, Mary may be keenly aware of how the boyfriend's income contributes to the household and might also see her mother's need for companionship. She could also be protecting her younger siblings from the boyfriend and in a new community where extended family is no longer available to assist with childcare. For all these reasons, Mary would (likely) be reluctant to disclose about her abuse, and ambivalent when she sees her mother's reaction. The CW worker will also be assessing the mother's ability to protect Mary and her siblings at this delicate stage of both assessment and investigation. Questions such as these emerge: If the abuse is substantiated, can the mother be an ally in removing the risk from the children or do the children need to be removed from the risk? What kind of assistance does mother need to work through this crisis? How can CW collaborate with law enforcement on the potential criminal aspects of this investigation? While these will be explored in the Legal and Ethical Considerations Section of this chapter, more information needs to be gathered from all family members at this point of the assessment and investigation process.

Both physical and behavioral indicators provide the CW professional with clues that a child is being physically/sexually or emotionally abused. Physical indicators may include bruises, lacerations, burns, fractures, head injuries, the presence of illness or disease, and internal injuries (Zastrow & Kirst-Ashman, 2012). The California Social Work Education Center (CalSWEC, 2013) noted that behavioral indicators are also referred to as trauma-related indicators. These may include self-protective behaviors in the form of social and physical isolation, excessive cleanliness or poor hygiene, and wearing layers of clothing. Self-protective behaviors are not uncommon in children who have experienced child sexual abuse such as in Mary's case. Trauma-related behaviors may also include hyperarousal, hypervigilance, startle responses, intrusive images and thoughts, and other symptoms associated with post-traumatic stress disorder (PTSD; CalSWEC, 2013). Children who experience trauma may experience PTSD which includes a set of symptoms such as feelings of fear and helplessness, reliving of the traumatic experience, and attempts to avoid reminders of the traumatic experience (Balaban, 2008; Farkas, 2004; Farmer, 2009).

In the case vignette described above, upon assessment and investigation, the allegations of child maltreatment in the form of child sexual abuse were substantiated. The social worker and law enforcement determined that the family unit could be preserved and that Mary could safely remain in the home of her mother. In many jurisdictions, a CW agency may provide services without Juvenile Court involvement, under some form of a voluntary family maintenance agreement; that is what was done here. While Josephine experienced initial disbelief, she demonstrated protective capacity by severing the relationship with Louis and enrolling the family in supportive and therapeutic services to address the traumatic effects of the abuse and her first reaction to the child's disclosure. The social worker and supervisor, as well as law enforcement, were satisfied that Josephine's actions alleviated immediate safety threats and the risk of future harm to all the children. It is important to note that some nonoffending parents do struggle with believing that abuse occurred, and this becomes an issue that can be better understood in therapy.

Diversity Considerations

According to the American Public Human Services Association (2011) CW workers can improve their practice with children, youth, and families by increasing their knowledge and appreciation of different cultures. Increased sensitivity to cultural differences can help workers more fully engage with families, better understand family actions and interactions, and make culturally appropriate case decisions. In addition to race and ethnicity, other aspects of culture that merit consideration include sexual orientation, gender identity, disability, class,

military affiliation, refugee and immigrant status, as well as religious and spiritual practices of families and individuals (American Public Human Services Association, 2011).

In the case scenario described in the beginning of the chapter, it is noted that the family is of Latino background. The family's perceptions of the sexual abuse, blame and responsibility, the use of coping strategies, and attitudes toward help seeking may be influenced by culture (which includes religion) and ethnicity. The concept of shame is powerful in traditional Latino cultures (Fontes, 2007). Fontes (2005) noted that some elements of shame are common to most victims of child sexual abuse regardless of their ethnicity and cultural background. However, the same author (2005, 2007) also noted that the shame around sexual abuse intersects with ethnic culture in many ways including beliefs related to responsibility for the abuse, failure to protect, fate, the concept of damaged goods, virginity, sexual taboos and pressures, predictions of a shameful future, revictimization, and the layers of shame produced by cultural oppression.

Josephine's reticence about sharing the sexual abuse disclosure with anyone outside the home could be perceived as denial; however, one would need to consider the possibility that her reticence is embedded in shame, her sense of responsibility and role in the events leading to the sexual abuse, failure to protect, and Louis's betrayal. The use of prayer can be viewed as an important aspect of Josephine's coping strategies and her reliance on spirituality as well as her perceived cultural beliefs and norms that such disclosures are kept within the family and home. Factors related to shame may also contribute to Josephine's attitudes about seeking help outside of the home and her ambivalence about the use of formal support systems.

Mary's ambivalence and confusion about her disclosure can be attributed to shame related to responsibility for the abuse, sexual taboos and a sense of having been damaged. Josephine's support, protective capacity, and her belief that the sexual abuse happened will be important factors in Mary's emotional and psychological recovery from trauma.

According to the standards of the National Association of Social Workers (NASW), cultural competence refers to "the process by which individuals and systems respond respectfully and effectively to people of all cultures, languages, classes, races, ethnic backgrounds, religions, and other diversity factors in a manner that recognizes, affirms, and values the worth of individuals, families, and communities and protects and preserves the dignity of each" (NASW, 2008, p. 11).

The issue of racial disproportionality in CW continues to provoke concern and discourse. A substantial amount of research has documented the overrepresentation of certain racial and ethnic groups, including African Americans and Native Americans, in the CW system when compared with their representation in the general population (Casey-CSSP Alliance for Racial Equity, 2006; Child Welfare Information Gateway, 2011; Derezotes, Poertner, & Testa, 2005; Hill, 2005, 2006; McRoy, 2005). While the extent of this overrepresentation varies significantly across different regions of the country, it exists at some level in virtually every locality. African American children are overrepresented in this country's CW system through each decision point, and their outcomes in the system are very different than the outcomes for white children (Belanger, Green, & Bullard, 2008).

According to CalSWEC (2012), racial disproportionality is compounded at certain decision points in the system. Disproportionality increases from referral to substantiation to placement. African American and Native American children are more likely to be referred to the CW system compared to white and Hispanic children (Magruder & Shaw, 2008; Mumpower, 2010; Needell et al., 2011). After assessment and substantiation of allegations, African American and Native American children are more likely to be placed in foster care than white children (AFCARS, 2008 as cited in Wells, Merritt, & Briggs, 2009; Needell et al., 2011; Perez, 2010). Additionally, after being in the CW system for 18 months, African American and Native American children are less likely to be reunified with their birth parents than white children (U.S. General Accounting Office, 2008; Needell et al., 2011; Perez,

2010). African American and Native American children are more likely to remain in foster care after 24 months (Needell et al., 2011). Native American children under ICWA are somewhat less likely to be adopted than other groups (Perez, 2010).

Careful examination of this issue, however, has concluded that although children of color are disproportionately represented within the CW population, research from the first three National Incidence Studies of Child Abuse and Neglect (NIS) found no relationship between race and the incidence of child maltreatment after controlling for poverty and other risk factors such as single parenthood (Sedlak & Broadhurst, 1996). However, the most recent NIS (NIS-4) indicated that African American children experience maltreatment at higher rates than white children in several categories of maltreatment (Sedlak et al., 2010). Bartholet (2009) postulates that African American families are disproportionately characterized by risk factors associated with maltreatment; this is precisely why they are overrepresented. Further, she maintains that they warrant the CW system's intervention and society should act to prevent the disproportionate maltreatment of African American children, and provide greater support to families at risk of falling into the dysfunction that result in maltreatment.

CalSWEC (2012) has taken a different position, noting that most CW decisions are presumed to be based on data documenting that maltreatment has occurred; however, decisions occur within a cultural context infused with race, gender and social class biases. According to CalSWEC (2012), cultural misinterpretations are inevitable when there are significant cultural and social class differences between professionals and the people they serve. They add that perceptions of neglect are highly susceptible to biased evaluations (CalSWEC, 2012).

The theory of racial microaggressions, which occur at the micro level, provides an explanation into potential manifestations of cultural misinterpretations and biases that occur at the various decision points described above. Sue et al. (2007) described racial microaggressions as "brief, subtle, and common place daily verbal, behavioral, or environmental indignities, whether intentional or unintentional, implicit or explicit, that communicate hostile, derogatory, or negative racial slights and insults toward people of color" (p. 271). The power of racial microaggressions lies in their invisibility to the perpetrator and oftentimes the recipient (Sue, 2005).

Sue et al. (2007) noted that "there is an urgent need for greater awareness and understanding for how microaggressions operate, their numerous manifestations in society, the type of impact they have on people of color, the dynamic interaction between perpetrator and target, and the educational strategies needed to eliminate them" (p. 273). Cultural competence training in CW has introduced the concept and use of cultural humility in practice (Hohman, 2013). Humility is having a sense that one's own knowledge is limited as to what truly is another's culture (Hohman, 2013). According to Ortega and Coulborn-Faller (2011), we are limited because we have unconscious stereotypes of others and tend to use stereotypes as a "safety net" to help explain behavior (as cited in Hohman, 2013). It is noted (Hohman, 2013) we are also limited as an individual cannot know everything about every culture and because clients are complex human beings who intersect in a variety of cultures, be it their race, sexual and gender identity, class, age, work or disability status. Hohman (2013) noted that cultural humility is about accepting one's limitations. According to Tervalon and Murray-Garcia (1998) those who practice cultural humility work to increase their self-awareness of their own biases and perceptions and engage in a lifelong self-reflection process about how to put these aside and learn from clients (as cited in Hohman, 2013). Ortega and Coulborn-Faller (2011) state that the social worker is not the expert but the learner and the self-reflection process enables the social worker to determine what attitudes and values keeps him or her from learning from the client (as cited in Hohman, 2013). Hohman (2013) noted that "clients are approached humbly and are viewed as collaborators in the helping process. Clients teach the social worker about their unique places at the intersections of their different cultures and the role of the social worker is to be willing to learn

about their experiences" (para. 3). Ortega and Coulborn-Faller (2011) wrote that it is this openness (humility) to learn that "frees" social workers from having to be experts and feel that they must know everything about various cultures (as cited in Hohman, 2013).

Intervention

An emerging trend in the 21st century is that social workers, including CW and clinical professionals, are more frequently utilizing EBP for the assessment and treatment planning of the children and families they serve (Child Welfare Information Gateway, 2013b). EBP involves identifying, assessing, and implementing strategies that are supported by scientific research, and integrating these with clinical expertise and the client/family's cultural and personal values (Shlonsky & Friend, 2007). State CW agencies are increasingly aware of the need to focus their resources on programs that have demonstrated results, especially for achieving outcomes as mandated by ASFA in the Federal Child and Family Services Review process (Child Welfare Information Gateway, 2013a). Thus the use of EBPs is a component of the process by which states are held accountable for setting and meeting outcomes to steadily improve their practice.

Cross-section integration of EBPs continues to emerge as there is greater collaboration among public CW agencies and purveyors of mental health services, particularly as children and families, as consumers, intersect both systems. Additionally, as the CW system is becoming more trauma focused, professionals are first, recognizing the traumatic nature of child maltreatment, second, acknowledging that interventions themselves can be traumagenic and third, recognizing that there is a need for fidelity to the treatment models of EBPs to assure they are effective in addressing these traumas.

The focus on preventing and treating early exposure to trauma, including child maltreatment, is grounded firmly in emerging science about its devastating impact on lifelong well-being. Abuse and/or neglect can derail a child's normal development, disrupt critical attachments, and impair social and emotional functioning (Perry, 2003). When it takes place, how long it lasts, and the presence or absence of protective factors affect the traumatic impact of maltreatment on a child. In addition to hindering healthy development in the short term, early exposure to trauma can have significant adverse effects across the lifespan and in multiple domains. Unaddressed, the impact of maltreatment on the developing brain compounds over time, limiting social and cognitive capacities that are essential to school success, future earning potential, and the ability to engage in healthy relationships (Perry, 2003). Research with the Adverse Childhood Experiences (ACE) study has shown that children who experience complex interpersonal trauma are more likely to have poor physical health as adults, and are at greater risk for many of the leading causes of early death, including diabetes, heart disease, and cancer (Anda, Butchart, Felitti, & Brown, 2010).

While the effects of childhood trauma can be profound, they can be minimized, and children can recover. As more is learned about how trauma affects children's well-being, researchers and professionals are developing increasingly effective methods for mitigating its harm. There is a rapidly growing array of evidence-based interventions that, when delivered with fidelity can help restore developmentally appropriate functioning and improve outcomes for children and youth who have experienced maltreatment (Administration for Children and Families, 2013). Examples of EBP in CW practice include Integrative Treatment for Complex Trauma (ITCT), Motivational Interviewing (MI), Structured Decision Making (SDM), Trauma-Focused Cognitive Behavioral Therapy (TF-CBT), and Parent-Child Interaction Therapy (PCIT). These last two were identified by the Kauffman Best Practices Project (2004) as being among the best practices for both helping children to heal from the impact of abuse and being likely to reduce the long term consequences of child maltreatment. Many of these approaches have been supported by one or more randomly controlled treatment outcome studies, demonstrating their efficacy. TF-CBT

is specifically designed to reduce children's negative emotional and behavioral responses to primarily sexual abuse, while it also addresses maladaptive beliefs (cognitive distortions) and supports parents' and caretakers' ability to respond to their child (Cohen & Mannarino, 2008). It accomplishes this through the use of psychoeducation, cognitive reframing, stress management techniques, and constructing the trauma narrative. Parental participation in parallel or conjoint treatment is essential. In the case of Mary, TF-CBT would utilize psychoeducation to normalize the typical reactions victims have to child sexual abuse experiences. It would be likely to label Mary's frequent showering because she feels "dirty" as a cognitive distortion and work with her to cognitively reframe her anxiety about this. Mary would be guided to use stress reduction techniques such as focused breathing, emotion identification and expression skills, and thought stopping and replacement. Mary would be enabled to construct the trauma narrative gradually; thus, the power of the abusive events would lessen its grip on her. As a result of her improved ability to talk about the events, she would begin to integrate the experience into her life and move forward. Josephine would be supported in helping Mary decrease her showering and in processing her own reaction to the disclosure because parental support is integral to this model. Students and CW workers can access online training on the TF-CBT model (see Internet Resources, on p. 196).

TF-CBT is not the only treatment approach that would be suitable for Mary. ITCT is a multi-modal, comprehensive treatment model that takes into account a range of psychological, social, and cultural issues while emphasizing the relationship with the therapist and focusing on interventions to enhance attachment relationships with the parent (Lanktree & Briere, 2013). Furthermore, this approach would require Josephine's active participation, likely probing her initial reaction to the disclosure. There are different yet similar versions of the approach for children and adolescents, and they each require frequent reassessments.

The challenge is integrating these interventions and models into every day practice; to this end, agency-based training must reflect this. Now evidence-based websites such as the California Evidence-Based Clearing House and The National Children's Traumatic Stress Network (see Internet Resources, on p. 196) have been developed to help CW workers easily access this information as they need it. Integrating EBPs like these into CW work would eventually reduce the recurrence of child maltreatment and potentially reduce caseloads.

One of the primary activities of child abuse or neglect investigations involves interviewing children, parents, and others who may have knowledge that can assist the investigation. Interviews may be conducted to gather information for assessments or to gather evidence for court use; the latter are called forensic interviews (Child Welfare Information Gateway, 2013c). An emerging movement in CW practice is the integration of narrative interviewing techniques in the investigation process. Incorporated within the spectrum of evidence-based intervention is the most well-known and widely studied interviewer training system known as the National Institute of Child Health Development (NICHD) Protocol. It was developed by a team of researchers, interviewers, police officers, and legal professionals with reference to child development issues, including linguistic capabilities, memory and suggestibility, forensic needs, interviewer behaviors, and the effects of stress and trauma (Lamb, La Rooy, Malloy, & Katz, 2011). More than a decade of research has shown that effective interviewer training can begin with the proper use of the NICHD Protocol because it allows interviewers to maximize the amount of information obtained from free-recall memory by using open-ended prompts (Lamb et al., 2011).

Transference and Countertransference Issues

A challenge in working with child abuse and neglect cases is related to transference and countertransference, particularly as there is an increased awareness of the traumatic nature of child maltreatment. Transference is the client's conscious or unconscious transfer of positive or negative feelings from a past relationship onto a helper. Countertransference occurs when the helper projects the same kinds of feelings onto the client, either consciously or unconsciously as well. Child maltreatment cases epitomize betrayal; older or adult caregivers have broken a child's trust, misused their power, and severely violated boundaries, particularly in child sexual abuse cases. Thus they are a minefield for countertransference, whether or not the CW worker actually had a similar experience, because identification with the betrayal that child abuse victims experience is not uncommon. It is important to consider that these reactions may be outside the scope of awareness (unconscious) so when a countertransference reaction is taking place, the CW worker might be tempted to react to the situation "as if" it had happened to him/ her or perhaps they might try to rework the situation "as if" it were happening again. For example, in the case vignette describing Mary's child sexual abuse, if the CW worker were to tell Mary how she should feel towards the perpetrator or become overly protective of Mary based on his/her own childhood experiences, these could be construed as countertransference reactions. This is why CW workers should discuss their reactions to clients with their supervisors, who can hopefully help them sort out these common reactions and chart a course that honors client self-determination and helps the SW worker become more self-aware. Boundary issues are particularly relevant in child abuse cases and the surfacing of countertransference issues precisely because of violations in trust, intimacy, and power. According to Harper and Steadman, the maintenance or dismissal of boundaries conveys messages regarding power, trust, and authority to clients (as cited in Flanagan, 2012).

The term secondary traumatization refers to the psychological trauma experienced by those in close contact with trauma victims (Figley, 2012). Secondary traumatic stress is defined as the natural consequence resulting from the helper's knowledge about a traumatizing event experienced by another person. Because this engenders stress, it is also discussed using either term (Figley, 2012).

Professionals who have their own history of trauma and those who have minimal clinical experience in working with traumatized clients are vulnerable to secondary traumatization (ACS-NYU Trauma Institute, 2012). In these situations, it can be easy to suppress one's emotions and begin distancing oneself from clients (Newell & McNeil, 2010). Forward thinking CW agencies have taken initiatives in reducing secondary trauma among CW staff who should be considered first responders because of the unpredictable nature of the task and the relative lack of physical and psychological protection they experience when they initiate an investigation (ACS-NYU Trauma Institute, 2011). An important element of supervision of CW professionals involves monitoring their emotional well-being, particularly in light of the distressing nature of child maltreatment cases.

Across the country, CW agencies increasingly offer coaching programs to assist staff as they make program improvements or implement new practices (Fixen, Naoom, Blasé, Friedman, & Wallace, 2008). The National Child Welfare Resource Center for Organizational Improvement (2012) has defined coaching as "a structured process in which a coach uses specific strategies to help learners improve their performance on the job and to contribute to improved agency practice and outcomes" (p. 3). The challenge of secondary traumatization can be an important discussion point as the concept of coaching becomes increasingly integrated into the role of supervision. Coster and Schwebel note that CW practitioners experience the stressors associated with emotionally charged cases in addition to the normal stressors of daily life (as cited in Flanagan, 2012). With this in mind, supervisors must ensure they are engaging in self-care to avoid burnout, particularly because they model these positive behaviors for their supervisees.

Legal and Ethical Concerns

CW professionals will face a variety of dilemmas in the course of their career. Some will be personal, some will be social, and others will be legal. None of these is necessarily an ethical dilemma, so they will be considered here separately. Many of the duties of a CW worker are imposed either by law or by court order (CalSWEC, 2012). It is incumbent upon CW agencies and professionals to remain current with each state's legal mandates that guide and inform practice. The states do differ on the authority they assign to either CW or law enforcement to remove children. Forty six states give specific powers to police officers to take legal custody of children without a court order; approximately 20 states extend that same authority to CW (Pence & Wilson, 1992). In practice, most jurisdictions strive to make these decisions jointly as a team for two reasons: Parents are less likely to react violently in the presence of the police and CW has the ability and authority to approve a relative on a temporary basis or utilize other licensed placements to receive the child. Thus the most effective approach to child maltreatment cases is through interagency coordination and planning (U.S. Department of Justice, 2014). In circumstances where the removal of a child occurs, the agency with authority may determine that exigent circumstances exist meaning that the situation requires immediate attention and leaving to obtain a court order and returning would put the child in an unsafe situation. Thus, when removal is needed, children are typically removed without a court order then a hearing is set to have a judge review the circumstances for removal. States vary in the time frame they set for obtaining retroactive judicial approval for the removal (Office on Child Abuse and Neglect, 2006b). During this window of time, a CW worker will assess if the child can safely return home or if what most jurisdictions call a "petition" will be filed with the Juvenile Court. This petition would allege that the child is described by the state's statute(s) as an abused or neglected child and would be in need of further placement or supervision. While this is happening, the perpetrator may be investigated and possibly arrested by law enforcement and referred to the District Attorney for criminal prosecution. A complexity of CW cases reveals itself here: these cases may simultaneously have a life in both the State's Juvenile Court System (civil) and the State's Criminal Court System. In the opening vignette, the CW worker would collaborate with law enforcement on the overall case investigation, including interviewing all the children, the decision on whether or not to remove them, and the seeking of a medical exam. Beyond this, law enforcement would be conducting its own investigation on the criminal aspect of the allegations and collaborating with the District Attorney on the filing of criminal charges.

Despite the public apprehension generated by the fear of a child's removal, in actuality, this does not happen very often. For example in 2007, in California approximately 490,000 children were accepted for a CPS investigation. In the end, about 33,000 were placed in out of home care for more than 8 days (Reed & Karpilow, 2009). This is a fairly low removal rate of about 7% for all cases accepted for an investigation. In fact, CPS is required, in accord with ASFA (1997), to make removal a last resort, and professionals must be able to demonstrate that they performed "reasonable efforts" to prevent the removal (Office on Child Abuse and Neglect, 2006a).

While the law and court orders guide aspects of CW practice, the National Association of Social Workers (NASW) has also established ethical standards that guide social work practice. Because CW has its roots in the social work profession, and some states actually proscribe that a percentage of the workforce have MSW degrees, it is important to examine the standards and core values of the *NASW Code of Ethics* (see Internet Resources, on p. 196) because so many specifically pertain to the protection of children, preservation of families, respect for persons, client self-determination and confidentiality.

It is essential that every social work professional understand that the social work profession has at its core some very deeply held values. These values in turn serve as the foundation for the ethical basis for practice, which in turn is the justification for the very existence of the profession and the interventions social workers undertake (CalSWEC, 2012).

MEZZO PERSPECTIVE

While many organizational issues compete for attention in public CW, the most compelling ones arise at the intersection of worker turnover/retention, caseload size and training. Direct line staff turnover is estimated to be 30%–40% annually. Indeed, with the average length of stay for a new worker being less than two years (USGAO, 2003) the agency welcomed Title IV-E training partnership with universities to train new workers. One facet of this partnership offered stipends for MSW education, requiring an MSW specialization in public CW (PCW) in exchange for a commitment to work in a PCW agency. To date, these partnerships that exist in almost every state have been successful in infusing the workforce with a substantial number of MSWs with CW preparation, who are more likely to remain in PCW employment compared to workers without this training (Weaver, Chang, Clark & Rhee, 2007).

In the case of Mary, it might be speculated that if her CW worker had an MSW education with Title IV-E training, he or she would have been well prepared to understand many of the issues already discussed: child sexual abuse dynamics, cultural considerations, collaboration with law enforcement, use of the NICHD Protocol, and involvement in EBP treatment. Although this kind of preparation encourages CW worker retention, if Mary and her siblings experience several workers due to turnover, it is easy to see how they might come to distrust the CW agency. Even more problematic, Mary and the siblings might generalize those feelings to other adults and be wary of future adult helpers.

Although many complaints contribute to turnover in PCW, the most readily understood is the issue of caseload size; it is the top complaint of workers across the country (Friend, 2012). Because of the complexity of concerns that surround child protection cases, the Child Welfare League issued a national standard of 12–15 children per worker (Children's Defense Fund and Children's Rights, 2006). It is worthy to note that this yardstick was established well before the requirements of ASFA were fully integrated into the CW system. Workload, or the amount of work and time it takes to successfully manage a case and complete non-casework responsibilities, is also a piece of this puzzle. In the first round of the ASFA-mandated Child and Family Services Reviews, about half the states noted that addressing workload and caseload issues would be part of their program improvement plan (Children's Defense Fund and Children's Rights, 2006).

These chronic problems contribute to organizational inefficiency and perceptions of ineffectiveness. In the classic and dreaded instance when a child dies, workers, supervisors and managers typically cite workload and caseload as prominent reasons why optimal services were not offered. These then often become a more divisive community issue, centering attention on why more was not done to prevent the tragedy. Many critical stakeholders operate with benefit of hindsight. Many times the media is involved in drawing the public's attention and galvanizing public opinion. Workers are sometimes placed on leave while an investigation is launched. In some communities, a panel of experts is convened to offer elected officials a blueprint for fixing the problem (Independent Child Death Review Panel, 2006; Los Angeles County, 2014). These high-profile experts then become a type of advocacy group who attempt to harness public opinion to put pressure on elected officials to make change happen. While CW managers may lament having solutions imposed on them, it is often the price paid for the cumulative neglect of line worker requests and patterns of worker turnover. It could also be argued that the fundamental reasons for these problems lies with constant underfunding of CW services. Thus the painful process that flows from a child's death to a community problem and on to an advocacy issue can sometimes bring about a change that will recalibrate service, training and even retention of the workforce.

Across many CW systems, high profile child fatalities have resulted in class action litigation as a strategy for holding CW agencies accountable to the provisions of ASFA. Lawsuit settlements and consent decrees generated further workforce training and improvements (Meltzer, Joseph, & Shookhoff, 2012). In fact, Mor Barak, Levin, Nissly and Lane (2006) contend that effective training is one factor that may facilitate the greater retention of qualified workers. If we define a qualified worker as properly trained with an educational background that prepared them for CW work or substantial practice expertise, then these are ideally the workers that should be retained. Research has shown that CW workers who are prepared express greater job satisfaction and contribute to lower turnover rates (Weaver et al., 2007). Qualitatively, many workers claim that the social support they receive from peers and supervisors, the opportunity for professional development, and the flexibility they have in managing the work all contribute to "liking" CW work and remaining on the job (Weaver et al., 2007).

MACRO PERSPECTIVE

This chapter has discussed several macro practice issues, three will be recapped here: ASFA as the federal foundation of all PCW services in the country, the attempts to ascertain the true incidence of child maltreatment nationally, and Title IV-E Partnerships as a method for attracting and training a qualified PCW workforce. These Partnerships are created when states draw down federal Title IV-E funds in order to contract with universities to train social work students in a child welfare specialization.

Established as law in 1997, ASFA codified requirements and set the tone for the delivery of PCW services in the United States. One important change was that permanency for children became ascendant, meaning that timelines for the performance of reasonable efforts to achieve reunification were shortened and CW workers were mandated to conduct what was identified as "concurrent planning." Parents and children receiving family reunification services now technically have only 12 months to achieve this before a more permanent solution will be seriously considered. For children age 3 and under, the timeline is only 6 months. This more permanent solution would emerge from concurrent planning efforts in which relatives and foster parents were encouraged to consider adopting the children in question while the parents simultaneously tried to achieve reunification within the shorter timeline. This inspired many candid discussions among the participants that included the effects of out-of-home care on child development, the consequences of failing to reunify in the specified time period, and the possibility of relinquishing parental rights to the child (D'Andrade, Frame, & Duerr-Berrick, 2006). Controversial at its first introduction, this concept has gained widespread acceptance and has facilitated shorter reunification periods as well as more kinship and foster parent adoptions (D'Andrade et al., 2006). In the opening vignette, had Mary and her siblings been removed from their home, the mother would have had 12 months to do what the case plan specified for reunification with the older two children, but only 6 months to do the same for the youngest child. Thus ASFA timelines are clearly driving the CW system to achieve permanency for children as early as possible, and they are underscoring the need for very young children to experience permanency.

Despite the many efforts to understand the true national incidence of child maltreatment documented in this chapter, it is still a struggle to utilize uniform definitions across states, ensure consistent reporting and enforce mandatory reporting. Beyond this, there is concern carefully documented by Bartholet (2014) in an address delivered at the Annual Colloquium of the American Professional Society on the Abuse of Children (APSAC), that alternative response cases, devised to allow flexibility, in some states, are not counted as incidents or investigations. It had been hoped that the National Incidence Surveys would resolve these issues, but more needs to be done to assure that PCW agencies are reaching all the children who need a response.

Finally, Title IV-E Partnerships across the nation have infused a substantial number of MSW prepared graduates into the PCW system. Although the research reflects that they are more likely to stay and experience job satisfaction (Weaver et al., 2007), retention rates may also be a reflection of the economy and the lack of available alternatives. A concerted effort needs to be made to reduce caseloads and enhance new supervisory and growth strategies such as coaching and skills training on EBPs.

CONCLUSION

This chapter has traversed many issues in the micro, mezzo and macro aspects of child welfare practice. Despite the intricacies and complexities of CW work, many social workers launch and continue their careers in this setting, so familiarity with the basic issues introduced here is essential.

In micro practice, many shifts in CW work have paralleled shifts in SW practice. For example, there is now an established consciousness about the cultural context for casework decisions across both areas of practice (Clark, 2003). The adoption of practice models that include families in the identification of strengths, problems, decisions, and evidence-based interventions is a strategy that promotes healing, reduces recurrences in child maltreatment, and potentially will reduce caseloads. The integration of trauma-informed and evidence-based practice strategies presents many opportunities for conjoint research at the intersection of CW and SW.

On a mezzo and macro practice level, SW and CW have been concerned about workforce retention, improved training and the reduction of caseloads. Title IV-E Partnerships with SW schools have enabled PCW systems to retain MSW practitioners and train the workforce to understand the delivery and accountability provisions of ASFA. While ASFA serves as a federal guideline, the provision of CW services will be delivered by an informed and culturally competent workforce that is responsive to all the issues presented in this chapter. The Internet Resources section that follows will provide the reader with information that expands on many of the concepts that were addressed here.

INTERNET RESOURCES

- American Profession Society on the Abuse of Children: http://www.apsac.fmhi.usf.edu/
- National Child Welfare Resource Center for Organizational Improvement: http://muskie.usm.maine.edu/helpkids/
- California Evidence Based Clearinghouse for Child Welfare: http://www.cebc4cw.org
- California Social Work Education Center: http://www.calswec.berkley.edu
- Children's Traumatic Stress Network: http://www.nctsn.org
- Casey Family Programs: http://www.casey.org
- Child Welfare League of America: http://www.cwla.org
- Futures Without Violence: http://www.futureswithoutviolence.org

- U.S. Department of Health and Human Services, Administration on Children, Youth, and Families: http://www.acf.hhs.gov/programs
- National Association of Social Workers: http://www.socialworkers.org
- Child Welfare Information Gateway: https://www.childwelfare.gov
- Integrative Treatment of Complex Trauma for Adolescents: http://keck.usc.edu/Education/Academic_Department_and_Divisions/Department_of_Psychiatry/Research_and_Training_Centers/USC_ATTC/ITCT-A.aspx
- TF-CBT Web: http://tfcbt.musc.edu/

DISCUSSION QUESTIONS

1. How do federal laws influence organizational policies and procedures, and how do policies and laws drive child welfare practice?

2. How can CW practitioners best impact racial disproportionality in child welfare systems at the micro practice level? Why is this important?

3. What are potential transference and countertransference issues that can arise in child welfare at the micro practice level? How can transference and countertransference issues potentially impact micro practice and outcomes for children and families? What can one do if/when one experiences a countertransference reaction with one's clients?

4. What are some of the organizational issues that impact practitioner retention rates in child welfare? What are some ideas for improving practitioner retention in child welfare?

5. Why are diversity considerations important in child welfare? Name at least five aspects of diversity that merit consideration at the micro, mezzo, and macro practice levels.

REFERENCES

ACS-NYU Trauma Institute. (2011). *The resilience alliance: Promoting resilience and reducing secondary trauma among child welfare staff.* Retrieved from http://www.nrcpfc.org/teleconferences/2011-11-16/Resilience_Alliance_Participant_Handbook_-_September_2011.pdf

ACS-NYU Trauma Institute. (2012). *Addressing secondary traumatic stress among child welfare staff: A practice brief.* Retrieved from http://www.nyc.gov/html/acs/downloads/providers_newsletter/aug08/addressing%20STS%20among%20child%20welfare%20staff%20practice%20brief.pdf

Administration for Children and Families. (2013). *Integrating safety, permanency, and well-being for children and families in child welfare. A summary of administration on children, youth, and families projects in fiscal year 2012.* Washington, DC: U.S. Department of Health and Human Services. Retrieved from http://www.acf.hhs.gov/sites/default/files/cb/acyf_fy2012_projects_summary.pdf

Adoption and Safe Families Act of 1997, Pub. L. No. 105–89, § 107 (1997).

American Public Human Services Association. (2011). *Practice model guidance. Positioning public child welfare guidance. Strengthening families in the 21st century.* Retrieved from http://www.ppcwg.org/practice-model-overview.html

Anda, R., Butchart, A., Felitti, V., & Brown, D. (2010). Building a framework for global surveillance of the public health implications of adverse childhood experiences. *American Journal of Preventative Medicine, 39*(1), 93–98. doi: 10.1016/j.amepre.2010.03.015

Balaban, V. (2008). Assessment of children. In E. B. Foa, T. M. Keane, M. J. Friedman, & J. A. Cohen (Eds.), *Effective treatments for PTSD: Practice guidelines from the International Society for Traumatic Stress Studies* (2nd ed., pp. 62–82). New York, NY: Guilford Press.

Bartholet, E. (2009). The racial disproportionality movement in child welfare: False facts and dangerous directions. *Arizona Law Review, 51*(4), 871. Retrieved from http://dash.harvard.edu/handle/1/2887034

Bartholet, E. (2014, June). *Differential response: A dubious experiment in child welfare.* Plenary session presented at Annual Colloquium of the American Professional Society on the Abuse of Children, New Orleans, LA.

Belanger, K., Green, D. K., & Bullard, L. B. (Eds.). (2008). Special issue: Racial disproportionality in child welfare. *Child Welfare, 87*(2).

Besharov, D. (1985). Doing something about child abuse: The need to narrow the grounds for state intervention. *Harvard Journal of Law and Public Policy, 8*(3), 539–589. Retrieved from http://heinonline.org

Brittain, C., & Equibel-Hart, D. (Eds.). (2004). *Helping in child protective services: A competency-based casework handbook.* Englewood, CO: American Humane Association.

California Social Work Education Center. (Ed.). (2012). *Framework for child welfare practice in California, Version 2.0.* California Common Core Curricula for Child Welfare Workers. Berkeley, CA: Author. Retrieved from http://calswec.berkeley.edu/framework-child-welfare-practice-california-version-20

California Social Work Education Center. (Ed.). (2013). *Child maltreatment identification part two: Sexual abuse and exploitation.* California Common Core Curricula for Child Welfare Workers. Berkeley, CA: Author. Retrieved from http://calswec.berkeley.edu/child-maltreatment-identification-part-2-sexual-abuse-and-exploitation-version-125

Casey-CSSP Alliance for Racial Equity. (2006). *Places to watch: Promising practices to address racial disproportionality in child welfare services.* Retrieved from http://www.cssp.org/publications/child-welfare/top-five/places-to-watch-promising-practices-to-address-racial-disproportionality-in-child-welfare.pdf

Charlesworth, L. (2007). Child maltreatment. In E. Hutchison, H. Matto, M. Harrigan, L. Charlesworth, & P. Viggiani (Eds.), *Challenges of living: A multidimensional working model for social workers* (pp. 105-139). Thousand Oaks, CA: Sage.

Charlesworth, L. W., Wood, J., & Viggiani, P. (2013). Middle childhood. In E. D. Hutchinson (Ed.), *Essentials of human behavior: Integrating person, environment, and the life course* (pp. 501–543). Thousand Oaks, CA: Sage.

Child Welfare Information Gateway. (2011). *Addressing racial disproportionality in child welfare.* Retrieved from https://www.childwelfare.gov/pubs/issue_briefs/racial_disproportionality/racial_disproportionality.pdf

Child Welfare Information Gateway. (2013a). *Evidence-based practice.* Retrieved from https://www.childwelfare.gov/management/practice_improvement/evidence/ebp.cfm

Child Welfare Information Gateway. (2013b). *Family-centered practice.* Retrieved from https://www.childwelfare.gov/famcentered

Child Welfare Information Gateway. (2013c). *Interviewing.* Retrieved from https://www.childwelfare.gov/responding/iia/investigation/interviewing.cfm

Children's Defense Fund and Children's Rights, Inc. (2006). *Components of an effective child welfare workforce to improve outcomes for children and families: What does the research tell us? Cornerstones for kids.* Retrieved from http://www.childrensrights.org/wp-content/uploads/2008/06/components_of_effective_child_welfare_workforce_august_2006.pdf

Choi, S., & Tittle, G. (2002). Parental substance abuse and child maltreatment literature review. Retrieved September 11, 2011, from http://www.cfrc.illinois.edu/publicationslr_20020501_ParentalSubstanceAbuseAndChildMaltreatment.pdf

Clark, S. (2003). The California collaboration: A competency-based child welfare curriculum project for master's social works. *Journal of Human Behavior in the Social Environment, 7*(1–2), 135–157.

Cohen, J., & Mannarino, A. (2008). Trauma-focused cognitive behavioral therapy for children and parents. *Child and Adolescent Mental Health, 13*(4), 162–185.

D'Andrade, A., Frame, L., & Duerr-Berrick, J. (2006). Concurrent planning in public child welfare agencies: Oxymoron or work in progress? *Children and Youth Services Review, 28*(1), 78–95.

Derezotes, D. M., Poertner, J., & Testa, M. F. (Eds.). (2005). *Race matters in child welfare: The overrepresentation of African American children in the system.* Washington, DC: Child Welfare League of America.

Farkas, B. (2004). Etiology and pathogenesis of PTSD in children and adolescents. In R. R. Silva (Ed.), *Posttraumatic stress disorders in children and adolescents* (pp. 123–140). New York, NY: Norton.

Farmer, R. (2009). *Neuroscience and social work practice: The missing link.* Thousand Oaks, CA: Sage.

Figley, C. (2012). Secondary trauma. In C. Figley (Ed.), *Encyclopedia of trauma: An interdisciplinary guide.* Thousand Oaks, CA: Sage.

Fixen, L. D., Naoom, F. S., Blasé, A. K., Friedman, M. R., & Wallace, F. (2008). *Implementation research: A synthesis of the literature.* Retrieved from http://nirn.fpg.unc.edu/sites/nirn.fpg.unc.edu/files/resources/NIRN-MonographFull-01–2005.pdf

Flanagan, A. Y. (2012). *Child abuse in ethnic minority and immigrant communities.* Sacramento, CA: CME Resource. Retrieved from http://www.netce.com/coursecontent.php?courseid=861

Fontes, L. A. (2005). *Child abuse and culture: Working with diverse families.* New York, NY: Guilford Press.

Fontes, L. A. (2007). Sin verguenza: Addressing shame with Latino victims of child sexual abuse and their families. *Journal of Child Sexual Abuse, 16*(1), 61–83.

Friend, C. (2012). Contributions to social work and child welfare by APSAC. Invited commentary for special 25 year anniversary issue. *APSAC Advisor, 1–2.*

Hill, R. B. (2005). *Overrepresentation of children of color in foster care in 2000.* Rockville, MD: Race Matters Consortium. Retrieved from www.racemattersconsortium.org/docs/whopaper7.pdf

Hill, R. B. (2006). *Synthesis of research on disproportionality in child welfare: An update.* CSSP-Casey Alliance for Racial Equity. Retrieved from http://www.cssp.org/reform/child-welfare/other-resources/synthesis-of-research-on-disproportionality-robert-hill.pdf

Hohman, M. (2013, September 13). Cultural humility: A lifelong practice [Web log comment]. Retrieved from https://socialwork.sdsu.edu/insitu/diversity/cultural-humility-a-lifelong-practice

Hutchison, E. D. (2013). *Essentials of human behavior: Integrating person, environment, and the life course.* Thousand Oaks, CA: Sage.

Independent Child Death Review Panel for Clark County Nevada. (2006). *Report of findings and recommendations: Child deaths 2001–2004.* Retrieved from http://dcfs.nv.gov/uploadedFiles/dcfsnvgov/content/Tips/Reports/Attachment04b.pdf

Kauffman Best Practices Project to Help Children Heal From Child Abuse. (2004). *Closing the quality chasm in child abuse treatment: Identifying and disseminating best practices.* Retrieved from http://www.chadwickcenter.org/Documents/Kaufman%20Report/ChildHosp-NCTAbrochure.pdf

Lamb, M. E., La Rooy, D. J., Malloy, L. C., & Katz, C. (Eds.). (2011). *Appendix: The National Institute of Child Health and Human Development (NICHD) protocol: Interview guide, in children's testimony: A handbook of psychological research and forensic practice.* Chichester, UK: John Wiley & Sons.

Lanktree, C. B., & Briere, J. (2013). Integrative treatment of complex trauma (ITCT) for children and adolescents. In J. D. Ford & C. A. Courtois, *Treating complex traumatic stress disorders with children and adolescents: An evidence-based guide* (pp. 143–161). New York, NY: Guilford Press.

Los Angeles County Blue Ribbon Commission on Child Protection. (2014). *The road to safety for our children.* Retrieved from http://ceo.lacounty.gov/pdf/brc/BRCCP_Final_Report_April_18_2014.pdf

Magruder, J., & Shaw, T. (2008). Children ever in care: An examination of cumulative disproportionality. *Child Welfare, 87*(2), 169–188.

McRoy, R. G. (2005). Overrepresentation of children and youth of color in foster care. In G. P. Mallon & P. McCartt- Hess (Eds.), *Child welfare for the 21st century: A handbook of practices, policies, and programs* (pp. 623–634). New York, NY: Columbia University Press.

Meltzer, J., Joseph, R. M., & Shookhoff, A. (2012). Introduction and preview. In J. Meltzer, R. M. Joseph, & A. Shookhoff (Eds.), *For the welfare of children: Lessons learned from class action and litigation.* Retrieved from http://files.eric.ed.gov/fulltext/ED536815.pdf

Mor Barak, M. E., Levin, A., Nissly, J. A., & Lane, C. J. (2006). Why do they leave? Modeling child welfare workers' turnover intentions. *Children and Youth Services Review, 28,* 548–577.

Mumpower, J. (2010). Disproportionality at the front end of the child welfare services system: An analysis of rates of referrals, hits, misses, and false alarms. *Journal of Health and Human Services Administration, 33*(3), 364–405.

National Association of Social Workers. (2008). *Code of ethics of the National Association of Social Workers.* Retrieved from http://www.socialworkers.org/pubs/code/code.asp

National Child Welfare Resource Center for Organizational Improvement. (2012). *Child welfare matters.* Retrieved from http://muskie.usm.maine.edu/helpkids/rcpdfs/cwmatters11.pdf

Needell, B., Webster, D., Armijo, M., Lee, S., Dawson, W., Magruder, J., Exel, M., . . . Henry, C. (2011). *Child* welfare services reports for California. Retrieved from http://cssr.berkeley.edu/ucb_childwelfare

Newell, J. M., & McNeil, G. A. (2010). Professional burnout, vicarious trauma, secondary traumatic stress, and compassion fatigue: A review of theoretical terms, risk factors, and preventive methods for clinicians and researchers. *Best Practice in Mental Health, 6*(2), 57–68.

Office on Child Abuse and Neglect. (2006a). *Child neglect: A guide for prevention, assessment and intervention.* Retrieved from https://www.childwelfare.gov/pubs/usermanuals/neglect/neglect.pdf

Office on Child Abuse and Neglect. (2006b). *Working with courts in child protection.* Retrieved from https://www.childwelfare.gov/pubs/usermanuals/courts/courts.pdf

Ortega, R. M., & Coulborn-Faller, K. (2011). Training child welfare workers from an intersectional cultural humility perspective: A paradigm shift. *Child Welfare, 90*(5), 27–49.

Pence, D., & Wilson, C. (1992). *The role of law enforcement in response to child abuse and neglect.* Retrieved from https://www.childwelfare.gov/pubs/usermanuals/law/index.cfm

Perez, A. (2010). *Policy analysis proposal regarding the Indian Child Welfare Act of 1978.* Retrieved from http://pqdtopen.proquest.com/doc/757011611.html?FMT=AI

Perry, B. (2003). *Effects of traumatic events on childhood: An introduction.* Retrieved from http://www.mentalhealthconnection.org/pdfs/perry-handout-effects-of-trauma.pdf

Reed, D., & Karpilow, K. (2009). *Understanding the child welfare system in California: A primer for service providers and policy makers.* Retrieved from http://www.ccrwf.org/wp-content/uploads/2009/03/final_web_pdf.pdf

Sedlak, A. J., & Broadhurst, D. D. (1996). *Executive summary of the third national incidence study of child abuse and neglect.* Retrieved from www.childwelfare.gov/pubs/statsinfo/nis3.cfm

Sedlak, A. J., McPherson, K., & Das, B. (2010). *Supplementary analyses of race differences in child maltreatment rates in the NIS–4.* Washington, DC: U.S. Department of Health and Human Services. Retrieved from www.acf.hhs.gov/programs/ opre/abuse neglect/natl incid/nis4_supp_analysis_race_diff_mar2010.pdf

Shlonsky, A., & Friend, C. (2007). Double jeopardy: Risk assessment in the context of child maltreatment and domestic violence. In A. R. Roberts & D. W. Springer (Eds.), *Handbook of forensic mental health with victims and offenders.* New York, NY: Thomas.

Sue, D. W. (2005). Racism and the conspiracy of silence. *Counseling Psychologist, 33,* 100–114.

Sue, D. W., Capodiluop, C. M., Torino, G. C., Bucceri, J. M., Holder, A. M. B., Nadal, L, & Esquilin, M. (2007). Racial microaggressions in everyday life: Implications for clinical practice. *American Psychologist, 62*(4), 271–286.

Tervalon, M., & Murray-Garcia, J. (1998). Cultural humility versus cultural competence: A critical distinction in defining physician training outcomes in multicultural education. *Journal of Health Care for the Poor and Underserved, 9*(2), 117–125.

U.S. Department of Health and Human Services, Administration for Children and Families, Children's Bureau. (2012). *Child maltreatment 2011.* Retrieved from http://www.acf.hhs.gov/programs/cb/research-data-technology/statistics-research/child-maltreatment

U.S. Department of Justice, Office of Justice Programs. (2014). *Law enforcement response to child abuse.* Retrieved from http://www.ojjdp.gov/pubs/243907.pdf

U.S. General Accounting Office. (2003). *Child welfare: HHS could play a greater role in helping child welfare agencies recruit and retain staff.* Retrieved from http://www.gao.gov/new.items/d03357.pdf

U.S. General Accounting Office. (2008). *African American children in foster care: HHS and congressional action could help reduce proportion in care.* Retrieved from http://www.gao.gov/new.items/d081064t.pdf

Weaver, D., Chang, J., Clark, S., & Rhee, S. (2007) Keeping public child welfare workers on the job. *Administration in Social Work, 3*(12), 5–25.

Wells, S. J., Merritt, L. M., & Briggs, H. E. (2009). Bias, racism and evidence-based practice: The case for more focused development of the child welfare evidence base. *Children & Youth Services Review, 31*(11), 1160–1171.

Zastrow, C. H., & Kirst-Ashman, K. K. (2012). *Understanding human behavior and the social environment* (9th ed.). Belmont, CA: Thomson Learning.

CHAPTER 15

Lifespan Perspective With Developmental Disabilities

Barbara Y. Wheeler, Amy D. Lyle, Catherine K. Arnold, Marian E. Williams, Karen Kay Imagawa, & Min Ah Kim

CHAPTER OBJECTIVES

- Articulate five core principles underlying services provided to individuals with developmental disabilities and their families;
- Describe and discuss three areas of assessment that may be needed when serving individuals with developmental disabilities, including the multiple components of family assessment when a family has a child with a developmental disability;
- Describe the structure of group work in the developmental disabilities field;
- Define the role of the social worker at the micro, mezzo, and macro levels of practice in addressing the needs of individuals with developmental disabilities and their families across the lifespan within the continuously changing social, economic, and demographic factors that impact public services.

CASE VIGNETTE

Naomi was the product of a full-term pregnancy, the second child of an Asian couple who had been trying to have another child for more than five years. Both parents were born in Asia and are in the United States on a permanent visa. Naomi's father came to California to go to school and continued to work for an American subsidiary of the company he worked for where he was born. After finishing school, he started his own business in advertising and travels to Asia regularly. He is the sole source of income for the family. Naomi's mother went to college in her birth country and worked until she started having children. Naomi's mother recalled her distress in the delivery room when Naomi didn't cry right away and a nurse asked her whether she had smoked or taken drugs during her pregnancy. A heart murmur was noted on the first day of life, and Naomi was discharged after two days with a referral for a cardiology consult. Her mother recalled, "On the way back home I started crying. My breast was hard, Naomi didn't feed well. My milk stopped. When I got Naomi home, she started turning blue and had difficulty breathing. They taught me to push her legs up when this happened. I don't know how I survived those days." After corrective surgery for a congenital heart defect, Naomi was still not able to hold up her head at 3 months of age and did not respond to loud sounds. When Naomi's mother communicated her concern about Naomi's delayed development to her pediatrician, she was reassured that delayed development was not unusual in children with heart defects, but Naomi's development continued to be a concern for her mother.

Naomi's mother eventually contacted her Lamaze instructor who she remembered also had a baby with a heart defect and learned about early intervention programs. At 8 months of age, Naomi began receiving Early Intervention (EI) services in a home-based program and later transitioned to a center-based program until 22 months of age. Naomi was in preschool when she had her first formal diagnostic assessment and was found to qualify for special education services based on a diagnosis of intellectual disability. The news was difficult, but both parents hoped she would catch up over time. When Naomi's mother observed her at school, she noted that Naomi seemed lost in class and she played by herself on the playground. Feeling the system was not responsive to her concerns, Naomi's mother began attending parent education and advocacy trainings. Although activism was not part of her cultural make-up, she learned much from other parents she met at trainings and support groups. She was nominated to attend the Partners in Policymaking program, a national training program for parents and adults with developmental disabilities to participate in shaping policy and the legislative process, which further launched her comfort and skills with advocacy. Three years later, Naomi's mother started a parent education and support group for Asian-speaking parents of children with disabilities.

During this time, Naomi's 12-year-old brother became increasingly bothered that he didn't see his mother as much as he used to, and he missed going to sporting events with his Dad and seeing his friends because he was expected to watch Naomi. He knew his parents counted on him to help out at home and remembered how his mother used to cry when she thought no one was around, so he thought it best to keep his worries to himself. He kept telling himself this wouldn't be forever.

When Naomi turned 18, she walked across the stage at graduation with the rest of her class, having earned a special diploma based on achieving her IEP goals. Her brother came home from graduate school to celebrate this important event. After graduation, Naomi, with the assistance and support of school transition staff, got a part-time paid employment experience at a nearby restaurant filling condiments, sorting silverware, and wiping down menus. The customers and her co-workers really enjoyed Naomi. During the afternoons she spent her free time at school with a male classmate from her life skills class. Transition program staff referred to him as Naomi's "boyfriend," which made her parents uncomfortable. The staff recommended that Naomi participate in a workshop about relationships, which included information about sexuality. Her parents had never considered the possibility of Naomi having an adult relationship with a peer.

INTRODUCTION

It is estimated that approximately 15% of the world's population (more than 1 billion people) live with some form of disability and, regardless of their country of residence, experience lower levels of health, education, employment, and income than people without disabilities (World Health Organization and the World Bank, 2011). Historical treatment of people with disabilities ranged from genocide to placement in large congregate institutions, segregated from society and vulnerable to abuse, neglect, and victimization (Hayden, 1997). In the United States, exposés of inhumane, sometimes horrific treatment in state institutions became a catalyst for organizing families and advocates to press for reform. Known as the deinstitutionalization movement, this steady, mounting effort continues today to close institutions and serve people with disabilities in the community (Parish & Lutwick, 2005). Over a 40-year period, the population of large institutions decreased by almost 75%, from 228,500 individuals residing in institutions in 1967 to 59,312 in 2008 (Lakin, Larson, Salmi, & Webster, 2010). In parallel fashion, the numbers of individuals living in the community increased from 78,173 to 321,025 (Salmi, Scott, Webster, Larson, & Lakin, 2010). Social workers have been prominent in facilitating these transitions and powering social change in the disability movement (Mary, 1998); however, with progress also comes new and emerging challenges and opportunities where social workers are again key players.

This chapter focuses on individuals with developmental disabilities (DD) and their need for lifelong, frequently complex supports and services. The skills, competence, and leadership of social workers are needed at the micro, mezzo, and macro levels of practice to support individuals with DD as the barriers to accessing quality services are many, available resources may be scarce, and the needs of individuals change as new opportunities for full participation in community life become available and as they age. A "developmental disability" is defined by the Developmental Disabilities Assistance and Bill of Rights Act of 2000 (DD Act) as a disability that is attributable to a mental or physical impairment, manifests before the age of 22, is expected to continue indefinitely, results in substantial functional limitations in three or more major life activities (i.e., self-care, receptive and expressive language, learning, mobility, self-direction, capacity for independent living, and/or economic self-sufficiency), and requires services or supports for an extended duration. It is estimated that 4.6 million Americans, roughly 1.5% of the population, has a DD (Larson et al., 2001). Common conditions include intellectual disabilities (formerly called mental retardation), cerebral palsy and other neuro-motor and/or mobility impairments, autism spectrum disorders, severe behavioral disorders, and certain genetic or chromosomal conditions. State laws can vary in criteria for eligibility for publicly funded programs and how services for individuals with DD are organized, funded, and delivered.

Disability is a broad term inclusive of an array of disabilities that manifest in ways that interfere with the individual's ability to engage in activities of daily living. Root causes of these disabilities include genetic disorders, perinatal factors and events, accidental or intentional trauma or injury, and environmental factors (e.g., lead ingestion from paint causing brain damage or lack of stimulation; Batshaw, Pelligrino, & Roizen, 2007).

DISABILITY NORMS, VALUES, AND PRINCIPLES

Fueled by a strong advocacy movement originally started by parents of children with DD and disability advocates in reaction to historical discrimination and exclusion of individuals with DD from public education and/or placed in large institutions, current service systems are shaped by the following core values and philosophical approaches, which are embedded in federal legislation and should be reflected in all levels of social work practice.

Choice, autonomy, independence, productivity, and responsibility (DD Act, 2000) describe the broad goals the system holds for people with DD. Each individual has a right to make *choices* about his or her life that are free of the undue influence of others (*autonomy* and *independence*). For those individuals who have severe intellectual disabilities, this value obliges the system to make every effort to provide opportunities for choices, ranging from where the person chooses to live to whether he can pick Jell-O or fruit for dessert. *Productivity* acknowledges the potential for all people to contribute to the civic and social activities of their chosen community. Reflecting this shifting value, national priorities are focusing on competitive employment and real jobs for people with disabilities—a sharp departure from sheltered workshops and day programs of times past (Office of Disability Employment Policy, 2013). *Responsibility* refers to a person's accountability for his or her actions and choices. If an individual chooses Jell-O for dessert and doesn't like it, he cannot throw it across the table in anger.

Community inclusion refers to the preference that individuals with disabilities receive services that support their participation in all aspects of community life, in contrast to serving and supporting them in segregated settings where they are only with other people with disabilities.

Least restrictive environment (LRE) refers to an individual's right to be served in environments which have the fewest constraints ("least restrictive") and are the most normalized (i.e., in the same settings where people without disabilities receive services; Pacer Center, 2009). Over time, LRE has become a core principle of all major disability legislation and argued in case law. For example, it was the key legal argument for the 1999 Olmstead Decision (*Olmstead v. L. C.*, 1999), which held that placing people with disabilities in a nursing home as their primary residence was a violation of their rights to be served in the "least restrictive environment."

Family-centered care refers to (1) seeing the family as the constant thread in the child's life and acknowledging the "expertise" of the family in the intimate details of the child's strengths, needs, and preferences, (2) actively seeking family input on perceived needs and proposed interventions, (3) responding to family concerns using a strengths-based, individualized approach, and (4) collaborating with families as equal partners in the planning, implementation, and evaluation of services (Family Voices, n.d.).

Person-centered planning is a process that empowers the individual with a DD to exercise "self-determination" by (1) placing the person at the center of the decision-making process, (2) providing information and support to assist the individual to make informed choices about their life (such as going to school, getting a job, or a change in residence), and participating in decisions regarding the type of services they will receive and who will provide them (Falvey, Forest, Pearpoint, & Rosenberg, 1997; O'Brien & Lyle O'Brien, 1998; Wehmeyer, 1998; see Person-Centered Planning under Internet Resources, on p. 215). These values reflect a paradigm shift that sees the "person" first and his or her potential, rather than his or her disability.

MICRO PERSPECTIVE: SERVING INDIVIDUALS WITH DD AND THEIR FAMILIES

Assessment

Early research on family adjustment to the birth of a child with a disability was likened to a grieving process (i.e., the loss of the dreamed-for child). Parental responses described in the literature included shock, helplessness, hopelessness, disappointment, denial, depression, guilt, anger, and shame. Some argued that feelings of "chronic sorrow" would be lifelong (Sen & Yurtserver, 2007; Wittert, 2002). In contrast, recent research has confirmed parents still report stress raising their child with a disability, but only a minority of them report adverse psychological, social, or familial outcomes, possibly reflecting the growing availability of community-based DD services and supports and changing societal views of the human potential of every individual regardless of the presence of a disability. Research in the U.S., Australia, Korea, Canada, and Europe has documented reports by parents and family members of the positive transformative benefits of having a family member with a disability, including stronger spousal/partner bonds, increased sensitivity to socially disenfranchised people, and insight about what is important in life (Scorgie, Wilgosh, & Sobsey, 2004). The family life management framework in contemporary social work practice which emphasizes family strengths and resilience as the norm is in full alignment with this paradigm shift, and is supported by research that demonstrates the important role parents can play as interventionists for their children (Dykens, Fisher, Taylor, Lambert, & Miodrag, 2014).

Family Assessment

At the time of the passage of the Support for Families of Children with Disabilities Act of 1994 (Part I of P.L. 103-3821), most states had already adopted legislation mandating family support services for families who have children with significant needs (Agosta & Melda, 1996). A family assessment utilizes a systems and ecological perspective to determine (1) the level of the family's understanding of the child's disability, (2) the strengths and needs of the child with a disability, all family members, and the family as a unit, (3) sources and perceived adequacy of the family's formal and informal network of services and supports (i.e., financial, material, social and emotional support) and (4) the family's capacity to advocate for the needs of the family member with a disability and the entire family (Agosta & Melda, 1996).

The family assessment and intervention process is key to unravelling how disability is viewed, familiarity and comfort with evidence-based practices, and capacity to navigate service systems (Gannotti, Kaplan, Handwerker, & Groce, 2004; Harrington & Kang, 2008; Mandell et al., 2009). Cultural differences, socioeconomic status and literacy levels may require alternative methods of soliciting information for the family assessment. An effective method called "narrative" interviewing has been used in research and also in clinical settings to capture "illness and disability" narratives (Mattingly & Garro, 2000). Unlike semi-structured interviews, which are focused on the linear collection of facts, narrative interviewing seeks to elicit stories about the experiences and perceptions of individuals using an unstructured conversational process. The stories elicited frequently reveal the personal and cultural meaning of information sought, such as perceptions of what is at stake and the motives, intentions, and desires that drive the actions of key family members (Mattingly & Garro, 2000; Mattingly & Lawlor, 2000). Much of the description in Naomi's vignette came from utilizing this approach with her mother.

Sibling Assessment

Siblings within a family have the potential to greatly impact each other's lives (McHale & Gamble, 1987; Seligman & Darling, 1997). Because the relationship between siblings will likely outlast the relationship each individual has with his or her parents by 20 years or more (Cicirelli, 1995) and is a potentially important resource in the long-term care and support of individuals with DD (Arnold, Heller, & Kramer, 2012), the nature and quality of sibling relationships represent an important component of the family assessment that should not be ignored.

Recent research on the needs and experiences of siblings of children with disabilities have found they are more engaged in caregiving tasks than their peers whose siblings do not have disabilities. Moreover, younger siblings have caregiving responsibilities for their older sibling with a disability more frequently than similar-age peers (Stoneman, 2001), a responsibility some question as possibly developmentally inappropriate. There is growing evidence that the needs of siblings may be overshadowed by their brother/sister with a disability, and as family members, siblings also have needs throughout the life cycle of the family. In the early years, siblings have expressed the need for information about their sibling's disability, how to interact with their sibling successfully, and how to respond to questions by their peers about their sibling with a disability (Arnold et al., 2012). They also wonder what their parents are feeling, what their parents expect of them, and how they can help their family (Gallagher, Powell, & Rhodes, 2006), issues raised in the case vignette by Naomi's brother.

As they get older, siblings report having to forego opportunities to spend time with their friends and attending after-school activities in order to meet their caregiving responsibilities more often than their peers (Stoneman, Brody, Davis, & Crapps, 1988).

But like Naomi's brother, not all siblings feel comfortable vocalizing these feelings. Sibling rivalry is a natural phenomenon in families (Banks & Kahn, 1997) and similarly reported in sibling relationships when one sibling has a disability (Stoneman et al., 1988). However, perceptions of a lack of fairness in family expectations have been documented, such as more lenient expectations of the sibling with a disability, which can be aggravated by having to forego personal social opportunities because of caregiving responsibilities (Meyer & Vadasy, 1994). In adulthood, siblings have reported concerns about continued expectations for caregiving of their adult sibling with a disability when they are trying to start their own families (Evans, Jones, & Mansell, 2001)—a conversation which is now influenced by the addition of a prospective new member of the family, their spouse/partner. The impacts of having a sibling with a disability (personal, social, and academic) and the common expectation of caregiving responsibilities that accompany their sibling role should be part of the family assessment. Open family conversations should be encouraged to maintain the social and emotional health of the family as a unit, in addition to the health of each family member. If not managed well, sibling development and their evolving attitudes toward their caregiving responsibilities may be negatively impacted as families move through the life cycle. The Sibling Need and Involvement Profile (SNIP; Senner & Fish, 2012) is a tool designed to assess the needs of siblings of people with DD and their current involvement.

In the case vignette, Naomi's older brother keeps his concerns to himself, and he could benefit from peer support to have a space to share his feelings with other siblings. Social workers can provide information to families about the importance of peer support opportunities for siblings throughout the lifecourse, beginning in their early years through adulthood. The more support siblings receive, the more likely they will remain involved in the support of their brothers and sisters with disabilities, especially as parents age and sibling caregiving roles transition. Anticipating this, social workers can encourage families to regularly have an ongoing dialogue about the future where all members of the family have a voice in the discussion and a choice in their potential role in the future using resources and information available about planning. (See Sibling Resources in the Internet Resources section on p. 215)

Screening and Assessment of Abuse, Neglect, and Victimization

Child maltreatment is a familiar issue for social workers because it occurs across all socioeconomic groups and in every community. Studies have reported that children with a disability are 1.7 to 3.4 times more likely to be victims of abuse or neglect than children without a disability (Sullivan & Knutson, 2000; U.S. Department of Health and Human Services, 2006), and they often experience multiple forms of maltreatment. Risk factors for the general population (e.g., poverty, parental substance abuse, violence in the home, social isolation, parental lack of knowledge of child development) also apply to children with disabilities. Because increased caregiver stress and/or frustration for families of children with disabilities have been found to be correlated with unmet medical, equipment, educational, and behavioral support needs (Sullivan & Cork, 1996), social workers should assess these areas during the family assessment and, as appropriate, assist families to coordinate, advocate for, and secure needed services.

Adults with DD are 2 to 4 times more likely to be victims of sexual or physical assault, robbery, fiduciary abuse, and/or neglect and may be especially vulnerable to interpersonal violence because they may not recognize danger, may not be able to protect themselves verbally or physically, and may be less inclined to resist unwanted behaviors because they are dependent on others for food, shelter, personal care and social interaction (Morrison et al., 2003; Petersilia, 2001). These contextual variables can lead to what has been called "social compliance" or "agreeing just to get along." Predatory offenders are skilled in playing on the vulnerability of people with disabilities to assure the silence of their victims, using strategies such as threatening that no one will believe them, that other workers at the home will get mad at them if the victim reports the abuse, or that the victim will have to leave their home and move to an institution if they make trouble (Morrison et al., 2003; Petersilia, 2001). A social worker's role as a mandated reporter in abuse cases of children and adults with DD is no different than her role working with the general population. Reports are made to the Child Welfare system (sometimes called Child Protective Services) or Adult Protective Services, social service programs provided by municipalities nationwide to serve children, seniors, and adults with disabilities who are in need of assistance. (See the section on Abuse, Neglect, and Victimization under Internet Resources.)

In the vignette, there were several junctures that might increase the risk for abuse. At birth, Naomi's mother indicated feeling distressed going home to care for an infant with medical problems. Social workers can intervene by assessing for postpartum depression and/or other psychosocial stressors, such as mother's potential feelings of limited social support, feelings of frustration, and isolation. By disability status, children with behavior disorders have been found to be at highest risk for abuse followed by those with speech/language disorders and intellectual disabilities, such as Naomi (Sullivan et al., 2000). If ignored, these feelings can escalate and increase the risk for potential child abuse. In early childhood, Naomi began receiving early intervention and other services involving more caregivers, which increased the opportunity for abuse or if caregivers are well trained, they could provide the advantage of more eyes to recognize signs of abuse. When Naomi reached adulthood, adult relationships and sexuality became a focus of dialogue and conversation. At this developmental juncture, social workers have the opportunity to advocate for programs that strengthen the adult's life skills and early teaching on normal sexual feelings and to educate the family and Naomi about staying safe when exploring new relationships.

Behavioral and Mental Health Assessment for Individuals With DD

Individuals with DD are two to four times more likely to have a co-occurring mental health condition than typically-developing individuals (Dekker, Koot, van der Ende, & Verhulst, 2002; Emerson, Einfeld, & Stancliff, 2010). The National Association for the Dually Diagnosed (NADD) provides education, advocacy and research to address the needs of this population. While some of the most common co-occurring mental health conditions include anxiety and disruptive behavior disorders, the full range of psychopathology exists in this population. The *Diagnostic Manual–Intellectual Disability* (Fletcher, Loschen, Stavrakaki, & First, 2007) provides criteria for mental health diagnoses contained in the *Diagnostic and Statistical Manual of Mental Disorders* (American Psychiatric Association, 2013), which has been adapted for individuals with intellectual disability. Many evidence-based treatments for mental health disorders have been found to be effective with individuals with DD (McIntyre & Abbeduto, 2008; Suveg, Comer, Furr, & Kendall, 2006). An important component of intervention is identifying possible reasons an individual with DD might exhibit challenging behaviors, including frustration associated with lack of functional communication, physical illness, loneliness, and unidentified abuse.

In the vignette, Naomi was described as playing by herself on the playground and seeming lost in class. A social worker could complete a mental health assessment to identify possible contributing factors to these difficulties (e.g., social anxiety or difficulty reading social cues). Instituting a prevention program would keep these underlying factors from escalating and leading to more severe mental health issues, requiring a higher level of intervention.

Diversity Considerations

Findings of racial, ethnic, and linguistic disparities and inequities have been found in studies of individuals who utilize every major public service system (i.e., health care, developmental disabilities, mental health, special education, and long-term care services; Bui & Takeuchi, 1992; Cauce et al., 2002; Kuhlthau, Nyman, Ferris, Beal, & Perrin, 2004; McCallion, Janicki, & Grant-Griffin, 1997;

Pruncho & McMullen, 2004; Ronsaville & Hakim, 2000; Weech-Maldonado, Morales, Spritzer, Elliott, & Hays, 2001). Using secondary data analysis of California's large public-use DD database, Harrington and Kang (2008) found African Americans, Asians and Pacific Islanders, Hispanics, and individuals from racial or ethnic groups other than non-Hispanic white had significantly lower odds (23% to 31% lower) of receiving any DD services through California's 21 regional centers, after controlling for need, age, and Medicaid status. For those who did receive services, regional center expenditures to purchase needed services for Hispanics, Asian/Pacific Islanders and African Americans were lower ($,3190 to $1,080 respectively) than was spent on non-Hispanic white clients. In a compelling article in the Los Angeles Times entitled *Warrior Parents Fare Best in Securing Autism Services* (Zarembo, 2011), investigative report Alan Zarembo reported that one potential reason for disparities in California's regional center system is the difference among parents who know how to strongly advocate for their children; not surprisingly the majority of these "warrior" parents were white middle class.

At the micro level, there were a number of examples of cultural differences surfacing throughout Naomi's life. Early on when Naomi's mother shared her concern about Naomi's delayed development to her pediatrician, she kept silent (not questioning authority) when she was told that this was normal for a child with a congenital heart defect and her instincts said otherwise. When Naomi was in school and her mother noticed her daughter seemed lost in class and played by herself on the playground, the response of school personnel was limited, but her mother did not feel comfortable advocating for a change of placement or additional services. When Naomi's brother showed subtle signs of difficulty in adolescence, these were missed because of the assumption of her culture that all the family members had a duty to help Naomi. The social worker has a critical role in helping to unravel the dissonance between service system values and the cultural values of its users. The strategy, narrative storytelling, identified earlier under the family assessment section,

is an excellent method for social workers working with Naomi's family to identify how their Asian culture impacted how they saw Naomi's disability, their understanding of what services they were entitled to and their comfort level using those services, how to navigate the system so they go the services they felt Naomi needed, and how to participate in the formal process used by schools, DD and other systems when they disagreed with what they were being offered. For many first generation families, this path of acculturation to the service system can take many years and specialized interventions (such as belonging to an ethnic focus parent support group) in order to address these culture-specific needs.

Intervention

Early Intervention

Part C of the Individuals with Disabilities Education Act (U.S. Department of Education, n.d.) provides grants to states and territories to implement a coordinated system of early intervention (EI) for infant and toddlers (0–2 years) who are at risk of having substantial developmental delays if intervention is not provided. Key to these programs is the assessment of the physical, cognitive, communication, social-emotional, and adaptive developmental needs of children 0–2 years, which informs the development and implementation of an Individualized Family Service Plan (IFSP) facilitated by the family's service coordinator, a role often held by a social worker. Services in the IFSP include but are not limited to special instruction, speech therapy, occupational therapy, physical therapy, psychological services, and family education and counseling. EI programs have been successful in assisting large number of children to avoid the need for special education or other special services once they are school age. Those identified with long-term service needs have been assisted to transition smoothly into special education and other service systems for which the child is eligible. Although Part C or Early Intervention grants are discretionary, every state operates an early intervention program. States vary in the designated state agency that administers this program (e.g., the state education agency, the state health and human services agency, or the state DD agency) and the names of EI programs vary across states (e.g., Early Intervention, Birth to Three, Early Start). There are numerous parent and family resources at the local, state, and national level. Social workers can play key roles in linking children and families with early intervention services and parent support and advocacy programs. Naomi's involvement in early intervention services from 8 to 22 months helped her to get an early start in addressing her developmental needs and to ensure that she was linked with preschool special education services. As was evident in our case vignette, Naomi's mother's connection to parent education, advocacy, and support resources in the community was life altering. (See Family Information and Support Programs under Internet Resources.)

Individuals With DD and Co-Occurring Mental Health Disorders

When an individual exhibits disruptive, aggressive, or self-injurious behaviors, a functional behavioral assessment is essential to carefully identify the antecedents of the concerning behaviors, the context in which the behaviors occur, and the factors that may be maintaining the behaviors in order to develop an effective behavioral intervention plan (Cipani & Schock, 2010). The functional behavioral assessment leads to a positive behavior support plan which is implemented in the school, in the home, and/or in the community, to reduce the disruptive behaviors and enable participation in meaningful community activities. (See Co-Occurring Mental Health Disorders under Internet Resources.)

Anxiety is commonly seen in individuals with DD, especially those with autism spectrum disorders. The most widely researched effective intervention for anxiety is cognitive-behavior therapy (CBT), which has also been shown to be effective with individuals with DD. In particular, the Coping Cat program shows promise for treating children with DD experiencing anxiety (Kendall & Hedtke, 2006). Some modifications that make CBT more effective

for those with DD include (1) spending more time teaching clients to recognize and interpret emotions (Anderson & Morris, 2006), (2) increasing the use of visual aids (White et al., 2010), (3) focusing on the behavioral aspects of the treatment (e.g. practicing coping skills such as relaxation during exposure therapy; Wood et al., 2009), and (4) increasing sibling/family involvement to encourage practice of new skills at home (Lang, Regester, Lauderdale, Ashbaugh, & Haring, 2010).

In the case of Naomi, a social worker could provide mental health consultation or intervention in the preschool setting to help increase her interactions with peers and development of friendships. For example, coaching Naomi in strategies to initiate social overtures could be effective in increasing her positive social interactions. An innovative mental health intervention social workers could use involves training peers to be "friendship ambassadors" who reach out to individuals who seem to be left out, rather than focusing on the individuals with disabilities themselves (Kasari, Rotheram-Fuller, Locke, & Gulsrud, 2012).

Transition to Adulthood: The Tension Between Independence and Risk

When a young person with DD reaches age 16, she or he begins an educational process called "transition" under special education law (U.S. Department of Education, Office of Special Education, 2007a, 2007b), which deliberately focuses on promoting greater independence, autonomy, and movement into adulthood, so that students with DD are prepared for adult life and accessing adult service systems when they leave high school. Some students leave high school with their general education peers at 18 years of age if they are graduating with a high school diploma. Others may continue to receive special education services up to 22 years of age, consistent with their alternative educational plan. During transition, youth and young adults learn to start identifying goals they want for their lives and how to achieve these. Goals should include all aspects of the youth's life including employment, community inclusion, health, independent living, housing and, increasingly post-secondary and college experiences. (See Transition Resources under Internet Resources.)

Key to learning the skills and knowledge to move into adulthood is the concept of self-determination, which refers to an individual participating actively in defining what she or he wants to do and how to get there. At the core of this concept is the belief that learning through experience is part of learning to determine aspects of your life, even when the individual might make mistakes. Some families believe the potential for harm associated with individuals making their own decisions is greater for their child with a disability because of compromises in their judgment about people and situations, a greater tendency to follow a persuasive individual, and worries about predators who may target people with disabilities because of these vulnerabilities, which has validity if there is no intervention to compensate for these behaviors. This can be more common for families who may come from other cultures and have less experience with their child's successful involvement with the mainstream system. As already noted, social workers are key to creating an open dialogue between these families and the service system. The introduction of increasingly challenging daily life experiences must be well thought through, rehearsed, with appropriate safety nets, with ultimate buy-in from diverse families who may have concerns. Social workers who use their negotiation skills with a sensitivity to cultural differences will be more likely to achieve meaningful buy-in. Exposure to "risks" should be developmentally appropriate, and culturally neutral, with each new decision or experience incrementally built on previous successes. Ideally, the child/youth who has the supports of their immediate family and/or extended circle, will have access to training and supported experiences to acquire the knowledge, skills, and experience to navigate difficult and unpredictable situations, building the individual's capacity to move into adult life.

Sexuality and Relationships

Although sexuality is a natural part of the human experience (Baxley & Zendell, 2005),

individuals with DD have been and continue to be denied sexual rights and expression (American Association on Intellectual and Developmental Disabilities, 2008; Hafner, 2005; Kempton & Kahn, 1991). The notable absence of direct, developmentally appropriate instruction about healthy sexual expression and the more nuanced social dynamics of intimate relationships (Eddy, 2007; Graham, Nelis, Sandman, Arnold, & Parker, 2011; Hafner, 2005) perpetuates this problem. With the requirement for the "least restrictive environment" in school, students with disabilities should have access to the same sex education classes available to their general education peers. Special education personnel should monitor these sessions and provide additional training to ensure that students with disabilities understood what was being taught in these sessions and have opportunities to apply and practice what is learned.

Naomi's family opted out of traditional sexuality education classes during her adolescent years because they believed she lacked the maturity to understand and apply the information and they were worried such training might introduce her to behaviors (e.g., intercourse), which they felt she was not ready for and also made them uncomfortable. Echoing these feelings, recent research (Pownall, Johoda, & Hastings, 2012) has shown that mothers of children with ID (all ethnicities) were more guarded in their attitudes about their child's readiness to learn about sex and contraception and engaging in intimate relationships, leading them to focus on their child's vulnerability and the need for training in staying safe rather than learning about normalized sexual development and expression. They also reported wanting more access to other parents, to talk to and support them in this stage of their child's development (Pownall et al., 2012).

In addition, Naomi's transition teachers had not done preparatory staging with Naomi's parents before they recommended the training on adult relationships and sexuality. The social worker played an important role at this juncture by engaging Naomi and her family in a discussion to create and define shared goals around this potential need, using a family-centered approach which integrated the cultural values of the family and a person-centered approach to insure that the plan developed reflected Naomi's preferences as well. After reviewing a number of curricula on the market (Baxley & Zendel, 2011; Couwenhoven, 2007; Hafner, 2005; Heighway & Webster, 2007; Wrobel, 2003), some written specifically for parents and caregivers while others written more generally for a broad audience (parents, teachers, or support staff), Naomi's mother chose Social Stories ™ (Gray, 2000), a curriculum which uses photographs, line drawings, and written scripts customized to the individual to teach basic personal hygiene routines or other social content in a step-wise manner because she felt Naomi would love to see herself in a story. The social worker met weekly with Naomi and her mom to develop social stories around the family's identified goals of "safe touch and privacy" that included photographs of Naomi to accompany the printed pictures from the curriculum. Naomi then chose to share the social story with her school team, who reinforced the concepts at school when they checked on her at work. With the success of this first effort, Naomi's parents agreed to include the school personnel in their future team meetings to plan the next topic of instruction.

Transference and Countertransference Issues

Although not studied widely, psychodynamic therapists have noted that the transference relationship may be stronger and occur more quickly when the client has an intellectual disability (Hurley, Tomasulo, & Pfadt, 1998). Just as in psychodynamic therapy with individuals without disabilities, the client may perceive the therapist as a friend, parent figure, or romantic partner and respond to them accordingly. Hurley and colleagues recommended reviewing the limits of therapy and clarifying the role of the psychotherapist up front in concrete and direct terms, to help the client develop a working relationship with the therapist. In Naomi's case, the social worker explained to Naomi that it was her job to advise and support Naomi and her family,

so as not to be confused with a friend, though they were certainly friendly and developed a good working relationship.

Due to the wide range of settings and the variety of roles a social worker might fulfill in working with individuals and families, it is imperative that professionals pay close attention to their own emotional reactions, both positive and negative, that may arise (Walsh, 2002). Professionals must be aware of their own values and biases in order to avoid bias caused by countertransference. It is important to consider the history of paternalism within the field of DD and balance the desire to protect people with disabilities against their right to live a full life in the community. Family members or service providers may, consciously or unconsciously, be uncomfortable with the person's greater independence and the potential risk that might bring. For some, issues of sexuality may carry personal meaning that may interfere with the professional's practice. In Naomi's case, if the social worker assisting her with sexuality education had experienced sexual abuse as a child, she may find herself preoccupied with teaching Naomi skills to protect against similar abuse, rather than teaching her to begin exploring her body and normal sexual feelings. It is critical to her practice that the social worker seek support and feedback through supervision and also through her own mental health provider (if being used) to maintain healthy boundaries with her client.

Legal and Ethical Concerns

Several legal and ethical concerns may come into play when working with individuals with DD across the lifespan. First, in rare circumstances when individuals have profound impairments in their decision-making capacity, alternative forms of decision making may be put in place (e.g., conservatorship, guardianship), which allow others to make decisions for them. A current controversial issue in the advocacy community is the overuse of guardianship for individuals with all levels of ID (Jameson et al., 2015). Families are being encouraged to consider less restrictive alternatives to guardianship/conservatorship such as powers of attorney, health proxies or advance directives (American Association on Intellectual and Developmental Disabilities, 2009), which can allow for different levels of decision making based on the issue at hand, rather than the traditional sweeping assumption that individuals who are conserved cannot make any decisions. It should also be noted that increasingly family members and friends are identifying ways to work with individuals with ID to help them manage their lives without the necessity of guardianship, but information on how to do this is not universally available.

Second, with core values related to choice, independence, productivity, and community inclusion, there is a growing debate over balancing the right to habilitation (training) and the individual's right to personal liberties (choice; Bannerman, Sheldon, Sherman, & Harchik,1990). The argument for habilitation over choice is supported by noting that individual choices (1) may not be safe or healthy (e.g., overeating, self-injury, going out alone and getting lost) or (2) may hinder the acquisition of critical independent activity (e.g., uncontrolled self-stimulation, napping, playing video games). The compelling argument in favor of giving the clients right to choose is that it is mandated by law; even a person with profound intellectual disabilities can make some kind of choice. The second argument is that making choices prepares individuals to live in a community where this is expected and which will be gratifying for individuals who learn to do this over time. Social workers can be key in articulating how to implement the law and conduct habilitation to help individuals to make "good" choices and to learn from the consequences of their choices.

Third, related to the sexuality training of Naomi in the vignette, there is still controversy over the rights of people to have sex and be parents (Aunos & Feldman, 2002). There is no law that prohibits an individual from having sex or getting pregnant; on the contrary, it is a basic civil liberty protected under the Constitution. Concerns about the adequacy of the parenting skills of an individual with intellectual disabilities have been tied to an overrepresentation of these individuals in child maltreatment cases (Feldman, 1994; Murphy & Feldman, 2002) and studies finding their children have an increased risk for DD, school and behavior problems (Murphy & Feldman, 2002). While the research is still inadequate, other studies have found that parents with intellectual disabilities can learn parenting skills and response to dangers, accidents, and childhood illness, but most studies suggest that these educational classes are not always adequate to lead to the best outcomes (Murphy & Feldman, 2002). Other studies have found parents with intellectual disabilities have reported positive views of parenting (something they like or love), but these same participants also acknowledged the challenges of parenting (Ehlers-Flint, 2002). More research is needed. From a societal and service perspective, a major ethical concern is the presumption of incompetence and limited and inappropriate services and supports for parents with ID and/or DD. Consequently, the specter of sterilization of individuals with DD as a protective mechanism continues in spite of this being illegal. Social workers are well postured to help protect the rights of individuals with DD to have intimate relationships with others and having children; as important, social workers have the competence to assure that programs to educate, support, and serve parents with DD and their children. As with many ethical issues, social work intervention is needed at the micro, mezzo, and macro levels.

MEZZO PERSPECTIVE: SOCIAL WORK GROUP PRACTICE

Promoting Family and Consumer Voice and Advocacy for Systems Change

During the 1970s and 1980s, a cascade of grassroots advocacy and the passage of disability laws marked a cultural shift in the disability community towards a focus on disability rights, parent and consumer advocacy, and community action.

Laws such as Section 504 of the Rehabilitation Act of 1973 (29 U.S.C. § 504) and the Education for All Handicapped Children Act (1975) emphasized the importance of providing accommodations and modifications to the environment, rather than focusing on "fixing" the person with a disability. The introduction of procedural safeguards in special education law (U.S. Department of Education, Office of Special Education, 2007a, 2007b) codified the rights of parents and youth in transition to participate in the educational decision-making process with the force of law behind it. Consequently, family members and individuals with DD gained unprecedented opportunities to have a voice in service decisions, and a national movement to establish parent education and support programs run by parents for parents was launched, some with a single disability focus (e.g., Down syndrome, cerebral palsy, autism), and others focusing on a developmental period or other basis for social networking. Naomi's mother went beyond the boundaries of her cultural comfort level when she engaged in the Partners in Policymaking program. Here she gained support and knowledge from other parents, but she also found her own, unique voice. It was empowering to meet with legislators about issues vital to their family, to tell their story, and join with other families to effect change. When parents of young children with disabilities have been asked who can best support them emotionally, their first choice is other parents who have similar life experiences (Santelli, Poyadue, & Young, 2001). The establishment of an effective family support network in the community and within states is critical to maintaining a family-centered system (Family Voices, n.d.). With this in mind, social workers may assist parent groups to organize into a county, regional, or statewide collaborative to address broad policy issues.

In addition, social workers can promote family representatives on the boards of community service agencies or encourage agencies to establish an advisory board consisting of family members or individuals with disabilities who represent the full range of people served by the program. It was Naomi's service coordinator (who is a social worker) who recommended Naomi's mother for participation in Partners in Policymaking; she was the only Asian in that cohort. Family members and self-advocates on advisory boards may encounter disagreements with the host organization over the boundaries of the board's influence. It is critical for social workers to help family members and self-advocates become comfortable deliberating these issues openly at meetings to ensure their full (rather than token) participation in shaping policy for the host organization.

Self-Advocacy Groups and Networks

Adults with DD continue to have limited opportunities for autonomy and decision making due to public attitudes and inadequate community supports to develop and support these skills (Heller, Harris, & Albrecht, 2012). Coinciding with the closing of institutions and movement of people with disabilities into the community, there has been a growing movement nationally for individuals with disabilities to join or organize into groups in order to leverage their individual power when advocating for reform at the macro or policy level. Research has demonstrated that participation in a self-advocacy group also reduces isolation, facilitates friendships and relationships, and facilitates learning basic and advanced social and leadership skills (Stoddart, 1998). While individuals from diverse cultures currently do not participate fully in the self-advocacy movement, Naomi's transition services should help position her for involvement in the self-advocacy movement over time. Social workers are uniquely qualified to promote the achievement of autonomy and self-determination in youth and adults with DD through their practice at the mezzo level focusing on organizing, facilitating and supporting self-advocacy groups and networks. (See Facilitating Advocacy Groups under Internet Resources.)

Decisions regarding group type, structure, processes and size must be made early to assure that the purpose or goals of the group will be attained

(Association for the Advancement of Social Work With Groups, 2010). There is controversy about the optimal combination of group members, with advantages and disadvantages for each type of group. Homogeneous groups allow an understanding of common barriers and shared life experience, mixed disability groups provide opportunities for members to increase their knowledge and awareness of their uniqueness and commonalities and to leverage their voice and influence in a cross-disability entity, and participating in groups with members who do not have disabilities allows a focus on issues that impact all citizens (e.g., employment, voting, poverty, housing discrimination, environmental hazards; Corrigan, Jones, & McWhirter, 2001).

Social workers may function as group facilitators, but in this role they should actively solicit group member expectations of the facilitator's role (See information on facilitator's role under Internet Resources.) With a focus on facilitating and maintaining a structure where group members can achieve group goals, group work should avoid directive guidance and instead support group reflections on decisions made by examining the real-life consequences that resulted. The social worker can help members to deconstruct self-doubt, self-blame, and feelings of inadequacy to build a solid foundation for self-efficacy, empowerment, and confidence, but she must avoid turning the group into a therapy session (Association for the Advancement of Social Work With Groups, 2010).

MACRO PERSPECTIVE: SYSTEMS CHANGE AND TRANSFORMATION
Promoting the Sibling Voice in Shaping Policy

The participation of siblings in shaping policy is a growing movement. The Sibling Leadership Network (SLN) was created in 2007 in response to a growing awareness of the important perspective and role that siblings play. The SLN compiles research on siblings, advocates for policies related to siblings, and connects siblings with information and peer support across the country. The Sibling Support Project is a national effort dedicated to the life-long concerns of brothers and sisters of people who have special health, developmental, or mental health concerns. (See the section on Siblings under Internet Resources.) Social workers have a key role as a promoter, facilitator, or consultant to strengthen these parent, consumer, and sibling-driven networks.

Addressing the Long-Term Care Needs of Individuals with DD: A Demographic Crisis

While the field continues to refine and reinvent what quality of life means for people with DD and how to achieve it, the success of the past 40 years in moving people with DD into communities and neighborhoods has fueled a crisis that requires macro social work interventions at many levels (Parish & Lutwick, 2005). Due to advances in medical care and technology, the average life expectancy of people with DD is now equal to people without disabilities (Roizen & Patterson, 2003); consequently, baby boomers with DD will need services at unprecedented numbers, at the same time their family caregivers are also aging and initiating contact for services. Naomi and her family will be in the cohort impacted by this demographic shift. Naomi's parents, her sibling, and Naomi may be part of the advocacy movement to prepare for this emerging need.

Social workers must work with other stakeholder groups to develop and implement a multimodal preemptive plan to reduce the increasing strain on the long-term care system. First, collaborations between aging and DD services can be built to leverage and coordinate services that support the aging adult with DD and his or her aging caregiver through comingled services that assure maximum health, independence, and productivity for both parties. The creation of the Administration on

Community Living (see Disability Policy Organizations under Internet Resources.) at the federal level will facilitate this integration as it is the new home for the Administration on Aging, Administration on Intellectual and Developmental Disabilities, the National Institute for Disability, Independent Living and Rehabilitation Research, and the Help America Vote Act. The next several years carries rich opportunities for social workers to prepare for America's aging population, including those who are aging with DD. Second, sustained political advocacy is needed in partnership with longstanding disability allies in every state (see Disability Policy Organizations under Internet Resources), to set guidelines for professional standards to assure a quality DD workforce, inform proposed legislation to address inequities or threats to meeting the needs of individuals with DD and their families, and forming cross-disability, cross-stakeholder coalitions to maximize the breadth and reach of political activity. Social workers can play a key role in building the capacity of organizations to understand their legal obligation to serve individuals with disabilities and then to facilitate personnel training to build competence in serving this population.

CONCLUSION

The implementation of disability law continues to change the landscape of services and supports for individuals with DD as almost every federal agency acknowledges the disabled as a subgroup of people they serve. At the heart of legislative changes are the core values and principles outlined in the Introduction to this chapter. As with all laws that define how things should be, social workers are and will be an essential part of the workforce at the micro, mezzo, and macro levels to ensure the spirit of the law is met. In a prophetic article published 15 years ago about the evolution of DD services since the 1960s, Mary (1998) lamented recent trends in social work student preference for micro practice as clinical social workers or psychotherapists over social work's historical emphasis on macro practice, engaging in advocacy and social activism on behalf of vulnerable populations. In actuality, the complexity presented by major demographic and economic shifts will require the skills of social workers at all levels of practice in order to shape innovative and transformative practices to serve and support individuals with DD, their birth and chosen family units, and the communities in which they choose to live.

INTERNET RESOURCES
Person-Centered Planning

- Inclusion Press: http://www.inclusion.com
- Imagine: http://www.dimagine.com
- The Learning Community for Person-Centered Practices: http://www.learningcommunity.us

Early Intervention

- Learn the Signs, Act Early: http://www.cdc.gov/ncbddd/actearly/index.html
- Make the First Five Count (Easter Seals): http://es.easterseals.com/site/PageServer?pagename=ntlc10_mffc_homepageasq

Family Information and Support Programs

- Parent-to-Parent USA: http://www.p2pusa.org/p2pusa/sitepages/p2p-home.aspx
- Family Voices: http://www.familyvoices.org/
- Family-to-Family Health Information Centers (F2F-HICs): http://www.familyvoices.org/admin/miscdocs/files/F2FBrochure_10-14-2010.pdf
- Parent Training and Information Centers (PTIs) and Community Parent Resource Centers (CPRCs): http://www.parentcenterhub.org/find-your-center/

Sibling Resources

- Sibling Leadership Network: http://www.siblingleadership.org
- Sibling Support Project: http://www.siblingsupport.org.
- Sibshops: http://www.siblingsupport.org

- Sibling Survival Guide: Indispensable Information for Brothers and Sisters of Adults With Disabilities: http://astore.amazon.com/thesib-suppro-20/detail/1606130137

Abuse, Neglect and Victimization

- National Child Abuse Hotline (Childhelp-Prevention and Treatment of Child Abuse): https://www.childhelp.org/hotline/
- National Adult Protective Services Association (NAPSA): http://www.napsa-now.org/get-help/

Co-Occurring MH Disorders

- National Association for the Dually Diagnosed (NADD): http://www.thenadd.org

Transition Resources

- Got Transition? http://www.gottransition.org/
- Think College: http://www.thinkcollege.net/
- Transition Health Care Checklist: Preparing for Life as an Adult: http://www.waisman.wisc.edu/cedd/pdfs/products/health/THCL.pdf

Facilitating Self-Advocacy Groups

- Advising Through Self-Determination: An Information Guide for Advisors: http://www.aucd.org/docs/Advising-Through-SD.pdf

Disability Policy Organizations

- Self-Advocates Becoming Empowered (SABE): http://www.sabeusa.org/
- Consortium for Citizens with Disabilities: http://www.c-c-d.org/
- National Disability Rights Network (NDRN): http://www.ndrn.org/index.php
- Association of University Centers on Disabilities Research, Education, Service (AUCD): http://www.aucd.org/template/index.cfm
- United Cerebral Palsy (UCP): http://ucp.org/
- The Arc: http://www.thearc.org/
- National Down Syndrome Society National Policy Center: http://www.ndss.org/Advocacy/About-the-NDSS-National-Policy-Center/

- National Alliance on Mental Illness (NAMI): http://www.nami.org/template.cfm?section=About_NAMI/
- Administration on Community Living: http://www.acl.gov/About_ACL/Index.aspx

DISCUSSION QUESTIONS

1. What are the needs of people with DD and their family members across the lifespan?

2. What are the barriers people with DD may encounter when seeking services and supports to meet their needs?

3. Discuss the changing demographics in the U.S. and how this will affect individuals with DD and the social service system that supports them.

4. What are challenges confronting individuals with DD exercising their right to the same rights and entitlements as people without disabilities, and what can be done to assure equity and parity for all?

5. What groups, if any, are at particular risk for being unserved/underserved as we move into the next decade of community inclusion?

REFERENCES

Agosta, J., & Melda, K. (1996). Supporting families who provide care at home for children with disabilities. *Exceptional Children, 62*(3), 271–282.

American Association on Intellectual and Developmental Disabilities (AAIDD). (2008). *Sexuality: Joint position statement of AAIDD and The Arc.* Washington, DC. Retrieved from http://aaidd.org/news-policy/policy/position-statements/sexuality.

American Association on Intellectual and Developmental Disabilities (AAIDD). (2009). *Guardianship: Joint position statement of AAIDD and The Arc.* Washington, DC. Retrieved from http://aaidd.org/news-policy/policy/position-statements/guardianship.

American Psychiatric Association. (2013). *Diagnostic and Statistical Manual of Mental Disorders* (5th ed.). Arlington, VA: Author.

Americans With Disabilities Act of 1990. U.S. Department of Education, Office of Civil Rights. Retrieved from http://www2.ed.gov/about/offices/list/ocr/docs/hq9805.html.

Anderson, S., & Morris, J. (2006). Cognitive behavior therapy for people with Asperger syndrome. *Behavioural and Cognitive Psychotherapy, 34*(3), 293–303. doi: 10.1017/S1352465805002651

Arnold, C. K., Heller, T., & Kramer, J. (2012). Support needs of siblings of people with developmental disabilities. *Intellectual and Developmental Disabilities, 50*(5), 373–382. doi:10.1352/1934-9556-50.5.373

Association for the Advancement of Social Work with Groups. (2010). *Standards for social work practice with groups.* Retrieved from http://www.aaswg.org/files/AASWG_Standards_for_Social_Work_Practice_with_Groups.pdf.

Aunos, M., & Feldman, M.A. (2002). Attitudes towards sexuality, sterilization, and parenting rights of persons with intellectual disabilities. *Journal of Applied Research in Intellectual Disabilities, 15,* 285–296.

Banks, S. P., & Kahn, M. D. (1997). *The sibling bond.* New York, NY: Basic Books.

Bannerman, D. J., Sheldon, J. B., Sherman, J. A., & Harchik, A. E. (1990). Balancing the right to habilitation with the right to personal liberties: The rights of people with developmental disabilities to eat too many doughnuts and take a nap. *Journal of Applied Behavior Analysis, 23*(1), 79-89.

Batshaw, M. L., Pellegrino, L., & Roizen, N. J. (Eds.). (2007). *Children with disabilities* (6th ed.). Baltimore, MD: Paul H. Brookes.

Baxley, D., & Zendell, A. (2005). *Sexuality education for children and adolescents with developmental disabilities: An instructional manual for parents or caregivers of and individuals with developmental disabilities.* Tallahassee, FL: Florida Developmental Disabilities Council. Retrieved from http://www.albany.edu/aging/IDD/documents/parent-workbook.pdf.

Baxley, D., & Zendell, A. (2011). *Sexuality across the lifespan: Sexuality education for children and adolescents with developmental disabilities: An instructional manual for family members of individuals with developmental disabilities.* Retrieved from: http://www.fddc.org/sites/default/files/file/publications/Sexuality%20Guide-Parents-English.pdf

Bui, K., & Takeuchi, D. T. (1992). Ethnic minority adolescents and the use of community mental health care services. *American Journal of Community Psychology, 20*(4), 403–417. doi:10.1007/BF00937752

Cauce, A. M., Domenech-Rodriguez, M., Paradise, M., Cochran, B. N., Shea, J. M., Srebnik, D., & Baydar, N. (2002). Cultural and contextual influences in mental health help seeking: A focus on ethnic minority youth. *Journal of Consulting and Clinical Psychology, 70*(1), 44–55. doi:10.1037/0022-006X.70.1.44

Cicirelli, V. G. (1995). *Sibling relationships across the life span.* New York, NY: Plenum Press.

Cipani, E., & Schock, K. M. (2010). *Functional behavioral assessment, diagnosis and treatment: A complete system for education and mental health settings.* New York, NY: Springer.

Corrigan, M. L., Jones, C. A., & McWhirter, J. J. (2001). College students with disabilities: An access employment group. *Journal for Specialists in Group Work, 26*(4), 339–349. doi:10.1080/01933920108413783

Couwenhoven, T. (2007). *Teaching children with Down syndrome about their bodies, boundaries, and sexuality.* Bethesda, MD: Woodbine House.

Dekker, M. C., Koot, H. M., van der Ende, J., & Verhulst, F. C. (2002). Emotional and behavioral problems in children and adolescents with and without intellectual disability. *The Journal of Child Psychology and Psychiatry, 43*(8), 1087–1098. doi:10.1111/1469-7610.00235

Developmental Disabilities Assistance and Bill of Rights Act of 2000. 42 U.S.C. § 15001.

Dykens, E., Fisher, M., Taylor, M., Lambert, W., & Miodrag, N. (2014). Reducing distress in mothers of children with autism and other disabilities: A randomized trial. *Pediatrics, 134*(2), e454–e463. doi:10.1542/peds.2013-3164

Eddy, K. (2007). *Sexuality and people with mental disabilities–The issues, the law, and the guardian.* Retrieved from http://www.guardianship.org/training_modules/Sexuality.pdf.

Education for All Handicapped Children Act, 1975. P.L. 94–142.

Ehlers-Flint, M. (2002). Parenting perceptions and social supports of mother with cognitive disabilities. *Sexuality and Disability, 20*(1), 29–51.

Emerson, E., Einfeld, S., & Stancliff, R. J. (2010). The mental health of young children with intellectual disabilities or borderline intellectual functioning. *Social Psychiatry and Psychiatric Epidemiology, 45*(5), 579–587. doi:10.1007/s00127-009-0100-y

Evans, J., Jones, J., & Mansell, I. (2001). Supporting siblings: Evaluation of support groups for brothers and sisters of children with learning disabilities and challenging behavior. *Journal of Learning Disabilities, 5*(1), 69–78. doi:10.1177/146900470100500107

Falvey, M., Forest, M., Pearpoint, J., & Rosenberg, R. (1997). *All my life's a circle: Using the tools: Circles, MAPS, and PATHS.* Toronto, Canada: Inclusion Press International.

Family Voices. (n.d.). *Definitions and principles of family-centered care.* Retrieved from http://www.familyvoices.org/admin/work_family_centered/files/FCCare.pdf.

Feldman, M. A. (1994). Parenting education for parents with intellectual disabilities: A review of outcome studies. *Research in Developmental Disabilities, 15*(4), 299–332.

Fletcher, R., Loschen, E., Stavrakaki, C., & First, M. (Eds.) (2007). *Diagnostic Manual—Intellectual Disability (DM-ID): A textbook of diagnosis of mental disorders in persons with intellectual disability.* Kingston, NY: NADD Press.

Friedman, C., Arnold, C. K., Owen, A., & Sandman, L. (2014). "Remember our voices are our tools:" Sexual self-advocacy as defined by people with intellectual and developmental disabilities. *Sexuality and Disability.* doi:10.1007/s11195-014-9377-1

Gallagher, P. A., Powell, T. H., & Rhodes, C. A. (2006). *Brothers & sisters: A special part of exceptional families* (3rd ed.). Baltimore, MD: Paul H. Brookes.

Gannotti, M., Kaplan, L., Handwerker, W. P., & Groce, N. E. (2004). Cultural influences on healthcare use: Differences in perceived unmet needs and expectations of providers by Latino and Euro-American parents of children with special healthcare needs. *Journal of Developmental and Behavioral Pediatrics, 25*(3), 156–165. doi:10.1097/00004703-200406000-00003

Graham, B., Nelis, T., Sandman, L., Arnold, K., & Parker, S. (2011). Promoting sexual citizenship and self-advocacy for people with intellectual and developmental disabilities: The sexuality and disability consortium. *The Community Psychologist, 44*(1), 8–11. Retrieved from http://www.scra27.org/files/4113/8557/6022/TCP_Winter_2011.pdf

Gray, C. A. (2000). *The new social story book: Illustrated edition.* Arlington, TX: Future Horizons.

Hafner, D. (2005). *S.A.F.E.: Safety awareness for empowerment: A training guide for safety at home, at work, and in public.* Retrieved from http://www.waisman.wisc.edu/cedd/pdfs/products/health/SAFE.pdf

Harrington, C., & Kang, T. (2008). Disparities in service utilization and expenditures for individuals with developmental disabilities. *Disability and Health Journal, 1*(4), 184–195. doi:10.1016/j.dhjo.2008.05.004

Hayden, M. E. (1997). Class action, civil rights litigation for institutionalized persons with mental retardation and other developmental disabilities. *Mental and Physical Disability Law Reporter, 21*(3), 411–423.

Heighway, S., & Webster, S. (2007). *S.T.A.R.S: Skills training for assertiveness, relationship-building, and sexual awareness.* Arlington, TX: Future Horizons.

Heller, T., Harris, S. P., & Albrecht, G. L. (2012). *Disability through the life course.* Los Angeles, CA: Sage.

Hurley, A. D., Tomasulo, D. J., & Pfadt, A. G. (1998). Individual and group psychotherapy approaches for persons with mental retardation and developmental disabilities. *Journal of Developmental and Physical Disabilities, 10*(4), 365–386. doi:10.1023/A:1021806605662

Individuals with Disabilities Education Act, 42 USC 1400 (1990).

Jameson, J. M., Riesen, T., Polychronis, S., Trader, B., Mizner, S., Martinis, J. & Hoyle, D. (2015). Guardianship and the potential of supported decision making with individuals with disabilities. *Research and Practice for Persons with Severe Disabilities,* 1–16. doi:10.1177/1540796915586189

Kasari, C., Rotheram-Fuller, E., Locke, J., & Gulsrud, A. (2012). Making the connection: Randomized controlled trial of social skills at school for children with autism spectrum disorders. *Journal of Child Psychology and Psychiatry, 53*(4), 431–439.

Kempton, W., & Kahn, E. (1991). Sexuality and people with intellectual disabilities: A historical perspective. *Sexuality and Disability, 9*(2), 93–111. doi:10.1007/BF01101735

Kendall, P. C., & Hedtke, K. (2006). *Cognitive-behavioral therapy for anxious children: Therapist manual* (3rd ed.). Ardmore, PA: Workbook.

Kuhlthau, K., Nyman, R., Ferris, T., Beal, A., & Perrin, J. (2004). Correlates of use of specialty care. *Pediatrics, 113*(3), e249–e255.

Lakin, K. C., Larson, S., Salmi, P., & Webster, A. (2010). *Residential services for persons with developmental disabilities: Status and trends through 2009.* Research and Training Center on Community Living, Institute on Community Integration/ UCEDD, College of Education and Human Development, University of Minnesota. Retrieved from http://rtc.umn.edu/docs/risp2009.pdf

Lang, R., Regester, A., Lauderdale, S., Ashbaugh, K., & Haring, A. (2010). Treatment of anxiety in autism spectrum disorders using cognitive behavior therapy: A systematic review. *Developmental Neurorehabilitation, 13*(1), 53–63.

Larson, S. A., Lakin, K. C., Anderson, L., Lee, N. K., Lee, J. H., & Anderson, D. (2001). Prevalence of mental retardation and developmental disabilities. *American Journal on Mental Retardation, 106*(3), 231–252.

Mandell, D. S., Wiggins, L. D., Carpenter, L. A., Daniels, J., DiGuiseppi, C., Durkin, M. S., ... Kirby, R. S. (2009). Racial/ethnic disparities in the identification of children with autism spectrum disorders. *American Journal of Public Health, 99*(3), 493–498. doi:10.2105/AJPH.2007.131243

Mary, N. L. (1998). Social work and the support model of services for people with developmental disabilities. *Journal of Social work Education, 34*(2), 247–260. doi:10.1080/10437797.1998.10778921

Mattingly, C., & Garro, L. C. (Eds.). (2000). *Narrative and the cultural construction of illness and healing.* Los Angeles, CA: University of California Press.

Mattingly, C. F., & Lawlor, M. C. (2000). Learning from stories: Narrative interviewing in cross-cultural research. *Scandinavian Journal of Occupational Therapy, 7*(4), 4–14. doi:10.1080/110381200443571

McCallion, P., Janicki, M., & Grant-Griffin, L. (1997). Exploring the impact of culture and acculturation on older families' care-giving for persons with developmental disabilities. *Family Relations, 46*(4) 347–357.

McHale, S. M., & Gamble, W. C. (1987). The role of siblings and peers. In J. Garbarino, P. E. Brookhauser, & K. J. Authier (Eds.), *Special children—Special risks* (pp. 47–68). New York, NY: Aldine De Gruyter.

McIntyre, L. L., & Abbeduto, L. (2008). Parent training for young children with developmental disabilities: Randomized controlled trial. *American Journal on Mental Retardation, 113*(5), 356–368.

Meyer, D., & Vadasy, P. (1994). *Sibshops: Workshops for siblings of children with special needs.* Baltimore, MD: Paul H. Brookes.

Morrison, L., Shinn, A. N., Wheeler, B., Kurtz, D., Miller, L., Jones, C., ... Callanan, K. (2003). *Abuse and neglect of adults with developmental disabilities: A public health priority for the state of California.* Retrieved from http://www.disabilityrightsca.org/pubs/701901.pdf

Murphy, N., & Elias, E. (2006). Sexuality of children and adolescents with developmental disabilities. *Pediatrics, 118*(1), 398–403. doi:10.1542/peds. 2006-1115

Murphy, G., & Feldman, M. A. (2002). Parents with intellectual disabilities. *Journal of Applied Research in Intellectual Disabilities, 15,* 281–284.

O'Brien, J., & Lyle O'Brien, C. (1998). *A little book about person-centered planning.* Toronto, Canada: Inclusion Press International.

Office of Disability Employment Policy. (2013). *ODEP accomplishments: 2009–2012. Real people, real impact.* Retrieved from: http://www.dol.gov/odep/pdf/2009-2012Accomplishments.pdf

Olmstead v. L. C., 527 U.S. 581 (1999).

Pacer Center. (2009). *Least restrictive environment (LRE): A simplified guide to key legal requirements.* Minneapolis, MN: Author. Retrieved from http://www.pacer.org/parent/php/php-c7.pdf

Parish, S. L., & Lutwick, Z. E. (2005). A critical analysis of the emerging crisis in long-term care for people with developmental disabilities. *Social Work, 50*(4), 345–354. doi:10.1093/sw/50.4.345

Petersilia, J. R. (2001). Crime victims with developmental disabilities: A review essay. *Criminal Justice and Behavior, 28*(6), 655–694. doi:10.1177/009385480102800601

Pownall, J. D., Johoda, A., & Hastings, R. P. (2012). Sexuality and sex education of adolescents with intellectual disability: Mothers' attitudes, experiences, and support needs. *Intellectual and Developmental Disabilities, 50*(2), 140–154. doi:10.1352/1934-9556-50.2.140

Pruncho, R. A., & McMullen, W. F. (2004). Patterns of service utilization by adults with a developmental disability: Type of service makes a difference. *American Journal on Mental Retardation, 109*(5), 362–378.

Rehabilitation Act of 1973, Pub. L. No. 93–112, 29 U.S.C. § 504 (1973).

Roizen, N. J., & Patterson, D. (2003). Down's syndrome. *The Lancet, 361*(9365), 1281–1289.

Ronsaville, D. S., & Hakim, R. B. (2000). Well child care in the United States: Racial differences in compliance with guidelines. *American Journal of Public Health, 90*(9), 1436–1443.

Salmi, P., Scott, N., Webster, A., Larson, S. A., & Lakin, K. C. (2010). Residential services for people with intellectual or developmental disabilities at the 20th anniversary of the Americans With Disabilities Act, the 10th anniversary of Olmstead, and in the Year of Community Living. *Intellectual and Developmental Disabilities, 48*(2), 168–171. doi:10.1352/1934-9556-48.2.168

Santelli, B., Poyadue, F. S., & Young, J. L. (2001). *The parent to parent handbook: Connecting families of children with special needs.* Baltimore, MD: Brookes.

Scorgie, K., Wilgosh, L., & Sobsey, D. (2004). The experience of transformation in parents of children with disabilities: Theoretical considerations. *Developmental Disabilities Bulletin, 32*(1), 84–110.

Seligman, M., & Darling, R. B. (1997). *Ordinary families, special children* (2nd ed.). New York, NY: Guilford Press.

Sen, E., & Yurtserver, S. (2007). Difficulties experienced by families with disabled children. *Journal for Specialists in Pediatric Nursing, 12*(4), 238–252. doi:10.1111/j.1744-6155.2007.00119.x

Senner, J., & Fish, T. (2012). Comparison of child self-report and parent report on the sibling need and involvement profile. *Remedial and Special Education, 33*(2), 103–109. doi:10.1177/0741932510364547

Stoddart, K. P. (1998). The treatment of high-functioning pervasive developmental disorder and Asperger's disorder: Defining the social work role. *Focus on Autism and Other Developmental Disabilities, 13*(1), 45–62.

Stoneman, Z. (2001). Supporting positive sibling relationships during childhood. *Mental Retardation and Developmental Disabilities Research Review, 7*(2), 134–142. doi:10.1002/mrdd.1019

Stoneman, Z., Brody, G. H., Davis C. H., & Crapps, J. M. (1988). Childcare responsibilities, peer relations, and sibling conflict: Older siblings of mentally retarded children. *American Journal on Mental Retardation, 93*(2), 174–183.

Sullivan, P., & Cork, P. M. (1996). *Developmental disabilities training project.* Omaha, NE: Center for Abused Children With Disabilities, Boys Town National Research Hospital, Nebraska Department of Health and Human Services.

Sullivan, P. M., & Knutson, J. F. (2000). Maltreatment and disabilities: A population-based epidemiologic study. *Child Abuse Neglect, 24*(10), 1257–1273. doi:10.1016/S0145-2134(00)00190-3

Suveg, C., Comer, J. S., Furr, J. M., & Kendall, P. C. (2006). Adapting manualized CBT for a cognitively delayed child with multiple anxiety disorders. *Clinical Case Studies, 5*(6), 488–510. doi:10.1177/1534650106290371

U.S. Department of Education. (n.d.). *Early intervention program for infants and toddlers.* Retrieved from http://www2.ed.gov/programs/osepeip/index.html

U.S. Department of Education, Office of Special Education. (2007a). *A guide to the individualized education program.* Retrieved from http://www2.ed.gov/parents/needs/speced/iepguide/index.html

U.S. Department of Education, Office of Special Education. (2007b). *Topic: Secondary transition.* Retrieved from http://idea.ed.gov/explore/view/p/,root,dynamic,TopicalBrief,17.

U.S. Department of Health and Human Services, Administration for Children and Families, Administration of Children, Youth and Families, Children's Bureau. (2006). *Child maltreatment 2004.* Washington, DC: U.S. Government Printing Office. Retrieved from http://www.acf.hhs.gov/programs/cb/stats_research/index.htm

Walsh, J. (2002). Supervising the countertransference reactions of case managers. *The Clinical Supervisor, 21*(2), 129–144. doi:10.1300/J001v21n02_09

Weech-Maldonado, R., Morales, L. S., Spritzer, K., Elliott, M., & Hays, R. D. (2001). Racial and ethnic differences in parents' assessments of pediatric care in Medicaid managed care. *Health Service Research, 36*(3), 575–594.

Wehmeyer, M. (1998). Self-determination and individuals with significant disabilities: Examining meanings and misinterpretations. *Research and Practice for Persons with Severe Disabilities, 23*(1), 5–16. Retrieved from http://kuscholarworks.ku.edu/dspace/bitstream/1808/6229/1/SD4A_Self-Determination%20and%20Individuals.pdf

White, S. W., Albano, A. M., Johnson, C. R., Kasari, C., Ollendick, T., Klin, A., . . . Scahill, L. (2010). Development of a cognitive-behavioral intervention program to treat anxiety and social deficits in teens with high-functioning autism. *Clinical Child and Family Psychological Review, 13*(1), 77–90. doi:10.1007/s10567-009-0062-3

Wittert, D. D. (2002). Parental reactions to having a child with disabilities. *Nursing Spectrum, 8*(17), 12–14.

Wood, J. J., Drahota, A., Sze, K., Har, K., Chiu, A., & Langer, D. A. (2009). Cognitive behavioral therapy for anxiety in children with autism spectrum disorders: A randomized controlled trial. *Journal of Child Psychology and Psychiatry, 50*(3), 224–234. doi:10.1111/j.1469-7610.2008.01948.x

World Health Organization and the World Bank. (2011). *The world report on disability-Summary.* Retrieved from http://www.gsdrc.org/go/display&type=Document&id=4193.

Wrobel, M. (2003). *Taking care of myself: A hygiene, puberty, and personal curriculum for young people with autism.* Arlington, TX: Future Horizons.

Zarembo, A. (2011, December 13). Warrior parents fare best in securing autism services. *The LA Times.* Retrieved from http://www.latimes.com/local/autism/la-me-autism-day-two-html-htmlstory.html

CHAPTER 16

Coping and Resilience in Youth After Exposure to Disaster

Leslie H. Wind

CHAPTER OBJECTIVES

- Understand the basic approach to mental health triage in the immediate aftermath of disasters;
- Determine when use of psychological first aid is appropriate in the immediate aftermath of disaster;
- Identify the key components of psychological first aid;
- Recognize and consider aspects of diversity such as age and race when utilizing psychological first aid.

CASE VIGNETTE

Connor is an 8-year-old African American male in the second grade who lives with his mother, Tanya, in New Orleans, Louisiana. He and his mother have lived with his grandmother since Connor was born, and his grandmother has been his primary caregiver while Tanya has been working at her full-time job. Connor saw his grandmother trip and tumble down the stairs during the Hurricane Katrina evacuation. He watched in horror, unable to move or speak, as she fell; her crumbled body lay still at the bottom of the stairs with blood seeping from her head and face. She died as a result of the fall.

Connor continued to stare at his injured grandmother, waiting for her to get up. He experienced minute shivers, extreme fear for his safety and the safety of his mother and grandmother, then numbness as he watched her unresponsive body. Tanya had to physically carry him down the stairs and out of the house. Connor and his mother were transported to an evacuation site where they were told they could stay for

---

a brief period of time. No other information was provided at the time of evacuation, and the evacuation center felt chaotic. Tanya began to worry that the flood would damage her home and that they might not be able to live there again. She also worried about how the disaster would affect her job. In response to the multiple losses experienced by both Connor and his mother, Tanya stated, "It's God's will."

INTRODUCTION

Disasters present significant and often overwhelming challenges for children and families. It has been estimated that as many as 14% of youth are exposed to a disaster in childhood (Becker-Blease, Turner, & Finkelhor, 2010). Hurricane Katrina has been identified as one of the deadliest hurricanes in United States history, flooding 80% of New Orleans, killing 1,833 people along the Gulf Coast, and resulting in $81 billion in damage (Knabb, Rhome, & Brown, 2006). The hurricane resulted in the displacement of a significant number of poor African Americans in New Orleans, many of whom had lived in intergenerational poverty (Bell, 2008). The growing literature on the traumatic effects of natural disasters on children and adolescents indicates symptoms of anxiety and depression (Groome & Soureti, 2004; McDermott & Palmer, 2002), posttraumatic play, increased arousal symptoms, regressive behavior, and functional impairment that can last years after exposure (Gurwitch, Pfefferbaum, & Leftwich, 2002; Gurwitch, Sitterle, Young, & Pfefferbaum, 2002; Koplewicz et al., 2002; Weems, Taylor, et al., 2010; Weisler, Barbee, & Townsend, 2006) with mixed findings regarding racial and ethnic differences. Some studies have found youth outcomes generally equal across racial groups (Garrison et al., 1995; Shannon, Lonigan, Finch, & Taylor, 1994; Vernberg, LaGreca, Silverman, & Prinstein, 1996), but in a review of the literature by La Greca and Silverman (2006), minority groups had more severe posttraumatic stress symptoms in the aftermath of disaster. While ethnic differences in outcomes may be due to a variety of risk factors, Norris and Alegria (2005) warn that ethnicity and culture are influential in determining help seeking behaviors, the availability/accessibility of assistance and the likelihood that help provided is effective. Individual, family, and social factors influence disaster reactions and the diverse ways in which children cope (Self-Brown, Lai, Thompson, McGill, & Kelley, 2013; Terranova, Boxer, & Morris, 2009). Resources that are both lost and available impact individual and family capacity to cope, including losses of physical resources and loved ones (Gerrity & Steinglass, 2003; Hobfoll, Freedy, Green, & Solomon, 1996). Families who lose their homes, those who lose their jobs, social support, and their sense of control often experience acute psychological distress (Freedy, Shaw, Jarrell, & Masters, 1992). The loss of a loved one may combine with multiple other losses thereby requiring the family to reorganize the family system (Walsh & McGoldrick, 2004). In combination, those exposed to the death of others (particularly the loss of a loved one), those who experience a sense of threat to their life or loss of physical resources, and challenges in obtaining information and resources are at greater risk for difficulty adapting to life after the disaster. Hope for the future (Hackbarth, Pavkov, Wetchler, & Flannery, 2012), the family's ability to effectively traverse the traumatic event (Hackbarth et al., 2012; Walsh, 2003), and those who turn to strong spiritual or religious beliefs for support (Pargament, Smith, Koenig, & Perez, 1998; Hackbarth et al., 2012) demonstrate more effective coping and greater resilience in the aftermath of disaster. This chapter links coping and resilience theories to empirical knowledge of child and family reactions to disaster, based on these factors and developmental and cultural contexts, and discusses the importance of triage and implementation of the multi-level psychological first aid (PFA) approach with children and families struggling with direct exposure to disasters.

Resilience is defined as positive adaptation by individuals and families despite adverse experiences (Cicchetti, 1996). *Risk factors* are individual characteristics, life experiences, or contextual variables that challenge positive adaptation and either increase the likelihood of the onset of a particular problem or promote the likelihood a problem will continue or be exacerbated. They may be individual characteristics, life experiences, or contextual variables. *Protective factors* are individual, familial, or extrafamilial characteristics that may compensate for vulnerability and increase resistance to risk by moderating the relationship between the risk factor and negative outcome (Fraser, Richman, & Galinsky, 1999). Availability of supportive resources, such as counseling, within a community is also known to increase resilience; loss of such resources is known to negatively impact coping (Hobfoll et al., 1996).

Coping generally refers to the way individuals attempt to reduce stress. Lazarus and Folkman (1984) define coping as "constantly changing cognitive and behavioral efforts to manage specific external and/or internal demands that are appraised as taxing or exceeding the resources of the person" (p. 141). Among children and adolescents exposed to natural disaster, those who engaged in negative coping strategies (e.g., blaming self or others) demonstrate higher levels of posttraumatic symptomatology compared to those with a more proactive style of coping (e.g., problem solving, engaging social support; Self-Brown et al., 2013; Vernberg et al., 1996).

Combining these two theories, adaptation to a stressful event will be based upon multiple factors, including individual and family factors as well as environmental risk and protective aspects. Individually, interpretation of the event as well as the particular coping strategies used are strongly influenced by developmental stage (Bingham & Harmon, 1996; Compas, Connor-Smith, Saltzman, Thomsen, & Wadsworth, 2001). Children, particularly young children, are egocentric and often will place blame on themselves when something bad occurs. Negative self-attribution and guilt related to trauma can increase posttraumatic stress symptoms (Resnick, 2001).

Children's adaptation can also be influenced by caregiver responses, previous exposure to trauma, and degree of physical and interpersonal exposure during the traumatic event. During disasters multiple members of a family may be exposed to trauma. Caregivers may struggle to recover from the crisis and are then less able to provide a secure environment for the child. This can be particularly true within the context of a temporary shelter environment. Parents' ability to cope in the aftermath of a disaster significantly contributes to a child's ability to cope with the event (Deering, 2000; Huzziff & Ronan, 1999; Norris, Friedman, & Watson, 2002; Ronan, 1997). Children who perceive their caregivers as having difficulty coping and discussing the event with them demonstrate reduced coping ability (Huzziff & Ronan, 1999). Due to their own distress, parents may fail to recognize their children's response to the event and cannot effectively help them with coping. Three types of exposure have been found to impact child outcomes in the aftermath of disasters: (1) previous traumatic exposure; (2) physical exposure; and (3) interpersonal exposure. Pfefferbaum and colleagues (2003) found that children with previous traumatic exposure to events such as accidents, natural disasters, violence, and or death exhibited greater posttraumatic stress symptoms. They also found that more intense peritraumatic reactions (e.g., a combination of physiological, cognitive, and emotional responses) following exposure to disasters may also contribute to poorer outcomes. The highest rates of posttraumatic responses have been reported to be related to interpersonal exposure that resulted in the violent loss of a loved one (Ayalon, 1993; Elbedour, Baker, Shalhoub-Kevorkian, Irwin, & Belmaker,1999; Trappler & Friedman, 1996). Children and adolescents who have lost someone significant in their lives such as a family member are more likely to exhibit arousal and fear (Pfefferbaum et al., 1999). In the immediate aftermath of a disaster, it is critical to assess the functioning of children, their caregivers, and the resources within their environment to determine the best course of support.

MICRO PERSPECTIVE

Butler, Panzer, and Goldfrank (2003) offer the individual assessment and triage protocol in Figure 16.1, focused on mental health needs in the aftermath of disaster.

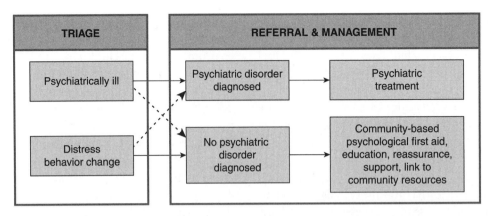

Figure 16.1 Post-Disaster Triage, Referral, and Management Based on Psychiatric Screening and Diagnosis

SOURCES: Butler, A. S., Panzer, A. M., & Goldfrank, L. R. (Eds.) (2003). Preparing for the psychological conse-quences of terrorism: A public health strategy. Committee on Responding to the Psychological Consequences of Terrorism. Washington, DC: National Academies Press. Post-Disaster Triage, Referral, and Management Based on Psychiatric Screening and Diagnosis (Developed by Carol C. North, M.D.)

The initial screen includes determination of any previous mental health diagnosis or distress and possible behavior change due to exposure to the disaster. If no psychiatric disorder is present, the authors recommend PFA, with its inclusion of ongoing assessment of child and family function-ing, education, reassurance, support, and linkage to community resources. For purposes of this chapter, it is assumed that both Connor and Tanya have no previous psychiatric diagnoses. Therefore, PFA would be an appropriate intervention.

Diversity Considerations

Youth and adolescents are at increased risk of having mental health problems if they live in low-income families (Stagman & Cooper, 2010). These individuals demonstrate poorer academic performance; higher rates of problematic behav-iors; and are more likely to be absent, suspended, or expelled, with the highest rates seen among African American youth compared to their Cau-casian peers (40% vs. 15%; Blackorby & Cameto, 2004). There is limited research on differences in traumatic reactions based on children's ethnic and religious backgrounds. Cultural and reli-gious beliefs and attitudes can shape the meaning

attributed to an event as well as assessment of the trauma related to disaster (Nader, 2004). Issues of diversity related to the vignette presented above are discussed throughout the remainder of the chapter.

Intervention With PFA

According to the *Psychological First Aid Field Operations Guide* (PFA *Field Guide*; Brymer et al., 2006), PFA is an evidence-informed approach used to assist youths, adults, and families immedi-ately after exposure to disasters or terrorism. The PFA *Field Guide* indicates that this intervention is designed to meet four standards: (1) consistency with research evidence on risk and resilience after exposure to trauma; (2) applicability and practi-cality in community settings; (3) developmentally appropriate intervention across the lifespan; and (4) culturally informed and flexible delivery of services.

PFA includes rapid assessment techniques to identify survivors' immediate concerns and needs, offers flexible supportive activities, and includes handouts with vital information that promote healthy recovery. An overview of the nine com-ponents (i.e., core actions) of PFA is provided in Table 16.1.

Table 16.1 Overview of Psychological First Aid Actions and Goals

Preparing to deliver psychological first aid	Know of the nature of the mass level event, current circumstances, type and availability of relief and support services
Contact and engagement	Respond to contacts initiated by survivors or initiate contacts in a nonintrusive, compassionate, and helpful manner
Safety and comfort	Enhance immediate and ongoing safety; provide physical and emotional comfort
Stabilization	Calm and orient emotionally overwhelmed or disoriented survivors
Information gathering: Current needs and concerns	Identify immediate needs and concerns; gather information; tailor psychological first aid interventions
Practical assistance	Offer practical help to survivors in addressing immediate needs and concerns
Connection with social supports	Help establish brief or ongoing contacts with primary support persons and other sources of support
Information on coping	Provide information about stress reactions and coping to reduce distress and promote adaptive functioning
Linkage with collaborative services	Link survivors with available services needed immediately in the future

SOURCES: Brymer et al. (2006, pp. 101–102).

Each of the core components are detailed below, as presented in the *Psychological First Aid Field Operations Guide* (Brymer et al., 2006). While some of the following sections of the chapter include application to the vignette, a more comprehensive summary of the application of PFA to the vignette is offered at the end of the chapter, emphasizing the fluidity of PFA.

Preparing to deliver PFA requires knowledge of the specific disaster, working effectively with the Incident Command System (ICS) framework specifying roles and decision making, understanding the setting and how to communicate with authorized personnel, and knowledge of available support services. In addition, accessing accurate information about what has happened and what is going to happen is critical to reducing survivors' distress and promoting resilience. A calm presence along with knowledge of and sensitivity to culture and diversity is required. Self-awareness of the worker's values and biases and how they may

or may not fit with survivors' culture, ethnicity, religion, and race will impact the quality of support provided. Planning and preparation of the worker assisting survivors, with consideration of the areas identified above, will contribute to worker self-care as well.

The first contact with disaster survivors is the foundation upon which attempts to be helpful will succeed or fail. It is critical the worker be respectful during introductions, that they provide their title and role, and consider the specific style of physical or personal contact that may vary according to the survivor's culture. If unfamiliar with the survivor's culture, workers should maintain a good physical distance, not make prolonged eye contact, or touch the survivor. Seeking guidance from a cultural leader is recommended. When working with families, it is also recommended that workers identify the spokesperson for the family and initially speak with them. Then, speak calmly and quietly and focus on determining any pressing issues that require attention. Medical concerns have the greatest priority. Before connecting with children or adolescents workers need to obtain parental permission to talk with their children. While challenging to protect confidentiality in the shelter context, it is important to follow mandated reporting laws, requirements of the Health Insurance Portability and Accountability Act (HIPAA), and provisions related to disaster and terrorism. Any questions should be discussed with the shelter supervisor.

Ensuring immediate environmental safety may require reorganization of the shelter. Inquiring about and obtaining assistance for survivor needs related to health or activities of daily living and ongoing assessment of potential harm to self or others, and symptoms of shock are needed to ensure safety. Providing information about what they can do next, what is being done to assist them, the current status of the disaster, support services available, common stress responses, methods of self-care and coping are helpful in comforting survivors. Addressing immediate concerns and needs reduces fears and promotes coping and resilience. Because caregivers are so crucial to children's sense of safety and comfort, reconnecting children and adolescents separated from their families is a priority. Acute grief reactions may accompany the loss of a loved one. Survivors may struggle with anger and sadness, guilt, have regrets about not being able to say "goodbye," and express wishful thinking about seeing their loved one again. Grief reactions are grounded in cultural beliefs and attitudes about death and memorials/funerals. Asking about any cultural or spiritual needs and encouraging families to engage in their own traditions will help provide survivors with mutual support, to seek meaning, and to manage their emotional reactions. Also, creating a designated area that is child-friendly, is monitored for safety, and includes activities that are calming will reduce anxiety and promote a sense of safety and comfort. Finally, helping caregivers to understand the importance of shielding their children from trauma reminders (e.g., media coverage of the disaster and reminding

parents to be aware of their conversations about the disaster when children and adolescents are nearby and clarify things said that might be upsetting) will promote positive coping and resilience.

Ongoing assessment to evaluate stabilization includes observing survivors for signs of disorientation. If such signs are present, it is important to determine if the individual has family or friends in the shelter, identify their primary concern. It is helpful to calmly and quietly offer suggestions to help them with manageable feelings, thoughts, and goals, and provide information that orients them to the shelter. Exposure to disasters can exacerbate pre-existing mental health conditions and some survivors may not have their prescribed medication(s). If so, it is critical to gather the following information for physician referral: current medications being taken, medication compliance, symptoms of substance abuse, and any ongoing medical conditions. To assist in gathering critical information, the PFA *Field Guide* provides a Survivor Current Needs form and PFA Provider Worksheet that can be helpful in documenting survivor needs and the PFA services provided. The information gathered includes questions about the nature and severity of survivors' experiences during the disaster; any losses or injury of a loved one or injury to themselves; concerns about the individual/family post-disaster circumstances and potential ongoing threats; any concerns about separation from or safety of loved ones; identification of preexisting medical or mental health conditions and any need for medication; losses related to home, pets, or work; strong feelings of guilt or shame; hurting oneself or others; availability of social support; prior alcohol or drug use; and prior exposure to trauma or prior loss of loved ones.

Once a survivor's needs and concerns are identified, a problem-solving plan is developed and information is provided to the survivors. Children can be included in the process and may benefit from the assistance of adolescents or adults as they attempt to implement their plans. Practical assistance includes first identifying the most immediate needs, then clarifying the need to better identify effective steps to address concerns, discussing an action plan, and then helping the survivor take action. However, ethnic differences in a survivor's perception of the need for help, availability and accessibility of help, and comfort with help-seeking are important considerations and will impact the adequacy of the services provided (Norris & Alegria, 2005).

Social support is known to enhance well-being and recovery following exposure to disasters (Brymer et al., 2006). Workers facilitate emotional support (via active listening, acceptance of an individual's or family's experience), promote a sense of social connection (e.g., a sense of common ground with others), of feeling needed and having the confidence to manage the challenges ahead. They seek to have others reassure survivors they can be relied upon for support/assistance, receiving information or advice (e.g., about what is happening in the community or in the shelter, how to do something related to positive coping), and physical and material assistance (e.g., assistance with paperwork or facilitating access to basic needs such as food, clothing, or medicine). Survivors often want to immediately contact family, close friends, and clergy. Assisting them in reconnecting with their support networks can facilitate recovery. Also helping survivors engage with available resources within the shelter (e.g., relief workers, other survivors), offering reading materials (e.g., local newspapers, fact sheets), and bringing survivors together in a group can provide needed information and social contact. Bringing children or adolescents together in same age groups for calming activities and problem solving ways to ask for what they need and to support others nearby will help them cope in the immediate aftermath of disaster.

Information on coping offers information about normal stress reactions within the disaster context and coping strategies to reduce distress and promote resilience. Survivors with significant exposure to trauma and loss are provided with psychoeducation about stress reactions, emphasizing that such responses are normal within the context of disaster. Letting them know that such reactions

that negatively impact daily functioning for more than a month indicate a need for psychological support is critical to supporting resilience after their sheltered experience. Differentiating three types of posttraumatic responses: (1) intrusive reactions; (2) avoidance and withdrawal reactions; and (3) physical arousal reactions helps them to recognize likely reactions as normal within the disaster context. Trauma reminders, loss reminders, and change reminders can also cause distress by evoking memories of the disaster. Grief reactions are also common, particularly among survivors who have lost a loved one or those who have lost their home, pets, or personal things. They may experience sadness, anger, regret, or disturbing dreams. Those who have lost a loved one may experience traumatic grief symptoms such as preoccupation with how the death could have been prevented and who was at fault. Physical reactions such as headaches, stomachaches, racing heart, and hyperventilation may be present. Youth in particular will vary in their ability to connect the events of the disaster to their emotions and physical responses. Talking with youth and adolescents about typical responses after a traumatic loss will help them to connect their experience and emotions. Providing basic information about methods of coping to both parent and youth or adolescent (e.g., relaxation techniques, reestablishing family routines, utilizing support groups, using calming self-talk, obtaining needed information, focusing on practical things that are doable in the present) will promote resilience. The PFA *Field Guide* provides handouts to help parents to manage anger responses, guilt or shame, sleep problems, or alcohol/substance abuse.

The last component of PFA seeks to link survivors of disaster with available services needed immediately or in the future. Referrals and facilitation of access to needed supports address medical or mental health problems, threats of harm to self or others, pastoral counseling when desired, and ongoing challenges with coping. Referrals may be new to the parent or child/adolescent or a reconnection to organizations that previously provided them with services.

Transference and Countertransference Issues

Marginalized groups, such as racial/ethnic minorities and those with low income, are known to be at greater risk for disaster exposure and poorer mental health outcomes (Hawkins, Zinzow, Amstadter, Danielson, & Ruggiero, 2009). Minority and low-income groups are often least likely and unable to evacuate prior to the disaster. Spence, Lachlan, and Griffin (2007) found that before Hurricane Katrina, only 64.5% of African Americans versus 85.5% of white respondents evacuated. Researchers posit that marginalized populations such as African Americans are often distrustful of the government and other authorities and more likely to heed warnings and information provided by those within their social networks (Eisenman, Cordasco, Asch, Golden, & Glik, 2007; Peguero, 2006).

Cultural beliefs impact individuals' behaviors and outcomes in both the pre- and peridisaster (immediate post-disaster) phases. For example, African Americans often hold a fatalistic perspective (e.g., a tendency to perceive events as being the result of external control vs. individual control). Some studies have found fatalism to be associated with failure to evacuate, increased disaster related distress, and a higher risk of PTSD (Elliott & Pais, 2006; Perilla, Norris, & Lavizzo, 2002). Finally, perceived discrimination, stigma regarding receipt of mental health services, a reliance on informal support networks and religious/spiritual activities all may contribute to help-seeking or receptiveness to assistance in the aftermath of disaster.

Racism in the United States was highlighted by Hurricane Katrina. Sixty percent of African Americans perceived race as a critical factor in the slow response to the disaster victims (Boyd-Franklin, 2008). Studies indicate that soon after Hurricane Katrina, ethnic minority adults in the Gulf region perceived greater discrimination than nonminorities. In addition, all adults residing in New Orleans perceived themselves as receiving less social support and greater discrimination than those along the Gulf coast of Mississippi (Weems et al., 2007). Boyd-Franklin (2008) cites 20,000 people at the Convention Center and 20,000 at the Superdome who were left without food or water; a large number of those were black. In addition, numerous African Americans lost their homes in New Orleans and knew they could not afford the cost of rebuilding. A review of 17 studies of the experiences of African Americans following Hurricane Katrina found that African American women were the most likely group to report mental health distress and disrupted relationships as well as strengthened faith and greater recognition of the importance of family (Laditka, Murray, & Laditka, 2010). Within the shelter, racial tension can escalate and create conflict between survivors and disaster responders (Weems et al., 2007). Consequently, African American survivors' assessments and outcomes are the result of the direct experience of the disaster itself and the inhuman conditions and racism experienced during the shelter experience.

In order to work effectively with African American families, Hines and Boyd-Franklin (1982) emphasize the importance of practitioners being able to consider the impact of the family's social, political, socioeconomic, and broader environmental conditions and how systems within their community may have intruded in their lives. Family members may be suspicious of responder's motives as they request personal information and permission to facilitate community support, reflecting an issue of trust grounded in a learned, survival response. Their ambivalence can influence engagement and cooperation throughout the implementation of PFA. The mental health responder working with Connor and Tanya will want to be sensitive to and explore how Tanya and Connor make sense of what has happened to them and to Connor's grandmother. They will want to consider how previous experiences with discrimination may impact their willingness to seek assistance and engage in PFA.

Disaster responders are exposed to repeated traumatic events and in their role as helpers may have strong countertransference reactions accompanied by a decreased ability to cope (Substance Abuse and Mental Health Services Agency [SAMHSA], 2007).

Depending on the responder's personal history and vulnerabilities, countertransference reactions could be related to survivor guilt, a sense of helplessness at not being able to protect child victims, developing an intolerance to the anguish of bereaved survivors, or questioning their own assumptions about faith or their world reality. Over-identification with disaster survivors may lead responders to be unable to maintain appropriate personal and professional boundaries, particularly if they desire to help by "fixing it" for others. Responders may also attempt to distance themselves from survivors' pain and rage. The PFA *Field Guide* and SAMHSA (2007) emphasize the importance of self-awareness, consultation, and supervision to assist responders in exploring their motivations for helping, recognizing boundary issues, examining personal prejudices and cultural stereotypes, and recognizing over-identification with survivors' emotions, how their own disaster experience is impacting helping others, and how their personal history may be interfering with their work. The PFA *Field Guide* offers responders suggestions for organizational care and self-care to reduce countertransference and promote responder resilience. The mental health professional working with Connor and Tanya will need to be open to self-exploration, maintain self-awareness, and seek consultation and support as needed to ensure they provide effective services.

Legal and Ethical Concerns

In the event of a natural disaster such as Hurricane Katrina, the American Red Cross has a cooperative partnership with local government to provide a range of services which include but are not limited to emergency sheltering, mental health support, and disaster welfare inquiry services. Legally, disaster mental health responders are covered under their professional liability malpractice insurance and the limitation to practice only within their state jurisdiction is waived during a public health emergency (National Association of Social Workers, 2014).

Soliman (2010) proposes an ethical framework emphasizing the importance of accountability, responsibility, equity, transparency, decision making capacity, risks/benefits, and confidentiality. The mental health professional providing PFA intervention with Tanya and Connor would need to be able to demonstrate competency that promotes their protection in the shelter environment. This requires knowledge of the shelter system and related systems such as the Incident Command Center, training in PFA, and utilization of consultation and supervision to address countertransference and burnout. In addition, the mental health professional would engage in transparency, providing clear, timely, and honest information to Tanya as it relates to the status of the disaster, status of family members, and shelter operation. The responder would also need to promote social justice by providing/facilitating equal opportunity for Tanya and Connor to request and access services and address any forms of discrimination, oppression, or social profiling. It is critical that responders consider all survivors' rights, providing adequate services and treat them with dignity and respect. Confidentiality can be extremely challenging within the shelter environment. The responder working with Tanya and Connor would need to make every effort to engage them utilizing procedures that protect their rights to confidentiality. The mental health professional will also need to obtain Tanya's permission for any referrals specifically made for Connor. The responder would also need to work with shelter managers to keep Tanya and Connor safe within the chaotic environment. For example, making sure there is supervision of the area designated for youth activities. All disaster responders must comply with the ethical and practice standards within their discipline and engage within the scope of their training.

MEZZO AND MACRO PERSPECTIVES

While the majority of social work practice in disasters is provided at the micro level with individuals and families, there are significant opportunities to promote human and community resilience and recovery through mezzo and macro level practices.

In the aftermath of disaster it is crucial for communities to have the ability to restore, and even improve, the health and social services networks as a means to promote resilience and well-being. The U.S. Department of Homeland Security (2013) provides a National Disaster Recovery Framework designed to support locally directed recovery efforts. In the pre-disaster stage, the focus is on preparedness, developing strategies supporting recovery in relation to bio-behavioral health and social services. The preparedness protocols incorporate principles of sustainability, resilience, and mitigation. In the post-disaster phase, this framework is designed to address barriers to recovery, establish communication forums for services providers, coordinate with other local and large scale partners to assess environmental health conditions, and restore the capacity for social services to meet the needs of the impacted community. At the mezzo level, social workers can play a key role through community organizing to support disaster services coordination that includes community assessment and services coordination of both formal and informal organizations. Pyles (2007) describes the community-based disaster management model (CBDM), a disaster recovery approach that highlights the importance of participation and linkages. This model emphasizes participation of vulnerable populations and outsiders who can offer supportive, indigenous leadership, strengthening the capacity of local communities, and linking disaster and development challenges with a focus on empowerment (Murphy & Cunningham, 2003). This model is consistent with a social work perspective of emergency management that includes diverse organizational representatives and leaders from the community. Harrel and Zakour (2000) identify the importance of representatives of informal community organizations that address the needs of vulnerable groups being involved in the planning process of emergency management. Social workers can be excellent community organizers. They have knowledge and expertise in multiple systems and institutions impacting residents and the community infrastructure as well as community assessment. Numerous factors, including

power, race, class, gender, and access to resources and information impact disaster recovery (Smith & Wenger, 2007). Social workers engaged in mezzo-level practice are concerned with supporting the social environment of individuals; support networks that include not only family and friends but social services organizations. Equal access to needed service systems is critical. In the aftermath of disasters, community and faith-based organizations (often termed NGOs) are instrumental in recovery, offering both short- and long-term services. Mobilization and coordination of these services, particularly for vulnerable populations can provide much needed continuity of care for disaster survivors (Zakour & Harrell, 2003). Coordination and implementation of interorganizational networks has proven to enhance the effectiveness of disaster services (Liu, Gillespie, & Murty, 2000). Social workers can effectively create linkages between vulnerable groups and service systems, engaging in a variety of roles such as advocacy and brokering. Individual and family recovery also requires that the community around them is functioning. Social workers can create collaborations among service systems as a means to support the accessibility of resources (Zakour & Harrell, 2003). Community organizing may also include coordinating volunteer programs that train and coordinating facilitation of psychological debriefings (Miller, 2003) as well as expand the capacity to rebuild and manage shelters and ensure safety (Zakour & Harrell, 2003).

At the macro level, the development of a comprehensive and effective system supporting human and community recovery requires advocacy that addresses both human and community vulnerability and recovery. Individual vulnerability is grounded in social structural factors that increase the likelihood of greater exposure to adverse conditions and poorer social, psychological, and health outcomes in the aftermath of disaster (Thomas & Soliman, 2002). Persons who are older, people of color, and children are disproportionately represented among low income populations, a primary factor associated with greater social vulnerability (Rogge, 2003). At the community level, vulnerability is based on demographic, historical, cultural, and ecological characteristics. Poverty level is negatively associated with community impact and recovery. Poorer communities tend to have fewer social service organizations and less developed disaster relief networks (Zakour & Harrell, 2003).

Social workers are bound by a Code of Ethics that demands awareness and response to social injustice. Vulnerable populations such as minority groups, children, and those with low income have historically experienced delays in receipt of disaster relief or diminished assistance (Soliman, 2010). Recognition and response to the differential burden faced by vulnerable groups in the aftermath of disaster must be considered at all phases of disaster planning and response. This is of paramount importance. Applying principles of distributive, procedural, and participatory justice, social workers advocate for at-risk disaster survivors' rights as class advocates (Murty, 2000). Being involved and advocating for the rights of vulnerable populations in both local and statewide pre-disaster assessment, mitigation, planning, and preparedness processes as well as post-disaster response will increase the likelihood of equitable and accessible services for at-risk groups. In addition, advocating for the building of the adaptive capacity of communities, utilizing a lens of empowerment, collaboration and innovation, social workers can effectively address social justice challenges to better meet the needs of vulnerable groups in the aftermath of disaster.

COMPREHENSIVE APPLICATION TO CASE VIGNETTE

Assessment and intervention at the individual level would be initiated for both Connor and his mother. According to the triage approach described, if neither Connor nor his mother is identified as having a mental health diagnosis they would be referred for PFA. If we assume that Connor has had a consistent, nurturing environment living with his grandmother and mother and that he and his mother have no prior psychological diagnoses PFA is recommended. Ongoing assessment of the needs and concerns of Connor and his mother would occur as part of PFA.

The worker would introduce themselves in a calm, warm, welcoming, and informal or "down to earth" manner. They would be respectful, speak to everyone present around the group, first asking adults their names and how they would prefer to be addressed (Boyd-Franklin, 2008) and then the youths or adolescents present. The worker would attempt to identify any specific needs requiring attention, particularly medical needs or those related to environmental safety within the chaotic shelter environment. Connor's mother needs to receive accurate information about the current disaster situation and what is being done both within the shelter and outside of the shelter as well as what to expect next. In the face of the traumatic loss, both Connor and his mother could experience denial, anger, guilt, and sadness (Webb, 2002).

In the vignette, Connor stared in horror as his grandmother fell. He experienced strong peritraumatic symptoms, and his mother had to carry him down the stairs. Due to the egocentricity of latency-stage youth, he may wonder whether he could have done something to prevent his grandmother from falling and feel guilty for not "saving" her. Connor might also take his mother's comment, "It's God's will," to mean he did something bad that led to God punishing him by taking his grandmother away from him. He may have limited ability to verbalize his feelings (Webb, 2002). The worker would engage Tanya (and possibly Connor) in identifying immediate concerns. Gaining Connor's mother's permission to talk with him individually may assist in identifying Connor's fears related to his experience of seeing his grandmother fall as well as any regrets, or wishful thinking that he might see his grandmother again. That said, it will be important for the worker to consider cultural and religious beliefs Tanya and Connor may have about death. While there is certainly diversity in beliefs about death and related rituals based on differences in religious affiliations, African Americans often see death as God's will or plan and that their loved one is with God. They are also likely to believe that they will be reunited in heaven, a belief that can help survivors feel an ongoing connection to their deceased loved one (Smith, 1999, 2002).

The worker will want to encourage Connor and Tanya to engage in their own traditions to the degree possible within the context of the shelter.

Within African American families, the cultural value of "being strong" can translate into opting to quietly manage the traumatic experience without tears or changes in activities of daily living. This could relate to concerns of feeling overwhelmed and being unable to manage the situation. However, within the African American community, open, public expression of grief is encouraged, particularly by women and children (Hines, 2004). It is likely that Tanya is greatly concerned about what has happened to her mother, her home, her job, and her ability to meet the needs of her son. Because the death of Connor's grandmother was unexpected, both Connor and his mother may struggle with anger, anxiety, and a sense of powerlessness (Hines, 2004). The worker can utilize the Survivor Current Needs form and PFA Provider Worksheet to document the family's needs and concerns, their particular experiences during the disaster (including the loss of Connor's grandmother), and availability of support. Connor's resilience will depend on the effectiveness of the coping strategies he and his mother use, any previous history of traumatic exposure, and his mother's ability to provide emotional support and a sense of safety in the environment. Fortunately, African American women have demonstrated their ability to meet the demands to guide their families through crises (Salahu-Din, 1996, as cited in Laurie & Neimeyer, 2008). The worker can support the family's sense of safety and comfort by identifying any cultural or spiritual needs. For example, within the African American culture it is important that the deceased be given a "send off" through which they can "go out in style" (Hines, 2004). Attending the funeral is tremendously important and the community is notified of the death by placing a wreath on the door of the deceased individual's home (Hines, 2004). It might be helpful to create an opportunity for Connor and Tanya to make some type of wreath in recognition of the loss of Connor's grandmother. Doing so reinforces both cultural rituals and supports the African American belief of maintaining connection to their loved one thereby supporting the grief process. Providing Tanya with psychoeducational information about coping for herself and Connor (e.g., the importance of shielding Connor from trauma reminders, calming activities, breathing and relaxation exercises) helps Connor to cope and Tanya to feel more empowered. Helping Tanya to interact with other relief workers and disaster survivors, and offering reading materials, and engaging her in a problem solving process to address the family's concerns are empowering and effective. The worker would utilize active listening, demonstrate acceptance of their experience, and offer any physical and material assistance needed. Tanya may want to contact family members, including biological family as well as fictive kin and clergy (Laurie & Neimeyer, 2008). If Connor's mother presented concerns of racism, Boyd-Franklin (2008) recommends encouraging the survivor to provide a story of their experience. If the worker is of a different racial group, to also ask how the survivor feels talking about racism with the worker, particularly if they are white can help to set a foundation for other core PFA actions (Boyd-Franklin, 2008).

A space designed for children that is monitored for safety and includes calming activities could also give Tanya time to herself without the demands of caring for Connor and support Connor's coping and adaptation. With Tanya's permission, the worker would meet with Connor to clarify his needs and concerns. Because youth vary in their ability to relate the disaster event to their emotions, helping them to understand their physical and emotional reactions to the disaster supports the coping process. The worker can ask Connor about physical sensations he experienced, suggest different feelings and let him pick those that fit for him, always using developmentally appropriate language. If Connor is able to participate in the problem solving process they can collaborate on a plan to address his concerns.

Throughout their time in the shelter the worker would engage in ongoing assessment observing Connor and Tanya, watching for any signs of disorientation or extreme distress and offering crisis support as needed, providing Tanya and Connor referrals and facilitating access to needed supports. During the maintenance phase of risk communication Tanya and Connor (as appropriate for his developmental age and coping capacity) need to be informed about what is happening outside of the evacuation center; the status of the disaster and what resources will be available to them during their stay at the evacuation center as well as planning for when they leave the center. Tanya needs accurate information in order to make good decisions about how they will determine the condition of their home and where they will live when they leave the evacuation center as well as if and when she can return to work. She may be at risk for relocation and may need help in reaching out to extended family to ensure a safe and secure living environment after leaving the shelter. Accurate communication and facilitation of outreach is critical to addressing the needs of families as they try to put their lives back together. Over time, Tanya and Connor may need assistance from multiple social service organizations to address longer term impacts due to loss of family, housing, and employment. They may need social workers to advocate on their behalf in order to access needed services. If a comprehensive, culturally sensitive system of social services has been developed prior to the disaster, or even initiated in the aftermath of the disaster, the likelihood they will obtain relevant, needed services is greatly enhanced.

CONCLUSION

Disasters devastate communities and create overwhelming challenges for individuals and families. Individuals and families may experience a range of physical and psychological impacts over time. Triage and assessment are critical as a foundation in determining a course of action that promotes best outcomes. For those without a diagnosed mental illness, PFA provides a research informed and culturally sensitive approach to meet the mental health needs of diverse children, adolescents, adults, and families thereby supporting resilience in the aftermath of disaster. Because the impacts of

disaster may include delayed emotional responses as well as long-term support needs related to housing, health, and employment, it is critical that social services linkages be available for extended periods and that the infrastructure and policies support both immediate and long-term accessibility to culturally relevant services.

INTERNET RESOURCES

- Federal Emergency Management Agency: http://www.fema.gov
- International Federation of Red Cross and Red Crescent Societies: Disaster Management: http://www.ifrc.org/en/what-we-do/disaster-management/
- National Center for Post-Traumatic Stress Disorder: http://www.ptsd.va.gov
- National Child Traumatic Stress Network: Psychological First Aid Field Guide: http://www.nctsn.org/content/psychological-first-aid
- Psychological First Aid Fact Sheet: http://store.samhsa.gov/shin/content/NMH05–0210/NMH05–0210.pdf

DISCUSSION QUESTIONS

1. How might intervention differ at the triage level?

2. How might implementation of psychological first aid vary with different racial/ethnic groups?

3. How might implementation of psychological first aid vary if caregivers and their children or adolescents are separated?

4. What would your particular challenges be in terms of managing personal biases and implementing psychological first aid?

5. How can social workers advocate for improvement of shelter conditions that support effective implementation of psychological first aid in the immediate aftermath of disasters?

6. What roles can social workers play at the mezzo and macro levels of practice to address the needs of vulnerable populations impacted by disasters?

REFERENCES

Ayalon, O. (1993). Posttraumatic stress recovery of terrorist survivors. In J. Wilson & B. Raphael (Eds.), *International handbook of traumatic stress syndromes* (pp. 855–866). New York, NY: Plenum Press.

Becker-Blease, K., Turner, H. A., & Finkelhor, D. (2010). Disasters, victimization and children's mental health. *Child Development, 81*(4), 1040–1052.

Bell, H. (2008). Case management with displaced survivors of Hurricane Katrina: A case study of one host community. *Journal of Social Service Research, 34*(3), 45–53.

Bingham, R. D., & Harmon, R. J. (1996). Traumatic stress in infancy and early childhood: Expression of distress and developmental issues. In C. R. Pfeffer (Ed.), *Severe stress and mental disturbance in children* (pp. 499–532). Washington, DC: American Psychiatric Press.

Blackorby, J., & Cameto, R. (2004). *Changes in school engagement and academic performance of students with disabilities.* In SEELS, *Wave 1 Wave 2 overview* (pp. 8.1–8.23). Menlo Park, CA: SRI International.

Boyd-Franklin, N. (2008). *African Americans and trauma: Lessons learned from disasters.* Melissa Institute. Retrieved from http://www.melissainstitute.org/documents/LessonsTrauma.ppt

Brymer, M., Jacobs, A., Layne, C., Pynoos, R., Ruzek, J., Steinberg, A., . . . Watson, P. (2006). *Psychological first aid: Field operations guide* (2nd ed.). Retrieved from http://www.nctsn.org

Butler, A. S., Panzer, A. M., & Goldfrank, L. R. (Eds.). (2003). *Preparing for the psychological consequences of terrorism: A public health strategy.* Committee on Responding to the Psychological Consequences of Terrorism. Washington, DC: National Academies Press.

Cicchetti, D. (1996). Child maltreatment: Implications for developmental theory and research. *Human Development, 39*(1), 18–39.

Compas, B. E., Connor-Smith, J. K., Saltzman, H., Thomsen, A. H., & Wadsworth, M. E. (2001). Coping with stress during childhood and adolescence: Problems, progress, and potential in theory and research. *Psychological Bulletin, 127*(1), 87–127. doi:10.1037/0033–2909.127.1.87

Deering, C. G. (2000). A cognitive developmental approach to understanding how children cope with disasters. *Journal of Child and Adolescent Psychiatric Nursing, 13*(1), 7–16. doi:10.1111/j.1744–6171.2000.tb00070.x

Eisenman, D. P., Cordasco, K. M., Asch, S., Golden, J. F., & Glik, D. (2007). Disaster planning and risk communication with vulnerable communities: Lessons from Hurricane Katrina. *American Journal of Public Health, 97*(Supp. 1), S109–S115.

Elbedour, S., Baker, A., Shalhoub-Kevorkian, N., Irwin, M., & Belmaker, R. (1999). Psychological responses in family members after the Hebron massacre. *Depression and Anxiety, 9*(1), 27–31.

Elliott, J., & Pais, J. (2006). Race, class, and Hurricane Katrina: Social differences in human responses to disaster. *Social Science Research, 35*(2), 295–321.

Fraser, M. W., Richman, J. M., & Galinsky, M. J. (1999). Risk, protection, and resilience: Toward a conceptual framework for social work practice. *Social Work Research, 23*(3), 131–143.

Freedy, J. R., Shaw, D., Jarrell, M. P., & Masters, C. (1992). Towards an understanding of the psychological impact of natural disaster: An application of the conservation resources stress model. *Journal of Traumatic Stress, 5*(3), 441–454.

Garrison, C. Z., Bryant, E. S., Addy, C. L., Spurrier, P. G., Freedy, J. R., & Kilpatrick, D. G. (1995). Posttraumatic stress disorder in adolescents after Hurricane Andrew. *Journal of the American Academy of Child & Adolescent Psychiatry, 34*(9), 1193–1201. doi:10.1097/00004583–199509000–00017

Gerrity, E. T., & Steinglass, P. (2003). Relocation stress following catastrophic events. In R. J. Ursano (Ed.), *Terrorism and disaster: Individual and community mental health interventions* (pp. 259–286). New York, NY: Cambridge University Press.

Groome, D., & Soureti, A. (2004). Post-traumatic stress disorder and anxiety symptoms in children exposed to the 1999 Greek earthquake. *British Journal of Psychology, 95*(3), 387–397.

Gurwitch, R. H., Pfefferbaum, B., & Leftwich, M. J. T. (2002). The impact of terrorism on children: Considerations for a new era. *Journal of Trauma Practice, 1*(3/4), 101–124.

Gurwitch, R. H., Sitterle, K. S., Young, B. H., & Pfefferbaum, B. (2002). Helping children in the aftermath of terrorism. In A. M. La Greca & W. K. Silverman (Eds.), *Helping children cope with disasters: Integrating research and practice* (pp. 327–357). Washington, DC: American Psychological Association.

Hackbarth, M., Pavkov, T., Wetchler, J., & Flannery, M. (2012). Natural disasters: An assessment of family resiliency following Hurricane Katrina. *Journal of Marital and Family Therapy, 38*(2), 340–351.

Harrell, E. B., & Zakour, M. J. (2000). Including informal organizations in disaster planning: Development of a range-of-type measure. *Tulane Studies in Social Welfare, 21/22,* 61–83.

Hawkins, A. O., Zinzow, H. M., Amstadter, A. B., Danielson, C. K., & Ruggiero, K. J. (2009). Factors associated with exposure and response to disasters among marginalized populations. In Y. Neria, S. Galea, & F. H. Norris (Eds.), *Mental health and disasters* (pp. 277–290). New York, NY: Cambridge University Press.

Hines, P. M. (2004). Mourning in African-American culture. In F. Walsh & M. McGoldrick (Eds.), *Living beyond loss: Death in the family* (2nd ed.; pp.125–130). New York, NY: W.W. Norton.

Hines, P. M., & Boyd-Franklin, N. (1982). Black families. In M. McGoldrick, J. K. Pearce, & J. Giordano (Eds.), *Ethnicity and family therapy* (pp. 84–107). New York, NY: Guilford Press.

Hobfoll, S. E., Freedy, J. R., Green, B. L., & Solomon, S. D. (1996). Coping in reaction to extreme stress: The roles of resource loss and resource availability. In M. Zeidner, & N. S. Endler (Eds.), *Handbook of coping* (pp. 322–349). New York, NY: John Wiley & Sons.

Huzziff, C. A., & Ronan, K. R. (1999). Prediction of children's coping following a natural disaster— the Mount Ruapehu eruptions: A prospective study. *Australasian Journal of Disaster and Trauma Studies,* 1. Retrieved from http://trauma.massey.ac.nz/issues/1999-1/huzziff1.htm

Knabb, R. D., Rhome, J. R., & Brown, D. P. (2006). *Tropical cyclone report, Hurricane Katrina, 23–30 August 2005.* Retrieved from http://www.nhc.noaa.gov/data/tcr/AL122005_Katrina.pdf

Koplewicz, H. S., Vogel, J. M., Solanato, M. V., Morrissey, R. F., Alonso, C. M., Abikoff, H., . . . Novick, R. (2002). Child and parent response to the 1993 World Trade Center bombing. *Journal of Traumatic Stress, 15*(1), 77–85.

Laditka, S. B., Murray, L. M., & Laditka, J. N. (2010). In the eye of the storm: Resilience and vulnerability among African American women in the wake of Hurricane Katrina. *Health Care for Women International, 31,* 1013–1027.

La Greca, A. M., & Silverman, W. K. (2006). Treating children and adolescents affected by disasters and terrorism. In P. C. Kendall (Ed.), *Child and adolescent therapy: Cognitive-behavioral procedures* (3rd ed.; pp. 356–382). New York, NY: Guilford Press.

Laurie, A., & Neimeyer, R. A. (2008). African Americans in bereavement: Grief as a function of ethnicity. *Omega: Journal of Death and Dying, 57*(2), 173–193.

Lazarus, R. S., & Folkman, S. (1984). *Stress, appraisal, and coping.* New York, NY: Springer.

Liu, L., Gillespie, D. F., & Murty, S. A. (2000). Service coordination as intergovernmental strategies in service delivery. *Tulane Studies in Social Welfare, 21/22,* 85–103.

McDermott, B. M., & Palmer, L. J. (2002). Postdisaster emotional distress, depression and event related variables: Findings across child and adolescent developmental stages. *Australasian and New Zealand Journal of Psychiatry, 36*(6), 754–761.

Miller, J. (2003). Critical incident debriefing and social work: Expanding the frame. *Journal of Social Service Research, 30*(2), 7–25.

Murphy, P. W., & Cunningham, J. V. (2003). *Organizing for community controlled development: Renewing civil society.* Thousand Oaks, CA: Sage.

Murty, S. A. (2000). When disaster strikes . . . The critical incident stress debriefing process. *Journal of Emergency Medical Services, 8*(1), 36–39.

Nader, K. O. (2004). Assessing traumatic experiences in children and adolescents: Self-reports of DSM PTSD Criteria B-D Symptoms. In J. P. Wilson, & T. M. Keane (Eds.), *Assessing psychological trauma and PTSD* (pp. 513–537). New York, NY: Guilford Press.

National Association of Social Workers (2014). *Social workers and disaster relief services.* Retrieved from http://www.socialworkers.org/ldf/legal_issue/200509.asp?back=yes

Norris, F. H., & Alegria, M. (2005). Mental health care for ethnic minority individuals and communities in the aftermath of disasters and mass violence. *CNS Spectrums, 10*(2), 132–140.

Norris F. H., Friedman, M. J., & Watson, P. J. (2002). 60,000 disaster victims speak: Part II. Summary and implications of the disaster mental health research. *Psychiatry, 65(3)*, 240–260.

Pargament, K. I., Smith, B. W., Koenig, H. G., & Perez, L. (1998). Patterns of positive and negative religious coping with major life stressors. *Journal for the Scientific Study of Religion, 37*, 710–724.

Peguero, A. (2006). Latino disaster vulnerability: The dissemination of hurricane mitigation information among Florida's homeowners. *Hispanic Journal of Behavioral Sciences, 28*(1), 5–22.

Perilla, J., Norris, F., & Lavizzo, E. (2002). Ethnicity, culture, and disaster response: Identifying and explaining ethnic differences in PTSD six months after Hurricane Andrew. *Journal of Social and Clinical Psychology, 21*(1), 20–45.

Pfefferbaum, B., Nixon, S. J., Tucker, P. M., Tivis, R. D., Moore, V. L., Gurwitch, R. H., . . . Geis, H. (1999). Posttraumatic stress responses in bereaved children after the Oklahoma City bombing. *Journal of the American Academy of Child and Adolescent Psychiatry, 38*(11), 1372–1379.

Pfefferbaum, B., North, C. S., Doughty, D. E., Gurwitch, R. H., Fullerton, C. S., & Kyula, J. (2003). Posttraumatic stress and functional impairment in Kenyan children following the 1998 American embassy bombing. *American Journal of Orthopsychiatry, 73*(2), 133–140.

Pyles, L. (2007). Community organizing for post-disaster social development: Locating social work. *International Social Work, 50*(3), 321–333.

Resnick, P. A. (2001). *Stress and trauma.* Philadelphia, PA: Psychology Press.

Rogge, M. E. (2003). The future is now: Social work, disaster management, and traumatic stress in the 21st century. *Journal of Social Service Research, 30*(2), 1–6.

Ronan, K. R. (1997). The effects of a 'benign' disaster: Symptoms of post-traumatic stress in children following a series of volcanic eruptions. *Australasian Journal of Disaster and Trauma Studies, 1*(1). Retrieved from http://www.massey.ac.nz/~trauma/issues/1997-1/ronan1.htm

Salahu-Din, S. N. (1996). A comparison of coping strategies of African American and Caucasian widows. *Omega: Journal of Death and Dying, 33*(2), 103–120.

Self-Brown, S., Lai, B. S., Thompson, J. E., McGill, T., & Kelley, M. L. (2013). Posttraumatic stress disorder symptom trajectories in Hurricane Katrina–affected youth. *Journal of Affective Disorders, 147*(1), 198–204.

Shannon, M., Lonigan, C. J., Finch, A. J., & Taylor, C. M. (1994). Children exposed to disaster: Epidemiology of post-traumatic symptoms and symptoms profiles. *Journal of American Academy of Child & Adolescent Psychiatry, 33*(1), 80–93. doi:10.1097/00004583–199401000–00012

Smith, G. P., & Wenger, D. (2007). Sustainable disaster recovery: Operationalizing an existing agenda. In H. Rodriguez, E. L. Quarantelli, & R. R. Dynes (Eds.), *Handbook of disaster research* (pp. 234–257). New York, NY: Springer.

Smith, S. H. (1999). "Now that mom is in the Lord's arms, I just have to live the way she taught me": Reflections on an elderly, African American mother's death. *Journal of Gerontological Social Work, 32*(2), 41–51.

Smith, S. H. (2002). "Fret no more my child . . . for I'm all over heaven all day": Religious beliefs in the bereavement of African American middle-aged daughters coping with the death of an elderly mother. *Death Studies, 26*(4), 309–323.

Soliman, H. (2010). Ethical considerations in disasters: A social work framework. In D. Gillespie & K. Danso (Eds.), *Disaster concepts and issues: A guide for social work education and practice* (pp. 223–240). Alexandria, VA: CSWE Press.

Spence, P. R., Lachlan, K. A., & Griffin, D. R. (2007). Crisis communication, race, and natural disasters. *Journal of Black Studies, 37*(4), 539–554.

Stagman, S., & Cooper, J. L. (2010). *Children's mental health: What every policymaker should know.* National Center for Children in Poverty. Retrieved from http://www.nccp.org/publications/pub_929.html

Substance Abuse and Mental Health Services Agency. (2007). *Mental health response to mass violence and terrorism.* Retrieved from http://www.pinalcountyaz.gov/publichealth/EmergencyPreparednessResponse/Documents/CDR/Stress%20Prevention,%20managment,%20intervention.pdf

Terranova, A. M., Boxer, P., & Morris, A. S. (2009). Factors influencing the course of posttraumatic stress following a natural disaster: Children's reactions to Hurricane Katrina. *Journal of Applied Developmental Psychology, 30*(3), 344–355. doi:10.1016/j.appdev.2008.12.017

Thomas, N. D., & Soliman, H. H. (2002). Preventable tragedies: Heat disaster and the elderly. *Journal of Gerontological Social Work, 38*(4), 53–66.

Trappler, B., & Friedman, S. (1996). Posttraumatic stress disorder in survivors of the Brooklyn Bridge shooting. *American Journal of Psychiatry, 153*(5), 705–707.

U.S. Department of Homeland Security. (2013). *National response framework* (2nd ed.). Retrieved from https://www.fema.gov/national-response-framework

Vernberg, E. M., LaGreca, A. M., Silverman, W. K., & Prinstein, M. J. (1996). Predictors of children's post-disaster functioning following Hurricane Andrew. *Journal of Abnormal Psychology, 105,* 237–248.

Walsh, F. (2003). Crisis, trauma, and challenge: A relational resilience approach for healing, transformation, and growth. *Smith College Studies in Social Work, 74*(1), 49–71.

Walsh, F., & McGoldrick, M. (2004). Loss and the family: A systemic perspective. In F. Walsh & M. McGoldrick (Eds.), *Living beyond loss: Death in the family* (2nd ed.; pp. 3–26). New York, NY: W.W. Norton.

Webb, N. B. (2002). The child and death. In N. B. Webb (Ed.), *Helping bereaved children: A handbook for practitioners* (pp. 19–44). New York, NY: Guilford Press.

Weems, C. F., Taylor, L. K., Cannon, M. F., Marino, R. C., Romano, D. M., Scott, B. G., . . . Triplett, V. (2010). Posttraumatic stress, context, and the lingering effects of the Hurricane Katrina disaster among ethnic minority youth. *Journal of Abnormal Child Psychology, 38*(1), 49–56.

Weems, C. F., Watts, S. E., Marsee, M. A., Taylor, L. K., Costa, N. M., Cannon, M. F., . . . Pina, A. (2007). The psychosocial impact of Hurricane Katrina: Contextual differences in psychological symptoms, social support, and discrimination. *Behaviour Research and Therapy, 45*(10), 2295–2306.

Weisler, R. H., Barbee, J. G. T., & Townsend, M. H. (2006). Mental health and recovery in the Gulf Coast after Hurricanes Katrina and Rita. *Journal of the American Medical Association, 296*(5), 585–588.

Zakour, M. J., & Harrell, E. B. (2003). Access to disaster services: Social work interventions for vulnerable populations. *Journal of Social Service Research, 30*(2), 27–54.

CHAPTER 17

Transition in Pediatric Oncology

Amber Denbleyker

CHAPTER OBJECTIVES

- Discuss the transition to adult health care providers for adolescent young adult survivors of pediatric cancer;
- Demonstrate that adolescent and young adult cancer survivors are a growing population and discuss why transition support and programs are essential in the overall success of these adolescents;
- Discuss how motivational interviewing and psychoeducational interventions support the transition to adult care;
- Review resources and formal supports available for adolescent and young adult cancer survivors and discuss how connecting survivors to these resources aids in the transition to adult care.

CASE VIGNETTE

Marco, a 17-year-old Mexican American male, was diagnosed with acute myeloid leukemia at age 15. After receiving four cycles of chemotherapy, he relapsed. As a last option to cure his disease, he and his mother met with the medical team to discuss a bone marrow transplant.

At the meeting, Marco was accompanied by his mother, a 54-year-old Mexican woman named Alma. Marco was estranged from his father, and there were no other family members disclosed at the time of the meeting. Alma was reserved and polite and was monolingual Spanish speaking. She asked very few questions during the conference, but it was clear she had a strong dedication to Marco and had a strong Catholic faith. Alma shared her history of mental health and health problems, including her own struggle with cancer and her current battle with depression and anxiety. She talked about the stressors in her life, including the struggles of parenting an adolescent, especially one with cancer.

Marco, like many teenagers, presented as private and uninterested in participating in the conference. Marco was receiving mental health services through the hospital and had been diagnosed with depression and anxiety. Marco did not want to talk about his life, his feelings, or what may happen to him as a result of the treatment. After both Marco and his mother signed the consents to proceed with treatment, Marco walked out of the room and his mother trailed behind him.

Marco was hospitalized on the bone marrow transplant unit and remained in an isolated room for five months, until he was stable enough to return home. He no longer had leukemia, but he still needed to follow very strict medical instructions, such as taking 15 pills a day, wearing a mask when leaving the house, eating a special diet, and remaining on isolation precautions. His mother assisted with his medical needs, always at his bedside in the hospital and then bringing him to the outpatient clinic for follow-up appointments. Marco was hospitalized for an infection about one month after he had initially returned home.

During this hospitalization, it was evident that his mother, Alma, had been neglecting her own needs, especially her health. Alma talked about the stress of balancing her own health with all of Marco's needs. She presented as tired, disheveled, anxious, and physically ill. After about two weeks into Marco's hospital stay, Alma was emergently admitted to the hospital and diagnosed with end-stage breast cancer; her prognosis was terminal. It was clear that Marco was going to lose his mother and that he would need a guardian in order to return home. Although Marco was placed in the legal guardianship of his 21-year-old sister, Marco was now going to be the primary person responsible for his health, his success, and his future. Now, more than ever, supporting Marco through this crisis, his grief, and his transition to adulthood would be vital to his overall success and future as a survivor of pediatric cancer.

INTRODUCTION

According to the American Cancer Society's data from 2014, an estimated 15,780 children and adolescents in the United States will receive a new cancer diagnosis (Ward, DeSantis, Robbins, Kohler, & Jamal, 2014). Over the last several decades, advances in medicine and treatment options for pediatric cancer have resulted in a significant improvement in patient survival (Olson, Hung, Bobinski, & Goddard, 2010). In 2012, it was estimated that there were approximately 58,510 survivors of childhood cancer living in the United States (Siegel et al., 2012). This progress in childhood cancer treatment has produced a large cohort of adolescent and young adult (AYA) survivors who have a very distinct set of health care and psychosocial needs.

Survivorship can have varying definitions and meanings for each individual cancer survivor. Survivorship can be described as the time after the cancer diagnosis. Some define it as being cancer free for a specific period of time, or the time from receiving the last cancer treatment (American Society of Clinical Oncology [ASCO], 2014). Because each individual survivor may have a different way of defining survivorship, it is important to assess how they define survivorship for themselves in order to determine the best way to support the survivor at each stage of their journey (ASCO, 2014).

The focus on survivorship in pediatric oncology arose from those who recognized that there are multiple dimensions to life after cancer and that many survivors' needs were not being met. With an increasing number of long-term childhood cancer survivors, it became evident that these AYA survivors faced various medical as well as psychosocial challenges, even years after treatment. In addition, survivors of childhood cancer eventually face the time when they transition to the adult health care setting. This transition process can present many new challenges.

Transition can be defined as "a multi-faceted, active process that attends to the medical, psychosocial and educational and vocational needs of adolescents as they move from child-focused to the adult focused health-care system" (Blum et al., 1993, p. 1). During this time of health transition, adolescents are also entering adulthood and developing their sense of independence, autonomy, and self-sufficiency. For cancer survivors, this process can be complicated by their past cancer experiences and the stress that accompanied their treatment course. The cancer experience may also affect their development, mental health, and interpersonal relationships. Often times, these adolescents are transitioning from a comfortable and predictable medical environment to an independent adult environment, where they are expected to be the primary manager of their own care. This new expectation makes it that more important to assist these adolescents in planning and preparing at every step of the transition.

The concept of transition has been established as a "major quality-of-care issue for pediatric and adult health care providers" (Kolb, 2009, p. 31). Transition has been a focus of attention for the past decade with increasing research evaluating different comprehensive transition models in hopes of developing the best ways to meet the unique needs of this population and assist adolescents with this process (Kolb, 2009). There is substantial research on the importance of transition and the connection with follow-up care, health outcomes, and an overall successful future for the AYA. Knowing how fragile and important this process can be for an adolescent, it is imperative that the health care team begins this process early on in order to provide each adolescent with the comprehensive support and guidance tailored to their needs.

Clinical social workers in a health setting play a crucial role in this transition process. Clinical social workers must be skilled at conducting biopsychosocial assessments, and implementing interventions such as motivational interviewing, and psychoeducation tailored to the psychosocial and health needs of each AYA. Many AYA cancer survivors do quite well with the transition to adulthood and adult care with the appropriate professional support and guidance.

MICRO PERSPECTIVE
Assessment

Understanding the transition from pediatric to adult health care within a developmental framework is essential. AYAs face unique challenges related to their development, identity, and autonomy and having cancer can intensify these issues. When AYAs are diagnosed with cancer and going through treatment they are often forced to become dependent on parents and other caretakers, which can often interfere with their natural adjustment to adolescence and the process of developing their newfound independence and autonomy (Kwak et al., 2013).

AYAs with cancer are particularly vulnerable to distress as a result of the intersection of disease and developmental stage (Kwak et al., 2013). There are several studies that look at the psychological outcomes of childhood cancer survivors. In the longitudinal study conducted by Brinkman and his team (2013), it was found that distress could emerge far past the original cancer diagnosis. In other studies by Zebrack et al. (2004, 2007) and Michel, Rebholz, von der Weid, Bergstraeeser, and Kuehni (2010), it was found that there were some AYAs who were at significant risk for experiencing emotional distress, including anxiety and depression. However, Zebrack and colleagues also found that these risks for experiencing distress were correlated to and compounded by varying other psychosocial limitations, such as socioeconomic status and health status.

In the longitudinal study conducted by Kwak and colleagues (2013), it was found that AYAs experience two main periods of significant distress, first at the time of diagnosis and then again at the time of their transition from active treatment to survivorship care. This affirms the importance of reassessing the adolescent's feelings, concerns about their future, and mental health functioning throughout their journey, even when anticipated distressing symptoms may have resolved. Detecting and understanding when AYAs experience distress and why it persists or changes can help social workers identify who is in need of psychosocial interventions and when and how to intervene (Kwak et al., 2013).

From diagnosis at the age of 15 through the next few years, Marco faced the psychosocial task of Erikson's identity vs. role confusion (Berzoff, Flanagan, & Hertz, 2011). During adolescence there is a focus on developing a sense of personal identity and sense of self (Berzoff et al., 2011). Adolescents often question the ideas and beliefs of others, gaining new insights about the world and who they are. When diagnosed, Marco was in the process of developing his sense of identity, merging his past experiences with his anticipated future. His cancer diagnosis and treatment process resulted in many unexpected developmental shifts and challenged the way he viewed himself in his environment. This change in roles forced him to be reliant on others, especially his mother, for most of his day-to-day functioning. During this time, he may have been confused about what was within his control and what he needed others to help with. Again, after his mother died, he was forced into a position where he assumed all responsibility for his own care. He remembered to take his medications by himself, he made it to doctors' appointments on his own, and he had to start planning how to manage his day-to-day life as well as his health care. These major events, such as his cancer and his mother's death, may have interfered with Marco's ability to have a fully formed sense of self. On the other hand, Marco may have had an adaptive response to the disruptions of his developing identity.

Ledlie (2007) recognizes that the first step to a successful health care transition is the assessment process. It is important for the social worker to initiate the discussion to help clarify and develop mutually agreed upon goals that are tailored to each adolescents needs. According to Kolb (2009), it is important for survivors who are in the transition process to meet "transition readiness criteria," which includes "developmental level, cognitive ability, medical condition, self-care skills, family functioning, social support system and self-advocacy" (p. 33). It is also important to assess the mental health history of the adolescent and his family, as

well as current symptoms of depression and anxiety, which are common in adolescents who have faced a life threatening illness. Data suggests that most physicians do not feel confident assessing for distress and few utilize a standardized process (Brinkman et al., 2013). This affirms the importance of having social workers, as the psychosocial experts within the multidisciplinary medical team, who are adequately trained on not only assessing for these risk factors but also being prepared to offer appropriate referrals for mental health evaluation and support.

Once Marco had finished his treatment and was being monitored regularly in the outpatient setting, it was time to establish goals towards transition. To begin this process, a transition assessment was completed by the social worker and included the assessment criteria mentioned above. It was clear that Marco was establishing a stronger sense of autonomy now that he managed most of his own care. He lacked strong family and social support. However his sister's new involvement was a source of strength to the situation. It was necessary to assess any current medical issues affecting his day-to-day functioning, including cognitive, physical limitations, and other challenges. Marco was very bright and appeared to have an adequate understanding of his medication requirements. However, he reported that he did not always consistently take his medications and struggled with motivation.

An assessment of his current mental health symptoms and mental health follow up was also important. Marco was seen weekly by the social worker for individual bereavement support to help cope with the loss of his mother, as well as increase his coping strategies to manage his symptoms of depression and anxiety. He was also seen by a psychiatrist once a month to manage his psychotropic medications. Marco reported that during times of significant stress he did not attend medical appointments and stopped taking his medication. Marco's self-report indicated that at times he struggled with medication adherence which was often times linked with increased symptoms of depression and anxiety. This assessment led the social worker to encourage Marco's ongoing participation in mental health services, as well as provide a referral to an adolescent cancer support group. Having a better understanding of Marco's level of transition readiness and capability, allowed the social worker to tailor the interventions that would ultimately contribute to his overall health success and psychosocial growth.

Diversity Considerations

Social workers recognize that diversity includes the "sociocultural experiences of people of different genders, social classes, religious and spiritual beliefs, sexual orientations, ages, and physical and mental abilities" (National Association of Social Workers [NASW], 2001, p.8). These are all important factors to consider when creating a unique and personalized transition plan. Culture often dictates how a patient understands their illness and informs how they would like to proceed with treatment and planning for the future. Significant cultural information should be taken into consideration when developing the patient's treatment plan and it is often the social worker who can ensure inclusion of this relevant cultural information into the multidisciplinary approach and treatment planning of each individual patient and family (Shanske, Arnold, Carvalho, & Rein, 2012).

To address these considerations proactively, the survivor could communicate directly with the health care provider about the unique needs and beliefs he or she has. It is important to assess the diversity and culture of each individual survivor and his or her family members because every survivor and family member has his or her own style of communicating, making decisions, and sharing information within the family.

Social workers should assess for the survivors needs over time, as many cancer survivors change their ideas and beliefs depending on their experiences and interaction with others and their environment. Social workers can apply their assessment skills by asking such questions as, "How do you and your family make decisions about your health care?" or "Do you have any specific cultural or religious beliefs that help guide your thoughts or decision making?"

Asking Marco and his family these questions, allowed the social worker to better understand the family's Catholic faith and how they rely on their faith to help them make decisions and cope with uncertainties and difficult times. When deciding to proceed with the optional treatment of a bone marrow transplant, his mother Alma indicated that she had complete faith in God and felt secure that God would take care of her son. It was evident that she felt a sense of comfort and security from her faith. Understanding Alma's faith provided the opportunity to involve the Spiritual Care Services within the hospital to provide support, prayer, and other religious practices during their hospital stays. Also, because it was assessed that the family had limited family support, the social worker encouraged Alma to reach out to her church community for additional support, which had strong Mexican-American Catholic affiliation.

In addition it was important to acknowledge the presence of language differences, especially when communicating with the health care team. It was important to ensure proper interpretation when communicating with Alma, as well as translation of written communication and psycho-educational materials. Understanding the specific learning needs, such as level of education, literacy level, and preferred learning style were all important factors to consider as well.

Following Alma's death, it was important to recognize the specific shift of the family's culture of decision making. The family transitioned from a family centered and family shared decision making process to an autonomous decision making process, with Marco driving the decision making.

Shanske et al. (2012) term social workers "cultural brokers" because social workers ensure that the patient and family's individual culture and perspectives are being respected, honored, and understood by the health care team. According to Hoffman (2004), cultural bias and misunderstanding can affect the quality of patient care. Understanding a patient's culture will result in an increased sense of respect for the patient's culture, as well as increase the trust the patient has in the medical team. This will ultimately strengthen the physician patient partnership, increasing the patient's participation in their own care and the likelihood of follow-up care and a successful transition (Hoffman, 2004).

In addition, the social worker can also assist families' in navigating very complex health care settings and provide appropriate referrals that are culturally appropriate and helpful. There are significant challenges in making resources available and accessible "across differences in culture, age, and literacy" (Hewitt & Ganz, 2007, p. 78). This challenge must be overcome, as it is those who are economically disadvantaged and face other discriminations, which are the most in need of community resources and referrals (Hewitt & Ganz, 2007). A study that looked at follow-up care for childhood cancer survivors confirmed that significant health disparities exist and engaging survivors in follow-up health care is challenging (Barakat, Schwartz, Szabo, Hussey, & Bunin, 2012). They confirmed that socio-demographic factors are considerable risk variables for reduced engagement in follow-up care (Barakat et al., 2012). Unfortunately, the reality is that there are survivors with poor access to quality health care because they live in poverty, have little or no health insurance, or are physically isolated from medical care (Hoffman, 2004). Meeting basic needs, such as transportation and access to medical insurance, are necessary before an adolescent can successfully participate in survivorship care.

Upon the initial meeting with Marco, it was very important to assess his and his family's cultural practices and beliefs. It was clear from the psychosocial assessment and medical chart review that his family was very low income and received public benefits such as Supplemental Security Income (SSI) from Marco's disability. They lived in a one bedroom apartment and used public transportation to get to the hospital. Marco and his family obtained medical care through the public health insurance programs Medi-Cal (Medicaid) and California Children's Services (CCS). As a result of the psychosocial assessment, multiple referrals were provided to alleviate some of the barriers the family faced, in order to ensure Marco's access to the needed treatment. There was also a strong level of social work advocacy to educate the medical team and advocate for culturally competent care and for the ongoing need for Spanish interpretation.

In addition to the underlying cultural identities that each AYA holds, AYA cancer survivors share a unique culture of survivorship. This encompasses such things as, "the uncertainty about the future, loss of the pre-cancer life, sense of abandonment by their pediatric health care team, . . . self-transcendence . . . and the circle of influence" (Hoffman, 2004, p. 178). At times it may be helpful for the AYA to identify with others who have similar experiences, thoughts, and feelings. Social workers can embrace this culture by connecting AYAs with the cancer survivorship community, while also recognizing individual needs and embracing differences. Social workers can provide psychoeducation on the benefits of participating in peer support activities that are aimed to promote healthy communication as well as link AYAs directly to these programs (Kent et al., 2013, p. 8).

Interventions

Social workers play a key role in transition planning. Social workers in a health setting, such as a hospital or outpatient clinic, are often the member of the health care team who are engaging AYAs in discussions about transition to adult care. Evidenced-based interventions such as motivational interviewing and psychoeducation are ways to engage AYA in these discussions, empowering the patients towards taking an active role in their own care, and providing them with the tools and skills necessary to do so.

Motivational Interviewing

According to Miller and Rollnick (2009), motivational interviewing (MI) is a "collaborative, person-centered form of guiding to elicit and strengthen motivation for change" (p. 129). Many social workers naturally practice MI in their work with clients by respectfully communicating and holding a non-judgmental approach. Specifically, MI can be applied when working with adolescents who are transitioning to adult care, as adolescents often experience challenges with the change process of transitioning. Transition to adult care is a time when adolescents are challenged to take on new roles, engage with new health care providers, and experience new expectations of their health. Because adolescents often struggle with communicating their feelings and being motivated for change, MI is a useful strategy to enhance the communication with the provider and empower the youth to develop their goals.

MI is a method for enhancing motivation for healthy behavior change (Naar-King & Suarez, 2011). Research demonstrates that motivation to change is related to improved self-care in terms of illness management behaviors and with increased engagement in health care (Naar-King & Suarez, 2011). This is particularly important with adolescent cancer survivors who may still require close medical follow up and are at risk for future health problems. Also, it is a time when the adolescent assumes a more active role in decision making and goal setting. As the young adult becomes increasingly more responsible for managing their own care, they can experience difficulties in following medical treatment recommendations and overall illness management skills. MI is a sensitive approach that builds on the internal motivation of the adolescent, while respecting their autonomy and valuing their perspective (Naar-King & Suarez, 2011). Some examples of this approach include minimizing pressures and demands and offering choices (Naar-King & Suarez, 2011).

MI was most helpful with Marco during the engagement process, as well as when addressing his poor adherence to medication. There were expected challenges as Marco took on more responsibilities after his mother died and nearing his transition to adulthood. Marco did not have a long history of making decisions or setting goals for himself so MI proved to be an effective intervention.

During the engagement process, the social worker practiced MI by demonstrating empathy and using a non-judgmental approach, while emphasizing the importance of collaboration. Often when AYAs are told to do something or feel pressured in any way, they resist or become more withdrawn. It was very important for the social worker to avoid statements telling Marco to do something, like to take his medication. It was also helpful to give Marco choices. For example, the social worker would say, "It seems you have a lot of medication to take. The doctor feels it's very important for you to take your medication. You have a choice to take the medication to protect your body or not take the medication and possibly develop an infection . . . perhaps you can talk to your doctor about these options or ask your doctor which ones are really important and if there are any medications that you can stop taking ." The social worker can also say, "I can help you explore what's going on, how you are feeling about it and how you want to handle this situation." This example shows how the social worker allowed the AYA to problem solve for himself by suggesting some talking points to continue the discussion. Ultimately, opening up the dialogue encourages the AYA's participation in his or her health care, which is essential for the transition process.

Psychoeducation

Also in this context of transitioning to adult care, psychoeducation is an intervention that encompasses health education, problem-solving strategies, and overall social-emotional support. Although physicians can also provide psychoeducation to increase the AYA's knowledge about their illness and treatments, social workers are experts at combining this knowledge with other forms of supportive counseling, including motivational interviewing.

Psychoeducational interventions are effective in promoting positive growth towards the transition to adulthood and adult care. Social workers can educate their patients and provide appropriate preparation for what to expect during the transition process in order to lessen the anxiety and fear of transitioning, as well as promote healthy decision-making and problem solving skills. Furthermore, psychoeducation prevents logistical and emotional barriers to the transition to adult care (Shanske et al., 2012).

As part of the transition process, the social worker provided Marco with specific anticipatory guidance of transitioning to an adult health care center. The differences between a pediatric center and adult center were reviewed with emphasis on ways to be prepared for the first visit to the adult center and questions to ask the new physician that specializes in care of adults. In addition, Marco developed a "health passport," a written, summarized health history that he was able to carry with him to his adult health care center appointments.

Another form of psychoeducation is to utilize transition questionnaires and checklists to determine what stage of the transition process the AYA is in. Kolb (2009) notes that these tools can be extremely helpful in assessing a patient's readiness for the transition process. It also assists providers in creating a unique individualized health care plan with each patient, allowing the AYA to guide the direction of change. It can also be helpful to provide AYA with transition timelines and health care skills checklists, so that they can be informed, active participants in their transition plan. (Kolb, 2009, p. 33). For example, Sawicki et al. (2009) confirmed that the Transition Readiness Assessment Questionnaire (TRAQ) is a validated tool to assess transition readiness and guide educational interventions to support transition. Marco completed the TRAQ and other transition checklists so that it could be determined what areas Marco excelled in and which needed strengthening.

It was difficult to engage Marco in transition discussion and planning. Up until his mother's death, he had not been faced with the position to manage his own care. It was important to create short-term goals that allowed Marco to be involved in his own care, but not place too much responsibility on him all at once. First, Marco was asked to describe his health history and his current medical needs. He was then asked to complete a transition questionnaire. This allowed the providers to see what knowledge areas needed strengthening.

However, it also allowed Marco to see which areas he already accomplished. It also allowed the medical team to focus on Marco's concerns and allowed him to guide the change process. This sense of accomplishment increased his self-efficacy and motivated Marco to be more involved in his care.

The use of technology, including the Internet and applications for smartphones, are becoming widespread in the cancer community. One of the most effective ways that survivors have experienced a positive transition and have been empowered to participate in their own care is through accessing online resources and supports. The Internet is a helpful way for the patient and family to engage in their care, monitor their progress, and plan for the future. Social workers assist the AYA in setting short-term and long-term goals individualized to their needs with the help of these online tools. For instance, Marco would bring his health passport on his smartphone to the clinic. This was a good way for him to record his health history and review his current treatment expectations, such as current medications and a list of current medical providers.

Despite the fact that there are ample cancer resources on the web and connecting patients to these resources is beneficial, there continues to be an unfortunate lack of knowledge and underutilization (Hewitt & Ganz, 2007). According to Blum, a systematic distribution of resources is strongly lacking in oncology care (as cited in Hewitt & Ganz, 2007). Within oncology clinics, it is rare to have a designated person who is responsible for distributing resources. It is commonly the social workers who provide the psychoeducation, including distributing information, linking patients and families to resources, and utilizing transition tools with their transition age patients. This form of psychoeducation drives the success in this special group of AYA. According to a study by *Cancer Practice* published in 2002, less than 60% of oncology professionals recommended support services or thought these types of services were helpful (as cited in Hewitt & Ganz, 2007). It is important to shift this way of thinking and encourage providers to take responsibility for ensuring their patients access to these resources.

Transference and Countertransference Issues

Pediatric cancer survivors often have very close long-term relationships with their medical team providers who have often been managing their care since diagnosis. Physicians, nurses, and even social workers who work in oncology often feel as though they have watched their patients grow up. Just as a parent may struggle with the "letting go" process, providers can also share the same experience. This countertransference process was especially complicated by the death of Marco's mother. This led many providers to feel an extreme sense of guilt due to the fact that he lost his mother. They may have unconsciously created a fantasy where they rescued Marco from his emotional pain and suffering, while curing his cancer (Malawista, 2004). The medical providers felt as though they needed to rescue Marco and treat him as if he was their own child. In addition, the providers experienced difficulties in setting limits and enforcing treatment recommendations because they felt "bad" or "guilty," that at the beginning there were no caregivers to help him manage his health care.

When the time comes for the adolescent to transition to increased independence and adulthood, providers often struggle to give up the control and management of their patient out of fear that it will result in a negative outcome for the patient. What providers often fail to recognize is that when they slowly relinquish control and responsibility it naturally projects that control and responsibility onto the adolescent. Since every survivor accomplishes tasks on an individual timeline, it is important for parents and providers to give the adolescent autonomy in a gradual process (Kolb, 2009). This process should not result in a sense of abandonment on either party, but instead should create a healthy way to foster growth and independence within the adolescent.

It is clear that the patient provider relationship and alliance is "central to a therapeutically successful transition process" (Shanske et al., 2012, p. 288). Social workers are trained in human development and behavior, attachment theories, and loss theories, all of which can be critical in driving transition forward. (Shanske et al., 2012). Social work theory tells us that the patient/provider relationship is "initiated, nurtured, and ultimately, terminated" (Shanske et al., 2012). The transition to adult care and to a new adult provider can result in a significant loss for both the patient and pediatric provider. It is important to acknowledge the loss of the relationship with the medical team, similarly to terminating with a psychotherapist (Menzer, 2011).

Patients may experience transference reactions when terminating a physician/patient relationship. Some feelings that may emerge are significant feelings of loss, abandonment, inadequacy, and guilt. Due to the attachment that occurs in the patient/provider relationship, it is possible that the patient may feel abandoned by the physician, especially if he or she has suffered a previous loss of someone significant in his or her life, as Marco experienced. Often patients want to please their doctors by having improved health, and often this improvement is beyond their control or in process, and patients may feel as if they are letting their physicians down or not living up to their expectations.

The pediatric provider must take an increased responsibility for self-awareness by being honest about their feelings (Shanske et al., 2012). It is essential to process the likely feelings of loss before they interfere with patient care and success. Failure to acknowledge this process may project a sense of doubt or uncertainty from the medical provider onto the adolescent that is unnecessary and can impede the transition process (Shanske et al., 2012). In addition, it can damage the ability to form healthy trusting relationships with future health care providers (Shanske et al., 2012).

It is important for the social worker to incorporate termination into their practice, as well as encourage the process within the entire health care team. The social worker on the medical team involved Marco in the transition discussion early, including the discussion of terminating with his pediatric providers. It was also necessary for the social worker to encourage Marco's primary oncologists to recognize that he would be leaving the cancer center and encourage his oncologist to provide a proper referral to an adult oncologist or cancer survivorship program.

Legal and Ethical Concerns

There are significant legal and ethical considerations throughout the transition process, including privacy, confidentiality, and informed consent (Shanske et al., 2012). Social workers have the clinical skills to assess the patient's developmental stage and level of understanding, which can help inform and influence how the medical team delivers care. The social worker can assist the medical team in understanding how much autonomy and decision making the patient should have. Also, the provider may decide to meet individually with their patients, without a guardian present, to respect the patient's privacy and encourage a trusting patient/physician relationship (Shanske et al., 2012). Although the legal age for medical consent is typically 18, it is important to involve patients in the decision-making process at a much earlier age, and offer them the ability to provide informed assent to treatment and medical plans (Shanske et al., 2012).

It is difficult to establish a definitive age to start the transition process, as AYA cancer survivors vary in the age at which they were when they were diagnosed and their developmental stage (Kolb, 2009). Some providers begin the transition discussion shortly after diagnosis, and others wait until the last moment when the AYA is forced to transition to an adult facility due to loss in insurance coverage or hospital and clinic requirements. Ignoring the transition process and failing to discuss the AYA's long-term follow-up plan openly and honestly, may produce a sense of false hope and expectations that the AYA will be able to obtain services at a pediatric institution well into adulthood. It is ethically irresponsible to inadequately prepare the AYA cancer survivor for the transition to adult care, as they will only face greater challenges without the proper preparation, planning and support.

When Marco's mother died, the health care team immediately responded to the uncertainty of who was going to assume the legal responsibility of guardianship and consent to treatment. Although Marco had shared that he had family in the area, no family had been present in the hospital for the past two years of his treatment. Through discussion with Marco, the health care team obtained the contact information for his 21-year-old sister who lived locally and elicited her support to take over the care of her brother and be the legal responsible party. The social worker assisted Marco's sister in the guardianship process and referred the family to local agencies to assist with court proceedings with temporary guardianship, which was upheld until Marco turned 18. Prior to Marco turning 18, the medical team creatively worked with this family to optimize the best health outcomes for Marco. The social worker assessed the barriers to attendance, such as the lack of a guardian to be present for appointments. The social worker provided the assessment that Marco was mature and independent enough to attend medical appointments by himself. Marco was at risk for missing his appointments if he was unable to come by himself. The medical team was able to obtain proper consents and provide the medical care needed.

MEZZO PERSPECTIVE: ORGANIZATION AND COMMUNITY

Medical social workers are often the team members that serve as the liaison to the community and who collaborate with other health care providers in a patient's life, including school personnel and employers. Most often it is the social worker who is educating and guiding patients and families on how to navigate health care systems and other community systems.

Supportive counseling, vocational counseling, and school interventions can mitigate the social, vocational, and academic life disruptions caused by cancer that may have extended into survivorship otherwise (Kwak et al., 2013). Social workers can ensure access to appropriate school services and encouraging adolescents to access educational support through Individualized Education Plans

(IEP), as well as planning for their future with planning for higher education and scholarship/financial aid opportunities. Social workers are also responsible for providing appropriate referrals to cancer support organizations, AYA support groups, and other peer opportunities.

Many patients undergoing intense cancer treatments have gaps in their education. School reintegration is a big part of the survivor experience, especially initially following the end of treatment. With social work support, guidance, and school advocacy, Marco was able to reintegrate into high school and complete his high school education. It was important that Marco received proper evaluation and support services through the school district. The medical social worker served as the liaison between the hospital and the school and provided the school with all the necessary medical history for the school to determine proper services. Marco's needs and the service goals were outlined in his IEP/504 plan, which ensured that despite some ongoing medical needs, he would receive an optimal education. IEP accommodations included involving the school nurse to monitor Marco's medications, adaptive physical education, staying out of the sun, and having time between classes.

MACRO PERSPECTIVE: POLICY ANALYSIS AND POLICY ADVOCACY

Cancer is a major public health problem in the United States, and AYA cancer survivors are a growing population with unique, long-term health care needs (Kirchoff, Lyles, Fluchel, Wright, & Leisenring, 2012). According to the National Cancer Institute, it is a national priority to focus on research that will improve outcomes for young cancer survivors (Kirchoff et al., 2012, p. 8).

Although transition planning is recognized as important to the health success of the AYA, it is not implemented often enough. Transitional care depends on research to inform how providers are trained, how care is delivered, and how much it is going to cost (Kolb, 2009, p. 39). It is evident

that there can be much difficulty accessing adult health care and specialized survivorship care and that there is a "lack of capacity for survivorship care within cancer treating institutions" (Keene, Hobbie, & Ruccione, 2007, p. 20). Many cancer centers see long-term survivors, but do not have a comprehensive survivorship program. According to Oeffinger and Wallace (2006), in 1997 only 53% of all institutions had a long-term follow-up (LTFU) program. Even less have the capacity to follow young children into adulthood (Prasad, Bowles, & Friedman, 2010, p. 374). It is projected that by 2020, there will not be an adequate number of oncologists available to provide patient care for the increasing demand of direct oncology service (Prasad et al., 2010). It is imperative that validated transition models are created to meet the needs of this increasing demand (Prasad et al., 2010).

Some AYA cancer survivors do transition into follow up with a primary care adult doctor following their cancer treatments (Kirchoff et al., 2012). A significant barrier to follow-up care for survivors can be a lack of adequate health insurance (Prasad et al., 2010). In Kirchoff et al.'s (2012) study, "uninsured AYA survivors faced the largest cost barrier to care, with 74% reporting forgoing care due to cost" (p. 7). In addition, there are often gaps in insurance coverage during the transition period due to AYA's type of insurance (e.g. public/private, parent's coverage, employer based coverage), creating a challenge for some AYAs to continue with care. Improvements in posttreatment access must be prioritized for this population. All types of health insurance, including private and public health insurance, should cover comprehensive cancer survivorship care that includes surveillance of late effects of cancer treatment. Efforts from the federal and state policy level are needed to promote the importance of health insurance in this population and ensure that all cancer survivors have access to adequate affordable health care (National Cancer Institute, 2006, p. iii).

The Adolescent and Young Adult Oncology Progress Review Group (AYAOPRG) report in 2006 "recognized an urgent need for education, training, and communication activities to raise awareness and recognition of the AYA population at both public and professional levels as a first step towards increasing national focus and resource allocation" (National Cancer Institute, 2006, p. ii). One way to increase awareness of resources is through awareness campaigns. Social workers can join advocacy efforts of groups seeking to expand coverage for cancer-related issues. Social workers can develop or support programs and initiatives to increase psychosocial support within cancer survivorship, including survivorship and community clinics and encourage them at their own institutions. Lastly, it is important for every member of the medical team, including social workers, to participate in education and training on survivorship care to advance their knowledge on current best practices.

Fortunately, once Marco's bone marrow transplant physicians decide he is ready for survivor care, he will be easily transitioned to an oncologist who specializes in survivor care and who can monitor possible late effects of cancer treatments. One of the benefits of having a comprehensive survivorship program in a pediatric institution, with a partnership with adult facilities, is that providers can ensure proper cancer survivorship medical care well into adulthood.

CONCLUSION

In conclusion, this chapter explores micro, mezzo, and macro perspectives that social workers in a pediatric or young adult health care setting can use to inform their social work practice with youth transitioning beyond cancer survivorship and into adult care. Two evidenced-based practices that have been found to be most helpful when working with this population are psychoeducation and motivational interviewing. These interventions can be used throughout the transition process, and help guide the youth towards their successful transition goals. Throughout this process it is imperative that social workers recognize the unique needs of this specific culture of AYA cancer survivors, while embracing their strengths and resilience. Lastly, social workers have a professional obligation to provide policy advocacy that leads to improved psychosocial programs and support throughout the cancer survivorship and transition process.

INTERNET RESOURCES

- American Cancer Society: http://www.cancer.org/
- Children's Oncology Group Long-Term Follow-Up Guidelines for Survivors of Childhood, Adolescent, and Young Adult Cancers (COG-LTFU Guidelines): http://www.survivorshipguidelines.org
- COG Family Handbook: http://www.childrensoncologygroup.org/media/COG_Family_Handbook.pdf
- Life After Cancer Treatment Guide: http://www.cancer.org/survivorshipguide
- Cancer Care: A Helping Hand: http://www.cancercare.org
- National Coalition for Cancer Survivorship (NCCS): http://www.canceradvocacy.org
- Cancer Survivor Toolbox: http://www.canceradvocacy.org/toolbox/
- The National Children's Cancer Society: Beyond the Cure: http://www.beyondthecure.org
- American Childhood Cancer Organization: http://www.acco.org
- Lance Armstrong Foundation: http://www.livestrong.org
- Planet Cancer: http://myplanet.planetcancer.org
- National Cancer Institute: http://www.cancer.gov/cancertopics/aya
- Facing Forward: A Guide for Cancer Survivors: http://www.cancer.gov/cancertopics/coping/life-after-treatment.pdf
- The Office of Cancer Survivorship: http://cancercontrol.cancer.gov/ocs/
- The Cancer Support Community: http://www.cancersupportcommunity.org
- American Society of Clinical Oncology People Living with Cancer Survivorship: http://www.cancer.net/survivorship
- CureSearch: http://www.curesearch.org
- Critical Mass: The Young Adult Cancer Alliance: http://criticalmass.org
- Association of Cancer Online Resources: http://www.acor.org

- National Healthcare Transition center: http://www.gottransition.org
- Navigating Cancer Survivorship: http://www.navigatingcancersurvivorship.org
- Triage Cancer: http://www.triagecancer.org
- Association of Oncology Social Work: http://www.aosw.org
- Passport For Care: An Internet Based Survivorship Care Plan: https://www.passportforcare.org/
- The Institute of Medicine Video: "From Cancer Patient to Cancer Survivor: Lost in Transition": http://www.youtube.com/watch?v=YhuqWM3dNAw
- LIVESTRONG Young Adult Alliance: http://www.livestrong.org/What-We-Do/Our-Actions/Programs-Partnerships/LIVESTRONG-Young-Adult-Alliance

AYA Cancer Support Resources

- Stupid Cancer: http://www.stupidcancer.org
- Seventy K: Survival Up: http://www.seventyk.org
- Planet Cancer: http://myplanet.planetcancer.org/
- Prepare to Live: http://www.preparetolive.org
- Starbright World: http://www.starbrightworld.org
- Teens Living With Cancer: http://www.teenslivingwithcancer.org
- Group Loop: http://www.grouploop.org
- The SAMFund: http://www.thesamfund.org
- Ulman Cancer Fund: http://www.ulmanfund.org
- Imerman Angels: http://www.imermanangels.org
- Cancer and Careers: http://www.cancerandcareers.org
- Cancer Care: http://www.cancercare.org
- FertileHope: http://www.fertilehope.org
- First Descents: http://www.firstdescents.org
- Athletes for Cancer: http://athletes4cancer.org
- Cancer Survivors Fund: http://www.cancersurvivorsfund.org
- Cancer Climber Association: http://www.cancerclimber.org
- Face2Face: http://www.nextstepnet.org/node/51
- Cancer Hope Network: http://www.cancerhopenetwork.org/

Additional Resources

- Transition Readiness Assessment Questionnaire: http://hscj.ufl.edu/jaxhats/traq/
- Healthy Survivorship application for smartphone for Young Adult Cancer Survivors: http://www.healthysurvivorship.org
- Cancer.net application for smartphone: http://www.cancer.net/navigating-cancer-care/managing-your-care/mobile-applications
- Cure Search: http://curesearch.org/CureSearch-CancerCare-App

DISCUSSION QUESTIONS

1. How do you see yourself using MI and psychoeducation with adolescent cancer survivors?

2. What are some barriers Marco may have faced during the process of transitioning to adult care?

3. How do you think policy can influence the way survivorship care is delivered?

4. What ethical or legal issues can you identify that may surface when working with AYA cancer survivors?

REFERENCES

American Society of Clinical Oncology. (2014). *Cancer survivorship: Trusted information about life after treatment* [Booklet]. Retrieved from www.cancer.net/survivorship.

Barakat, L. P., Schwartz, L. A., Szabo, M. M., Hussey, H. M., & Bunin, G. R. (2012). Factors that contribute to post-treatment follow-up care for survivors of childhood cancer. *Journal of Cancer Survivorship, 6,* 155–162. doi 10/1007/s11764–011–0206–6

Berzoff, J., Flanagan, L., & Hertz, P. (2011). *Inside out and outside in: Psychodynamic clinical theory and psychopathology in contemporary multicultural context.* Lanham, MD: Rowman & Littlefield.

Blum, R. W., Gareel D., Hodgman C. H., Jorissen, T. W., Okinow, N. A., Orr, P. P., & Slap, G. B. (1993). Transition from child-centered to adult health-care systems for adolescents with chronic conditions. A position paper of the Society for Adolescent Medicine. *Journal of Adolescent Health, 14*(7), 570–576.

Brinkman, T. M., Zhu, L., Zeltzer L. K., Recklitis, C. J., Kimberg, C., Zhang, N., . . .Krull, K. R. (2013). Longitudinal patterns of psychological distress in adult survivors of childhood cancer. *British Journal of Cancer,109*(5), 1373–1381.

Hewitt, M., & Ganz, P. A. (2007). *Implementing cancer survivorship care planning. A National Coalition for Cancer Survivorship and Institute of Medicine national cancer policy forum workshop.* Lance Armstrong Foundation and The National Cancer Institute. Washington, DC: National Academies Press.

Hoffman, B. (2004). *A cancer survivor's almanac: Charting your journey* (2nd ed.). Hoboken, NJ: Johan Wiley & Sons.

Keene, N., Hobbie, W., & Ruccione, K. (2007). *Childhood cancer survivors: A practical guide to your future* (2nd ed.). Sebastopol, CA: O'Reilly Media .

Kent, E. E., Wilder Smith, A., Keegan, T. H. M., Lynch, C. F., Xiao-Cheng, W., & Harlan, L. C. (2013). Talking about cancer and meeting peer survivors: Social information needs of adolescents and young adults diagnosed with cancer. *Journal of Adolescent and Young Adult Oncology, 2*(2), 44–52. doi: 10.1089/jaya0.2012.0029

Kirchhoff, A. C., Lyles, C. R., Fluchel, M., Wright, J., & Leisenring, W. (2012). Limitations in health care access and utilization among long-term survivors of adolescent and young adult cancer. *Cancer, 118*(23), 5964–5972. doi: 10.1002/cncr.27537

Kolb, M. (2009). Life after pediatric cancer: Easing the transition to the adult primary care provider. *Clinical Journal of Oncology Nursing, 13*(6), 30–40.

Kwak, M., Zebrack B. J., Meeske, K. A., Embry, L., Aguilar, C., Block, . . . Cole, S. (2013). Trajectories of psychological distress in adolescent and young adult patients with cancer: A 1-year longitudinal study. *Journal of Clinical Oncology, 31*(17), 2160–2166. doi:10.1200/JCO/2012.45.9222

Ledlie, S. W. (2007). Methods of assessing transition health care needs. In C. L. Betz & W. M. Nehring (Eds.), *Promoting health care transitions for adolescents with special health care needs and disabilities* (pp. 119–136). Baltimore, MD: Paul H. Brookes.

Malawista, K. L. (2004). Rescue fantasies in child therapy: Countertransference/transference enactments. *Child and Adolescent Social Work Journal, 21*(4), 373–386.

Menzer, E. (2011). *Perceived lack of control and learned helplessness: The effects on transition to adult health care.* PCS Grand Rounds. Los Angeles, CA: Children's Hospital Los Angeles.

Michel, G., Rebholz, C. E., von der Weid, N. X., Bergstraeeser, E., & Kuehni, C. E. (2010). Psychological distress in adult survivors of childhood cancer: The Swiss Childhood Cancer Survivor study. *Journal of Clinical Oncology, 28*(10), 1740–1748.

Miller, W. R., & Rollnick, S. (2009). Ten things that motivational interviewing is not. *Behavioural and Cognitive Psychotherapy, 37*(2), 129–140.

Naar-King, S., & Suarez, M. (2011). *Motivational interviewing with adolescents and young adults.* New York, NY: Guildford Press.

National Association of Social Workers. (2001). *Standards for cultural competence in social work practice.* Washington, DC: NASW Press.

National Cancer Institute. (2006). *Closing the gap: Research and care imperatives for adolescents and young adults with cancer.* Report of the Adolescent and Young Adult Oncology Progress Review Group. Bethesda, MD: Author.

Oeffinger, K. C., & Wallace, W. H. (2006). Barriers to follow-up care of survivors in the United States and the United Kingdom. *Pediatric Blood Cancer, 46*(2), 135–142.

Olson, R., Hung, G., Bobinski, M., & Goddard, K. (2010). Prospective evaluation of legal difficulties and quality of life in adult survivors of childhood cancer. *Pediatric Blood Cancer, 56*(3), 1–5. doi: 10.1002/pbc.22777

Prasad, P. K., Bowles T., & Friedman, D. L. (2010). Is there a role for a specialized follow-up clinic for survivors of pediatric cancer? *Cancer Treatment Reviews, 36*(4), 372–376. doi: 10.1016/j.ctrv.2010.02.014

Sawicki, G. S., Lukens-Bull, K., Yin, X., Demars, N., Huang, I. C., Livingood, W., . . . Wood, D. (2009). Measuring the transition readiness of youth with special healthcare needs: Validation of the TRAQ—Transition Readiness Assessment Questionnaire. *Journal of Pediatric Psychology, 36*(2), 16–71.

Shanske, S., Arnold, J., Carvalho, M., & Rein, J. (2012). Social workers as transition brokers: Facilitating the transition from pediatric to adult medical care. *Social Work in Health Care, 51*(4), 279–295.

Siegel, R., DeSantis, C., Virgo, K., Stein, K., Mariotto, A., Smith, T., & Ward, E. (2012). Cancer treatment and survivorship statistics, 2012. American Cancer Society. *CA: A Cancer Journal for Clinicians, 62*(4), 220–241. doi:10.3322/caac.21149

Ward, E., DeSantis, C., Robbins, A., Kohler, B., & Jamal, A. (2014). Childhood and adolescent cancer statistics, 2014. *CA: A Cancer Journal for Clinicians, 64*(2), 83–103.

Zebrack, B. J., Gurney, J. G., Oeffinger, K., Whitton, J., Packer, R.J., Mertens, A. . . . Zeltzer, L. K. (2004). Psychological outcomes in long-term survivors of childhood brain cancer: A report from the childhood cancer survivor study. *Journal of Clinical Oncology, 22*(6), 999–1006.

Zebrack, B. J., Zevon, M. A., Turk, N., Nagarajan, R., Whitton, J., Robison, L. L., & Zeltzer, L. K. (2007). Psychological distress in long-term survivors of solid tumors diagnosed in childhood: A report from the childhood cancer survivor study. *Pediatric Blood Cancer, 49*(1), 47–51.

CHAPTER 18

Autism Spectrum Disorder

Samih Samaha

CHAPTER OBJECTIVES

- Define autism spectrum disorder;
- Provide tips on diagnosing autism spectrum disorder;
- Discuss current evidence-based interventions;
- Critically analyze clinical social worker involvement.

CASE VIGNETTE

Nolan is 5 years old and lives in a loving family of Asian American decent. Nolan will be assessed through a systems theory, meta-framework lens. He lives with his father, mother, and three younger brothers (see Appendix A). Extended family, specifically a maternal aunt and maternal grandmother, do visit at times and stay over to help with family chores as needed. Nolan is the oldest of the children, with the next child, P, being one year younger; the third child, D, being 2 years younger; and the last child, J, is the newborn. His father and mother are very caring and loving, have a strong, supportive marriage, and both work from home on a home business. Nolan was referred for behavioral therapy when he was 5. He was diagnosed with autism spectrum disorder (ASD) at the age of 4.

BIOLOGICAL

Nolan was born through normal vaginal delivery, in a hospital, at full term and with no birth complications. There were no biological abnormalities noted on the birth records regarding the mother or child during the prenatal care exams. The mother was not on any medication nor did she abuse any drugs throughout the pregnancy. This was mother's first child at age 27. Father was also healthy during her pregnancy. Father reported smoking about three packs of cigarettes a week during the pregnancy. Father was 29 when Nolan was born. There is, however, history of ASD within this family. The mother's oldest brother has a child who is also diagnosed with ASD, although evaluated on a lower level of severity than Nolan. Lastly, Nolan's sibling P is also diagnosed as moderately severe on the ASD scale, and child D is diagnosed as mildly impacted. The newborn, J, seems to be developing appropriately. Mother reported that by the time Nolan was diagnosed, P was already born and also being assessed and D was starting to show signs, albeit extremely mild. Nolan started therapy at 5, P at 4, and D between 2 and 3 as they were all recommended for early intervention services once Nolan was diagnosed.

DEVELOPMENTAL

From birth to 2 years of age, Nolan appeared to be developing and meeting milestones appropriately. Gross motor skills were developing appropriately. He was able to hold his head up on his own, roll over, point, reach and then grasp objects, and eventually crawled and started walking. The parents noted that between 2–3 years of age he just seemed hyperactive and unfocused. They stated that around 2, he started to become withdrawn from his family and showed little to no advances in verbal communication. Baird, Douglas, and Murphy (2011) and Greenspan and Wieder (2006) discussed that many symptoms of ASD become more apparent around age 2 as the developmental gaps between typically developing children and those who aren't become more evident. The parents described it "like a switch turned off and he [Nolan] changed." Nolan is considered to fall on the ASD severity scale level 3. This is considered severely impacted and needing a great amount of assistance to function. The parents further noted that while other children started paying attention to each other, parallel playing and reciprocating, Nolan remained on the sidelines, fixated by shapes, colors, and other visual stimulation. They reported he would stare at a toy train up close for minutes on end or cover his ears and scream because of loud noises.

INTERVENTION

Nolan was referred to behavioral therapy at age 4. Nolan had one behavioral specialist hired by a private, for-profit agency funded by Regional Centers, working with him on improving his table manners, communication skills, and ability to sit and work for periods of 5–10 minutes at a time, in preparation for school. Nolan's receptive and expressive language is severely impaired. He is unable to regulate himself or his behaviors and is extremely aggressive. He will scream, bite, kick, and, more often, will run away to avoid difficult tasks. He has a history of running out of the house and into dangerous situations. He was being taught using the Picture Exchange Communication System (Pyramid Educational Consultants, 2013) to use pictures and eventually words as a form of communication instead of grabbing things, yelling, hitting, or running toward or away from objects, tasks, and people. The main method of instruction was applied behavior analysis (Applied Behavior Analysis [ABA], 2013) at the time, supplemented by floortime therapies modified from the Greenspan model as outlined in the Greenspan and Wieder (2008) book. Physically, Nolan did not have any abnormalities and was, by all accounts, a physically healthy boy. A psychiatrist, however, was assessing him at that time, and antipsychotic medication was becoming more a possibility; later into school age, it became a reality.

INTRODUCTION

Autism spectrum disorders (ASD) have no clear cause(s) at this time. The general consensus in research, however, is to intervene as early as possible upon onset of symptoms or formal diagnosis of ASD (National Institute of Mental Health [NIMH], 2015). Children who display symptoms, as observed by the frontline staff interacting with them, should immediately see a trained professional in order to be accurately diagnosed (Baird et al., 2011). Since parents are usually the gatekeepers to allowing first access to assess children, they should always discuss questions regarding symptoms with their pediatricians at the first sign. Other people who would also have access to children and should be trained to spot symptoms of ASD include daycare teachers, mental health professionals, and social workers. Therefore, part of the goals for this chapter is to help identify the frontline staff with access to the children served, including parents, to begin facilitating the early intervention process as quickly as possible. A large part of proper diagnosing and intervening is to make sure to take into account all presenting symptoms, especially those related to possible comorbidity with other mental health issues and any other biopsychosocial roots of the behaviors, in order to provide a complete picture of the child from a systems perspective. Post diagnosis, this "systems map" of the client will assist in identifying what type of evidence-based practice works best for this family and ultimately for the child. Furthermore, as all the systems involved become more apparent, the worker should be able to identify the transference and countertransference issues that might impede the success of the therapies. Ultimately, part of the process for social workers helping families to make long-term plans for the family and child is that they will also be bringing ASD awareness at the micro, mezzo, and macro levels to promote stronger support systems.

Definition and Diagnosis

NIMH (2015), the article by Baird et al. (2011), and the *Diagnostic and Statistical Manual of Mental Disorders* (DSM-5; American Psychiatric Association, 2013) all help us define ASDs as persistent impairments in reciprocal social communication and interactions. The child must at least exhibit impairments in his or her ability to initiate and reciprocate social communication and interaction with others in order to be considered to be on the autism spectrum. In children, that presents as the inability to initially participate in parallel and then consequently reciprocal play with peers, follow simple directions from adults, and communicate their needs to those adults using clear verbal communication. The above references also note that once the primary domain criterion in social deficits is met, secondary criteria also need to be present to confirm ASD diagnosis and are in the more physical behavioral domain. These physical behaviors are classified as restricted repetitive patterns of motion. The individuals manifest the behaviors when they show a limited range of participation in special interests or activities. For example, the child will not reciprocate play with peers; instead, he will sit in front of a TV for hours and watch the same show repetitively, engaging in "self-stimulatory" behaviors such as humming, flapping his hands, or pacing back and forth and walking in circles as he attempts to self-regulate (ABA, 2013; Greenspan & Wieder, 2008; National Institute for Health and Clinical Excellence, 2011).

DSM-5 Diagnostic Criteria

The following is a summary of the diagnostic criteria as outline in the DSM-5. The manual states that for the ASD category to be considered, the two domains mentioned above (social and physical behavioral deficits with specific symptoms), must be assessed and met. The DSM-5 also notes that the symptoms must be pervasive and begin in childhood. Also note, the main changes from the DSM-IV is that in the DSM-5, what were previously four separate disorders are now one disorder labeled ASD, and ASD is now diagnosable on a spectrum of varied symptom severities, under those two core domains.

First, all three of the following persistent deficits in social communication and social interaction across contexts, not accounted for by general developmental delays, must be present: (1) deficits in social and emotional reciprocity, which means children exhibit abnormal social communication approaches, fail to maintain back and forth flow of conversation about shared interests, and exhibit a lack of initiation and response to social interactions; (2) deficits in nonverbal communication, such as poor eye contact and body language or deficits in understanding and use of nonverbal communication (i.e., total lack of facial expression or gestures); and (3) deficits in developing and maintaining relationships and friendships with others, appropriate to developmental level and outside the relationships with primary caregivers.

The second list of criteria to meet is the physical behavioral symptoms. When two of the four symptoms listed in the DSM-5 under this second domain are met, children fall on the physical behavioral ASD spectrum. The symptoms are generally addressed under the category of restricted, repetitive patterns of behavior, interests, or activities. The first and most obvious symptoms are usually the stereotyped or repetitive speech, motor movements, or use of objects, such as simple motor stereotypes, echolalia, repetitive use of objects (toys, books, utensils, etc.), or idiosyncratic phrases. The second symptom is an excessive adherence to routines. Basically this looks like ritualized patterns of verbal or nonverbal behavior or excessive resistance to change (e.g., motoric rituals, insistence on the same route or food, repetitive questioning, or extreme distress at small changes). The third set of symptoms under this category is highly restricted, fixated interests that are abnormal in intensity or focus (e.g., strong attachment to or preoccupation with unusual objects, excessively circumscribed or perseverative interests). The fourth set of symptoms is hyper- or hypo-reactivity to sensory input. This is also exhibited as unusual interest in sensory aspects of environment (e.g., apparent indifference to pain/heat/cold, adverse response to specific sounds or textures, excessive smelling or touching of objects, fascination with lights or spinning objects).

The symptoms exhibited by the child must be present in early childhood but may not become fully manifest until social demands exceed his or her limited capacities. What this tells us is that even though children might be considered to fall on the ASD spectrum, we are unable to properly assess symptoms until they start manifesting, and this happens when social demands are made on the children. This is one reason why many children are diagnosed late or only when they begin preschool or kindergarten. Those are usually the times when the social demands on the children to socialize and make friends begin to exceed their social capacities. Finally, these symptoms together must limit and impair everyday functioning. For example, for a child to be able to function in everyday life, the child will need to be able to sit down for extended periods of time to work or eat, verbally communicate his needs, and not participate in self-stimulatory behaviors that affect his everyday ability to function in the home and community. An individual who is unable to do that will not be able to successfully navigate the community, will be diagnosed with ASD, and will require assistive supplemental services in order to thrive in the social environment.

Not all the outlined symptoms above will occur at the same time or under the same environmental conditions. Each child's ecology is different, and practitioners must also take into account context and environment to accurately diagnose ASD. Child development experts and clinicians must be aware of the symptoms in their context as they work with children in order to be able to diagnose early and effectively; for example, cultural contexts vary between children. Finally, a worker must pay particular attention to the spectrum of autism. There are varying severities and forms of autism, and the NIMH and DSM-5 describe them as having different levels of intensity; Level 1 is the lowest and level 3 requires the highest level of support to function.

Post Diagnosis

Intervention should begin immediately following diagnosis of the disorder. This includes also completing a psychiatric evaluation, doing comorbidity assessments, and then providing the child with intensive behavioral, play, and social skills training therapies (NIMH, 2015). In California, for example, the majority of these services are provided by Regional Centers and private agencies that supply the resources, such as therapists. Private donations, public school districts, or early intervention programs as guaranteed by the California Lanterman Act usually are the main sources of funding for these services (California Department of Developmental Services, 2013). Check services in your jurisdiction for differences. Once a diagnosis is made in California, a child 3–5 years old or younger will be serviced by funding from their closest Regional Center early intervention program. Then, for school-age children 5 and older, school psychologists will begin the process of providing services by assessing them in the school environment. Once that assessment is complete, services then are provided by the public school districts and as agreed upon in an Individualized Education Plan (IEP) created when school officials, parents, and therapists meet to discuss the results of the assessment of the child's needs. This process is illustrated in the vignette presented earlier in the chapter.

MICRO PERSPECTIVE

Consideration at the micro system level must not only show how interventions and interactions affect the client, but also highlight the reciprocal effects of the transactions between the systems, for example, how the client's behaviors and reactions also affect the social worker and the therapeutic approaches. That general approach is accurately highlighted by the intersectional model of assessment (Springer, Hankivsky, & Bates, 2012), which tells us we must take into account how a client's attributes or characteristics, such as gender, age, disability, race, diagnosis, socioeconomic status (SES), and education, on the micro level, contribute to or hinder his or her ability to access and benefit from resources from the other systems involved. In this case, Nolan is a male, 5 years old, diagnosed with severe ASD, and is of Asian American descent and from a family with limited resources. All these highlighted intersectional attributes can then be broken down individually to explain how the client faces obstacles to care.

Being a child, he is limited to participating in only what his parents are able to provide him. The SES and educational level of his parents also affect access to therapeutic services. A family with minimal resources relies on publicly funded services, and many times that limits choices for them compared with a family who has the resources to access any service they choose. Because his parents are of low SES, we can deduce that Nolan will not have the access to resources a family with high SES would. As a result, he presumably would not be going to private doctors but instead to community health clinics that might provide only emergency or basic medical care as opposed to more long-term, personally tailored preventative care. In fact, that is what we see here. Nolan was born in a hospital and had access to prenatal care because his mother was working at an accounting firm during the pregnancy, but after his birth, his mother stopped working and lost her health insurance. The father had a home-based business of buying and selling computer parts online, but that salary was not enough to support the family and provide them with all the medical care they needed. As a result, Nolan visited doctors at medical clinics, but infrequently. He was taken to community clinics for vaccinations and only when he was sick. They did not have access to a regular pediatrician or even daycare centers where other professionals could assess the child at an early age for developmental delays. The mother also needed to stay home with the child, further limiting exposure to the community professionals who might have been able to spot symptoms. Because of her inexperience as a new mother, Nolan's mother did not know the signs and symptoms of developmental delay and neglected to take the child in for any assessments until the signs were unavoidable between ages 3–4.

Diversity Considerations

Being of Asian American descent, Nolan's race and culture also play a big role in the ability to gain access to resources (Mandell, Listerud, Levy, & Pinto-Martin, 2009). Research has been consistent in showing racial disparities in access to resources for historically disenfranchised communities. Although cultural differences are socialized into communities and into templates that guide individual interactions, they can serve as barriers to improving quality of life for the disenfranchised. When a minority race, such as Asian Americans, is attempting to gain access to services, their socialized cultural traits might not be assessed appropriately for services if the assessment tools being used were created to service only the dominant populations. This is what is referred to as competency in the field of social work. For example, it might be appropriate for a person of Asian descent, in her own culture, to be expected to stay quiet or act "shy" in the presence of strangers or people in position of authority, as a sign of respect. The family might have feared speaking up to doctors they encountered or challenging authority when it came to discussing their child's needs, creating a barrier for proper diagnosis and early intervention. Additionally, for people with ASDs being assessed with Western assessment tools, cultural traits could be misconstrued as a sign of social impairment. That intersection of attributes and the negative currency between the systems as a result of this cultural characteristic can also make proper diagnosis difficult. For Nolan, this could have been another reason why he was diagnosed so late. Being unfamiliar with cultural differences while trying to assess an individual could lead to incorrect, late, or general under- or overdiagnosing of a disorder, based solely on misinterpreted cultural social cues (Mandell et al., 2009).

The same concept can be applied to gender. For ASD, behavioral problems such as poor social skills or inattention can be interpreted differently for males and females (Mandy et al., 2012). Mandy et al. note that males are actually more likely to be diagnosed with ASD than females. This can be interpreted in many ways, one of which is any behavioral problem in boys, whether it falls on the ASD criteria or not, can be interpreted as ASD when naturally, boys might just be "acting like boys." This pattern has been researched for ADHD, but the same principle can be ported to ASD as some of the hyperactivity in ADHD is also present in ASD. For example, males who misbehave and show attention deficits might be quickly diagnosed with ADHD. Rivet and Matson (2011) add to that and discuss how the comorbidity in females between ASD and other learning and intellectual impairments may act as a hindrance to proper diagnosis of ASD in females. They explain that a possible reason why females are less likely to be diagnosed with ASD is that they do not exhibit learning impairments along with their ASD symptoms; therefore, clinicians underdiagnose them with ASD versus males, who do show learning impairments more readily. This, in effect, is telling us that males are more likely to be diagnosed with ASD than females because they show behavioral and learning impairments, while females show behavioral impairments but do not necessarily exhibit learning deficits that impact their daily lives.

Comorbidity

This discussion of comorbidity and proper diagnosis of ASD goes further. Nolan was eventually diagnosed with multiple disorders besides ASD. Getting a proper diagnosis was very time consuming and difficult. Simonoff et al. (2008) tell us that in fact, ASD is rarely a standalone diagnosis. Many times ASD is associated with other psychiatric disorders. The authors found that 70% of people with ASD have one comorbid mental disorder, and about 40% have two. Nolan was assessed by one psychiatrist who really got to know him between the ages of 6–10 and was not only able to diagnose him with severe ASD, but she found comorbidity for ADHD and a possibility of mild epilepsy that might have been the cause for his violent psychotic episodes. Bolton et al. (2011) tell us about the prevalence of epilepsy comorbidity with ASD, and how it can be easily overlooked because it doesn't always lead to grand mal seizures and professionals don't readily screen for epilepsy. It could be that the person is only experiencing minor brain seizures that might go unnoticed if it wasn't for the behavioral symptoms he exhibits. A seasoned practitioner will understand comorbidity and look at the outward symptoms and assess for inward answers. A novice, perhaps an inexperienced professional, will be looking for symptoms and moments when a child seems to lose focus and stare blankly, for example. Said child's body might feel stiff and when the seizure is over, the child will experience a moment of disorientation when he or she will be confused by the environment, which might result in aggressive behavior.

Nolan experienced exactly those symptoms and was eventually prescribed three antipsychotic medications by his psychiatrist because the behaviors seemed out of his and his therapists' control. One medication was for the ADHD, one for seizures, and one for the general psychotic episodes. Further down the line, the diagnosis of severe mental retardation (now intellectual disability) was also finalized as an umbrella term to encompass his general developmental delays, and ASD was also kept. Last, Nolan also has a sleeping problem (that is being treated with melatonin) and has an extremely restricted diet: He refuses to readily eat anything beyond chicken nuggets, French fries, and rice (which quite possibly could be compounding his developmental delays with malnutrition or food allergies that affect general moods). Therefore, it is easy to see why a systemic approach to diagnosing is critical to properly understand the disorder so that targeted interventions can be utilized more effectively. Nolan, for example, could be "misbehaving" on any particular day due to a mini seizure, or lack of sleep, or poor nutrition, or he might be having a psychotic episode, none of which would be immediately recognizable as the antecedent to the behavior if the system is not looked at as a whole.

Interventions

The primary, non–medication-based interventions currently used to shape behaviors in individuals diagnosed with ASD are play therapy and ABA (Greenspan & Wieder, 2006). Psychiatric medications; special diets (e.g., gluten or dairy free); and physical, occupational, and speech therapies are some of the varied supplemental therapies many families have been seeking in the treatment of their children's ASD (Levy & Hyman, 2008). The key again with all these therapies, however, is early intervention, in order to find the most effective

regimen of therapies that works for each child and produces the most positive results.

ABA is used to train daily tasks and specific behavioral reactions to actions using researched and proven behavioral learning theories (ABA, 2013). Play therapy is a style of working with children that involves being "in the moment" with them, playing and interacting in ways that enhance and promote reciprocal interaction (Greenspan & Wieder, 2006). The social worker always needs to remember that when working with people diagnosed with ASD, the worker must focus on developing strong rapport and trust with them before anything else. They are, above all, people and children like anybody else and demand the same respect and acknowledgment as everyone around them. Although they might not readily exhibit it, they are very aware of their environment, even if they do have difficulties participating. It is extremely frustrating for anyone to feel misunderstood, especially so for someone who is unable to communicate it with others due to disabilities. The natural reaction for children diagnosed with ASD is to walk away from someone who just "doesn't understand them," as it naturally would be with anyone, so make sure when working with someone who is diagnosed with a social or developmental impairment to utilize all verbal and nonverbal communication cues in order to develop that trust and rapport. Once trust and rapport is established, only then can the therapeutic techniques designed specifically for the individual be implemented and prove successful and meaningful to the therapist and client.

Assistive technology is another aspect of the micro-level interventions that have been expanding rapidly over the years. It refers to the use of assistive tools and technologies at the disposal of the client, in order to provide them with external compensation for internal deficits. These tools are also called augmentative and alternative communication devices and teaching or supportive tools and strategies. These include modified computers, keyboards, mouses, enhanced software, mobile device applications, or text-to-speech devices that assist clients with ASD to more effectively communicate with their social environment. For example, Nolan would carry around a text-to-speech device on which he would type words or sentences, such as, "I want drink," and the device would read it aloud to the adults in his vicinity, alerting them of his needs. Eventually, picture communication software was installed on his computer and subsequently an application on his digital tablet (iPad) for him to use when he is unable to verbalize needs was also utilized. He would click a picture and it would verbalize his needs. These services are changing rapidly as technology advances; therefore, they are a very important part of any modern intervention program, so it is critical that social workers stay up-to-date and informed on assistive technologies as enhancements to any therapeutic process.

Last, in behavioral therapy, the social worker is constantly looking for the function of the behavior to know how to address it. The function of a behavior is simply the "why" behind how the person is behaving or responding to his environment. Besides utilizing skills and theories learned in Human Behavior in the Social Environment (HBSE) classes, the best evidence-based practice methodology for working with children diagnosed with ASD is the ABC model of identifying a behavior function. This methodology is clearly outlined in behavioral therapy theories studied in social work and in ABA classes.

ABC stands for antecedent (A) to the behavior (B) and the consequences (C) of that behavior (ABA, 2013). For example, Nolan would randomly begin to scream in the middle of a classroom and hit someone. For weeks the social worker was unable to explain or predict this behavior, and it became extremely frustrating for both the child and therapist to go anywhere outside the classroom, such as to assemblies or into quiet libraries. So for a month the ABCs of the screaming were charted daily. Every time Nolan would burst out in a scream, the social worker logged it and noted the consequences and reactions taken by everyone around the child. The hypothesis was to identify whether the screaming was just an attention-seeking behavior or a reaction to something aversive in his environment. If it turned out to be an attention-seeking behavior,

any reaction on the part of the social worker would only be serving to reinforce this negative behavior, so it was crucial to find the cause. The social worker wanted to know whether this behavior was a result of his inability to communicate an aversive environmental factor that was causing him discomfort, such as noises from peers, or difficulty performing a table task, or even just basic hunger and thirst. When the antecedents, behaviors, and consequences were tallied up at the end of the month, they were input into an Excel worksheet and graphed. The resulting graphs provided insight as to the antecedents of the behavior so the social worker could determine how to best intervene and then provide the appropriate consequence/reinforcement for the behavior in order to shape it, change it, or eliminate it. The graph showed a spike in screaming behaviors on the days after Nolan did not get much sleep. It helped the team reach the conclusion that Nolan was tired, frustrated, and agitated. We began asking the parents to alert the team on the days Nolan was lacking sleep, so that he would be given more breaks in the day and allowed extra time to complete assignments.

Transference and Countertransference Issues

Gibson (2006) and Greenspan and Wieder (2006) state that for any clinician to provide effective therapy and a healthy environment for a client, he or she must be very aware of his or her challenges and limitations with the work. This concept can be summed up as another part of social worker competence. Part of that competence is being aware of issues of transference and countertransference. These are two of the biggest obstacles faced by clinicians and clients reciprocally, and in therapy they can play a major role in promoting or hindering therapeutic success.

Transference. Working with Nolan, transference happens when he becomes immediately defensive at the sight of a therapist because he's learned over the years that therapists don't seem to understand him and are only there to "make him do things he doesn't want to do," and he should avoid them. This, in fact, was the exact response Nolan demonstrated to any new therapist coming into his life. His prior experience with therapy was that it was a negative and aversive force in his life. Therapists seemingly only came to see him to make him sit at a table for hours, do repetitive ABA-style behavioral training, and try and shape his behaviors with primary reinforcements. For example, a past therapist would come into the home in the afternoon while Nolan was watching a favorite television show. The therapist would walk into the room and announce that it was time for "work" and the TV should be turned off. Anyone who is abruptly told to stop a favored activity would react the same way and become upset at the proposition, and Nolan would, in fact, become upset at this demand. Then when he became upset, he would be punished for his actions and told he was not allowed to yell or hit. In effect, he was being told to not only abruptly stop what he was doing, but that his feelings of frustration were invalid and he was not even allowed to communicate them. The downfall to not building rapport and being where the client is was not recognizing that Nolan was just communicating his frustration in the best way he knew how.

Then, being already upset, Nolan would be expected to comply with directions to sit at a table for an undefined period of time, doing repetitive ABA activities to learn what, to him, were meaningless words and social interactions. Nolan would be asked to receptively identify objects by pictures, then asked to expressively name them, and then he would be rewarded with a primary reinforcer such as chips. Imagine how it feels being controlled with primary reinforcements to do unwanted or meaningless things. General consensus in the field is that primary reinforcement should never or rarely be used with people. It is inappropriate to control access to food or water and then expect a person to trust the therapist. It begins to create an atmosphere of tension between client and therapist, and negative behaviors will usually end up escalating. As an example of this, the therapists viewed Nolan's hitting, screaming, or running away from them as defiance and a negative behavior that needed punishment, when in fact he was just communicating a need to escape what, to him, was a negative environment he was unable to comprehend. This is why building rapport and trust with people who have social, learning, and communication impairments is crucial to effective clinical long-term therapy. This transference on the part of the client ultimately created extra barriers with future therapists and further slowed the therapeutic process unnecessarily.

Countertransference. Countertransference happens when the recipient of Nolan's behaviors would react to him based on his or her own experience with these behaviors. For example, analysis of the initial therapists working with Nolan would reveal that their countertransference toward his seemingly inappropriate defiant behavior might have occurred because the behaviors reminded them of their own upbringing, in which they were punished for defying their parents' directions. The therapist's natural reaction might have been to just punish Nolan for screaming, without really taking the time to assess the situation to find out if Nolan was actually being defiant or he just did not understand what the therapists wanted from him. Generally, social workers are trained to react to a client's actions and need to be self-aware enough to be able to understand the functions of their behaviors as well. Making that basic socialized mental shift from thinking Nolan was being defiant to thinking he might just be confused can help the social worker react in more adaptive ways that defuse a traumatic situation. More experienced therapists would begin by entering the room, talking to Nolan, sharing in his experience (the TV program), then waiting for a more respectful opportune time to begin placing restrictions on the activity and allow Nolan time to regulate his emotions and process and act on the demands placed upon him (McKay et al., 2004).

MEZZO PERSPECTIVE

We must now move from the micro systems up to the mezzo—communities and agencies involved in the client's life also play a big role in his success or failure. The various mezzo systems at play in Nolan's life in California are the Regional Centers that provide the home therapy, the Los Angeles Unified School district that will provide therapy and assistance at school, and the multitude of agencies in the community that will provide the ancillary services. These ancillary services include occupational therapy, physical therapy, socialization clubs, summer camp programs for children with disabilities, respite agencies to assist the families with babysitting services and, for older individuals, educational tutoring and job training centers to assist with the transition to adulthood. It is important to identify the mezzo systems at play not only because of the need to tap all available resources and educate families on their services, but because it is also important to assess barriers to access of care. Simply knowing that an agency exists to assist a client is not enough to produce results. Clients must be able to access those services, and social workers play a major role in that process.

Regional Centers (RC; California Department of Developmental Services, 2013), for example, are meant to be all-encompassing nonprofit centers that are primarily geared toward providing services for individuals with developmental disabilities. There are multiple RC locations to service different areas of California. For each state, the worker should follow the funding trail and look for similar umbrella agencies that provide similar services. RCs in California are funded by the government's Department of Developmental Services (DDS), which even has an Early Start early intervention program for children with developmental impairments who are 0–36 months of age. Private providers of services (therapists) can also contract with DDS and provide services directly to individuals and bill DDS for the services. That is an example of the mezzo's interface, an energy transaction between the micro and macro systems to provide care. Children who are believed to be inappropriately developing and are under 5 years of age are referred to a RC for assessment and the RC contracts with an outside agency in the child's area for individual or group home services. RCs fund the services for the clients, including home

therapy, respite care, social skills training, and anything else that is specific to that individual's out-of-school needs. Quarterly reports are written to the RC by the therapists apprising them of the progress being made with the child, of any regression, and to justify continued funding and services.

The school districts, on the other hand, are then meant to take over services when children are 5 and older and enroll in public school. As part of a district's umbrella of support systems, they are responsible for providing a child with developmental impairments with any services needed to assist him in gaining access to the same education all other children have access to. The process usually involves first the teacher or parent identifying that the child is in need of extra services because he or she might begin performing below grade and developmental level expectations. Supportive services range from providing after school tutoring, to providing remedial assistance outside the classroom to help the student catch up to peers, to providing the student with a personal assistant who will shadow the child's activities throughout the school day. Public schools are also responsible for providing physical and occupational therapies. These therapies are needed to assist the child in learning gross motor skills such as how to participate in school physical education classes, peer play on the yard, lining up for lunch, as well as learning fine motor skills such as how to grasp writing objects and scissors and practice various other fine and gross motor skills needed to succeed in school. Once a need is identified, an IEP meeting is scheduled, and all the adults involved in the child's life will meet to discuss all services that would benefit the child and implement a plan of action to mitigate the gap between the student and his or her peers. These meetings would usually involve the school psychologist, private therapists, psychiatrists, teachers, school administrators, attorneys, social workers, and family members.

Nolan's services included home-based play therapy through an RC, respite care for babysitting, an IEP at school that called for a personal assistant, placement in an autism-specific classroom (because he was severely autistic), physical and occupational therapies, speech therapy, and a specialized physical education program designed for individuals with developmental impairments. All these services were provided to the child on a continuous basis. His services were funded by the RC in home after school (which was funded by DDS), the local city government that budgeted the school district's funds during the day at school, and by a permanent disability Supplemental Social Security Income monthly stipend because he was given permanent disability status by the state of California. Last, this classification qualified Nolan for state Medi-Cal (Medicaid) insurance to pay for all his medical needs thereafter.

MACRO PERSPECTIVE

On the macro level, government policy directly affects clients through laws and regulations that can either hinder or promote access to services by historically underrepresented populations. As discussed in the case study vignette, Nolan's family is not wealthy enough to be able to provide for all his needs privately. His other three siblings also all need varying levels of assistance, as they are all diagnosed with varying severities of ASD. For a family like Nolan's family, not having key legislations such as the federal Americans With Disabilities Act (ADA) of 1990 and the California state Lanterman Developmental Disabilities Services Act (Frank D. Lanterman Regional Center, 2013), becoming functional contributing members of the home and the communities might have been impossible. Despite how the economy and funding might fluctuate over time, the Acts mentioned above will always make it illegal for any person, agency, or community or local government to discriminate against people with disabilities and block them from accessing the services they need to live life and participate in society the same as everyone else (U.S. Department of Justice, 2015; Frank D. Lanterman Regional Center, 2013). This, on a macro level, should legally guarantee access to services to any individual in need of specialized assistance.

The ADA, a federal law, prohibits the discrimination against people with disabilities for employment considerations, state and local government services and access to public accommodations (U.S. Department of Justice, 2015). This is a major piece of legislation both for direct access to services and to the allocation of local funding for and the regulation of assistive services for people with developmental impairments. For specific state-by-state legislation and funding, please access local government websites or offices. Federally there are some programs that can be accessed, such as the Medicaid and Social Security assistance programs for the nation's disabled, which provide the federal share of funding needed for services. Also on a federal level, special education services funding under the Individuals With Disabilities Education Act (IDEA) are provided to public schools in addition to the state funds. Therefore again, although states might differ in their respective set of services they provide, on a federal macro system level, programs do exist to provide assistance for the disabled.

At the California state government macro system level at least, the Lanterman Act of 1969 afforded California's disabilities communities the right to legal protection for access to services and supports they need. It outlines for regional centers and service providers what type of help and services people with disabilities can obtain (Frank D. Lanterman Regional Center, 2013). (See Lanterman Act in the Internet Resources section below.)

For Nolan, those key pieces of macro-level legislations not only insure that he will have access to the services he needs as a child, but that he will continue to benefit from this assistance well into adulthood, as he begins to train for a job, prepare for independence, or at a worst case scenario, continue to require further intensive services to maintain a dignified human life (Howlin, Goode, Hutton, & Rutter, 2004). Additionally, aging with a developmental impairment usually does not get easier with time (Happé & Charlton, 2012), requiring more assistance and services in order to maintain a quality of life close to what was enjoyed as a younger adult. Many times individuals with disabilities require even more specialized attention, services, and training in order to participate in activities we all take for granted and to maintain their quality of life into late adulthood. Nolan will require specialized assistance and training for the rest of his life. His brothers, who were diagnosed and treated earlier, will have a better chance at assimilating into adulthood than Nolan. The combination of late intervention, severe developmental delays, and comorbid diagnoses make Nolan a potential candidate for lifetime assistance, which without the persistence of politicians, activists, and social workers, would not have been possible.

CONCLUSION

ASD intervention is a complicated and intricate balance of best practices aimed at enhancing the lives of those on the spectrum. A keen awareness of the disorder and how it manifests in the person's environment is key to a complete and holistic accurate assessment. Interventions that are tailored to the specific needs of the individual will yield the best results, and developing a strong rapport with the client before implementation of interventions will go a long way in decreasing anxiety and stress in the therapeutic relationship and increasing success. As seen throughout this chapter, that concerted effort between all the systems at play is critical to ensuring success in all aspects of a person's life. Just as intersectional theoretical approaches inform us of the different attributes of individuals that affect behavior, systems theory informs social work practice that the micro, mezzo, and macro all interact and work together and can all be attributed to successes or failures experienced in one's lifetime. Therefore, continued advocacy and lobbying on behalf of children like Nolan, people with disabilities, and the disenfranchised are a key responsibility of the work we do and can go beyond the individual therapeutic supports we provide clients on a daily basis.

INTERNET RESOURCES

- Autism Speaks: http://www.autismspeaks.org
- Assistive Technology: http://www.autismspeaks.org/family-services/resource-library/assistive-technology
- What Is Assistive Technology? http://www.autism-community.com/education/assistive-technology/

- Autism Research Institute: http://www.autism.com
- Individuals With Disabilities Education Act: http://idea.ed.gov
- Lanterman Developmental Disabilities Services Act: http://www.lanterman.org/lanterman_act
- American Psychiatric Association: DSM-5: http://www.dsm5.org
- Information About Regional Centers: http://www.dds.ca.gov/RC/Home.cfm
- World Health Organization: http://www.who.int
- U.S. Department of Education: http://www.ed.gov
- Autism NOW Center: http://www.autismnow.org
- Autism Internet Modules: http://www.autisminternetmodules.org
- A Parent's Guide to Autism Spectrum Disorder: http://www.autismweb.com
- Autism Transition Handbook: http://www.autismhandbook.org/index.php/Web_Resources
- Autism Society: Online Courses and Tutorials: http://www.autism-society.org/living-with-autism/how-the-autism-society-can-help/online-courses-and-tutorials/

DISCUSSION QUESTIONS

1. What is ASD and what are its symptoms?

2. When and how should diagnosing begin, and why is that important to client success?

3. What are some examples of evidence-based practice interventions shown to work with ASD clients?

4. What is the social worker's role in the ASD support system?

5. How do the micro, mezzo, and macro systems affect (positively or negatively) a client's future success?

REFERENCES

American Psychiatric Association. (2013). *Diagnostic and Statistical Manual of Mental Disorders* (5th ed.). Arlington, VA: Author.

Americans With Disabilities Act of 1990, Pub. L. No. 101-336, 104 Stat. 328 (1990).

Applied Behavior Analysis (ABA). (2013). *Autism speaks.* Retrieved from http://www.autismspeaks.org/what-autism/treatment/applied-behavior-analysis-aba.

Baird, G., Douglas, H. R., & Murphy, M. S. (2011). Recognizing and diagnosing autism in children and young people: Summary of NICE guidance. *British Medical Journal, 343,* d6360. doi: 10.1136/bmj.d6360

Bolton, P. F., Carcani-Rathwell, I., Hutton, J., Goode, S., Howlin, P., & Rutter, M. (2011). Epilepsy in autism: Features and correlates. *The British Journal of Psychiatry 198*(4), 289–294.

California Department of Developmental Services. (2013). *Information about regional centers.* Retrieved from http://www.dds.ca.gov/RC/Home.cfm

Frank D. Lanterman Regional Center. (2013). *The Lanterman Developmental Disabilities Services Act.* Retrieved from http://www.lanterman.org/lanterman_act.

Gibson, J. (2006). Disability and clinical competency: An introduction. *The California Psychologist, 6,* 5–10.

Greenspan, S., & Wieder, S. (2006). *Infant and early childhood mental health: A comprehensive developmental approach to assessment and intervention.* Arlington, VA: American Psychiatric Association.

Greenspan, S., & Wieder, S. (2008). *Engaging autism: Using the floortime approach to help children relate, communicate and think.* Cambridge, MA: Da Capo Press.

Happé, F., & Charlton, R. A. (2012). Aging in autism spectrum disorders: A mini-review. *Gerontology, 58*(1), 70–78.

Howlin, P., Goode, S., Hutton, J., & Rutter, M. (2004). Adult outcome for children with autism. *Journal of Child Psychology and Psychiatry, 45*(2), 212–229.

Individuals With Disabilities Education Act, 20 U.S.C. § 1400 (2004).

Levy, S. E., & Hyman, S. L. (2008). Complementary and alternative medicine treatments for children with autism spectrum disorders. *Child and Adolescent Psychiatry Clinics of North America, 17*(4), 803–820. doi: 10.1016/j.chc.2008.06.004

Mandell, D. S., Listerud, J., Levy, S. E., & Pinto-Martin, J. A. (2009). Race differences in the age at diagnosis among Medicaid-eligible children with autism. *Journal of the American Academy of Child and Adolescent Psychiatry, 41*(12), 1447–1453.

Mandy, W., Chilvers, R., Chowdhury, U., Salte, G., Seigal, A., & Skuse, D., (2012). Sex differences in autism spectrum disorder: Evidence from a large sample of children and adolescents. *Journal of Autism and Developmental Disorders, 42*(7), 1304–1313. doi: 10.1007/s10803–011–1356–0

McKay, M. M., Hibbert, R., Hoagwood, K., Rodriguez, J., Murray, L., Legerski, J., & Fernandez, D. (2004). Integrating evidence-based engagement interventions into "real world" child mental health settings. *Brief Treatment and Crisis Intervention, 4,* 177–186.

National Institute of Mental Health. (2015). Retrieved from http://www.nimh.nih.gov/health/topics/autism-spectrum-disorders-asd/index.shtml

National Institute for Health and Clinical Excellence. (2011). *Autism: Recognition, referral and diagnosis of children and young people on the autism spectrum.* Clinical guideline 128. Retrieved from http://guidance.nice.org.uk/CG128

Pyramid Educational Consultants. (2013). *Picture Exchange Communication System (P.E.C.S.).* Retrieved from http://www.pecsusa.com

Rivet, T. T., & Matson, J. L. (2011). Review of gender differences in core symptomatology in autism spectrum disorders. *Research in Autism Spectrum Disorders, 5*(3), 957–976.

Simonoff, E., Pickles, A., Charman, T., Chandler, S., Loucas, T., & Baird, G. (2008). Psychiatric disorders in children with autism spectrum disorders: Prevalence, comorbidity, and associated factors in a population-derived sample. *Journal of the American Academy of Child and Adolescent Psychiatry, 47*(8), 921–929.

Springer, K. W., Hankivsky, O., & Bates, L. M. (2012). Gender and health: Relational, intersectional, and biosocial approaches. *Social Science and Medicine, 74*(11), 1661–1666.

U.S. Department of Justice. (2015). *Information and technical assistance on the Americans With Disabilities Act.* Retrieved from http://www.ada.gov

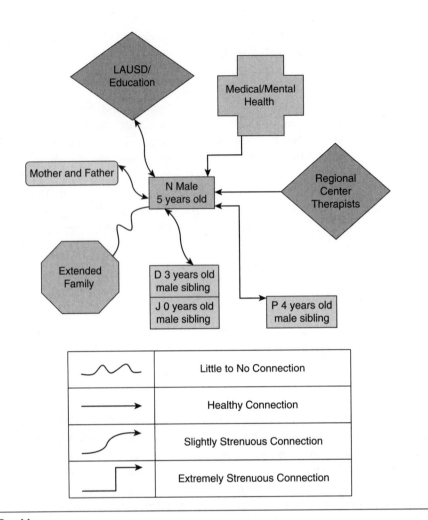

Appendix A Eco Map

CHAPTER 19

Intimate Partner Violence

Elizabeth Eastlund & Susan Hess

CHAPTER OBJECTIVES

- Explore the prevalence and dynamics of intimate partner violence;
- Understand the effects of early childhood trauma and its relation to intimate partner violence in adulthood;
- Identify practical and emerging strategies, such as trauma-informed care, for working with victims of intimate partner violence and their children;
- Explain countertransference when working with victims of intimate partner violence and creating wellness for the treating social worker.

CASE VIGNETTE

Rosa, age 23, and her 3-year-old daughter Glenda both reside in a 45-day intimate partner violence emergency shelter. La Paloma Shelter was the only shelter that would accept Rosa because she did not have a legal immigration status to reside in the U.S., and she had been using illicit drugs. Rosa was born and raised in El Salvador to a father and mother who both suffered from alcoholism. Rosa excelled in school and followed all of the rules at home because punishment was severe when the rules were broken. Rosa was sexually abused from 6 to 10 years of age by her male cousin who was of the same age. She would later witness his murder by a neighbor. At the age of 11, Rosa was left alone quite often as both parents worked. Rosa and her two older sisters, who were ages 15 and 16, began experimenting with alcohol, drugs, and sex.

When Rosa was 12, her mother checked herself into a rehabilitation center to treat her alcoholism. During this time, Rosa's father presented with depression and attempted suicide by cutting his wrists in front of Rosa. Subsequently, her father also went into a rehabilitation center, and Rosa resided with her maternal grandmother.

Later, Rosa was expelled from school in El Salvador due to engaging in physical altercations. Eventually, Rosa ran away from her grandmother's home and at age 18, she met a man and crossed the U.S. border into California, where she began to work as a sex worker.

In California, Rosa entered a relationship with an old friend from El Salvador who was gang affiliated. Within three months, Rosa was being physically, emotionally, and sexually abused. The relationship continued for several years. Several times, Rosa attempted to end the relationship and was physically assaulted. The last incident resulted in Rosa being severely injured and hospitalized. Rosa learned that she was pregnant from the rape of this last incident. Rosa stopped using illicit drugs and obtained a restraining order; however, she began to see him secretly without telling her friends or family who were also residing in the U.S.

Rosa ended the relationship once she gave birth to her daughter and relocated to live with a friend and began to work as a housekeeper. At this time, her ex-partner located her and physically assaulted her in front of their daughter. A neighbor called the police and Child Protective Services was contacted. Child Protective Services called approximately 12 shelters prior to Rosa and her daughter being accepted at La Paloma Shelter.

INTRODUCTION

Intimate partner violence (IPV) is a pervasive social issue affecting one in four women in the United States and is one of the most chronically underreported crimes. According to the U.S. Department of Justice, "about 55% of domestic violence [is] reported to police" (Truman & Morgan, 2014, p. 9). Females are most often victimized by someone they know, while males are most often victimized by a stranger (Catalano, 2004).

The term *IPV* is more widely used than the term *domestic violence* as it is more inclusive in recognizing the different types of intimate relationships, including sexual minorities. In a trauma-informed care system, which will be described later in this chapter, the person receiving services is viewed as actively participating in her own care and in partnership with the service provider; therefore, the term *participant* is used rather than *client*. Although both men and women experience IPV, the vast majority of victims are women, and this chapter is written from the perspective of females as victims (Rennison, 2003).

Many different types of abuse can occur within intimate relationships. The dynamics of IPV follows a pattern of escalating abuse that can become life threatening, and at times it does end with the victim being murdered by her intimate partner. IPV is characterized by power and control, specifically one intimate partner exerting power and control tactics over the other. The Duluth Model was created by the Domestic Abuse Intervention Programs in the early 1980s and provides a framework defining the various types of abuse that may be present in IPV. A physical assault rarely occurs without other elements of abuse present, such as verbal and emotional abuse. The power and control wheel outlines the various types of abuse with power and control at the center, including physical and sexual assault; using intimidation; using emotional abuse; using isolation; minimizing, denying, and blaming; using children; using male privilege; using economic abuse; using coercion and threats (Domestic Abuse Intervention Programs, n.d.).

Lenore Walker first defined the "cycle of violence" in 1979. The cycle of violence describes a pattern of three distinct phases that occur in IPV: the tension-building phase; the acute battering episode; and the honeymoon phase. Each relationship is different, and although the time in which couples experience the full cycle varies, there is a definite pattern that is described by many victims of IPV (Walker, 2009). The most commonly asked question is "Why does the victim stay?" Instead, we should be asking "Why do batterers abuse?" Victims or survivors often describe that they remember the love that existed prior to the abuse and do not necessarily want the relationship to end; they want the abuse to end. This is exemplified when Rosa would see the person who had abused her and not disclose this information to her friends or family.

Research confirms a correlation between IPV and adverse childhood experiences. Data suggests staggering evidence of the short- and long-term outcomes including health, social, and economic risks that result from childhood exposure to IPV. Childhood abuse, neglect, and exposure to other traumatic stressors, termed *adverse childhood experiences* (ACE), are common (Felitti et al., 1998). This is clearly depicted in the film *Healing Neen* (Stromer & Cain, 2010), in which Felitti and others state the prevalence of traumatic experiences among various populations: Ninety percent of individuals in the public mental health system have been victims of trauma; 85% of girls in the juvenile justice system have been victims of early physical or sexual abuse; 87% of women who are homeless have been the victims of early childhood abuse; and 50% of women in substance use programs report histories of incest.

Social workers can benefit from understanding the impact of ACE on future outcomes with regard to health and social problems. Felitti (2013) suggests a direct link between ACE and adult onset of chronic disease, depression, alcohol use, illicit drug use, suicide, IPV, and early death among many other health, social, and emotional problems. Additionally, in order to fully understand the neurological impact of ACE, it is recommended to integrate the ACE Questionnaire in the treatment plan for each participant (see Assessment, below).

Felitti (2013) suggests sharing the results within treatment groups to create support and reduce isolation among participants. It is critical that IPV systems integrate trauma-informed care and nonviolent parenting as an intervention to address ACE. Rosa's multiple childhood adversities suggest a link to her alcohol and illicit drug use and being in an abusive intimate partner relationship. All of these experiences could negatively impact her daughter, Glenda, both in the present and in terms of long-term outcomes.

Having an understanding of trauma and attachment theories and how a participant's traumatic experiences have affected their ability to function in the present is essential. "Adults' responses to children during and after traumatic events can make an enormous difference in these eventual outcomes—both for good and ill" (Perry & Szalavitz, 2006, p. 3). For example, it would be critical that Rosa receive empathy from a safe adult regarding the trauma of her parents using alcohol and not living in the home. Traumatic experience includes a real or perceived threat to a person's well-being. Judith Herman (1997) described traumatic events as those that "overwhelm the ordinary systems of care that give people a sense of control, connection, and meaning" (p. 33). Rosa presented with symptoms of complex trauma and the impact of exposure to multiple traumatic events often occurring within the caregiving system over an extended period of time. The National Child Traumatic Stress Network (n.d.) further describes elements of complex trauma as including "an invasive, interpersonal nature, and the wide-ranging, long-term impact of this exposure." Symptoms include difficulty concentrating, isolation from friends and family, irritability, nightmares, exaggerated startled reflex, intrusive thoughts, and feeling constantly on guard. Rosa reports that she began to use drugs to suppress these overwhelming symptoms. Making a formal diagnosis as part of conducting an assessment will be described later in this chapter.

The traumatic experience of IPV is complicated by the relationship between the person who was abusive and the victim. One of the greatest forms of abuse is that the person who was abused can become emotionally dependent on the person who abused through a process called trauma bonding (Bancroft, 2002). Women often experience much confusion and anxiety about missing the person who was abusive, which is often compounded by a common practice in which IPV shelters discourage women from talking about their conflicted feelings for the person who was abusive. This is exemplified when Rosa met with the person who was abusive after she filed for a restraining order and didn't disclose this to her friends or family. Responses to trauma are normal reactions to abnormal circumstances. It is imperative to understand the impact of trauma neurologically so that behaviors are understood with compassion and the presenting symptoms are addressed in order to decrease recidivism rates. It is not as simple as saying, "Do not see your batterer" (D'Anniballe, 2013). It is critical to understand the neurobiology of trauma and the presenting symptoms in order to decrease the recidivism rates. (For further information on neurobiology and trauma, The Child Trauma Academy provides free online training on "the amazing human brain and human development." Please see the Internet Resources section at the end of this chapter).

MICRO PERSPECTIVE

Examining Rosa's presenting problem, a social worker can utilize a trauma-informed framework. Trauma-informed care (TIC) begins with attempting to assist the participant in developing her own understanding of safety and providing education on emotional regulating techniques. It is important for social workers to utilize a strengths-based approach in order to identify the participant's coping abilities. TIC assesses for trauma across the lifespan to gain an understanding of the various types of trauma the participant has experienced. Often victims of IPV have experienced multiple traumas, beginning from an early age. The ACE Questionnaire can be used to identify the various ACEs a victim has experienced over her lifetime (www.acestudy.org). Implementation of crisis intervention techniques allow for

rapid assessment and development of a therapeutic relationship, identification of goals, and exploration for continued safety.

Assessing a victim's risk of lethality from her perpetrator and continued abuse is paramount. Campbell (1986) developed a 20-question "Danger Assessment" that examines factors common in women who had been murdered by their intimate partners. It provides a four-point scale range that includes variable danger, increased danger, severe danger, and extreme danger. The Danger Assessment assists practitioners in providing education to the participant regarding the potential level of lethality (Campbell, 1986).

In addition, it is recommended to assess for the diagnosis of Posttraumatic Stress Disorder (PTSD). Symptoms of PTSD are most commonly seen among victims entering IPV services. Rosa often presented with symptoms of anxiety and depression, and her ambivalence to appear in court to request a restraining order was due to fear of seeing her former partner. PTSD falls under the category of Trauma and Stressor-Related Disorder in the DSM-5 (American Psychiatric Association [APA], 2013). The criteria for PTSD includes exposure to actual or threatened death, serious injury, or sexual violence (Criterion A); re-experiencing of the trauma (Criterion B); avoidance of stimuli associated with traumatic events (Criterion C); negative alterations in cognitions and mood associated with traumatic events (Criterion D); heightened arousal symptoms (Criterion E; APA, 2013).

It is critical for a social worker to continuously assess for child safety and to provide referrals and follow up to see whether Rosa is receiving services for possible addiction. Additionally, shelters often encourage participants to contact the local District Attorney to inform them that Rosa and Glenda are residing at a shelter and will be receiving services, to prevent the person who perpetrated the violence from filing kidnapping charges. Throughout the assessment, it is vital to explore the social and family supports, such as a faith-based organization, that could be sources of support in order to prevent isolation.

Diversity Considerations

It is critical to consider diversity while working with victims of IPV. Recognizing Rosa's cultural influences is a critical principle of TIC. Many terms have been used to examine culture and diversity, including *cultural sensitivity, multicultural,* and *cultural competency.* It is important to incorporate ongoing training for staff working with culturally diverse populations in order to be mindful of and understand the social worker's own potential biases. A broad and more critical definition of culture refers to shared experiences that develop and evolve according to changing social and political landscapes, including race, ethnicity, gender and gender identity, sexual orientation, class, immigration status, location, time, and other axes of identification understood within the historical context of oppression (Warrier, 2005). It is vital to understand historical trauma such as the social and political impact of the civil war in El Salvador. Understanding the complexities by which men and women are socialized and how society responds to domestic violence in El Salvador (and in the United States) is essential to understanding the fear that Rosa may experience in relation to appearing in court (as well as her hesitation to be involved in the legal system, given her undocumented status).

Competency in the delivery of services has to be developed at both the individual and the organizational level in an effort to balance standardization with flexibility. It is recommended that organizations develop policies and protocols that clearly show the need for developing competency at all levels (Warrier, 2005). The criteria to be accepted into an IPV agency is often discriminatory for males, adolescent boys, participants who identify as sexual minorities, participants who use alcohol or illicit drugs, participants who have a mental health diagnosis, or participants who do not have legal documents to reside in this country. Racial microaggressions are daily verbal, behavioral, or environmental indignities, whether intentional or unintentional, that conveys hostile, derogatory, or negative racial slights and insults toward people of color (Sue et al., 2007). IPV agencies often rationalize the reasons for these microaggressions, such as saying male participants will retraumatize the female participants or adolescent boys are sexually active and will impose their sexuality on the females in the shelter; asking what if the person who identifies as a sexual minority creates discomfort for other participants or begins to develop feelings for another participant. Agencies often state they do not have the resources or training to treat participants with a mental health diagnosis or who use alcohol or illicit drugs, or that a participant who does not have her legal documents to reside in this country will not be able to work or attend school, which is a requirement of many shelters. This is exemplified when Child Protective Services called approximately 12 shelters in the local area to find a shelter for Rosa that would accept a woman who did not have legal papers to reside in this country. Due to the complicated nature of immigration law and obtaining legal status for victims, it is recommended the social worker provide referrals to legal aid organizations or the Salvadoran Consulate to determine if Rosa is eligible to apply for immigration status. The social worker can provide a referral to an interpreter if Rosa needs one for the meeting with the attorney.

Intervention

TIC is a paradigm shift and emerging framework within the IPV field. Essentially, TIC seeks to do no additional harm through the provision of services to victims of IPV. According to Harris and Fallot (2001), the core values of TIC are safety, trustworthiness, choice, collaboration, and empowerment.

The TIC approach provides a foundation for service provision that ensures all participants are provided with respect, choice, autonomy, and that the service provider works in partnership to develop a service plan that best fits the needs of the participant and her family. The TIC approach ensures that social workers have a basic understanding of trauma and its effects and encourages flexibility and adaptability to the needs of each individual and family being served. The Substance Abuse and Mental Health Services Administration's (SAMHSA) National Center for Trauma-Informed Care describes the paradigm shift in service provision from one that asks "What's wrong with you?" to one that seeks to understand "What happened to you?" (SAMHSA, 2015).

TIC is based in trauma theory and seeks to assist victims in stabilizing their current crisis, empower victims to understand their options, create hopefulness, and build a foundation for growth and change. The National Center for Trauma-Informed Care provides guidance for trauma-specific interventions that address the consequences of trauma and generally follow key principles:

> The survivor's need to be respected, informed, connected and hopeful; the intersection between trauma and symptoms of trauma; the need to work in a collaborative way with survivors, family and friends of the survivor, and other human service organizations in a manner that will empower survivor. (SAMHSA, 2015, para. 6)

Herman (1997) described the stages of trauma treatment in her book *Trauma and Recovery,* which includes safety and stabilization, remembrance and mourning, and reconnecting. It is essential to establish safety prior to processing a traumatic event or series of events, as in the case of IPV. Establishing safety begins by focusing on control of the body and gradually moves externally to the environment. It is recommended that Rosa first pay attention to her basic health needs, regulation of sleep, eating, exercise, management of post-traumatic symptoms, and control of self-destructive behaviors. Following would be the establishment of environmental safety such as financial security, mobility, and the development of social support (Herman, 1997). Assisting participants in identifying what safety means to them, both physical and emotional safety, is the beginning of the process toward healing from trauma. Recognizing the need for the survivor to grieve the loss of her relationship is an important component in the healing process.

Often in the context of providing services to survivors of IPV, practitioners focus on safety and recovery and miss the critical step of grieving in the healing process. While the experience of IPV is horrific, practitioners must recognize and validate that the traumatic event occurred within the context of an intimate relationship. Mourning the loss of the relationship, however violent it became, is essential in the healing process. Finally, reconnecting with self and through creating new relationships allows the participant to move beyond the role of victim. This final phase of treatment focuses on reconnecting with everyday life (Herman, 1997).

Some evidenced-based practices (EBP) can be helpful when participants are in a stable emotional state and once safety has been established; however, different aspects of various modalities are used to meet the various needs and stages of trauma of the participants, providing options and choices for the survivor and providing the flexibility that is essential in a trauma-informed system. Najavits (2002) developed Seeking Safety to assist victims experiencing symptoms of PTSD who also have substance abuse issues; it can be adapted to working with participants of IPV who may not meet the criteria for PTSD or are actively using substances. (In Rosa's case, she may not meet the full criteria for PTSD, and although she denies current illicit drug use, she had a history of drug and alcohol use and thus this approach may be suitable for her.) Seeking Safety has been translated into Spanish and can be utilized with victims who are monolingual Spanish speaking. Seeking Safety is an EBP that has been widely adopted by many IPV agencies. Seeking Safety can be implemented as an individual intervention or within group setting and consists of 25 distinct sessions. Seeking Safety is recognized as an EBP on the SAMHSA Registry. Seeking Safety focuses on the potential of a participant rather than on her pathology. It is an action-oriented and informational intervention that includes elements of CBT, psychodynamic theory, and self-help traditions. The topics are evenly divided among cognitive, behavioral, and interpersonal domains with the overall goal of providing an integrative approach to treating participants who have experienced interpersonal trauma. The main principle of the Seeking Safety intervention is safety. Each of the 25 distinct sessions explores a safe coping skill. Examples of safe coping skills include: detaching from emotional pain, compassion, recovery thinking, setting boundaries in relationships, and self-nurturing (Najavits, 2002). Rosa can be invited to practice simple grounding techniques to detach from emotional pain. Group sessions follow a specific format that includes a brief check-in; a quotation to introduce the safe coping topic and begin the discussion phase of the session; relating the topic to the participants' lives; and a check-out in which participants are able to describe what they are taking from the session as well as identifying and exploring community resources to assist them with their ability to cope.

Nonviolent parenting is an evidence-informed and early intervention to ACE such as witnessing IPV. Nonviolent parenting is based on attachment theory and recognizes the impact of the caregiver-child relationship on the child's developing brain and the effects of disrupted attachment. There is strong evidence to suggest attachment behavior comes to be organized within an individual is influenced by the kinds of experiences the child has in his or her family of origin (Bowlby, 1988). Brain research and an understanding of the importance of emotional intelligence and empathy suggest that we deeply question the paradigm that has been perpetuated as the basis of parenting. Growing evidence in the fields of neuroendocrinology and developmental science established that violence exposure can be detrimental to children of all ages (Garner & Shonkoff, 2012).

Although many people assume that infants and young toddlers will not remember or do not understand, and thus will not be damaged by IPV exposure, memories of this experience are imprinted on the brain and profoundly affect neurodevelopment for children of all ages (Wagner & Malmberg, 2008). Thus, infants and very young children can be affected negatively from exposure that may be more difficult to identify.

Nonviolent parenting teaches parents to use emotion words to describe their child's behavior. For example, Rosa might say, "Glenda you are looking down at the ground and are talking so softly. Are you feeling worried?' When parents help their children develop a language for their emotions, as well as recognize and cope with strong emotions, children gain a sense of mastery over them. This helps the child develop the skills to manage their behavior and mood (Katz & Windecker-Nelson, 2006). A calm and supportive approach helps children regulate their emotions. It also helps them learn that their environment is safe and that they can trust the adults around them, establishing the foundation for teaching alternative, pro-social strategies for expressing emotions, including providing the vocabulary to describe their emotions (Hodas, 2006).

Nonviolent parenting steps away from the mainstream philosophy about raising children, in which adults are in control and use their power over children; parenting is about the adult's demands, rather than the child's needs or emotions. Cultural considerations with regard to parenting will need to be explored as Rosa may have been raised within the dominant paradigm, which could include corporal punishment. Any child-raising practice that hurts the mind, body, or spirit of a child is harmful and impacts brain development. This includes physical punishment, manipulation, blaming and shaming, as well as using praise and rewards to control behavior. The term *compulsive compliance* describes the children's fear of their parents, which leads them to do whatever they are told, immediately and unthinkingly (Kohn, 2005). Mainstream philosophy about child raising can be compared to the cycle of violence with children. The child is often in fear regarding the parents commands and if she/he will receive a reward or punishment. This is clearly a dangerous strategy as the brain retains the feelings that are repeated (Siegel & Hartzell, 2004).

Nonviolent parenting recognizes the effects of trauma in both children and adults (neurological, social, emotional, cognitive and physical). It is recommended that participants receive support from a qualified professional especially if one is socially isolated. "An unresolved issue can make us quite inflexible with our children and often unable to choose responses that would be helpful to their development" (Siegel & Hartzell, 2004, p. 28). Siegel and Hartzell described a safe stable and nurturing relationship with a caring adult is a source of strength for the child's developing mind which is supported by attachment theory. Neuroscientists now tell us that it is not what happened to children that will decide their future outcomes, it is how children make sense of what happened to them.

A commitment to nonviolence is an essential intervention in an IPV service agency because the service provider-survivor relationship is based on equality which parallels the parent child relationship. A service provider or social worker will not use punitive interventions that emphasize power differential that echoes the power over paradigm the participant had experienced prior to entering the shelter. For example, providing Rosa with choices throughout the 45 days she is residing at La Paloma empowers her to make the best decision for her and Glenda. It is recommended that Rosa be given the choice of which support services will most benefit her and Glenda. In addition, if there is a day that Rosa does not wish to attend support services, it is critical she have the choice to not attend as this is a clear example of self-determination. It is recommended the social worker explore social supports Rosa has in her life and provide the necessary referrals, such as transportation, to ensure her support systems are included in her treatment plan.

Transference and Countertransference Issues

The prevalence of trauma related experiences in the general population informs us that those working in the IPV field have likely experienced their own trauma (Felitti et al., 1998). Seventy percent of the 17,000 participants experienced at least one type of trauma, resulting in an ACE score of 1, and 87% experienced more than one traumatic experience. ACE scores of 4 or more resulted in four times the risk of emphysema or chronic bronchitis, more than four times the likelihood of depression, and 12 times the risk of suicide. ACE scores are also correlated with early initiation of smoking and sexual activity, adolescent pregnancy, and risk for IPV (Felitti et al.,1998).

At the very least, many workers have known someone who has been or is currently being affected by IPV. It is important that staff is supported in developing awareness of their own trauma responses and how their work with victims affects them as well as understanding how the participant relates to the social worker (e.g., transference reactions). Laura van Dernoot Lipsky (2009) offers a guide for understanding how this work affects social workers and other service providers and offers a framework to address the impact of working with trauma survivors in her book *Trauma Stewardship: An Everyday Guide to Caring for Self While Caring for Others*. It is essential to recognize and address the effects of listening to traumatic narratives on a daily basis and to implement strategies toward wellness in order to prevent burnout, vicarious trauma, and secondary traumatic stress.

Regular reflective supervision (RS) meetings with supervisees provide an opportunity to ensure competency of service providers. It is recommended that meetings are confidential where supervisees can openly discuss the difficulty of working with children and families, many of whom have experienced trauma. RS is characterized by consistency, collaboration, and reflection (Weatherston, Weigand, & Weigand, 2010). It is also indicated that RS is a collaboration between the supervisor and the supervisee to equalize the power dynamics during the supervision session. The supervisee will have choice and control within the supervision process.

RS is a paradigm shift from the traditional supervisory experience where the focus may be on a crisis and/or administrative responsibilities to focusing on the values and beliefs of the provider in order to prevent burn-out, vicarious trauma and secondary trauma. In the situation with Rosa and Glenda, ideally the supervisee would explore his/her values/beliefs regarding Rosa and Glenda's trauma to avoid projective identification if the supervisee had experienced or witnessed IPV. It is critical for supervisors to provide a safe confidential space to debrief with a supervisee as prevention to vicarious trauma, secondary trauma and burnout.

A trauma-informed culture expects that managers and supervisors working in IPV agencies are in partnership with the staff they supervise, developing and supporting plans for their own wellness. It is critical that staff have an understanding of their coherent narratives and their histories of trauma in order to be aware of possible countertransference. Staff who are immigrants or have histories of drug use may over-identify with Rosa. Exploring one's countertransference is also critical in the prevention of vicarious trauma, secondary trauma, and burnout (Van Dernoot Lipsky, 2009).

Legal and Ethical Concerns

Obtaining restraining orders and family law issues are the main legal concerns facing victims of violence. It is important to note that mandatory reporting laws vary from state to state; contact the state board to determine whether social workers are required to report suspected child abuse when a child has witnessed domestic violence. Additionally, health care professionals are mandated to report IPV to law enforcement in some states (Futures Without Violence, n.d.). Cooperating with a criminal prosecution case can be difficult for victims and retraumatizing on many levels, as the victim is asked to share her story in detail multiple times. In working with families who have experienced IPV, the main ethical dilemmas that emerge often involve working with children. It is critical to be mindful of the impact on brain development and child development specifically when the child has visitation with the person who perpetrated the violence. It is recommended that Rosa ask for Glenda to be represented by a guardian ad litem who understands the neurological impact on youth who have witnessed IPV. If the court determines that these visitations will impact the child adversely; it can be requested through the courts that the visits be monitored. Staff working in IPV agencies regularly report to child protective service agencies when a child has witnessed violence in their homes. This can be either a positive or negative experience for the family depending on the level of involvement by child protective

services. Often victims are held to a higher level of accountability than their abusers and threats to remove the children are common if the victim does not engage in IPV-specific services, including entering an emergency shelter. Other times child protective services provides additional supports and protection to the family that is attempting to leave a violent home.

MEZZO PERSPECTIVE

The National Network to End Domestic Violence (NNEDV) estimates there are nearly 2,000 IPV organizations in the U.S. providing a range of support services to victims including: individual and group counseling, legal services, advocacy, children's support services, emergency shelters, and transitional housing programs in the United States. The availability of services varies from urban versus rural settings and often requests for service go unmet. NNEDV conducts an annual survey to collect information about services being provided by IPV agencies during a 24-hour period and the amount of service needs that go unmet. In 2011, NNEDV's Domestic Violence Counts survey reported over 10,000 unmet requests for services in one day.

Addressing IPV requires a multidisciplinary response as many different systems are involved in identifying and addressing IPV, including law enforcement, health care professionals, children's protective services, courts, and IPV specific organizations. IPV organizations are often encouraged, if not required, to enter into collaboration with their local law enforcement organization and health care providers. A number of urban areas have created formal collaborations between law enforcement and IPV organizations. The Domestic Abuse Response Teams (DART) provide victims with direct access to an IPV organization by having responding officers directly connect with an IPV hotline with the victim present. During Rosa's last physical assault by her partner, the responding officers contacted La Paloma shelter, and Rosa was able to speak to an advocate who assisted her with the shelter intake process.

MACRO PERSPECTIVE

Since the 1970s, thousands of organizations have been created in the United States to address the complicated issues associated with IPV. Services for victims generally focus on emergency housing, transitional living programs, counseling, advocacy and case management services, legal services, and children's programming. The availability of services often is not sufficient to meet the need for those seeking services.

The Violence Against Women Act (VAWA, 2013) is a landmark federal legislation that provides a comprehensive approach to address violence against women through improving the criminal justice response, holding offenders accountable, and providing a range of funding for services for victims. VAWA has made it possible for victims to obtain necessary services and has reduced the number of IPV homicides ("Fact Sheet: The Violence Against Women Act," 2012).

ACE clearly needs to be integrated into organizational policies to avoid re-traumatization. It is essential to recognize and address organizational disparities that adversely affect underserved communities as they prohibit equal access to emergency and transitional shelters. Integrating the ACE questionnaire into IPV shelters, may increase understanding among shelter staff and improve access to victims with complex trauma. Violence against women and the movement toward implementing TIC has become a priority of the U.S. government. Since the enactment of the VAWA in 1994, there have been three reauthorizations further enhancing and increasing the amount of protections for victims and their families. The most recent reauthorization in 2013 includes language recognizing sexual minorities as having challenges in accessing services, and it protects them from discrimination while providing current service providers resources to encourage increased accessibility. VAWA also provides protections for immigrants who are victims of the crime of IPV an opportunity to apply for temporary U.S. residency under a U visa when the victim is cooperating in the investigation and prosecution of certain crimes. The U visa provides immigrants temporary legal residency status and the ability to work for four years.

In 1995, the Office of Violence Against Women was created to provide oversight and technical assistance for programs being funded by VAWA. SAMHSA created the National Center for Trauma-Informed Care (NCTIC) in 2005 to provide technical assistance and build awareness regarding the implementation of TIC in programs serving persons with substance abuse and/or mental health issues. NCTIC recognizes that the vast majority of persons seeking services through mental health and substance abuse programs have experienced trauma at some point in their lives and encourages programs to create TIC cultures. The *Organizational Self-Assessment: Adoption of a Trauma-Informed Practice* is recommended to be administered to the shelter staff where Rosa and her daughter are residing. The *Organizational Self-Assessment* is designed for organizations interested in improving their policies, procedures, practices, and social and physical environment to reflect the guiding principles of a trauma-informed care organization.

CONCLUSION

In conclusion, this chapter explores the various aspects of IPV and the ability of social workers to accurately assess, diagnose, and intervene to assist participants in their healing process, as well as addressing issues relating to the effects of ACE and addressing the interventions of nonviolent parenting and Seeking Safety. Agencies addressing IPV can implement a TIC system in an effort to ensure that services are provided in such a way as to not cause additional harm to the participant. The TIC system includes establishing safety, trust, and providing choice to effectively collaborate with participants in empowering them with the tools needed to move beyond the effects of IPV. Additionally the TIC system recognizes the importance of effective supervision in identifying and addressing the effects of burnout, vicarious trauma, and secondary traumatic stress among staff. The mezzo and macro perspectives of IPV include recognizing the need for collaboration among various systems such as law enforcement, health care, child protective services and IPV organizations. The landmark Violence Against Women Act has established national recognition and a funding stream to address the complex issues related to IPV.

INTERNET RESOURCES

- R3 App (Recognize, Respond, and Refer to Domestic Abuse): https://itunes.apple.com/us/app/r3-app/id491452316
- California Partnership to End Domestic Violence: http://www.cpedv.org
- National Network to End Domestic Violence: http://www.nnedv.org
- Ohio Domestic Violence Network: http://www.odvn.org
- Washington State Coalition Against Domestic Violence: http://www.wscadv.org
- Adverse Childhood Experiences (ACE) Study: http://www.cdc.gov/ace/index.htm
- SAMHSA's National Center for Trauma-Informed Care: http://www.samhsa.gov/nctic/
- The Office of Violence Against Women: http://www.ovw.usdoj.gov
- Danger Assessment: http://www.dangerassessment.org
- Echo Parenting and Education: http://www.echoparenting.org
- Multiplying Connections: http://www.multiplyingconnections.org
- Rainbow Services: http://www.rainbowservicesdv.org
- Sanctuary Model: http://www.sanctuaryweb.com/sanctuary-model.php
- The Duluth Model, Power & Control Wheel: http://www.duluth-model.org

DISCUSSION QUESTIONS

1. What are the challenges and benefits of integrating TIC with someone who has experienced IPV?

2. Why is it important to explore attachment parenting models with survivors of IPV?

3. How can social workers address unsafe coping strategies without using judgment?

4. How can countertransference impact the relationship with a participant?

5. What would be a trauma-informed strategy when supporting Rosa and her daughter upon their arrival at the shelter?

6. How would a social worker integrate the five principles of a trauma-informed system into the agency or with a specific participant?

REFERENCES

American Psychiatric Association. (2013). *Desk reference to the diagnostic criteria from DSM-5.* Arlington, VA: Author.

Bancroft, L. (2002) *Why Does He Do That? Inside The Minds Of Angry And Controlling Men.* New York: The Berkley Publishing Group.

Bowlby, J. (1988). *A secure base parent-child attachment and healthy human development.* New York, NY: Basic Books.

Campbell, J. (1986). *The danger assessment.* Retrieved from http://www.dangerassessment.org.

Catalano, S. (2004). *Criminal victimization 2013. Bureau of Crime Statistics, National crime victimization survey.* Retrieved from http://www.bjs.gov/content/pub/pdf/cv03.pdf

D'Anniballe, J. (2013, April). *The neurobiology of trauma and implications for healing.* Paper presented at the meeting of House of Ruth, Pomona, California.

Domestic Abuse Intervention Programs. (n.d.). *Power and control wheel.* Retrieved from http://www.theduluthmodel.org/pdf/PowerandControl.pdf.

Fact sheet: The Violence Against Women Act. (2012). *The White House.* Retrieved from http://www.whitehouse.gov/sites/default/files/docs/vawa_factsheet.pdf

Felitti, V. (2013, March). *The intersections between adverse childhood experiences, trauma informed care and nonviolent child raising.* Paper presented at Changing the Paradigm, a conference conducted by Echo Parenting and Education, Los Angeles, CA.

Felitti, V. J., Anda, R. F., Nordenberg. D., Williamson, D. F., Spitz, A. M., Edwards V. . . . Marks, J. S. (1998). Relationship of childhood abuse and household dysfunction to many of the leading causes of death in adults: The Adverse Childhood Experiences (ACE) Study. *American Journal of Preventive Medicine, 14*, 245–258.

Futures Without Violence. (n.d.). *Mandatory reporting of domestic violence to law enforcement by health care providers: A guide for advocates working to respond to or amend reporting laws related to domestic violence.* Retrieved from http://www .futureswithoutviolence.org/userfiles/Mandatory_ Reporting_of_DV_to_Law%20Enforcement_by_ HCP.pdf

Garner, A., & Shonkoff, J. (2012). Early childhood adversity, toxic stress, and the role of the pediatrician: Translating developmental science into lifelong health. *Pediatrics, 129*, e224–231.

Harris, M., & Fallot, R. (2001). *Using trauma theory to design service systems.* Indianapolis, IN: Jossey-Bass.

Herman, J. (1997). *Trauma and recovery the aftermath of violence—from domestic abuse to political terror.* New York, NY: Basic Books.

Hodas, G. (2006). *Responding to childhood trauma: The promise and practice of trauma informed care.* Retrieved from http://www.dpw .state.pa.us/ucmprd/groups/public/documents/ manual/s_001585.pdf.

Katz, L. F., & Windecker-Nelson, B. (2006). Domestic violence, emotion coaching, and child adjustment. *Journal of Family Psychology 20*, 56–67.

Kohn, A. (2005). *Unconditional parenting.* New York, NY: Atria Books.

Najavits, L. (2002). *Seeking safety: A treatment manual for PTSD and substance abuse.* New York, NY: Guilford Press.

National Child Traumatic Stress Network. (n.d.) *Complex trauma.* Retrieved from http://www .nctsn.org/trauma-types/complex-trauma

Perry, B., & Szalavitz, M. (2006). *The boy who was raised as a dog.* New York, NY: Basic Books.

Rennison, C. M. (2003). *Crime data brief: Intimate partner violence, 1993–2001.* Bureau of Justice Statistics. Retrieved from http://www.bjs.gov/ index.cfm

Siegel, D., & Hartzell, M. (2004). *Parenting from the inside out.* New York, NY: Penguin Group.

Stromer, T. (Producer) & Cain, L. (Director). (2010). *Healing Neen.* [Motion Picture]. Retrieved from http://healingneen.com/buy-dvd

Substance Abuse and Mental Health Services Administration. (2015). *National Center for Trauma-Informed Care and Alternatives to Seclusion and Restraint (NCTIC).* Retrieved from http://www.samhsa.gov/nctic

Sue, D. W., Capodilupo, C. M., Torino, G. C., Bucceri, J. M., Holder, A. M. B., Nadal, K. L., & Esquilin, M. (2007). Radical microaggressions in everyday life: Implications for clinical practice. *American Psychologist, 62*, 271–286. doi: 1037/0003–066x.62.4.271

Truman, J., & Morgan, R. (2014). *Nonfatal domestic violence: 2003-2012.* Washington, DC: U.S. Department of Justice. Retrieved from http:// www.bjs.gov/content/pub/pdf/ndv0312.pdf

Van Dernoot Lipsky, L. (2009). *Trauma stewardship: An everyday guide to caring for self while caring for others.* San Francisco, CA: Berrett-Koehler.

Violence Against Women Reauthorization Act of 2013. Pub. L. No. 113–4, 127 Stat. 54; 42 USC §13701 (2013).

Wagner, A. (Producer), & Malmberg, R. (Director). (2008). *First impressions: Exposure to violence and a child's developing brain.* [Motion Picture]. Sacramento, CA: Office of the Attorney General.

Walker, L. A. (2009). *The battered woman syndrome* (3rd ed.). New York: Springer.

Warrier, S. (2005). *Culture handbook.* San Francisco, CA: Family Violence Prevention Fund. Retrieved from http://www.futureswithoutviolence.org/ userfiles/file/ImmigrantWomen/Culture%20 Handbook.pdf

Weatherston, D., Weigand, R., & Weigand, B. (2010). Reflective supervision: Supporting reflection as a cornerstone for competency. *Zero to Three, 31*(2), 22–30. Retrieved from http://www.zerotothree .org/about-us/areas-of-expertise/zero-to-three-journal/31-2.pdf

CHAPTER 20

Working With Gang-Involved/Affiliated Youth

Robert Hernandez

CHAPTER OBJECTIVES

- Understand the interaction of violence and youth gangs by looking at the historical and social factors that lead to the formation of gangs in the United States;
- Explore the images and challenges faced when working with this population and the influence of diversity on gang culture and peer development;
- Understand the influence of interactions between individuals, families, groups, organizations, communities, institutions, and larger systems on gang involvement;
- Understand current practice, research, and policies dealing with gang activity in communities such as Los Angeles.

CASE VIGNETTE

M. J. is a young man struggling with gang affiliation and a substance use disorder. M. J. is a 16-year-old Latino male residing in the inner-city streets of Los Angeles who has been raised the majority of his childhood and teen years by his maternal grandparents. M. J.'s grandmother died three months ago due to medical issues she had been struggling with for the past few years. It is also documented that M. J.'s aunt, who is sister to his biological father, recently died in an automobile accident. Feedback from the family indicates there has been a noticeable change in M. J.'s demeanor. M. J. has isolated himself from the family, which is more apparent than ever before. Also, M. J. has been smoking marijuana in his room and coming home under the influence of substances, usually marijuana and alcohol. M. J.'s mother is 33 years of age. M. J.'s stepfather is the biological father to M. J.'s siblings and is 35 years of age. M. J. has two stepsisters, 12 and

10 years of age. M. J. also has an 8-year-old half-brother from his mother and stepfather. For the past few years, they have lived with M. J.'s maternal grandparents. During the formative years of M. J.'s childhood, M. J.'s mother was in and out of the picture due to issues of substance abuse. M. J.'s biological father has been in state prison since M. J. was a toddler. The family does not talk about the father's incarceration. M. J.'s grandparents have done their best to provide a nurturing, caring home for M. J.; however, over the years M. J. has distanced himself from the family due to the unstable relationship with his parents and stepfather. It is documented that growing up M. J. was an aggressive child, instigating fights in the neighborhood and at school, which has found him suspended from school several times. M. J. lives in an area in Los Angeles that is impacted by gangs. Several of the friends M. J. grew up with since grade school are gang involved.

M. J. was recently put on probation for shoplifting and has a scheduled court date in three months to determine whether he will remain on probation, be placed in a residential facility, or be detained in juvenile hall. M. J. has a history of smoking marijuana and must test clean for drug use as part of his conditions of probation. M. J. challenges authority figures, more so when they are female. M. J. has no real connection to his family. The only form of communication that occurs in M. J.'s household is when arguments take place. M. J. repeatedly declines to follow up with any activities suggested by the referring case manager, who happens to be female. The case manager works for a community-based gang intervention agency in Los Angeles. Social workers are housed in this agency and are used to better assist the social and emotional needs of this population. M. J. was referred to the agency by his probation officer after his recent arrest. M. J. is not engaged in any outside activities except for his association with a local gang. M. J. and the family have no record of prior treatment for substance abuse and/or mental health disorders.

INTRODUCTION

A main concern for the case described in the above vignette is the label of "gang affiliation." With punitive measures set in place by the state of California and other states over the span of more than 30 years, there has been a drastic increase of inner city youth coming into regular contact with the juvenile justice system. What was supposed to be a measure to deter juveniles from entering the prison system had an adverse effect, resulting in a disproportionate number of juveniles of color entering prison (Wahlberg & Neale, 2008). The term *gang* carries' harsh penalties, with several enhancements based solely on one's identification or supposed identification with a gang.

One of the biggest challenges that exist when servicing this population is the definition of a gang. Researchers to date continue to struggle with defining a gang. In California, the legal definition of a gang is

Any ongoing organization, association or group of three or more persons, whether formal or informal, having as one of its primary activities the commission of [crime (including fights, intimidation, and threats)], having a common name or common identifying sign or symbol, whose members individually or collectively engage in or have engaged in a pattern of criminal activity. (National Institute of Justice, 2011, para. 5)

Once juveniles have the label "gang member" placed on them, it affects their legal rights, impacts their ability to attend school and the types of services they can qualify for, and is a barrier to employment opportunities.

M. J. has never been officially "jumped" in or "initiated" into a gang. He associates with local youth he was raised with ever since elementary school and middle school. Some of these youth may have ties to an official "gang," while others do not. M. J. has been identified as a gang member by law enforcement officials due to his association with his neighborhood friends.

According to well-known gang researcher Ronald Huff (1993), youth groups, also known as "gangs," are an active part of youth development, albeit an extreme manifestation. Other researchers have argued that gangs represent a subversive response to the standards set by the identified dominant culture for that society, especially when youth experience challenges identifying with the dominant culture (Schaefer, 2001; Yinger, 1960).

The process of becoming identified as a gang member is a challenge in itself, outside of the traditional process, which usually consists of being "initiated" into the gang through various means, the most common being "jumped in"—a physical beating by the gang for a certain amount of time (keep in mind that this is not always the case).

Over the years, law enforcement have used stop-and-frisk strategies that consist of gathering data from adolescents and recording it on a Field Identification (FI) card. The procedure used by law enforcement usually consists of random stop and frisk encounters with youth on the streets, followed by a series of questions. If law enforcement feels a youth is affiliated with a gang based on specific tattoos, who he associates with, or nicknames they feel identify the youth with a gang, they will then determine the youth to be gang involved or affiliated (About the YJC, n.d.). Youth who go through this type of process with law enforcement, such as M. J., often report nothing ever happening to them other than being asked a series of questions and immediately being released after this barrage of questioning. Further exploration indicates that this data makes its way to the Cal-Gang database, which is a statewide database that allows police to track and share information about alleged gang members (Muniz, 2012). This creates several concerns due to the fact that this type of procedure relies heavily upon biased opinions determining whether or not a juvenile is a gang member or associates with a gang. Anecdotal field data indicates youth reporting to court for a first-time offense are often surprised to learn that there is documentation that profiles them to be gang involved, such as in M. J.'s case.

Being a youth identified as a gang member has several repercussions. In many cases, gang enhancements provide youth with additional penalties since the state of California has a zero tolerance toward gang membership, so what may be a first-time offense of shoplifting is now seen as a gang crime, with higher penalties than a civilian crime. This dichotomy is due, in large part, to the Street Terrorism Enforcement and Prevention Act of 1988, also known as the S.T.E.P. Act, which enhances a defendant's charges if he is associated with an "urban terrorist group" (California Penal Code §186.32). In M. J.'s case, his first stint in juvenile hall's holding tank for shoplifting created an atmosphere of hardened survival to identify himself with a gang based on where he resides. The question "Where you from?" by other juveniles while in detainment in and of itself placed M. J. as being a part of a gang, forcing M. J. to claim the neighborhood gang where he lives. Once identified as being gang involved, M. J. will now be associated with a particular gang in the community by other youth who were in detainment with M. J. Studies indicate that youth alliance with a gang actually strengthens by 88% once entering detention (National Gang Intelligence Center, 2011). It is these types of nuances and challenges that stigmatize youth coming from underserved urban communities. A better understanding of this dynamic will allow the social worker to better serve this population, which society has come to label as "gang members." There is a clear distinction to keep in mind: A youth who has formally been initiated into a gang and is "putting in work" for the gang is considered to be *gang involved*, whereas a youth who is *gang affiliated* hangs out with possible members of a gang, but he is not officially in the gang or "putting in work" for the gang.

It is important for the social worker to have a sound knowledge of some of the root causes of gang formation. This will allow the social worker to see beyond the imagery found in media—which tends to influence society as to how to deal with gangs, resulting in suppressive types of strategies and approaches—and to use more wellness and healing types of interventions. Research shows that of the identified gang population within the United States, only 3%–4% are violent members; the rest are not. Nonviolent members are largely engaged in drug use/abuse and other forms of juvenile delinquency, such as truancy and vandalism (National Gang Center, 2012). It is important for the social worker to learn about the youth's culture and how that plays out within his or her social structure (e.g., dress, music, art, peer association, values, rituals, customs, etc.). Gang researchers commonly assess gangs through five traditional gang domains: individual, family, peer, school, and community/neighborhood. However, the lens applied through these five gang domains is from a criminal perspective, understood to be criminogenic risk factors (Aarons, Smith, & Wagner, 2009). This type of approach excludes the person-in-the-environment concept, which is a foundation of the social worker ideology and method of operation. This calls for the social worker to apply a holistic ecological framework to delve deeper than the symptom of gang involvement or association. A full scale biopsychosocial assessment must be administered by the social worker to identify areas impacting and influencing the youth who has been identified to be a gang member.

Meeker (2003) has found that often it is society who labels a youth as a gang member. Considerations to ponder as a social worker are how often perceptions of individuals and attire, coupled with specific ethnic background or even where they live conjures up so many false beliefs and pretenses that can have detrimental effects when servicing this vulnerable population. By these assumptions, a youth's identity becomes distorted, neglecting any unique challenges hindering the psychosocial level of functioning of the youth.

Understanding the culture of the community will provide better insight into the socialization experience for youth living in a gang-saturated community. Assessing certain trends in attire, music, slang, and peer association will lessen the assumptions that is typically made that a youth is a gang member based on his look and how he carries himself. In working with youth considered to be gang involved, it is important to allow them to tell their story. Providing a safe, nonjudgmental space for youth to freely talk of their experiences encourages a forum predicated upon respect. Anecdotal field data of personal testimony of active and former gang-involved youth show a constant theme of fighting due to feeling "disrespected." There tends to be a common theme among gang-involved youth, best summarized as the strong desire to feel respected through intimidation, if needed.

For several underserved communities and their families, specifically those who have a history of migration to this country, the fabric of an oppressed group may include the culture of gangs. For several immigrant communities and groups, migration to the United States, especially out west, was met by severe racism and discrimination (Diego Vigil & Yun, 2002). The ability to acculturate to the dominant culture came with severe criticism and opposition by the larger communities, where attacks historically were made on certain ethnic groups in the form of psychological and physical abuse (violence, rape, and murder). This resulted in a subversive reaction to the dominant culture, resulting in a push back. This type of culture clash spawned what renowned gang researcher James Diego Vigil (1983) calls "multiple marginality." Current literature that draws upon the work of Diego Vigil discusses the concept of multiple marginality as it relates to street socialized youth and the development of "gangs." Looking at micro-historical and macro-structural frameworks, Diego Vigil found that three agents of social control (family, school, law enforcement) directly influence the degree of gang formation for street-socializing youth. Any distortion/breakdown within these agents of social control, coupled with financial stressors, segregation, language barriers, immigration, and other ecological factors such as trauma, are what makes peers and street models more attractive to youth (Diego Vigil & Yun, 2002).

An ecological risk factor that is a pivotal barrier for this population is violence-related trauma. Violence-related trauma is defined as any relationship, process, or condition by which an individual or a group violates the physical, social, and/or psychological integrity of another person or group.

From this perspective, violence inhibits human growth, negates inherent potential, limits productive living, and ultimately causes death. Studies conducted nationwide show a 22% increase in trauma exposure for youth living in underserved communities (Basheer & Hoag, 2014). Studies indicate 30% of urban youth develop Posttraumatic Stress Disorder (Saigh, 1991). Work from Diego Vigil (1983) indicates the prevalence of psychological barriers for youth and families from underserved communities where current studies indicate a positive association with community violence–related trauma (Foy & Goguen, 1998).

It is this process that prompts groups living within these communities to adapt to certain living conditions. The added strain on these community systems presents traumatic experiences for youth navigating these systems, as alluded to previously by Diego Vigil and Yun (2002) in the form of psychological barriers. At the same time, underground economic systems start to develop as a means of survival (Huff, 2002), with the uptake of violence as a means of power and influence to survive within these neglected communities. Every youth has basic needs for feelings of self-worth, identity, acceptance, recognition, companionship, belonging, purpose, and security. When families, schools, churches, and communities do not meet these needs, gangs may. Gangs can often supply what traditional systems have failed to provide, like love, affirmation, encouragement, hope, and a chance. Gangs then act as surrogate families (Communities in Schools, 2006).

In a broad sense, systems have failed to assist troubled youth in need of guidance to develop a positive self-identity. Some have found what psychologist Erik Erikson describes to be a greater sense of identity through being alienated or in severe delinquency that is found in gangs (Diego Vigil, 1983). Further research indicates that ego development begins in early childhood. Family and environmental factors for children contribute to the formation of their meaning of self. It is assumed that presenting problems within this stage of development will affect later stages of development (Erikson, 1956). Gang members' early ego formation creates difficulty in achieving a healthy sense of identity and self-identification, especially if exterior factors such as poverty, drugs, family dysfunction, and other institutions such as schools and law enforcement and community have negatively affected their lives, making for a problematic "psychosocial moratorium." The psychosocial moratorium is a time of free experimentation when, psychologist and psychoanalyst Erik Erikson (1956) believes, one goes through a period of trying multiple identities. It is during the moratorium that peers and street models become more important to gang members (Diego Vigil, 1983).

Gangs commonly consist of the most marginalized and troubled youth who exhibit features of conduct disorder that is closely affiliated with antisocial behaviors and oppositional defiance. These youth commonly experience issues with depression, revealed as acting out behavior, attention deficit hyperactivity disorder, anxiety, mood disorders, and signs of PTSD (Krans, 2013). They tend to exhibit poor coping skills, low self-esteem and self-worth, and experience issues of loneliness, isolation, and low frustration tolerance (Krans, 2013).

Society as a whole, along with law enforcement, may place assumptions on an adolescent's ethnic identity. Often there are misperceptions of youth to be gang involved and violent based on their families' or friends' affiliation with a gang (Zastrow & Kirst-Ashman, 2012). This is the most harmful approach a social worker can take when working with vulnerable youth populations such as gang-involved youth. It is prejudgments that can revictimize the youth's experience when working with systems that have already negatively influenced their self-concept.

All individuals form impressions of who they think they are. This personal impression of one's unique attributes and traits, both positive and negative, is known as *self-concept* (Zastrow & Kirst-Ashman, 2012). One must feel good about oneself to be confident, productive, and enjoy life experiences. This concept is also often associated with self-esteem. For several gang-involved youth, the process to building a positive self-identity has been stunted due to a number of reasons. Several of the youth have been under strain and duress while attempting to navigate systems that have directly influenced their experiences. Studies indicate alarming rates of trauma exposure for several of the minority youth groups coming from these underserved communities, which impacts the development of their self-concept. It is crucial for social workers to assess for strengths currently being exhibited by the gang-involved youth, to increase internal and external capacity for the youth and family members. For years the response to treating gang members in the U.S. has been facilitated in large part by law enforcement suppression-oriented practices (Klein, 1995). This has brought about a rise in gang membership and prevalence of gang crime, violence, prisons, and prisoners (Klein, 1995). These short-term suppression-oriented practices and approaches are often ineffectual and lead to high rates of recidivism (Klein, 1995).

In order to effect long-term transformational change, it is important that youth treatment programs address the impacts of trauma on healthy youth development, with a focus on increasing positive self-concept. Keep in mind that self-concept refers to a person's judgment of his or her own value. Gang members suffer from issues of low self-esteem and low self-worth. Improving an individual's self-concept is often a therapeutic goal as a means of empowerment, especially for this population. This in itself can have huge implications as it relates to the decrease in violence.

MICRO PERSPECTIVE

Assessment

When working with adolescents of color, society's labels need to be examined. Often African Americans and Latinos are perceived as defiant when exhibiting acting-out behaviors, as in the case of M. J. In this instance, it is noted that three months ago, M. J. endured the loss of his grandmother and his aunt within a few weeks of each other. His behavior could be seen as PTSD or Acute Stress Disorder rather than defiance. The practitioner may want to further examine and assess M. J.'s diagnosis of Conduct Disorder and Substance Use Disorder, ruling out Cannabis Abuse and Alcohol Abuse. The practitioner can also rule out PTSD, Acute Stress Disorder, Mood Disorder, and Anxiety Disorder. It is important to identify if the substance use by M. J. increased after the death of his grandmother and aunt. Further examination of the impact of grief and loss on M. J. and his family is necessary to gain better insight into the family dynamics.

For several youth coming from high rates of trauma-exposed communities, the social worker must be mindful when assessing the youth, taking into account the environmental strain which may be creating psychological and emotional barriers to the youth due to systemic breakdown. Diego Vigil (1983) indicates that adolescence is a period of life when a person's identity goes through marked changes, physically and mentally, and there are also greater societal expectations. Early life experiences; social, cultural, and environmental conditions; and agents of socialization must be accounted for when assessing this process (Diego Vigil, 1983).

As in the case of M. J., the ecosystems perspective assumes that human needs and problems are generated by the transactions between people and their environments (Robbins, Chatterjee, & Canda, 2012). M. J.'s lack of attachment to his biological parents presents an insecure setting. To understand an individual's problems, the social worker must understand her client's environmental context and how it impacts the actions, beliefs, and choices of the individual. The fact that M. J. was raised by his grandparents, his father has been in prison since he was a toddler, and his mother struggled with substance abuse during his formative years can present issues of "grief and loss" for M. J. The messages received by his environment can impact this grieving process, resulting in issues of disenfranchised loss and traumatic separation. Research indicates when a family member is not permitted to grieve due to public shaming (disenfranchised loss), it positions them to mourn in isolation without family support (Werner-Lin & Moro, 2004). For children, the inability to grieve becomes more apparent, making the child invisible (Werner-Lin & Moro, 2004), which in M. J.'s case may be impacting his overall healthy sense of self. The fact that the family does not talk of M. J.'s father's incarceration emphasizes this point even more. Additional literature by Pynoos (1993) highlights the linkage between childhood trauma and the parent's incarceration and its relationship to later life pathologies.

Diversity Considerations

Diversity issues like language, culture, racial differences, and residential settings are concerns that need to be addressed when implementing treatment interventions, program designs, as well as policy making. Cultural competency for social workers is critical. With this in mind, literature points to the importance of having appropriate facilitators or mediators to help all systems work together (Meeker, 2003). It is recommended that gang members be included in the treatment planning process with the youth and family, to lessen the social and cultural distance (Meeker, 2003). It is also recommended that collaboration take place between the systems impacting the youth and families. This can include law enforcement and other ethnic groups, to rid the process of the "us and them" stigma that exists for these communities. These steps can facilitate empowerment for vulnerable groups to work through their healing process. It can also bring about a culture where youth are no longer viewed as gangsters but as strong individuals who are vested in their communities (Elizalde & Ramirez, 2006).

In the case of M. J., practitioners of the same ethnic background and gender could be utilized to work and engage with M. J. and his family. Part of the treatment planning may also include former gang members who are employed by the agency working with M. J. and are violence intervention specialists, which we will explore in further detail later in this chapter. This strategy can create stronger and faster rapport building with M. J. and the family. Incorporating this type of approach is mindful of the culture and subcultures he and his family may be navigating. The hope is to build M. J.'s and the family's social capital to continue to promote resiliency for M. J. and his family, all the while seeking opportunities for empowerment.

Interventions

A multisystemic approach to addressing street violence and the reduction of gang activity is highly recommended when working with conduct-related disorders that are most commonly found in gang members (Henggeler et al., 1998). This treatment model assists to strengthen families, promote resiliency, encourage youth away from antisocial peer groups, work to increase school performance, and incorporate the practices and traditions of their indigenous social support system found in the community (Henggeler et al, 1998).

The inclusion of the evidence-based practice intervention Multi-Systemic Therapy (MST) would involve a systems and socioecological approach. Assessments would be conducted within each adolescent's home, school, and community. Information would come from a wide array of resources, such as parents, siblings, teachers, probation officers, case workers, and others in the community who interact with the adolescent who is receiving services. This is to ensure ecological validity. The family and the adolescent would agree upon the treatment goals that fit the identified problem. The implementation of the goals would be provided by a designated person within each system: the home, school, and community. Because this approach is multidimensional, other therapies may be needed. Behavioral, cognitive, and various other therapies and interventions could be used with adolescent receiving MST as identified needs arise while exploring each system (Henggeler et al., 1998).

MST uses a home-based model of service delivery approach facilitated by the agency social worker (Fain, Greathouse, Turner, & Weinberg, 2014). The identified MST social worker working the case would use the youth's family, peers, school, neighborhood, and any additional identified social support networks to work through the stages of positive change with the youth. The goal in MST is to improve client functioning in multiple systems by preventing gang activity, arrest, incarceration, and/or out-of-home placement. MST also seeks to provide parents and caregivers with the tools needed to work through their youth's challenges while empowering the youth to cope with various environmental stressors such as family, peer, school, and community hardships (Fain et al., 2014). Once referred, clients and their families undergo an intensive home-based treatment practice ranging from 4 months to a year of service. Therapy sessions are usually conducted weekly for about 75 minutes, in the home. In addition, the practitioner must be on call when not interfacing with the family to conduct crisis intervention (e.g., in the school or community setting). During treatment, the client and his or her family seek to gain the skills and resources needed to become empowered. It is important for the social worker to join with the family while reviewing problem-solving strategies to acquire the skill sets to deal with day-to-day conflicts. Effective communication skills need to be covered and examined with the family. This process encourages communication between parent(s) and youth. Community resources and their utilization also need to be covered. This increases the client's and family's ability to overcome barriers of accessibility. Various positive socialization skills should be addressed, depending on the need to assist the youth in daily interactions with school, peers, and the community (Schaeffer & Borduin, 2005).

Evidence-based practices such as psychoeducation need to be incorporated into the family sessions and individual sessions with the youth, ranging from substance use/abuse, addiction, education, to mental health issues. As part of the treatment, it is important that flexibility on the part of the social worker is maintained. They can follow up with a youth who may be incarcerated or placed out of the home during time of treatment in order to maintain the therapeutic relationship. By focusing on the relationship of interactions that take place between multiple systems and the individual,

changes in behavior can directly alter the environment and individual's responsiveness to those changes. The primary goal would be to empower the youth and family by providing the skills and resources needed to overcome barriers that prevent effective system functioning. This approach is also community based, which promotes positive change by working with the strengths of each system (Schoenwald, Borduin, & Henggeler, 1998). When practitioners focus on the combination of complex multiple systems impacting the youth (e.g., family, peer, school, community) and try to change the negative factors that impede development, the behavior and functioning of the youth may produce positive changes. It has been identified that MST has been an effective treatment modality for several adolescents and families from various culture and socioeconomic backgrounds who need the skills and resources to be resilient. For full empowerment of MST to take place, literature indicates that MST also addresses barriers to effective parenting, such as parental drug use and parental mental health issues (Boxer, 2011). Antisocial youth, juvenile offenders, and gang-affiliated youth are populations who have benefited most. For juvenile offenders, it has been "one of the best available treatment approaches for youth who have mental health treatment needs and are involved in the juvenile justice system" (National Mental Health Association, 2004, p. 5). Evaluations conducted by the National Mental Health Association have shown that MST reduces long-term rates of rearrests by 70% and out-of-home placements by 64% (National Mental Health Association, 2004). In addition, it has been shown to decrease mental health problems for serious juvenile offenders (National Mental Health Association, 2004).

Within the last decade, what has become an informed evidence practice as a supplement to MST is the use of gang interventionists under the Community-Based Gang Intervention Model.

The Community-Based Gang Intervention Model is a two-pronged approach that increases the safety of the overall community by addressing the violence in a comprehensive and cost-effective manner: It directly reduces gang violence and provides holistic, integrated human services. The Community-Based Gang Intervention Model is an integrated approach of service delivery that addresses the various systemic and institutional barriers that gang-involved youth and their families encounter in their daily lives. Community-based gang intervention consists of a variety of activities that focus on and engage active and former gang members, their close associates, and gang members in and returning from confinement. This specific approach is conscientious of the fact that gang-involved youth and their families require specialized intensive and comprehensive services that address the unique issues encountered by youth when they become involved with gangs. Service providers should have a history, experience, or specific training in effectively working with gang-involved youth and their families. This work must be specifically tailored to these communities where the service providers work collaboratively and directly with youth and their families under the premise of a strengths-based approach.

This type of treatment modality is culturally competent and would fit well with youth and families who associate with gangs. The use of a gang intervention specialist (GIS) would allow the practitioner working with M. J. to assess M. J.'s level of involvement with the local gang. Understanding M. J.'s *embeddedness*, a term used by some researchers to describe ones' level of gang involvement, can allow the practitioner to better determine what types of treatment modalities to implement, such as psychoeducational skill-building efforts to increase M. J.'s resiliency to stand independent of gang activity. Also having a good understanding of the gang dynamic would increase the type of safety measures to operate from and how to best use the gang intervention specialist. More than often the GIS has a "trusting" relationship with the local neighborhood gangs as part of his or her community peace building efforts. This is what makes the use of GIS workers so powerful: the credibility they carry from the streets, also known as the "License to Operate."

The uniqueness of this approach, based on practiced informed evidence, is that GIS bring their own gang experiences and knowledge to the heart of the intervention with the gang-involved youth (Huff, 1993). Almost all of the GIS are former gang members. They are a group of individuals who have transformed their lives and have dedicated themselves to helping the community reduce gang violence. The experience from the street has made rapport building and engagement a significant component in servicing this population identified as gang-involved youth. This component has been a barrier for several professional practitioners; for example, law enforcement has relied on the collaboration with GIS to prevent gang retaliations. The ability to build client rapport is the primary practice skill that makes this approach unique. This skill has enabled outreach to become an exclusive intervention for building bridges in the community to curtail gang violence (Huff, 1993).

GIS are not new to this country. In Los Angeles and elsewhere, they were a key element in social agency and community development work in the 1960s and 1970s (Huff, 1993). What is relatively new is how the Community-Based Gang Intervention Two-Pronged Approach operates. It was implemented as the Community-Based Gang Intervention Model for the City of Los Angeles in February 2008, and it takes a comprehensive intergrative service delivery approach. This policy not only defines what gang intervention is, but actually acts as a guide on how services need to be rendered to produce postive results when servicing gang-involved youth and their families. The Model provides hardcore, specialized, street-based mediation and mitigation to stop or prevent violence between gangs and the concurrent redirection of individual gang members and their families in ways that bring progress to themselves and their communities in a holistic manner (Cárdenas, 2009). Prong I is the immediate cease fire and stoppage of community violence. Prong II consist of access to a wide array of supportive services for youth and their families involved in gangs (see Figure 20.1).

Rapport building is strongly emphasized and the point of focus throughout this approach. Building trust and alliance with the client and family can help the progression of treatment. Engaging

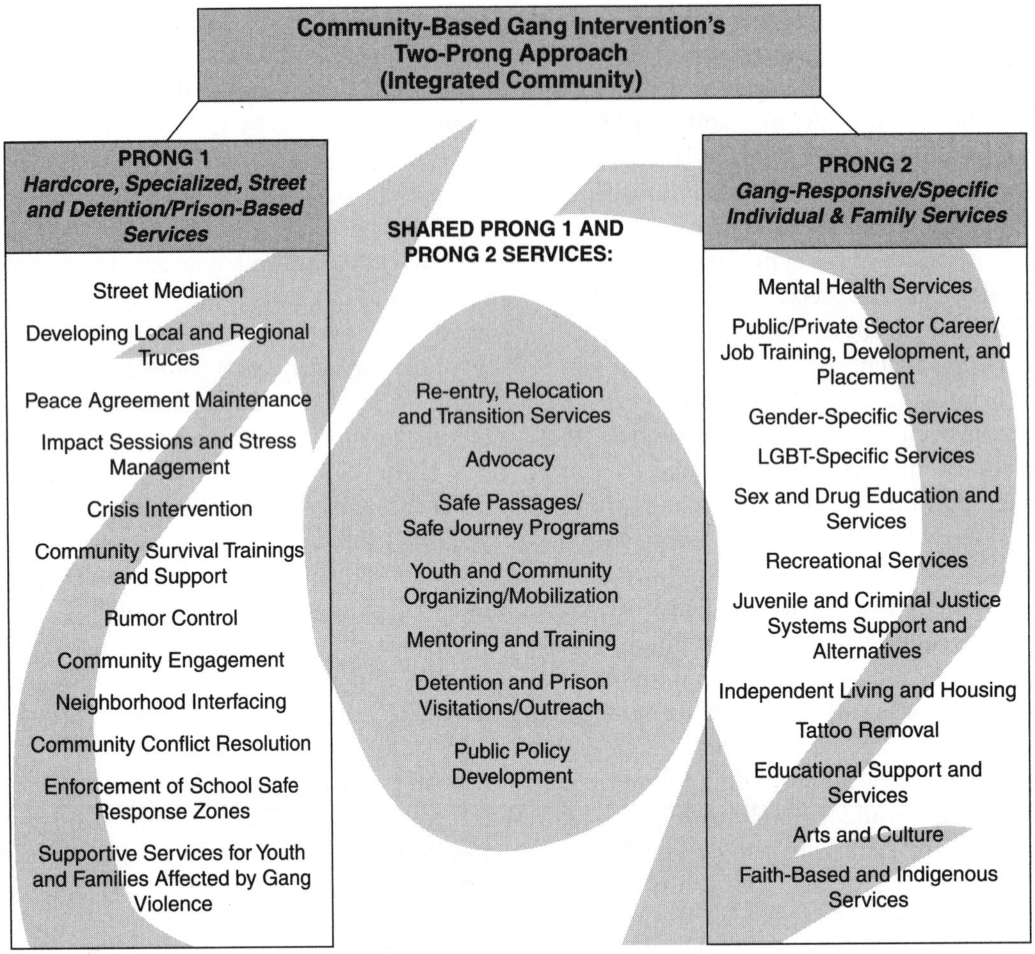

Figure 20.1. Community-Based Gang Intervention Model

SOURCE: Community Based Gang Intervention Act, H.R. 2669, 113th Cong. (2013).

the client to accept mental health services or services known to heal individuals from high rates of trauma exposure is crucial and needs to be a key focus during treatment. Building trusting relationships with clients is strongly encouraged which should be facilitated by a GIS practitioner. Clients will be in direct contact with a social worker or therapist upon referral along with a GIS practitioner. A GIS practitioner plays a significant role as a liaison in the beginning stages of the therapist and client interface. A GIS utilizes a nontraditional clinical approach when working with this population due to the sensitivity of rapport building

(see Figure 20.2). Issues of safety are usually a concern with social workers. This is why it is vital to have a GIS assist the social worker when interfacing with the gang-involved youth and family until treatment is securely in place and committed to by the youth and family.

The implementation of the Community-Based Gang Intervention Two-Pronged Approach takes a multisystems approach, operating on an interactional framework that incorporates prevention, early intervention, intervention, and re-entry. One of the primary goals would be to empower the youth and family by providing the

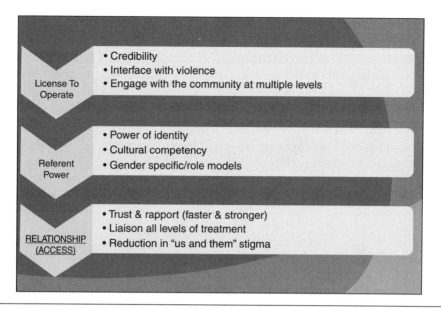

Figure 20.2. Gang Intervention Specialist Level of Engagement

SOURCE: Estrada and Hernandez (2011).

skills and resources needed to overcome barriers that prevent effective system functioning that is found on Prong II.

In working with M. J., the fluidness of the therapeutic relationship held by a social worker allowed for the creativeness of using boxing as part of the therapeutic process. Understanding the idea of promoting violence is a concern raised by other professionals; nevertheless, boxing showed effectiveness to build on an area of interest expressed by M. J. and allowed the strengthening of a therapeutic process to ensue. Twice a week work outs at a local gym consisted of hitting the punching bag while M. J. unknowingly was processing his frustrations with his family, specifically his mother as he punched the bags harder. This led to a half a year processing at the boxing gym to later in the year processing the day-to-day challenges with his family on M. J.'s front porch. The gym was still used once a week as a sheer motivator to keep physically fit. Much of the processing now occurs in more formal areas, such as his house and school. Incorporating MST, if available within the agency, would be an effective modality that would enhance the treatment

modality by creating stronger relationships in M. J.'s ecosystem and increasing the resource capacity of M. J. and his family. This would prime M. J. and his family for long-standing change.

Transference and Countertransference Issues

When working with this population, the issue of safety becomes a real concern for social workers because community gang violence is a reality. The influence of the media portraying these youth as violent does not help with this issue and often can impede the therapeutic process, especially if the social worker has limited knowledge working with this population and their communities. However, the double-edged sword here is if one is familiar with these communities and population and comes from the same ethnic makeup, the tendency can be to over-identify with the youth and struggle with clear boundaries. The youth may also experience issues of transference, closely identifying with the therapist, especially if they are the same ethnic make-up and sex. It is important for the social worker to have clear boundaries and role identification as it relates to the validity of the treatment. The social worker is modeling appropriate actions, behaviors, and responses to the youth and his family in all the settings the youth is navigating to influence positive change. How the social worker interacts with the youth is key, learning body language and positioning; understanding the culture and traditions as well as the subculture of youth gangs is imperative to lessen the fear factor.

A place of vulnerability can be an engaging factor. Often the youth's appearance, which may include tattoos, can be intimidating. When servicing M. J., the noticeable tattoos on his hands and arms could cause him to be perceived as a full-pledge gang member; however, with further assessment by the GIS worker, it was determined that none of M. J.'s tattoos were gang related. Not having gang-related tattoos can strengthen the ability to better service M. J. as he navigates his conditions of probation and the legal system. As the social worker continues to build trust and rapport with this population, it is important to increase the external resource capacity for the youth. Since mistrust of others is a key challenge for this population, once trust is established there becomes a tendency for this population to feel dependent upon their social worker, making loyalty strong, which can present a problem when terminating the case. As in the case of M. J., it would be important to identify external formal and informal resources where he can establish trusting healthy relationships and bonds moving forward. This would lessen the feeling of loyalty to one person, which can create unhealthy dependency. The overall goal is to achieve empowerment.

MEZZO PERSPECTIVE: COMMUNITIES IN SCHOOLS

It must be emphasized that rapport building is the most difficult area to achieve when working with gang-involved or street-socializing youth. The idea of working alongside a gang intervention specialist is one that fuses nontraditional practices with traditional practices and is one of the promising approaches. This strategy incorporates the services of gang intervention specialist to effectively administer services to gang involved youth to increase public safety. An example of this approach has been implemented in one of the country's premier gang intervention agencies, Communities in Schools (CIS). CIS is a nonprofit social service agency located in North Hills in the San Fernando Valley. CIS is an organization committed to combating gang and youth violence in the community by offering prevention, early intervention, intervention, and reentry services to youth 10–25 years of age and their families. CIS offers a wide range of social services to youth, such as tattoo removal, educational development, after school activities, job development, mentoring/tutoring, case management, a series of sporting events, programming in detention facilities, and yellow tape protocol, which consist of a GIS being first on the crime scene at a gang homicide and conducting rumor control to stem the violence and provide responsive services to the victim's family, gender-specific services, individual and family counseling, peace mediation efforts, and a host of other services including yearly peace marches throughout the city in neighborhoods that are saturated with gang violence. It is this type of comprehensive integrative service delivery model that allows access to treatment for a neglected population.

MACRO PERSPECTIVE: POLICY IMPLICATIONS

Youth gangs have existed in the United States as far back as the 1800s, primarily consisting of immigrant Irish, Jewish, Italian, German, and Polish populations. For the 21st century, according to the Office of the National Gang Center (NGC, 2011) the ethnicity of youth in gangs is African American, (35.3%); Hispanic,(46.2%); Caucasian, (11.5%); and (7%) Other.

There is an estimated 1,076 active gangs in the City of Los Angeles, with more than

80,000 identified individuals considered to be gang involved. Gang violence in the past five years has resulted in thousands of violent crimes, including homicides, felony assaults, rape, and robberies. For example, over the last 10 years, there has been more than 5,752 gang-related homicides. During the last five years, there was an increase in the number of youth gangs in Los Angeles, which led to the spending of millions of taxpayer's' dollars on increased law enforcement, juvenile justice systems, and other related costs such as hospitalizations (Cárdenas, 2009).

The growing gang population is an issue that affects not only those living in urban communities, but the larger facets of our society. With the recent statistics of California being ranked as 49th in the nation for education spending while at the same time being number one in prison spending is having a direct impact on our nation's youth and overall prosperity of our country. Current cost to incarcerate just one youth per year is estimated to be anywhere from $95,000 to $250,000 per year (California Department of Finance, 2015). At the same time studies show evidence of effective interventions that directly reduce recidivism rates by 77%, at a lower cost of $7,000 to $ 12,000 a year per youth, which results in an estimated savings of up to $238,000 per youth a year (National Mental Health Association, 2004). Incarceration rates continue to quadruple which has been documented since the 1960's (Alexander, 2012). In California alone 21 prisons were built between 1982 and 2001 but only three universities were built during that same time (About the YJC, n.d.). Using ecological theory to illuminate the effects on youth today and the exploration of how to better serve this population is crucial for the success of vulnerable youth.

Over the past decade continuous efforts have been made by cities such as Los Angeles to reduce community gang violence. The Los Angeles City Council has undergone evolutionary approaches that have attempted to curtail gang violence. Nevertheless, there has been a moderate drop in gang violence and gang crime; however, we have seen an increase in the number of gangs and gang membership in the City of Los Angeles and County of Los Angeles (National Gang Intelligence Center, 2011). Suppression efforts have been seen as an adverse reaction to this strategy by only spreading the problem (i.e., the implementation of gang injunctions). Reports have shown that these efforts have not remedied the problem but rather left the city to address and evaluate current gang reduction strategies in Los Angeles. Los Angeles has made huge strides within the last few years by coordinating its efforts in addressing the issue of gang violence by stopping the duplication of services and requiring accountability for funding of programs addressing gang violence.

At the core of this restructuring is a historical statute authored by more than 20 organizations and individuals labeled as the "Best of the Best" in regard to working with the issue of community gang violence for the City of Los Angeles. Spearheaded by then–Council member Cárdenas of District 6, the adoption of the Community-Based Gang Intervention Two-Pronged Approach was voted into policy by City Council unanimously in February 2008 as the Gang Intervention Model for the City of Los Angeles. A few months later the Office of Gang Reduction Youth Development (GRYD) was established by the Mayor's office that incorporated the model into its strategy.

The Community-Based Gang Intervention Two-Pronged Approach shows a high degree of cultural competency as it relates to the youth and individuals being identified as gang involved by society and keeps the community's issue of being labeled as violent into consideration when intervening in a community. In July 2013, Congress member Cárdenas presented juvenile crime prevention legislation to Congress and to the House of Representatives, which highlights the Community-Based Gang Intervention Two-Pronged Approach, under the Community-Based Gang Intervention Act (H.R. 2669). On September 13, 2013, the bill was referred to the House of Education and the Workforce Subcommittee on Early Childhood, Elementary, and Secondary Education where it lies dormant. Legislation such as this is a proactive approach that will aid youth such as M. J. by providing access to care. The effectiveness of this legislation is that it was created by those most impacted by the social issues of gangs. It's relevancy rings true for youth such as M. J. who can relate to this practice-driven approach. It takes into consideration the environmental factors faced by M. J. and his family. It is also mindful of M. J.'s experience as a youth attempting to develop in a gang-impacted area of the city where youth have limited options within their control. The legislation provides hope to reach those deemed unreachable. It can also be seen as an investment, saving this country extraordinary amounts of taxpayers' money with a return of prosperity.

CONCLUSION

It is within the social workers oath to pursue social change, particularly with and on behalf of vulnerable, oppressed individuals and groups of people. These efforts of social change by social workers consist of, but are not limited to issues of poverty, unemployment, discrimination, violence, and other forms of social injustices (National Association of Social Workers, 2014). Furthermore, social workers have the capacity to influence policy and research through a practice-driven approach by identifying the root causes of social issues such as gangs. In addition, social workers should use successful program outcomes to seek policy changes and lobby for increased funding that can be directed to supporting gang interventions such as the Community-Based Gang Intervention Two-Pronged Approach. Once data collection and analysis has been completed, results of these evaluations can be applicable to the social work practice because it will provide the framework for future program-driven evidence-based models when working with gang-involved youth among other marginalized populations.

INTERNET RESOURCES

- Office of Juvenile Justice and Delinquency Prevention: Model Programs Guide: http://www.ojjdp.gov/mpg/

- U.S. Department of Justice Office of Justice Programs: http://www.iir.com/nygc/publications/gang-problems.pdf
- National Gang Center: http://www.national-gangcenter.gov/
- OJJDP Comprehensive Gang Model: http://www.nationalgangcenter.gov/
- A Guide for Understanding Effective Community Based Gang Intervention: http://www.atty.lacity.org/stellent/groups/electedofficials/@atty_contributor/documents/contributor_web_content/lacityp_006140.pdf
- Street Gangs Media: http://www.streetgangs.com
- National Gang Crime Research Center: http://www.ngcrc.com/

DISCUSSION QUESTIONS

1. What are the effects of mass incarceration rates on communities of color?

2. Discuss the socialization process for gang members.

3. Do you feel culture plays a role in gang membership?

4. Please highlight any risk factors you feel contribute to youth joining gangs.

5. How can policy create joint actions, or inactions, that exacerbate the gang problem?

REFERENCES

Aarons, J., Smith, L., & Wagner, L. (2009). Dispatches from Juvenile Hall: Fixing a Failing System. New York, NY: Penguin Books.

About the YJC—Mission and history. (n.d.). *Youth Justice Coalition*. Retrieved from http://www.youth4justice.org/about-the-yjc/history

Alexander, M. (2012). *The new Jim Crow: Mass incarceration in the age of colorblindness.* New York: The New Press.

Basheer, A., & Hoag, C. (2014). *Peace in the hood: Working with gang members to end the violence.* Nashville, TN: Turner.

Boxer, P. (2011). Negative peer involvement in multisystemic therapy for the treatment of youth problem behavior: Exploring outcome and process variables in "real-world" practice. *Journal of Clinical Child & Adolescent Psychology, 40,* 848–854.

California Department of Finance. (2015). *Budget.* Retrieved from http://www.ebudget.ca.gov

Cárdenas, T. (2009). *A guide for understanding effective community-based gang intervention, Vol. II.* Los Angeles: City of Los Angeles.

Communities in Schools. (2006). *Handbook.* Los Angeles, CA: Author.

Community Based Gang Intervention Act, H.R. 2669, 113th Cong. (2013).

Diego Vigil, J. (1983). Chicano gangs: One response to Mexican urban adaptation in the Los Angeles area. *Urban Anthropology, 12*(1), 45–75.

Diego Vigil, J., & Yun, S. C. (2002). A cross-cultural framework to understand gangs: Multiple marginality and Los Angeles. In C. R. Huff (Ed.), *Gangs in America* (3rd ed., pp. 161–174). Thousand Oaks, CA: Sage.

Elizalde, T. M., & Ramirez, G. A. (2006). Effective intervention with gangs and gang members. *The School Services Sourcebook, 50,* 529–546.

Erikson, E. H. (1956). Ego identity and the psychosocial moratorium. *New Perspectives For Juvenile Delinquency, 356,* 1–23.

Estrada, J. N., & Hernandez, R. A. (2011, February). *Understanding the historical context of gang culture: A socio-economic approach challenging current gang theory and intervention practices.* Lecture conducted from Kaiser Permanente, Baldwin Park, CA.

Fain, T., Greathouse, S. M., Turner, S., & Weinberg, H. D. (2014). *Is multisystemic therapy (MST) effective for Hispanic youth? An evaluation of outcomes for juvenile offenders in Los Angeles County.* Santa Monica, CA: RAND Corporation. Retrieved from:= http://www.rand.org/pubs/research_briefs/RB9791

Foy, D. W., & Goguen, C. W. (1998). Community violence-related PTSD in children and adolescents. *The National Center for Post-Traumatic Stress Disorder PTSD Research Quarterly, 9*(4), 1–5.

Henggeler, S. W., & Schoenwald, S. K. et al. (1998). *Multisystemic treatment of antisocial behavior in children and adolescents.* New York, NY: Guilford Press.

Huff, C. R. (1993). *Gangs in the United States: The gang intervention handbook.* Champaign, IL: Research Press.

Huff, C. R. (Ed.). (2002). *Gangs in America* (3rd ed.). Thousand Oaks, CA: Sage.

Klein, M. W. (1995). *The American street gang.* New York, NY: Oxford University Press.

Krans, B. (2013). *Gang members hit high levels of mental illness.* Retrieved from http://www.healthline.com/health-news/mental-gang-members-suffer-from-high-rates-of-mental-illness-071213

Meeker, J. W. (2003). Fear of gang crime: A look at three theoretical models. *Law & Society Review, 37*(2), 425–456.

Muniz, A. (2012). *Tracked and trapped: What's wrong with California's gang databases and gang injunctions?* Retrieved from http://www.youth4justice.org/wp-content/uploads/2012/12/TrackedandTrapped.pdf

National Association of Social Workers. (2014). *Social workers' ethical responsibilities to the broader society.* Retrieved from http://www.socialworkers.org/.

National Gang Center. (2011). *2011 national youth gang survey analysis.* Retrieved from http://www.nationalgangcenter.gov/survey-analysis/demographics

National Gang Center. (2012). *2012 National Youth Gang Survey analysis.* Retrieved from http://www.nationalgangcenter.gov/Survey-Analysis/Prevalence-of-Gang-Problems

National Gang Intelligence Center. (2011). *2011 national gang threat assessment: Emerging trends.* Retrieved from http://www.fbi.gov/stats-services/publications/2011-national-gang-threat-assessment

National Institute of Justice. (2011). *What is a gang? Definitions.* Retrieved from http://www.nij.gov/topics/crime/gangs/Pages/definitions.aspx

National Mental Health Association. (2004). *Mental health treatment for youth in the juvenile justice system: A compendium of promising practices.* Bethesda, MD: Author. Retrieved from https://www.nttac.org/views/docs/jabg/mhcurriculum/mh_mht.pdf

Pynoons, R. S. (1993). Traumatic stress and developmental psychopathology in children and adolescents. In J. A. Arditti (Ed.), *Parental incarceration and the family: Psychological and social effects of imprisonment on children, parents, and caregivers.* New York, NY: New York University Press.

Robbins, S. P., Chatterjee, P., & Canda, E. R. (2012). *Contemporary human behavior theory* (3rd ed.). New Jersey, NJ: Allyn & Bacon.

Saigh, P. A. (1991). The development of posttraumatic stress disorder following four different types of traumatization. *Behaviour Research and Therapy, 29*, 213–216.

Schaeffer, C. M., & Borduin, C. M. (2005). Long-term follow-up to a randomized clinical trial of multisystemic therapy with serious and violent offenders. *Journal of Consulting and Clinical Psychology, 73*(3), 445–453.

Schaefer, R. T. (2001). *Sociology* (7th ed.). Boston, MA: McGraw-Hill.

Schoenwald, S. K., Borduin, C. M., & Henggeler, S. W. (1998). Multisystemic therapy: Changing the natural and service ecologies of adolescents and families. In M. Epstein, K. Kutash, & A. Duchnowski (Eds.), *Outcomes for children and youth with behavioral and emotional disorders and their families: Programs and evaluations best practices* (pp. 485–511). Austin, TX: Pro-ed.

Vigil, J. D. (1983). Chicano gangs: One response to Mexican urban adaptation in the Los Angeles. *Urban Anthropology, 12*(1), 45-75.

Wahlberg, M., (Producer) & Neale, L. (Director). (2008). *Juvies.* [Motion Picture]. Santa Monica, CA: Chance Films.

Werner-Lin, A., & Moro, T. (2004). Unacknowledged and stigmatized losses. In J. A. Arditti (Ed.), *Parental incarceration and the family: Psychological and social effects of imprisonment on children, parents, and caregivers.* New York, NY: New York University Press.

Yinger, J. M. (1960). Contraculture and subculture. *American Sociological Review, 25*(5), 625–635.

Zastrow, C., & Kirst-Ashman, K. K. (2012). *Understanding human behavior and the social environment* (8th ed.). Belmont, CA: Thomson Learning.

CHAPTER 21

Adolescent Bullying

Nadia Mishael

CHAPTER OBJECTIVES

- Identify the various forms of bullying that impact adolescents;
- Identify the physical, psychological, and social effects of bullying;
- Describe evidence-informed interventions for individuals and school-based interventions;
- Understand how state and federal legislation on bullying is part of larger systemic attempts to combat bullying.

CASE VIGNETTE

Alicia is a slim, petite, and frail-looking brunette. "I didn't realize that I'd been pulling my hair out," she said, as she struggled to find words. Alicia was in the 10th grade attending a public high school, until four months ago. Previously recognized as a talented artist and student, Alicia's functioning had deteriorated. Now, two large bald spots mark the crown of her head, a visible symbol of her distress and anguish. She exhibits severe anxiety, and throws up several times a week, triggered by thoughts of having to go to public places. She was pulled out of school by her mother as a result of being bullied. She is currently being homeschooled.

Alicia is a 16-year-old Hispanic female of Cuban descent. Her parents have been married for 18 years. According to Alicia's mother, her husband works long hours as manager of a custodial company, "so I feel like a single parent." Alicia has no siblings.

After Alicia began the 10th grade, her mother reported several incidents of harassment by other students, including name calling and spreading rumors, to the school principal, but "nothing was done." In a school that appears to be segregated by differences in financial standing and cultural backgrounds, Alicia's mother believes, "It was clearly a case of the haves and have-nots." Alicia's family did not have the financial stability that others in the community enjoyed. Without school support, Alicia's mother felt helpless in her efforts to support Alicia, so she pulled her out of school.

Alicia participated in two counseling sessions with a social worker in a private practice. The family maintained HMO health insurance and with the recommendation of her primary care physician, Alicia took the opportunity to see someone for help. Her mother felt that the social worker, despite good intentions, "made everything worse," and Alicia felt more helpless than before. Alicia was told she "must be on medication" to treat her severe anxiety, "should not have been pulled out of school," and "should return to school as soon as possible." As a result, both mother and daughter felt hesitant about resuming therapy.

INTRODUCTION

"Young people deserve the opportunity to learn and grow and achieve their potential without having to worry about the constant threat of harassment."

—*President Barack Obama*

Bullying is an epidemic problem. It has an extreme adverse impact on the psychosocial functioning of adolescents. Dan Olweus was recognized as a pioneer and founding father of research on bullying problems. In 1970, Olweus started a large-scale project which is now regarded as the first scientific study on bullying problems in the world. Emerging research on the prevalence of bullying demonstrates a continuing pattern of bullying among adolescents which includes physical attacks, spreading rumors, and cyberbullying, a relatively new and ominous threat in the 21st century. Certain minority groups, such as adolescents who are disabled and sexual minorities, are at an even higher risk. The effects of bullying on adolescents is tremendous, and may be long-standing. Some of the effects include anxiety, PTSD, depression and suicidal ideation.

Evidenced-based approaches to prevention and intervention of bullying have been found to be efficacious. At a macro level, state and federal legislation addressing bullying has been enacted and amended to address the growing and changing needs of this population. Many resources exist to help victims and school administration to combat bullying, including a variety of Internet sites providing information and services on both a local and national scale. The case of Alicia is presented to exemplify the effects of bullying on an adolescent girl and various treatment approaches that may be implemented to assist adolescents in similar situations.

Bullying or peer victimization is repeated unwanted and aggressive behavior that involves real or perceived power imbalances. Adolescent bullying may take many forms: physical, verbal, and relational or social. Physical bullying (e.g., hitting, pushing, and kicking) and verbal bullying (e.g., name calling and teasing) are usually considered to be a direct form, while relational bullying refers to an indirect form of bullying, such as social exclusion and spreading rumors. (U.S. Department of Health & Human Services, n.d.).

The percentages of students involved in bullying can vary according to the definition that is applied. Hughes, Middleton, and Marshall (2009) noted that most students did not report bullying to an adult at school or parent, suggesting that the prevalence may be much higher. A nationally representative survey found that approximately 28% of students ages 12 to 18 reported being bullied at school (Robers, Zhang, Truman & Snyder, 2012). A 2007 National Crime Victimization Survey supplement found that 32% of students ages 12 to 18 reported being bullied at school. According to the National Education Association (2012), approximately 160,000 U.S. students miss school each day because they are being bullied.

Cyberbullying has emerged as a common form of adolescent bullying and occurs when the bully uses the Internet, cell phones, or other devices to send or post messages, videos, or photos intended to hurt or embarrass another person (The National Crime Prevention Council, 2008). Researchers estimate that about 20% of teens have been the victim of cyberbullying at some point in their lifetime (Smith et al., 2008). A 2011 Youth Risk Behavior Surveillance Survey found that 16% of high school students (grades 9–12) were electronically bullied in the past year (National Crime Prevention Council, 2013; U.S. Department of Health and Human Services, n.d.).

Research shows that more males than females admit to bullying, and more females said they were victims than males. Studies have consistently shown that boys are more likely to be involved in physical and verbal forms (direct bullying), whereas girls are more involved in the relational form (indirect bullying; Center for Disease Control [CDC], 2011). While boys tend to employ physical means, such as hitting or kicking, girls more frequently use a range of indirect aggressions, including social ostracism (Besag, 2006).

No single factor puts an adolescent at risk of being bullied, however, certain vulnerable populations, including lesbian, gay, bisexual, or transgendered (LGBT) adolescents and adolescents with disabilities, are at a higher risk of being bullied. Sexual minority students face a pervasive problem with a specific set of challenges. According to the Gay, Lesbian and Straight Education Network (GLSEN), more than 8 out of 10 sexual minority students experience harassment at school each year because of their sexual identity (orientation), and 6 out of 10 because of their gender expression. Sexual identity or orientation refers to erotic and/or affectional disposition to the same and/or opposite sex (Gonsiorek, Sell, & Weinrich, 1995). Gender expression refers to stereotypical roles and behaviors associated with each sex, reflected in a range of characteristics distinguishing between masculinity and femininity. Gender is a culturally

determined construct that helps us to distinguish generally between men and women (Eitzen & Sage, 2003). In the United States, men are expected to be tough and physically strong, whereas women are expected to be nurturing and subservient (Eitzen & Sage, 2003).

Adolescents with disabilities such as physical disabilities or intellectual developmental disorders are at an increased risk of being bullied. For example, the prevalence rates of bullying for adolescents with autism spectrum disorders were 46.3% (Sterzing, Shattuck, Narendorf, Wagner & Cooper, 2012). Studies show that students with both visible and nonvisible disabilities are subject to more bullying than nondisabled peers and that boys with disabilities are bullied more often than girls. Reported forms of bullying include name-calling, teasing, physical attacks, and taking belongings. Many students with disabilities have significant challenges with social skills or traits of their disability. Such students can be at particular risk for bullying and victimization (Carter & Spencer, 2006; Dawkins, 1996).

Students who are chronic targets of bullying experience more physical and psychological problems than nonbullied peers. According to Klomek, Marrocco, Kleinman, Schonfeld, and Gould (2007), students who are victims of bullying in or away from school are two to three times more likely to be depressed. Research also suggested that bullying victims are more likely to be lonely, anxious, have low self-esteem, experience headaches, stomachaches, have poorer school performance, and think about or attempt suicide. Distress among victims is highest among victims of both cyberbullying and school bullying (Klomek et al., 2007; Schneider, O'Donnell, Stueve, & Coulter, 2012).

The impact of bullying does not stop in adolescence. Long-term effects on bullied teens may include diminished self-esteem and depression. Victims of prolonged bullying will eventually become either withdrawn or aggressive and, in extreme cases, suicidal or violently retaliatory (Garrett, 2003). Research suggests that adults who were bullies or victimized as adolescents are at greater risk for psychiatric problems, such as anxiety, depression, substance abuse and suicide as adults (Copeland, Wolke, Angold, & Costello, 2013).

A multisystem approach utilizing evidence-based practice in prevention and intervention that involves the victim, family, school and community is necessary to reduce rates of bullying and its effects. Evidence-based interventions such as various forms of cognitive behavioral therapy have shown to be effective for victims like Alicia who experience traumatic events. Cognitive Behavioral Intervention for Trauma in Schools (CBITS) is an effective school-based program (Jaycox, 2003). Also, anti-bullying programs that have been established for use by teachers, special education professionals, and school counselors are essential for systemic change. Research shows that peer intervention is the most effective way to stop bullying long term (Hawkins, Pepler & Craig, 2001).

The Columbine High School shooting in 1999 was the first of many high-profile incidents of violent behavior that appeared to implicate bullying as an underlying cause (Greene, Michael, & Ross, 2005). The incident provoked a wave of new legislative action within state legislatures that aimed to reduce bullying on school campuses or to mitigate its effects. The trend was later fueled by a number of highly visible suicides among school-age children and adolescents that were linked to chronic bullying and sexual harassment, attracting national attention to the issue (Marr & Field, 2001; Higgins, 2013).

In August 2010, policy makers, researchers, educators, corporate leaders, and others met in Washington, DC, for the first-ever Federal Partners in Bullying Prevention Summit, hosted by the U.S. Department of Education. Summit sponsors and participants pledged their commitment to working together to draft a national strategy to reduce and prevent bullying. In his opening remarks, Secretary of Education Arne Duncan made clear that dealing with bullying—and the related issues of ensuring students feel safe and have a school free of disruption—is fundamental to education (The White House, 2011).

MICRO PERSPECTIVE
Assessment

It is important to do a thorough biopsychosocial assessment when working with adolescents. Adolescent victims may develop different types of physical, emotional, or behavioral problems in response to traumatic experiences. Areas to consider in assessment include the adolescent's physical well-being, emotional state, behavioral patterns, familial functioning, peer support and academic performance.

An assessment of an adolescent's overall physical well-being is beyond the scope of a social worker's competence. A referral to a medical doctor should be considered in cases where an adolescent expresses physical symptoms, even if the social worker suspects that the symptoms are psychosomatic. Some physical symptoms may include stomachaches, headaches and migraines, frequent illnesses such as viral infections, colds, chest, ear, and throat infection; irritable bowel syndrome; and skin problems such as eczema (Garrett, 2003).

The psychological, emotional and social impact of bullying is often more difficult to recognize and contend with than the resultant physical ailments. The strategies employed to exclude, ostracize, ridicule and demoralize victims are very sophisticated and can leave enduring scars (Rivers, Duncan, & Besag, 2007). Affective problems may include sadness, fear, anxiety or anger. Some adolescents may develop depression, substance use problems, or PTSD. Evidence indicates that adolescents who do not cope well with major and minor life events and do not have family and peer support are more likely to have suicidal ideation (Mazza & Reynolds, 1998). Attempted or completed suicide may be precipitated by shameful or humiliating experiences, such as being bullied.

Peer relationships are the most studied social determinant of bullying involvement. Victims have fewer friends and are rejected by classmates more than noninvolved peers, leaving victims of bullying more vulnerable to aggressive peers (Spriggs, Iannotti, Nansel, & Haynie, 2007). Additionally, students who are more socially anxious, submissive, or withdrawn are more likely to be victimized (Perren & Alsaker, 2006). Adolescents who have fewer high-quality friendships are more likely to be victimized (Bollmer, Harris, & Milich, 2006). Conversely, having a best friend is related to decreases in victimization (Hodges, Boivin, Vitaro, & Bukowski, 1999).

The family and social systems are important components of adolescent functioning and coping. Wang, Iannotti, and Nansel (2009) contend that parental support may protect adolescents from various forms of bullying. In contrast, an adolescent who has poor familial relationships will be at greater risk (Demaray & Malecki, 2003; Khatri & Kupersmidt, 2003). Secure parental relationships are negatively correlated with some forms of peer victimization (Coleman & Bird, 2003; Veenstra et al., 2005). According to Flouri and Buchanan (2002), a father's involvement in his child's life appears to protect the child from extreme forms of victimization.

Changes in an adolescent's academic performance also need to be noted in an assessment. A drop in grades is often an early sign of other psychosocial stressors in an adolescent's life. Cornell, Gregory, Huang, and Fan (2013) contend that students who are bullied become less engaged in school and their grades and test scores decline.

As noted in Garrett (2003), teens like Alicia who become repeated victims of aggression tend to be quiet and shy in temperament. Victims tend not to retaliate or make any assertive responses to the initial aggression, which is then repeated by the bullies. Alicia seemed to have turned most of her angst and anxiety inward. She was socially withdrawn and experienced feelings of isolation and abandonment. She exhibited low self-esteem, anhedonia, and feelings of hopelessness and helplessness. Given her psychological presentation, an assessment of Alicia's suicidal risk took

precedence. She reported that she had thoughts of "taking some pills and being done with it, or stabbing myself in the chest," but also affirmed that she knew she could never do it because "I am too chicken." She also did not want to hurt her mother.

Alicia's mother had taken her to see her physician many times since her crisis began. According to her physician, Alicia's many physical symptoms appeared to stem from her anxiety. Nevertheless, he continued to test for possible intestinal viral infections which may have caused her nausea and stomachaches.

Alicia's functioning at school and her overall academic performance have been severely compromised by her experience. "She was a hard working student and interested in learning, but it all went out the door," said her mother. Being home-schooled meets the academic requirements set for graduation; however, Alicia missed much of the experiential components of going to high school and attending a real class.

Diversity Considerations

Victimization as a result of a child's race or ethnicity does occur, but the precise way in which that demographic variable plays a role is less clear (Boulton, 1995; Nansel et al., 2001; Seals & Young, 2003). Research indicates that prevalence rates of bullying victimization vary for African American youth based on the wording of the measures. African American youth may have differing conceptions of bullying victimization and therefore may underreport their victimization experiences (American Educational Research Association [AERA], 2013). Research suggests that the relationship may be less about race per se and more about whether a child is part of the racial minority at his or her school. Graham and Juvonen (2002) found that being part of a racial group that is in the numerical minority at school may lead to more victimization; however, victims may feel more loneliness and social anxiety when they are in a classroom where most students are of the same ethnicity as the victims (Bellmore, Witkow, Graham, & Juvonen, 2004).

In the early 1990s estimates of homophobic bullying in U. S. schools ranged from 33% to 49% (Berril, 1992). Homophobic bullying does not just affect students who are gay and lesbian; it can also affect students who do not conform to gender stereotypes (Rivers et al., 2007). Teenage boys who are physically underdeveloped in comparison to their peers and those who are less confident speaking out may be labeled queer. Among girls, those who liked sports or those who do not express interest in boys may be labeled "lesbian" (Rivers et al., 2007). A 2001 survey of middle and high school students found that 44% of female students and 20% of male students had a fear of being sexually harassed (Harris Interactive, 2001).

Being disabled is another diversity factor that puts students at greater risk for being bullied. According to Rose and Espelage (2012), students with disabilities are twice as likely to be identified as victims as are students without disabilities. Victimization may be predicted by the severity of the disability. Students with more severe disabilities, such as autism, are at a higher risk (Rose, 2010).

Alicia is a second-generation Hispanic of Cuban origin. Though initially accepted and embraced by other students, who became her friends, Alicia's ethnic background became one of the aspects targeted by those who bullied her. Text messages referring to Alicia being a "Mexican loser" were sent to her and posted on social media sites. It is common among those who are naive and uninformed about the vast diversity amongst Hispanics to group all as "Mexicans," discounting the rich heritage among various different backgrounds.

Latina adolescents experience depression and suicidal ideations in a disproportionate manner compared to their non-Latina counterparts (Romero, Wiggs, Valencia, & Bauman, 2013). After controlling for depressive symptoms, Romero et al. (2013) found that Latina adolescents who have been bullied were 1.5 times more likely to attempt suicide compared to those who have not been victims. Researchers suggest that stress associated with victimization may create internalizing problems, such as depression or anxiety, and for minority adolescents, feelings of victimization, including the cultural challenges associated with feeling connected to one's own heritage and discrimination (Romero et al., 2013). These stressors appear to be disproportionately experienced by females (Peskin, Tortolero, Markham, Addy, & Baumler, 2007; Romero et al., 2013).

Intervention

Unlike a time-limited traumatic event, bullying or peer victimization may be chronic and ongoing. Therefore, intervention must be provided at several different systemic levels: a combination of anti-bullying strategies at the school and more supportive modalities to allow the student to regain self-esteem and confidence and simultaneously focus on school work.

Osofsky (1999) studied the ability of children and youth to bounce back in the face of community violence and war. The most critical protective factor for a child is a strong, positive relationship between the child and a competent, caring adult (Osofsky,1999). The therapist must provide a holding environment, a safe place where the adolescent patient can freely express herself or himself and experience containment and tolerance (Osofsky, 1999).

Trauma-Focused Cognitive Behavioral Therapy (TF–CBT) is an evidence-based therapy designed to help 3- to 18-year-olds overcome the negative effects of traumatic life events. TF–CBT aims to treat serious emotional problems such as posttraumatic stress, fear, anxiety, and depression by teaching children and parents new skills that can be used to process thoughts and feelings resulting from traumatic events (Cohen, Mannarino, Berliner, & Deblinger, 2000).

TF–CBT combines cognitive behavior and family theory and adapts them to the treatment of traumatic events. TF–CBT is based on the theory that people have difficulty processing the complex and strong emotions that result from exposure to single or multiple traumatic events. Typically, TF–CBT is implemented as a brief intervention, usually lasting from 12 to 18 weekly sessions (Cohen et al., 2000).

Parents and caregivers play a critical role in treatment. TF-CBT operates through the use of a parental treatment component and several child–parent sessions. In this way, the parent could learn more optimal, supportive skills to help. The parent–child session would ideally encourage the adolescents to discuss the traumatic events directly with their parent and allow both to communicate concerns and feelings more openly (Cohen et al., 2000).

The components of TF-CBT are summarized by the acronym PRACTICE, which stands for **P**sychoeducation and parenting skills; **R**elaxation skills; **A**ffective regulation skills; **C**ognitive coping skills; **T**rauma narrative and cognitive procession of the traumatic events; **I**n vivo mastery of trauma reminders; ongoing **C**hild-parent sessions; and **E**nhancing safety and future development trajectory (Cohen & Mannarino, 2008).

It is also important to implement appropriate interventions at school. The Cognitive-Behavioral Intervention for Trauma in Schools (CBITS) program is a school-based group and individual intervention that has been used with students from 5th grade through 12th grade who have witnessed or experienced traumatic life events (CBITS, n.d.). Stein et al. (2003) describe CBITS as a standardized cognitive-behavioral group intervention protocol that aims to significantly decrease symptoms of depression and PTSD in students who are exposed to trauma. The treatment can be effectively delivered in school campuses by trained school-based mental health clinicians.

The CBITS 10-session protocol begins with Session 1 and an introduction of group members, and a discussion of reasons for participation. Session 1 sets the tone for how the rest of the group is going to work. The goal is to make sure that the group is engaged and that group members want to come back. An icebreaker game may be used to give members the sense that they are in a place where they can talk to others about their experiences. Clinicians may use this opportunity to point out similarities and commonalities (CBITS, n.d.).

Confidentiality can be a big issue in the schools, particularly among the school staff who may not be used to working with clinicians and staff who don't understand the appropriate clinical boundaries. In most circumstances, the school staff will need to be educated about the process. A confidentiality contract is provided to students in the first session, and students generally are respectful of the boundaries. If there is a breach, the group discusses and decides how they want to handle it and whether or not they want the person who violated the rules to be able to stay in the group. This gives the other group members a greater sense of control (CBITS, n.d.).

In Session 2, the objectives of the group are explained and members are educated about common reactions to stress and trauma. Relaxation training is also provided to help combat anxiety. Between Session 2 and Session 6, there are also individual sessions that focus on imagined exposure to a traumatic event. The imagined exposure can then be brought out through drawing and writing exercises in group sessions (Stein et al., 2003).

Sessions 3 and 4 are focused on cognitive restructuring. Members are taught about the linkage between thoughts and feelings, and introduced to ways to combat negative thinking. It is useful to have had individual sessions with the student before Session 5, so that the clinician has familiarity with some of the details of the traumatic event. Group members construct a fear hierarchy, and learn alternative coping strategies (CBITS, n.d.).

Sessions 6 and 7 involve group exposure to traumatic memory through drawing, writing and verbalizing a part of the story, and in vivo imaginal exposure. It's important to utilize all three modalities across the two groups. Each group member has a unique individual experience within the group setting (CBITS, n.d.).

Session 8 and 9 involve social problem solving. Given the real problems that adolescents may face, taking the time to look at options for handling difficult situations and managing social, academic, or familial problems can be a powerful tool (Kataoka, Langley, Wong, Baweja, & Stein, 2012). In the sessions covering problem solving, it is important to link feelings, thoughts and actions, by working through examples and listing potential actions one could take, and making links to the underlying thoughts and feelings. The types of situations may include a teacher yelling at the student or parents fighting with each other. The clinician will engage the student in brainstorming options or solutions, rating each option in terms of how effective it may be in solving the problems (Kataoka et al., 2012).

Session 10 is the final session, and includes a graduation ceremony. Group members are also taught relapse prevention. Research has shown that students who participate in the program have significantly fewer symptoms of PTSD, depression, and psychosocial dysfunctions (CBITS, n.d.). In some situations, there are students who may have a series of traumatic events, for example, ongoing domestic violence. In other cases, some students may continue to be symptomatic or may have comorbid issues. If this is recognized in the group process, clinicians should make the appropriate referrals that need to be made (CBITS, n.d.).

Parents are encouraged to participate and learn how they can best help their child during the implementation of CBITS. Often, parents know what their child is exposed to and the impact it is having, but they don't know how to help him or her. Also, it can be very helpful for teachers in the classroom to understand some of the challenges their students face and learn how to better address them. Parents and teachers must be able to support the child because when CBITS ends after 10 weeks, these other people in the child's life are going to have to be there to provide support and to help enhance the child's resilience (CBITS, n.d.).

Short-term, time-limited psychotherapy has proved to be the most effective approach to treatment with traditional Hispanic adolescents and their families. The therapy should be present-oriented and address the here and now of the situation (Markowitz et al., 2009).

Alicia's case is complex in that she has experienced significant trauma with symptoms including anxiety, depression, psychosomatic symptoms and suicidal ideation. A psychodynamic conceptualization of the case offered insight into the nature of the therapeutic relationship and transference and countertransference issues that emerged; and cognitive-behavioral theory and interventions were utilized to address dysfunctional thoughts and problematic behaviors associated with Alicia's reaction to being victimized (Hoch-Espada & Lippmann, 2000).

Alicia had become agoraphobic, fearful of being outside of the home and interacting with anyone who may hurt her (American Psychiatric Association, 2013). Her thinking pattern had become rigid and she was unable to entertain any proposed outings. The original traumatic events that occurred seemed to have been replaced with new and unwarranted fears of what may happen to her in the future.

A critical ingredient in Alicia's therapy was her mother's continued support. Over time, Alicia felt more comfortable to discuss the events that had transpired. She was able to express the hurt and shame she felt, and slowly began to externalize some of these feelings in her writing and drawing. Alicia and her mother both noticed that the more Alicia expressed her thoughts and feelings about the past, the less stomachaches she had.

Alicia needed to gain mastery over her environment. Taking risks by going out with family and friends, and possibly visiting her old school would help her accomplish this goal. In one of the later sessions, Alicia imagined going back to her old school. She confessed that she loved her school. With careful analysis of her thoughts and feelings, Alicia began to realize that she did not really fear going back to school; she feared and was angry with three specific students at her school.

Transference and Countertransference Issues

The client's tendency to approach connection with another person in a certain way will manifest in an initial interview and must be factored into the clinical understanding of the client (McWilliams, 1999). In order to accurately assess a case, a social work practitioner must be able to use his or her countertransference to understand the client's reenactment of unresolved relationships in the therapeutic relationship. In addition, the practitioner must have sufficient self-awareness to discern which aspects of the relationship are formed by the client's projection and which are not.

Countertransference issues are of particular importance in work with victims because they tend to revolve around frightening aspects of the therapists' life that are often unconscious and difficult to deal with, such as fears of violence, abandonment, and helplessness (Dalenber, 2000). Traumatized clients sometimes evoke a desire, on the therapist's part, to step outside of the therapeutic boundaries to intervene and "save" the client. In fact, what victimized clients really need is a therapist who can maintain appropriate boundaries and thereby prove that the client is not helpless, nor are they responsible for or deserve the victimization (Dalenber, 2000).

In the early stages of psychotherapy with adolescents, therapists frequently find themselves doing much of the work. This situation may lead to angry feelings on the part of the therapist, and if not understood, could interfere with the treatment process. Therapists must ask numerous questions; extend themselves to the client; try to avoid the development of long silences, at least in the beginning; and wait patiently for the time when interpretations can be made (Dalenber, 2000). A therapist's angry feelings are often associated with the sensation that they are doing much of the work, and getting little in return.

Countertransference can lead the therapist under the guise of giving comfort to repeat the trauma of the previous experience and to re-traumatize the patient (Dalenber, 2000). For example, the therapist may find her or himself taking an overly rigid, punitive stance or tone with some clients.

It is essential for therapists to practice ethically, and be able to honestly identify and confront any biases that may be present on their end. If biases are not confronted, they may lead to the development of distancing defense mechanisms between the client and the therapist (Rothe, 2004).

Because a cross-cultural client-therapist dyad existed in the treatment of Alicia, the clinician would be remiss not to analyze the client's projections. Given the traumatic experiences Alicia had encountered with predominantly Caucasian students, it was necessary to be aware of the potential transference dynamic early in therapy.

Alicia's unresolved feelings toward the authority figures at her school would also be expected to emerge in the transference. Understandably, Alicia was suspect of assistance she was supposed to receive from an outsider and, at least unconsciously, wondered whether the therapist would victimize or abandon her as well. The evolution of the therapeutic relationship and distinct and contrasting experiences of the therapist during the early diagnostic phase versus later phases of therapy attenuates the fact that there was transference (McWilliams, 1999). Alicia was reluctant and resistant to therapy. Initially she did not trust the therapists' motives. Later in therapy, Alicia was deeply invested in working with the therapist and eager to achieve her goals.

Legal and Ethical Concerns

Schools have a legal responsibility to provide a safe learning environment for students. According to the U.S. Department of Education (2011), most U.S. states have passed anti-bullying laws, and if the school district does not take reasonable, appropriate steps to end the bullying or harassment of a child, the district may be violating federal, state, and local laws.

School counselors and school social workers are an integral part of school-based crisis management, suicide prevention, and post intervention efforts. However, intervention with students may present a number of legal and ethical challenges to counselors as well as other school faculty, administration and staff. Counselors who work with adolescents must consider their confidentiality rights while simultaneously appreciating the right of parents to be appraised of their children's clinically-related development. For example, parents of minors must be notified when an adolescent is determined to be at risk for a suicide attempt. Confidentiality is not possible or required in this circumstance, as the welfare of the adolescent is the most important consideration (Remley & Herlihy, 2001).

Approximately 160,000 students stay home each day to avoid bullying (NEA, 2012). However, compensatory education laws require students to attend school. Many states allow parents to home school, so long as it provides an "equivalent education," or teach for an equivalent period of time (Buss, 2000). It is estimated that at least one million children are homeschooled each year (Buss, 2000).

Finally, issues of bullying can be dealt with at the legal level. Furniss (2000) suggests taking into consideration the nature of the act, extent of the harm caused, and the intention of the offender. Furniss (2000) also warns that claimants may face a complex situation when they decide to litigate about bullying issues, due to existing barriers to successful litigation, having resulted so far in very few successful claims in courts.

Alicia's emotional state and ability to self-regulate was a clinical and ethical issue. She presented with severe depressed mood and a sense of hopelessness. Thus, suicidal risk was considered from a legal and ethical standpoint throughout treatment.

Alicia's parents have not pursued any legal recourse in their daughter's situation. Alicia's mother felt that she learned about her rights "too late" and did not want to cause additional emotional harm to Alicia by pursuing matters with the school. Her mother wanted to focus on helping Alicia heal, and feared that any investigative probes into Alicia's case would be more harmful than helpful. Alicia has been homeschooled for over a year. Though one of the therapeutic goals is for her to return to school, her enrollment will be based on her readiness and selection of a new school.

MEZZO PERSPECTIVE

The school system plays an enormous part in the lives of adolescents. Schools are ultimately responsible for protecting children, and in many instances, they are culpable when they do not. The school's role in preventing and intervening when bullying occurs is paramount to the functioning of its students. Studies reflect that parents are unaware of bullying and talk about it on a limited basis (Olweus, 1993), with teachers seldom talking to their class about bullying (Charach, Pepler, & Ziegler, 1995). Few students feel that adults will help, and they feel that when adults do help, it is ineffective and makes things worse (Charach et al., 1995).

A California student survey revealed that the reasons for harassment or bullying on school property include race, ethnicity, national origin, religion, gender, sexual identity (orientation), and physical or mental disability (Furlong, Greif, & Austin, 2005). Unfortunately, many school staff have not been trained in how to prevent and stop bullying and harassment, which includes failing to prevent students from targeting another student. As many as one-third of teachers report feeling untrained to handle bullying (Harris & Willoughby, 2003).

AERA (2013) suggested the implementation of teacher training and ongoing professional development on different ways to intervene when bullying occurs. In addition, Laminack and Wadsworth (2012) contend that bullying behavior is less likely to emerge in classrooms where all students feel valued, have a sense of belonging, and a sense of significance to the community. School-level policies and practices, such as hall monitoring and enforcement of rules against peer intimidation, are often key components in bullying prevention and intervention. Smith (1997) argued that schools should have a clear policy regarding bullying. This policy should be compatible with the development of a climate and a culture that disapproves of bullying (Smith, 1997). Advocacy on the part of a social worker becomes paramount in cases involving bullying. Parents are often not informed of their legal rights and option to contact the U.S. Department of Education, Office of Civil Rights. Some parents may not be able to advocate for their child because they do not have adequate resources. Others may not speak English or may be intimidated by the thought of having to navigate through the bureaucracy in the school system and community organizations.

Parents may obtain the school's anti-bullying policy and file a report with the school if their child is being bullied. Alicia's mother had determined that her child was being bullied and did speak to the principal about the issue. However, she did not pursue it further or file a report. The principal needs to determine whether the incident mandates notice to law enforcement or disciplinary action.

Though the principal was mandated to file a report when alerted about bullying or harassment (Higgins, 2013), it is possible that he did not take the complaint about Alicia seriously enough. According to Bradshaw and Waasdorp (2009), staff members significantly underestimate the number of students who are frequently involved in bullying. In addition, although most students believe their school is not doing enough to prevent bullying, most staff feel their efforts are adequate (Bradshaw & Waasdorp, 2009). Regardless of reasons offered or substantiated, it appears that the school failed Alicia.

MACRO PERSPECTIVE
Policy Analysis

Federal bullying prevention legislation has been introduced every year since 2003, when Congresswoman Linda Sanchez (D-CA) first introduced the Safe Schools Improvement Act (SSIA). Over the course of 10 years, support for federal anti-bullying legislation has grown, garnering bipartisan support and the endorsement of SSIA.

From 1999 to 2010, there were more than 120 bills enacted by state legislatures nationally that have either introduced or amended education or criminal statutes to address bullying and related behaviors in schools. In 2010, 21 new bills were passed and eight additional bills were signed into law through April 30, 2011 (U.S. Department of Education, 2011).

The state of Georgia became the first state to pass bullying legislation in 1999, which required schools to implement character education programs that explicitly addressed bullying prevention. Since that time, there has been a wave of new legislation at the state level to define acts of bullying in the school context and to establish school or district policies that prohibit bullying behavior.

According to the U.S. Department of Education (2011), there are 46 states with anti-bullying laws in place. Thirty-six states have provisions that prohibit cyberbullying and 13 have statutes that grant schools the authority to address off-campus behavior that creates a hostile school environment. In 2011, there were four remaining states (Hawaii, Michigan, Montana, and South Dakota) without anti-bullying legislation. As of 2012, Montana was the only state that had no anti-bullying law in place (www.bullypolice.org).

California's newest anti-bullying law, "Seth's Law"—named after 13-year-old Seth Walsh, who committed suicide after being harassed about his sexual identity (orientation)—took effect on July 1, 2012. Seth's Law strengthens existing state anti-bullying laws to help protect all California public school students. According to the American Civil Liberties Union of California, Seth's Law requires schools to update their anti-bullying policies and programs, and it focuses on protecting students who are bullied based on their actual or perceived sexual orientation and gender identity/gender expression.

Gendered harassment must be addressed in accordance with federal guidelines that are part of Title IX. In October 2010, the U.S. Department of Education's Office for Civil Rights issued guidance to all school districts in the form of a "Dear Colleague" letter. In this letter there was clear wording regarding how Title IX applies in such cases. Title IX prohibits sexual harassment and gender-based harassment of all students, regardless of the actual or perceived sexual orientation or gender identity of the harasser or target (Education Amendments of 1972).

The distinctions between bullying and harassment are important because they have different legal implications. When bullying behaviors constitute harassment or discrimination against a protected class (e.g., one defined by religion, race, disability, gender, nationality, ethnicity, or sexual orientation and association with a person or group with one or more of these actual or perceived characteristics), the U.S. Department of Education Office of Civil Rights (OCR) and the U.S. Department of Justice Civil Rights Division may become involved. Alicia was harassed based upon her ethnicity, sex, and national origin, and as such, further legal action could have been taken on her behalf to protect her civil rights.

The launch of the website www.bullying.org allows for a more centralized and accessible site for federal resources on bullying for victims (U.S. Department of Health and Human Services, n.d.). Alicia's mother was unaware of these resources. She confessed that she would have done things very differently if she had known more about her daughter's rights.

Policy Advocacy

Many organizations are in place to help advocate for victims of bullying and better policies. Bully Police USA, Inc. (www.bullypolice.org), a watch-dog organization advocating for bullied children, posts ratings of all U.S. states (from A to F). It provides links to each state's legislative contact, and encourages citizens to ask for assistance and to voice concerns. Twenty-one states received less than an "A" rating due to their anti-bullying policies in schools. For example, Montana was rated an "F" because they tried to pass an anti-bullying law but it was shut down. California currently has a "B" because they have an anti-bullying law, but it is still missing some key points.

Stopbullying.org presents a detailed protocol to help parents advocate for their children. They recommend that the parent contact the teacher, school counselor, school principal, school superintendent and the State Department of Education. If the school does not adequately address a problem based on race, color, national origin, sex, disability, or religion, parents are encouraged to contact the State School Superintendent; State Department of Education; U.S. Department of Education, Office of Civil Rights; and U.S. Department of Justice, Civil Rights Division.

CONCLUSION

Adolescent bullying is a pervasive problem that requires systematic prevention and interventions at the micro, mezzo and macro levels. Emerging research and alarming news reports have transformed the idea that bullying is merely a rite of passage, or a normal and inevitable part of growing up. "Kids will be kids" is no longer an acceptable retort for the many victims, families, schools and communities impacted by bullying.

The psychosocial effects of bullying can be devastating and longstanding. Certain minority groups, such as disabled adolescents, are at an even greater risk. Evidence-based interventions such as cognitive behavioral therapy have been shown to be efficacious for victims of bullying. In order to address the problem of bullying more globally evidenced-based approaches at schools and in communities are necessary components of systemic change.

Legislation continues to be enacted and amended to support the prevention and intervention of bullying. The inclusion of legislation directed at cyberbullying reflects the evolving needs of this population. Numerous resources and Internet sites are available to educate and help victims of bullying, and aid schools to prevent and combat bullying.

Alicia made several attempts to attend a different school. She finally succeeded at the task of entering the school grounds. However, her anxiety escalated and she was not able to tolerate sitting inside a classroom for more than five minutes. Because her ultimate goal was to graduate high school, Alicia and her mother decided that the best approach for her was to continue being homeschooled.

Alicia continued to attend weekly psychotherapy sessions, and demonstrated tremendous improvement in her overall psychosocial functioning. She made several new friends online, and enjoyed going out with them to concerts and the mall. Alicia also began to draw again. She experimented with new mediums, and for the first time, used color in her portraits, a symbolic representation of her evolution and growth.

Alicia was able to ascribe a different meaning to the traumatic events that had transpired. She ultimately credited her greater self-understanding and acceptance to the experience of being bullied. Alicia also felt that she had found direction in her life. She planned to go to college and pursue a career in mental health in order to assist children and teens facing similar issues.

INTERNET RESOURCES

- Stopbullying.gov: http://www.stopbullying.gov
- Bullying.org: http://www.bullying.org
- Stop Bullying Now: http://www.stopbullying-now.hrsa.gov/adults
- Abilitypath: http://www.abilitypath.org
- American Federation of Teachers: http://www.aft.org
- Centers for Disease Control: http://www.cdc.gov
- Cyberbullying: http://www.cyberbullying.org
- Gay, Lesbian & Straight Education Network: http://www.glsen.org
- National Education Association: http://www.nea.org
- Not in Our School: http://www.niot.org/nios
- PACER's National Bullying Prevention Center: http://www.pacer.org/bullying
- Public Broadcasting Service: http://www.pbs.org
- National Parent-Teacher Association: http://www.pta.org
- The Trevor Project: http://www.thetrevorproject.org

DISCUSSION QUESTIONS

1. How do you define bullying?

2. What populations are at greater risk for being bullied?

3. What are some important areas to consider when conducting an assessment of a student who has been bullied?

4. What micro and mezzo prevention and intervention approaches should be implemented to stop bullying on school campuses?

5. How can policy effect change in this area?

REFERENCES

American Educational Research Association. (2013). *Prevention of bullying in schools, colleges and universities: Research report and recommendation.* Washington, DC: Author.

American Psychiatric Association. (2013). *Diagnostic and statistical manual of mental disorders* (5th ed.). Arlington, VA: Author.

Bellmore, A. D., Witkow, M. R., Graham, S., & Juvonen, J. (2004). Beyond the individual: The impact of ethnic context and classroom behavioral norms on victims' adjustment. *Developmental Psychology, 40,* 1159–1172.

Berril K. (1992). Antigay violence and victimization in the United States: An overview. In G. Herek & K. Berril (Eds.), *Hate crimes: Confronting violence against lesbians and gay men* (pp. 19–45). Thousand Oaks, CA: Sage.

Besag, V. E. (2006). *Understanding girls' friendships, fights and feuds: A practical approach to girls' bullying.* England: Open University Press.

Bollmer, J. M., Harris, M. J., & Milich, R. (2006). Reactions to bullying and peer victimization: Narratives, physiological arousal, and personality. *Journal of Research in Personality, 40*(5), 803–828.

Boulton, M. J. (1995). Patterns of bully/victim problems in mixed race groups of children. *Social Development, 4,* 277–293.

Bradshaw, C. P., & Waasdorp, T. E. (2009). Measuring and changing a "culture of bullying." *School Psychology Review, 38*(3), 356–361.

Buss, E. (2000). The adolescent stake in the allocation of education control between parent and state. *The University of Chicago Law Review, 67*(4), 1233–1289.

Carter, B. B., & Spencer, V. G. (2006). The fear factor: Bullying and students with disabilities. *International Journal of Special Education, 21*(1), 1.

CBITS. (n.d.), *Cognitive behavioral intervention for trauma in schools.* Retrieved from https://cbitsprogram.org

Centers for Disease Control and Prevention. (2011). *Bullying among middle school and high school students.* Retrieved from http://www.cdc.gov/mmwr/preview/mmwrhtml/mm6015a1.htm

Charach, A., Pepler, D., & Ziegler, S. (1995). Bullying at school: A Canadian perspective: Survey of problems with suggestions for intervention. *Education Canada, 35*(1), 12.

Cohen, J. A., & Mannarino, A. P. (2008). Trauma-focused cognitive behavioral therapy for children and parents. *Association for Child and Adolescent Mental Health, 13*(4), 158–162.

Cohen, J. A., Mannarino, A. P., Berliner, L., & Deblinger, E. (2000). Trauma-focused cognitive behavioral therapy for children and adolescents: An empirical update. *Journal of Interpersonal Violence, 15*(11), 1202–1224.

Coleman, P. K., & Byrd, C. P. (2003). Interpersonal correlates of peer victimization among young adolescents. *Journal of Youth and Adolescence, 32,* 301–314.

Copeland, W. E., Wolke, D., Angold, A., & Costello, E. J. (2013). Adult psychiatric outcomes of bullying and being bullied by peers in childhood and adolescence. *JAMA Psychiatry, 70*(4), 419–426. doi:10.1001/jamapsychiatry.2013.504

Cornell, D., Gregory, A., Huang, F., & Fan, X. (2013). Perceived prevalence of teasing and bullying predicts high school dropout rates. *Journal of Educational Psychology, 105*(1), 138–149. doi:10.1037/a0030416

Dalenber, C. J. (2000). *Countertransference and the treatment of trauma.* Washington, DC: American Psychological Association.

Dawkins, J. L. (1996). Bullying, physical disability and the pediatric patient. *Developmental Medicine and Child Neurology, 38*(7), 603–612.

Demaray, M. K., & Malecki, C. K. (2003). Perceptions of the frequency and importance of social support by students classified as victims, bullies, and bully/victims in an urban middle school. *School Psychology Review 32*(3), 471.

Education Amendments of 1972, Title IX, 20 U.S.C. § 1681 (1972).

Eitzen, D. S., & Sage, G. H. (2003). *Sociology of North American sports* (7th ed.). Madison, WI: McGraw-Hill.

Flouri, E., & Buchanan, A. (2002). Life satisfaction in teenage boys: The moderating role of father involvement and bullying. *Aggression and Behavior, 28,* 126–133. doi: 10.1002/ab.90014

Furlong, M. J., Greif, J. L., & Austin, G. (2005). Harassment. In S. W. Lee (Ed.), *Encyclopedia of school psychology* (pp. 233–237). Thousand Oaks, CA: Sage.

Furniss, C. (2000). Bullying in schools: It's not a crime, is it? *Education and the Law, 12*(1), 9–29.

Garrett, A. G. (2003). *Bulling in American schools: Causes, prevention, interventions.* Jefferson, NC: McFarland & Company.

Gonsiorek, J. C., Sell, R. L., & Weinrich, J. D. (1995). Definition and measurement of sexual orientation. *Suicide & Life-Threatening Behavior, 25,* 40–51.

Graham, S., & Juvonen, J. (2002). Ethnicity, peer harassment, and adjustment in middle school: An exploratory study. *Journal of Early Adolescence, 22,* 173–199.

Greene, M. B., Michael, B., & Ross, R. (2005). *The nature, scope, and utility of formal laws and regulations that prohibit school-based bullying and harassment.* Persistently Safe Schools. The National Conference of the Hamilton Fish Institute on School and Community Violence. Retrieved from http://www.fas.org/sgp/crs/misc/R42652.pdf

Harris Interactive. (2001). *Hostile hallways: Bullying, teasing, and sexual harassment in schools.* New York, NY: American Association of University Women. Retrieved from http://history.aauw.org/aauw-research/2001-hostile-hallways

Harris, S., & Willoughby W. (2003). Teacher perceptions of student bullying behavior. *ERS Spectrum, 21*(13), 4–11.

Hawkins, L. D., Pepler, D. J., & Craig, W. M. (2001). Naturalistic observations of peer interventions in bullying. *Social Development, 10*(4), 512–527.

Higgins, N. (2013). Bullying is the new harassment, but are our students any more protected? *Northeastern University Law Journal, 5*(1), 133–152.

Hoch-Espada, A. L., & Lippmann, J. (2000). Integrating cognitive behavioral therapy into a psychodynamic framework. *Cognitive and Behavioral Practice, 7*(3), 350–356.

Hodges, E., Boivin, M., Vitaro, F., & Bukowski, W. M. (1999). The power of friendship: Protection against an escalating cycle of peer victimization. *Developmental Psychology, 35,* 94–101.

Hughes, P. P., Middleton, K. M., & Marshall, D. D. (2009). Students' perceptions of bullying in Oklahoma public schools. *Journal of School Violence, 8*(3), 216–232.

Jaycox, L. H. (2003). *Cognitive-behavioral intervention for trauma in schools.* Longmont, CO: Sopris West Educational Services.

Kataoka, S., Langley, A., Wong, M., Baweja, S., & Stein, B. (2012). Responding to students with PTSD in schools. *Child & Adolescent Psychiatry Clinics* of North America, 21(1), 119–120. doi:10.1016/j.chc.2011.08.009

Khatri, P., & Kupersmidt, J. B. (2003). Aggression, peer victimization, and social relationships among Indian youth. *International Journal of Behavioral Development, 27*(1), 87–95. doi:10.1080/01650250244000056

Klomek, B. A., Marrocco, F., Kleinman, M., Schonfeld, I. S., & Gould, M. S. (2007). Bullying, depression, and suicidality in adolescents. *Journal of the American Academy of Child & Adolescent Psychiatry, 46*(1), 40–49.

Laminack, L. L., & Wadsworth, R. M. (2012). *Bullying hurts: Teaching kindness through read alouds and guided conversations.* Portsmouth, NH: Heinemann.

Markowitz, J. C., Patel, S. R, Balan, I. C., Bell, M. A., Blanco, C, Yellow, M., & Lewis-Fernandez, R. (2009). Toward an adaptation of interpersonal psychotherapy for Hispanic patients with DSM-IV major depressive disorder. *The Journal of Clinical Psychiatry, 70*(2), 214–222.

Marr, N., & Field, T. (2001). *Bullycide: Death at playtime.* Oxfordshire, UK: Success Unlimited.

Mazza, J. J., & Reynolds, W. M. (1998). A longitudinal investigation of depression, hopelessness, social support, and major and minor life events and their relation to suicidal ideation in adolescents. *Journal of Suicide and Life-Threatening Behavior, 28*, 358–374.

McWilliams, N. (1999). *Psychoanalytic case formulation.* New York, NY: Guilford Press.

Nansel, T. R., Overpeck, M., Pilla, R. S., Ruan, R. S., Simons-Morton, B., & Scheidt, P. (2001). Bullying behaviors among U.S. youth: Prevalence and association with psychosocial adjustment. *Journal of the American Medical Association, 285*, 2094–2100.

National Crime Prevention Council. (2008). *Cyberbullying.* Retrieved from http://www.ncpc.org/topics/cyberbullying

National Crime Prevention Council. (2013). *What is cyberbullying?* Retrieved from http://www.ncpc.org/topics/cyberbullying/what-is-cyberbullying

National Education Association. (2012). *Nation's educators continue push for safe, bully-free environment.* Retrieved from http://www.nea.org/home/53298.htm

Olweus, D. (1993). *Bullying at school.* Cambridge, MA: Blackwell.

Osofsky, J. D. (1999). The impact of violence on children and youth. *Domestic Violence and Children and Youth, 9*(3), 33–49.

Perren, S., & Alsaker, F. D. (2006). Social behavior and peer relationships of victims, bully-victims, and bullies in kindergarten. *The Journal of Child Psychology and Psychiatry and Allied Disciplines, 47*, 45–57.

Peskin, M. F., Tortolero, S. R., Markham, C. M., Addy, R. C., & Baumler, E. R. (2007). Bullying and victimization and internalizing symptoms among low-income black and Hispanic students. *Journal of Adolescent Health, 40*(4), 372–375.

Remley, T. P., & Herlihy, B. (2001). *Ethical, legal, and professional issues in counseling.* Upper Saddle River, NJ: Merrill/Prentice Hall.

Rivers, I., Duncan, N., & Besag, V. E. (2007). *Bullying: A handbook for educators and parents.* Westport, CT: Pager.

Robers, S., Zhang, J., Truman, J., & Snyder, T. (2012). *Indicators of school crime and safety: (2011).* Washington, DC: National Center for Education Statistics, U.S. Department of Education, U.S. Department of Justice Office of Justice Programs. Retrieved from http://www.bjs.gov/content/pub/pdf/iscs11.pdf

Romero, A. J., Wiggs, C. B., Valencia, C., & Bauman, S. (2013). Latina teen suicide and bullying. *Hispanic Journal of Behavioral Sciences, 35*, 159–173.

Rose, C. A. (2010). Bullying among students with disabilities: Impact and implications. In D. L. Espelage & S. M. Searer (Eds.), *Bullying in North American schools: A socio-ecological perspective on prevention and intervention* (2nd ed., pp. 34–44). Mahwah, NJ: Lawrence Erlbaum.

Rose, C. A., & Espelage, D. L. (2012). Risk and protective factors associated with the bullying involvement of students with emotional and behavioral disorders. *Behavioral Disorders, 37*, 133–148.

Rothe, E. M. (2004). Hispanic adolescents and their families: Sociocultural factors and treatment considerations. *Adolescent Psychiatry, 28*, 251–278.

Schneider, S. K., O'Donnell, L., Stueve, A., & Coulter, R. (2012). Cyberbullying, school bullying, and psychological distress: A regional census of high school students. *American Journal of Public Health, 102*(1), 171–177.

Seals, D., & Young, J. (2003). Bullying and victimization: Prevalence and relationship to gender, grade level, ethnicity, self-esteem, and depression. *Adolescence, 38*, 735–747.

Smith, P. (1997). Bullying in life-span perspective: What can studies of school bullying and workplace bullying learn from each other? *Journal of Community and Applied Social Psychology, 7*, 249–255.

Smith, P. K., Mahdavi, J., Carvalho, M., Fisher, S., Russell, S., & Tippett, N. (2008). Cyberbullying: Its nature and impact in secondary school pupils. *Journal of Child Psychology and Psychiatry, 49*(4): 376–385. doi: 10.1111/j.1469–7610.2007.01846.x

Spriggs, A. L., Iannotti, R. J., Nansel, T. R., & Haynie, D. L. (2007). Adolescent bullying involvement and perceived family, peer and school relations: Commonalities and differences across race/ethnicity. *The Journal of Adolescent Health, 41*(3), 2283–2293.

Stein, B. D., Elliott, M. N., Tu, W., Jaycox, L. H., Kataoka, S. H., Wong, M., & Fink, A. (2003). A mental health intervention for schoolchildren exposed to violence. *Journal of the American Medical Association, 290*(5), 603–611.

Sterzing, P. R., Shattuck, P. T., Narendorf, S. C., Wagner, M., & Cooper, B. P. (2012). Bullying involvement and autism spectrum disorders: Prevalence and correlates of bullying involvement among adolescents with an autism spectrum disorder. *Archives of Pediatric and Adolescent Medicine, 166*(11), 1058–1064. doi: 10.1001/archpediatrics.2012.790

U.S. Department of Education. (2011). *U.S. Education Department releases analysis of state bullying laws and policies* [Press release]. Retrieved from http://www.ed.gov/news/press-releases/us-education-department-releases-analysis-state-bullying-laws-and-policies

U.S. Department of Health and Human Services. (n.d.). *What is bullying?* Retrieved from http://www.stopbullying.gov/what-is-bullying/related-topics/index.html

Veenstra, R., Lindenberg, S., Oldehinkel, A. J., De Winter, A. F., Verhulst, F. C., & Ormel, J. (2005). Bullying and victimization in elementary schools: A comparison of bullies, victims, bully/victims, and uninvolved preadolescents. *Developmental Psychology, 41*, 672–682.

Wang, J., Iannotti, R. J., & Nansel, T. R. (2009). Four forms of school bullying behaviors among U.S. adolescents and their association with sociodemographic characteristics, parental support, and friends. *Journal of Adolescent Health, 45*(4), 368–375.

The White House. (2011). *Press briefing by Press Secretary Jay Carney, Domestic Policy Council Director Melody Barnes, and Secretary of Education Arne Duncan* [Press release]. Retrieved from http://www.fednews.com

CHAPTER 22

Crisis Intervention With Adolescent Victims of Sexual Assault

Kristen Zaleski

CHAPTER OBJECTIVES

- Describe the principles of crisis work with adolescent victims of sexual assault;
- Explain the neurobiological components of how a trauma can interfere with identity development during adolescence;
- Explain the basic tenets of psychological first aid and how to use them with an adolescent victim of sexual assault;
- Differentiate between the cultural, neurobiological, psychological, and family characteristics of adolescent sexual trauma and how social workers can be instrumental in beginning the healing process.

CASE VIGNETTE

Robbie is a 16-year-old gay male of mixed ethnicity who presents to the emergency room for a forensic sexual assault exam. He describes meeting a 21-year-old man online and beginning a relationship with him two months ago. Last night was the first time they had met in person. Robbie remembers going to dinner and drinking a beer in the car on the way to a movie. He then blacked out and was sexually assaulted by his date. When Robbie returned home, he told his parents and immediately reported the assault to the police. As part of the sexual assault investigation, Robbie has been brought to the hospital to undergo a DNA evidence exam and receive prophylaxis medication to prevent sexually transmitted diseases.

Robbie is met by the social worker to provide support and obtain the details around the sexual assault for the police report. Robbie admits to feeling ashamed and embarrassed and is unsure if he wants other people to know what happened. He questions if he even wants to follow through with the police report. He shares that he is afraid that other people at his school will find out about his assault and spread rumors about him. He is also afraid his parents are angry at him for keeping the date with the older man a secret and blames himself for being "so stupid." He states, "Being gay is hard enough; I don't know how I am going to deal with this, too."

INTRODUCTION

Working with an adolescent victim of sexual trauma in a crisis setting is a challenging experience for a new social worker. Providing supportive, ethical, and competent social work practice is essential for the recovery of the adolescent victim. In a very brief period of time, the social worker has an obligation to help the traumatized adolescent begin their journey of healing, assist with forensic evidence collection, the police interview, provide family crisis therapy, and help re-stabilize the social network of the trauma victim that promotes the post-assault healing. The various roles involved in the aftermath of an adolescent sexual assault is a juggling act that involves a multitude of providers from the social welfare and medical systems, as well as many legal authorities such as the interviewing police officer, the detective, and district attorney. This can be overwhelming for the victim. This chapter will explore the various elements involved in the medical and psychological responses to a sexual assault, and discuss the unique features of Robbie's case to showcase how important social work services are to promoting trauma resolution for the long term.

MICRO PERSPECTIVE

Adolescent Psychosocial Development

According to Erikson (1968), the adolescent psychosocial stage spans ages 12 to 18. Erikson argued that the *psychosocial crisis* of the adolescent in Western society was resolved when the adolescent successfully forms a lasting identity and strong sense of self-worth. If the adolescent encounters social isolation and trauma during these formative years, the end result is often low self-esteem and what Erikson termed *identity confusion*. Thus, stress or trauma during this stage carries significant implications for the adolescent throughout the lifespan. Sexual trauma has a destabilizing effect on the psyche of the teen; this creates the potential for identity confusion and shifts in a teenager's sense of mastery and safety within his or her social world (Mishne, 2001; Pervanidou, Kolaitis, & Chrousos, 2011). As a result, it is important for clinicians to understand the risks that trauma can present to an adolescent in this developmental stage.

An example of how identity confusion can begin is illustrated in Robbie's vignette. Robbie identifies as being gay and longs for a romantic relationship. As a result, he met a man online and agreed to meet in person. He also decided to drink a beer with his date, and concealed these things from his parents. Each of these elements illustrate that Robbie is still testing the bounds of his sexuality, his relationship with his parents, and his social values. As a result of the perpetrator's actions, Robbie is experiencing shame and guilt that are key elements to his sense of self-worth and esteem. This can inhibit his ability to establish his sense of self-worth. If Robbie interprets this trauma to mean he is at fault for the sexual assault, this can alter his sense of safety in the world (Mackay, 2002).

One traumatic occurrence can be an obstacle to healthy adolescent identity development and can stall or prevent the maturation of adult independence, self-reliance, and the ability to self-care. For instance, teenagers who have a history of sexual abuse have difficulties with physical and emotional intimacy in their relationships (Feiring, Simon, Cleland, & Barrett, 2013). Trauma increases the propensity to enter violent dating relationships (either as a victim or aggressor) with teens that harbor a history of unresolved sexual assault (Briley, 2004; Smith, Leve, & Chamberlain, 2006). Substance abuse is also found to be higher with teens who have a history of trauma (sexual or other) as compared their peers who have no trauma history (Danielson, 2010). Research shows that both male and female adolescents are more promiscuous than their non-traumatized peers (Smith, Leve, & Chamberlain, 2006). Cavanaugh (2013) found that female teenagers with a history of posttraumatic stress are seven times more likely to engage in unprotected sexual intercourse, suggesting trauma can impact long term sexual health and self-care.

In addition to creating risks for healthy identity and relationship development, trauma can contribute to negative health and mental health outcomes. The most common mental health problems experienced with adolescent victims of trauma are depression and posttraumatic stress disorder (Hirth & Berenson, 2012). Additionally, research shows that childhood trauma increases the likelihood of being diagnosed with an anxiety disorder, chronic somatic complaints and disorders, and physical illness such as chronic fatigue syndrome, asthma, heart disease, and diabetes (Buckingham & Daniolos, 2013).

The negative outcomes described above are understood when one considers how a trauma can impact the brain. The immediate aftermath of a sexual trauma is a salient time for a social worker to understand the young person in front of them and tailor their intervention according to each unique situation. In Robbie's case, the social worker will have to cater the social work intervention to Robbie's trauma symptoms, which include self-blame, shame, and self-doubt, while reinforcing Robbie's identity development of being gay and being an autonomous teenager. This is a delicate balance in a crisis setting, and the social worker can draw upon the knowledge of adolescent neurobiology to inform the next steps in the emergency department. This is will be discussed in the following section.

The adolescent brain has more potential to be influenced by trauma than most other times of the lifespan (Karlsson & Karlsson, 2010; Romer & Walker, 2007). Crisis workers dealing with sexual assault need to develop an understanding of the neurobiological underpinnings that can influence the severity and duration of the effects of the trauma.

Adolescent Neurobiology

By the age of five the human brain is 95% of its adult size. During infancy, the brain has an explosion of neuronal growth that will develop into pathways for emotional and cognitive development (Schore, 2003). The first five years is a crucial time for brain development and an infant with "good enough" parenting will rapidly develop language and physical skills. Hebbian theory, named after Donald Hebb in 1949, is a theory of synaptic plasticity that describes how neurons that "fire together, wire together" (p. 66; Shatz, 1992) and become more permanent in the brain's architecture. In other words, if one neuron causes another neuron to fire, and they do so repeatedly, the two neurons tend to connect more strongly. The neural architecture of the brain depends on this neural pruning, where the more frequently reinforced neuronal experiences become entrenched and less active neural pathways are pruned away (Applegate & Shapiro, 2005).

Adolescence is another time in a person's life where the opportunity to re-wire emotional and cognitive states occurs with a greater salience than any other time in development. Around the time of puberty (sometime between ages 11 and 12) the adolescent will once more experience a rapid neural pruning. So, two teens who spend equivalent time playing video games or soccer respectively will have different physical and cognitive abilities refined for their adult years. This is good news for teenagers who had negative life experiences during early childhood. Positive emotional experiences during adolescence can begin to repair some earlier damage. That is, a teen who experienced profound sadness as an infant but has experienced life as more happy and fulfilling as a teenager will have the opportunity to create stronger neural circuitry in order to hard wire happier experiences. Additionally, if sadness or fear is experienced less, then those negative emotions will decrease their neural connectedness, and lose prominence. This in turn allows for the positive neural connectedness (emotions) to be more prominent, creating a happier person to enter adulthood (Casey & Jones, 2010; Schore, 2003).

The nervous system is controlled by the brain, specifically the brain stem, and reacts to the emotional experiences that the person may encounter. The fight, flight, freeze response is directly related to the nervous system's activation in the wake of stress. That is, when an individual is faced with danger, the nervous system will activate sympathetic responses such as fighting the danger or running away, as a protective mechanism to prevent traumatization, injury, and death (Applegate & Shapiro, 2005). If the person is trapped, such as being overpowered during a sexual assault, the brain stem may shift the body into a parasympathetic state which results in the freeze response (Levine, 1997). This response results in the person feeling like they cannot move or run away and as a result they may mentally dissociate from the traumatic event.

Many sexual assault survivors will report experiences where they felt out of their body during the trauma event. Some individuals will have full memory of the assault and others will not. For most sexual assault victims, the freeze response serves as a "last resort" defense and prevents the assailant from hurting them further and causing substantial physical injuries which could have happened if the victim kept fighting. Understanding this biologically adaptive response (it is present in reptiles and mammals too) is important for sexual assault victims to understand. During the investigation of the assault authority figures will ask why the victim did not fight back. This has potential to create feelings of shame in the victim if he or she does not understand that their body did not allow them to have a choice in this mechanism.

While the adolescent brain is experiencing a rapid growth spurt in the neurobiological sense their social environment is also expanding. Teens have a wider variety of choices in front of them as compared to the childhood stages. The adolescent becomes preoccupied with social engagements, school demands, adjusting to their changing body shape and size, and becomes more interested in peer relationships than ever before (Tallman, 1961). Within this new world are perilous options for them, many of which may contain significant risks that the teen brain cannot yet understand or appreciate. Engaging in unprotected intercourse, experimenting with drugs, and participating in dangerous physical activities are temptations most adolescents will encounter at one point during their development. There is evidence to show that an adolescent brain may even be wired to enjoy risk taking opportunities. Sanders (2013) reports how "Neuroimaging studies demonstrate that adolescents may experience greater emotional satisfaction with risk-taking behavior" (p. 355). As a result, teenagers find themselves in more life-threatening, and ego-threatening, situations more often than most adults.

Social workers who provide support to adolescents must have a grasp on how to allow a teenager to experiment safely and to allow for the teenager to talk about their thrill-seeking behaviors. Hornberger (2006) states,

> Those counseling adolescents must understand that certain levels of experimentation in lifestyles and social behavior characterize normal adolescence. Risk taking is a normal part of human development. People will not grow and change without taking risks and experiencing success and failure. Helping adolescents discover their areas of competence and helping them achieve a reasonable level of self-confidence is key to healthy identity development. (p. 243)

Mental health researchers believe that adolescent risk-taking is a necessary part of forming identity. The key to successful identity formation is not whether they succeed or fall behind with the risks they decide to engage in, but how they feel about the consequences that will happen after the risky behavior is performed. When an adolescent has the fortune to find a support system that can help him or her understand their feelings, while at the same time provide an environment of safety and security, the better it is for the adolescent's brain as it shapes neural circuitry. In the case of Robbie, empathic intervention from the social worker (and other support personnel in the ED) is essential to help him feel more at ease and less fearful. Robbie reports fear that his peers will find out about his sexual assault, he is worried his parents are angry, and he is questioning his sense of safety in general. These issues must be attended to during the crisis as a key transformative intervention to help shape positive coping with Robbie's brain in the wake of the traumatic event.

Assessment

In the Robbie vignette, he met an older man on the Internet for a date, and the older man took advantage of the risk Robbie was taking, and sexually assaulted him. Robbie's sense of mastery over his world, and his resulting self-esteem, can be negatively altered. The support in the wake of the crisis from his relationships, such as peers or authority figures, can help shape his ability to process the negative event and not have it alter his sense of independence (Symonds, 2010). Consequently, if Robbie's self-blame is not resolved, the resulting shame, self-loathing, and regret can influence his neurobiology toward a more negative emotional state that has the potential to linger for his lifetime. A proper biopsychosocial assessment will assist a social work practitioner with identifying the salient issues the trauma has stirred within the adolescent's psyche and how the worker can begin to assist in the crisis setting.

Sexual Identity

Attention to sexual identity is crucial in working with sexual assault survivors. Robbie is beginning to identify himself as a sexual being, and a sexual assault will often affect the clarity with which he sees himself. Thus, the already difficult questions related to sexual identity in this developmental stage may become even more challenging for a victim of sexual assault.

Research tells us that gay-identified youth, when compared to heterosexual or even racial identity formation, have a much harder time finding role models in their communities to help them develop a healthy sense of self (Rosario, Schrimshaw, Hunter, & Braun, 2006). In fact, most lesbian, gay, bisexual, transgender, queer, and intersexed (LGBTQI) youth are not raised in accepting communities that support and reinforce their sexual identity. Being sexually assaulted can "reawaken a conflict on sexual orientation" that had been previously resolved (Dunn, 2012, p. 3442). For Robbie's social worker, attention to his sexual identity is almost as crucial as the trauma work itself. As Dunn (2012) suggests,

> Men who experience homophobic abuse are helped by accepting a victim identity, but only if they can quickly move on from it by reconstructing a masculine gay (nonvictim) identity. This process can be facilitated by agencies such as the police and victim services, provided they help men exercise agency in "fighting back"; that is, resisting further victimization and recovering. (p. 3442)

Further, sexual identity is important within the context of virginity for all youth. If the sexual assault was the first sexual encounter, it is important for the teenager to understand his or her virginity is not taken away. Many adolescent sexual assault counselors will reinforce that virginity is a choice, not a physical commodity that can be stolen by a perpetrator. Reinforcing this fact to an adolescent can help him or her feel less victimized and more in control of his or her body.

Social work conversations about sexual identity should complement the developmental age the teenager appears to be and also the cultural and religious framework with which the client identifies. Often, chaplains in hospitals and the client's religious figures will talk to the client about sexual identity and virginity after an assault. Further, having a similar conversation with the parents of the teenager is also an important intervention around sexual identity and virginity. The sooner the teenager feels in control of his or her body once again, and that the adults around him or her support that control, the faster his or her nervous system can recalibrate and recover from the trauma.

Mental Health History

In addition to understanding the client's sexual history, the social work clinician should also gather information on the client's mental health history. Studies show that adolescents who develop depression will be less empathically attuned to themselves and others and will also engage in suicidal preoccupation (Black & Possel, 2013).

Talking with Robbie about his history of depression and accompanying suicidal thoughts is always an important area to explore. Additionally, Robbie's history or potential to hurt himself in a non-lethal way is another important assessment issue. Self-injury can take many forms, such as restrictive eating, binging and purging, cutting or burning his body, and even engaging in reckless physical activities. It is important to assess whether there is any history of acting out in these ways and help Robbie understand what he might be feeling that may precede these behaviors. With that in mind, it is important to note that research indicates having a history of self-injury does not necessarily predispose them to suicide attempts (Zetterqvist, Lundh, & Sveden, 2013). However, teenagers with no history of trauma rarely engage in self-injury. It is the teenager who has experienced neglect, trauma, or what researchers term as "adverse life events" that most typically demonstrate such behaviors (Tormoen, Rossow, Larsen, & Mehlum, 2013; Zetterqvist et al., 2013). As with any social work biopsychosocial assessment, it is important to take into account all risk factors, such as socioeconomic status, history of abuse, family history of mental illness, and the teenager's self-reports of how he or she copes with stress or conflict.

Diversity Considerations

LGBTQI individuals face specific challenges in adolescence. The teenage years are often the time that the LGBTQI individual may decide to "come out" to parents and social groups (Ford, 2003). The coming out process is a delicate one for most teenagers, involves a unique shift in identity development, and often involves fear of others not accepting their identity. If the coming out process is experienced with little support, studies show serious adolescent development issues can be impacted such as identity confusion, low self-esteem, depression, alienation, withdrawal, substance abuse, and indulgence in self-destructive behavior (Ford, 2003). The lack of acceptance can take a dramatic toll on the nervous system of adolescents, causing some to develop symptoms of Posttraumatic Stress Disorder (PTSD; D'Augelli, Grossman, & Starks, 2006). Studies have also shown a higher proportion of LGBTQI adolescents have been bullied when compared to their heterosexual peers (Beckerman & Auerbach, 2014), which also contributes to the increase in PTSD symptomology. For more information on bullying, please see Chapter 21.

Marshall et al. (2013) analyzed more than 12,000 adolescent health reports from The National Longitudinal Study of Adolescent Health to see if there were any differences in depression and suicide within adolescents who identified as "sexual minorities" (p. 1245). Their results indicated greater depressive symptoms and suicidal thoughts with sexual minority youth in early adolescence. The authors also found that once those symptoms emerged they lasted from adolescence into adulthood (Marshall et al., 2013). As Robbie was expressing to his social worker in the vignette, "being gay is hard enough." Having a social worker understand the unique challenges facing sexual minority youth and explore this issue up front in the treatment process can be beneficial to psychological identity development.

Crisis Intervention

Crisis intervention is a skilled intervention practice that allows the clinician to see "which factors of the crisis need to be punctuated to adequately address the crisis—which parts of the clients' story are drawn into the foreground or dropped in the background" (Miller, 2011, p. 39). This chapter highlights the important "punctuation" marks around adolescent sexual assault related to identity formation (i.e., sexual identity, social relationships, and mental health) and how the neurobiology of a trauma can affect these elements. With these important variables in mind, the focus will now shift to how crisis intervention can be performed within this context.

Psychological first aid (PFA) is an evidenced-based practice that has eight "core actions" to treating a person in crisis: contact and engagement, safety and comfort, stabilization, information gathering, practical assistance, connection with social supports, information on coping support, and linkage with collaborative services (Ruzek, Brymer, Jacobs, Layne, Vernberg, & Watson, 2007). The goal, as with any crisis technique, is to return the client back to pre-trauma functioning.

In the case of Robbie, the objective of the "contact and engagement" phase means the clinician would need to establish quick rapport and communicate to Robbie that he is safe and able to talk freely without judgment. As the rapport is built, the clinician would focus on the "safety and comfort phase" which involves educating Robbie about why he is in the hospital, helping him understand the forensic interview, and attend to any other of Robbie's concerns regarding his physical and emotional well-being. Sometimes, seeing law enforcement of the Department of Children Services social workers can evoke fear that the adolescent is in trouble. For instance, Robbie might fear he will be in trouble for drinking alcohol or lying to his parents. The clinician should assess if these are concerns for Robbie and help him to understand how each professional is there to take care of his needs. A sexual assault can also leave physical injuries that a person in crisis may not disclose immediately. The social worker should try to address any physical discomfort before the mental health intervention begins. This is the important piece of stabilization in PFA.

The next phase of PFA is to gather information and explore the most salient issues to Robbie. In the vignette, he identified his biggest concerns as his friends finding out he was assaulted (and also debating on whether to file the police report because of that fear) and he is also concerned he is in trouble with his parents. These issues should be the first to be explored and help Robbie to explain to you his concerns. Often, this may involve his family where a discussion can be facilitated that he is not in trouble and his parents are not angry with him.

Another way to help with Robbie's concern is to involve the reporting police officer to explain confidentiality around sexual assault reporting. Victims of sexual assault, and all minors under the age of 18, are protected from public crime reports making it impossible for Robbie's peers to know he was a victim of a trauma. Both interventions mentioned can involve both Robbie's parents and the reporting officer. These are examples of the next few elements of PFA that include practical assistance and connection with social supports. This is discussed further in the mezzo section of this chapter. Referrals to sexual assault counseling centers and lesbian, gay, bisexual, transgendered, queer, and intersexed (LGBTQI) groups would be the final element of PSA that involves linking the client to supportive referrals when he has completed the services your agency provides.

If time allows, the clinician could explore areas of self-blame that can negatively affect his trauma symptoms such as sexual identity confusion, fear of bullying by peers, and drug use or abuse. Crisis intervention techniques do not need to take a lot of time to perform, but a good alliance with the adolescent client is necessary to solicit the self-blame and shame that is so often prominent in a victim's post assault reactions. Once the clinician has assessed the "punctuated" areas following the trauma and allowed Robbie to consider more realistic cognitive constructions of the events, the work of involving law enforcement and parents can begin. The final PFA intervention will be to refer Robbie to support networks that can reinforce that sense of safety and self-acceptance that the clinician has introduced during the crisis work. These aspects are discussed next.

MEZZO PERSPECTIVE

This section will discuss issues that arise in the crisis work with adolescents and can be important when applying PFA. As with any social work intervention, it is important to always be aware of the presenting issues of the client and the nature of the assault. An assessment with a youth who was sexually assaulted by a family member will proceed differently than a youth who was sexually assaulted by a stranger. Every sexual assault case is unique and the social worker's training will be important in guiding how to assess the abuse. The following discussion will explore the major issues at a mezzo level that confront a traumatized youth, regardless of the details.

Law Enforcement

A victim under the age of 18 will come into contact with many investigative personnel who will all ask similar questions about the assault. This process can be retraumatizing and often revictimizing for the adolescent (Tavkar & Hansen, 2011).

If possible, the best way to minimize the risk is to wait for law enforcement and child welfare representatives to arrive so all personnel can listen to the story at once. Some agencies employ the ideal strategy of using a one way mirror to allow for a single interviewer to be in the room asking the questions. If this is not possible, it is important to take steps to ensure information is efficiently and quickly shared with other professionals to reduce the risk of re-traumatization. Whatever the scenario, it is important for the social worker to provide crisis intervention and support first before hearing the narrative of the assault.

For the teenager, the interview with protective agencies can be the most threatening and have the greatest toll on the adolescent's sense of shame and embarrassment. Having a social worker alongside the adolescent during the police process is important and often necessary. The police investigators, though competent and protective, are used to interviewing suspects as opposed to victims. As a result, the interview can feel like an interrogation for a victim of any age, let alone a teenager who is biologically predisposed to experience high levels of shame already. Officers often ask victim-blaming questions such as, "Why didn't you fight the assailant off?" or "Why didn't you say no?" If the teenager was acting in secrecy, such as Robbie in the vignette, the police will ask about the reason for secrecy and attempt to rule out the possibility that the teenager is just accusing the assailant of assault to get out of trouble with his parents. It is the officers' duty to protect the assailant from being wrongly accused and they will ask questions to ascertain the facts of the alleged assault. With a social work advocate present during the police interview, the teen can have someone who can explain the purpose of the questions and make attempts to decrease the level of shame the teen can experience by this process. In the case of Robbie, having the social worker prepare him for the interview and provide some psychoeducation about why the officer may ask what appear to be blaming questions can be important in helping him understand the officer is only following interview protocol and is not blaming him for the assault.

Working With Parents of Adolescent Victims

Parents, or guardians, of adolescents can present in varying degrees of anger, sadness, and shock as they support the teen with the sexual trauma. An important role for the social worker is to assist the parent in decreasing the shame and blame felt by the adolescent, despite the parent's emotional reactions. As with any stage of grief and loss, the teen will fluctuate through anger and depression as well as denial and acceptance. The parent(s) must be educated about the normal emotional hills and valleys and allow the teen to experience them safely. The parent should be encouraged to talk to their teen in the aftermath to help him understand how the trauma has impacted him emotionally and help them establish a positive identity that does not involve shame or self-blame around the assault. That may be uncomfortable for some parent(s) who have a history of unresolved trauma in their own history and are unfamiliar with what "normal" emotional expression may look like. Working with families is critical in supporting the traumatized adolescent in reducing risk behaviors and depression. Stanik, Riina, and McHale (2013) found that within African American two-parent families, "greater maternal warmth was associated with less risky behaviors for sons and more paternal warmth and shared time with fathers were associated with less risky behaviors in youth" (p. 597).

Further, some parents become focused on what the teen did wrong, such as lying to go out on the date, and lose sight of the bigger issue that the teen was a victim of a crime. If possible, engage the family support system and respond to the most salient concerns. This could be in the form of a phone call or a family session in a hospital room. A social worker can be an important asset to the family system by providing empathic interventions to the parents' concerns. If time allows during a social work visit, bringing the teen and parent together to talk about their emotions and fears can help align the dyad to continue to empathically and emotionally expressive dialogue at home. These issues will be reinforced in the outpatient psychotherapy the teen and family will receive in the future.

For many teenagers, hearing their parent tell them "it's not your fault" can dissolve a lot of shame and self-blame. Most teens will not admit that their parents' support has a lot of power in the wake of a trauma. If the social worker can encourage this kind of empathic attunement between the teenager and the parent(s), this can assist in repairing the damage that the trauma has inflicted.

Utilizing an appropriate agency's resources to provide support to both the parent and the teen are important during this time. Resources may include pamphlets on normal emotional responses to grief, loss, and trauma, as well as referrals to mental health social workers that can see them in the longer term. School social workers are great referral sources for this kind of work.

In the case of Robbie, the social worker may decide to meet with Robbie's parents first to understand how they are feeling about the assault and how their son's honesty and sexual identity are intertwined in the parents' assessment of blame. The social worker may provide some psychoeducation about sexual assault and, if necessary, reassign the blame for the assault to the assailant, not the victim. Then, a conjoint session is also important for the social worker to realign the parents and Robbie together and help them find a path to traumatic healing as a family.

Transference and Countertransference Issues

It is important to remember that working with trauma survivors will often bring up countertransference reactions within the social worker. If the clinician has a history similar to Robbie's (LGBTQI identity, trauma history, etc.), he or she will need to be aware of his or her personal biases and not allow them to interfere with Robbie's care. Additionally, if the social worker has any judgment or personal beliefs about Robbie's choices or lifestyle, the ethical social worker will not let this be known to Robbie.

Besides the trauma, violence, and abuse in the social worker's personal life, he or she must battle the unfortunate reality that trauma can happen to anyone, at any time. Having good supervision from a licensed clinician is important in processing the ways in which the natural, personal reactions to trauma may get in the way with the helping process. Research shows that mental health clinicians who work in crisis settings have an increased risk of developing trauma reactions (called *vicarious trauma*) or even PTSD from their work with clients, despite never having experienced a trauma firsthand (Finklestein, Stein, Greene, Bronstein, & Solomon, 2015). Further, maintaining professional boundaries is an important step in shielding oneself from the trauma the client is discussing. However, research shows that when a social worker is experiencing stress from working with a traumatized client, boundaries can often become impacted (Cohen & Collins, 2012). Vicarious trauma research also shows that having good support from an employer, and most important a supervisor, can help buffer the effects of traumatic exposure for mental health clinicians (Bell, Kulkarni & Dalton, 2003; Finklestein et al., 2015).

Often, there are traumatic experiences that trigger countertransference, and personal psychotherapy is needed to untangle the personal reactions to the client's needs and concerns. Acknowledging that trauma affects the nervous systems of everyone involved, including the paid professionals, and allowing for emotional release is important. Part of providing ethical social work practice is knowing when the social worker may need extra attention and support from his or her supervisor, or a trusted friend or therapist, to help decompress from the stress that trauma work can bring.

MACRO PERSPECTIVE

In 1974, Congress enacted the first federal law on child sexual abuse titled the Child Abuse Prevention and Treatment Act of 1974 (CAPTA; Child Welfare Information Gateway, 2011). This legislation was groundbreaking at the time as the government began to acknowledge child abuse as a cultural problem with widespread implications. Before 1974, victims of child abuse were largely without advocates and abuse reporting did not exist. Accordingly, CAPTA provided money to states to develop child protective agencies that would investigate and protect abused children. The Child Abuse Prevention and Treatment Act of 1974 also created the National Center on Child Abuse and Neglect (NCCAN) to research and disseminate grant funding to the states in order to empower state governments to provide the best child welfare possible. The law also set forth a minimum standard to define child abuse, which all states accepting grant funds would be required to adopt.

Mandated reporting standards vary from state to state. Social workers are mandated in all 50 states to report the crime of sexual abuse of a minor under laws governing child abuse. The sexual assault report is often three pronged: alerting social welfare or child protective services (CPS), contacting the police department, and notifying the parents of the minor that they were a victim of a crime. The order of social work interventions will differ according to state and local guidelines and protocols used by varying agencies.

Understanding the macro forces within the American legal culture is essential in providing competent social work care for sexual assault victims.

Even though individual states have their own administrative and legal mandates for child sexual assault, the federal government issues requirements and offers funding to support the states' efforts in prevention and treatment. Social workers are important conduits to helping victims of violence access services that are available to them. In Robbie's case, he has a right to have a person accompany him to all investigative interviews and even on the witness stand, if the assailant is prosecuted in court. Additionally, victim services in each state may give financial assistance to victims of violence to help them pay for counseling and other legal fees that they may incur. Last, Robbie's abuse, though not at the hand of a relative, will still need to be cross-reported to child protective services. The social worker can help Robbie and his family understand their rights as victims and prepare them for the road ahead.

CONCLUSION

Sexual assault currently affects 1 in 5 girls and 1 in 20 boys, with the most common age being between 7 and 13 years old (Truman, 2011). However, most statisticians agree that the majority of sexual assaults on youth go unreported. Working with adolescent sexual assault requires a unique set of clinical skills that can be developed in even the most novice clinician. Following the guidelines outlined in this chapter will enhance the workers' interventions to dispel any shame and self-blame that can alter an adolescents' world for the lifetime.

INTERNET RESOURCES

- Rape, Abuse, and Incest National Network (RAINN): http://www.rainn.org
- Pandora's Project: http://www.pandys.org/lgbtsurvivors.html
- Rape Treatment Center: http://www.911rape.org
- Office of Juvenile Justice and Reporting: http://www.ojjdp.gov/
- The National Child Traumatic Stress Network: http://www.NCTSN.org
- The Headington Institute (receive a certification in vicarious trauma training): http://www.headington-institute.org

DISCUSSION QUESTIONS

1. Why is adolescence a vulnerable time for developing a lifetime of trauma symptoms?

2. What are the basic tenets of psychological first aid?

3. What unique issues of identity development are important to explore after a sexual trauma in adolescence?

4. What kind of macro issues are involved in sexual trauma in adolescence?

5. What are appropriate referrals to provide to an adolescent who has been sexually victimized?

REFERENCES

Applegate, J., & Shapiro, J. (2005). *Neurobiology for clinical social work: Theory and practice.* New York, NY: W.W. Norton & Company.

Beckerman, N. L., & Auerbach, C. (2014). PTSD as aftermath for bullied LGBT adolescents: The case for comprehensive assessment. *Social Work in Mental Health, 12*(3), 195–211.

Bell, H., Kulkarni, S., & Dalton, L. (2003). Organizational prevention of vicarious trauma. *Families in Society [H.W. Wilson - SSA], 84*(4), 463.

Black, S., & Possel, P. (2013). The combined effects of self-referent information processing and ruminate responses on adolescent depression. *Journal of Youth and Adolescence, 42*(8), 1145–1154. doi: 10.1007/s10964–012–9827-y

Briley, J. P. (2004). *Trauma responses, abuse history, and exposure to violence as risk factors in adolescent sex and non-sex offenders* (Doctoral dissertation). Retrieved from ProQuest Information & Learning.

Buckingham, E., & Daniolos, P. (2013). Longitudinal outcomes for victims of child abuse. *Current Psychiatry Reports, 15,* 342–349. doi: 10.1007/s11920–012–0342–3

Casey, B., & Jones, R. (2010). Neurobiology of the adolescent brain and behavior. *Journal of the American Academy of Child and Adolescent Neurobiology, 49*(12), 1189–1285. doi:10.1016/j.jaac.2010.08.017

Cavanaugh, C. (2013). Brief report: The influence of posttraumatic stress on unprotected sex among sexually active adolescent girls and boys involved in the child welfare system of the United States. *Journal of Adolescence, 36*(5), 835–837.

Child Welfare Information Gateway. (2011). *About CAPTA: A legislative history.* Washington, DC: U.S. Department of Health and Human Services, Children's Bureau.

Cohen, K., & Collins, P. (2012). The impact of trauma work on trauma workers: A metasynthesis on vicarious trauma and vicarious posttraumatic growth. *Psychological Trauma: Theory, Research, Practice, and Policy, 5*(6), 570–580. doi:10.1037/a0030388

Danielson, C. (2010). Risk reduction for substance use and trauma-related psychopathology in adolescent sexual assault victims: Findings from an open trial. *Child Maltreatment,15*(3), 1077–5595.

D'Augelli, A. R., Grossman, A. H., & Starks, M. T. (2006). Childhood gender atypicality, victimization, and PTSD among lesbian, gay, and bisexual youth. *Journal of Interpersonal Violence, 21*(11), 1462–1482. doi: 10.1177/0886260506293482

Dunn, P. (2012). Men as victims: "Victim" identities, gay identities, and masculinities. *Journal of Interpersonal Violence, 27,* 3442-3467. doi: 10.1177/0886260512445378

Erikson, E. H. (1968). *Identity: Youth and crisis.* New York, NY: Norton.

Feiring, C., Simon, V., Cleland, C., & Barrett, E. (2013). Potential pathways from stigmatization and externalizing behavior to anger and dating aggression in sexually abused youth. *Journal of Clinical Child and Adolescent Psychology, 42*(3), 309–322. doi:10.1080/15374416.2012.736083

Finklestein, M., Stein, E., Greene, T., Bronstein, I., & Solomon, Z. (2015). Posttraumatic stress disorder and vicarious trauma in mental health professionals. *Health and Social Work, 40*(2), e25–e31. doi:10.1093/hsw/hlv026

Ford, V. E. (2003). Coming out as lesbian or gay: A potential precipitant of crisis in adolescence. *Journal of Human Behavior in the Social Environment, 8*(2–3), 93–110. doi: 10.1300/J137v08n02_06

Hebb, D. O. (1949). *The organization of behavior.* New York, NY: Wiley.

Hirth, J. M., & Berenson, A. B. (2012). Racial/ethnic differences in depressive symptoms among young women: The role of intimate partner violence, trauma, and posttraumatic stress disorder. *Journal of Women's Health, 21*(9), 966–974. doi: 10.1089/jwh.2011.3366

Hornberger, L. (2006). Adolescent psychosocial growth and development. *Journal of Pediatric and Adolescent Gynecology, 19*(3), 243–246. doi:10.1016/j.jpag.2006.02.013

Karlsson, L., & Karlsson, H. (2010). Trauma and the adolescent brain. *Nordic Journal of Psychiatry, 64*(1), 33. doi: 10.3109/08039480903576749

Levine, P. A. (1997). *Waking the tiger: Healing trauma: The innate capacity to transform overwhelming experiences.* Berkeley, CA: North Atlantic Books.

Mackay, J. L. (2002). A psychodynamic understanding of trauma and adolescence: A case study. *Southern African Journal of Child and Adolescent Mental Health, 14*(1), 24–36. doi: http://dx.doi.org/10.1080/16826108.2002.9632421

Marshall, M., Dermody, S., Cheong, J., Burton, C., Friedman, M., Aranda, F., & Hughes, T. (2013). Trajectories of depressive symptoms and suicidality among heterosexual and sexual minority youth. *Journal of Youth and Adolescence, 42*(8), 1243–1256. doi: 10.1007/s10964–013–9970–0

Miller, G. (2011). *Crisis intervention primer.* East Orange, NJ: Wiley.

Mishne, J. M. (2001). Psychological trauma in adolescence: Familial disillusionment and loss of personal identity. *The American Journal of Psychoanalysis, 61*(1), 63–83. doi: http://dx.doi.org/10.1023/A:1002757409710

Pervanidou, P., Kolaitis, G., & Chrousos, G. (2011). Neurobiology of posttraumatic stress disorder in childhood and adolescence. In L. Sher & A. Vilens (Eds.), *Neurobiology of post-traumatic stress disorder* (pp. 137–152). Hauppauge, NY: Nova Biomedical Books.

Romer, D., & Walker, E. F. (2007). *Adolescent psychopathology and the developing brain: Integrating brain and prevention science.* Oxford, NY: Oxford University Press.

Rosario, M., Schrimshaw, E., Hunter, J., & Braun, L. (2006). Sexual identity development among gay, lesbian, and bisexual youths: Consistency and change over time. *Journal of Sex Research, 43*(1), 46–58. doi:10.1080/00224490609552298

Ruzek, J., Brymer, M., Jacobs, A., Layne, C., Vernberg, E., & Watson, P. (2007). Psychological first aid. *Journal of Mental Health Counseling, 29*(1), 17–49.

Sanders, R. A. (2013). Adolescent, psychosocial, social, and cognitive development. *Pediatrics in Review, 34*(8), 354–359. doi:10.1542

Schatz, C. (1992, September). The developing brain. *Scientific American, 267*(3) 60–67. Retrieved from http://www.scientificamerican.com/magazine/sa/1992/09-01/

Schore, A. (2003). *Affect regulation and disorder of the self.* New York, NY: W.W. Norton & Company.

Smith, D. K., Leve, L. D., & Chamberlain, P. (2006). Adolescent girls' offending and health-risking sexual behavior: The predictive role of trauma. *Child Maltreatment, 11*(4), 346–353. doi: 10.1177/1077559506291950

Stanik, C., Riina, E., & McHale, S. (2013). Parent-adolescent relationship qualities and adolescent adjustment in two-parent African American families. *Family Relations, 62,* 597–608. doi: 10.1111/fare.12020

Symonds, M. (2010). The "second injury" to victims of violent acts. *The American Journal of Psychoanalysis, 70*(1), 34–41. doi: 10.1057/ajp.2009.38

Tallman, F. F. (1961). *Treatment of emotional problems in office practice.* University of California Medical Extension Series (pp. 50–61). New York, NY: McGraw-Hill.

Tavkar, P., & Hansen, D. J. (2011). Interventions for families victimized by child sexual abuse: Clinical issues and approaches for child advocacy center–based services. *Aggression and Violent Behavior, 16*(3), 188–199.

Tormoen, A., Rossow, I., Larsen, B., & Mehlum, L. (2013). Nonsuicide and self-harm in adolescents: Differences in kind and degree? *Social Psychiatry and Psychiatry Epidemiology, 48*(9), 1447–1455.

Truman, J. (2011). Criminal Victimization 2010. Bureau of Justice Statistics Bulletin. Washington D.C.: Bureau of Justice Statistics. Retrieved from http://www.bjs.gov/index.cfm?ty=pbdetail&iid=2224

Zetterqvist, M., Lundh, L, & Sveden, C. (2013). A comparison of adolescents engaging in self-injurious behaviors with and without suicidal intent: Self-reported experiences of adverse life events and trauma symptoms. *Journal of Youth and Adolescence, 42,* 1257–1272. doi: 10.1007/s10964–012–9872–6

CHAPTER 23

Adolescents in Juvenile Detention

Brandon Burton

CHAPTER OBJECTIVES

- Learn best practices when assisting youth in detention centers;
- Explore the challenges facing youth who are housed in juvenile justice facilities with regard to receiving appropriate and gender-specific services to assist them in rehabilitation;
- Discuss current statistics and subsequent outcomes for youth in detention;
- Demonstrate how the intervention of multisystemic therapy has been proven to assist imprisoned youth and their families to help youth stabilize and reorient themselves to society while also lowering the juvenile detention recidivism rate.

CASE VIGNETTE

Yvette spoke through high security, double-plated glass via the type of sturdy handset found on now defunct public pay telephones scattered in short supply around various metropolitan areas. Her time to talk with her social worker was limited. Yvette, with a 1-year-old child, was being charged with homicide and is currently held in a high-security detention center. Yvette is a 17-year-old Hispanic female who has no immediate family to support her. Her grandfather, who will be taking custody of Yvette's 1-year-old son, does not want to have a relationship with her nor does he want Yvette's son to be involved with her now or in the future. It is too far off to tell whether or not the juvenile court will find Yvette guilty of her alleged crime and whether they will transfer her case to adult court. She is essentially alone and trying to survive in her new environment while also trying to do what is best for her son. She is confused and angry. She is among numerous adolescent detainees in a place where camaraderie comes with a price. Yvette lives each day in her detention facility afraid for her life and afraid of being sexually and physically accosted by either the other inmates or by the staff. Even if Yvette is found innocent, she will still be alone and need help with basic social services.

As a public child welfare social worker visiting inmates, the official job is often to interview and document statements for court. Seldom are social workers there to provide mental health services, unless particularly employed within a justice facility. Yvette began to sense that the social worker was not there to judge her but was there to assess as well as to be therapeutic, a skill often disregarded in child welfare interactions. As she sat there in her bright orange jumpsuit and her somewhat matted hair, she asked, "Will I ever get to see my son again?"

Though the social worker couldn't answer the question with any certainty, a therapeutic alliance with Yvette began to be established through the telephone by using empathy via tone of voice, eye contact, and effective listening. Yvette has a long history of involvement with the child welfare system where sexual and physical abuse was the unfortunate foundation of her traumatic childhood, yet she is not being offered any type of mental health supportive services. Yvette and the social worker were suddenly plunged back into their respective worlds as the loudspeaker screeched that visiting time was over. As they said goodbye and hung up their telephone receivers, a sea of young girls in identical prison uniforms, followed closely by imposing male guards, quickly swallowed Yvette into their fast-moving, anxious current down the hall. Yvette disappeared behind metal gates that slammed shut, cutting them off from society's view.

INTRODUCTION

Detained youth housed in juvenile detention facilities remain one of the most underserved and forgotten populations in the United States. Though originally established to intervene and defend children's best interests, the juvenile justice system has all too quickly metamorphosed into the same type of disciplinary core consistent with the adult criminal justice institution (Greenwood & Turner, 2011). This is not to say that adults who are also imprisoned do not also qualify for such forgotten members of society, but youth who were once troubled and who were once held or incarcerated were once thought of as being able to be rehabilitated. It was simply expected that society would be there to help them follow a steadier path by offering mental health, educational, and vocational services while housed in youth facilities. In fact, the tenets of the juvenile justice system rested in a foundation of evaluating children and adolescents differently than adults due to developmental differences and whereby a more sensitive judicial ruling toward offending children could be enacted

(Steinberg, 2009). In fact, the tide has changed from considering rehabilitation to demanding correction in regard to our nation's youth. Lee and Ameen (2012) argue that youth reoffend at a rate of 50% to 80%, which can only suggest a bleak future for detained youth not currently receiving adequate services to augment rehabilitation into society. Evidence has shown that by locking up detained youth without also providing them with the help required to regain their lives, society is not only endorsing injustice to our youth, but also encouraging youth to return to prison as adults with no hope of becoming respected citizens.

Youth often receive adult-like sentences by either being housed in adult facilities because of lack of funding in the juvenile justice system, or due to the direct-file process, which commits youth to being tried as adults. Society in recent decades moved from a rehabilitative mindset toward offending youth to a more punishing principle, whereby youth who committed any type of offense were now categorized as crimes and no longer simply "delinquent." In fact youth were now being designated as adults accompanied by proportional disciplinary action against them (Steinberg, 2009, p. 48). This seems to be a separate problem, where the main concern should be that adolescents are not yet adults and should simply not be treated as such; regardless of their crimes. There would be those who would disagree that if a youth commits murder, for instance, that the offending youth, regardless of age, should be tried and sentenced as an adult. Such an argument is without credible reports that such an approach would benefit the youth or public safety in general. In fact, trying youth as adults has shown to produce ill outcomes for all concerned. By evaluating and drawing from empirical data and research, the juvenile justice system procedures can begin to change from within. It is not reasonable for society to expect all offending youth to never commit crimes, whether serious or not, due to the complexities involved in all human behavior. It would be beneficial to treat children and adolescents as such before making life-changing judgments that will severely impact this youth population for a lifetime to come (Steinberg, 2009).

The disparity of detained youth minorities remains the most glaring of problems in the juvenile justice setting. Where blacks and whites are concerned, there remains a tremendous discrepancy in regard to detained youth and youth within the general population, where blacks make up 40% of juvenile justice facilities but only account for 15% of the overall youth population. Whites, on the other hand, consist of 35% of the juvenile justice population, but they make up 56% of the total youth population. There are overt "racial inequalities" in all aspects of the juvenile justice system (Lee & Ameen, 2012, p. 99). Not only do youth of color, who are also detained, face institutionalized racism from all facets of the juvenile justice system, from the law enforcement booking to judicial proceedings, they must also confront racism in environments outside of the juvenile justice settings as they return to their communities to attend school or obtain employment. Engel, Abulu, and Nikolov (2012) found the arrest rate for robbery was 10 times higher for African Americans compared to Caucasian youths. Therefore, as they

enter the correctional facility upon arrest, many of them are not previously determined to have mental health needs and therefore, they may go undetected. This is important to address in order to help them while they are incarcerated, to be reformed as much as possible.

Although girls housed in detention facilities are rarely discussed in the literature, both boys and girls who are in detention will be addressed in this chapter with current statistics for both. When evaluating offending youth's outcomes while in detention or upon release, detained girls remain a population severely needing quality interventions and rehabilitative efforts. Though there has been an increasing amount of adolescent females entering into the juvenile justice system, we do not have enough research or data to understand exactly why. In fact, between 1991 and 2003, the number of females sentenced to custody increased 52%, which makes up almost one-third of all juvenile arrests. We need to analyze why this is occurring and how we can change such a trend (Odgers, Robins, & Russell, 2010). Though the number of juvenile crimes is declining, the number of juvenile crimes involving girls is increasing at alarming rates. A key area to study is why there is an increase in female juvenile crime arrests and a decrease in male arrests in certain categories. For example, in 2009, females were responsible for 17% of juvenile violent crime arrests, 36% of juvenile property crime arrests, and 44% of the juvenile larceny-theft arrests. This is an increase from 2008, when female juvenile arrests, accounted for 30% of all juvenile arrests. While crimes like simple assaults, larceny-theft, and driving under the influence increased in females from the years 1998 to 2008, the data shows a decrease in overall juvenile crime but an increase in certain crimes by females under the age of 18, especially in the categories of "petty" crime (Engel et al., 2012, p. 341).

Girls in detention are also not protected from being transferred to adult prisons. There is relatively few, if any, gender-specific interventions being employed for girls housed in detention facilities and they are among some of the most needy due to the amount of mental health severity conditions and physical health risks that they face. A large percentage of males, and an even greater percentage of girls, in detention facilities have "one or more psychiatric disorders," (Abram et al., 2013, p. 1). The statistics on female adolescents detained in correctional facilities show that more than 90% were sexually active and 75% claimed they had sexual intercourse by the age of 13. In another study done on 197 girls in the system, nearly one-third had been pregnant, and more than half of them reported not using a condom in their last sexual experience. In addition, 20% of these girls claimed that they had sex with the intent to become pregnant, and 40% reported that the sex was casual and not part of a committed relationship. These are very high-risk behaviors for female adolescents, and, therefore, it is no surprise that these studies document high rates of HIV and STDs compared to male adolescents in custody and nonoffending females (Odgers et al., 2010). The method of simply housing girls in nonintervention type of chambers, without also providing them with quality health screening and time-limited interventions, has the potential to cause debilitating harm.

Juvenile detention facilities and staff also need to be better equipped at serving the detained adolescent population, especially youth of color and girls, by offering culturally sensitive services, hiring more qualified staff members, and offering training to such staff members to learn how better to handle and deal with detained youth without re-traumatizing them and exacerbating their mental and physical barriers. In order to expand the notion of more sensitive treatment of offending youth from all disciplines, such as law enforcement, detention, legal proceedings, and medical and psychological professionals, it would behoove a staff person working with detained youth to be aware of the many differences and cognitive developments that are forming, and in constant flux, within all children and adolescents (Steinberg, 2009).

Among the most glaring is the fact that social work practitioners are not as prevalent within juvenile justice environments and settings as they were in the past. There was what seemed to be a mass exodus of the social work profession from juvenile justice environments. What is currently left are a handful of psychiatrists, who are of course adequately trained and skilled in treating adolescents, but who are small in number to be able to adequately serve detained youth who have ample mental health needs. Social workers have skills that transcend other disciplines in that the approach to an individual does not solely rest on that individual, but seeks to connect a bridge of concerned and appropriate family and community members who can support the individual in a more positive direction where alienation and depression will be lessened by youth who are confined in detention.

MICRO PERSPECTIVE
Assessment

Adolescents' mental health needs are not being met, nor is there an adequate flow of information to and from their families and communities. Instead, children are kept at a distance and not able to access their own mental health treatments or legal proceedings. If a particular youth has family members who are able and willing to advocate and assist obtaining answers from the juvenile justice system's myriad rules, regulations, and procedures, then there is some relief on the part of the child. Most often, however, detained youth must fend for themselves. Their mental status and medication requirements, for instance, go unattended by staff and receive little attention in regard to helping the youth return to their regular medication regime, should they have one.

Some groups think that there is a window of opportunity for providing health maintenance for these adolescents living on the social edge by delivering targeted health services. For instance, encouraging the involvement of pediatricians and adolescent health care specialists to cooperate and work together on the improved plan for the implementation of medical services for these at risk youth is often recommended. There have also been recommendations by the National Commission on Correctional Health Care (NCCHC) to screen at the point of intake of these juveniles into the correctional facility in order to assess mental and physical health disorders. This is a proactive approach, rather than a reactive approach. Currently, services are only provided when they are recognized and they often go undetected and therefore, not addressed appropriately (Odgers et al., 2010, p. 441). Empirical studies have shown that detained youth, either diagnosed upon entry or prior, who present with psychiatric disorders remain vastly untreated from any type of mental health specialist (Abram et al., 2013).

Detained youth experience trauma in much higher percentages than the nonoffending youth population: more than 90%. Additionally, more than 60% of both girls and boys have seen violent acts firsthand (Abram et al., 2013, p. 7). Such "childhood traumatic victimization[s]" could be considered a direct link to juvenile delinquency (Ford, Chapman, Mack, & Pearson, 2006, p. 13). By first considering that the vast majority of detained youth experience emotional distress due to witnessing traumatic events, we can then help provide a more sensitive and trauma-informed system of care in the hopes to forge a bridge to rehabilitation into a successful reintegration into their community (Ford et al., 2006).

Substance abuse is a common factor among juvenile offenders who enter the juvenile justice system. Often, youth who are considered juvenile delinquents are also more prone to being involved in having substance use disorders in some capacity. Female youth detainees have twice the rate of substance use disorder and male youth detainees report three times the rate of substance use disorder when compared to the general non-offending high school youth population (Abram et al., 2013).

To date, Yvette has had one child, and aside from the grief and loss that she and her son endure, she has also disclosed to have had unprotected sex as early as age 13. This is not uncommon with girls in juvenile detention. Lederman, Dakof, Larrea, and Li (2004) argue that female young offenders engage in "high risk" sexual activity at a very early age, often before reaching the age of 15 (p. 323).

Psychoeducation that relates to safe sex practices, as well as planned parenting, is not a regular supportive service offered in detention. In fact, "female-focused" services in juvenile detention that would address common issues related to the female offender population, including "individual and family therapy, pregnancy, and HIV prevention," are universally not being offered, nor are girls in detention settings being approached in a humanistic manner by eliciting and empowering their individual strengths (Lederman et al., 2004, p. 332).

Therefore, girls are not being steered toward empowerment while they are in detention, nor are they being taught about physical or sexual safety issues. Yvette lived in poverty and suffered from a plethora of abuse growing up and relocated from foster homes to group homes until finally running away. She has never been officially diagnosed but based on her experiences of traumatic victimization, it would be a fairly safe bet that she would be a candidate for posttraumatic stress disorder (PTSD), as well as substance use disorder, since it was established in her case file that she had a history of methamphetamine use and gang activity where she disclosed to have been a witness to countless violent acts, as well as committing them herself. Despite this fact, Yvette claims that she was never diagnosed when in the child welfare system nor currently within the juvenile detention setting. This hindrance is what needs to be addressed at the time detained youth are brought in by law enforcement and placed in a juvenile detention location. Instead of being re-traumatized by being placed in a high-security holding tank, which was mainly staffed by male prison guards, it would be more beneficial to assess offending youth, like Yvette, by conducting a mental health screening and physical health examination.

Diversity Considerations

According to Arya (2011), African American youth make up only 17% of the total youth population, yet they make up 30% of those arrested and 62% of those youth tried in the adult criminal system. African American youth are nine times more likely than White youth to receive an adult prison sentence. There is a similar pattern with the Latino youth population, which is 43% more likely to be moved into the adult correctional system and 40% more likely to be incarcerated. Native youth also have a higher rate at about 1.5 times more likely to enter the adult criminal justice system and courts compared to white youth and 1.84 times more susceptible to being incarcerated in an adult prison. In relation to the overall population, African American and Latino/a youth make up the majority of the juvenile justice population. The rates, in fact, are alarming in that from all aspects of the juvenile justice system youth of color are being convicted and imprisoned in much greater numbers than non-Hispanic, white youth.

Not only are minority youths overrepresented in the juvenile justice system, but also female adolescents are becoming a much larger populace when it comes to arrests and sentencing of young persons. Though both genders suffer a lack of supportive and health services while in detention, and both experience high rates of recidivism, girls have a more complex array of mental health problems, which place them at even greater risk than boys for having less positive outcomes upon release. In fact, the female population in the criminal justice system have high rates of mental health problems and history of drug and physical abuse which makes them more vulnerable to engaging in illegal behaviors (Odgers et al., 2010). There are efforts being made to address the mental health aspect of incarcerated girls, but efforts have been minimal.

Interventions

Evidence-based interventions tailored for detained youth are readily available, but are not employed in any large number in the juvenile justice system. Henggeler and Schoenwald (2011) estimate that only 5% of youth detainees are offered the opportunity to partake in an evidence-based treatment. Though federal and state initiatives have only recently begun to focus on the implementation of the utilization of more evidence-based interventions, progress is slow. This is primarily due to funding and lack of data. Evidence-based intervention practices with offending youth are hardly new, but most have not been offered in any large-scale fashion nor have outcomes for such participating youth been studied universally (Henggeler & Schoenwald, 2011).

Henggeler and Schoenwald (2011) found that one of the most well-known and most studied evidence-based interventions with the detained youth is multisystemic therapy (MST), which has garnered significant positive outcomes; mostly the reduction of recidivism. MST engages a community, as well as a family approach embracing the specific individual circumstances of the offending youth in treatment. This process builds pods of positive networks for the youth and the youth's family to draw upon for assistance and support as opposed to being isolated and alienated; a feeling most exacerbated for youth who are released back into the community from detention. The foundation of MST intervention fuses a treatment plan for a youth's specific obstacles, alongside therapy sessions, which occur within a youth's own environment and community. MST incorporates utilizing cognitive behavioral therapeutic techniques while tending to the needs of a youth's caregiver(s) in order to bolster empowerment in parenting approaches. Psychoeducation is a large component in the MST paradigm where educating youth to better communicate and function together as a unit is an important goal. MST takes into account the individual and environmental stressors that exist for a client and, figuratively and literally, meets clients where they are at by working with clients within their own communities to more comprehensively engage with clients, build rapport, and foster their empowerment (Letourneau et al., 2009).

MST identifies series of subsystems for youth, such as family, peers, teachers, and community members who all will play a part in the actual treatment modality. Empowerment of the youth is established early on via these various stakeholders and, as such, is in alignment with "Bronfenbrenner's theory of social ecology" and can positively influence and affect the state of being in the youth (Henggeler & Schoenwald, 2011, p. 6).

In addition to constructing support for the youth, erected from their own natural environments, MST provides cognitive behavioral therapy for the youth while also offering tools and resources for the youth's parent(s) to help empower their child while also empowering their own parenting practices in a more positive way. As minority youth are overrepresented in the juvenile justice system on all counts, MST has been shown successful with youth of color, as it is a culturally sensitive evidence-based practice (EBP). What makes MST such a powerful intervention to apply to the detained youth population is that it has been shown to be effective cross-racially and cross-ethnically (Lipsey, 2009). As Yvette has no family to provide support during her detainment or after her adjudication, a mental health intervention could significantly improve her chances of becoming self-sufficient. As she has not seen a physician, psychiatrist, or a trained mental health practitioner to assess what her mental and physical needs might be, it might be expected for her to have feelings of hopelessness. The majority of detained youth, especially youth of color and girls, are not offered screening or assessments for pre-existing mental health or physical health issues. As there is a predominance of juveniles in detainment who suffer from psychiatric disorders (often having more than one disorder), it is imperative that the juvenile justice system changes its practices. Interventions focusing on rehabilitative approaches have been proven effective and have better long term results, as opposed to those concerned with corrective and controlling elements (Lipsey, 2009).

Transference and Countertransference Issues

Transference and countertransference issues cannot be avoided or predicted with clients. However, social workers can empower their practice as well as enhance their alliance with clients by tuning into the general societal attitudes often projected upon youth housed in detention facilities. For instance, the term *delinquent,* regularly used by the public and juvenile justice to refer to detained

youth and adolescents, has negative connotations that can further alienate detainees from society, keeping them misunderstood by others who do not consider the youth's psychological struggles and trauma history and often think of them as simply experiencing family troubles and being rebellious (Pearson, 2009). The social worker must approach this reality conjointly and openly discuss such attitudes with clients in detention to help prevent a client's potential transference of negative emotions and attitudes onto the social worker. In the same regard, avoiding blanket statements that discredit the potential of youth who are caught up in the juvenile justice system—and referring to detained youth by name and, as such, enabling them to begin to advocate for themselves for who they are and what they would like to become—is important to alleviate any potential countertransference stemming from the social worker.

Because every detained youth has a plethora of different experiences that have shaped who he or she is, it can be difficult to know whether a client is experiencing transference with his or her social worker. Therefore, it is vital, after a solid foundation of trust and rapport has been built, to address and discuss one's clinical observations with clients. Asking how clients are feeling and effectively reflecting back to the client what is being perceived can be a very effective strategy in working through potential transference issues with clients in a sensitive and yet direct manner.

In detention facilities, there is an element of distrust that detained youth and their families may feel about a social worker or mental health practitioner who is working with the youth and their family. Mainly this is due to legal concerns on the part of the youth and the family that the social worker or practitioner may reveal confidential information to the juvenile court that the youth or family members think could harm the circumstances of the youth. It would be wise to engage with the youth and family members and to discuss this topic of potential concern with them. Though time may be limited and trust issues prevalent, there is always time to establish rapport with youth, as well as to address any concerns about therapy sessions impacting the youth's legal proceedings (Engel et al., 2012).

Additionally, and similar to transference potentialities, a social worker cannot know for certain when or whether countertransference with a given client may surface. However, social workers who are self-aware will be more effective at preventing the kind of countertransference that disrupts the therapeutic process with clients. Self-awareness is not only key to reducing struggle in a client's life while also encouraging healing, but also to being successful at working with detained youth and their families in order to forge a concrete alliance with both client and their family members, if they are ready. For instance, the social worker providing service to Yvette in detention can choose to align with Yvette by relating to her as a human being requiring help and intervention, interdependent of the justice system's description of her and her alleged crime, or the social worker can choose to only see what is written about her on paper or what the popular opinion of Yvette may be. The social worker with self-awareness and empathy will be more successful in aligning with the client as well as counteracting transference or countertransference issues.

Legal and Ethical Concerns

According to Arya (2011), the United States has structured systems in place for the treatment of offending youth compared to offending adults, and since about 100 years ago when a juvenile justice system was conceived, the nation is sorely lacking in such a definitive separation between a child and an adult. Most offending youth begin in the juvenile justice settings. Consequently, a great deal of them end up being tried as adults which severely hinders their growth as emerging adults and creates a quagmire for the safety of both the offending children and the society at large. Youth of color are the ones who paid the price mostly for this new criminalization of our nation's youth as most juveniles were arrested for minor status offenses such as running away, curfew violations, and other various nonserious offenses. Since that time, things have shifted in the public opinion area, which has slowly been influencing public policy to stop arresting youth for nonserious infractions. It seems that a positive change, albeit slow in the political arena, is at hand for offending youth being offered consideration, at least, that rehabilitative services would benefit youth and society greatly, where 90% of citizens believe that a less corrective approach for offending youth can help the youth from committing crimes again (Arya, 2011). Yvette and her child could benefit from such shifting public opinion in order to stay free from any continued involvement with the juvenile justice system.

MEZZO PERSPECTIVE

The juvenile justice system could improve greatly if it had better practices that were tailored for servicing the mental health and physical needs of detained youth. Detained youth should be provided with quality evidence-based interventions that give them the tools to better regulate their emotions and teach them self-empowerment practices, such as having better understanding of their legal standing and mental health diagnoses. The more they are prevented from having access to treatment and quality services, the less likely they will become a nonoffending adult (Ford et al., 2006). A staff trained in cultural awareness and sensitivity to maltreatment and neglect could help the experience of youth who are in detainment. Communication between juvenile detention facilities, child welfare, juvenile courts, law enforcement, and child attorneys could also assist youth to better navigate the legal proceedings as well as help their families to gain some form of understanding of what is happening with their child. In the case of Yvette, the lack of substantial communication between law enforcement and child welfare is detrimental to her case as well as to her young son and his future upbringing. A more consistent linkage, whereby communication flows freely between child welfare and law enforcement, would greatly assist Yvette and her family.

MACRO PERSPECTIVE

Interventions for detained youth are not free. Federal and state financial programs irregularly provide monetary funding to employ evidence-based programs such as MST. Though the effective type of interventions like MST are not habitually used within juvenile detention facilities, one can imagine the effectiveness of such interventions based on statistical data and the lower rate of recidivism. Pearson (2009) advocates that by offering youth detainees both therapeutic and community services that the rates of recidivism decrease and where hope and outcomes for offending youth increase. There is much work to be done in regard to any evidence-based intervention being used in detention facilities to any large degree. The alternative is much worse. Recidivism rates skyrocket, which creates a more costly situation for taxpayers, but mostly youth are simply held in detainment and transferred either to more secure juvenile facilities or to adult prisons. It makes clear financial sense to invest the time, energy, and staff power to implement EBP programs with detained youth. Greenwood (2008) argues that adult criminals normally have had previous juvenile crime records and such a cyclical pattern of crime not only debilitates victims, but also creates turmoil within the economy where "billions of dollars" funnel into the criminal justice system each year (p. 186). It is there that they often remain with little hope of being released back to the community, just as Yvette has little hope of being offered quality interventions and services which would relate directly to the reduction of her likely recidivism, if in fact, she is ever released.

In December of 2010, legislative steps were taken by California Senate and Assembly members to address the issue of youth serving time in prison for life without the option of parole (LWOP). What was developed was Senate Bill 9: Fair Sentencing For Youth. Senate Bill 9 (SB 9) "authorizes" a prisoner who was under the age of 18 at the time of his/her "committing offense," and who had received a sentence to life without parole, the opportunity to file a "petition for re-sentencing." What SB 9 does is afford youth a potential opportunity for obtaining a lesser sentence after serving their minimum time in prison and after showing positive progress while in prison.

Not only is it important to gain perspective about what adolescents are experiencing on a behavioral, cognitive, and societal level, it is just as imperative to consider that adolescents are not adults. There are developmental deficiencies in adolescents when compared to adults to be able to conduct basic and responsible societal functioning in the world. According to Steinburg (2009), the cognitive development of youth stops by age 16 for the most part, but in other influential areas of the brain there are ongoing malleable and budding processes that do not take complete shape until approximately age 22. Inability to evaluate long-term consequences, uncontrollable impulsivity, and being more prone to peer influence are among the most noted. As Wolf and Gutierrez (2012) argue, another complexity in addition to developmental needs of all young adults in detention, is the fact that the arrest rate of females is higher than it has been historically, while the arrests of male youth are down. What needs to be offered in detention are gender-specific services for both male and female offenders. Social workers, such as the one working with Yvette, can help to advocate for their clients by seeking out alternative service providers in a given community who can address such gender-specific needs of detainees. Additionally, social workers can create alliances with those in detention facilities to work together towards offering more client-centered services. Collaboration with clients and community members alike has a better chance of overall success than a social worker working in isolation and in a non-collaborative approach.

CONCLUSION

Working with youth who are housed in detention facilities, like Yvette, present unique challenges that stem from public policy restrictions, a lack of standardized training of qualified mental health practitioners and programs, as well as a pervasive negative public attitude toward minors who offend. If there is to be any hope at rehabilitating youth who are stuck in the quagmires of the juvenile justice system, a universal approach that embraces quality and data-driven interventions, such as MST, must be employed. Advocacy groups must be realistic, yet tenacious, at striving for youth empowerment and justice. Funding must be allocated in a fair fashion as opposed to simply building more prison systems where youth are often housed with adult inmates. Though such daunting tasks may seem insurmountable there seems to be a shift, albeit slowly, in returning to a system of care that is leaning more toward healing the nation's youth as opposed to hindering their progress.

INTERNET RESOURCES

- Equal Justice Initiative: http://www.eji.org/
- The Children's Defense Fund: http://www.childrensdefense.org/
- The National Center for Juvenile Justice: http://www.ncjj.org
- National Criminal Justice Reference Service: https://www.ncjrs.gov/
- Office of Juvenile Justice and Delinquency Program: http://www.ojjdp.gov/
- National Center for Youth Law: http://www.youthlaw.org/juvenile_justice

DISCUSSION QUESTIONS

1. Why do you suppose juvenile detention centers turned away from treating youth with compassion and evidence-based mental health services and began leaning toward a punitive, adult-like approach?

2. How can society expect emerging adults, such as Yvette, to be rehabilitated to re-enter society successfully when the majority of detention centers do not have trained staff on site to assist?

3. Should the very nature of adolescence be taken into account when prosecuting youth and determining whether or not to place them in adult or juvenile settings? Where is the line drawn, if any?

4. How, and in what ways, can social work with at-risk youth prevent them from entering the juvenile justice environment?

5. Do the needs and services of girls in detention facilities differ from those of boys? If yes, how? If no, why not?

REFERENCES

Abram, K., Teplin, L., King, D., Longworth, S., Emanuel, K., Romero, E., . . .Olson, N. (2013). *Working for youth justice and safety.* Washington, DC: Office of Juvenile Justice and Delinquency Prevention.

Ameen, E., & Lee, D. (2012). Vocational training in juvenile detention: A call for action. *The Career Development Quarterly, 60,* 98–108.

Arya, N. (2011). *State trends: Legislative changes from 2005 to 2010: Removing youth from the adult criminal justice system.* Washington, DC: Campaign for Youth Justice.

Engel, L., Abulu, J., & Nikolov, R. (2012). Psychopharmacological treatment of youth in juvenile justice settings. In E. L. Grigorenko (Ed.), *Handbook of juvenile forensic psychology and psychiatry* (pp. 341–355). New York, NY: Springer Science + Business Media.

Ford, J., Chapman, J., Mack, M., & Pearson, G. (2006). Pathways from traumatic child victimization to delinquency: Implications for juvenile and permanency court proceedings and decisions. *Juvenile and Family Court Journal,* 13–26.

Greenwood, P. (2008). Prevention and intervention programs for juvenile offenders. *The Future of Children, 18*(2), 185–210.

Greenwood, P., & Turner, S. (2011). *Crime and public policy.* New York, NY: Oxford University Press.

Henggeler, S., & Schoenwald, K. (2011). Evidence-based interventions for juvenile offenders and juvenile justice policies that support them. *Social Policy Report, 25*(1), 1–28.

Lederman, C., Dakof, G., Larrea, M., & Li, H. (2004). Characteristics of adolescent females in juvenile detention. *International Journal of Law and Psychiatry, 27,* 321–337.

Letourneau, E., Henggeler, S., Borduin, C., Schewe, P., McCart, M., Chapman, J., & Saldana, L. (2009). Multisystemic therapy for juvenile sexual offenders: One-year results from a randomized effectiveness trial. *Journal of Family Psychology, 23*(1), 89–102.

Lipsey, M. (2009). The primary factors that characterize effective interventions with juvenile offenders: A meta-analytic overview. *Victims and Offenders, 4,* 124–147. doi: 10.1080/15564880802612573

Odgers, C., Robins, S., & Russell, M. (2010). Morbidity and mortality risk among the "forgotten few:" Why are girls in the justice system in such poor health? *Law of Human Behavior, 34,* 429–444. doi: 10.1007/s10979–009–9199–3

Pearson, G. (2009). Frontline reports. *Psychiatric Services, 60*(12), 1690–1690.

Steinberg, L. (2009). Adolescent development and juvenile justice. *The Annual Review of Clinical Psychology, 5,* 47–73.

Wolf, A., & Gutierrez, L. (2012). It's about time: Prevention and intervention services for gang-affiliated girls. *The California Cities Gang Prevention Network, 26,* 1–7.

PART III

Social Work Practice
Interventions With Diverse Communities in the U.S. and Global Action

CHAPTER 24

Public Health Social Work

Julie A. Cederbaum, Eddie Hu, & Heather A. Klusaritz

CHAPTER OBJECTIVES

- Develop an understanding of the context of social work practice within a public health framework;
- Learn the history of public health social work;
- Identify ways in which the Affordable Care Act (ACA) influences opportunities for public health social work;
- Learn how public health social workers provide services in the 21st century.

CASE VIGNETTE

Ramble, Missouri, is a mid-size town located just outside the large metropolitan area of St. Louis. Although surrounded by lush farmland, Ramble has a large number of fast food restaurants, a climbing obesity rate, and limited access to fresh fruits and vegetables outside of those purchased in national chain supermarkets. Community leaders, health providers, public health social workers, and community members work together to ameliorate this issue. Using a three-pronged lens—micro, mezzo, and macro—they work to identify the problems contributing to the issue. From the micro perspective, they note the issue is individual food consumption behaviors, particularly limited intake of fresh fruits and vegetables. Next, the mezzo lens highlights the issue of access: The community is a food desert, lacking access to fresh fruits and vegetables. The problem from a macro perspective is two-fold: The area lacks an ordinance related to number of fast food establishments and there are no established community areas for access to fresh fruits and vegetables (like a farmer's market). With the goals of primary, secondary, and tertiary prevention within their Ramble community, the coalition sprang into action. Their collective action created a solution to increase health and wellness among Ramble community members, stimulated fruit and vegetable intake, generated income for local farmers, and established a permanent farmer's market for the Ramble community.

INTRODUCTION

The implementation of healthcare reform in the United States has created a new opportunity to not only treat illness, but also focus on reducing health disparities through prevention. It is well established that along with genetic predisposition and environmental exposures, individual adoptions related to diet, exercise, tobacco, alcohol, and other substance use, among other risk behaviors, are the root causes of many of the chronic health conditions that cost the United States billions of dollars annually (American Public Health Association, 2013; DeVol & Bedroussian, 2007; Robert Wood Johnson Foundation, 2013b). The Group for Public Health and Social Work initiatives (2011) defines public health social work as "a contemporary, integrated, transdisciplinary approach to preventing, addressing, and solving social health problems" (para 3). This statement highlights prevention along with intervention and utilizes research, policy, and advocacy, along with clinical approaches to promote resilience and reduce risk. Based on the definition, public health and social work are natural collaborators; further partnership can increase provision of services at both the individual and population levels (Van Pelt, 2009).

Public health and social work share common goals "to improve the health, welfare, and social well-being of society-at-large" (Keefe & Evans, 2013, p. 5). Social justice is the driving force for public health and social work; both professions strive to enhance the lives of the disadvantaged and disenfranchised. Public health and social work share the same passion, utilizing tools such as social action and advocacy to change people's lives on individual, community, organizational, and legislative levels. Further, public health and social work have complementary skills and have become increasingly reliant on one another. Public health professionals are focused on epidemiology as an approach to understanding the health of a community, but they have become aware of how an individual's psychosocial experience influences his or her health. Social workers, most often practicing at the tertiary level, recognize the difficulties of providing intervention (services) after the problem has occurred and recognize the value and need for prevention of issues, not just solutions. Although the approaches are varied, the complimentary nature is critical in taking a holistic approach to ameliorating social issues that influence health and quality of life. Because public health social work takes a transdisciplinary approach to addressing and resolving social health problems (Boston University, n.d.), there are many opportunities to become change agents within the framework. Focused on resilience and a strengths-based approach to the promotion of health and reduction of risk (Boston University, n.d.), professionals from each discipline are practicing around the globe and serving all populations. Public health social workers are working as elected officials, researchers, advocates, educators, and program evaluators in all countries to enhance the lives of the disadvantaged (Keefe & Evans, 2013). This rest of the chapter discusses the history of public health social work and ways in which academicians and practitioners in the field can promote transdisciplinary collaboration to increase recognition and coordination of services (Ruth et al., 2008).

History

The disciplines of public health and social work are some of the oldest professions. Public health dates back to the 19th century when John Snow, a physician, helped stop the cholera outbreak of 1848 in London by using systematically collected data from neighborhoods that were most affected by the outbreak; he proved that the cholera epidemic was caused by contaminated water (Rothman, 2012). Dr. Snow also devised methods to locate where the first few cases of cholera had occurred; the work led to the development of new sanitation methods to dispose of waste. It is because of this that individuals today see public health practice as disease control and surveillance, advocating for vaccinations, health education, and promotion (Keefe & Evans, 2013). Like public health, the profession of social work also dates back to the 19th century. However, the impact of social work in the health arena was more grounded in its roots of social action. For example, Dorothea Dix, a well-known activist in the 1840s, saw that people who were suffering from mental disorders who could not care for themselves were lacking a place that could provide care for them. She lobbied state legislature and the United States Congress vigorously to create the first American mental asylum (Viney & Zorich, 1982). Later, Jane Addams, Lillian Wald, and many other activists led numerous political movements to improve health and services for women, children, and other disenfranchised populations (Buhler-Wilkerson, 1993; Lundblad, 1995). Based on this history, social work in the United States came to be known for providing services to individuals along with advocating for change in communities (Keefe & Evans, 2013).

Along with humanization of mental illness, it was in the areas of infectious disease control, maternal and child health, child abuse and neglect prevention, and the creation of settlement houses that public health social work can really be said to have emerged as an independent approach to practice, with efforts targeting changes to the health and well-being of the underserved (Ruth & Sisco, 2008). The creation of the Federal Children's Bureau in 1912 is an early example of how the U.S. government invested in public health social work (Kotch, 2005). This agency, set up to promote maternal and child health, was heavily staffed by social workers whose goal was the prevention of negative outcomes. The passage later of Medicare and Medicaid is another reflection of ways in which public health social workers' efforts contributed to policy change. During this time, and through most of the century, the public health approach was highlighted in the social work literature (Roskin, 1980). Efforts were also made to infuse a prevention model into social work education (Wilkinson, Rounds, & Carr-Copeland, 2002). However, it was the civil rights movement (and related social justice successes) that resulted in an increase in the number of public health social work programs and the presence of social workers in key health initiatives (Ruth & Sisco, 2008).

Current Status of Public Health Social Work

More recent history has seen a shift in the priorities of public health social workers. In the 1980s there was a shift of focus; new initiatives highlighted the AIDS epidemic, substance abuse, violence, and aging (Moroney, 1995). Social work literature has contributed to understanding these areas over the last 35 years; social activism among public health social workers continues to influence research agendas (including those of the National Institute of Health) as well as policy changes, including the Americans With Disabilities Act (1990), Mental Health Parity and Addiction Equity Act (2008), and, most recently, the Patient Protection and Affordable Care Act (2010). These priorities map on well to Healthy People 2020, the U.S. government's decade-long initiative to improve the health and well-being of its citizens (U.S. Department of Health and Human Services, 2013). Particularly, the Healthy People 2020 initiatives of access to health, educational and community-based programs, health-related quality of life and well-being, injury and violence prevention, mental health and mental disorders, older adults, social determinants of health, and substance abuse provide continued opportunities for public health social workers to influence health and wellness.

The Patient Protection and Affordable Care Act

With the passing of the Patient Protection and Affordable Care Act, commonly known as the ACA, the demand for social workers trained in health care has increased. Under the ACA, millions of uninsured Americans now have access to health care. This landmark legislation shifts the focus to ambulatory/community-based delivery models of care. Furthermore, the ACA emphasis on disease prevention through established clinical care will increase the demand for public health social workers trained in health prevention and education. Essentially, the ACA aims to reform the health care delivery system in the United States by expanding health insurance coverage to millions of the currently uninsured, limiting health disparities, reforming insurance, and implementing changes in financing and delivery of care (Patient Protection and Affordable Care Act, 2010).

The ACA and Implications for Social Work Practice

Health care reform will bring changes to the health care delivery system while providing opportunities for social workers, especially practitioners focused on service delivery in health settings. One of the features of the ACA is the 10 essential health benefits. Any new health insurance plan is mandated to provide these 10 benefits (i.e., ambulatory patient services; emergency services; hospitalization, such as surgery; maternity and newborn care; mental health and substance use disorder services, including behavioral health treatment; prescription drugs; rehabilitative and habilitative services and devices; laboratory services; preventive and wellness services and chronic disease management; and pediatric services; Centers for Medicare & Medicaid Services, 2013b). Coordinated and integrated care is the another core health care system change under the ACA. Coordinated and integrated care means integrating both general and behavioral health care in a systematically coordinated way to help individuals affected by both mental and substance abuse disorders. These individuals are more likely to experience premature death from complications of mental and substance abuse disorders or from untreated and preventable chronic illness resulting from poorer health habits associated with substance abuse or mental illness. Many of these individuals' health issues are treated in emergency care settings (Cederbaum, Guerrero, Mitchell, & Kim, 2014; French, Fang, & Balsa, 2011; Wu et al., 2012); increasing access to and use of primary care services can be navigated by social workers, helping high need/high risk individuals traverse the complex health care system (Centers for Medicare

& Medicaid Services, n.d.; Substance Abuse and Mental Health Services Administration, n.d.).

Public health social work practice is a natural fit for the ACA. Social workers possess the skills to provide coordinated and integrated care to clients, particularly through case management. The National Association of Social Workers (2013) defines case management as "a process to plan, seek, advocate for, and monitor services from different social services or health care organizations and staff on behalf of a client" (p. 13). Additionally, social work practice focuses on "person in environment" and takes a strengths-based approach to help clients achieve desired health outcomes. Furthermore, social workers trained in public health can use skills including assessment, assurance, and policy development to help reduce health disparities, assist clients, and advocate for change in the community and/or health care settings (Darnell, 2013, Keefe & Evans, 2013; Spitzer & Davidson, 2013).

Intervention

The strength of public health social workers is that they work on primary, secondary, and tertiary levels to address different health determinants to ensure that better care is provided to individuals (Keefe & Evans, 2013). Public health social workers focus on primary prevention and health promotion; in addition, they are aware of and incorporate culturally relevant care at all levels (macro, mezzo, and micro). Practitioners target communities to change the norms that influence individual behavior, along with their direct practice with individuals. Public health social workers employ social epidemiology and are aware of social determinants of health (behavioral and otherwise) and how these factors affect communities. They utilize technologies, such as Geographic Information Systems to promote healthy food access for children and women who are living in a food desert (defined as "areas that lack access to affordable fruits, vegetables, whole grains, low-fat milk, and other foods that make up a full and healthy diet"; Centers for Disease Control and Prevention,

2012 para 1; Walker, 2010; Widener, Metcalf, & Bar-Yam, 2011). Moreover, public health social workers conduct community assessments to identify the strengths and weaknesses of a particular community to reduce community health problems and, in turn, empower community members. In addition, they tackle community health problems through policy development and assurance to advocate, implement, and serve the community. Because of the many ways in which public health social workers intervene, it is challenging to identify any one way in which interventions are accomplished. The most valuable factor about the approach is its person-in-environment methods to changing both individuals and the systems they live within.

APPLICATION TO VIGNETTE

The goals of the efforts in Ramble, Missouri, were to facilitate changes for individuals and the community, which in turn would influence policy changes to effect sustainable changes to the food environment. This section details ways in which public health social work practitioners can facilitate changes to influence tertiary care, as well as influence primary and secondary prevention.

Micro Perspective

The goal at the micro level for the Ramble project was to modify the eating behaviors of community members, specifically by increasing vegetable intake. In addition to issues of access, familiarity with certain vegetables, comfort with preparation of those vegetables, and openness to trying new foods was deemed limited by community members. As such, the intervention on the individual level was focused on increasing access to and comfort with preparing food, with the goal of increasing vegetable intake. In the Ramble project, this was accomplished in a number of ways. Coalition members took a two-fold approach: First, they increased accessibility by (1) placing the farmer's market close to the health care facility where patients were accessing services and (2) providing

patients with vouchers that could be utilized at the farmer's market to purchase healthy fruits and vegetables. Both increased the feasibility of uptake by consumers. Second, coalition members put together a free cookbook with recipes that utilized the vegetables available for purchase at the farmer's market. Many were "old favorites" with a new take, highlighting how easy it could be to integrate more vegetables into their diet and influence their health.

Mezzo Perspective

As noted above, by working closely with a community-based health clinic (where medical professionals provide screening and medical care), the coalition identified a farmer's market location close to the health clinic. This not only brought a much-needed resource for fruits and vegetables into the community, it decreased the access issues that might make utilization of the market more difficult. A second strategy was to engage with local farmers. Because they were surrounded by a lush farmland, coalition team members engaged farmers to sell their vegetables at the farmer's market. For farmers, it was an opportunity to sell their goods locally (generating needed revenue) and for community members, farmers provided access to locally grown vine-ripened food.

Macro Perspective

Although agreement from the town of Ramble was needed for the land use by the weekly farmer's market, this was only one approach to system-level change. To understand the ways in which utilizing the farmer's market was making an impact on the lives of the individuals in Ramble, coalition members created an evaluation system. At each weekly farmer's market, data were collected from both consumer and farmers. Consumers were asked about eating habits, changes in diet, items purchased, and items that were most valued. To compliment this data, vendors provided information on weekly sales (amount of each type of fruit/vegetables sold). Using this data, coalition members were able to make an assessment of behavior changes at the individual (micro) level, as well as assess the economic influence of sales of locally grown foods on the income of local farmers (mezzo level).

PROGRAM PLANNING AND EVALUATION

Aside from using intervention, public health social work practice also involves program planning and evaluation. Most public health social workers, at some point in their career, will be involved with program planning and evaluation, and thus, it is important to be knowledgeable about the process. "Planning an effective program is more difficult than implementing it . . . good planning skills are prerequisite to programs worthy of evaluation" (Minelli & Breckon, 2009, p. 137). Effective planning and evaluation involves time, effort, practice, and training; most experienced public health social work practitioners and other health professionals still find program planning challenging because of the diverse work settings, resources, and populations (McKenzie, Neiger, & Thackeray, 2013).

Systematic planning is important for a number of reasons. First, planning requires the program designer to think about the future and try to anticipate possible problems that the program might encounter. Second, planning can bring community members or other program stakeholders together; this increases acceptance and enhances program transparency. Third, planning is empowering. Because of the extensive work that goes into a comprehensive program plan, once decision makers (e.g., administrator of an organization) approve the plan, practitioners/planners and implementers are empowered to provide the program. When all stakeholders are involved in the process and the comprehensive plan is approved, public health social workers eliminate the uncertainties that might hinder the program momentum. Last, planning helps program implementers and practitioners/planners know where they stand in the organization and provides structure and support for their roles (McKenzie et al., 2013).

Generally, developing an effective program requires planning. Planning has five steps: (1) assessing needs, (2) setting goals and objectives, (3) developing an intervention, (4) implementing the intervention, and (5) evaluating the results (McKenzie et al., 2013). Each step should be well thought out during the planning stages to ensure its efficiency and increase the likelihood that the program actually reaches the target population, providing relevant, evidence-based intervention. Prior to the setting of goals and objectives, public health social work practitioners should conduct some pre-planning activities; this gives practitioners direction in their planning and allows stakeholders to participate and give input. Understanding the community is also important to the planning process. Allowing stakeholders (e.g., target population) to be involved with planning will provide a much clearer picture of how the presenting problem is experienced by the target community or population. If practitioners assume they "know" the target community, it will likely lead to insufficient planning, which, in turn, results in an ineffective intervention (McKenzie et al., 2013).

During the planning process, practitioners/ planners should keep evaluation in mind. There are three types of evaluations: (1) formative (conducted prior to the intervention to gain information for program development or improvement), (2) process (conducted during the intervention to ensure the intervention is being administered as designed), and (3) summative (conducted after the intervention to gain insight into its outcome and impact; McKenzie et al., 2013). Each type of evaluation is essential to the success of the program. Stakeholders put tremendous effort (e.g., funds, time) into the creation/establishment of a program; evaluation is a way to show whether a program should be continued or eliminated or how it may be improved (e.g., quality, reach, and product). Evaluation can also affect policy decisions, raise awareness, and help improve future interventions (McKenzie et al., 2013).

The Centers for Disease Control and Prevention established a framework for program evaluation (1999), which includes six steps and four standards (see Figure 24.1). Step 1 involves engaging stakeholders. These should include individuals who (1) will implement the program, (2) be affected by the program, and (3) will use the evaluation results. In Step 2, the program is described. This is often done using a diagram/graph to show how the program will effect change. Step 3 is when the focus on the evaluation begins. Public health social work practitioners/planners will state the reasons for evaluation, including who will use the results and how the results will be analyzed. In Step 4 evidence is gathered. In this stage, practitioners/planners decide which method(s) will be used to collect evidence and what those sources of evidence may be. Step 5 includes the justification of the evidence gathered; practitioners/planners will compare evidence against standards of acceptability to judge the worth of the program. In the last step (Step 6), the goal is to ensure the lessons have been learned. In this step, practitioners/planners should make sure that end users (i.e., stakeholders) have access to evaluation data and that feedback is received from stakeholders. The four standards of effective evaluation are used as guidelines to decide among different evaluation options, all of which must meet (1) the minimum level of utility (useful

to users); (2) feasibility (pragmatic and viable); (3) propriety (ethical); and (4) accuracy (findings are considered correct; CDC, 1999).

The Changing Climate of Social Work Practice and Health Care Delivery

This ACA legislation will require trained social workers to assist with navigation through a complex insurance marketplace and continuing shifts in community-based health care delivery models. Occupational growth for public health social workers is expected to rise 33% by 2020; the need for social workers who provide services in outpatient care settings is expected to increase even more (48%; U.S. Department of Labor Bureau of Labor Statistics, 2010). A major shift because of ACA legislation, well suited for a public health social work perspective, is the increased focus on disease prevention, including efforts that engage communities in preventive services (Koh & Sebelius, 2010). Public health social work has the opportunity to engage in prevention activities across the spectrum. At the very root of health care

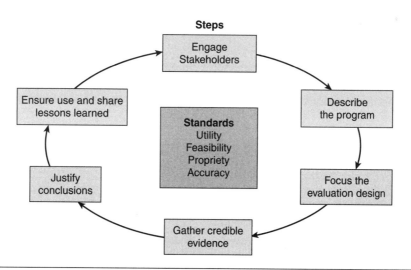

Figure 24.1 The CDC Framework of Program Evaluation

SOURCE: Centers for Disease Control and Prevention (1999).

reform is the recognition of a need for a conceptual shift from a health care system that focuses on the treatment of disease, injury, and disability to a health care system focused on primary and secondary prevention. The ACA's provisions that expand access to care through the Medicaid expansion, the Individual Mandate, and the Health Insurance Marketplace form the foundation for the needed pendulum swing to primary prevention. These provisions create tremendous demand for health care professionals trained in facilitating access to care, health insurance navigation and advocacy, and client empowerment. As the initial rollout of the Marketplace demonstrated, obtaining health insurance is a complex process that requires a high level of health literacy. Public health social workers are primed to engage with the previously uninsured population and assist clients through the complicated enrollment process. Further, social workers will need to be on the frontlines of advocacy activities to continue to push for further expansion of Medicaid in states where Medicaid remains at the pre-ACA coverage levels and millions of Americans remain without the health insurance critical for them to engage in preventive care (Kaiser Family Foundation, 2014).

Once individuals have insurance, public health social workers continue to be an essential component of the post-ACA health care workforce. The ACA also focuses on models of care that improve quality and lower cost. Many of these models of care, such as Accountable Care Organizations and the Patient Centered Medical Home (PCMH), require interdisciplinary care teams with values and patient care goals well-aligned with social work. PCMH is a model of care that is focused on comprehensive, relationship-based care of the whole person, with an emphasis on care coordination across settings and superb access to quality care (U.S. Department of Health & Human Services, n.d.). PCMH requires care teams take into account the multiple systems that impact a patient's ability to achieve health outcome goals, work to bridge care gaps, integrate primary and behavioral health care, and focus on the care of the whole person. Social workers are an integral part of this model

of care, helping to navigate patient transitions and facilitate community-based care, intervening at the individual, family, community and systems levels. Social workers also have a professional orientation uniquely suited to help the interdisciplinary care team understand the patient perspective and respect patient agency and health care goal setting.

Finally, the ACA's focus on Accountable Care Organizations (ACOs) reducing readmission rates provides another opportunity for social work. ACOs are a network of providers, clinics, and hospitals that collaborate to provide coordinated care for a population of patients and strive to reduce duplication of services, prevent medical errors, and improve quality outcomes (Centers for Medicare & Medicaid Services, 2013a). ACOs receive financial compensation for patient care that meets quality benchmarks. ACOs are centered on primary care medical homes that have interdisciplinary care teams, including social workers, and focus on an integration of primary and behavioral health care. Social workers in the ACO model can be engaged in a variety of care delivery opportunities. From clinical therapeutic behavioral health care, to health system navigators, to members of community-based care teams, to leaders of care teams designed to improve transitions in care, social workers are a vital part of the ACO model (National Association of Social Workers, 2011). In order to reduce costs, one of the primary goals of hospitals, both those engaged in ACOs and those that have not yet adopted this model of care, is reducing readmission rates. Section 3025 of the ACA added section 1886(q) to the Social Security Act, establishing the Hospital Readmissions Reduction Program. Under this program, the Centers for Medicare and Medicaid Services is required to reduce payments to hospitals with excess readmissions within 30 days for patients discharged with a diagnosis of Acute Myocardial Infarction (AMI), Heart Failure (HF) and Pneumonia (PN). In order to decrease readmissions, hospitals are focused on improving discharges for these patients and ensuring that once the patients leave the hospital they have a comprehensive care plan in place and that any risks to readmission have been mitigated. At the core of these discharge interventions are social workers who assess risks to readmission such as gaps in insurance coverage, difficulty navigating follow-up appointments, or gaps in transportation or social supports and who then work to develop a care plan that closes these gaps and continues to coordinate community-based care for the patient. Initial models of care with social work at the core are reporting success (The Advisory Board Company, 2013).

Educating Public Health Social Work Practitioners

The U.S. Department of Labor's Bureau of Labor Statistics (2010) estimates that social workers' employment (all forms of practice) will grow as much as 25% in the next decade. However, in spite of the growing demand for public health social workers, the education of this discipline continues to lag behind. A study conducted by Klusaritz, Cederbaum, Traube, Kim, and Seo (in press) of Master of Social Work (MSW) programs that have a concentration in health noted that in 2010, only 49 of the 200 accredited MSW programs in the United States had a health concentration—a small increase since 1982. In addition, more universities are offering Masters in Public Health, but only a third of those programs offer MSW/MPH degrees. Dual training in social work and public health would fill the expected shortage of specially trained individuals who can meet the health and wellness needs of the newly insured.

Interprofessional Education and Collaboration

The World Health Organization (2010) notes that,

Interprofessional education occurs when students from two or more professions learn about, from and with each other to enable effective collaboration and improve health outcomes. Once students understand how to work interprofessionally, they are ready to enter the workplace as a member of the collaborative practice team. This is a key step

in moving health systems from fragmentation to a position of strength. (p. 10)

Key to the success of public health social work is this learning and practice through an interprofessional lens. Here we highlight ways in which social workers in community-based health settings might work to strengthen these collaborations and maximize health and wellness through this multifaceted approach.

Utilizing an interprofessional approach requires the sharing of information, partnerships in practice, balancing of power differentials, interdependency, and a process orientation that promotes communication (D'Amour, Ferrada-Videla, San Martin Rodriguez, & Beaulieu, 2005). These characteristics help maximize team effectiveness, which may be seen by group members as a clear and valuable role on the team, open communication, resource equity, and presence of autonomy (Morrison, 2007). This collaborative model, when undertaken effectively, allows for increased skills among all team members and increases the delivery of high quality care (Bridges, Davidson, Soule Odegard, Maki, & Tomkowiak, 2011). Social work practitioners can help build and be a part of interprofessional teams; they bring to the effort leadership and communication skills that can help foster the critical elements needed for successful collaborations. These include accountability, coordination of activities, effective communication, ongoing cooperation, individual autonomy, and trust and respect among team members (Canadian Interprofessional Health Collaborative, 2010, as cited in Bridges et al., 2011).

Although interprofessional (previously referred to as interdisciplinary) collaboration (Bronstein, 2003) is not a new concept, the growing push for interprofessional education (Robert Wood Johnson Foundation, 2013a) has seen renewed efforts to define the role of social workers within collaborative teams (see Crawford, 2012; Leathard, 2013). Social work training programs need to work toward a number of changes that will facilitate training of interprofessionals. These include (1) coordinating interprofessional experiences;

(2) leadership and teaching by interdisciplinary faculty; and (3) training experiences that afford students the opportunities to engage and work within interprofessional teams (Bridges et al., 2011). For continued learning opportunities related to the role of social work practitioners in interprofessional and interagency collaboration, visit the Social Care Institute for Excellence (2009).

CONCLUSION

This chapter has provided an overview of public health social work, with an emphasis on how practitioners can make change at the individual, family, community, and systems levels. With the emphasis in the ACA on interprofessional collaboration, public health social workers are charged with creating a strong intrinsic social work identity that accounts for the ways in which social work practitioners interact with and influence the health and well-being of the systems in which we engage. Reframing our efforts to include, along with a tertiary approach to client care, an emphasis on prevention will help to propel social workers to the forefront of the dynamic shift in health care delivery.

INTERNET RESOURCES

- American Public Health Association: https://www.apha.org/
- National Public Health Week: http://www.nphw.org
- Public Health Social Work: http://publichealthsocialwork.org/
- Certified Social Worker in Health Care:http://www.socialworkers.org/credentials/specialty/c-swhc.asp

DISCUSSION QUESTIONS

1. What are the ways in which public health social work has influenced clinical practice in health care and health-related settings?

2. What elements of the public health social work approach are important to include in

foundation social work curricula to ensure that all social workers understand primary, secondary, and tertiary care?

3. How might policy changes like ACA influence the ways in which public health social workers practice?

4. What are the ways in which public health social workers can prioritize health and well-being to influence policy agendas?

5. In what ways might any social worker collaborate with public health practitioners to make individual and systems-level changes utilizing a multi-pronged micro, mezzo, and macro approach (as seen in Ramble)?

REFERENCES

The Advisory Board Company. (2013). *How a hospital used social workers to cut readmissions.* Retrieved from http://www.advisory.com/daily-briefing/2013/09/30/how-a-hospital-used-social-workers-to-cut-readmissions

Americans With Disabilities Act of 1990, Pub. L. No. 101–336, 104 Stat. 328 (1990).

American Public Health Association. (2013). *Public health and chronic disease: Cost saving and return on investment.* Retrieved from http://www.apha.org/NR/rdonlyres/9A621245-FFB6-465F-8695-BD783EF2E040/0/ChronicDiseaseFact_FINAL.pdf

Boston University. (n.d.). *What is PHSW? Public health social work.* Retrieved from http://publichealthsocialwork.org

Bridges, D. R., Davidson, R. A., Soule Odegard, P., Maki, I. V., & Tomkowiak, J. (2011). Interprofessional collaboration: Three best practice models of interprofessional education. *Medical Education Online, 16,* 1–10. doi:10.3402/meo.v16i0.6035

Bronstein, L. R. (2003). A model for interdisciplinary collaboration. *Social Work, 48,* 297–306.

Buhler-Wilkerson, K. (1993). Bringing care to the people: Lillian Wald's legacy to public health nursing. *American Journal of Public Health, 83,* 1778–1786.

Canadian Interprofessional Health Collaborative. (2010). *A national interprofessional competency* framework. Retrieved from http://www.cihc.ca/files/CIHC_IPCompetencies_Feb1210.pdf

Cederbaum, J. A., Guerrero, E. G., Mitchell, K. R., & Kim, T. (2014). Utilization of emergency and hospital services among individuals in substance abuse treatment. *Substance Abuse Treatment, Prevention, and Policy, 9*, 1–16. doi:10.1186/1747-597X-9-16

Centers for Disease Control and Prevention. (1999). Framework for program evaluation in public health. *Morbidity & Mortality Weekly Report, 48*(RR-11), 1–35.

Centers for Disease Control and Prevention. (2012). *A look inside food deserts.* Retrieved from http://www.cdc.gov/features/fooddeserts/

Centers for Medicare & Medicaid Services. (n.d.). *Coordinating your care.* Retrieved from http://www.medicare.gov/manage-your-health/coordinating-your-care/coordinating-your-care.html

Centers for Medicare & Medicaid Services. (2013a). *Accountable Care Organizations (ACO).* Retrieved from http://cms.hhs.gov/CCIIO/Programs-and-Initiatives/Other-Insurance-Protections/mhpaea_factsheet.html

Centers for Medicare & Medicaid Services. (2013b). *What does marketplace health insurance cover?* Retrieved from https://www.healthcare.gov/what-does-marketplace-health-insurance-cover

Crawford, K. (2012). *Interprofessional collaboration in social work practice.* Thousand Oaks, CA: Sage.

D'Amour, D., Ferrada-Videla, M., San Martin Rodriguez, L., & Beaulieu, M. (2005). The conceptual basis for interprofessional collaboration: Core concepts and theoretical frameworks. *Journal of Interprofessional Care, 19*(1), 116–131.

Darnell, J. S. (2013). Navigators and assisters: Two case management roles for social workers in the Affordable Care Act. *Health & Social Work, 38*(2), 123–126.

DeVol, R., & Bedroussian, A. (2007). *An unhealthy America: The economic burden of chronic disease.* Retrieved from http://www.sophe.org/Sophe/PDF/chronic_disease_report.pdf

French, T. F., Fang, H., & Balsa, A. I. (2011). Longitudinal analysis of changes in illicit drug use and health services utilization. *Health Services Research, 46*, 877–899.

Group for Public Health Social Work Initiatives. (2011). What is PHSW? Retrieved from http://publichealthsocialwork.org/?page_id=2

Kaiser Family Foundation. (2014). *The coverage gap: Uninsured poor adults in states that do not expand Medicaid.* Retrieved from http://kff.org/health-reform/issue-brief/the-coverage-gap-uninsured-poor-adults-in-states-that-do-not-expand-medicaid

Keefe, R. H., & Evans, T. A. (2013). Introduction to public health social work. In American Public Health Association (Ed.), *Handbook for public health social work* (pp. 3–20). New York, NY: Springer.

Klusaritz, H. A., Cederbaum, J. A., Traube, D. A., Kim, K. H., & Seo, B. (in press). Where is health in social work? *Social Work in Health.*

Koh, H. K., & Sebelius, K. G. (2010). Promoting prevention through the Affordable Care Act. *New England Journal of Medicine, 363*, 1296–1299.

Kotch, J. (2005). *Maternal and child health: Programs, problems, and policy in public health.* Boston, MA: Jones & Bartlett.

Leathard, A. (Ed.). (2013). *Interprofessional collaboration: From policy to practice in health and social care.* London, UK: Routledge.

Lundblad, K. S. (1995). Jane Addams and social reforms: A role model for the 1990s. *Social Work, 20*(5), 661–673. Retrieved from http://go.galegroup.com.libproxy.usc.edu

Mental Health Parity and Addiction Equity Act of 2008, Pub. L. No. 110–343 (2008).

McKenzie, J. F., Neiger, B. L., & Thackeray, R. (2013). *Planning, implementing, and evaluating health promotion programs: A primer* (6th ed.). San Francisco, CA: Pearson Benjamin Cummings.

Minelli, M. J., & Breckon, D. J. (2009). *Community health education: Settings, roles, and skills* (5th ed.). Sudbury, MA: Jones & Bartlett.

Moroney, R. M. (1995). Public health services. In R. L. Edwards (Ed.), *Encyclopedia of social work* (19th ed., pp. 1967–1973). Washington, DC: NASW Press.

Morrison, S. (2007). Working together: Why bother with collaboration? *Work Based Learning in Primary Care, 5*, 65–70.

National Association of Social Workers. (2011). *Accountable Care Organizations (ACOs): Opportunities for the social work profession*. Retrieved from http://www.socialworkers.org/assets/secured/documents/practice/health/ACOs%20Opportunities%20for%20SWers.pdf

National Association of Social Workers. (2013). *Standards for social work case management*. Retrieved from http://www.naswdc.org/practice/naswstandards/casemanagementstandards2013.pdf

Patient Protection and Affordable Care Act, 42 U.S.C. § 18001 et seq. (2010).

Robert Wood Johnson Foundation. (2013a). *Push for interprofessional education picks up steam: Health professions accreditors take steps to ensure educational programs prepare students to participate in team-based care*. Retrieved from http://www.rwjf.org/en/about-rwjf/newsroom/newsroom-content/2013/11/push-for-interprofessional-education-picks-up-steam.html

Robert Wood Johnson Foundation. (2013b). *Return on investments in public health: Saving lives and money*. Retrieved from http://www.rwjf.org/content/dam/farm/reports/issue_briefs/2013/rwjf72446

Roskin, M. (1980). Integration of primary prevention into social work practice. *Social Work, 25*, 192–196.

Rothman, K. J. (2012). Pioneers in epidemiology and public health. In *Epidemiology: An introduction* (2nd ed., pp. 8–22). New York, NY: Oxford University Press.

Ruth, B. J., & Sisco, S. (2008). Public health social work. In T. Mizrahi & L. E. Davis (Eds.), *Encyclopedia of social work* (20th ed.). New York, NY: Oxford University Press.

Ruth, B. J., Sisco, S., Wyatt, J., Bethke, C., Bachman, S., & Markham Piper, T. (2008). Public health and social work: Training dual professionals for the contemporary workplace. *Public Health Reports, 123*, 71–77.

Social Care Institute for Excellence. (2009). *An introduction to interprofessional and inter-agency collaboration*. Retrieved from http://www.scie.org.uk/publications/elearning/ipiac

Spitzer, W., & Davidson, K. (2013). Future trends in health and health care: Implications for social work practice in an aging society. *Social Work in Health Care, 52*(10), 959–986. doi: 10.1080/00981389.2013.834028

Substance Abuse and Mental Health Services Administration. (n.d.). *What is integrated care?* Retrieved from http://www.integration.samhsa.gov/about-us/what-is-integrated-care

U.S. Department of Health and Human Services. Agency for Healthcare Research and Quality. (n.d.). *Defining the PCMH*. Retrieved from http://pcmh.ahrq.gov/page/defining-pcmh

U.S. Department of Health and Human Services. Office of Disease Prevention and Health Promotion. (2013). *Healthy people 2020*. Retrieved from http://www.cdc.gov/nchs/healthy_people/hp2020.htm

U.S. Department of Labor. Bureau of Labor Statistics. (2010). *Occupational outlook handbook, 2010–11 edition, social workers*. Retrieved from http://www.bls.gov/oco/ocos060.htm

Van Pelt, J. (2009). Social work and public health—perfect partners. *Social Work Today, 9*(1), 28. Retrieved from http://www.socialworktoday.com/archive/011909p28.shtml

Viney, W., & Zorich, S. (1982). Contributions to the history of psychology: XXIX. Dorothea Dix and the history of psychology. *Psychological Reports, 50*, 211–218.

Walker, R. E. (2010). Disparities and access to healthy food in the United States: A review of food deserts literature. *Health & Place, 16*, 876–884.

Widener, M. J., Metcalf, S. S., & Bar-Yam, Y. (2011). Dynamic urban food environments: A temporal analysis of access to healthy foods. *American Journal of Preventative Medicine, 41*(4), 439–441. doi: 10.1016/j.amepre.2011.06.034

Wilkinson, D., Rounds, K. A., & Carr-Copeland, V. (2002). Infusing public health content into the social work curriculum. *Journal of Teaching in Social Work, 22*(3/4), 139–154.

World Health Organization. (2010). *Framework for action on interprofessional education and collaborative practice*. Geneva: Author. Retrieved from http://whqlibdoc.who.int/hq/2010/WHO_HRH_HPN_10.3_eng.pdf

Wu, L. T., Swartz, M. S., Wu, Z., Mannelli, P., Yang, C., & Blazer, D. G. (2012). Alcohol and drug use disorders among adults in emergency department settings in the United States. *Annals of Emergency Medicine, 60*, 172–180.

CHAPTER 25

The Engineering of Social Work in Communities

Eugenia L. Weiss & Diana Pineda

CHAPTER OBJECTIVES

- Discuss the initiative of the Grand Challenges for the social work profession;
- Describe how social workers can collaborate with engineers to promote social causes in communities;
- Identify the use of electronic mobile devices/applications (apps) in social work practice;
- Explain how the University of Southern California's Welcoming Practices program can use technology to assist children and families with school transitions.

INTRODUCTION

"Engineering" in the title of this chapter has a double meaning: It is a metaphor for the retooling of social work practice and education in the 21st century, and it refers to the application of technology in cross-collaborative work to reach vulnerable client communities. This retooling involves two factors. First, it will bolster a labor force that is capable of transacting in multiple dimensions of social work practice by being able to design multitheoretical and evidence-based integrative intervention plans that take into account the totality of an individual (e.g., behavioral, spiritual, emotional, cognitive, biological aspects) within his or her context (e.g., social systems, culture, community, ecology, economics, organization, and the political; Forte, 2014). Second, it will address the Grand Challenges for Social Work Initiative proposed by the American Academy of Social Work and Social Welfare (http://www.aaswsw.org). The Grand Challenges for Social Work is an agenda for our profession that involves "inquiry, innovation, testing, and application" and "creative and effective means of dealing with social problems and opportunities," which includes incorporating science and technology (Sherraden et al., 2014, p. 1). The Grand Challenges for Social Work was inspired by the 2008 work of the National Academy of Engineering, who sought to merge academics and practitioners in the field of engineering through innovative solutions to practical problems facing our world in the 21st century (e.g., clean and efficient sources of energy and fuel, access to clean water, preventing nuclear disasters, and cyberspace security, to name a few; http://www.engineeringchallenges.org; Uehara et al., 2014). The identified challenges and proposed solutions are field dependent. For instance, several areas have been suggested by the participants in the Grand Challenges for Social Work committee, such as addressing the nation's problems with housing insecurity and reducing poverty, as well as the prevention of mental and behavioral problems in children and youth (Uehara et al., 2014).

> By the end of the day, participants [in the Grand Challenges Committee] were in agreement that the creation of a grand challenges for social work initiative might both galvanize the profession and create transdisciplinary communities of innovators who work together to accomplish shared and compelling societal goals. Grand challenges could capture the interest of the general public while advancing the science and practice of social work. Participants acknowledged that adopting a grand challenges approach has risks: it places demands on individuals and organizations—and success is not guaranteed. Yet the potential benefits may greatly outweigh the risks. The history of social work offers many examples of great achievements, such as the Children's Bureau infant mortality campaign and the Program of Assertive Community Treatment, which can serve as models for addressing contemporary grand challenges. If the practical issues involved in developing grand challenges could be overcome, the approach would offer social work a tremendous opportunity to enhance social justice and individual well-being. (Uehara et al., 2014, p. 2)

This historical movement in the field of social work in terms of change and redefining our role is something that has been contemplated for a few years now, as quoted from Elizabeth Clark, Executive Director of NASW, on the Social Work Congress, the meeting of leaders in the social work profession (NASW, 2010):

> The social work profession is expected to grow faster than average over the next eight years and we must prepare a new generation of social workers to step into the roles and shoes of those of us who

are retiring in the next decade. We are also facing huge social and economic upheaval so we will use the Congress to encourage leaders in our profession to step up and be heard, Clark said. That is why this year's theme [2010]—Reaffirm, Revisit and Reimagine the Profession—is so fitting. (para. 4)

SOCIAL WORK AND ENGINEERING

Interdisciplinary education in social work and engineering in the training of students has been proposed as a burgeoning area of education in developing innovative solutions to address global and community challenges (see Gilbert, 2014 for a review). The University of Southern California's new initiative, Welcoming Practices That Address Transition Needs of Military Students in Public Schools (Welcoming Practices), led by Astor and associates, is an example of an innovative and technology-based approach through a novel collaborative partnership between the School of Social Work and School of Engineering, incorporating graduate students from both programs (Astor, Benbenishty, Gilreath, & Jacobson, 2014). This is a prime illustration of how two very different fields are uniting to solve a problem and prevent the disruptions that often occur when children and adolescents transition from one school to another school in a different community. The initiative will create electronic applications (i.e., mobile devices, apps on phones and tablets) that will enable parents and students to register for a new school with the appropriate documentation before they arrive at the school and become connected with school and community supports as they transition from one school to another. The program is funded by the Department of Defense Education Activity (DoDEA) and was developed by a consortium of school districts in Southern California as a way to connect military families who are faced with multiple transitions as they relocate between military installations across the nation; however, the transition program will serve all children and families who are entering new schools to better prepare them to integrate into communities. The technology is meant to facilitate and ease the stress of such transitions while also offering on-the-ground supports, such as transition welcoming centers located in the schools (Astor, Benbenishty, Gilreath, et al., 2014).

The Welcoming Practices program developed as a result of the Building Capacity consortium data that highlighted transitions as a major challenge that students in public schools face (Astor, Benbenishty, Wong, & Jacobson, 2014). After review of the data, literature, and analysis of resources in schools, particularly in San Diego and Riverside Counties of Southern California, the Welcoming Practices team developed this prevention model as an innovative approach to address transitions and provide supports as soon as a student arrives at a new school.

Initially, the goal of the Welcoming Practices program was to increase academic achievement, belonging, and well-being of military-connected students through the use of technology in public school districts. However, the program was modified to be a universal model to include all new students experiencing the same transition challenges. This model was conceptualized as a way to greet new students using technology that informs schools about the new incoming student while helping with transition issues. The technology includes a web registration tool available on Android and iOS phones or tablets that expedites the registration process. The process is presented in a user-friendly manner for parents to register students before their move rather than handing in paper registration once they arrive at campus, which can delay school placements (Astor, Benbenishty, Gilreath, et al., 2014). For example, this innovative program would benefit a family moving from Fort Bliss, Texas, to San Diego, California, by allowing them to begin the online registration process for a school they plan to enroll their child in before arriving in California, which eases the transition and saves parents' time while allowing time for the school to prepare, plan for, and welcome the new student.

The technology also provides an opportunity to assess the transitioning family's needs and to provide appropriate resources with an integrated mobile application. The mobile app will provide resources to parents and their families that are customized based upon location of schools and the type of resource users are interested in. The users, in this case, are parents and students. If parents have not already completed a profile through the web registration, the mobile app will direct parents to complete a profile and select resources they would be interested in, either for their child or for themselves. The app then generates a list of resources based on their selection and profile (Astor, Benbenishty, Gilreath, et al., 2014). For example, a parent registering her child for school can indicate her interest in afterschool tutoring or afterschool sports and clubs on the web registration resource menu. Thus, at the touch of a smartphone, parents can also seek out resources quickly for themselves, such as the nearest health clinic or counseling center, with details about the agency, and they can connect directly to that agency via the information included on the app profile (i.e., resource type, address, telephone number, etc.). Such resources will address issues from bullying in schools to academic help to mental health, substance abuse, and many other needs. It is traditional for social workers to have a comprehensive list of resources available for clients; however, having access to customized resources at the touch of a button on a phone embodies the shift in social work as technology becomes more available and accessible.

In addition to the Welcoming Practices online registration platform and connecting to various resources, the mobile app will connect to transition centers at the schools and student programs that welcome the newly transitioned student. According to Astor, Benbenishty, Gilreath et al. (2014), these transition welcoming centers will have a school team member known as a navigator, who will welcome and help guide the new student and his or her family. From a micro social work perspective, working with the client—in this case, the student and his or her family—provides an opportunity for the navigator to develop a sense of rapport and relationship with the family while assessing any needs the family might identify. For example, at one transition welcome center that is based near the district office, the navigator provides new students and families with a welcome kit.

From a social work mezzo perspective, connecting families to their community through the web mobile app enhances social supports for families who may feel disconnected from their communities. For example, the mobile app can provide resources for students and parents looking for sports or social clubs, such as the Student to Student (S2S) leadership clubs in schools or parent groups (Astor, Benbenishty, Gilreath, et al., 2014). Having access to such resources fosters a sense of community and a sense of belonging for both the student and parents.

From a broader and macro perspective, social workers need to incorporate information and communication technologies (ICTs) into their practice. NASW and the Association of Social Work Boards (2005) developed standards regarding the use of technology in social work practice. "Social workers need ICT competencies in order to effectively lead different types of social change initiatives or collaborate with professions of other disciplines who are using ICTs as part of existing strategies" (Perron, Taylor, Glass, & Margerum-Leys, 2010, p. 67). Furthermore, Craig and Lorenzo (2014) posit from a health social work perspective that

> social workers must proactively adapt and harness the potential of ICT or risk being left behind, which ultimately would impact vulnerable patient populations as well as the profession as a whole. Even more importantly, ICT may allow for the emergence of innovative interventions within social work when focused on empowering patients and their families. (p. 847)

Craig and Lorenzo (2014) provide recommendations to engage social workers in utilizing ICT based on a distillation of the literature, such as including social workers in the development and design of new technologies, proving social workers with training on the use of ICT, developing clear guidelines and ethical considerations, and investing in research initiatives associated with ICT and social work best practices.

The Welcoming Practices program is still in its early phase, with a completed prototype of the web registration tool and mobile app (see Appendices A and B for screen shots of the app map and resources). However, the predicted outcome is that the transition process for students and families will be less stressful and less traumatic with proactive strategies using the web registration tool to register a child in school online and using the mobile app for the convenience of connecting to on-the-ground student programs and resources. As far as serving clients, the app is not meant to replace social workers as "there will never be an app that does social work as we know it, but there are apps that may help social workers and other clinicians work more efficiently and effectively" (Getz, 2012, p. 8). The social work profession has been traditionally slow to adopt technologies for various reasons, for instance, lack of technological literacy and "fears of de-professionalization" (Craig & Lorenzo, 2014, p. 854). However, Craig and Lorenzo noted that the issues of greater concern have to do with potential breaches of client confidentiality through the use of technology and whether or not client populations have equal access based on sociodemographic factors (i.e., the "digital divide").

The preventative model that Welcoming Practices presents is not only for social work practice but is applicable to research and engaging in an evidence-based practice process that includes evaluation (Rubin, 2013). Using the mobile app and online surveys of parents, the Welcoming Practices consortium of schools will have access to large samples of data that will serve to not only evaluate the effectiveness of the program but guide future prevention and intervention efforts. The data gathered from this project will inform researchers on social behaviors and student-based outcomes and will provide greater insight into the use of technology to impact parent engagement in the schools and communities (Astor, Benbenishty, Gilreath et al., 2014).

Social workers today need to collaborate with other disciplines, particularly in the area of emerging ICTs, in order to develop innovative approaches to working with vulnerable populations. Such practices are seen in the Welcoming Practices program, in which social worker researchers collaborated with engineers to develop an innovative program and strategies that will reach clients and provide optimal services. In this case, a group of app developer engineers designed an online web registration platform and web resource app to meet the needs of newly transitioned students and their families in schools. In designing the web platform, a user-centered approach was used whereby social workers' perspectives were included from the start of the web design and every step of the way. Based on technology and social work research, participatory approaches to technology design relies heavily on the user—in this case, the client (parent and students)—and the social work perspective (Gillingham, 2014). The functionality and design of the web registration and mobile app was created with input from social workers and feedback from stakeholders. Social workers participated in the testing and validation of the web mobile app. This process involved continued communication through web meetings, online forum groups, development of a resource database, planned timeline of a prototype, and problem solving. According to Astor, Benbenishty, Gilreath et al. (2014), the resource database was created by a team led by social work researchers in Welcoming Practices who mapped out resources for student and families based upon the school/district environment, military/veteran supports, community supports, and national resources. The collaboration proves insightful for both groups and meaningful in developing real-world solutions that will address the needs of these new students and their families while creating a welcoming environment. With the advancement of technology, this is a time more than ever that social work needs to collaborate with other disciplines, such as engineering, to integrate technology to best serve clients in a more effective and timely manner informed by evidence-based practices.

Geographical Information Sciences (GIS) is another area of technology that social work is beginning to learn from and apply to practice and research. GIS uses technology to analyze geographical locations in a meaningful way through visualization and spatial sciences. Social workers have mapped out geographic locations by hand, but the use of "GIS technology can benefit social work by (1) continuing and strengthening the social survey tradition; (2) providing a framework for understanding human behavior; (3) identifying community needs and assets; (4) improving the delivery of social services; and (5) empowering communities and traditionally disenfranchised groups" (Hillier, 2007, p. 205). In the Welcoming Practices program, a team mapped out thousands of resources for the clients (Astor, Benbenishty, Gilreath et al., 2014). GIS will be included as a way to analyze resources in the community for planning purposes of on-the-ground programs. GIS can provide benefits to social work and evidence-based practices if we utilize the technological tools and train more social workers in their use and application (Felke, 2006). USC's School of Social Work program has taken the lead in training master's-level social worker students in GIS. This will equip a new group of social workers with the ability to map out and effectively analyze communities, which will add to redefining the profession. According to Hillier (2007), "social workers have a critical role to play in ensuring that GIS and other technologies are used to promote the social welfare of all people" (p. 215).

CONCLUSION

Using technology in innovative programs that reach vulnerable clients, such as the Welcoming Practices program, and in preparing our social work students/ trainees, combined with cultivating interdisciplinary partnerships, is not only needed for redefining social work but is critical for sustaining and promulgating the profession. Social work traditionally has been behind the curve when it comes to the use of technology, but with the explosion of an information society and rapid technological advances, in order to remain relevant when technology is being used both professionally and socially, social workers at all levels need to adapt their role and redefine the profession through the use of technology and in collaboration with other disciplines, and this is where social workers can begin to address the Grand Challenges of today and tomorrow.

INTERNET RESOURCES

- American Academy of Social Work and Social Welfare: http://www.aaswsw.org
- Building Capacity and Welcoming Practices: http://buildingcapacity.usc.edu/
- USC Institute of Creative Technologies: http://ict.usc.edu/

DISCUSSION QUESTIONS

1. Discuss how an app can be helpful from a micro, mezzo, and macro social work perspective and what the issues or challenges are at each level of practice.

2. What do you think are the Grand Challenges facing the nation today (from a social work perspective), and what ideas do you have to solve them that would include interdisciplinary collaborations?

3. Why are social workers sometimes hesitant with regard to incorporating technology in their practice, and how can you address any barriers or ethical considerations?

4. What are some innovative ways that GIS could be used in social work?

5. What are the strengths and limitations of incorporating technology in your own practice?

REFERENCES

Astor, R. A., Benbenishty, R., Gilreath, T., & Jacobson, L. (2014). *Welcoming practices in military-connected schools: Annual report year 1.* Los Angeles: USC School of Social Work.

Astor, R. A., Benbenishty, R., Wong, M., & Jacobson, L. (2014). *Building capacity in military-connected schools: Annual report year 4.* Los Angeles: USC School of Social Work.

Craig, S. L., & Lorenzo, M. V. C. (2014). Can information and communication technologies support patient engagement? A review of opportunities and challenges in health social work. *Social Work in Health Care, 53,* 845–864.

Felke, T. P. (2006). Geographic information systems: Potential uses in social work education and practice. *Journal of Evidence-Based Social Work, 3*(3–4), 103–113.

Forte, J. A. (2014). *An introduction to using theory in social work practice.* New York, NY: Routledge.

Getz, L. (2012). Mobile app technology for social workers. *Social Work Today, 12*(3), 8.

Gilbert, D. J. (2014). Social work and engineering collaboration: Forging innovative global community development education. *Journal of Social Work Education, 50*(2), 292–304.

Gillingham, P. (2014). Electronic information systems and social work: Who we are we designing for? *Practice,* 1–14.

Hillier, A. (2007). Why social work needs mapping. *Journal of Social Work Education, 43*(2), 205–221.

National Association of Social Workers. (2010, April 21). *2010 social work congress will explore ways to develop new generation of social workers* [Press release]. Retrieved from http://www.socialworkers.org/pressroom/2010/042110 Congress.asp

National Association of Social Workers & Association of Social Work Boards. (2005). *NASW and ASWB standards for technology and social work practice.* Retrieved from http://www.socialworkers.org/practice/standards/NASWTechnologyStandards.pdf

Perron, B. E., Taylor, H. O., Glass, J. E., & Margerum-Leys, J. (2010). Information and communication technologies in social work. *Advances in Social Work, 11*(2), 67–81.

Rubin, A. (2013). *Statistics for evidence-based practice and evaluation* (3rd ed.). Belmont, CA: Brooks/Cole.

Sherraden, M., Barth, R. P., Brekke, J., Fraser, M., Madersheid, R., & Padgett, D. (2014). *Social is fundamental: Introduction & context for grand challenges for social work.* (Grand Challenges for Social Work Initiative, Working Paper No. 1). Baltimore, MD: American Academy of Social Work & Social Welfare.

Uehara, E. S., Barth, R. P., Olson, S., Catalano, R. F., Hawkings, J. D., Kemp, S., . . . Sherraden, M. (2014). *Identifying and tackling grand challenges for social work.* (Grand Challenges for Social Work Initiative, Working Paper No. 3). Baltimore, MD: American Academy of Social Work & Social Welfare.

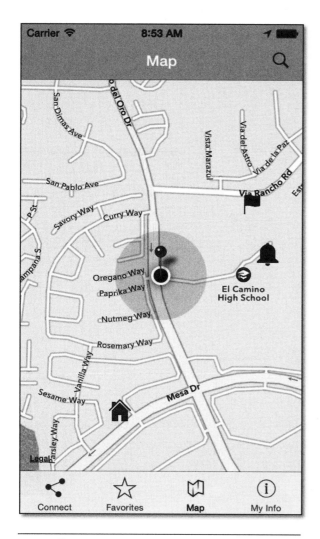

Appendix A   Screenshot of Map via Mobile App
SOURCE: Astor, R.A., Benbenishty, R., Gilreath, T., Jacobson, L. Welcoming Practices in Military-Connected Schools.

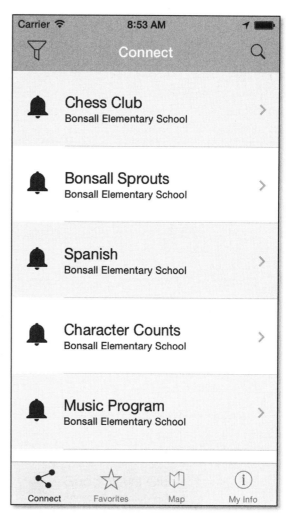

Appendix B   Screenshot of Resource Menu through Mobile App
SOURCE: Astor, R.A., Benbenishty, R., Gilreath, T., Jacobson, L. Welcoming Practices in Military-Connected Schools.

CHAPTER 26

Mental Health Promotion Among African Americans

Krystal Hays & Karen D. Lincoln

CHAPTER OBJECTIVES

- Describe African Americans' unique mental health profile and experiences with mental health services;
- Provide an overview of various preventive initiatives for mental health used with African Americans to target those most at-risk for developing a mental disorder;
- Highlight clinical mental health treatment with African Americans, including culturally competent services and cultural adaptations that take into consideration the historical context, cultural norms, experiences related to race, and religious preferences of African American clients;
- Explain how mental health promotion can be a strategy to address mental health issues among African Americans while focusing on positive mental health instead of mental illness.

CASE VIGNETTE

Ingrid Jackson is a 62-year-old African American woman. Ms. Jackson is generally healthy, well-groomed, about 30 pounds overweight, and takes medication for hypertension. She has health care coverage through her employer and recently visited her primary care physician complaining of headaches, upset stomach, and insomnia, which have been getting progressively worse over the past three months. After completing her physical exam, her physician found no medical cause for her complaints. The physician went on to ask about potential sources of stress in her life and suggested that emotional problems could explain her symptoms. Ms. Jackson replied, "There's nothing I'm dealing with that God can't handle." Her physician gave her informational pamphlets about stress and depression as well as a list of local mental health providers. Ms. Jackson denied having "mental problems" and didn't follow through with the information.

Ms. Jackson has been divorced for more than 15 years and lives alone in a duplex apartment in Los Angeles, CA. She has had no desire to date or have a romantic relationship, saying, "I can do bad all by myself." She does, however, feel very lonely at times. She has two sons, both in their 40s, who she sees or talks to on the telephone a few times a month. She has three grandchildren, who she sees about once a month. Both of Ms. Jackson's parents have been deceased for years, and she has two sisters and one brother who she sees regularly, making sure to spend holidays and most birthdays together. However, last month she did not attend her sister's Memorial Day cookout, telling her family, "I just don't feel like being bothered."

Ms. Jackson currently works for the County of Los Angeles and hopes to have enough financial stability to retire in a few years. Overall, she enjoys her job but finds administrative changes to be stressful. She has two co-workers with whom she feels close and confides in; however, one of them was laid off six months ago because of reduced County budgets. Ms. Jackson reports being afraid that she, too, will lose her job, telling her co-workers, "I am too close to the end to start over. If they cut me too I don't know what I'll do." At work she has grown increasingly tired, distracted, and irritable over the last several months, which may be symptoms of a mood disorder.

Ms. Jackson's spiritual life is very important to her. Feeling ashamed after her divorce, Ms. Jackson left the church she attended with her husband and sought a new place of worship, hoping to gain friendship and support. She has been a member of her current historically black Baptist church for 13 years. She has been active in several ministries—including music, hospitality, and outreach—throughout the years, at times attending services or meetings several times a week. She admits to being overwhelmed with church duties at times but, overall, feels a great sense of fulfillment through service and has developed supportive relationships with other parishioners. Lately, however, Ms. Jackson has only attended services a few times a month and has not participated in her normal committee meetings, complaining to her church friends that she doesn't "feel well."

INTRODUCTION

Despite similar or lower prevalence rates of most mental disorders among African Americans compared to other racial and ethnic groups, racial disparities in mental health remain. For example, following the initial onset, the burden of depression is greater for black Americans compared to non-Hispanic whites (Williams et al., 2007). Black Americans also have more severe, persistent, and disabling depressive episodes compared to whites (Bailey et al., 2009; Williams et al., 2007) and present to primary care with more depressive symptoms than does any other racial or ethnic group (Dwight-Johnson, Unutzer, Sherbourne, Tang, & Wells, 2001). Effective treatments exist for many mental disorders, but less than half of persons who meet criteria for a mental disorder receive any treatment (Wang et al., 2005). This gap

between need and use of mental health services is more pronounced among African Americans (e.g., Harris, Edlund, & Larson 2005; Wang et al., 2005). Moreover, the difference between need and service utilization has widened over time despite recent increases in mental health service use among the U.S. population overall (Kessler et al., 2005).

African Americans, like Ms. Jackson, possess many cultural strengths and resources that have allowed them to overcome historical and enduring discrimination, poverty, and other social injustices. However, some strengths and protective factors, such as strong kinship networks and high religious involvement, might also be barriers to addressing mental health issues. For instance, there continues to be cultural stigma associated with mental illness (Gary, 2005), lack of trust in service providers (Whaley, 2001), and reliance on religious coping (Chatters, Taylor, Jackson, & Lincoln, 2008) that might prevent many African Americans from addressing mental health issues and engaging in prevention and treatment interventions. Emotional problems often manifest as physical illness and are managed through primary care providers or informal sources of support, like church and family (González, Alegría, Prihoda, Copeland, & Zeber, 2011). However, if symptoms are left unrecognized or unmanaged, mild mood disorder symptoms can worsen and develop into major depression. The story of Ms. Jackson exemplifies the kind of experience many African Americans have with mental and emotional problems. Throughout this chapter we will explore the state of mental health among African Americans, describe prevention and treatment interventions, and present *mental health promotion* as a promising strategy to address mental health issues in African American communities.

MENTAL HEALTH AMONG AFRICAN AMERICANS

African Americans are not necessarily at greater risk than non-Hispanic whites for clinical psychiatric disorders (King & Williams, 1995). However, by virtue of differences in racially-patterned life circumstances, African Americans are excessively and disproportionately exposed to a variety of psychosocial stressors (e.g., economic deprivation, violent neighborhoods, racial discrimination) that are risk factors for mental health problems (Mizell, 1999). In addition, mental disorders are highly comorbid with medical conditions (Goodell, Druss & Walker, 2011) and African Americans have high rates of chronic health conditions which increases their risk for mental disorders. According to the Centers for Disease Control and Prevention (CDC, 2010), heart disease, cancer, stroke, diabetes and kidney disease were the leading causes of death for blacks in 2006; all of which are comorbid with mental health disorders like depression, schizophrenia, anxiety and bipolar disorder (Davidson et al., 2001; Allison & Mentore., 1999; Dixon et al., 1999; Herrán et al.,

2000; McElroy, Frye, & Suppes, 2002; Üçok & Polat, 2004; Cassidy et al., 1999; Allebeck, 1989).

Despite greater exposure to risk factors, epidemiologic studies suggest that there are similar or lower prevalence rates of most mental disorders among African Americans compared to non-Hispanic whites (Kessler & Berglund, 2005). These findings, to some degree, pose barriers to the inclusion of African Americans in mental health research, proper diagnosis and treatment because they are assumed to be a low-risk population. However, the focus on relatively low prevalence rates for common mental health problems and low treatment rates obscure disparities due to undertreatment and inappropriate treatment of severe, persistent, and disabling severe mental illness (SMI) among African Americans.

Effective interventions can play a major role in preventing and changing the course of mental illness. However, mental health promotion is needed prior to the onset of mental health problems to encourage and increase protective factors and healthy behaviors that can help prevent the onset of mental disorder as well as reduce risk factors that can lead to the development of mental health problems. Without intervention, whether it be prior to the onset of mental health problems (e.g., promotion, prevention) or after onset (e.g., treatment), many African Americans with persistent mental health problems will experience difficulty with securing and sustaining educational opportunities, employment, housing and supportive relationships (Bowie, Leung, & Reichenberg, 2008). African Americans with mental disorders are also vulnerable to experimentation and abuse of alcohol and illicit drugs, especially among males, as well as heavy smoking, and unhealthy dietary practices, which can result in a host of chronic health conditions and years of life lost. Finally, African Americans with comorbid chronic health conditions, such as diabetes, cardiovascular disease and congestive heart failure, have high rates of chronic major depressive disorder, a combination that decreases overall functioning and quality of life, and is associated with poor overall treatment adherence and higher mortality (Lin, Katon, & von

Korff, 2004). So, treatment is indeed a crucial aspect in the recovery process.

Prevalence of Mental Disorders Among African Americans

Epidemiological studies such as the National Study of American Life (NSAL), National Comorbidity Survey (NCS), and the National Comorbidity Survey-Replication (NCS-R), provide important information about the national prevalence rates of mental disorder for African Americans. For example, these studies report lower prevalence rates for lifetime mood disorders (e.g., major depressive disorder, bipolar disorder) for African Americans compared to non-Hispanic whites (Breslau et al., 2006). However, some research has suggested that the course and persistence of these disorders may be more chronic for blacks than for non-Hispanic whites (Williams et al., 2007). Recent findings from the NSAL reported lower lifetime prevalence rates for major depressive disorder (MDD) for African Americans and Caribbean blacks, compared to non-Hispanic whites (Williams et al., 2007). Findings also revealed similar risk profiles for MDD for African Americans and Caribbean blacks. Importantly, both groups had higher risk for the persistence of MDD compared to whites, greater impairment due to MDD, and were less likely than non-Hispanic whites to receive treatment that met the current guideline for mental health care (González et al., 2007; Melfi, Croghan, Hanna, 2000). Moreover, stigma of mental illness is active in African American communities and is rarely addressed in ethnic and racial minority communities (Whitehead, 1992) which can impact whether one seeks help for mental health problems (Hines-Martin, Malone, Kim, & Brown-Piper, 2003).

Mental Health Disparities

Comparatively, much more attention on mental health disorders and treatment has been paid to non-Hispanic whites than to African Americans. The status of depression among African Americans is a particularly under-researched area (Emslie, Ridge, Ziebland, & Hunt, 2006), in part because of the generally higher levels of depression, anxiety and other disorders, like schizophrenia reported among non-Hispanic whites. As a consequence, many mental disorders among African Americans often go unrecognized, undiagnosed and untreated. Tragically, undiagnosed depression, in particular, diminishes quality of life and can result in suicide; since the mid-1980s rates of suicide among African American men, in particular, have increased appreciably (Griffith & Bell, 1989; Joe, Baser, Breeden, 2006; Poussaint & Alexander, 2000).

Persistence and disability associated with mental illness, in many cases, can be combated by early diagnosis, which requires symptom recognition, proper treatment, and utilization of services. Unfortunately, racial disparities still exist in these areas. For example, there is strong evidence that African Americans are less likely than non-Hispanic whites to receive a proper diagnosis (Interian, Ang, & Gara, 2011; WHO, 2007). There are a number of reasons for misdiagnosis of African Americans, in particular, such as white norms that perpetuate stereotypes of African Americans that focus on perceptions of dangerousness and overweighting of putative psychosis that in a considerable number of cases results in clinical uncertainty and error (Adebimpe, 1981; Carrington, 2006). Research indicates that African Americans are often diagnosed with schizophrenia by white clinicians due to an underestimation of mood symptoms, even when these symptoms are evidenced by patients (González,, Tarraf, Whitfield, & Vega, 2010; Parks, Svendsen, Singer, Foti, & Mauer, 2006). There appears to be a tendency for some clinicians to place greater importance on (psychotic) symptom severity, personal ruminations, linguistic expressions, idioms of distress, and behaviors presented by African American patients or family members compared to inferences based on a criteria-based patient assessment (González et al., 2010).

Although there have been significant advances in the development of evidence-based mental health interventions, there are no systematic ongoing dissemination and implementation strategies embedded in existing services to address disparities in mental health care, and little rigorous data to establish their effectiveness for African Americans with SMI (Cabassa, Ezell, & Lewis-Fernandez, 2010). Consequently, in addition to much needed improvements in diagnosis and treatment, mental health promotion efforts are crucial for preventing the onset of mental disorder among African Americans and reducing the burden on individuals, families and communities.

MENTAL HEALTH PREVENTION AND INTERVENTION WITH AFRICAN AMERICANS

Since the 1990s, research efforts have shifted from a singular focus on treatment of mental illness to prevention in vulnerable populations (Cuijpers, Van Straten, & Smit, 2005). Research findings suggest that current treatment modalities, such as psychotherapy and pharmacotherapy, cannot avert the burden that mental illness causes to individuals, families, and communities, including increased morbidity and mortality (Andrews & Wilkinson, 2002). Accordingly, one way to lessen the burden is to prevent new cases of mental disorder from occurring (Andrews & Wilkinson, 2002), which is the goal of prevention efforts (Cuijpers et al., 2005). There are several types of prevention initiatives that specifically target African Americans. These initiatives have occurred at national, state and local levels. The purpose of this chapter is not to critically examine all prevention programs that target African Americans but instead, illustrate the variety and general effectiveness of recent strategies to prevent mental illness in this population. Limitations of current prevention and treatment strategies will also be presented.

Macro-Level Prevention Efforts

In 2008, the Substance Abuse and Mental Health Services Administration (SAMHSA) reported that 6% of African Americans aged 18–25 had a mental illness in the past year for which only 44.8% received treatment (SAMHSA, 2010).

These findings prompted SAMHSA, the Ad Council and the Stay Strong Foundation to develop a national advertising campaign titled, "Stories that Heal." This campaign targeted African Americans 18–25 years of age with the goal of promoting recovery from mental health problems by "encouraging, educating, and inspiring young people to talk openly" (SAMHSA, 2010). The campaign featured radio, print, public service announcements and videos of African Americans sharing their stories about mental illness or emotional problems and overcoming by seeking the appropriate treatment and with the support of family, friends, and community. The videos were simulcast at universities across the country and popular television outlets. The campaign ran through 2010 and information is now archived on the SAMHSA website and YouTube. Although the outcomes of the campaign were not released, this initiative was one of the first ad campaigns to target African Americans in addressing mental health issues at the national level.

Mezzo-Level Prevention Efforts

In 2004, California voters passed the Mental Health Services Act (MHSA) to eliminate socioeconomic and racial/ethnic mental health disparities through a culturally competent mental health care system, prevention of mental illness, early intervention and state-of-the-art treatment to promote recovery and wellness for persons with mental illness. (UC Davis Center for Reducing Health Disparities, 2009). Following this initiative, the University of California at Davis developed a Center for Reducing Health Disparities (CRHD) which takes a multidisciplinary and collaborative approach to address inequities in health access and quality of care. In 2006, the CRHD launched a project to conduct focus groups with historically underserved communities to collect data about participants' attitudes and beliefs about mental health and their mental health concerns, and to identify the types of prevention programs most appropriate for these communities. The Center released brief reports summarizing the findings and suggestions for developing prevention efforts within each minority community.

African American focus group participants identified violence, family disruption, drug and alcohol use, suicide, and homelessness as their greatest mental health-related concerns (UC Davis CRHD, 2009). Some of the factors identified by participants as correlates of these mental health concerns were poverty, racism and discrimination, stigma, police harassment and brutality. Participants also identified barriers to receiving mental health services, including the scarcity of affordable, timely, and culturally appropriate services and mistrust of mental health service agencies. Important strengths of African American communities were also described, including resilience and the importance of community-based organizations, churches, and schools. Identifying strengths is important, as they can be instrumental for addressing mental health challenges in underserved and under-resourced communities (UC Davis CRHD, 2009). Finally, the CRHD outlined six recommendations that were identified by participants for how their concerns and identified barriers can be addressed to prevent mental illness in African American communities, including (1) education programs about drug abuse, prevention and treatment, (2) parenting programs, (3) mentorship, sports, career training, and social programs for youth, (4) programs to motivate members of the community to engage in community advocacy, (5) more community activities to create a sense of union and power, and (6) programs to help the homeless address their mental health, substance abuse, food, housing, and medication needs.

The goals of the CRHD report were to voice the opinions and needs of communities that have been underserved and to educate policymakers on the mental health issues that are important to these communities. Consequently, each county in California developed their own unique MHSA plans which included prevention and early intervention programs that were culturally responsive (California Department of Health Care Services, 2012).

Micro-Level Prevention Efforts

Extant literature on the prevention of mental illness among African Americans is limited and there are an increasing number of preventative interventions for mental illness targeting older adults. The African American older adult population is expected to increase by 104% by 2030 (U.S. Department of Health and Human Services, 2012). This increase in the population also means an increase in mental health problems and chronic health conditions that are already prevalent among African American older adults. Further, African American older adults have less access to services (Smith Black, Rabins, German, McGuire, & Roca, 1997); are more likely to use informal sources (e.g., family, friends, church members) for help with mental health and emotional problems (Mays, Caldwell, & Jackson, 1996); and when they do use formal services, they are more likely to seek treatment in primary care clinics versus specialized mental health clinics (Areán & Ayalon, 2005).

In order to help improve access to appropriate mental health care for older African Americans, specialized prevention interventions have been developed. Sriwattanakomen et al. (2008) designed a randomized control trial using Problem Solving Treatment in Primary Care (PST-PC) with 22 older African Americans with mild depressive symptoms. PST-PC is a manualized intervention found to be effective for treating late-life depression (Arean & Hegel, 2008). The specific skills gained through the intervention include problem solving, normalizing problems in life, increased belief in one's ability to solve problems (i.e., self-efficacy), identifying emotional and physiological cues to depression, and using the "stop and think" technique (Sriwattanakomen et al., 2008). The intervention is structured over 6–8 sessions lasting 30 minutes to one hour with the goal of preventing participants from developing major depressive disorder. Initial feedback from participants and subject retention for the intervention were promising. However, the actual effectiveness of the intervention was undocumented and thus, it is difficult to assess its impact. Researchers have demonstrated that there is often a significant gap between the evidence of an intervention's effectiveness and its actual implementation in communities (Bero, Grilli, Grimshaw, & Harvey, 1998). So, although this type of intervention has been found to reduce the incidence of depression in the general population of older adults, it remains unclear whether older African American will similarly benefit.

CULTURALLY ADAPTED CLINICAL INTERVENTIONS

Clinical Assessment

In 2006, the American Psychological Association's Presidential Task Force on Evidence-Based Practice broadened the definition of clinical mental health intervention to include assessment, which is a key element that precedes appropriate treatment (APA, 2006). Currently, there remain a number of limitations with regard to clinical assessment of mental health disorder among African Americans. One fairly serious limitation is the fact that most commonly used assessment tools were standardized on white, middle-class samples, thus largely ignoring racial and cross-cultural differences in psychopathology (Dana, 2002). Additionally, the need for cultural competence and evidence-based practices are critical issues for the future of mental health services delivery for African Americans. For example, racism has been identified as the primary factor to explain way African Americans are less likely than non-Hispanic whites to receive treatment that meets the current guideline for depression care (González et al., 2010). Further, Snowden (2003) notes that beliefs and actions of individual clinicians may be biased and based on unfounded assumptions about the mental health status and treatment expectations of African Americans.

Although the literature around providing culturally competent clinical assessment is limited, Whaley and Davis (2007) offer suggestions for clinicians to consider. First, clinicians must understand the meaning of culturally competent care which they define as a set of problem-solving skills where cultural sensitivity is critical. Specific steps clinicians must take in the assessment phase (and beyond) include (1) understand how an individual's heritage and cultural adaptations interplay to shape their behavior; (2) use the knowledge you've gained about an individual's heritage and adaptation challenges to guide your assessment, diagnosis, and treatment plan; and (3) internalize the processes so it becomes a routine part of your clinical skill set.

Here, the main message is that an individual's current behavior and psychopathology cannot be separated from their history and cultural experiences. For a clinician working with an African American client appropriate assessment must begin with an exploration of the client's history, racial identity, and cultural norms. The client's current behaviors must be contextualized within their cultural and historical experiences. Further, the clinician must attempt to be acutely aware of their own individual biases and cultural sensitivity that will undoubtedly impact the therapeutic relationship. Last, assessment tools must be used judiciously and evaluated for their cultural sensitivity and appropriateness for African Americans.

Clinical Interventions

In a meta-analysis of 76 mental health interventions, Griner and Smith (2006) found that culturally adapted interventions are generally effective. The specific aspects of cultural adaptation that were effective in treatment include (1) having groups of same-race participants, (2) race-matching of therapist and client, (3) incorporating explicit cultural values into treatment, (4) collaboration between clinicians and client's family and/or community, and (5) ensuring that services are accessible and located in the client's community (Griner & Smith, 2006).

One example of an intervention that has been adapted to meet the needs of African American clients is a patient-centered depression intervention in primary care (Cooper et al., 2013). This intervention targeted African Americans with depression and incorporated adaptations, including (1) utilizing African American case workers, (2) addressing cultural and health care access issues with clients, and (3) using culturally tailored depression materials (Cooper et al., 2013). Although the cultural targeting enhanced access and patients' experiences, the culturally adapted intervention did not prove to be more effective than standard care (Cooper et al., 2013). The authors suggest that African American clients may be hesitant to engage in traditional depression treatment, even with cultural adaptations, and that future research must address this limitation (Cooper et al., 2013).

Gaps and Limitations

There has been an increased focus on mental health treatment and interventions in recent years. However, there is a paucity of interventions to prevent and treat mental illness among African Americans. Many prevention and treatment programs for African Americans are underdeveloped, and some of those that do exist have not yet produced findings regarding their efficacy or effectiveness. In addition, prevention programs aimed at reducing mental health disparities among African Americans that do not also consider the impact of social determinants of health (e.g., education, income, job opportunities, neighborhood conditions, poverty) run the risk of being inadequate. Thus, current prevention and treatment efforts for African Americans should be expanded to include mental health promotion as a way to integrate social determinants of mental disorder with prevention and intervention. The following section defines mental health promotion, discusses current initiatives targeting African Americans, and suggests appropriate models of intervention.

MENTAL HEALTH PROMOTION

In 2005, the World Health Organization released a report outlining the state of mental health promotion and calling for more attention on the promotion of mental health throughout the globe. In this report, health promotion was defined as actions and advocacy that address the range of determinants of health which include helping people to adopt healthy lifestyles and encouraging actions that create living conditions and environments that support health (WHO, 1998). In addition, mental health promotion is identified as an integral part of health promotion that involves intervening at the micro, mezzo, and macro levels, including developing healthy communities, improving individuals' social skills, their ability to manage life, and their emotional resilience (Fledderus, Bohlmeijer, Smit, & Westerhof, 2010).

In order to fully understand mental health promotion, it is important to understand a key component—the emphasis on determinants of "positive mental health" rather than solely the avoidance of mental disease. The goal of mental health promotion is positive mental health, which is defined as "a state of well-being in which the individual realizes his or her own abilities, can cope with the normal stresses of life, can work productively and fruitfully, and is able to make a contribution to his or her community" (WHO, 2001, para 1). An individual and/or community that has positive mental health is not only free from mental illness but demonstrates mental and emotional fitness (WHO, 2005). Mental fitness is the goal of mental health promotion because of the potential to both prevent the debilitating effects of mental disorder and advance mental and emotional well-being.

The focus on determinants of positive mental health is an important distinction of mental health promotion because it separates it from traditional notions of mental health prevention and treatment. Mental health promotion should be understood as a "higher level" construct that includes both prevention and treatment activities but also addresses the upstream determinants of health which are associated with positive mental health and mental illness. Mental health promotion is ideal for addressing the limitations of mental health prevention and treatment previously described in this chapter because it is a holistic approach and targets higher level determinants of health.

Among African Americans specifically, mental health promotion promises to reduce disparities and improve the mental health of individuals and communities in a way that existing initiatives and interventions cannot because of the focus on "upstream" factors. Studies consistently demonstrate that disadvantaged populations, as indexed by black race and low socioeconomic position, have greater exposure to stress over the life course (Karlsen & Nazroo, 2002; Turner & Lloyd, 1999). African Americans, who live in more segregated, disorganized and dangerous neighborhoods, are exposed to more traumatic events and chronic stress than whites (Williams & Collins, 2001; Diez Roux 2003; Turner & Avison, 2003; Turner & Lloyd, 1999). Accordingly, their risk for diagnosable mental disorders associated with stress exposure, such as major depression, is particularly elevated. Mental health promotion efforts focus on the structural factors (e.g., discrimination, poverty, segregation) that lead to stress and ultimately cause the cascade of effects at subsequent levels (e.g., mezzo and micro) that are associated with and often lead to mental distress and mental illness among African Americans.

Mental Health Promotion With African Americans

The opening case example of Ms. Jackson highlights the complexity of mental and emotional issues faced by many African Americans. Although Ms. Jackson exhibits depressive symptomology she does not identify as being mentally ill nor is she open to accessing professional mental health services to improve her mental health. She is likely to not see the need to address the topic of mental illness until her symptoms become much worse and her functional impairments increase. Like many other African Americans, Ms. Jackson prefers to use spirituality and informal support to manage her symptoms (Woodward et al., 2008) and seems to hold negative attitudes toward mental illness and its treatment (Gary, 2005). Because of barriers like cultural stigma, traditional prevention and treatment efforts will likely fail to improve Ms. Jackson's health as she is unlikely to engage in interventions focused on mental illness. A mental health promotion framework, would broaden the scope and reach of interventions designed to improve the mental health of African Americans like Ms. Jackson. Here we will present three major

components of a comprehensive mental health promotion model which include (1) moving beyond a focus on mental illness toward a focus on health and well-being, (2) utilizing community and cultural strengths to promote health, and (3) encouraging collaboration between mental health professionals and trusted community resources.

First, mental health promotion encourages professionals to shift their thinking from treating mental illness toward facilitating emotional and psychological health (Jané-Llopis, Barry, Hosman, & Patel, 2005) This kind of approach may be more attractive to individuals like Ms. Jackson who would be more receptive to improving their mental health rather than identifying and treating a mental illness. Through a mental health promotion lens, professionals must be aware of the larger level social determinants that impact health. Ethnic minorities with a mental illness face a "double stigma" because of their racial status and mental diagnosis (Gary, 2005). Thus instead of trying to reduce stigma so that African Americans will accept traditional mental health treatment the goal should be to acknowledge the cultural stigma and work within that frame to encourage improved mental health. This could include such things as helping an individual identify what mental health means to them and helping them to identify and engage in positive activities (i.e., prayer, cooking, dancing) that will help facilitate improved emotional well-being.

Second, mental health promotion with African Americans should incorporate community and cultural strengths such as faith and religion. A large body of literature on religion consistently shows that African Americans have higher rates of religious involvement and religious coping than other ethnic groups (Chatters, Taylor, McKeever Bullard, & Jackson, 2009; Taylor et al., 2009; Chatters et al., 2009; Taylor, Chatters, & Jackson, 2007; Cooper, Brown, Thi Vu, Ford, & Powe, 2001). Religion is often regarded as an important cultural resource for many African Americans and has been identified as a protective factor that promotes physical (Strawbridge et al., 2001) and mental health

(Nooney & Woodrum, 2002). Religion often shapes the attitudes and behaviors of many African Americans toward mental health. Studies have shown that when facing mental or emotional difficulties, many African Americans prefer to seek help from their spiritual leader or pastor rather than a mental health professional (e.g., psychiatrist, social worker, mental health provider) (Neighbors, 1998; Matthews et al., 2006). Therefore a comprehensive mental health promotion model for African Americans must recognize and incorporate faith, spirituality, and religion at all levels of intervention.

Third, a mental health promotion model necessitates increased collaboration between professional mental health services and trusted community resources. Although mental health promotion focuses on promoting mental well-being it recognizes that formal treatment may be necessary for some as a means to improved mental health. However, simply making treatment available does not ensure that African Americans who need services will access them. To facilitate the use of appropriate mental health care there must be collaboration between formal service providers and trusted community organizations (Barry, Domitrovich, & Lara, 2005). Black churches are just one example of an enduring and trusted organization in the African American community (Lincoln & Mamiya, 1990). It has been suggested that black churches are a feasible setting for mental health promotion because of their spiritual nature and organizational structure (Hankerson & Weissman, 2012). Additionally, church-based interventions are appropriate for African Americans because they are tailored to emphasize black culture and spirituality (Hankerson & Weissman, 2012).

There are very few examples of efforts that utilize this comprehensive approach to mental health promotion with African Americans. The Joy of Living: Keeping Healthy Mentally program, however, exemplifies mental health promotion that targets African Americans and incorporates the three components described above (Crewe, 2007). Joy of Living is an education program developed by the Mental Health Association of the District of Columbia to improve the mental health of older African Americans and is specifically designed to address the unique needs and life experiences of African American older adults (Crewe, 2007). This program was developed with the assumption that African American elders possess skills and resources that have facilitated their ability to overcome challenges such as racism and discrimination over the course of their lives (Crewe, 2007).

The four key elements of the program are (1) partnership with trusted community organizations, (2) use of culturally competent staff, (3) the inclusion of faith, and (4) the use of a self-help model through sharing circles. The program has three 2-hour workshops that address topics related to health, mental health, memory loss, and depression and was held at various faith-based and senior center sites. Early outcomes of the intervention were promising as participants gave positive feedback about their experience and reported increased knowledge and skills regarding mental health and help-seeking (Crewe, 2007). Joy of Living does not seek only to prevent or treat illness but focuses on improving mental health and well-being which is at the heart of a mental health promotion model. It also builds on individual and community strengths and incorporates the importance of faith and religion.

MULTI-LEVEL PRACTICE IMPLICATIONS

The information provided in this chapter has many implications for social work practice at the micro, mezzo, and macro levels of intervention.

Micro-Level Implications

To explore micro-level issues, we can return to the vignette about Ms. Jackson. The story of Ingrid Jackson is an example of an African American older adult who does not fit the diagnostic criteria for any particular mental disorder but may be at risk of developing a disorder. Given her symptoms—social withdrawal, lack of interest in work, insomnia, loneliness, irritability, poor memory, and worry—it is possible that Ms. Jackson has mild depression. However, these symptoms did not significantly impact her ability to function, as she continued to maintain her job, housing, and health. Thus, her need for mental health treatment or intervention is not necessarily obvious to her or to others. From a mental health promotion perspective the goal for Ms. Jackson should be to not only decrease her current symptoms of mental illness but also improve her overall mental health. There are specific behavioral actions that Ms. Jackson can take to improve her mental health such as increased exercise, meditation, engaging in meaningful and enjoyable activities (without overcommitting herself), and getting educated about positive mental health and mental disorder.

Like many African Americans with emotional problems, Ms. Jackson went to her primary care physician for help. She also complained of physical ailments instead of mental or emotional problems, which is a common among African Americans (Snowden, 2001). That is, mental health problems among African Americans often manifest as somatic symptoms, such as stomach problems, headaches, or general physical pains (Das, Olfson, McCurtis, & Weissman, 2006). Consequently, it is important that health care providers are culturally competent and educated about how mental health problems are exhibited and described by African Americans. Primary care settings therefore, are important enter points to implement mental health promotion efforts, including awareness and education about mental illness, linkages and referrals to mental health providers.

Additional points of intervention are Ms. Jackson's social network and her religious involvement. Ms. Jackson is connected to several social resources (e.g., family, work, church) which could all serve as sources of social support and provide opportunities to implement mental health promotion efforts. Because of the importance of religion in her life, Ms. Jackson can seek support from her pastor to address her mental health problems. Empirical studies indicate that African Americans are more likely to seek help from their pastor when experiencing personal problems than psychiatrists,

psychologists, social workers or doctors (Chatters et al., 2011; Veroff, Kulka, & Douvan, 1981; Taylor et al., 2000) with positive results (Pargament, Koenig, Tarakeshwar, & Hahn, 2004; Neighbors, 1998; Young, Griffith, & Williams, 2003). Clergy are consulted for a variety of psychological issues, many of which are consistent with their ministerial and religious training (e.g., bereavement, comforting the sick and "shut in"). In addition, some members of the clergy have received training in pastoral counseling and can provide therapy services at no cost to congregants and often within the context of a longstanding relationship. Church members are also important and available sources of support for Ms. Jackson (Chatters, Taylor, Lincoln, & Schroepfer, 2002; Taylor et al., 2000; Krause et al., 2002). Church members provide an array of instrumental, material, and informational support (e.g., financial assistance, transportation, leads on employment opportunities) as well as spiritual and emotional support, including encouragement, prayer and sharing religious experiences through personal testimonies. Finally, Ms. Jackson can engage in religious coping—a form of cognitive reframing or psychological adjustment—to deal with her emotional problems, including prayer, asking others to pray for her, redefining the stressor within a religious framework, using her faith to decide how to cope with her situation or seeking control through a partnership with God. A religious approach to addressing her emotional problems is one recommendation for Ms. Jackson. Pastoral counseling may be appropriate however, not all pastors receive training in this area. In this case, it is important for pastors to refer their congregants to a culturally competent mental health professional or a church-based or faith-based program in the community. Such referrals are better facilitated if church leaders are connected to mental health service providers. Outreach and engagement strategies are useful in this regard.

Although mental health promotion efforts provided through informal sources of support such as church and family might be sufficient for improving Ms. Jackson's mental health, it is important for her and for members of her support network to consider and identify formal sources of support such as clinical intervention, if her symptoms do not improve or worsen. A social work professional who works with Ms. Jackson would need to be aware of the stigma around mental illness that is prevalent among African Americans and be able to address it (Gary, 2005). In order to do this effectively, a mental health professional who works with Ms. Jackson should be culturally competent, regardless of his or her race. When working with African American clients, like Ms. Jackson, clinicians should not assume that they understand their cultural experiences but instead engage in an open discussion about their ethnic background, faith, experiences of discrimination, beliefs and attitudes about mental illness, and other issues that will impact their ability to engage in treatment. It is also suggested that clinical interventions used with Ms. Jackson be culturally appropriate for African Americans. Culturally adapted interventions like those described in this chapter can be employed as a way to ensure that culturally competent services are being provided.

Mezzo Level Implications

At the mezzo level, implications for social work practice are at the community level. In addition to church- or faith-based mental health promotion programs like the one described in this chapter, increased collaboration between social service agencies, mental health service providers, health care providers, churches, and other community advocacy groups is needed. There are a variety of reasons that African Americans are less likely to seek formal mental health services compared to other racial or ethnic groups (e.g., stigma, mistrust, discrimination). Therefore, partnerships between mental health providers and trusted community agencies and organizations are essential to developing mental health promotion initiatives that will be acceptable to African Americans. For Ms. Jackson, this could mean having additional opportunities through her place of employment or church to be educated about mental health promotion and

ways to live a healthier life. She could have access to appropriate referrals for mental health providers that already have established relationships with her existing social networks. These opportunities can facilitate the receipt of mental health care by Ms. Jackson and support her behavior change that will lead to better mental health.

Issues of access are also important to consider at the mezzo level. Access to mental health services can be impacted by social and institutional factors. Family and community beliefs and attitudes regarding mental health can adversely affect an individual's help-seeking behavior and thus, pose barriers to access. In addition, difficulty identifying and/or locating mental health and supportive services as well as institutional factors such as long wait times, enrollment limitations or lack of culturally competent staff, can also pose barriers to access (Hines-Martin et al, 2003). Financial resources and health care coverage can also impact one's ability to obtain formal services as well as the type of services for which an individual is eligible. Fortunately for Ms. Jackson, she has health insurance through her employer that would most likely cover some level of mental health care if she were to request it. However, there may be other social or institutional barriers, such as the beliefs of members of her social network or the quality of services in her neighborhood that could impact her ability to access treatment.

Macro Level Implications

Macro level implications for social work include policy and advocacy issues related to mental health and disparities. As discussed above, social determinants of health such as health care access, poverty, unemployment, under employment, low education, lack of educational opportunities, and poor neighborhood conditions are all correlates of poor mental health and important issues that advocates and policy makers should address in order to reduce mental health disparities. Ms. Jackson could benefit from employment policies that promote positive mental health (Jané-Llopis et al., 2005).

Examples of mental health promoting workplace policies include lowering workload, ergonomic improvements, and improving role clarity and social relationships (Jané-Llopis et al., 2005).

When considering macro level implications of mental health promotion one must examine policies that affect access to health care. The goal of the Affordable Care Act is to improve health and reduce disparities by "investing in prevention and wellness, and giving individuals and families more control over their own care" (USHHS, 2011). Further, the law will increase access to health care coverage to millions of Americans who otherwise would not have it (www.healthcare.gov). This ultimately means that many African Americans who are currently uninsured will have access to affordable mental health care. Increased access is significant because without access to mental health care, efforts to improve outreach to African Americans and reduce disparities in mental health would be hampered.

CONCLUSION

The case of Ms. Jackson raises many implications for mental health practice. A thorough understanding of structural, cultural, gender, socioeconomic, and age-specific behaviors are important for practice with African Americans. Acknowledging the strength and resilience of the individual and knowledge gained by their lived experience is essential for a mental health promotion plan that is relevant and respectful. Community-based services that are accessible, culturally sensitive and congruent will enhance the quality of life for African Americans across the life course. Such services designed specifically for African Americans in natural settings are likely to be more positively perceived and utilized.

The importance of cultural competence, culturally adapted interventions, and community collaboration, especially with churches and faith groups, has been highlighted in this chapter. African Americans are less likely to utilize formal mental health services even when they have

access. Thus, a collaborative model that includes trusted community-based organizations will be especially important in meeting the needs of African Americans. It is also essential to recognize the various intervention points including formal mental health services, primary care, churches, communities, and families in the provision of mental health services.

INTERNET RESOURCES

- Administration on Aging: http://www.aoa.gov/
- Black Psychiatrists of America: http://www.bpainc.org/
- Health Care Reform: https://www.healthcare.gov/
- Mental Health Ministries: http://mentalhealth-ministries.net/
- The Office of Minority Health: http://minority-health.hhs.gov/
- SAMHSA Stories that Heal: http://www.samhsa.gov/samhsanewsletter/Volume_18_Number_2/MentalIllnessAfricanAmericans.aspx; https://www.youtube.com/watch?v=9aovOZVc5jI; https://www.youtube.com/watch?v=k30vb5ct_CU; https://www.youtube.com/watch?v=6dt_T3Uoims
- Center for Disease Control: Healthy People 2020: http://www.healthypeople.gov/2020/default.aspx
- California MHSA: http://www.dhcs.ca.gov/services/mh/Pages/MH_Prop63.aspx
- CDC Evidence Based Interventions: http://nccd.cdc.gov/DCH_CHORC/
- Mental Health America: http://www.mentalhealthamerica.net/
- National Alliance on Mental Illness (NAMI): http://www.nami.org/
- World Health Organization: Mental Health: http://www.who.int/topics/mental_health/en/

DISCUSSION QUESTIONS

1. What are some of the risk factors for poor mental health that are faced by African Americans?

2. African Americans face specific challenges in gaining access to mental health services. What are some of these challenges?

3. How can prevention and treatment interventions be tailored to meet the needs of African Americans?

4. What makes mental health promotion unique from traditional mental health prevention and treatment models?

5. What are some of the key elements in a comprehensive mental health promotion model?

REFERENCES

Adebimpe, V. (1981). Overview: White norms and psychiatric diagnosis of black patients. *American Journal of Psychiatry, 138*(3), 279–285.

Allebeck, P. (1989). Schizophrenia: A life-shortening disease. *Schizophrenia Bulletin, 15*(1), 81.

Allison, D., & Mentore, J. (1999). Antipsychotic-induced weight gain: A comprehensive research synthesis. *American Journal of Psychiatry, 156*(11), 1686–1696.

Andrews, G., & Wilkinson, D. D. (2002). The prevention of mental disorders in young people. *The Medical Journal of Australia, 177*, S97–S100.

APA Presidential Task Force. (2006). Evidence-based practice in psychology. *The American Psychologist, 4*(61), 271.

Areán, P., & Ayalon, L. (2005). Assessment and treatment of depressed older adults in primary care. *Clinical Psychology: Science and Practice. 12*(3), 321-335.

Areán, P., & Hegel, M. (2008). Effectiveness of problem-solving therapy for older, primary care patients with depression: Results from the IMPACT project. *The Gerontologist, 48*(3), 311.

Bailey, R., Blackmon, H., & Stevens, F. (2009). Major depressive disorder in the African American population: Meeting the challenges of stigma, misdiagnosis, and treatment disparities. *Journal of the National Medical Association, 101*, 1084–1089.

Barry, M. M., Domitrovich, C., & Lara, M. A. (2005). The implementation of mental health promotion programmes. *Promotion & Education, 2*, 30–6, 62, 68.

Bero, L., Grilli, R., Grimshaw, J., & Harvey, E. (1998). Closing the gap between research and practice: An overview of systematic reviews of interventions to promote the implementation of research findings. *British Medical Journal, 317*(7156), 465–468.

Bowie, C., Leung, W., & Reichenberg, A. (2008). Predicting schizophrenia patients' real-world behavior with specific neuropsychological and functional capacity measures. *Biological Psychiatry, 63*(5), 505–511.

Breslau, J., & Aguilar-Gaxiola, S. (2006). Specifying race-ethnic differences in risk for psychiatric disorder in a USA national sample. *Psychological Medicine, 36*(1), 57–68.

Cabassa, L., Ezell, J., & Lewis-Fernandez, R. (2010). Lifestyle interventions for adults with serious mental illness: A systematic literature review. *Psychiatric Services, 61*(8), 774–782.

California Department of Health Care Services. (2012). Mental health services act (Proposition 63). Retrieved August 26, 2013 from http://www.dhcs.ca.gov/services/mh/Pages/MH_Prop63.aspx

Carrington, C. (2006). Clinical depression in African American women: Diagnoses, treatment, and research. *Journal of Clinical Psychology, 62*(7), 779–791.

Cassidy, F., Ahearn, E., & Carroll, J. (1999). Elevated frequency of diabetes mellitus in hospitalized manic-depressive patients. *American Journal of Psychiatry, 156*(9), 1417–1420.

Centers for Disease Control, Office of Women's Health. (2010). *Leading causes of death in females, United States, 2006.* Retrieved from http://www.cdc.gov/nchs/nvss/mortality_tables.htm

Chatters, L., Taylor, R, Jackson, J., & Lincoln, K. (2008). Religious coping among African Americans, Caribbean blacks and non-Hispanic whites. *Journal of Community Psychology, 36*(3), 371–386.

Chatters, L., Taylor, R., Lincoln, K., & Schroepfer, T. (2002). Patterns of informal support from family and church members among African Americans. *Journal of Black Studies, 33*(1), 65–85.

Chatters, L., Taylor, R., McKeever Bullard, K., & Jackson, J. (2009). Race and ethnic differences in religious involvement: African Americans, Caribbean blacks and non-Hispanic whites. *Ethnic and Racial Studies, 32*(7), 1143–1163.

Chatters, L., Mattis, J. S., Woodward, A., Taylor, R. J., Neighbors, H. W., & Grayman, N. (2011). Use of ministers for a serious personal problem among African Americans: Findings from the National

Survey of American Life (NSAL). *American Journal of Orthopsychiatry, 81*(1), 118–127. doi:10.1111/j.1939–0025.2010.01079.x

Cooper, L. A., Brown, C., Thi Vu, H., Ford, D. E., & Powe, N. R. (2001). How important is intrinsic spirituality in depression care? *Journal of General Internal Medicine, 16*(9), 634–638.

Cooper, L. A, Ghods Dinoso, B. K., Ford, D. E., Roter, D. L., Primm, A. B., Larson, S. M., & Wang, N.-Y. (2013). Comparative effectiveness of standard versus patient-centered collaborative care interventions for depression among African Americans in primary care settings: The BRIDGE Study. *Health Services Research, 48*(1), 150–174. doi:10.1111/j.1475–6773.2012.01435.x

Crewe, S. E. (2007). Joy of living: A community-based mental health promotion program for African American elders. *Journal of Gerontological Social Work, 48*(3/4), 421–438.

Cuijpers, P., Van Straten, A., & Smit, F. (2005). Preventing the incidence of new cases of mental disorders. *The Journal of Nervous and Mental Disease, 193*(2), 119–125. doi:10.1097/01.nmd.0000152810.76190.a6

Dana, R. H. (2002). Mental health services for African Americans : A cultural/racial perspective. *Cultural Diversity and Ethnic Minority Psychology, 8*(1), 3–18. doi:10.1037//1099–9809.8.1.3

Das, A., Olfson, M., McCurtis, H., & Weissman, M. (2006). Depression in African Americans: Breaking barriers to detection and treatment. *Journal of Family Practice, 55*(1), 30–39.

Davidson, S., Judd, F., & Jolley, D. (2001). Cardiovascular risk factors for people with mental illness. *New Zealand Journal of Psychiatry, 35*(2), 196–202.

Diez Roux, A. (2003). Residential environments and cardiovascular risk. *Journal of Urban Health, 80*(4), 569–589.

Dixon, L. (1999). Dual diagnosis of substance abuse in schizophrenia: Prevalence and impact on outcomes. *Schizophrenia Research, 35,* S93–S100.

Dwight-Johnson, M., Unutzer, J., Sherbourne, C., Tang, L., & Wells, K., (2001). Can quality improvement programs for depression in primary care address patient preferences for treatment? *Medical Care, 39*(9), 934–944.

Emslie, C., Ridge, D., Ziebland, S., & Hunt, K. (2006). Men's accounts of depression: Reconstructing or resisting hegemonic masculinity? *Social Science & Medicine, 62*(9), 2246–2257.

Fledderus, M., Bohlmeijer, E. T., Smit, F., & Westerhof, G. J. (2010). Mental health promotion as a new goal in public mental health care: A randomized controlled trial of an intervention-enhancing psychological flexibility. *American Journal of Public Health, 100*(12), 2372. doi:10.2105/AJPH.2010.196196

Gary, F. A. (2005). Stigma: Barrier to mental health care among ethnic minorities. *Issues in Mental Health Nursing, 26*(10), 979–999. doi:10.1080/01612840500280638

González,, H., Tarraf, W., Whitfield, K. E., & Vega, W. A. (2010). The epidemiology of major depression and ethnicity in the United States. *Journal of Psychiatric Research, 44*(15), 1043–1051.

González, H., Whitfield, K., West, B., Williams, D., Lichtenberg, P., & Jackson, J. (2007). Modified-symbol digit modalities test for African Americans, Caribbean Black Americans, and non-Latino whites: Nationally representative normative data. *Archives of Clinical Neuropsychology, 22*(5), 605–613.

González,, J. M., Alegría, M., Prihoda, T. J., Copeland, L. A., & Zeber, J. E. (2011). How the relationship of attitudes toward mental health treatment and service use differs by age, gender, ethnicity/race and education. *Social Psychiatry and Psychiatric Epidemiology, 46*(1), 45–57. doi:10.1007/s00127–009–0168–4

Goodell, S., & Druss, B., & Walker, E. R. (2011). *Mental disorders and medical comorbidity.* Princeton, NJ: Robert Wood Johnson Foundation.

Griffith, E., & Bell, C. (1989). Recent trends in suicide and homicide among blacks. *Journal of the American Medical Association, 262*(16), 2265–2269.

Griner, D., & Smith, T. B. (2006). Culturally adapted mental health intervention: A meta-analytic review. *Psychotherapy, 43*(4), 531–548. doi:10.1037/0033–3204.43.4.531

Hankerson, S. H., & Weissman, M. M. (2012). Church-based health programs for mental disorders among African Americans: A review. *Psychiatric Services, 63*(3), 243–249. doi:10.1176/appi.ps.201100216

Harris, K., Edlund, M., & Larson, S. (2005). Racial and ethnic differences in the mental health problems and use of mental health care. *Medical Care, 43*(8), 775–784.

Herrán, A., Amado, J., García-Unzueta, M. T., Vázquez-Barquero, J. L., Perera, L., González-Macías, J. (2000). Increased bone remodeling in first-episode major depressive disorder. *Psychosomatic Medicine, 62*(6), 779–782.

Hines-Martin, V., Malone, M., Kim, S., & Brown-Piper, A. (2003). Barriers to mental health care access in an African American population. *Issues in Mental Health Nursing, 24,* 237–256. doi:10.1080/01612840390160775

Interian, A., Ang, A., & Gara, M. (2011). The long-term trajectory of depression among Latinos in primary care and its relationship to depression care disparities. *General Hospital Psychiatry, 33*(2), 94–101.

Jané-Llopis, E., Barry, M., Hosman, C., & Patel, V. (2005). Mental health promotion works: A review. *Global Health Promotion, 12*(2), 9–25. doi:10.1177/10253823050120020103x

Joe, S., Baser, R., & Breeden, G. (2006). Prevalence of and risk factors for lifetime suicide attempts among blacks in the United States. *Journal of the American Medical Association, 296*(17), 2112–2123.

Karlsen, S., & Nazroo, J. (2002). Relation between racial discrimination, social class, and health among ethnic minority groups. *American Journal of Public Health, 92*(4), 624–631.

Kessler, R., & Berglund, P. (2005). Lifetime prevalence and age-of-onset distributions of DSM-IV disorders in the National Comorbidity Survey Replication. *Archives of General Psychiatry, 62,* 593–602.

King, G., & Williams, D. (1995). Race and health: A multidimensional approach to African-American health. *Society and Health,* 93–130.

Krause, N. (2002). A comprehensive strategy for developing close-ended survey items for use in studies of older adults. *Journal of Gerontology Biological Psychological Science and Social Science, 57*(5), s263 -s274.

Lin, E., Katon, W., & von Korff, M. (2004). Relationship of depression and diabetes self-care, medication adherence, and preventive care. *Diabetes Care, 27*(9), 2154–2160.

Lincoln, C., & Mamiya, L. (1990). *The black church in the African American experience.* Durham, NC: Duke University Press.

Matthews, A. K., Corrigan, P., Smith, B., & Aranda, F. (2006). A qualitative exploration of African Americans' attitudes toward mental illness and mental illness treatment seeking. *Rehabilitation Education, 20*(4), 253–268.

Mays, V., Caldwell, C., & Jackson, J. (1996). Mental health symptoms and service utilization patterns of help-seeking among African American women. In H. Neighbors & J. Jackson (Eds.), *Mental health in black America* (pp. 161–176). Thousand Oaks, CA: Sage.

McElroy, S., Frye, M., & Suppes, T. (2002). Correlates of overweight and obesity in 644 patients with bipolar disorder. *The Journal of Clinical Psychiatry, 63*(3), 207–213.

Melfi, C., Croghan, T., & Hanna, M. (2000). Psychiatric briefs. *Journal of Clinical Psychiatry, 61,* 16–21.

Mizell, C. (1999). Life course influences on African American men's depression: Adolescent parental composition, self-concept, and adult earnings. *Journal of Black Studies,* 467–490.

Neighbors, H. (1998). The African American minister as a source of help for serious personal crises: Bridge or barrier to mental health care? *Health Education & Research, 25*(6), 759–777.

Nooney, J., & Woodrum, E. (2002). Religious coping and church-based social support as predictors of mental health outcomes: Testing a conceptual model. *Journal for the Scientific Study of Religion, 41*(2), 359–368. doi:10.1111/1468–5906.00122

Pargament, K. I., Koenig, H. G., Tarakeshwar, N., & Hahn, J. (2004). Religious coping methods as predictors of psychological, physical and spiritual outcomes among medically ill elderly patients: A two-year longitudinal study. *Journal of Health Psychology, 9*(6), 713–730.

Parks, J., Svendsen, D., Singer, P., Foti, M., & Mauer, B. (2006). *Morbidity and mortality in people with serious mental illness.* Alexandria, VA: National Association of State Mental Health Program Directors.

Poussaint, A., & Alexander, A. (2000). *Lay my burden down: Unraveling suicide and the mental health crisis among African-Americans.* Boston: Beacon Press.

Smith Black, B., Rabins, P. V., German, P., McGuire, M., & Roca, R. (1997). Need and unmet need for mental health care among elderly public housing residents. *The Gerontologist, 27*(6), 717–728.

Snowden, L. (2001). Barriers to effective mental health services for African Americans. *Mental Health Services Research, 3*(4), 181–187.

Snowden, L. (2003). Bias in mental health assessment and intervention: Theory and evidence. *American Journal of Public Health, 93*(2), 239–243.

Sriwattanakomen, R., Ford, A., Thomas, S., Miller, M., Stack, J. A., Morse, J. Q., & Reynolds, C. (2008). Preventing depression in later life: Translation from concept to experimental design and implementation. *American Journal of Geriatric Psychiatry, 16*(6), 460–468. doi:10.1097/JGP.0b013e318165db95

Strawbridge, W., Shema, S., Cohen, R., & Kaplan, G. (2001). Religious attendance increases survival by improving and maintaining good health behaviors, mental health, and social relationships. *Annals of Behavioral Medicine, 23*(1), 68–74.

Substance Abuse and Mental Health Services Administration. (2010, March/April). Take action in your community. *SAMHSA News,* pp. 1–20.

Sue, S. (1977). Community mental health services to minority groups: Some optimism, some pessimism. *American Psychologist, 32*(8), 116.

Taylor, R. J., Chatters, L. M., Bullard, K. M., Wallace, J. M., & Jackson, J. S. (2009). Organizational religious behavior among older African Americans: Findings from the National Survey of American Life. *Research on Aging, 31*(4), 440–462. doi:10.1177/0164027509333453

Taylor, R. J., Chatters, L., & Jackson, J. (2007). Religious and spiritual involvement among older African Americans, Caribbean blacks, and non-Hispanic whites: Findings from the national survey of American life. *The Journals of Gerontology Series B: Psychological Sciences and Social Sciences, 62*(4), S238–S250.

Taylor, R. J., Ellison, C. G., Chatters, L. M., Levin, J. S., & Lincoln, K. D. (2000). Mental health services in

faith communities : The role of clergy in black churches. *Social Work, 45*(1), 73–87.

Thompson, V. L. S., Bazile, A., & Akbar, M. (2004). African Americans' perceptions of psychotherapy and psychotherapists. *Professional Psychology: Research and Practice, 35*(1), 19–26. doi:10.1037/0735–7028.35.1.19

Turner, R., & Avison, W. (2003). Status variations in stress exposure: Implications for the interpretation of research on race, socioeconomic status, and gender. *Journal of Health and Social Behavior,* 488–505.

Turner, R., & Lloyd, D. (1999). The stress process and the social distribution of depression. *Journal of Health and Social Behavior,* 374–404.

UC Davis Center for Reducing Health Disparities. (2009). *Building partnerships: Conversations with African Americans about mental health needs and community strengths* (pp. 1–16).

Üçok, A., & Polat, A. (2004). Cigarette smoking among patients with schizophrenia and bipolar disorders. *Psychiatry and Clinical Neurosciences, 58*(4), 434–437.

U.S. Department of Health and Human Services. (2011). *National healthcare disparities report* (pp. 1–248). Rockville, MD: Author.

U.S. Department of Health and Human Services. (2012). *A profile of older Americans: 2012.* Washington, DC: Author.

Veroff, J., Kulka, R., & Douvan, E. (1981). *Mental health in America: Patterns of help-seeking from 1957 to 1976.* Retrieved from http://www.getcited.org/pub/102083331

Wang, P., Lane, M., & Olfson, M., Pincus, H., Wells, K., & Kessler, R. (2005). Twelve-month use of mental health services in the United States: Results from the National Comorbidity Survey Replication. *Archives of General Psychiatry, 62*(6), 629–640.

Whaley, A. L. (2001). Cultural mistrust and mental health services for African Americans: A review and meta-analysis. *The Counseling Psychologist, 29*(4), 513 -531. doi:10.1177/0011000001294003

Whaley, A. L., & Davis, K. E. (2007). Cultural competence and evidence-based practice in mental health services: A complementary perspective.

The American Psychologist, 62(6), 563–574. doi:10.1037/0003–066X.62.6.563

Whitehead, M. (1992). The concepts and principles of equity and health. *International Journal of Health Services, 22*(3), 429–445.

Williams, D., & Collins, C. (2001). Racial residential segregation: a fundamental cause of racial disparities in health. *Public Health Reports, 116*(5), 404 -416.

Williams, D., & Haile, R., González, H., Neighbors, H., Baser, R., & Jackson, J. (2007). The mental health of Black Caribbean immigrants: Results from the National Survey of American Life. *American Journal of Public Health, 97*(1), 52–59.

Woodward, A. T., Taylor, R. J., Neighbors, H. W., Chatters, L. M., & Jackson, J. S. (2008). The use of professional services and informal support among African Americans and Caribbean Blacks with a mental disorder. *Psychiatric Rehabilitation Journal, 59*(11), 1292–1298. doi:10.1176/appi.ps.59.11.1292

World Health Organization. (1998). Health promotion glossary. Geneva: Author.

World Health Organization. (2001). *World health report 2001: Mental health: New understanding, new hope.* Geneva: Author.

World Health Organization. (2005). *Promoting mental health: Concepts, emerging evidence, practice.* Geneva: Author.

World Health Organization. (2007). *World health statistics 2007.* Geneva: Author. Retrieved from http://www.who.int/whr/2001/en/

Young, J. J. L., Griffith, E. E. H., & Williams, D. D. R. (2003). The integral role of pastoral counseling by African-American clergy in community mental health. *Psychiatric Services, 54*(5), 688–692.

CHAPTER 27

Sexual Minorities

Jeremy T. Goldbach & Shannon L. Dunlap

CHAPTER OBJECTIVES

- Develop an awareness of the history of LGBT and civil rights;
- Identify common terms used in the LGBT community;
- Learn how to complete a biopsychosocial assessment that includes sexual orientation and gender identity as well as the use of inclusive language when assessing and building rapport with clients;
- Gain a deeper understanding of the contextual, interpersonal, and individual factors that impact health and wellness among sexual minority youth and adults.

CASE VIGNETTE

Toby is a 15-year-old Latino and Native American young man. He has been referred by his high school to a local mental health clinic for evaluation of suicidal ideation with no specific plan. Toby has also been missing school three to five days per week for the last three months, placing him at risk for repeating 10th grade. Drugs and alcohol have been suspected by both the school and his mother. Toby was adopted at birth. Toby was raised in a conservative religious family. Toby has two younger brothers and one sister who are all much younger than Toby at 3.6 years, 2 years, and 6 months, respectively. Toby's siblings are not adopted. Toby's father has moved out of the home on numerous occasions and most recently has been living in another apartment for the last four months. Toby's mother is working nights cleaning office buildings, and Toby is responsible for taking care of all of his siblings while his mother works. Toby's father does not provide financial assistance at this time.

Toby has experienced chronic bullying since elementary school and has changed schools five times between middle and high school as a result of bullying. Toby is now in an alternative high school. Toby has thought about suicide and has recently written notes to his teachers and principal about thoughts of killing himself and not wanting to be "here" anymore. Toby identifies as bisexual, and his gender presentation changes depending on many environmental and social factors. Toby's assigned sex at birth was female, but his internal gender is male. Toby does not live as a boy full time due to the stigma that he experiences within family, neighborhood, church, and school. Toby has few friends who are supportive and only presents and identifies as a boy at home when alone or with his mother or siblings, or when out of his neighborhood with certain supportive friends. Toby's adoptive father has no idea that Toby's gender is male. Toby's mother states that she is supportive but often uses both pronouns (he, she) and is inconsistent with what name she calls him, even in private. His school counselor is aware of Toby's gender identity but also uses "Tamara," his birth name, to refer to Toby. Toby currently does not receive medical or psychosocial support regarding his personal experience as a boy or his social and familial navigation of gender identity. Toby also has not been exposed to or referred to resources regarding sexual and gender orientation within school or community.

When Toby was 13, he started presenting as male in his room and when going out with friends. Prior to this, he preferred to play with toys and preferred playing games that were seen as socially inconsistent with "typical" preferences of his assigned sex. As an early teenager, Toby told his mother that he was bisexual. Toby's mother requested that Toby not disclose to his father. Instead, Toby's mother called the priest at their church who came to the home talk to Toby about the "sins" of homosexuality. When Toby is in his father's presence, in the neighborhood, and in most social and familial situations, he presents as female and uses the name Tamara. Toby's siblings call him Tammy. After the lecture by the priest, Toby started cutting himself and withdrawing to his room when home. Toby is sometimes gone from home for two to three days at a time. When he was 13 years old, he started smoking marijuana a few times a week. Currently, Toby uses marijuana daily.

INTRODUCTION

Much of what clinicians do involves the use of a label or a terminology. Labels represent one method for conforming to a universal language that can be replicated and understood by others within the field. However, many questions and concerns about the use of labels often occur when working with sexual minority clients who identify as lesbian, gay, bisexual, or transgender (LGBT). For instance, does placing a check in the "LGBT" box or the "heterosexual" box really capture a person's sexual orientation or sexual identity? Similarly, who decides the gender of the client, even when the client appears, on the surface, to have a gender that matches what the social worker believes to be their biological sex? What are the benefits and risks of lumping the "T" with the "LGB"? And why when a baby is born do people ask "what is the gender?" as if that young person has already developed a gender identity?

First, and perhaps most important, it is OK for the social worker not to have the answer. In fact, not assuming the answer is often the best approach. The "alphabet soup" of identity labels (including terms such as homosexual, gay, queer, lesbian, butch, femme, bisexual, transgender, pansexual, two-spirited, intersex, same-gender-loving, heterosexual, straight, gender fluid, gender queer, cisgender, stud, stem, ze/hir, questioning) often seem daunting, especially when we want to be sure we appropriately use and understand this language with the clients we serve. It would be impossible to list or even define all the sexual and gender identity labels used today; and there is no reason to do so. This chapter is intended to be a guide for social workers while they unpack the terminology and history of the LGBT community, and to help them understand the context of a rich cultural experience when deciding on best intervention approaches. This chapter is not intended as a finite immutable tutorial of when, where, why, how, and to whom labels should be used. While it helps to have some working knowledge of the general meaning behind the terms, in the end every person constructs their own identity labels and define them for themselves. To make matters potentially more confusing for the clinician, identities and labels may change as people evolve, grow and mature. By saying that this changes, it does not mean that sexual orientation or gender is a continually fluid process, nor does it mean that if it is fluid, it is so *only* for people who are not heterosexual. It does mean, however, that the experience and expression of sexual and gender identity is mutable, and if the social worker treats this as otherwise (such as the way racial or ethnic identity is considered) they may miss out on the richness of a client's life experience.

Defining the LGBT Community

Most estimates suggest that LGBT persons represent approximately 3% to 5% of the general population in the United States (Gates & Newport, 2012; Marshal et al., 2008). In school-aged youth under age 18, self-report rates are approximately 3% (Garofalo, Wolf, Kessel, Palfrey, & DuRant, 1998). It is possible that fewer youth identify as LGB because of uncertainty about how they will identify later in life (Savin-Williams, 2001). When offered a range of reporting choices about sexuality, approximately 25% of 12 year olds report they are "unsure" of their sexual orientation. This rate decreases significantly by age 18, when only about 5% report uncertainty (Remafedi, Resnick, Blum, & Harris, 1992; Robinson, 1994). It is evident that there is great diversity within the "LGBT" community. In fact, the "community" is more accurately made up of a number of smaller communities that coalesce around two constructs; sexual orientation (attractions, identities, and behaviors) and gender

identity (male, female, third gender) fall outside traditional heterosexual norms or sex-defined gender. This section will help you to understand the variety of constructs that should be considered in social work practice with sexual minorities.

Sexual Orientation

Individuals engaging in same-sex sexual behaviors or reporting same-sex attractions have been documented across a wide range of historical periods and cultural experiences (Blackwood, 1986). In the early 1900s, sexual orientation was described in terms of psychology and behavior (Sell, 1997). As early as 1905, Freud began to publish on sexuality, identifying the defining characteristic of sexual orientation as the sex an individual is compared with the sex of an individual to whom the individual is attracted (of note, Freud did not believe that homosexuality was an illness that could be changed or fixed; Lewes, 1988).

Also during this time, researchers began to recognize that gender roles, expression, and sexual behaviors were not parts of the same construct but multiple aspects of one's sexual identity. Many regard the work of Alfred Kinsey (Kinsey, Pomeroy, & Martin, 1948; Kinsey, Pomeroy, Martin, & Gebhard, 1953) as the first attempt to identify sexuality along a continuum rather than a binary (i.e., heterosexual *or* homosexual), placing individuals on a six-point sexuality scale ranging from "exclusively heterosexual"(0) to "exclusively homosexual" (6). This early work of Kinsey and his colleagues helped us to understand that *sexual behavior* is a continuum that may change over time.

More recently, a sophistication of defining sexual orientation has grown beyond this to include dimensions of *attraction* (i.e., who a person finds attractive; Janssen, Everaerd, Spiering, & Janssen, 2000); *romantic beliefs* (i.e., who a person is romantically interested in; Diamond, 2003, 2005) and *identity* (i.e., how an individual identifies; Kauth & Kalichman, 1995). Given this complexity, a number of definitions have emerged. In the early 1990s, sexual orientation was defined as "the direction of sexual feelings or behaviors toward individuals of the opposite sex, same sex, or combination of the two" (LeVay, 1993, p. 158; Sell, 1997). According to the American Psychological Association (2011), sexual orientation is defined as "the sex of those to whom one is sexually and romantically attracted" (p. 1). Still others have tried to embrace all of these dynamic constructs, stating that sexual orientation is an enduring emotional, romantic, sexual or affection, attraction or nonattraction to other people; sexual orientation is fluid and people use a variety of labels to describe their sexual orientation ("Safe zone resource manual," 2013).

As a practitioner, it is likely most helpful to recognize that individuals may answer the following questions in a variety of ways. It is important that social workers remember sexual orientation and sexual identity are often used synonymously and how and when they are used in the context of assessment, rapport building and treatment may depend on the client. Sexual identity is often defined as how one identifies or describes their sexual orientation. This can be the labels that people use to describe more specifically their sexual orientation. How clinicians assess sexual orientation and sexual identity can be different by race/ ethnicity, age, gender, or region of country.

Historically, women have often felt excluded from language that had been predominately focused on the experiences of gay men (Sell, 1997). Although the term *gay* is often used generally to describe sexual attraction toward a person of the same gender, this term is commonly associated with people of a male gender as opposed to female gender. *Lesbian*, on the other hand, is commonly described as a woman who is attracted or has affection for someone of the same gender. *Bisexual* is a term that is used to describe "attraction and/or affection for people of the same or other genders." However, these definitions are not inclusive of all language used to describe sexual orientation. For example, some may describe themselves as *pansexual*, or as having an attraction to and affection for all genders and sexes. Others may define themselves as *asexual*, or not having attraction to any gender. However, this does not necessarily mean

that people who are asexual don't have sex, as many do. Recognizing that an individual's sexual orientation or sexual identity label does not, then, define one's sexual behavior is a critical component of social work practice with this population. Thus, if during an assessment a female client discloses that all of her sexual partners have been male, this does not necessarily mean that she identifies with a heterosexual orientation or identity. Table 27.1 offers a brief list of common self-labels and definitions.

Gender Identity

Gender is also an important element of identity. Gender and sex can be related (although do not have to be) and are not synonymous. According to the University of California at Berkeley Gender Equity Resource Center, gender can be defined as a socially constructed system of classification that ascribes qualities of masculinity and femininity to people. On the other hand, sex is "a medical term designating a certain combination of gonads, chromosomes, external gender organs, secondary sex characteristics and hormonal balances" ("Definition of Terms," 2013, para 65). Gender is a socially constructed, emotional, expressed and internal experience of masculinity and/or femininity along the spectrum that can be inclusive or exclusive of both male and female. Gender can include expression, identity, behavior, role, and feelings. Toomey and colleagues (2010) state that gender-nonconforming individuals, such as boys who are more feminine than other boys or girls who are more masculine than other girls, can be described as those who transgress social gender norms. These social norms are often dominant societal expectations passed down over time and often oppress those who may not ascribe to such expectations. Sex, on the other hand, is biologically defined and describes physiological aspects of body only. Recently, gender has been used to describe the sex of an individual. However, since gender is a socially constructed and personal experience, it is more accurate to refer to the sex of a baby as opposed to the gender, assuming that a baby may not have awareness of gender at such a young age.

Table 27.1 Common Terminology and Definitions

Terminology	Definition
Asexual	A sexual orientation of those who are not sexually attracted to others or do not feel a desire for partnered sexuality.
Bisexual	A term to describe the sexual orientation and affectionate attraction for both people of the same gender and the other gender.
Cisgender	Gender identity or gender role that society considers to be aligned with assigned sex at birth.
Gay	An umbrella term that can be used for both men and women. It describes the emotional and/or physical attraction to or sexual orientation toward people of the same gender.
Gender	Different than sex assigned at birth. A social and personal construct that is used to categorize people and self as man, woman, or another identity.
Gender Expression	Expressing self either in dress or behavior that is socially considered to be feminine, masculine, or somewhere in between.
Gender Nonconforming	Not subscribing to socially constructed gender expression or roles.
Gender Queer	Gender role or identity outside the dominant societal expectations for one's assigned sex; can be beyond genders or a combination of genders.
Heterosexuality	A sexual orientation of those who are physically and emotionally attracted to people of a gender that is not their own.
Intersex	Those who develop (without medical or pharmaceutical intervention) the primary and secondary sexual characteristics that do not fit exactly the societal and medical classification of male or female.
Lesbian	One who identifies as a woman and is physically and emotionally attracted to others of the same gender.
LGBT	An acronym used for lesbian, gay, bisexual, and transgender.
Pansexual	Used to described people who are emotionally and sexually attracted to all genders and sexes.
Queer	A term that is and can be used by anyone regardless of sexual and gender orientation for many different sexual or gender-related reasons. Some still do consider this offensive due to historical use of this term as derogatory. Recently reclaimed as an umbrella term.
Sex	A characterization as male, female, or intersex based on genitalia at birth.
Transman	Can be used to describe a female to male transgender person. Can capture the gender identification or lived experience as a trans person.
Transgender	A person whose gender identity, expression, or role is outside the male/female binary or whose gender does not fit with the dominant societal expectations of assigned sex at birth.
Transwoman	Can be used to describe a male to female transgender person. Can capture the gender identification or lived experience as a trans person.

By preschool, most children have a strong concept of gender and are able to label their own and other's gender (Toomey et al., 2010). Those who conform to socially constructed gender roles are often reinforced to maintain those roles by society, while those who do not conform may face criticism within various community and familial settings. Egan and Perry (2001), suggested that "by middle childhood, a strong concept has developed regarding the degree to which they typify their gender category; degree of connection with gender assignment; whether they are free to explore cross-sex options or are compelled to conform to gender stereotypes; and whether their own sex is superior to another" (p. 459). Pressure to conform and shame often create oppressive experiences for many younger and older people alike who are gender nonconforming, are exploring their gender, or whose gender identity is not consistent with their assigned sex.

Gender nonconformity is defined as not conforming to society's expectations of gender expression based on the gender binary, expectations of masculinity and femininity, or how society feels they should identify their gender ("LGBTQIA Resource Center Glossary," 2014). Transgender, on the other hand, can be defined as a psychological self (i.e., gender identity) differing from the social expectations for the physical sex they were born with or a gender identity that does not fit within dominant-group social constructs of assigned sex and gender; having no gender or multiple genders. It is important to highlight that gender identity and sexual identity, can be related but are not always. A transgender female (some choose to identify this way if they were born with female body parts but identify with and/or live life along the male or masculine spectrum) who is attracted to a female may identify as heterosexual, lesbian, queer, or any other sexual identity. Regardless of a client's outward presentation or gender identity, it is always helpful to ask them how they describe their sexual orientation despite socially constructed ideas around the directional link between gender and sexual identity.

Finally, despite the recent popularity around using the word "queer," it is important to note that people of various ages and ethnic/racial backgrounds may not embrace the use of this word given historical significance and discriminatory use. Similarly, although the term "same-gender-loving" is sometimes used by African Americans (primarily men) to describe attraction to people of the same gender ("LGBTQIA Resource Center Glossary," 2014), this does not mean that all African Americans use this term to describe themselves. Therefore, before trying to assume gender identity, sexual orientation, or identity labels, it is always better to ask the client directly and use the words that they use for themselves.

Assessing sexual orientation or gender/sexual identity can bring up anxiety for both the client and the practitioner. The therapeutic relationship, however, may be the only place that someone feels safe to talk about sexuality, particularly those components of sexuality that have been seen as taboo or inappropriate in the general population. Creating a non-judgmental space where one can explore the dynamic aspects of sexuality is one essential task in developing and maintaining the therapeutic relationship, particularly with those who have experienced or are fearful of stigma. Demonstrating flexibility in helping the individual define and understand their experience of their sexual and gender identity is often more important than knowing the terminology.

A Brief History of the LGBT Movement

Clients may (or may not) recognize that they come from a rich and extensive social justice history that may affect their behavioral health in ways they do not fully understand. The experience of being a part of a minority group, and the knowledge passed down as a result of minority group membership, can foster a strong and healthy sense of self as well as increase stress that in turn may impact their likelihood of poverty and substance use, mental health concerns, and risk for HIV and other disease transmission (Fullilove et. al., 1990; Fullilove, 2006). Additionally, given the association between the LGBT community and HIV/AIDS (described in further detail below), stigma is a significant component of LGBT identity, and represents an important place for social work intervention.

While a number of significant events occurred before this time, most historians agree that the galvanization of the modern gay and lesbian movement occurred in June of 1969. Stonewall, a gay bar that sold alcohol in New York City and primarily catered to gay and lesbian patrons was raided by police and shut down, described by police as a "display of public morality" (Lisker, 1969). After arresting the bar staff and several patrons of the bar the crowd in the street began to riot. Over the next few weeks the Gay Liberation Front (GLF) was formed, a first attempt to organize around gay rights. Even in the earliest stages of the movement, the sexual behaviors of LGBT individuals were at the forefront of this fight for civil rights. Activists sought equal rights including protection in jobs and police interactions, the repeal of sodomy laws, and new legislation against discrimination at the local and national level (Bianco, 2000). Prior to Stonewall, early activists primarily relied upon picket lines organized by groups such as the Mattachine Society of New York and Daughters of Bilitis, under the collective East Coast Homophile Organizations (ECHO).

In the 1970's, a sense of liberation (which included sexual liberation) came to the gay communities of the United States. Mass numbers of gay men and women were moving to San Francisco, where an openly gay man, Harvey Milk, had been elected to city supervisor. Additionally, public sex venues (i.e., bathhouses) began opening throughout major cities (Binson, Woods, Pollack, Paul, Stall, & Catania, 2001). Although gay men were increasingly coming down with venereal diseases, due to new sexual acts such "Oral-Anal contact" (Centers for Disease Control [CDC], 1981a), most illnesses could easily be cured, resulting in the infrequent use of protection (Darrow, 1981). At this time in history, condoms were generally used to prevent pregnancy only, and gay men were not at risk for that.

The movement quickly slowed, however, in the early 1980s when the first outbreak of HIV was discovered and labeled. In 1981, the "gay cancer" and shortly after "GRID" or Gay-Related Immune Disorder (as it was known at this time) was noticed only in gay men and medically as Kaposi Sarcoma or other opportunistic infections (Altman, 1982; Cichocki, 2006). Although cases had been increasing since the late 1970s, the CDC did not issue an official recognition of the disease until June 5, 1981, when a number of gay men were becoming symptomatic and gravely ill. Initially this report was named "Pneumocystis pneumonia in homosexual men—Los Angeles," but the CDC was reluctant to include the reference to homosexual men for fear of tagging an outbreak to the community and causing further prejudice. So, all references to homosexuality were dropped from the report (Cohen, 2001; CDC, 1981a). The first CDC report to link the disease with gay men was on July 4, 1982 (CDC, 1981b).

Wrapped in the historical context of the first outbreaks of HIV are unique implications for working through historical trauma and stigma. For example, the negative attention of the disease served as early fuel for extremist "evidence" against homosexual practices. A Gallup poll in 1985 found that 37% of Americans stated their opinion about LGBT individuals changed for the worse, with only 4% feeling sympathetic or undecided (Associated Press, 1985). As sexuality (and associated sexual behaviors) was central to the experience of being a gay man, there was a heightened sensitivity within the LGBT to the CDC response given to it.

Before HIV/AIDS was irrefutably recognized as an illness that disproportionately affected gay men, most men and women did not adhere to recommendations about changing their sexual behaviors (Cohen, 2001). Although HIV/AIDS related deaths and illness were quickly rising, many gay men believed that the new "crisis" was simply a heterosexual plot to undermine the sexual liberation of the gay community, especially as the disease was initially called the "gay cancer" and was so strongly associated to the group. Then, in the 1990s, the concept of survivor's guilt also surfaced (Odets, 1994). This clinical phenomenon occurred in gay men who had seen their friends become diagnosed with HIV and die of AIDS, while they remained healthy. The PTSD-like symptoms occurred, as Agnos (1990) stated, from the "simple fact that by 1990, more San Franciscans had died of AIDS than died in the four wars of the 20th century, combined and tripled" (p. 1). The needs of HIV-positive individuals in the 1990s left HIV-negative gay men without social support and feeling guilty for even considering their own needs in the midst of the epidemic (Odets, 1994).

Contemporary Issues Facing LGBT Individuals

When working with an individual whose gender and sexual orientation and attraction lies outside the dominant societal expectations (defined here as LGBT), it is helpful to understand the health disparities they may face. While research on the LGBT community remains somewhat limited (Hughes & Eliason, 2002), a number of social factors, such as personal networks, social capital, cultural context and social network have an impact on behavioral health outcomes found among the population (Poundstone, Strathdee, & Celentano, 2004). Some research limitations including convening a generalizable sample, as well as those related to oversimplification of the "LGBT community" as described earlier in this chapter. As a social worker reading about the various disparities, remember that although often referred to as a broader "LGBT" group, the subgroups of this community (i.e., lesbians, gay men, etc.) find that their experiences and issues differ substantially from each other. For example, there is a social stigma ascribed to drinking among women in general (Lisanky, 1958), which may be impactful for lesbians as well but would not apply to gay men's drinking behaviors. That said, there are a number of mental and behavioral health disparities that exist within the LGBT community that should be assessed for when working with LGBT clients. These include health care disparities; alcohol, tobacco, and other drug use; depression; anxiety; and suicide risk. A longer discussion of the impact

that HIV/AIDS has had on the LGBT community is also included in Chapter 3 in this volume.

Mental Health and Substance Use Disparities

A number of behavioral health disparities exist among LGBT individuals. These include suicide (Fergusson, Horwood, & Beautrais, 1999; Freidman, 2010), emotional problems, major depression and anxiety disorder (Bailey, 1999), as well as substance use (Halkitis et al., 2005; Kubicek, McDavitt, Carpineto, Weiss, Iverson, & Kipke, 2007). Evidence indicates that lesbian and bisexual women are more likely than heterosexual women to experience traumatic events such as child abuse and neglect (Alvy, 2013; Austin et al., 2008; D'Augelli, 2003; Roberts, Gilman, Breslau, Breslau, & Koenen, 2010) and report higher rates of alcohol use (Hughes, Sathe, & Spagnola, 2010) and other substances (Cochran et al., 2004). Although most studies collapsed lesbian and bisexual women into a single category, recent studies have found bisexual women are at especially high risk of both substance use and mental health problems (Bostwick et al., 2010; McCabe et al., 2009; Wilsnack et al., 2008).

In light of a number of suicides by adolescents across the US, more attention has also been paid to the substance use and mental health patterns of LGBT adolescents. These youth face both conventional challenges of adolescence along with increased stress of being LG or questioning their sexuality. Sexual minority youth report high rates of discrimination, verbal and physical abuse and negative social consequences for revealing their sexuality (Haas et al., 2011). Adolescents who identify as gay or lesbian report nearly three times the rate of substances use from their heterosexual peers (Russell, Driscoll, & Truong, 2002), and are more likely to use multiple substances simultaneously (Garofalo et al., 1998) increasing their risk for adverse health outcomes (Marshal et al., 2008). A substantial literature has also linked experiences of loss of peer relationships and victimization in school (e.g., bullying, violence) to negative mental health and suicidal behavior (Bontempo & D'Augelli, 2002; Friedman, Koeske, Silvestre, Korr, & Sites, 2006; Friedman, Marshal, Stall, Cheong, & Wright, 2008; Goodenow, Szalacha, & Westheimer, 2006; Russell & Joyner, 2001). Hershberger, Pilkington, and D'Augelli (1997) found in their study of 194 LGB youth that loss of friends due to sexual orientation was one of the strongest predictors of a recent suicide attempt.

Practitioners should also focus their attention on the coming out experience when working with sexual minority adolescents. The experience of coming out to family can be especially stressful, with perhaps two-thirds of youth find the process *somewhat* or *extremely troubling* (Pilkington & D'Augelli, 1995). Among youth, studies indicate suicide attempts as high as 53% (Anhalt & Morris, 2008; Haas et al., 2011; McDaniel, Purcell & D'Augelli, 2001) contrasted with 7.1% of youth in general (Lewinsohn, Rohde, & Seeley, 1996). Families also appear to be primary influencers of mental health outcomes for youth. A number of studies have found an association between parental rejection and suicide attempt (D'Augelli et al., 2005; Liu & Mustanski, 2012; Ryan, Huebner, Diaz, & Sanchez, 2009). Further, sexual minority adolescents are disproportionately represented among homeless youth across the United States, suggestive of the frequent occurrence of family rejection (Ray, 2006).

A Framework for Understanding and Reducing Disparities

While recognizing that the mental and behavioral health outcomes described above do not apply to all LGBT individuals, these disparities should not go unnoticed and a framework for practice with this population is helpful. These poor outcomes are commonly attributed to the presence of intensely stressful circumstances. Stress theory posits that as major life events and chronic circumstances accumulate, an individual becomes less equipped to adapt, adjust and tolerate continued

life stress experiences (Brown & Harris, 1978). Like the experiences that increase stress, other experiences can buffer against negative outcomes, such as the perception of strong social support (Cohen & Wills, 1985). In practice, stress theory is often extended to individuals who are part of disadvantaged groups (e.g., women, ethnic minorities; Kessler, 1979; McLeod & Kessler, 1990) as minority individuals repeatedly show increased psychological vulnerability when compared to their majority group peers (Cervantes et al., 2011; Thoits, 1991). An expansive literature, particularly among racial/ethnic minority groups, finds minority-specific stress experiences to lead to increases in suicidal ideation and behavior (Fortuna et al., 2007; Zayas, Lester, Cabassa, & Fortuna, 2005), supported by emerging conceptual models of suicide (Zayas, 2011).

More recently, the tenets of stress theory have been applied to sexual minorities. As Meyer (1995, 2003) explains, there is an association between an array of social and psychological stressors related to being part of a sexual minority group (i.e., minority stress theory; MST). Hughes and Eliason (2002) describe these as experiences of stigmatization from being a sexual minority, along with their influence on behavioral health. The MST suggests that the mental health outcomes of sexual minorities are impacted by a number of distal and proximal stress experiences each that can be the focus of intervention. Distal stressors are those that occur in the environment in the form of negative experiences such as discrimination, homophobic events, and victimization because of sexual orientation. Proximal stressors occur within the individual and include internalized negative attitudes towards homosexuality, internalization of discomfort with sexuality, and emotional distress related to concealment, rejection and acceptance by others (Meyer, 2003; Rosario, Schrimshaw, Hunter, & Gwadz, 2002; Rosario, Rotheram-Borus, & Reid, 1996). Proximal and distal stressors are interrelated. For example, when internalized, minority stress can encourage negative societal attitudes in an individual, pressure to hide their feelings of sexuality and strongly discordant belief systems (e.g., adopting strong religious convictions against homosexuality; DiPlacido, 1998; Shidlo, 1994).

MICRO PERSPECTIVE

Assessment

A comprehensive assessment of gender identity and sexual orientation/identity will take time and may evolve as trust is built. Each client is different with regards to their trust in the therapeutic system and relationship given any previous experiences with trust across various social and institutional systems. Therefore, it's OK if a client chooses not to disclose or talk about gender or sexual orientation right away.

However, even if a client does not plan on disclosing right away (or ever for that matter), it feels more validating to use neutral terms during the initial phase of assessment. So, when assessing gender identity, sexual orientation/identity, and sexual history, it is important to refrain from using terms such *girlfriend* or *boyfriend,* unless those are the terms by a particular client. In an initial phase of assessment with a client who initially presents as female, using inclusive language often leaves the door open for future conversation around sexual partners and sexual identity. Also, avoid using slang because many young people can see right through that. Let them tell you what words, terms, or phrases they use to describe their partners/girlfriends/boyfriends, if they have any.

Regarding gender, despite feeling 100% sure of a client's gender and gender identification, it is still important to use inclusive terminology, and it's OK to be up front about that. Asking direct questions regarding preferred pronouns, gender, and preferred names other than a name given at birth opens the door for clients to talk about their authentic selves. Additionally, it is also important to recognize that if a client reports sex with one gender only, that does not define sexual identity, attraction, or orientation. Sexual orientation and attraction may be different than who they are having sex with or have had sex with during their lifetime.

Lastly, be cautious to assume that a gender or sexual identity outside of cisgender or heterosexual identity warrants an intervention. It is important to distinguish between what is a problem for the clinician/practitioner and what is of concern to the client. Likewise, if a client identifies as heterosexual, be cautious not to assume that this does not warrant intervention now or in the future. Just because a client's gender maybe outside the binary or inconsistent with assigned sex, this does not mean that this is what the client feels is distressing or is the priority. Lastly, assessment regarding sexual or gender identity must primarily include elements of social, family, and institutional stigma or discrimination as well as internalized homophobia or transphobia. As it is not the gender or sexual identity itself that is problematic but the experience of this within various micro-, mezzo- and macrosystems.

Considering the vignette, Toby may be responding to how he has been socialized within various systems. Often heterosexual and cisgender-norming language, pressures, and expectations can create early experiences of dissonance with an internal gender that is inconsistent with these normative messages. Both implicit and explicit messages regarding gender-specific behavior, presentation, and roles are communicated early in life and persist into adulthood. Family, peer, and religious expectations, coupled with school and school district climate and policies as well as community and neighborhood culture and norms, interact to influence the daily experience of youth similar to Toby. What would life be like for Toby if his family were supportive? If he had a strong connection to similar peers? If he lived in a community with easy access to an LGBT Center or Gay-Straight Alliance (GSA)?

Parent Involvement

This may depend on organizational culture or rules. However, it may be necessary to make the argument that it is not emotionally or physically safe for a client to involve parents. Sometimes building family relationships may not be appropriate at the time of this intervention. Or maybe family involvement is safe and necessary, but when and how depends on many factors, including agency policy. Family involvement may depend on a client's age and readiness, harmful aspects of the relationship and/or readiness of family members. Separate sessions with a client and separate sessions with family initially may be essential, but confidentially between family members is necessary. Or, if possible, certain non-supportive family members may need a referral to another practitioner within your organization, or if necessary outside your organization. Regardless, many young people who face LGBT-related discrimination or abuse within their family may struggle with safely attaching to family, siblings, friends, and partners. If, after an assessment, a goal of treatment is to improve a specific relationship (improve communication, support, emotional connection), an attachment approach to building and maintaining safe relationships, enhancing validating/supportive communication, and feeling connected to safe others may be considered.

Direct Service (Intervention) Considerations

Given that identifying as LGBT is not a disorder, no specific treatment approaches have provided evidence specifically for use with LGBT clients. As always, clinicians are advised to match their treatment approach to the specific client, their clinical diagnosis, the available evidence, and the client's culture and personal characteristics. Given the importance of personal desires and culture in treatment outcomes, this construct does warrant some attention.

Although LGBT individuals report high rates of substance use, mental health concerns, and trauma, their experiences in treatment settings is not well understood. Some research has indicated that lesbian women are less likely to seek help for substance use problems (Corliss, Grella, Mays, & Cochran, 2006). To our knowledge, only one study has explored differences at treatment

entrance between sexual minority and heterosexual women (Cochran & Cauce, 2006). This study found that sexual minority women (lesbian, bisexual, and transgender) were more likely to present to treatment with a heroin dependence, used at higher frequencies, had more mental health hospitalizations, were more frequently homeless, reported higher rates of domestic violence and used medical services less frequently. Studies have also found lesbian and bisexual women who enter substance abuse treatment to be less likely to complete (Senreich, 2009).

Generally, authors have suggested that these disparate treatment outcomes can be attributed to treatment environments that are not supportive of sexual minorities (Hellman, Stanton, Lee, Tytun, & Vachon, 1989; McDermott, Tyndall, & Lichtenberg, 1989) or social workers that quietly assume heterosexuality in their patients (Willging et al., 2006). Indeed, Senreich (2009) found that lesbian women in treatment felt less connected and satisfied with treatment than heterosexual women, and report that their sexual orientation negatively impacted their treatment experience. A number of general population studies have linked treatment success to client/social worker rapport.

With regard to social worker competence, Eliason and Hughes (2004) found that regardless of urban or rural setting, no differences existed for practitioners in their reported comfort of treating sexual minority clients, and no differences in knowledge about pertinent issues such as internalized homophobia, legal problems, the coming out process, or prevalence of substance use. However, countertransference that bring up feelings of internalized homophobia or transphobia as well as projection of practitioner feelings onto client can thwart the rapport building process and can influence treatment goals. Continued supervision to address these feelings early within the client relationship may be crucial. Additionally, many young people who have experienced gender-based or sexual orientation-based harassment within various settings may have experienced these events cumulatively throughout their life. Cumulative stress, not just the experience of one traumatic event, may increase risk for depression, anxiety, and PTSD symptoms. A thorough assessment of frequency, duration, and longevity of these minority stress experiences, coupled with an assessment of social and family support systems available within your client's life will help you develop an overall picture of emotional symptoms impacting the client and will subsequently inform appropriate treatment options. Only a handful of older studies have examined whether "gay specific" treatment settings are better for sexual minority participants (Paul et al., 1996; Driscoll, 1982). Further, the differences that may exist in these treatment facilities also remain unclear, as a recent national survey of these specialized facilities found few differences from those provided through general programs (Cochran, Peavy, & Robohm, 2007). Taken together, the available literature seems to hypothesize (while perhaps not with a substantial evidence base) that ensuring cultural and linguistic competency in the treatment of LGBT clients is an important factor in predicting treatment outcomes. With regard to Toby, rapport building and maintenance is one of the most imperative therapeutic approaches. Toby has likely felt isolated within his family and social support systems; thus, building trust and developing a therapeutic bond will create a safe place for Toby to openly express and process the stressors in his life. Building trust and a safe space will also provide him a place to map out how he wants to navigate his identity and potential transition within various relationships and settings.

MEZZO PERSPECTIVE

Schools have an opportunity to create an ideal place for safety and social change in the area of LGBT acceptance. However, hetero-normative education in schools causes great distress for students who do not conform directly to socially acceptable sexual norms. These students are, therefore, at increased risk for dangerous relationships and interactions. It is necessary that one-sided, biased, heterosexist education be stopped and a more inclusive model be utilized. The opportunity exists to help adolescents develop a positive sexual identity through a supportive school climate and inclusive sexual education programs. These improvements to both curriculum and school culture can bridge the gap for LGBT students to feel accepted, understood, and equipped to navigate social and intimate relationships.

In order to create safety, schools can create a "diversity room," which can serve as a center of tolerance and promoter of acceptance of all sexual, gender, ethnic, and religious identities in the school. This center would be able to address specific needs and problems for students, ranging from harassment issues to fear of violence, and it could help teach youth both compassion and problem solving. In addition, the director of this center would be responsible for creating a normative cultural of acceptance by educating students and teachers on diversity, the negative effects of harassment, and the long-term benefits of a positive school climate.

Schools also need to begin to recognize the importance of GSA meetings in their districts. Many schools have chosen to ignore the needs of their LGBT population by not allowing GSAs to exist. This is to the utmost harm of the LGBT student, as well as the straight ally student who chooses to advocate for the needs and rights of gay youth. Parents for Lesbian and Gays (PFLAG) is an organization that could also be utilized in school systems to help appropriately initiate these systems into curriculum. This national system of community has the ability to be compassionate to parents as well as understanding of the nature of their LGBT children. When incorporated, PFLAG would be an effective meeting place for both educated LGBT parents to meet and parents of newly out gay children to learn and gain support.

Lastly, GSAs are continually developing strategies to make schools safe not only for gay, lesbian, and bisexual youth but transgender youth as well. In general, schools across the country have a long way to go toward acceptance and support of transgender youth. Many transgender youth do not feel their needs are met through youth-led organizations such as the GSA. However, many GSAs are developing steps to ensure that the needs of transgender youth are being recognized and supported.

School Recommendations

This may depend on the political, ethnic/racial, and religious makeup of the community. Disclosure or coming out should not be the ultimate goal. It is important for a client to have allies and support at school, and the counselor or a supportive teacher/adult identified by the client may be a good place to start. Additionally, a particular client may not want to be the poster child at school, but at the same time, empowerment is key. So, let them feel in control of their school environment and how they feel they want to navigate that. The experience of navigating sexual and/or gender identity at school is not a one-size-fits-all approach. As social workers, part of the challenge is to know when to advocate with or on behalf of clients, when and how to empower them to take the lead, and when to continue to assess and wait. If a client's preferred gender pronouns or authentic (chosen) name is not being used by teachers at school, despite the client's request, the shared decision to take further action may be necessary. However, when possible, clients should be empowered to lead this process as is safe and appropriate. In the case of Toby, developing a plan to advocate with him for his needs must be balanced with his emotional and physical safety. If and when he decides to disclose his authentic gender identity or start any transition process at school, a thorough assessment of his formal and informal resources and support system as well as the general culture within the school should be considered and included in his overall plan. Additionally, it's critical to encourage him to take the lead and decide how he wants to advocate for himself and what role he would like his social worker to play.

Other Resources

First, let's not assume that access to as many resources as possible is a good thing. It may be helpful to first understand the resources, if any, that a client is open to or wanting to access. Suggesting different resources may feel helpful, but it is always important to recognize that it may take time to determine an appropriate referral and readiness for that resource. When a client is ready, check out your local Gay Straight Alliance (GSA) for some advice on resources in the schools or community. Also, it may be that a GSA or LGBT organization is not what a client wants or needs at that time. There may be other organizations that a client may be interested in, based on their interest or needs. Additionally, it is essential to ensure that the resources are supportive and would be a safe and accepting place for a client. Just because a community resource is associated with an LGBT cause does not mean it's the best or most supportive resource for a client. Some may look good on paper, but it can be essential to talk with various community resources to really get a sense of culture within to determine how emotionally and physically safe a client would be there.

MACRO PERSPECTIVE

Intervention at a social policy level to combat heterosexism directed toward youth requires multiple steps to ensure all schools afford their students a safe educational environment in which they can experience interpersonal growth and self-discovery. Because much of a school's curriculum is determined by state-wide policy, a major step in intervention requires changes at the government level.

The first step in social policy is to establish state-wide nondiscrimination policies throughout the country in order to protect the rights of all students, whether they identify themselves as heterosexual, homosexual, bisexual, transgendered, or are still questioning their sexual orientation. Not only will these laws instill a system in which respect for differences is mandatory, it will give those students who are discriminated against an avenue of defense. Furthermore, it is imperative that all local or state education laws that expressly forbid teachers from discussing gay and transgender issues (including sexual health and HIV/AIDS awareness) in a positive light (known as "no promo homo laws") are eliminated. These policies create an environment in which free thought is suppressed and personal identities are forced into repression.

Beyond nondiscrimination laws, policy should be redirected away from abstinence-only education and toward the funding of comprehensive sexual education curriculums in which students are afforded accurate information regarding safe sex, condom effectiveness, and sexuality. Without other school-based sexuality organizations, such as GSAs, comprehensive sexual education may be the only place in which adolescents are given LGBT resources and information. Because much of the funding for state-run abstinence education comes from the federal government, advocacy should be directed not only toward members of state Congresses but also federal Congress. Furthermore, consequences for noncompliance must be introduced at the policy level in order to address the instillation of heterosexist ideals throughout school systems. Without policy, schools are free to choose their curriculums, and many will choose a "no-promo-homo" approach.

Additionally, schools can and should develop policies to ensure the dignity and safety of their transgender students. First, teachers and school administration should enact policies mandating that teachers use the chosen names and gender pronouns of transgender youth. Most important, since locker rooms and bathrooms are major areas in the school where transgender youth are bullied or harassed, schools need to ensure that these spaces are safe and supportive. Gender-neutral bathrooms and changing areas are essential to mitigate verbal, physical, and sexual harassment. School GSAs can contribute by developing more inclusive programming that creates a positive and normative culture of acceptance and support for transgender youth at school. GSAs can also create a space where transgender voices are heard and validated, where LGBT youth work with their heterosexual allies to celebrate diversity in their schools.

Likewise, calling upon local LGBT centers or the American Civil Liberties Union (ACLU) may also be necessary on a district level or higher level to ensure the needs and rights of LGBT young people are being upheld. Finally, many young LGBT people face harassment by other students at school. Calling upon other local resources, such as a local ACLU, may be necessary to ensure that antiharassment policies and protocol are developed and implemented within the school system. For Toby, information is power, and helping him learn and know his rights and legal resources empowers him to make well-informed decisions regarding his education and how he wants to advocate for his safety and needs. Knowing his rights and resources helps him decide how he wants to navigate various settings and develop strategies to overcome barriers and gain the self-efficacy needed to determine his goals and dreams.

CONCLUSION

The purpose of this chapter was to help clinicians understand the importance of identity, labels, and to reflect on the variety of terminology that might be helpful in the clinical setting when working with LGBT individuals. Working with clients that are different from us, particularly when that difference may (or may not!) be causing additional stress that contributes to their behavioral health, can be anxiety provoking.

After reading this chapter, social workers should feel comfortable answering some of the questions we began with. Readers should recognize that simply placing a check in the "LGB" box or the "heterosexual" box does not fully capture a person's sexual orientation or sexual identity? These constructs are unique and complicated, just as all of the lives of clients we see are. Readers should also feel comfortable recognizing that they, as social work practitioners, should not feel obligated to determine a person's gender, regardless of the way the person presents on the surface. Further, readers should understand that gender and sexual orientation are related but separate constructs, and that biological sex does not determine the gender of an individual.

Readers should take from this chapter the permission to ask clients how they would like to be addressed and the pronouns they prefer when considering both their sexual orientation and gender. While clinicians want to appropriately use and understand this language with the clients we serve, we recognize that it would be truly impossible to list or define all the sexual and gender identity labels used today; and there is no reason to do so. While it is helpful to have some knowledge of these identity terms, every client (and individual in the world) has the right to construct their own identity labels and define them for themselves. Above all, however, readers should recognize that the experience and expression of sexual and gender identity is mutable in each and every person (not just LGBT individuals!), and this diversity truly brings richness to all of our experiences, to be seen as a strength rather than a deficit in the lives of our clients.

INTERNET RESOURCES

- American Civil Liberties Union: Understanding rights for LGBTQ youth at school and work: http://www.aclu.org
- Trevor Project: A national organization that provides suicide prevention and crisis intervention to LGBT youth 13–24 years of age: http://www.thetrevorproject.org
- Gay-Straight Alliance: A support program within schools for LGBTQ youth and their allies, including a unified stance against homophobia and transphobia. Important to talk to local GSA to determine if this group within a particular school meets the needs of transgender young people: http://www.gsanetwork.org
- T.U.F.F. (Trans United with Family and Friends): Financial assistance for gender-affirming medical interventions for transgender and gender-variant individuals: http://www.tufforg.com, or e-mail tufforg@gmail.com to request more specific information
- Transforming Family: A Los Angeles–based family support group creating a positive environment for children, adolescents, and their families to explore gender identity: http://www.transformingfamily.org
- The Los Angeles Gay and Lesbian Center: Provides a broad array of services for LGBTQ youth and adults. The Center is the largest LGBT+ center in the world: http://www.laglc.org

- The Center Long Beach: Provides social support and mental health counseling to LGBT youth as well as housing and legal advocacy support/resources: http://centerlb.org/social-support-groups
- Children's Hospital Los Angeles Adolescent Medicine: HIV testing and services: Testing, support and medical care for youth 13–24 and the Center for Transyouth Health and Development (meeting the emotional/social support, medical needs, and gender-affirming medical interventions for transgender youth): http://www.chw.org

DISCUSSION QUESTIONS

1. How do you identify your sexual orientation?

2. Who are you most attracted to sexually? Romantically?

3. What types of individuals do you most often engage in sexual behaviors with?

4. Have you ever thought of your gender and sex as different things?

REFERENCES

Agnos, A. (1990). *Plenary address.* Sixth International Conference on AIDS, June 20, 1990, San Francisco, CA.

Altman, D. G. (1982). Statistics in medical journals. *Statistics in Medicine, 1,* 59–71.

Alvy, L. M. (2013). Sexual identity group differences in child abuse and neglect. *Journal of Interpersonal Violence, 28*(10), 2088–2111.

American Psychological Association. (2011). *Practice guidelines for LGB clients: Guidelines for psychological practice with lesbian, gay, and bisexual clients, adopted by the APA Council of Representatives, February 18–20, 2011.* Retrieved from http://www.apa.org/pi/lgbt/resources/guidelines.aspx

Anhalt, K., & Morris, T. L. (2008). Parenting characteristics associated with anxiety and depression: Exploring the contribution of multiple factors. *Journal of Early and Intensive Behavioral Intervention, 5,* 122–137.

Associated Press. (1985). *Studds says Reagan has shown little concern over AIDS*. Retrieved from http://www.apnewsarchive.com/1985/Studds-Says-Reagan-Has-Shown-Little-Concern-Over-AIDS/id-f985ab6ba6d6fc4ff37ebb0ba0aa657b

Austin, S. B., Jun, H. J., Jackson, B., Spiegelman, D., Rich-Edwards, J., . . . Corliss, H. L. (2008). Disparities in child abuse victimization in lesbian, bisexual, and heterosexual women in the Nurses' Health Study II. *Journal of Women's Health, 17*, 597–606.

Bailey J. M. (1999). Homosexuality and mental illness. *Archives of General Psychiatry, 56*, 887–888.

Bianco, D. (2000). *Gay essentials: Facts for your queer brain*. New York City, NY: Alyson Books.

Binson, D., Woods, W. J., Pollack, L., Paul, J., Stall, R., & Catania, J. A. (2001). Differential HIV risk in bathhouses and public cruising areas. *American Journal of Public Health, 91*, 1482–1486.

Blackwood, E. (1986). Breaking the mirror: The construction of lesbianism and the anthropological discourse on homosexuality. In E. Blackwood (Ed.), *The many faces of homosexuality: Anthropological approaches to homosexual behavior*. New York, NY: Harrington Park Press.

Bontempo, D. E., & D'Augelli, A. R. (2002). Effects of at-school victimization and sexual orientation on lesbian, gay, or bisexual youths' health risk behavior. *Journal of Adolescent Health, 30*, 364–374. doi: 10.1016/S1054–139X(01)00415–3

Bostwick, W. B., Boyd, C. J., Hughes, T. L., & McCabe, S. E. (2010). Dimensions of sexual orientation and the prevalence of mood and anxiety disorders in the United States. *American Journal of Public Health, 100*(3), 468–475.

Brown, G. W., & Harris, T. (1978). *Social origins of depression: A study of psychiatric disorder in women*. New York: Free Press.

Centers for Disease Control. (1981a). Kaposi's sarcoma and pneumocystis pneumonia among homosexual men: New York City and California. *Morbidity and Mortality Weekly Report, 30*(25), 305–308.

Centers for Disease Control. (1981b). Pneumocystis pneumonia: Los Angeles. *Morbidity and Mortality Weekly Report, 30*(21), 250–252.

Cervantes, R. C., Fisher, D. G., Córdova, D., & Napper, L. E. (2011). The Hispanic Stress Inventory-Adolescent Version: A culturally informed psychosocial assessment. *Psychological Assessment. Psychological Assessment, 24*(1), 187–196. doi: 10.1037/a0025280

Cichocki, M. (2006). An HIV timeline—The history of HIV. *About.com Guide, 12*, 1–4.

Cochran, B. N., & Cauce, A. M. (2006). Characteristics of lesbian, gay, bisexual, and transgender individuals entering substance abuse treatment. *Journal of Substance Abuse Treatment, 30*(2), 135–146.

Cochran, B. N., Peavy, K. M., & Robohm, J. S. (2007). Do specialized services exist for LGBT individuals seeking treatment for substance misuse? A study of available treatment programs. *Substance Use & Misuse, 42*, 161–176.

Cochran, S. D., Ackerman, D., Mays, V. M., & Ross, M. W. (2004). Prevalence of non-medical drug use and dependence among homosexually active men and women in the U.S. population. *Addiction, 99*, 989–998.

Cohen, J. (2001). *Shots in the dark: The wayward search for an AIDS vaccine*. New York, NY: W.W. Norton & Company.

Cohen, S., & Wills, T. A. (1985). Stress, social support, and the buffering hypothesis. *Psychological Bulletin, 98*, 310–357.

Corliss, H. L., Grella, C. E., Mays, V. M., & Cochran, S. D. (2006). Drug use, drug severity, and help-seeking behaviors of lesbian and bisexual women. *Journal of Women's Health, 15*(5), 556–568.

Darrow, W. W. (1981). Social and psychologic aspects of sexually transmitted diseases: A different view. *Cutis, 27*, 307–316.

D'Augelli, A. R. (2003). Lesbian and bisexual female youths aged 14 to 21: Developmental challenges and victimization experiences. *Journal of Lesbian Studies, 7*(4), 9–29.

D'Augelli, A. R., Grossman, A. H., Salter, N. P., Vasey, J. J., Starks, M. T., & Sinclair, K. O. (2005). Predicting the suicide attempts of lesbian, gay, and bisexual youth. *Suicide & Life-Threatening Behavior, 35*(6), 646–660.

Definition of Terms. (2013). University of California at Berkeley Gender Equity Resource Center. Retrieved from http://geneq.berkeley.edu/lgbt_resources_definiton_of_terms

Diamond, L. M. (2003). What does sexual orientation orient? A biobehavioral model distinguishing romantic love and sexual desire. *Psychological Review, 110*(1), 173–192.

Diamond, L. M. (2005). From the heart or the gut? Sexual-minority women's experiences of desire for same-sex and other-sex partners. *Feminism and Psychology, 15,* 10–14.

DiPlacido, J. (1998) Minority stress among lesbians, gay men and bisexuals: consequence of heterosexism, homophobia and stigmatization. In G. Herek (Ed.), *Stigma and sexual orientation* (pp. 138–159). Thousand Oaks, CA: Sage.

Driscoll R. (1982). A gay-identified alcohol treatment program: A follow-up study. *Journal of Homosexuality, 4,* 123–142.

Egan, S. K., & Perry, D. G. (2001). Gender identity: A multidimensional analysis with implications for psychosocial adjustment. *Developmental Psychology, 37*(4), 451–463.

Eliason, M. J., & Hughes, T. L. (2004). Substance abuse counselor's attitudes about lesbian, gay, bisexual, and transgender clients: Urban versus rural counselors. *Substance Use and Misuse, 39*(4), 625–644.

Fergusson, D. M., Horwood, J., & Beautrais, A. L. (1999). Is sexual orientation related to mental health problems and suicidality in young people? *Archives of General Psychiatry, 56,* 876–880.

Fortuna, L., Perez, D., Canino, G., Sribney, W., & Alegría, M. (2007). Prevalence and correlates of lifetime suicidal ideation and attempts among Latino subgroups in the United States. *Journal of Clinical Psychiatry, 68*(4), 572–581.

Friedman, M. (2010). *N.J. Assembly, Senate pass anti-bullying bill of rights in wake of Tyler Clementi's death.* Retrieved from http://www.nj.com/news/index.ssf/2010/11/nj_assembly_passes_anti-bullyi.html

Friedman, M. S., Koeske, G. F., Silvestre, A. J., Korr, W. S., & Sites, E. W. (2006). The impact of gender-role nonconforming behavior, bullying, and social support on suicidality among gay male youth. *Journal of Adolescent Health, 38*(5), 621–623.

Friedman, M. S., Marshal, M. P., Stall, R., Cheong, J., & Wright, E. R. (2008). Gay-related development, early abuse and adult health outcomes among gay males. *AIDS and Behavior, 12,* 891–902.

Fullilove, M., Fullilove, R., Haynes, K., & Gross, S. (1990). Black women and AIDS prevention: A view towards understanding the gender rules. *The Journal of Sex Research, 27*(1), 47-64.

Fullilove, R. (2006). *African Americans, health disparities and HIV/AIDS: Recommendations for confronting the epidemic in black America.* Washington, DC: National Minority AIDS Council.

Garofalo, R., Wolf, R. C., Kessel, S., Palfrey, J., & DuRant, R. H. (1998). The association between health risk behaviors and sexual orientation among a school-based sample of adolescents. *Pediatrics, 101,* 895–902.

Gates, G., & Newport, F. (2012). *Special report: 3.4% of U.S. adults identify as LGBT: Inaugural Gallup findings based on more than 120,000 interviews.* Retrieved from http://www.gallup.com/poll/158066/special-report-adults-identify-lgbt.aspx

Goodenow, C., Szalacha, L., & Westheimer, K. (2006). School support groups, other school factors, and the safety of sexual minority adolescents. *Psychology in the Schools, 43,* 573–589. doi:10.1002/pits.20173

Haas, A., Eliason, M., Mays, V., Mathy, R., Cochran, S., D'Angelli, A., & Clayton, P. (2011). Suicide and suicide risk in lesbian, gay, bisexual, and transgender populations: Review and recommendations. *Journal of Homosexuality, 58*(1), 10–51.

Halkitis, P. N., Green, K. A., Remien, R. H., Stirratt, M. J., Hoff, C. C., . . . Wolitski, R. J. (2005). Seroconcordant sexual partnerings of HIV-seropositive men who have sex with men. *AIDS, 19*(S1), S77–S86.

Hellman, R. E., Stanton, M., Lee, J., Tytun, A., & Vachon, R. (1989). Treatment of homosexual alcoholics in government-funded agencies: Provider training and attitudes. *Hospital and Community Psychiatry, 40,* 1163–1168.

Hershberger, S. L., Pilkington, N. W., & D'Augelli, A. R. (1997). Predictors of suicide attempts among gay, lesbian, and bisexual youth. *Journal of Adolescent Research, 12,* 477–497.

Hughes, A., Sathe, N., & Spagnola, K. (2010). *State estimates of substance use from the 2007–2008 National Surveys on Drug Use and Health.* Rockville, MD: Substance Abuse and Mental Health Services Administration.

Hughes, T., & Eliason, M. (2002). Substance use and abuse in lesbian, gay, bisexual, and transgender populations. *The Journal of Primary Prevention, 22,* 263–298.

Janssen, E., Everaerd, W., Spiering, M., & Janssen, J. (2000). Automatic cognitive processes and the appraisal of sexual stimuli: Towards an information processing model of sexual arousal. *Journal of Sex Research, 37,* 8–23.

Kauth, M. R., & Kalichman, S. C. (1995). Sexual orientation and development: An interactive approach. In L. Diamant & R. D. McAnulty (Eds.), *The psychology of sexual orientation, behavior, and identity.* Westport, CT: Greenwood Press.

Kessler, R. C. (1979). Stress, social status, and psychological distress. *Journal of Health and Social Behavior, 20,* 259–272.

Kinsey, A. C., Pomeroy, W. B., & Martin, C. E. (1948). *Sexual behavior in the human male.* Philadelphia, PA: W. B. Saunders.

Kinsey, A., Pomeroy, W., Martin, C., & Gebhard, P. (1953). *Sexual behavior in the human female.* Philadelphia: W. B. Saunders.

Kubicek, K., McDavitt, B., Carpineto, J., Weiss, G., Iverson, E. F., & Kipke, M. D. (2007). Making informed decisions: How attitudes and perceptions affect the use of crystal, cocaine, and ecstasy among young men who have sex with men. *Journal of Drug Issues, 37,* 643–674.

LeVay, S. (1993). *The sexual brain.* Cambridge, MA: MIT Press.

Lewes, K. (1988). *The psychoanalytic theory of male homosexuality.* New York: Simon and Schuster.

Lewinsohn, P. M., Rohde, P., & Seeley, J. R. (1996). Adolescent suicidal ideation and attempts: Prevalence, risk factors, and clinical implications.

Clinical Psychology: Science and Practice, 3(1), 25–46.

LGBTQIA Resource Center Glossary. (2014). UCDavis Lesbian Gay Bisexual Transgender Queer Intersex Asexual Resource Center. Retrieved from http://lgbtqia.ucdavis.edu/lgbt-education/lgbtqia-glossary

Lisanky, E. S. (1958). The etiology of alcoholism: The role of psychological predisposition. *Quarterly Journal of Studies on Alcohol, 21,* 314–343.

Lisker, J. (1969). Homo nest raided, queen bees are stinging mad. *The New York Daily News,* July 6. Retrieved from http://www.yak.net

Liu, R. T., & Mustanski, B. (2012). Suicidal ideation and self-harm in lesbian, gay, bisexual, and transgender youth. *American Journal of Preventive Medicine, 42*(3), 221–228.

Marshal, M. P., Friedman, M. S., Stall, R., King, K. M., Miles, J. . . . Gold, M. A. (2008). Sexual orientation and adolescent substance use: A meta-analysis and methodological review. *Addiction, 103,* 546–556. doi: 10.1111/j.1360–0443.2008.02149.x

McCabe, S., Hughes, T., Bostwick, W., West, B., & Boyd, C. (2009). Sexual orientation, substance use behaviors and substance dependence in the United States. *Addiction, 104,* 1333–1345.

McDaniel, J. S., Purcell, J., & D'Augelli, A. R. (2001). The relationship between sexual orientation and risk for suicide: Research findings and future directions for research and prevention. *Suicide and Life Threatening Behavior, 31,* 84–105.

McDermott, D., Tyndall, L. W., & Lichtenberg, J. W. (1989). Factors related to counselor preference among gays and lesbians. *Journal of Counseling and Development, 68,* 31–35.

McLeod, J. D., & Kessler, R. C. (1990). Socioeconomic status differences in vulnerability to undesirable life events. *Journal of Health and Social Behavior, 31*(2), 162–172.

Meyer, I. H. (1995). Minority stress and mental health in gay men. *Journal of Health and Social Behavior, 36*(1), 38–56.

Meyer, I. H. (2003). Prejudice as stress: Conceptual and measurement problems. *American Journal of Public Health, 93,* 262–265.

Odets, W. (1994). Survivor guilt in seronegative gay men. In S. Cadwell, R. Burnham, Jr., & M. Forstein, M. (Eds.), *Therapists on the front line* (pp. 453–471). Washington, DC: American Psychiatric Press.

Paul, J. P., Barrett, D. C., Crosby, G. M., & Stall, R. D. (1996). Longitudinal changes in alcohol and drug use among men seen at a gay-specific substance abuse treatment agency. *Journal of Studies on Alcohol, 57,* 475–485.

Pilkington, N. W., & D'Augelli, A. R. (1995). Victimization of lesbian, gay, and bisexual youth in community settings. *Journal of Community Psychology, 23,* 34–56. doi: 10.1002/1520-6629(199501)23

Poundstone, K. E., Strathdee, S. A., & Celentano, D. D. (2004). The social epidemiology of human immunodeficiency virus/acquired immunodeficiency syndrome. *Epidemiologic Reviews, 26*(1), 22–35.

Ray, N. (2006). *Lesbian, gay, bisexual and transgender youth: An epidemic of homelessness.* New York: National Gay and Lesbian Task Force Policy Institute and the National Coalition for the Homeless. Retrieved from http://www.thetaskforce.org/downloads/reports/reports/HomelessYouth_ExecutiveSummary.pdf

Remafedi, G., Resnick, M., Blum, R., & Harris, L. (1992). Demography of sexual orientation in adolescents. *Pediatrics, 89*(4), 714–721.

Roberts, A. L., Gilman, S. E., Breslau, J., Breslau, N., & Koenen, K. C. (2010). Race/ethnic differences in exposure to traumatic events, development of post-traumatic stress disorder, and treatment-seeking for post-traumatic stress disorder in the United States. *Psychological Medicine, 40,* 1–13.

Robinson, K. E. (1994). Addressing the needs of gay and lesbian students: The school counselor's role. *The School Counselor, 41,* 326–332.

Rosario, M., Rotheram-Borus, M. J., & Reid, H. (1996). Gay-related stress and its correlates among gay and bisexual male adolescents of predominantly Black and Hispanic background. *Journal of Community Psychology, 24,* 136–159.

Rosario, M., Schrimshaw, E. W., Hunter, J., & Gwadz, M. (2002). Gay-related stress and emotional distress among gay, lesbian, and bisexual youths: A longitudinal examination. *Journal of Consulting and Clinical Psychology, 70,* 967–975.

Russell, S. T., & Joyner, K. (2001). Adolescent sexual orientation and suicide risk: Evidence from a national study. *American Journal of Public Health, 91,* 1276–1281.

Ryan, C., Huebner, D., Diaz, R. M., & Sanchez, J. (2009). Family rejection as a predictor of negative health outcomes in white and Latino lesbian, gay and bisexual young adults. *Pediatrics, 123*(1), 346–352.

Safe zone resource manual. (2013). UC Davis Lesbian Gay Bisexual Transgender Queer Intersex Asexual Resource Center. Retrieved from http://lgbtqia.ucdavis.edu

Savin-Williams, R. C. (2001). *Mom, Dad, I'm gay: How families negotiate coming out.* Washington, DC: American Psychological Association.

Sell, R. L. (1997). Defining and measuring sexual orientation: A review. *Archives of Sexual Behavior, 26*(6), 643–658.

Senreich, E. (2009). A comparison of perceptions, reported abstinence, and completion rates of gay, lesbian, bisexual, and heterosexual clients in substance abuse treatment. *Journal of Gay & Lesbian Mental Health, 13*(3), 145–169. doi:10.1080/19359700902870072

Shidlo, A. (1994). Internalized homophobia: Conceptual and empirical issues in measurement. In B. Greene & G. Herek (Eds.), *Lesbian and gay psychology: Theory, research and clinical applications.* Thousand Oaks, CA: Sage.

Thoits, P. A. (1991). Gender differences in coping with emotional distress. In J. Eckenrode (Ed.), *The social context of coping.* New York, NY: Plenum.

Toomey, R. B., Ryan, C., Diaz, R. M., Card, N. A., & Russell, S. T. (2010). Gender nonconforming lesbian, gay, bisexual, and transgender youth: School victimization and young adult psychosocial adjustment. *Developmental Psychology, 46,* 1580–1589. doi:10.1037/a0020705

Willging, C. E., Salvador, M., & Kano, M. (2006). Unequal treatment: Mental health care for sexual and gender minority groups in a rural state. *Psychiatric Services, 57,* 867–870.

Wilsnack, S. C., Hughes, T. L., Johnson, T. L., Bostwick, W. B., Szalacha, L. A., Benson, P. B., et al. (2008). Drinking and drinking-related problems among heterosexual and sexual minority women. *Journal of Studies on Alcohol and Drugs, 69*(1), 129–139.

Zayas, L. H. (2011). Latinas attempting suicide: When cultures, families, and daughters collide. New York, NY: Oxford University Press.

Zayas, L. H., Lester, R. J., Cabassa, L. J., & Fortuna, L. R. (2005). Why do so many Latina teens attempt suicide? A conceptual model for research. *American Journal of Orthopsychiatry, 75,* 275–287.

CHAPTER 28

Intergenerational Trauma and Indigenous People

Hilary N. Weaver

CHAPTER OBJECTIVES

- Describe intergenerational trauma and its impact on indigenous peoples in the United States;
- Review general principles for interventions and apply them in a case example;
- Articulate the importance of trauma-informed care;
- Identify resources to further understanding of the intergenerational trauma experiences of Native Americans.

CASE VIGNETTE

Marjorie is a 43-year-old Cheyenne woman who lives in Denver, Colorado. She has two of her own children, ages 17 and 15, living at home and also has custody of her teenage daughter's infant twins while she is in residential treatment for methamphetamine use. Marjorie's husband is also Cheyenne. He has been violent toward her and the children and has been in prison for eight years for killing a police officer during a drug raid at their home. Marjorie's father left the family when she was an infant and she has no recollection of him. Her mother drank heavily and was found frozen to death in a snowbank after a night of drinking. Marjorie has been a heavy drinker since her early teens and has used marijuana and cocaine regularly but has been working to remain sober and drug free for the last six months with the help of a Native American 12-step program, under threat of having the twins removed from her home. In spite of her struggles, Marjorie is committed to keeping her family together and providing stability for the children in her care.

Working with a social worker at a local agency, she has identified the following steps and priorities: In order to ensure that her home remains drug free and safe for the children in her care, she will develop a "map" of the people in the family's social environment and work to strengthen healthy connections with family members and friends living a healthy lifestyle. She and her social worker will develop a genogram to examine the multigenerational patterns of violence and substance abuse within her family. They will reflect on the family stories, discussing both the healthy and unhealthy behaviors as well as the environmental and historical factors that shaped, limited, and facilitated the lifestyles of family members. Marjorie will read books that recount Cheyenne history from a Cheyenne perspective, and this reading will inform discussions with her social worker about how trauma has affected her community, family, and herself. Marjorie will attend her community's annual commemoration of the Sand Creek massacre, journal about her experiences, and discuss her reflections with her social worker. As their work together progresses, Marjorie will be able to articulate what it means to be a healthy Cheyenne woman and develop a specific plan for reaching that goal. As part of her journey toward physical and spiritual healing, Marjorie is considering participating in next year's Sand Creek Massacre Spiritual Healing Run, which takes place at the massacre site 160 miles southeast of Denver, Colorado. Marjorie's social worker presents her with a poster of the well-known Cheyenne saying, "A nation cannot be defeated until the hearts of its women are on the ground." This provides a foundation for an ongoing discussion about resilience in the face of adversity and providing a healthy foundation for the generations to come.

INTRODUCTION

In recent decades, social workers and other helping professionals have begun to grapple with the impact of intergenerational or historical trauma on indigenous populations (Braveheart, 1999; Faimon, 2004; Gone, 2009; Whitbeck, Adams, Hoyt, & Chen, 2004). The terms *historical trauma* and *intergenerational trauma* are used interchangeably in the literature and throughout this chapter. Historical trauma can be defined as "cumulative trauma over both the lifespan and across generations that results from massive cataclysmic events … [manifesting in symptoms such as] depression, self-destructive behavior, substance abuse, ancestral pain, fixation to trauma, somatic symptoms, anxiety, and chronic bereavement" (Braveheart, 1999, p. 111).

Likewise, the terms *Native Americans* and *indigenous peoples* are used interchangeably throughout this chapter. While the term *indigenous peoples* is broader than *Native Americans,* it reflects connections to other populations around the world that are increasingly recognized in North America. Although this chapter provides content on indigenous peoples in the United States, many of the concepts discussed here are relevant to indigenous peoples in Canada and other parts of the world.

The key to understanding historical trauma is recognizing that events from the past are relevant to current circumstances. When massive trauma occurs in a population, the experiences of that generation do not end with them. Rather, the trauma they experienced is passed to subsequent generations, thus the term *intergenerational trauma.* Although subsequent generations did not experience the initial trauma directly, their life experiences are nevertheless shaped by those of their parents, grandparents, and ancestors.

Historical trauma often results in unresolved grief that has been described as a soul wound (Duran, 2006) or an injury to the spirit (Smith, 2003). For indigenous peoples, trauma and the resulting sequelae have been inflicted by colonization. The resulting soul wound, in turn, enhances vulnerability for a variety of social and health maladies. A complex connection is hypothesized between historical trauma and health, including connections between trauma and diabetes, antisocial personality disorders, metabolic syndrome, substance abuse, and hypertension (Estrada, 2009). Indeed, historical trauma is often seen as part of the explanatory framework for high rates of substance abuse, violence, and suicide in Native American communities (Morgan & Freeman, 2009).

AN OVERVIEW OF INTERGENERATIONAL TRAUMA

Historical or intergenerational trauma can occur when a population is exposed to persecution and large scale losses such as massacres, genocide, ethnic cleansing, enslavement, colonization, and pandemics. This large-scale trauma typically occurs in populations that experience a power disadvantage and subsequent oppression. This power disadvantage is often systematic and institutionalized. Structural factors in society enable and perpetuate intergenerational trauma.

Massive trauma has been experienced by various populations throughout history. Indeed, no single population has a monopoly on being the oppressed or the oppressor. Early historical trauma theories were based on examinations of the Jewish Holocaust during World War II. There are also preliminary explorations of the impact of Spanish colonialism and Anglo American neocolonialism on Mexicans and Mexican Americans in the Southwest as factors leading to intergenerational trauma (Estrada, 2009), but these theoretical positions need further empirical exploration. Likewise, some scholars describe the legacy of slavery as a basis for intergenerational trauma in African Americans (Eyerman, 2001; Leary, 2005), but a review of the literature reveals little research in this area to date.

Even though early scholarly explorations of historical trauma began with Jewish populations and some scholars extended this concept to other groups, by and large, the majority of contemporary theory and research on historical trauma is based on the experiences of Native Americans. For many years it has been well documented that Native Americans disproportionately suffer from psychological distress as well as a variety of social and health disparities (Barnes, Adams, & Powell-Griner, 2010; Mehl-Madrona & Mainguy, 2014). Researchers and helping professionals now consistently associate this distress with the trauma inherent in colonization (Duran, 2006; Yellow Horse Brave Heart & DeBruyn, 1998). Because a structurally reinforced power imbalance is typical of colonial situations, indigenous populations, including Native Americans, while certainly not the only populations who have experienced massive trauma, provide a prime example of intergenerational trauma.

Intergenerational trauma is typically conceptualized in sequential stages beginning with a massive trauma. After an initial event there is a trauma response in the first generation. Later the trauma response is transmitted to subsequent generations. As intergenerational trauma theory becomes more sophisticated, according to this author, it is important for researchers and clinicians to move beyond a simple, linear stage approach.

In critically thinking about and further refining this theory, it is important to recognize that massive events are not the only source of trauma in a population. For example, racism is typically an ongoing experience not easily characterized in terms of a single event or even a series of events. It is important to explore the impact of ongoing oppression on a trauma response. Likewise, exploration of how a group's trauma history (e.g., that experienced by Native Americans) links to more individualized trauma histories (e.g., those experienced by combat veterans and victims of violent crimes) is needed. Indeed, as the theoretical and empirical basis of intergenerational trauma coalesces, many areas are ripe for further exploration and elucidation.

The term *historical trauma* suggests that intergenerational trauma is a legacy of events that happened in the past. It is clear, however, that racism and oppression are ongoing phenomena. Indeed, many indigenous scholars point out that colonization and its effects continue to exist and are not simply history (Hart & Rowe, 2014; Wilson & Yellow Bird, 2005).

Contemporary expressions of physical and psychological violence, including microaggressions, may continue to instigate and perpetuate trauma. Microaggressions, brief, denigrating messages that people of color often experience in everyday interactions, are a common form of contemporary racism (Hernandez, Carranza, & Almeida, 2010). Microaggressions may include name calling, avoidance, minimizing, denying, or invalidating someone's thoughts, feelings, and experiences. Many people of color are constantly bombarded with microaggressions leaving them with feelings of self-doubt, frustration, and isolation. People who experience microaggressions may also be hesitant to respond, as many of these insults may be deemed unintentional or outside the awareness of the instigator (Hernandez et al., 2010).

In March 2014, an active dialogue ensued on a Listserv of indigenous social work educators, resulting in an extensive list of microaggressions they had personally experienced or witnessed. The microaggressions regularly experienced by indigenous peoples compound previous trauma. For example, statements that acknowledge the injustices that occurred in the past while minimizing the contemporary implications of injustice compound trauma and inhibit healing; much like the adage "adding insult to injury."

Additionally, contemporary events may continue to create trauma for future generations. For example, the large numbers of indigenous women that continue to disappear in Canada, often referred to as the "Stolen Sisters," creates ongoing trauma in indigenous communities. Often these women are found murdered. Sometimes they are not found at all (Amnesty International, 2009). While an Amnesty International investigation that resulted in the *No More Stolen Sisters* report focused on indigenous women in Canada, violence against Native women is also common in the United States as they document in their *Maze of Injustice* report (Amnesty International, 2007). Violence against indigenous women is just one example of contemporary trauma that will leave its legacy for future generations.

Examining the Intergenerational Trauma Experiences of Native Americans

While any population can experience intergenerational trauma, there may be relevant cultural considerations common to Native American populations that contribute to a predisposition toward intergenerational trauma. For example, Native American cultures typically emphasize a collective sense of identity in which the group is prioritized over the individual. This sense of interconnectedness may reinforce a sense that what happens to one member of a group has an effect on other members. This worldview also has intergenerational implications (Weaver & Congress, 2010).

Much of the devastation experienced by indigenous peoples in the Americas was due to the introduction of new diseases for which they had no immunities (Stiffarm & Lane, 1992). While some of this was an unintentional result of colonists transmitting diseases previously unknown in the Americas, in some cases it was deliberate and amounted to germ warfare (d'Errico, 2013). The deliberate nature of this population decimation compounds trauma.

Broken treaties and erosion of promises, including invasion of land retained by indigenous peoples, was a betrayal that added to other traumatic experiences. In December 1890, the United States Cavalry surrounded and disarmed Chief Bigfoot of the Lakota and his band of approximately 350 people, the majority of whom were women and children. Four hundred seventy troops and 30 scouts set up Hotchkiss rapid-fire artillery guns on the hill overlooking the Native American encampment. Fighting broke out and more than 200 Lakota people were killed within minutes, including fleeing women and children shot up to three miles from the camp (Venables, 2004). The Wounded Knee Massacre is often cited as the last major confrontation between the U.S. military and Native Americans.

The 1890s were a transitional time indigenous populations were greatly reduced and largely confined to reservations. It became financially feasible to turn from warfare to assimilationist social policies designed to eliminate indigenous cultures, languages, and spirituality; a practice often considered to be cultural genocide (Lazarus, 1991).

Boarding schools and allotment were some of the most prominent examples of assimilation policies. By the late 1800s it became official U.S. policy to remove Native American children from their homes and communities and educate them in residential schools, often long distances from their homes. Richard Pratt, a former military Captain and founder of the infamous Carlisle boarding school, is credited with the slogan that became associated with all boarding schools, *Kill the Indian, Save the Man* ("Kill the Indian," 2014). In other words, the schools were designed to eradicate indigenous cultures as a way to make indigenous peoples just like anyone else and suitable for integration into American society, thus eliminating Native Americans as distinct peoples.

Likewise, the United States developed a policy of dividing Native lands and distributing them to individuals as a way to eliminate communal ownership, undermine collectivist, extended family networks, and free up "excess" land (i.e., those parts of reservations not specifically delegated to individuals) for white settlement (Venables, 2004). This policy, commonly known as allotment, was conducted under the Dawes Act of 1887. The Act also contained a provision that allotted land would be temporarily held in trust, thus enacting a federal trusteeship over Native people until they were deemed competent. This policy remained in effect until the 1934. Although the policy was repealed before being enacted on all reservations, it resulted in a loss of 63% of all Native land holdings (Venables, 2004). This huge loss of land and the concomitant attacks on the communal nature of indigenous societies was a major source of trauma.

At this same time of tremendous trauma, indigenous strengths and coping mechanisms were undermined. In 1883, the Indian Religious Crimes Code banned the practice of indigenous ceremonial practices. This ban was put in place as another component of the plan of assimilation and cultural destruction (Venables, 2004). This denial of traditional coping mechanisms like spirituality not only inhibited healing from trauma but was traumatic in and of itself.

Assaults seemed to come from all sides. Compounding population decimation, loss of land, and attacks on culture, objects of spiritual and cultural significance were plundered by souvenir hunters, museums, universities, and wealthy collectors. This plunder included grave robbing and failure to relinquish sacred objects and remains of ancestors (American Indian Ritual Object and Repatriation Foundation, 1996).

While the losses suffered by Native Americans are often thought of as happening long ago, they continued well into the 20th century. In 1964, the Army Corps of Engineers built Kinzua Dam, resulting in the inundation of 10,000 acres, or 1/3 of Allegany Reservation in western New York State (Seneca Nation of Indians, 2015) as well as destruction of all the Cornplanter Tracts, the last remaining Native lands in Pennsylvania (Hauptman, 1986). Discussions in preparation for the Kinzua project were drawn out for years, thus producing significant stress and trauma, even before the land was taken through eminent domain. Ultimately, 160 families were displaced, substantial prime farming land was lost, access to medicine plants was obliterated, and key community institutions such as the school and the Longhouse, the center of Haudensaunee spiritual activities, were destroyed. Bulldozing homes happened quickly, sometimes before families had an opportunity to remove their possessions (Bilharz, 1998). As indigenous peoples often see land as a defining part of their identity, residents displaced from flooded areas have experienced fracturing of their community-specific identities (Williams, 2007).

That the project was supposedly conducted in the name of "progress" reinforced the psychological trauma of being expendable and undesirable in the eyes of the United States. Indeed, the relocation bill for the Kinzua project included a rider requiring the

Seneca to draft a termination plan for putting an end to the tribe as a legal entity under federal trust responsibility. . . . The fact that the United States could break one of the oldest treaties signed with a Native nation left the Seneca and other Native people feeling completely vulnerable and unsupported. The dam became a symbol that the U.S. could and would act with total impunity and disregard for those living within its territories. (Weaver & Congress, 2010, p. 220)

Indeed, the pain and atrocities experienced by Native Americans are monumental. Rather than continuing to list assault after assault, the point is to give the reader a sense that traumatic experiences were numerous, often made worse by the fact that they were deliberately inflicted and traditional coping mechanisms were prohibited. The sense of a collectivist identity and connection to ancestors helps facilitate and perpetuate intergenerational trauma.

Particularly poignant is the way many indigenous people articulate their experience of trauma as an injury to the spirit. Mabel Kudralook Smith, an Inupiaq woman from Barrow, Alaska, clearly articulates her own experiences which reflect the experiences of many others:

I saw for the first time that I carried within my spirit the suffering of my people as well as myself. That was part of the deepest part of my pain. It's like I inherited the pain of the preceding generations that came before me, like an illness that is hereditary, an illness that is transmitted to each successive generation as long as I silently bear it within me. (Smith, 2003, p. 85)

The Social, Biological, and Spiritual Impact of Historical Trauma

Preliminary research is beginning to identify significant connections between historical trauma and social, biological, and spiritual indicators of well-being. For example, Estrada (2009) posited that historical trauma lays the foundation for socioeconomic status. Trauma sequelae such as lower educational achievement, poverty, unemployment, and underemployment are reinforced through structured and institutionalized oppression, discrimination, and racism. A complex connection is hypothesized between historical trauma and health. For example, historical and social events lead to institutions and perceptions that are racist and discriminatory toward people of color. These, in turn, negatively influence eligibility for health insurance and access to health care. Limited access to healthcare leads to more health problems (Estrada, 2009).

Studies indicate there may also be biological changes as a result of trauma (Perry, 2001; Van der Kolk, 1994). Cumulative intergenerational stress may trigger a "psychobiological stress response mechanism that influences neuroendocrine hyperactivity, autonomic and metabolic responses, and the immune system" (Estrada, 2009, p. 335), thus leading to diabetes, antisocial personality disorders, metabolic syndrome, substance abuse, and hypertension.

The psychological impact of historical trauma can also be devastating. Mabel Kudralook Smith (2003) spoke of her childhood in a family immersed in alcoholism as demonstrated in the following quote:

Inside I developed feelings of shame, insecurity, confusion, abandonment, rejection, isolation, anger, and fear. Trauma causes a series of emotions to be generated, then blocks the release of these emotions. These hard emotions got pushed down deep inside, buried inside, covered by layer upon layer of scar tissue from childhood as years go by. When they are turned inward and stuffed deep inside, these intense, hard emotions cause destructive behaviors. For example, anger turned inwards becomes rage, and rage is an emotion that is self-destructive. One becomes powerless. There was no opportunity to express anger in a safe environment so it stayed inside and became something worse and it hurt me. (p. 84)

Historical trauma is often thought of as part of the explanatory framework for substance abuse, violence, and suicide in Native American communities (Braveheart, 1999; Duran, 2006).

In other words, the inability to recover from past trauma leads to current problems. This historical unresolved grief or soul wound has been inflicted by colonization. Trauma, both historical and contemporary, leads to intergenerational accumulation of risk for poor mental health status for Native Americans. For example, Native Americans experience a 30.6% rate of past month binge drinking and 11.2% rate of illicit drug use compared to rates of 24.5% and 7.9% in the general population (Substance Abuse and Mental Health Services Administration, 2010). Native Americans also have the highest rates of suicide of any group: 18.2 per 100,000. This is about twice the national average (US Department of Health and Human Services, 2010). While suicide rates vary significantly across regions and tribal groups, suicide among Alaska Natives is 117% higher than any other Native American group (Morgan & Freeman, 2009).

MICRO PERSPECTIVE

Assessment

As noted above, a growing body of literature indicates that substance abuse, violence, and suicide may be symptomatic of intergenerational trauma. The implication of this connection is that practitioners encountering these issues in their clients should also look for signs of intergenerational trauma in the assessment process.

Assessing the nature and effects of intergenerational trauma has not been standardized, however two measures have recently been developed, the Historical Loss Scale and the Historical Loss Associated Symptoms Scale. These scales measure typical losses experienced by Native Americans, how they are thought about in the present, and symptoms that may result from contemplating these losses (Ehlers, Gizer, Gilder, Ellingson, & Yehuda, 2013). It should be noted that more work is needed to develop and test historical trauma constructs as well as the scales developed to measure them (Walls & Whitbeck, 2012). While still relatively new, these tools may prove useful for clinicians.

Assessments for historical trauma should include a family history that will enable the practitioner to identify how current problems fit with intergenerational patterns. It may be helpful to use intake forms to begin gathering this information. For example, some social agencies that focus on assisting indigenous clients have a question on their intake form that asks if the prospective client or any member of his/her family have attended boarding schools.

Looking for intergenerational patterns of violence, substance abuse, child removal or other key social issues can be an important part of the assessment process. This would be important in the case described in this chapter. Tools such as eco-maps and genograms can facilitate this process. Completing these tools with a client or assigning them to a client as "homework" can also bridge assessment with the therapeutic process, as using such tools may lead to "ah ha" moments. Use of these tools can be informative in helping Marjorie's social worker better understand her and her situation. Reviewing the results of these assessment tools can also help Marjorie gain insight into her own behaviors including patterns of behavior that she shares with members of her family and community.

Examining community and tribal history may also reveal important information that sheds light on a client's experiences. While some of this information may be gleaned directly from the client, there may also be times when a client is unfamiliar with or has been misinformed about events that happened in the community or tribe. Uncovering this information may be therapeutic for Marjorie and other clients like her as well as informative for the assessment process. Indeed, there are times when assessment and intervention go hand in hand. Clearly it is important for Marjorie's social worker to explore strengths that have enabled her to survive a violent family situation, keep custody of her children thus far, and seek help through a 12-Step program and from a social worker.

While the nature of assessing for intergenerational trauma leads helping professionals to identify traumatic events, it is important to remember that an individual's life experiences cannot be summarized by simply understanding traumatic events and reactions to them. Indeed, the social work profession has always emphasized the importance of strengths. Assessments must include uncovering strengths and resilience as well as areas of dysfunction.

General Principles for Interventions

A review of the literature reveals several general principles that apply to interventions for intergenerational trauma, regardless of whether the intervention takes place on a micro or macro level. Remembering and mourning are both critical factors in recovery. Through these mechanisms, painful burdens can be released. As one survivor of intergenerational trauma stated, "In order for you to heal you need to share your pain. In order to share my pain, I need to name it. In saying what it is accurately, I can deal with it" (Smith, 2003, p. 84). She described her healing process as a journey, a quest for learning. She felt the need to search to find the source of her deep pain and emptiness.

> Slowly at first, I turned my gaze inward and saw one layer at a time. At first, the way was dark and unknown, and I was determined to walk into that dark void to confront that deeply injured spirit that had been grieving for so long. What made me stronger than my fear was a yearning in my heart to be whole again. (Smith, 2003, p. 85)

In Marjorie's case, the social worker can assist her in reviewing and reflecting on the various traumatic events that have happened in her family and tribe. Recognizing these events and finding non-destructive ways to mourn and grieve are part of the therapeutic process.

Another core principle for intergenerational trauma interventions is that recalling and retelling history from an indigenous perspective bears witness. Often, historical events are recorded and recounted from the perspective of colonizing forces. For example, from an indigenous perspective, the 1890 events at Wounded Knee were a massacre that devastated the Lakota people and had ripple effects across many indigenous nations. On the other hand, some Americans commemorated the event as a great victory that resulted in soldiers receiving Medals of Honor.

> The fact that many Americans cheered the massacre and saw it as a positive event denied the Lakota their own understanding of what had happened. The massacre was typically portrayed as a glorious battle where the forces of good had triumphed over evil savages, thus supporting the interests of the United States and the American people. Only in recent years have Native people been able to claim/reclaim their own perspectives. (Weaver & Congress, 2010, p. 217)

Recalling what happened from an indigenous perspective is often overshadowed by an intergenerational legacy of shame, guilt, and distrust. Some stories of trauma are not shared because of this sense of shame or because the experience is unspeakable. This may lead to indigenous perspectives ultimately being lost and trauma being internalized. The imposition of colonial ideas and censorship of indigenous knowledge results in self-doubt and delegitimizes indigenous survivors' own experiences. At times the promotion of a non-indigenous perspective on traumatic experiences may be deliberate. "In order to escape accountability for his crimes the perpetrator does everything in his power to promote forgetting. Secrecy and silence are the perpetrator's first line of defense" (Faimon, 2004, p. 241). If secrecy fails, then perpetrators often attack the credibility of the victim, deny, minimize, or rationalize the event. Suppression of the truth perpetuates and compounds the experience of trauma. As Marjorie attends her tribe's commemoration of the Sand Creek Massacre, she can hear her people's story retold from an indigenous perspective. This can be empowering and help validate that the atrocities were real and facilitate moving toward mourning and healing.

Allies are important in counteracting silencing and denial. This can be a key role for social workers and other helping professionals. There must be acknowledgment of genocide, telling and retelling of stories, remembering what happened. While acknowledgment of the traumatic events is important, it is crucial that this is done in affirming ways that are not retraumatizing. The social worker, particularly if he/she does not share Marjorie's Cheyenne background, can play an important role in acknowledging the power of the trauma that has affected Marjorie and many Native American people.

Empowering survivors counteracts feelings of helplessness. As one survivor stated, "If I can release the rage within me, I can make room for a teachable spirit. I can relearn how to nurture understanding, how to extend care and compassion to others. If I can get that far, I can have intimacy" (Smith, 2003, p. 86). In Marjorie's case, participating in the Cheyenne remembrance of the Sand Creek massacre provides a supportive context for validating the pain associated with this atrocity and facilitating moving beyond the trauma.

Empowerment can serve as a framework for interventions for intergenerational trauma. The experiences that produce trauma typically leave those who experience them feeling as if they have little if any control over their situation. Likewise, the minimizing and denying of the atrocities experienced by indigenous peoples often undermines and devalues indigenous perspectives of both historical and contemporary traumatic events. Conversely, empowerment approaches can validate indigenous perspectives and reinforce the resilience of indigenous peoples.

Interventions that incorporate indigenous perspectives and knowledge are not only empowering but are also effective (King, 2011; Mehl-Madrona & Mainguy, 2014). Put another way, best practices for working with Native American clients often involve culturally grounded approaches. Just as the historical denial of indigenous cultures resulted in trauma and inhibited traditional coping mechanisms and healing, reincorporation of culture is therapeutic.

There are many different helping practices that are grounded in Native American cultures. The choice of intervention depends on the client's needs. Sometimes Native American cultural elements are integrated into mainstream practices. For example, many reservations and urban areas have Native-specific Twelve Step programs like the one mentioned in the case example. Some Native Americans for whom culture resonates strongly find comfort in traditional ceremonies like the Sweat Lodge. Mehl-Madrona and Mainguy (2014) reviewed how culture can be effectively integrated in a variety of health and mental health services tailored for Native Americans.

True healing from intergenerational trauma requires more than simply alleviating symptoms. It is important to move beyond the basics such as achieving sobriety and preventing suicide to embracing a healthy lifestyle. Helping must involve healing and developing skills for living life in balance (Coyhis & Simonelli, 2008). Effective interventions for intergenerational trauma involve integration of cultural strengths with clinical knowledge. The emphasis must be on ongoing wellness rather than remediation of disease.

Transference and Countertransference Issues

Social work that involves cross-cultural interactions can bring up additional issues of transference and countertransference. For example, if Marjorie's social worker is white, there may be a tendency to associate him or her with the oppressive forces that have colonized indigenous territories. Conversely, a white social worker may feel some level of guilt for the way that Native Americans have been treated and bring these feelings into the working relationship. If the social worker and client are both from oppressed groups there may be a tendency for one to see the other as an ally based on this presumed connection.

In the examples above, the social worker-client relationship can become clouded by perceptions of the other. It is important that social workers be vigilant about their own reactions to and feelings about clients and make sure that these do not influence helping relationships. Likewise, the social worker should be attentive to how the client may be perceiving him/her and call attention to this, as necessary.

In working with clients like Marjorie who have experienced trauma, social workers need to be attentive to issues of vicarious traumatization and compassion fatigue. Listening to stories like Marjorie's can be difficult and painful. It is important that social workers develop good skills in stress management and self-care so that they can be fully present in listening to and helping their clients.

Legal and Ethical Concerns

As Marjorie's case illustrates, trauma is a significant issue in the lives of some Native Americans. While not legal issues, per se, this case does raise some ethical considerations. Given the pervasiveness of trauma and growing scholarship on trauma-informed care, some would say that a trauma informed approach is required for ethical, responsible social work practice.

The considerable social and health disparities suffered by Native Americans can be traced to both historical and ongoing colonization (Freeman, Iron Cloud-Two Dogs, Novins, & LeMaster, 2004). Colonization provides the foundation for the pervasive violence and substance abuse illustrated by Marjorie's case. An increasing number of social workers see decolonization (i.e., raising awareness and challenging oppressive attitudes and colonial structures), as an ethical imperative (Gray, Coates, Yellow Bird, & Hetherington, 2013; Wilson & Yellow Bird, 2005).

It is clear that intergenerational trauma is not a thing of the past for many Native Americans. The social work profession is built on a foundation of serving disenfranchised populations and striving for social justice. Ethical practice for serving Marjorie as well as many other clients involves confronting continuing injustice, ongoing trauma, and oppression.

MEZZO PERSPECTIVE

The principles of Trauma Informed Care (TIC) provide important guidance for interventions as well as design of service systems. Trauma informed systems are those in which all components have been reconsidered and evaluated in light of a basic understanding of the role that violence plays in the lives of people seeking mental health and addictions services (Harris & Fallot, 2001).

There are five basic principles to be considered in providing trauma informed services: safety, trustworthiness, choice, collaboration, and empowerment. Studies of Adverse Childhood Experiences (ACE) reveal that traumatic childhood experiences are common, regardless of population, and that they have lasting implications for the health and well-being of adults (Centers for Disease Control [CDC], 2013). As illustrated by Marjorie's case and documented by extensive literature, traumatic experiences are common in many Native American families and communities.

These findings have implications for practitioners, administrators, and policy makers. Practitioners should keep in mind the principles of safety, trustworthiness, choice, collaboration, and empowerment throughout their work with clients. Maximizing these principles can be crucial in engaging and enhancing the effectiveness of work with clients who have experienced trauma. Likewise, administrators and policy makers must consider these principles in designing and implementing effective services. Many social agencies and programs have been designed without this awareness and sensitivity and have further traumatized some clients (Harris & Fallot, 2001).

People who design programs and implement services at agencies where Native American clients seek assistance should be aware of intergenerational trauma and should consider this in their planning. For example, it is important to consider how to provide an environment that feels safe and welcoming for clients like Marjorie. Fostering feelings of safety can involve things such as location of the agency, how waiting and interviewing rooms are set up, and presence of security guards. Fostering trustworthiness can involve elements such as a social worker following through with keeping appointments and making promised referrals, insuring that Marjorie receives the thoughtful attention that she deserves, and that her story is treated with respect. Both the agency and the social worker should be able to offer Marjorie choice in the type of services that she receives. Collaboration and empowerment are key social work principles, as are choice and trustworthiness, but there are times when the ways that agencies are set up or services are delivered undermine these principles. Clients who have experienced trauma, like Marjorie, are most likely to benefit from services in agencies that are attentive to the principles of trauma informed care.

The body of scholarship on ACE and trauma-informed care share many of the same basic ideas as scholarship on intergenerational trauma, yet, these areas of study have rarely been approached in an integrated manner. Practitioners would do well to draw from both bodies of literature to more effectively serve indigenous clients.

MACRO PERSPECTIVE

The Wounded Knee massacre served as a capstone summarizing many losses experienced by the Lakota and other indigenous peoples. Traditionally, in Lakota culture, a death is mourned for a year, then it is time to carry on with living, unencumbered by grief. At the time of the Wounded Knee massacre, however, traditional spiritual practices were banned and coping mechanisms severely compromised. It was not possible to grieve, then resume life as usual. As the hundredth anniversary of Chief Bigfoot and his band's travels to Wounded Knee approached, several traditional Lakota spiritual leaders and activists thought it appropriate, not only to commemorate the massacre but to provide a mechanism for the Lakota people to acknowledge and begin to let go of the grief built up over generations. Indeed, using the concept that one is connected to one's ancestors, it was decided that what was needed was *Wiping the Tears of Seven Generations*. In 1990 and every year since, riders retrace Chief Bigfoot's journey to promote remembering and healing. On these memorial rides, Lakota are joined by other Native people and allies from many backgrounds.

Likewise, the losses suffered by the Seneca have led to significant trauma, yet every fall a commemoration ceremony is held where community members alive when land was taken for Kinzua Dam gather with younger generations to *Remember the Removal*. Coming together to remember what happened and tell the story from a Seneca perspective is cathartic. In this way the healing continues (Weaver & Congress, 2010).

Both the *Kinzua Remembrance* and the *Wiping the Tears of Seven Generations* provide grassroots examples of collectivist healing efforts. Leaders within these communities have brought together people affected by these acts in ways that promote remembrance, validate an indigenous perspective of these events, and promote healing. A similar opportunity is available to Marjorie to gather with Cheyenne people and their allies to commemorate the Sand Creek Massacre.

CONCLUSION

This chapter has reviewed various issues related to intergenerational trauma and Native Americans. Intergenerational trauma is an important issue with implications for the well-being of many indigenous people. While historical trauma theories have experienced significant development in recent decades, it is clear that empirical validation and evidence-based practice require further development.

The inhumanity of the past has left scars for many people. Past atrocities continue to affect the well-being of many Native people. Speaking honestly about atrocities is a prerequisite to healing. Social workers have a role to play in validating indigenous perspectives and experiences of trauma and helping clients move toward healing. It is also important to note that inhumanity is not a thing of the past. Rather, contemporary trauma will leave its intergenerational legacy.

Social workers have a role to play in challenging injustice and oppression. Ultimately, while it is important to promote healing, prevention must become the primary mechanism for addressing trauma. In other words, we need to recognize and confront contemporary disparities, racism, and injustice of all kinds, thus promoting a more balanced, just, and peaceful world and interrupting the cycle of intergenerational trauma once and for all.

INTERNET RESOURCES

- The Takini Network: http://historicaltrauma .com
- KIFARU Wiping the Tears of Seven Generations: https://www.youtube.com/playlist?list=PL724E DD436CB7A4EC
- White Bison: http://whitebison.org
- The Indian Country Child Trauma Center, part of the National Child Traumatic Stress Network funded by SAMHSA: http://www.icct.org

DISCUSSION QUESTIONS

1. How do contemporary expressions of physical and psychological violence, including microaggressions, instigate and perpetuate trauma?

2. What are some contemporary events that are creating additional trauma for future generations of indigenous people?

3. How might social workers apply the principles of trauma-informed care to re-envision service delivery systems?

4. How can social workers from a variety of backgrounds serve as allies for indigenous peoples in ways that promote justice and mitigate trauma?

5. What are the implications of providing clinical interventions for intergenerational trauma when empirical validation of assessment tools and interventions is still in its infancy?

REFERENCES

American Indian Ritual Object Repatriation Foundation. (1996). *Mending the sacred circle: A Native American repatriation guide.* New York, NY: Author.

Amnesty International. (2007). *Maze of injustice: The failure to protect indigenous women from sexual violence in the USA.* London, UK: Author.

Amnesty International. (2009). *No more stolen sisters: The need for a comprehensive response to discrimination and violence against indigenous women in Canada.* London: Author. Retrieved from http://www.amnesty.ca

Barnes, P. M., Adams, P. F., & Powell-Griner, E. (2010). *Health characteristics of the American Indian or Alaska Native adult population: United States, 2004–2008.* National Health Statistics Report, 20. Retrieved from http://www.cdc.gov

Bilharz, J. A. (1998). *The Allegany Senecas and the Kinzua Dam: Forced relocation through two decades.* Lincoln: University of Nebraska Press.

Braveheart, M. (1999). Oyate ptayela: Rebuilding the Lakota Nation through addressing historical trauma among Lakota parents. *Journal of Human Behavior in the Social Environment, 2,* 109–126.

Centers for Disease Control and Prevention. (2013). *The adverse childhood experiences study.* Retrieved from http://www.cdc.gov/ace/

Coyhis, D., & Simonelli, R. (2008). The Native America healing experience. *Substance Use and Misuse, 43,* 1927–1949.

d'Errico, P. (2013). *Jeffrey Amherst and smallpox blankets.* Retrieved from http://www.nativeweb .org/pages/legal/amherst/lord-Jeff.html

Duran, E. (2006). *Healing the soul wound: Counseling with American Indians and other native peoples.* New York, NY: Teachers College Press.

Ehlers, C. L., Gizer, I. R., Gilder, D. A., Ellingson, J. M., & Yehuda, R. (2013). Measuring historical trauma in an American Indian community sample: Contributions of substance dependence, affective disorder, conduct disorder and PTSD. *Drug and Alcohol Dependence, 133*(1), 180–187.

Estrada, A. L. (2009). Mexican Americans and historical trauma theory: A theoretical perspective. *Journal of Ethnicity in Substance Abuse, 8*(3), 330–340.

Eyerman, R. (2001). *Cultural trauma: Slavery and the formation of African American Identity.* Cambridge, MA: Cambridge University Press.

Faimon, M. B. (2004). Ties that bind: Remembering, mourning, healing historical trauma. *American Indian Quarterly, 28*(1/2), 238–251.

Freeman, B., Iron Cloud-Two Dogs, E., Novins, D. K., & LeMaster, P. L. (2004). Contextual issues for strategic planning and evaluation of systems of care for American Indian and Alaska Native communities: An introduction to Circles of Care. *American Indian & Alaska Native Mental Health Research: The Journal of the National Center, 11*(2), 1–29.

Gone, J. P. (2009). A community-based treatment for Native American historical trauma: Prospects for evidence-based practice. *Journal of Consulting and Clinical Psychology, 77*(4), 751–762.

Gray, M., Coates, J., Yellow Bird, M., & Hetherington, T. (2013). *Decolonizing social work.* Farnham, UK: Ashgate Press.

Harris, M., & Fallot, R. D. (2001). *Using trauma theory to design service systems.* San Francisco, CA: Jossey-Bass.

Hart, M. A., & Rowe, G. (2014). Legally entrenched oppressions: The undercurrent of First Nations peoples' experiences with Canada's social welfare policies. In H. N. Weaver (Ed.), *Social issues in contemporary Native America: Reflections from Turtle Island* (pp. 23–41). Farnham, UK: Ashgate Press.

Hauptman, L. M. (1986). *The Iroquois struggle for survival: World war II to red power.* Syracuse, NY: Syracuse University Press.

Hernandez, P., Carranza, M., & Almeida, R. (2010). Mental health professionals' adaptive responses to racial microaggressions: An exploratory study. *Professional Psychology: Research and Practice, 41*(3), 202–209.

"Kill the Indian and Save the Man": Capt. Richard H. Pratt on the Education of Native Americans. (2014). *History Matters.* Retrieved from http://historymatters.gmu.edu

King, J. (2011). Reclaiming our roots: Accomplishments and challenges. *Journal of Psychoactive Drugs, 43*(4), 297–301.

Lazarus, E. (1991). *Black hills, white justice: The Sioux Nation versus the United States government, 1775-the present.* New York, NY: HarperCollins.

Leary, J. D. (2005). *Post traumatic slave syndrome: America's legacy of enduring injury and healing.* El Segundo, CA: Upton Press.

Mehl-Madrona, L., & Mainguy, B. (2014). Culture is medicine that works. In H. N. Weaver (Ed.), *Social issues in contemporary Native America: Reflections from Turtle Island* (pp. 187–202). Farnham, UK: Ashgate Press.

Morgan, R., & Freeman, L. (2009). The healing of our people: Substance abuse and historical trauma. *Substance Use and Misuse, 44,* 84–98.

Perry, B. D. (2001). *Violence and childhood: How persisting fear can alter the developing child's brain.* Retrieved from https://www.ChildTrauma.org

Seneca Nation of Indians. (2015). Retrieved from https://sni.org/government/territories/#1365

Smith, M. K. (2003). A recovery story that heals. *Arctic Anthropology, 40*(2), 83–86.

Stiffarm, L. A., & Lane, P., Jr. (1992). The demography of Native North America: A question of American Indian survival. In M. A. Jaimes (Ed.), *The state of Native America: Genocide, colonization, and resistance* (pp. 23–53). Boston: South End Press.

Substance Abuse and Mental Health Services Administration. (2010). *The NSDUH Report: Substance use among American Indian or Alaska Native adults.* Rockville, MD: Author.

U.S. Department of Health and Human Services. (2010). Surveillance for violent deaths: National violent death reporting system, 16 states, 2007. *Morbidity and Mortality Weekly Report, 59*(SS-4), 1–50.

Van der Kolk, B. (1994). *The body keeps the score: Memory and the evolving psychobiology of posttraumatic stress.* Retrieved from http://www.trauma-pages.com/vanderk4.htm

Venables, R. W. (2004). *American Indian history: Five centuries of conflict and coexistence.* Santa Fe, NM: Clear Light.

Walls, M. L., & Whitbeck, L. B. (2012). Advantages of stress process approaches for measuring historical trauma. *The American Journal of Drug and Alcohol Use, 38*(5), 416–420.

Weaver, H. N., & Congress, E. (2010). The ongoing impact of colonization: Manmade trauma and Native Americans. In A. Kalayjian & D. Eugene (Eds.), *Mass trauma and emotional healing around the world: Rituals and practice for resilience and meaning-making* (pp. 211–226). Santa Barbara, CA: Praeger.

Whitbeck, L. B., Adams, G. W., Hoyt, D. R., & Chen, X. (2004). Conceptualizing and measuring historical trauma among American Indian people. *American Journal of Community Psychology, 33*(3/4), 119–130.

Williams, V. (2007). *The Kinzua Dam controversy* (Master's thesis). Retrieved from ProQuest

Dissertations and Theses database. (UMI No. 1444012)

Wilson, W. A., & Yellow Bird, M. (2005). *For indigenous eyes only: A decolonization handbook.* Santa Fe, NM: School for Advanced Research Press.

Yellow Horse Brave Heart, M., & DeBruyn, M. (1998). The American Indian holocaust: Healing historical unresolved grief. *American Indian Alaska Native Mental Health Research, 8*(2), 56–78.

CHAPTER 29

The Suicidal Military Client

Fred P. Stone

CHAPTER OBJECTIVES

- Explain how to assess a military client for suicidality;
- Describe evidence-based interventions to use with suicidal military clients;
- Gain an appreciation of the cultural and community issues surrounding suicide in the military;
- Identify the policies and programs used to combat suicide in the military.

CASE VIGNETTE

Growing up in a small rural community, John R. never considered joining the military. He came from a lower-income farming family, and his home was chaotic and sometimes abusive. His father spent most of his time at home drinking beer, often several six packs a night, and if agitated, he would physically lash out at his wife and three sons. When John was 16, he and his mother and two brothers went to live with his maternal grandparents, but he did not adjust well to his new home. He was a poor student and dropped out of high school his senior year. He spent most of his time playing video games, drinking beer, and smoking marijuana. He was arrested twice for public intoxication, and his mother and grandparents insisted that he leave their home. With few options, he decided to join the U.S. Army in 2006. His drug use and arrests could have disqualified him from service, but the military needed recruits and granted him a moral waiver allowing him to enlist. After completing his Basic Combat and Advanced Individual Training at Fort Leonard Wood, Missouri, he was assigned to Fort Bragg, North Carolina, as an 88M, Motor Transport Specialist. To his surprise, he enjoyed Army life. He had many close friends and a serious relationship with a civilian woman, Candace, from the neighboring town.

Within a year, John was sent to Baghdad, Iraq, where he drove transport trucks on convoys to outposts around the city. On several occasions, his convoy was attacked, and John began to feel anxious even when he was in the relative safety of the base. During his fourth month, John's Humvee was struck by an Improvised Explosive Device. He was the only one of four soldiers in the vehicle to survive. Injuries to his neck and legs required his evacuation to a local military clinic followed by an aeromedical evacuation flight to Ramstein Air Base, Germany. John fully recovered from his physical injuries, but he suffered from severe anxiety related to the attack. He was diagnosed with post-traumatic stress disorder (PTSD) and returned to Fort Bragg. Candace was excited for John to return, and the first few weeks of their reunion were the best of his life, he told a friend. But John was still troubled. He dreaded going to work each day because he had to work on vehicles that were constant reminders of the attack. He also felt shunned by other soldiers who had heard that he had to return from Iraq because of PTSD. He was often mocked and accused of malingering by his supervisors. John attended individual and group therapy sessions with a civilian social worker on the base, but he rarely made any comments. He refused to drive and had problems sleeping. His drinking increased, but he was able to avoid using illicit drugs. Because of the severity of his symptoms, he expected to be discharged from the military.

Candace became frightened of John's mood swings and substance abuse. They broke up, and she refused to return his calls. John's symptoms increased, but he did not tell his social worker or anyone else, fearing that the social worker and others would either fail to understand his problems or reject him. One night after drinking heavily, John wrapped a zip tie around his neck and tried to suffocate himself. He left a short note that said he was sorry for "being a burden to everyone."

Luckily, his roommate walked in on John only moments after he wrenched the zip tie. The roommate cut the tie and called 911. John was transported to the base emergency room.

INTRODUCTION

The United States military was once a model of suicide prevention, with military suicide rates lower than civilian rates. This has changed dramatically during the past decade. The military's suicide rate rose from 10.3 per 100,000 in 2001 (Ramchand, Acosta, Burns, Jaycox, & Perin, 2012) to 22.7 per 100,000 in 2012 (Smolenski et al., 2013).

This chapter examines suicide in the U.S. military from micro, mezzo, and macro perspectives. From the micro perspective, it explains how to assess and treat a military client for suicidality and discusses some of the special considerations in working with this population and problem. The mezzo section looks at some of the military cultural and community influences on suicide, and the macro section examines the policies surrounding these issues. A case vignette introduced at the beginning of this chapter illustrates these perspectives.

The Centers for Disease Control and Prevention (CDC; 2010) estimates that 105 people kill themselves each day in the United States. Suicide is the 10th leading cause of death and among the top five causes of death for those between the ages of 10 and 54 (CDC, 2010). In 2013, suicide was the second leading cause of death of active duty military members, accounting for 28.5% of deaths (Armed Forces Health Surveillance Center, 2014). A poll of Operation Iraqi Freedom (OIF) and Operations Enduring Freedom (OEF) veterans found one-third had contemplated suicide (Briggs, 2013). Other research has found that 12% of active duty members have seriously considered suicide (Bray et al., 2009). The suicide rate among OIF and OEF combat veterans is lower than the rate for veterans who never deployed to a combat zone in these conflicts (Leardmann et al., 2013; Bush et al., 2013).

Suicide rates among veterans are also high. Veterans are twice as likely to commit suicide as non-veterans (Kaplan, Huguet, MacFarland, & Newsom, 2007).

MICRO PERSPECTIVE

Social workers need to assess risk and protective factors for suicide with every client. These factors are the foundation for assessing suicidal risk.

Risk Factors

Risk factors are variables that are often associated with suicidal thoughts and intentions. Ramchand et al. (2014) found three kinds of risk factors—internal, external, and societal. The internal risk factors include prior suicide attempts, mental and substance abuse disorders, depression, and anxiety (Ramchand et al., 2014). History of physical or sexual abuse and traumatic life events are external factors associated with suicide (Ramchand et al., 2014). Societal factors include the availability of firearms and suicide of others (Ramchand et al., 2014).

Several risk factors are particularly relevant to military clients. These factors include mental illness, substance abuse, history of being abused, and failed relationships. Mental illness is strongly associated with suicide (Cavanagh, Carson, Sharpe, & Lawrie, 2003), and several studies have found significant levels of depression and anxiety among military members. Barlas, Higgins, Pflieger, and Diecker (2013) found 9.6% of active duty military members had symptoms of "high depression" (p. ES-11) and 16 % had significant levels of anxiety. Around 15% of soldiers and marines returning from combat tours in Iraq and Afghanistan have met the criteria for depression (Tanielian & Jaycox, 2008). Fourteen percent of returning deployers screened positive for PTSD and 19% for traumatic brain injury (Tanielian & Jaycox, 2008).

Substance abuse is also a risk factor for suicide. Goldsmith, Pellman, Kleinman, and Bunney (2002) estimated that between 20% and 30% of people who commit suicide are intoxicated at the time of their deaths. The military tacitly endorses alcohol use. Military members below the age of 35 are more likely to be heavy drinkers (defined as 14 drinks per week for males/7 drinks for females per week) than their matched civilian counterparts (Barlas et al., 2013). Patterson, Jones, Marsh, and Drummond (2001) discovered that substance abuse was a contributing factor in 54% and 77% of U.S. Air Force aviator suicide attempts and deaths, respectively.

Childhood trauma has been associated with suicide (Afifi et al., 2008), and military members who have experienced childhood abuse are at an increased risk for suicide. Perales, Hallway, Forys-Donahue, Speiss, and Millikan (2012) found that 61.2% of soldiers with suicidal behavior had experienced childhood trauma.

The military has seen a significant increase in divorce rates since the attacks of 11 September 2001 (Negrusa, Negrusa, & Hosek, 2014), and failed relationships have also been associated with military suicides. Bush et al. (2013) discovered that 51% of those who committed suicide and those who attempted it had a history of failed spousal or intimate relationship and 30% had failed relationships within 30 days of their attempt. Divorced/separated members had a 24% higher suicide rate than single, never married members (Armed Forces Health Surveillance, 2012).

Protective Factors

Social workers should also assess factors that protect clients from committing suicide. These protective factors should be assessed as thoroughly as risk factors, and social workers should never assume that the absence of risk factors is the same as the presence of protective ones (Simon, 2011a). In the military, the presence of an intimate partner (Skopp, Luxton, Bush, & Sirotin, 2011) or strong social network (Pietrzak et al., 2010) has been shown to be protective factors. Limiting access to lethal means may also protect service members from attempting suicide. Some military specialties have ready access to weapons which may be correlated with higher rates of suicide in those specialties (Martin, Ghahramanlou-Holloway, & Lou, 2009). Reducing the ability to impulsively access a firearm has been shown to reduce suicides by firearms (Shenassa, Rogers, Spalding, & Roberts, 2004).

Cultural and religious prohibitions against suicide may serve as protective factors (Defense Centers of Excellence, 2010; Simon, 2011a) as well as strong coping skills and hope for the future (Defense Centers of Excellence, 2010; Simon, 2011a).

In the case presentation, John displayed a number of risk factors that should have placed him at a high risk for suicide. He had endured abuse as a child and had a history of substance abuse. John also had PTSD and depressive symptoms. With the loss of his girlfriend and his alienation at work, John had almost no support network, and he had no apparent protective factors. John's social worker should have regularly evaluated John for suicidal ideations.

Assessing Military Clients for Suicide

A proper assessment ensures that clients are fully evaluated and the important elements of suicidality are examined (Simon, 2011b). This assessment includes an evaluation of risk and protective factors as well as suicidal ideations and intent.

Military clients, however, may be reluctant to discuss these factors because they fear the significant negative consequences, either real or imagined, for revealing suicidality. The military may remove suicidal members from serving in sensitive positions because suicidality may indicate a "defect in judgment or reliability" (Department of the Army, 2014, p. 2). Sensitive positions are those that an impairment or misconduct could jeopardize national security (Department of the Army, 2014). Revealing suicidality may also result in being stigmatized as "crazy" by a client's coworkers and supervisors, and being suicidal will likely result in a mental health evaluation that can lead to a discharge from the military.

The lack of confidentiality makes these perceptions understandable even if exaggerated. The Department of Defense (DoD) requires mental health professionals (including social workers) in military settings to report crimes and fitness for duty.

These factors make assessment challenging and a proper systematic assessment even more important. Social workers should keep in mind that the more seriously clients are considering suicide the less likely they are to self-disclose (Apter, Horesh, Gothelf, Graffi, & Lepkifker, 2001).

Therapeutic Alliance

A strong therapeutic alliance can overcome these reporting barriers, but presents a number of challenges when working with suicidal clients (Schechter, Goldblatt, & Maltsberger, 2013). One of the challenges is balancing empathetic listening and regular suicide assessments. It may seem odd to ask about suicide when clients have not brought it up during their session (Schechter et al., 2013).

Social workers tend to overestimate their therapeutic alliance and assume that clients trust them enough to fully disclose. They should not accept deference and respect as a sign of a strong therapeutic relationship especially in military settings. The power of therapeutic alliance can also be overestimated. Although it is widely considered to reduce suicidality, there is no evidence that supports this belief (Simon, 2011a).

Assessing Suicidal Ideation and Intent

Social workers should directly ask whether or not a client has had thoughts of killing himself or herself. Clients who actively endorse suicidality should be encouraged to enter a psychiatric hospital voluntarily. If the client refuses, social workers should take steps to have the client involuntarily committed. The U.S. military essentially follows the same rules for commitment as the civilian community (DoD, 2013).

Clients will sometimes make vague comments about suicidality such as "I don't want to be here" or "I just wish I were dead." These passive endorsements must be followed up with specific inquiries on clients' intentions and plans. Clients with specific plans even without the intention to carry them out are at greater risk. Social workers should ask if clients have a method in mind, but also if they have access to other methods; the method of choice may be different (Shea, 2009).

Military clients will usually be reluctant to discuss suicidality because they may view suicidal thoughts as a sign of weakness (see Shea, 2009). Feeling weak is particularly stigmatizing in the hyper-masculine culture of the military. A number of studies have shown the perception that others will perceive them as "weak" is one reason that military members avoid mental health care (Wright et al., 2009; DoD Task Force, 2010). Hoge et al. (2004) found that 65% of combat soldiers and marines who met the screening criteria for a mental disorder reported that that they would avoid mental health services because "I would be seen as weak" (p. 21).

Social workers can overcome this reluctance by acknowledging these feelings and reassuring the client that it takes courage to discuss difficult topics. They can point to a number of military members who have shown incredible strength and courage, but who also sought mental health services. For example, Army Staff Sergeant Ty Carter received the Medal of Honor for his actions in combat, but he also struggled with PTSD symptoms (Shane, 2013).

Clients may avoid discussing their suicidal thoughts because they do not believe that the therapist can help them (Shea, 2009). Hoge et al. (2004) found this present in 38% of their sample of soldiers and marines who screened positive for a mental disorder. Social workers should directly address these concerns.

Social workers should also assess for past suicide attempts. Although most completed suicides occur on the first attempt, research shows a 40 to 50 fold increased risk of dying by suicide among those that have made a previous attempt (Harris & Barraclough, 1997).

Military members may be hesitant to reveal a history of suicide attempts. In the military, suicide attempts carry a heavy stigma, more so than in the civilian community. A history of suicidal behavior can disqualify a person from joining the military. As a result, recruits might not have divulged this information during their screening process and may be reluctant to reveal this information even during therapy. If the suicide attempt becomes known, commanders, supervisors, and coworkers will likely carefully watch the member and potentially reveal the attempt to other workers. In the U.S. Air Force, military members "who are judged to be a moderate or higher level of risk for psychological decompensation of significant maladaptive behavior" are labeled high risk (U.S. Air Force, 2011, p. 22). Clients who are moderately to severely suicidal are considered high risk and regular reports will be made to their commanders (U.S. Air Force, 2011).

Despite these concerns, social workers should be persistent and direct when assessing prior suicide attempts. They should not immediately believe the client's characterization of an attempt. Suicide attempts can be a source of shame, and clients may minimize the attempt or reframe it. Other people may even support this reframing in an effort to comfort themselves. Clinicians should avoid minimizing prior attempts and instead explore not only the attempt, but also the elements surrounding the attempt. Clinicians should also discuss some of the ways that the client overcame the feelings that precipitated the event.

John attended regular individual and group therapy sessions. His social worker initially assessed John for suicidal ideations, but John vehemently denied any thoughts of harming himself. After his attempt, he admitted that he had long considered suicide, but he was afraid to admit it. The social worker failed to regularly assess John because he felt that he had a good relationship with him. In other words, he overestimated the power of his therapeutic alliance. As a result, the social worker did not regularly reassess John and was not persistent when the risk factors clearly showed that John was at a high risk.

Intervention

Social workers should consider two types of interventions—crisis intervention and a continuing therapy model. The crisis intervention model is for clients who are acutely suicidal or are assessed to be at a high risk for suicide despite denials of suicidal intent. This model assumes that the client's suicidality is time limited, and the focus is on keeping the client alive until the crisis is resolved and longer term therapy implemented (Pulakos, 1993).

In the crisis intervention model, social workers should focus on saving the client's life. This may include supporting involuntary admission to a hospital and soliciting the support of family or friends in monitoring the client (Pulakos, 1993). Military social workers have an advantage in using crisis intervention because they can rely on a military member's command to assist in monitoring the client even without the client's permission. One disadvantage, however, is that military members who are new to a base or not located near family may not have family or friends available to watch the client and report concerns.

During the crisis, social workers should focus on helping clients see positive possibilities and reinforcing emotional attachments with others (Leenaars, 1994). The social worker needs to build rapport and listen to the client's crisis and problems. They should also highlight other positive possibilities in the client's life (Leenaars, 1994). The primary goal is for the client to develop hope for a better future or at least one without acute psychological pain.

Crisis intervention is a short-term solution, although occasionally social workers may have to return to using it if the client returns to acute suicidal ideations or intent. The longer-term solution is continuing psychotherapy.

A number of psychotherapies purport to reduce suicidality, but "there is a lack of strong evidence for any interventions in preventing suicide or suicide attempts" (Department of Veterans Affair & Department of Defense (VA/DoD), 2013, p. 88). The strongest evidence supports using cognitive behavioral therapy (CBT). In a meta-analysis, Tarrier, Taylor, and Gooding (2008) found strong evidence that CBTs, particularly problem-solving therapy and dialectical behavior therapy (DBT), reduced suicidal thoughts and behaviors. Hawton, Taylor, Saunders, and Mahadevan (2011) found problem-solving therapy more effective than controls in helping suicidal clients, and Brown et al. (2005) found that CBT lowered levels of depression, hopelessness, and suicidal ideation.

Rudd (2012) analyzed the effective elements of CBT for treating suicidal clients and found six common elements. Effective interventions for suicidality are easy to understand, focus on treatment compliance, teach skills, emphasize self-reliance, guarantee access to mental health services, and use extensive documentation (Rudd, 2012, pp. 596–597).

Rudd et al. (2015) developed a brief cognitive behavioral therapy (BCBT) for military members and veterans that has been shown to significantly reduce suicidality. BCBT focuses on three phases—orientation, skill focus, and relapse prevention. In the orientation phase, the military client commits to therapy and agrees to among other things show up to therapy on time, complete homework, and honestly and actively participate in treatment. The client and social worker develop a crisis and safety plan, and the client makes a commitment to living agreement. The client also focuses on goals beyond simply reducing suicidality, and he or she along with the social worker create a "survival kit." The kit consists of items that focus hope for the client and may include photos, letters, or other items that are meaningful. The skill focus and relapse prevention phases focus on self-management and emotional regulations. These skills include problem solving techniques, mindfulness, cognitive appraisal, and relaxation training (Rudd, 2012).

BCBT has several advantages that may appeal to military clients. Military members may have limited opportunities for long-term psychotherapy, and this intervention may improve participation in therapy (Rudd, 2012). A lack of time has been cited as a reason that military members avoid mental health services (Kim, Britt, Klocko, Riviere, & Adler, 2011; Hoge et al., 2004). BCBT may also appeal to military clients who prefer the structured approach which is similar to other elements of military life.

BCBT would be a perfect choice to help John. One of the problems with John's previous therapy was that it was unstructured and consisted primarily of people talking about their problems. BCBT will instead provide John with a number of skills to help him cope with feelings of anxiety and depression. John will also create a survival kit with photos of Candace and his family to remind him that others value him. Thwarted belongingness and perceived burdensomeness have been shown to increase suicidality (Van Orden et al., 2010), and the survival kit should help John avoid these feelings.

Diversity Issues

The U.S. military is dominated by white males, so it is no surprise that they account for the overwhelming majority of suicides. A review of military suicides from 1998 to 2011 found that 95% were male and 70% were white/non-Hispanic (Armed Forces Health Surveillance Center, 2012). The rates of suicide among women were almost a quarter of that of males, 15.3 versus 4.1 per 100,000 (Armed Forces Health Surveillance Center, 2012). Minorities had lower rates of suicide than whites (Armed Forces Health Surveillance Center, 2012).

There are some differences between gender groups. Benda (2005) found significant differences between male and female veterans: Female veterans' risk factors included childhood trauma, depression, and relationship problems, while men's factors were related to substance abuse, combat, and work-related problems.

Currently, there is no data on suicide rates in the military for members who are sexual minorities (gay, lesbian, bisexual, or transgender). The prohibition against gays and lesbians openly serving in the military was repealed in 2011, but transgender members are still prohibited from serving. Even with the repeal, gay and lesbian military members may be reluctant to reveal their sexual identity.

In the general population, gay and bisexual men have higher rates of suicide, especially in their earlier years (Paul et al., 2002). One of the risk factors is a hostile environment (Paul et al., 2002). The military has historically been hostile to homosexuality (Dunivin, 1994), and there is still stigma associated with being gay or lesbian in the hypermasculine military culture. Gays and lesbians often fear being rejected by mental health professionals, and social workers in military settings should focus on making mental health services welcoming to this group.

Attending therapy may undermine the religious convictions for some service members. In their view, admitting that they have thought about killing themselves may be equivalent to losing their faith (Rickgarn, 1990). Social workers should acknowledge and support positive religious beliefs because these may act as a protective factor against suicide. Colucci and Martin (2008) found that spirituality and religiosity may reduce suicidality, but they cautioned that some elements of religiosity may also increase it. For example, some religions condemn homosexuality or the act of killing which creates guilt. Social workers should not assume that a religious client who endorses his or her religious prohibitions against suicide is necessarily at less risk than others.

Transference and Countertransference Issues

Social workers will often experience negative transference from military clients. Military members often view seeking mental health services as a personal weakness and stigmatize those who seek help (Hoge et al., 2004; Kim et al., 2011). Studies show that 18% to 38% of military members do not trust mental health professionals (Hoge et al., 2004; Kim et al., 2011). Social workers should expect many military clients to view mental health professionals as either incompetent or a threat. They are viewed as incompetent because many military members do not believe that psychotherapy is effective or necessary (Kim et al., 2011). Military members may see social workers as a threat because they may recommend that members be discharged from the service. Social workers can lessen the impact of these transference issues by acknowledging these concerns and being empathetic with their military clients' situation. If the transference is strongly negative, social workers should explore the underlying issues that are causing the client's negative reactions (Gelso, Hill, & Kivlighan, 1991).

Working with suicidal clients can be particularly frustrating for social workers and promote countertransference (Maris, Berman, & Silverman, 2000, p. 512). It is not uncommon for social workers to experience hate, anxiety, fear, and malice toward suicidal clients (Maris et al., 2000; Rudd, Joiner & Rajab, 2001).

Many people, including medical staff, have negative views of suicidal clients. Medical staff may threaten to withhold treatment to punish or coerce cooperation from suicidal clients (Hawton et al., 2011). Social workers in military setting may become frustrated that a client who has successfully completed rigorous training and has access to resources continues to feel hopeless. These social workers may internalize the masculine warrior paradigm (Dunivin, 1994) themselves and expect military members to display toughness in the face of adversity. No amount of training or life experience, however, can fully prepare someone for all of life's challenges. Military members are as susceptible to depression and other mental health issues as any other population.

Other issues may also arise, such as a social worker becoming upset at hearing what a service member saw or did in combat. A recent case involving a social work intern highlights this issue. The social work intern interviewed a client who discussed the accidental death of a child during combat operations in Iraq. The intern became so upset that she began to vomit in front of the client. Needless to say, the client did not feel that he could work with this social worker. The social worker was just another person who would reject him for what he did.

Finally, social workers may have personal issues with suicide. They might have attempted suicide themselves or had a family member or friend who killed himself or herself. It is vital that social workers explore their thoughts and feelings on suicide before working with suicidal clients (Maris et al., 2000).

John's social worker was a civilian, and when the group discussed combat, he looked visibly uncomfortable. This impression was one of the reasons that John refused to discuss his combat experiences. John's social worker blamed John for being resistant, but it was the social worker's behavior that created the resistance. Social workers should always be sensitive to how their personal views and beliefs, even if unspoken, may impact their clients' cooperation with therapy.

Legal and Ethical Concerns

Regardless of the setting, social workers often must breach confidentiality to prevent an actively suicidal client from attempting suicide. In the military, however, the standard for breaching confidentiality is even lower. For example, in the U.S. Air Force, a client who deemed to be at moderate or high risk of suicide is categorized at high interest and notifications of the client's status as high interest are given to the client's primary care provider and command representative (U.S. Air Force, 2011). The intent of this instruction is to heighten the awareness of the client's command so that he or she can more closely monitor the client. Although this notification process is intended to protect the client from self-harm, it raises a serious ethical dilemma for social workers. Unless the client is actively suicidal, this process would constitute a breach of confidentiality in the civilian sector. The lack of confidentiality around suicide in the military may also be an additional barrier for clients accessing services or motivate military clients to seek care from civilian mental health providers that are not affiliated with the military. See Daley (2013) and Simmons and Rycraft (2010) for further information on ethical dilemmas when working with veterans, military members, or their families.

MEZZO PERSPECTIVE

Military settings offer some advantages over civilian settings in regards to dealing with the problem of suicide. The military community is sensitive to suicidality and provides a host of services and assistance. Active duty military members have access to mental health care, and each service has a suicide prevention program. Most military installations have programs for families and couples as well as financial management and aid programs that can help solve material problems that may contribute to suicidal behavior.

The military can also force a member to undergo a mental health evaluation. A commander can order a Command Directed Evaluation if a member's psychological state affects his or her "ability to carry out the mission" (Defense Centers of Excellence, n.d.). Although the goal is assessing fitness for duty, a well-done evaluation can provide an opportunity for a member to discuss his or her problems and seek treatment. Members who are a threat to themselves or others or suffering from a severe mental disorder can also be ordered to undergo this evaluation (DoD, 2013).

The military has unique programs and policies that can help identify suicidal members and prevent suicides. For example, the DoD is encouraging the use of gun locks to prevent potentially suicidal clients from using their firearms (Lyle, 2013). Military members can give the locks to friends or family to avoid the impulsive use of the weapon.

The Air Force has developed the Limited Privilege Suicide Prevention Program that allows military members who are under investigation and become suicidal to meet with a mental health professional with increased confidentiality (DoD Task Force, 2010). In theory, the program allows airmen to discuss their crimes and other issues without the information being disclosed to legal authorities. Anecdotally, the program appears to have varied degrees of success. The interpretation of the regulation has resulted in different uses of the program at different bases.

After John's attempt, he was hospitalized and given a Command Directed Evaluation. The evaluation confirmed the John suffered a number of mental health problems including depression and substance abuse. It, however, did not recommend a discharge. Instead, it recommended that John receive treatment for his PTSD, TBI and alcohol abuse problems. Up to this point, John had not actively participated in his treatment, but the attempt made it impossible to deny to his social worker or himself that he had to face his problems. John entered an outpatient substance abuse program. He also worked with his social worker to address his other problems. After four months of treatment, John remained sober and most of his PTSD and depressive symptoms were gone. He was able to resume his full duties with the Army and is hopeful that he will be able to remain in the military for many more years. If John separates from the military, he may be eligible for care through Veterans Health Administration. He may also qualify to use the Vet Centers. The Vet Centers provide services for veterans who have served in war zones.

MACRO PERSPECTIVE

Each military branch has its own suicide prevention program. Although there are some variations between the programs, the branches share many of the same elements. All focus on raising awareness through education. In particular, they educate their members on the signs of suicidality and encourage them to intervene to help distressed military members. Military members returning from deployment are specifically monitored for mental health problems (DoD, n.d.).

The military also has a robust surveillance system that tracks suicides and suicide attempts. *The Department of Defense Suicide Event Reporting* (DODSER) allows the leadership in the DoD to monitor trends in and between the different branches of the military (DoD Task Force, 2010).

There have been a number of evaluations of the military suicide prevention programs. RAND found that there was little evidence of their effectiveness (Ramchand et al., 2011). It criticized the military for failing to adequately promote self-care. The DoD Task Force on the Prevention of Suicide by Members of the Armed Forces commended the branches for their programs and initiatives but found that the "rapid establishment of these initiatives resulted in a lack of cohesion and coordination" (DoD, 2010, p. ES-3).

Both the RAND report and DoD Task Force noted that there is some evidence that the Air Force Suicide Prevention Program (AFSPP) had been effective. Knox et al. (2010) examined suicide rates between 1981 and 2008 and found that there was a significant decrease in suicides after implementation of the AFSPP in 1997. The Substance

Abuse and Mental Health Services Administration (as cited by Ramchand et al., 2011) supported the claim of AFSPP's effectiveness and lists it as an evidence-based practice to reduce suicides. Unfortunately, the gains made by AFSPP did not appear to last because the rates quickly returned to previous levels (DOD Task Force, 2010).

John attended an Army suicide prevention training, but it did not prevent him from making a suicide attempt. The central tenet of the Army suicide prevention program is Ask, Care, Escort (ACE), which encourages each soldier to watch out for other soldiers who might be in distress or show signs of mental illness or suicidality and escort them to help (Ramchand et al., 2010). John, however, was isolated from his fellow soldiers, who appeared to show little concern for him or his well-being.

CONCLUSION

Suicide is a serious problem in the U.S. military. Social workers working with military members need to focus on the risk and protective factors associated with suicide and pay special attention to those factors most associated with military suicides. The key to helping suicidal military members is a thorough assessment and proper interventions. Social workers also need to know the programs that are available to military members and the military system. Knowing how to navigate the military mental health system and other programs can help social workers to provide the best care. Social workers also need to understand their own potential countertransference issues and the role of diversity concerns in mental health.

Working with suicidal clients in any setting is challenging. In the military system, social workers have the opportunity to provide high quality services and turn around the increasing problem of suicide in the U. S. Armed Forces.

INTERNET RESOURCES

- U.S. Army: http://www.armyg1.army.mil/hr/suicide/default.asp

- U.S. Navy and Marine Corps: http://www.med.navy.mil/sites/nmcphc/health-promotion/psychological-emotional-wellbeing/Pages/suicide-prevention.aspx; http://www.usmc-mccs.org
- U. S. Air Force: http://www.afms.af.mil/suicideprevention/
- Defense Centers of Excellence: Suicide Prevention: http://www.dcoe.health.mil/Families/Suicide_Prevention_Warriors.aspx
- Real Warriors Campaign: http://www.realwarriors.net/

DISCUSSION QUESTIONS

1. How significant is the problem of suicide among military members and veterans?

2. What are some of the risk factors associated with suicide among military members and veterans?

3. Discuss some of your countertransference issues related to suicide.

4. What are the most important elements in assessing and treating a military client who is suicidal?

5. What are some policy changes that you believe the Pentagon should institute to help prevent suicide?

REFERENCES

Afifi, T. O., Enns, M. W., Cox, B. J. Asundson, G. J. G., Stein, M. B., & Sareen, J. (2008). Population attributable fractions of psychiatric disorders and suicide ideation and attempts associated with adverse childhood experiences. *American Journal of Public Health, 98*(5), 946–952.

Apter, A., Horesh, N., Gothelf, D., Graffi, E., & Lepkifker, E. (2001). Relationship between self-disclosure and serious suicidal behavior. *Comprehensive Psychiatry, 43*(1), 70–75.

Armed Forces Health Surveillance Center. (2012). Deaths by suicide while on active duty, active and reserve components, U.S. Armed Forces, 1998–2011. *Medical Surveillance Monthly Report, 19*(6), 7–10.

Armed Forces Health Surveillance Center. (2014). Surveillance snapshot: Manner and cause of death, active duty component, U. S. Armed Forces, 1998–2013. *Medical Surveillance Monthly Report, 21*(10), 21–23.

Barlas, F. M., Higgins, W. B., Pflieger, J. C., & Diecker, K. (2013). *2011 Health-related behaviors survey of active duty personnel.* Washington, DC: US Department of Defense. Retrieved from http://www.murray.senate.gov

Benda, B. (2005). Gender differences in predictors of suicidal thoughts and attempts among homeless veterans that abuse substances. *Suicide & Life-Threatening Behavior, 35,* 106–116.

Bray, R. M., Pemberton, M. R., Hourani, L. L., Witt, M., Olmstead, J. M., Brown, J. J., … Bradshaw, M. (2009). *2008 DoD behavioral health survey.* Washington, DC: U.S. Department of Defense. Retrieved from http://www.tricare.mil/tma/2008HealthBehaviors.pdf

Briggs, B. (2013, August 8). 30 percent of Iraq, Afghanistan veterans have mulled suicide: Survey. *NBC.com.* Retrieved from http://usnews.nbcnews.com

Brown, G., Ten Have, T., Henriques, G., Xie, S., Hollander, J., & Beck, A. (2005). Cognitive therapy for the prevention of suicide attempts: A randomized controlled trial. *Journal of the American Medical Association, 294*(5), 563–570.

Bush, N. G., Reger, M. A., Luxton, D. D., Skopp, N. A., Kinn, J., Smolenski, D., & Gahm, G. A. (2013). Suicides and suicide attempts in the U.S. military, 2008–2010. *Suicide and Life-Threatening Behavior, 43*(3), 262–273.

Cavanagh, J. T. O., Carson, A. J., Sharpe, M., & Lawrie, S. M. (2003). Psychological autopsy studies of suicide: A systematic review. *Psychological Medicine, 33*(3), 395–405.

Centers for Disease Control and Prevention. (2010). *Ten leading causes of death and injury.* Retrieved from http://www.cdc.gov/injury/wisqars/LeadingCauses.html

Colucci, E., & Martin, G. (2008). Religion and spirituality along the suicidal path. *Suicide & Life-Threatening Behavior, 38*(2), 229–244.

Daley, J. (2013). Ethical decision making in military social work. In A. Rubin, E. Weiss, & J. Coll (Eds.), *Handbook of military social work* (pp. 51–66). Hoboken, NJ: Wiley.

Defense Centers of Excellence (n.d.). Command directed evaluations. Retrieved from http://www.dcoe.health.mil/Content/Navigation/Documents/Command%20Directed%20Evaluations.pdf

Defense Centers of Excellence (2010). *Risk and protective factors.* Retrieved from http://www.med.navy.mil/sites/nmcphc/Documents/health-promotion-wellness/psychological-emotional-wellbeing/dcoe-protective-risk-factors.pdf

Department of Defense. (n.d.). *Post-deployment health reassessment (PDHRA) program (DD Form 2900).* Retrieved from http://www.pdhealth.mil/dcs/pdhra.asp

Department of Defense. (2010). *The challenge and the promise: Strengthening the force, preventing suicide and saving lives. Final report of the Task Force on the Prevention of Suicide by Members of the Armed Forces.* Retrieved from http://www.sprc.org/library_resources/items/challenge-and-promise-strengthening-force-preventing-suicide-and-saving-live

Department of Defense. (2013). *Department of Defense instruction 6490.04: Mental health evaluations and members of the military services.* Retrieved from http://www.dtic.mil/whs/directives/corres/pdf/649004p.pdf

Department of the Army. (2014). *Army Regulation 380–67: Personal security program.* Retrieved from http://www.apd.army.mil/pdffiles/r380_67.pdf

Department of Veterans Affairs & Department of Defense. (2013). *VA/DoD practice guidelines.* Retrieved from http://www.healthquality.va.gov/guidelines/MH/srb/VADODCP_SuicideRisk_Full.pdf

Dunivin, K. O. (1994). Masculine culture: Change and continuity. *Armed Forces and Society, 20*(4), 531–547.

Gelso, C. J., Hill, C., & Kivligan, D. M. (1991). Transference, insight, and the counselor's intentions during a counseling hour. *Journal of Counseling and Development, 69*(5), 428–433.

Goldsmith, S. K., Pellman, T. C., Kleinman, A. M., & Bunney, W. E. (Eds.). (2002). *Reducing suicide: A national imperative.* Washington, DC: National Academies Press.

Harris, E. C., & Barraclough, B. (1997). Suicide as an outcome of mental disorders: A meta-analysis. *British Journal of Psychiatry, 170*, 205–228.

Hawton, K., Taylor, T. L., Saunders, A., & Mahadevan, S. (2011). Clinical care of deliberate self-harm clients: An evidence-based approach. In R. O'Connor, S. Platt, & J. Gordon (Eds.), *International handbook of suicide prevention: Research, policy, and practice*. Hoboken, NJ: Blackwell Reference Online. Retrieved from http://www.blackwellreference .com

Hoge, C. W., Castro, C. A., Messer, S. C., McGurk, D., Cotting, D. I., & Koffman, R. L. (2004). Combat duty in Iraq and Afghanistan, mental health problems, and barriers to care. *The New England Journal of Medicine, 355*(1), 13–22.

Kaplan, M. S., Huguet, N., MacFarland, B. H., & Newsom, J. T. (2007). Suicide among male veterans: A prospective population-based study. *Journal of Epidemiological Community Health, 61*, 619–624.

Kim, P. Y., Britt, T. W., Klocko, R. P., Riviere, L. A., & Adler, A. B. (2011). Stigma, negative attitudes about treatment, and utilization of mental health care among soldiers. *Military Psychology, 23*, 65–81.

Knox, K. L. (2008). Epidemiology of the relationship between traumatic experiences and suicidal behaviors. *PTSD Research Quarterly, 19*(4), 1–3. Retrieved from http://www.ptsd.va.gov/professional/ newsletters/research-quarterly/v19n4.pdf

Knox, K. L., Pflanz, S. Talcott, G. W., Campise, R. L., Lavigne, J. E., Bajorska, A., . . .Caine, E. D. (2010). The U.S. Air Force suicide prevention program: Implications for public health policy. *American Journal of Public Health, 100*(12), 2457–2463.

Leardmann, C. A., Powell, T. M., Smith, T. C., Bell, M. R., Smith, B., Boyko, E. J., . . . Hoge, C. W. (2013). Risk factors associated with suicide in current and former U.S. military personnel. *Journal of the American Medical Association, 310*(5), 496–506.

Leenaars, A. A. (1994). Crisis intervention with highly lethal suicidal people. *Death Studies, 18*, 341–360.

Lyle, A. (2013, March 21). Officials uphold commitment to suicide prevention solutions. *Armed Forces Press Service*. U.S. Department of Defense. Retrieved from http://www.defense.gov/news/newsarticle .aspx?id=119597

Maris, R. W., Berman, A. L., & Silverman, M. M. (2000). Treatment and prevention of suicide. In R. W. Maris, A. L. Berman, & M. M. Silverman (Eds.), *Comprehensive textbook of suicidality* (pp. 509–535). New York, NY: Guilford Press.

Martin, J., Ghahramanlou-Holloway, M., & Lou, K. (2009). A comparative review of U.S. military and civilian suicide behavior: Implications for OEF/OIF suicide prevention efforts. *Journal of Mental Health Counseling, 31*(2), 101–118.

Negrusa, S., Negrusa, B., & Hosek, J. (2014). Gone to war: Have deployments increased divorces? *Journal of Population Economics, 27*, 473–496.

Patterson, J. C., Jones, D. R., Marsh, R. W., & Drummond, F. E. (2001). Aeromedical management of U.S. Air Force aviators who attempt suicide. *Aviation, Space, and Environmental Medicine, 72*, 1081–1085.

Paul, J. P., Catania, J., Pollack, L., Moskowitz, J., Canchola, J., Mills, T., . . . Stall, R. (2002). Suicide attempts among gay and bisexual men: Lifetime prevalence and antecedents. *American Journal of Public Health, 92*(8), 1338–1345.

Perales, R., Hallway, M. S., Forys-Donahue, K. L., Speiss, A., & Millikan, A. M. (2012). Prevalence of childhood trauma among U.S. army soldiers with suicidal behavior. *Military Medicine, 177*(9), 1034–1040.

Pietrzak, R. H., Goldstein, M. B., Malley, J. C., Rivers, A. J., Johnson, D. C., & Southwick, S. M. (2010). Risk and protective factors associated with suicidal ideation in veterans of Operations Enduring Freedom and Iraqi Freedom. *Journal of Affective Disorders, 123*, 102–107.

Pulakos, J. (1993). Two models of suicide treatment: Evaluation and recommendations. *American Journal of Psychotherapy, 47*(4), 603–612.

Ramchand, R., Acosta, J., Burns, R. M., Jaycox, L. H., & Perin, C. G. (2011). *The war within: Preventing suicide in the U.S. military*. RAND: Center for Military Health Policy Research. Retrieved from http://www .rand.org/pubs/monographs/MG953.html

Rickgarn, R. L. (1990). Risk assessment of the suicidal religious person: Some suggestions. *Counseling & Values, 35*, 73–76.

Rudd, M. D. (2012). Brief cognitive behavioral therapy for suicidality in military populations. *Military Psychology, 24*, 592–603.

Rudd, M. D., Bryan, C. J., Wertenberger, E. G., Peterson, A. L., Young-McCaughan, S., Mintz, J., . . . Bruce, T. O. (2015). Brief cognitive-behavioral therapy effects on post-treatment suicide attempts in a military sample: Results of a randomized clinical trial with 2-year follow-up. *The American Journal of Psychiatry, 172*(5), 441–449. doi:10.1176/appi .ajp.2014.14070843

Rudd, M. D., Joiner, T., & Rajab, M. H. (2001). *Treating suicidal behavior: An effective, time-limited approach.* New York, NY: Guilford Press.

Schechter, M., Goldblatt, M., & Maltsberger, J. T. (2013). The therapeutic alliance and suicide: When words are not enough. *British Journal of Psychotherapy, 29*(3), 315–328.

Shane, L. (2013, August 26). Latest medal of honor recipient to focus on PTSD. *Stars and Stripes.* Retrieved from http://www.stripes.com/news/us/latest-medal-of-honor-recipient-to-focus-on-ptsd-1.237464

Shea, C. W. (2009). Suicide assessment. *Psychiatric Times, 26*(12). Retrieved from https://www.psychiatrictimes .com/display/article/10168/1491291

Shenassa, E. D., Rogers, M. L., Spalding, K. L., & Roberts, M. B. (2004). Safer storage of firearms at home and risk of suicide: A study of protective factors in a nationally representative sample. *Journal of Epidemiology & Community Health, 58,* 841–848.

Simon, R. I. (2011a). Assessing protective factors against suicide. *Psychiatric Times, 28*(8), 35–37.

Simon, R. I. (2011b). Improving suicide risk assessment. *Psychiatric Times, 28*(11), 16–21.

Simmons, C. A., & Rycraft, J. R. (2010). Ethical challenges of military social workers serving in a combat zone. *Social Work, 55*(1), 9–18.

Skopp, N. A., Luxton, D. D., Bush, N., & Sirotin, A. (2011). Childhood adversity and suicidal ideation in a clinical military sample: Military unit cohesion and intimate relationships as protective factors. *Journal of Social and Clinical Psychology, 30*(4), 361–377.

Smolenski, D. J., Reger, M. A., Alexander, C. L., Skopp, N. A., Bush, N. E., Luxton, D. D., & Gahm, G. A. (2013). *DoDSER: Department of Defense suicide event report/calendar year 2012 annual report.* Retrieved from http://t2health.dcoe.mil/sites/default/files/dodser_ar2012_20140306_0.pdf

Tanielian, T., & Jaycox, L. H. (Eds.). (2008). *The invisible wounds of war: Psychological and cognitive injuries, their consequences, and services to assist recovery.* RAND: Center for Military Health Policy Research. Retrieved from http://www.rand.org/pubs/monographs/MG720.html

Tarrier, N., Taylor, K., & Gooding, P. (2008). Cognitive-behavioral intervention to reduce suicide behavior: A systematic review and meta-analysis. *Behavior Modification, 32*(1), 77–108.

U.S. Air Force. (2011). *Air Force instruction 44–172: Mental health.* Retrieved from http://static .e-publishing.af.mil/production/1/af_sg/publication/afi44–172/afi44–172.pdf

Van Orden, K. A., Witte, T. K., Cukrowicz, K. C., Braithwaite, S. R., Selby, E. A., & Joiner, T. E. (2010). The interpersonal theory of suicide. *Psychological Review, 117*(2), 575–600. doi:10.1037/a0018697

Wright, K. M., Cabrera, O. A., Adler, A. B., Bliese, P. D., Hoge, C. W., & Castro, C. A. (2009). Stigma and barriers to care in soldiers post combat. *Psychological Services, 6*(2), 108–116.

CHAPTER 30

Global Social Work

Murali D. Nair

---   ---

CHAPTER OBJECTIVES

- Identify the values of the social work profession from a global perspective;
- Explore the internationality of social work;
- Define the roles of Community-Based Organizations (CBOs) and Nongovernmental Organizations (NGOs) in social work;
- Outline details that should be considered when considering international volunteering and employment.

---   ---

INTRODUCTION

With the technological advances that have been made within the last two decades, communication between nations has become more interconnected. With the press of a button or the click of a remote, a person can find out what is happening on the other side of the world. In addition to facilitating communication, technology has resulted in more economic and resource interdependence. The tourism industry, for example, which has emerged as its own form of economy in many smaller nations, is based on the business of people from outside those communities (Becker, 2011). The exchange of resources and the effect this exchange has on international economies is one matter that is of the utmost importance for those with an interest in global social work. As citizens of the United States, many of us have been privileged to not want for many things. Though it is often restricted and/or difficult to access, health care and access to shelters are available even to those living in poverty in the United States. The United States, among various other elite nations, makes up one-eighth of the world's population, yet we utilize seven-eighths of the world's resources (Laughlin, 2006). Conversely, this means that the remaining seven-eighths of the world's population accesses one-eighth of the world's resources. This social inequity is something that social workers are committed to rectifying, as delineated by the values that govern the social work profession.

SOCIAL WORK VALUES
National Association of Social Workers

The National Association of Social Workers (NASW) developed a Code of Ethics and standards that dictate the values that need to be upheld by anyone holding the title of "social worker" in the United States. These standards, values, and Code are incorporated into the curricula of all accredited social work programs.

The values of the social work profession are six-fold: (1) service; (2) social justice; (3) dignity and worth of the person; (4) importance of human relationships; (5) integrity; and (6) competence (NASW, 2008). Although service may seem to be an obvious core value of social work because the majority of work takes place in the field and is therefore service based, it is important to acknowledge its inclusion as the foremost value. However, social justice can be argued to be of the utmost importance as it implies not only the aiding of a person but, specifically, the aiding of a person to decrease the disparity or disadvantages he or she faces. To do this aiding successfully, a person must have respect for the importance of personal relationships and an individual's worth and dignity. It is only by building respectful, egalitarian relationships using effective communication that a social worker will be able to effectively carry out his or her job. In order to uphold the aforementioned values, it is crucial that social workers understand their role and duty to their clients by becoming culturally, socially, and ethically competent. Being competent is the only way to act in accordance with social work values and a sense of integrity.

International Social Work Values

The United States is governed by one entity (NASW) in the matter of social work values, ethics, and standards, but globally there are a plethora of organizations that contribute to international social work standards and mission. The International Federation of Social Workers (IFSW), the International Association of Schools of Social Work (IASSW), as well as the International Council on Social Welfare (ICSW) are but a few of the organizations that focus on social work philosophies. The IFSW (2012) has defined social work as follows:

> The social work profession promotes social change, problem solving in human relationships and the empowerment and liberation of people to enhance well-being. Utilising theories of human behavior and social systems, social work intervenes at the points where people interact with their environments. Principles of human rights and social justice are fundamental to social work. (para. 3)

From this definition, similarities between domestic standards and international standards can be observed. Either implicitly or explicitly, these standards speak both to service and to social justice. Moreover, American emphasis on an individual's dignity and worth as well as the importance of human relationships is akin to the internationally upheld idea of empowering and liberating clients. Finally, competence (and integrity, to a certain degree) are alluded to on the international level in that social workers are expected to apply well-established theories to their work with clients and systems. It is clear that worldwide, standards are focused upon giving power and control to the individual or community being serviced.

The Global Sullivan Principles (GSP)

Expanded upon by Reverend Dr. Leon Sullivan in 1999, the Sullivan Principles were transformed into the Global Sullivan Principles (GSP; Kercher, 2007). These principles act as a code of conduct for workers worldwide (Kercher, 2007). The GSP consist of eight principles. These principles are aimed at promoting corporate social responsibility, but some principles can be applied to the communities workers are in and not just to the employees/workers and business partners. The first principle is to support human rights and the second principle is to promote equal opportunity. These principles are similar to the ICSW and NASW value of social justice and respect for human relationships. Comparable to the ICSW and NASW value to respect human worth and dignity is the GSP indicating that in order to do the highest quality of work, corporations must collaborate with the communities in order to provide the best service.

IMPORTANCE OF GLOBAL SOCIAL WORK

Social work is derived from a rich and far-reaching history, traced all the way back to 590 AD in the form of charitable organizations and religious institutions (Gilleard, 2007). However, traditional social work originated in the 19th century in response to (relative) poverty and social problems that arose as a byproduct of the Industrial Revolution. Since then, social work has grown in scope and evolved into a profession that functions on three levels: the macro, the mezzo, and the micro. It is social workers' ability to approach issues from these three different perspectives that makes them uniquely qualified to work both on a national and global scale. Although social problems such as the AIDS epidemic, chronic unemployment, limited and inadequate access to health care, and the ever-present impact that poverty has have on cultural, social, or geographical boundaries, leadership from an array of disciplines is needed (i.e., medical, political, economic, etc.), including leadership from social work (Ife, 2001; Nair, 2013, 2014). In addition to social workers' unique training with regard to the scope of the issue or population, social workers have the unique ability to tolerate discomfort and be culturally cognizant (owing to the values and principles discussed previously). These capacities qualify social workers for the hard work that needs to be done internationally, more so than people representing other professions.

Global social work is becoming an increasingly attractive field because of the increased attention that is being paid as a result of the wide influence that the media plays in our society.

With the lightening-fast dissemination of news articles, video/audio clips, and photographs via the Internet, citizens of all countries are being made aware of what is happening around the world. Social problems such as poverty, unemployment, water scarcity, terrorism, racism, homophobia, and natural disasters that have been linked to climate change have reared their heads across the globe ("Top 10 Most Urgent Problems," 2013). In addition, social workers are immersed in work with refugees; health, academic, and vocational training programs to further social development and longevity; as well as with advocating women's rights and gay rights (Nair, 2013, 2014). At the end of this chapter, a list of Internet Resources is provided for further individual investigation. Global social work has gained clout because people are now aware of what needs to be changed, can identify the regions that are most in need of aid, and are eager to contribute.

TYPES OF GLOBAL SOCIAL WORK

For those seeking to participate in global social work, it is important to note that there are a number of avenues to take to become involved. Participation in cultural exchange programs, international volunteering, or working (paid or unpaid) alongside nongovernmental organizations (NGOs), community-based organizations (CBOs), or internationally recognized organizations are among the many ways to engage in international social work. A resource list for each of these forms of involvement is provided on p. 433. However, before investigating all of these options, each involvement type will be covered in more depth for a holistic understanding.

Cultural Exchange Programs

Cultural exchange programs are synonymous with travel abroad programs through institutions of higher learning. Cultural exchange programs allow students and/or individuals to become immersed in the local culture as a result of their living in new communities. Participants are typically expected to attend classes, with lectures delivered in the region's native tongue. In addition to being exposed to the language in an academic setting, participants are often encouraged to travel throughout the area, explore their surroundings, partake in the local cuisine and customs, and in most senses, adhere to the adage, "When in Rome, do as the Romans do." In fact, programs such as the Critical Language Scholarship (CLS) Program require applicants to write about these exact matters. Below is an example of the CLS (2013) program application:

> The CLS Program is an intensive, group-based overseas learning environment. While on the program, you may frequently be exhausted from adapting to a new environment, studying intensively, attending mandatory cultural activities that may not always align perfectly with your interests, building new relationships with people from the host country and your CLS peers, and functioning day-to-day in another language. What aspects of the CLS Program do you expect will be the most challenging for you? How will you meet these challenges? (p. 18)

Participants are encouraged to give themselves over to and immerse themselves in the culture of the country they are in. This provides participants with a richer, hands-on experience of the culture as opposed to the stilted understanding they would glean from reading about the culture. Moreover, immersing oneself into the culture as true citizens live provides a realistic platform for understanding the challenges the locals face in accessing human services. With this knowledge, participants are able to develop ideas for improving systems in that community.

Applying the knowledge they have gained from their experiences abroad of the uniformity of basic human needs, students are better equipped to begin their careers. These types of programs are becoming increasingly popular in the United States because their value is becoming more apparent to educators and employers. Recent counts indicate that at least 866 organizations are offering study abroad or internship opportunities through at least 4695 programs (GoAbroad, 2013). According to reports from the 2011–2012 academic year,

approximately 283,300 American students had studied abroad, a record high for students from the United States (Thomas & Norton, 2013).

International Volunteering Programs

International volunteering programs function similarly to cultural exchange programs. The two differ in that one is geared toward students and the other toward professionals/those no longer in school. They allow individuals to gain a complex understanding of the culture they are immersed in and the opportunity to foster their passion for global social work matters. International volunteering programs help participants to overcome and surpass cultural barriers (Nair, 2013, 2014).

These types of programs are among the most popular because they are flexible (sometimes time sensitive) and volunteer opportunities can be identified within various institutions and programs (e.g., The Council on International Programs, International Partners in Mission, and Inter Action). Religious institutions, for example, offer their members the chance to travel for brief periods to other countries and do intensive work. Building houses, setting up health clinics/vaccination tents, or even raising money for other countries to invest in their own business and social services are among the many ways volunteer programs provide aid abroad. Laughlin (2006) has also reiterated that to do international social work, you do not have to devote years of your life or abandon your life at home. Rather, it is possible to contribute to international social work in small intensive bursts of time.

Nongovernmental Organizations (NGOs)

Nongovernmental organizations (NGOs) play a controversial but large role in global social work as they are often responsible for the health and human service needs of specific countries. NGOs are commonly referred to as nonprofit agencies and function at the local level. Depending on what the organization's specific mission is, they can provide assistance to communities on topics ranging from public health, family planning, and vocational training to child-focused care and training. Primarily, the NGO's role is to help empower members of the community in order for them to take the reins of their own lives (Clairborne, 2004; Nair, 2013, 2014). This is relevant to social work because it is in keeping with the NASW's Code of Ethics regarding respecting the client's self-determination.

NGOs are among the fastest-expanding entities in both developing and developed countries (Nair, 2013, 2014). These organizations are typically called for because they are filling a void in services that the government is incapable of or insufficiently providing. Funding for NGOs is typically acquired through the governments of the countries they are located in. However, this is becoming a problem as the government and other funding sources come to expect NGOs to become internally sustainable, which is close to impossible because they are afforded such limited resources (Nair, 2013, 2014).

Community-Based Organizations (CBOs)

Community-based organizations (CBOs), otherwise known as grassroots organizations, are key to global social work. Laughlin (2006) believes that becoming involved with CBOs is the best way to participate in global social work as it offers volunteers insight into the community on a "down and dirty" level. CBOs are run *by* community members *for* community members. CBOs have three main goals: (1) their proceeds and services are directed only to their members; (2) similarly, they are community oriented, aiding their community exclusively; and (3) they make sure that their work in helping the community and the community members intersect (Nair, 2013, 2014).

International Organizations

International organizations are those that operate on a global scale (Nair, 2013, 2014). Some of these international organizations are specifically aimed at social issues and are therefore of particular relevance to social workers looking to work or volunteer abroad. Examples of international organizations that have social work underpinnings include professional organizations, domestic agencies, as well as those within the United Nations such as The International Federation of Social Workers, The Agency for International Development, The Peace Corps, United Nations Children's Fund, World Health Organization, United Nations Fund for Population Activities, and United Nations High Commission for Refugees. Each of these organizations works to rectify or improve a social issue impacting a large subset of the world's population, making their work vital.

General Volunteering

While international volunteering programs and cultural exchange programs are more formal immersion programs, general, informal volunteering programs offer five main experiences. First, like all of the other types of involvement and organizations, they enable participants to completely immerse themselves in a new culture. Second, they expand upon education in an informal manner. Third, they act as an arena for networking and relationship/community building with members of the other country, assuming that everyone is driven to volunteer for the same intrinsic, altruistic reasons. Fourth, they offer the informal volunteering experience abroad that will come in handy when applying for formal abroad opportunities that require previous direct practice. And finally, the challenges faced in adapting to a new culture and the services provided during the volunteer period will help further personal growth and development.

CONSIDERATIONS

If any of the following options sound appealing, there are some things to consider when trying to identify what type of program or where one would like to work. Volunteering and traveling abroad can be a rewarding experience but it all depends upon a person's ability to embrace and consider a number of factors, which will be discussed in the section that follows.

First, as has been alluded to in the above sections, dealing with social issues of such a complex nature requires special personality characteristics. According to Ann Laughlin (2006), the founder and director of GoAbroad, attitude is the most critical aspect that recruiters and organizations will consider when searching for volunteers or employees. Going into any social work arena, abroad or domestic, it is vital to remember that the worker is no better than the people he or she is serving. Disrespecting the dignity and worth of the served community will negatively impact overall effectiveness. Laughlin (2006) suggests that forming relationships of mutual partnership, learning, and teaching is the best way to go about work and to respect the clients' experiences. It is imperative to try not to impose prejudiced beliefs; to help those in need, instead focus on offering assistance and be open to collaboration (Nair, 2013, 2014).

Second, Laughlin (2006) suggests searching for work opportunities with a general agenda as opposed to with a specific plan; or, if searching within a specific area of interest, make sure the geographic region has a need for your interest and particular skill set. For instance, going into an area where there is a plethora of social problems to address, clinically oriented workers' first instincts may be to offer counseling services. However, in reality, dealing with poverty or unemployment may be the more urgent need. Another example of when the worker's agenda may not be in line with the more salient need in the community is following a disaster. Disaster relief, as Pyles (2007) posits, typically focuses on trauma counseling of community members, and the rebuilding of the community is left to the monetary funds raised by charitable organizations. Disaster relief fails to focus on the social worker's macro abilities to organize and plan (Pyles, 2007). Overall, the ability to hone in on where a community's most dire need lies could be a social worker's biggest advantage when locating an abroad position.

Safety is a consideration that should be one of the top priorities as it may determine eligibility for certain abroad opportunities. Certain countries that are located in war zones or are high risk for terrorist attacks may require extra precautions. Americans tend to be privileged and are often seen as arrogant, giving them a less than desirable reputation in many countries; this may impact the reaction of the locals toward outsiders. Nair (2013, 2014) reminds readers that by checking travel.state. gov, American citizens can access warnings from the U.S. Department of State about countries to avoid or exercise extreme caution in.

Additionally, health is something that should be taken into account when investigating different abroad opportunities. Being cognizant of vaccinations that are required is an important aspect. The Centers for Disease Control and Prevention provide information on the vaccinations needed, and local health concerns can be easily uncovered and demystified.

Finally, after determining the correct organization and travel experience (i.e., examining the associated costs, reviewing and meeting all of the position/ volunteer requirements or qualifications, etc.), it is important to examine the cultural characteristics of the community. Specifically, it is beneficial to investigate the role that religion plays in the region, as well as taking into account the degree of development the region has undergone. The role of religion could influence the food the locals eat, their medicinal practices, and their acceptance of certain treatment services. Meanwhile, the degree of development should be considered because it may be taxing if you are not mentally prepared for an extreme lack of "modern comforts" (Nair, 2013, p. 120).

CONCLUSION

Because of technological advances, widespread dissemination of information through the media, and the interdependence of countries for resources and economics, the field of global social work has never been more popular. Social workers are in the unique position of having the micro, mezzo, and macro skills to effect change on a holistic level.

Many of the social problems countries are facing are being encountered at a global scale. As such, interdependence and aid from one country to another will likely increase. Volunteers, domestic and foreign, will continue to play a pivotal role in the coming years (Healy, 1997).

INTERNET RESOURCES
Issues of Importance

- Environment and Sustainable Growth: http://www.iaia.org
- Health: http://www.who.int/en/
- International Social Development: http://sodeit.org/
- Social Work with Refugees: A Growing International Crisis: http://www.unhcr.ch
- Women's Rights: http://www.womens-rights.org/
- U.S. Department of Health and Human Services: http://www.hhs.gov

Cultural Exchange Programs

- http://www.studyabroaddirectory.com

NGOs

- The Alliance for Arab Women: http://www.allianceforarabwomen.org
- The Amrita Organization: http://www.amrita.org
- The Centre for the Development of People: http://www.cedepghana.tripod.com

International Organizations

- The Agency for International Development: http://www.usaid.gov
- The International Council on Social Welfare: http://www.icsw.org
- The International Federation of Social Workers: http://www.IFSW.org
- The Peace Corps: http://www.peacecorps.gov
- U.N. Fund for Population Activities: http://www.un.org/popin
- U.N. High Commission for Refugees: http://www.UNHCR.ch

- United Nations Children's Fund: http://www.UNICEF.org
- World Health Organization: http://www.WHO.int

General Volunteering

- McMillon, B., Cutchins, D., & Geissinger, A. (2009). *Volunteer vacations: Short-term adventures that will benefit you and others.* Chicago, IL: Chicago Review Press.
- ACDI/VOCA: http://www.volunteeroverseas.com
- Amigos de las Americas: http://www.amigoslink.org
- Amizade Limited: http://www.amizade.org
- Association for all Speech Impaired Children: http://www.afasic.org/uk
- CARE International: http://www.care-international.org
- Global Citizens Network: http://www.globalcitizens.org
- Global Opportunities: http://www.globalvolunteernetwork.org
- Global Service Corps: http://www.globalservicecorps.org
- Global Volunteers: http://www.globalvolunteers.org
- Habitat for Humanity International: http://www.habitat.org
- How to Live Your Dream of Volunteering Overseas: http://www.volunteeroverseas.org
- InterAction: http://www.interaction.org/jobs/index.html
- International Employment Hotline: http://www.internationaljobs.org
- International Partners in Mission: http://www.ipm-connections.org
- International Volunteer Directory: http://www.VolunteerAbroad.com
- Japan-U.S. Community Education & Exchange: http://www.jucee.org
- Operation Cross Roads Africa: http://www.igc.org/oca
- Opportunities Abroad: http://www.cabroad.u-net.com
- Studying, Working, and Volunteering Abroad: http://www.transabroad.com
- The International Volunteer Programs Association: http://www.volunteerinternational.org

- Unitarian Universalist Service Committee: http://www.uusc.org
- United Nations Volunteers: http://www.unv.org
- Volunteers Abroad: http://www.volunteer-abroad.com
- Volunteer Opportunities Directory of the Catholic Network of Volunteer Service: http://www.cnvs.org
- Volunteers for Peace: http://www.vfp.org

International Employment

- Idealist: http://www.idealist.org
- International Employment: http://www.jobsabroad.com & http://www.teachabroad.com
- International Employment Hotline: http://www.internationaljobs.org
- Overseas Jobs: http://www.overseasjobs.com

DISCUSSION QUESTIONS

1. Social inequity is something that social workers are committed to rectifying. What are some disparities you can identify from your community of origin?

2. Service and social justice were identified as similarities among domestic and international standards of social work values. What are some others?

3. Turn on the TV or open your Internet browser to the latest world news. What social problems can you identify? How can you as a social worker make a difference?

4. Identify a cultural exchange program that interests you. What are the specific details regarding preparing yourself for such a program?

5. Conduct a search in your area (or an area of interest). How many NGOs and CBOs can you identify? What (if anything) does this reflect about the area?

REFERENCES

Becker, K. (2011). *Developing nations see huge gains in tourism revenue*. Retrieved from http://www.gadling.com/2011/05/26/developing-nations-see-huge-gains-in-tourism-revenue/

Claiborne, N. (2004). Presence of social workers in nongovernmental organizations. *Social Work, 49*(2), 207–218.

Critical Language Scholarship. (2013). *Critical Language Scholarship 2014 program application*. Retrieved from https://ais.americancouncils.org/cgi-bin/WebObjects/AIR.woa/wa/login?brand=cls

Gilleard, C. (2007). Old age in Byzantine society. *Ageing and Society, 27*(5), 623–642.

GoAbroad. (2013). *Study abroad programs, reviews & scholarships abroad*. Retrieved from http://www.goabroad.com/study-abroad

Healy, L. M. (1997). International social welfare: Organizations and activities. In R. Edwards & G. J. Hopps (Eds.), *Encyclopedia of social work* (pp. 1499–1510). Washington, DC: NASW Press.

Ife, J. (2001). *Human rights and social work*. New York, NY: Cambridge University Press.

International Federation of Social Workers. (2012, March). *Statement of ethical principles*. Retrieved from http://ifsw.org/policies/statement-of-ethical-principles/

Kercher, K. (2007). Corporate social responsibility: Impact of globalization and international business. *Corporate Governance eJournal*, 1–12.

Laughlin, A. (2006). International social work: Rising to the challenge. *The New Social Worker, 13*(2), 4.

Nair, M. (2013). Global perspective on volunteering: Opportunities and challenges. In *Engaged learning*. Los Angeles, CA: Figueroa Press.

Nair, M. (2014). International social work practice. In *Evidence-based macro practice* (pp. 372–389). Wheaton, IL: Gregory.

National Association of Social Workers. (2008). *Code of ethics of the National Association of Social Workers*. Retrieved from http://www.socialworkers.org/pubs/code/code.asp

Pyles, L. (2007). Community organizing for post-disaster social development: Locating social work. *International Social Work, 50*(3), 321–333.

Thomas, C., & Norton, S. K. (2013, November 21). U.S. should be thankful for international students.

National Geographic. Retrieved from http://news. nationalgeographic.com/news/2013/11/131121-international-students-study-abroad-education-peace-culture/

Top 10 most urgent problems in the world. (2013, March 26). *Top-10-List.org.* Retrieved from http://top-10-list.org/2013/03/26/top-10-most-urgent-problems-world/

CHAPTER 31

Trafficking and Modern-Day Slavery

A Case Study of the Philippines

Annalisa Enrile & Wilhelmina De Castro

CHAPTER OBJECTIVES

- Develop an understanding of the scope of trafficking and modern-day slavery and the role of social workers in these situations;
- Describe various forms of trafficking and modern-day slavery;
- Examine the issue of trafficking and modern-day slavery from a case study perspective, examining the experience and response of one country;
- Understand the role of the social worker at micro, macro, and mezzo levels and extrapolate patterns of advocacy and intervention in global and local contexts.

CASE VIGNETTE

Alma is a 9-year-old girl who has been living on the streets of Olongapo City, next to the Subic Bay Freeport. She was found scavenging on the streets and accused of being a pickpocket by a local business-man. When she was taken to the police station, a woman from the advocacy group Buklod saw her and demanded that the police release her for lack of evidence. She then approached Alma and took her to Buklod to help her get services.

Alma was born the eldest of four children in an urban poor tenement in Olongapo City. Her mother was a dancer in a club and does not know who Alma's father is, but it is apparent that Alma is half African American. She is one of the many Amerasian children in the Philippines. Alma began working in the club

---

when she was 5 years old, selling cigarettes and candy. She had to do this because her mother began to get sick and needed help for the smaller children. When she was 6 years old, her mother passed away. Alma does not know what her mother's illness was. She and the other children were sent to live with an "aunt and uncle," though Alma is not sure what the blood relation is. Alma became a maid for the family and was not able to attend school. When she turned 7, her "uncle" sold her to a foreigner sex tourist who said he would pay "top dollar" for a virgin child. Alma was sent with him and never saw her siblings again.

After she was raped, she was then sold to a brothel, where she was forced to have sex with men who "liked children." One night when she was 8 years old, one of her rapists gave her a $20 bill and told her to buy some cigarettes for him. He told the guard at the brothel that it was okay. Alma made a run for it and hid under a house for two days, scared that they would find her. She continued to hide in the shadows for months, scavenging for food when she could, trying to avoid any area near the brothel, until she was caught.

After Alma was brought to Buklod, she did not speak. She would not make eye contact and shied away when people tried to touch her. However, she did not move, staying still as a statue, when she was given a bath and dressed. She also did not show any emotion when a doctor was called to examine her. Her silence lasted for 16 days, and then she was given a doll. She went to her room to play with the doll, where the social worker was surprised to find it naked, with its hair torn, and black magic marker all over its body. When Alma was confronted she refused to look at the social worker. The social worker persisted in asking why Alma ruined the doll, to which Alma quietly responded, "That's not a doll; that's me."

INTRODUCTION

Images of bound hands reaching out between jail cell bars, of women cowered into corners, and of children barefoot and crying have become the symbols of human trafficking and modern-day slavery. The U.S. State Department estimates anywhere from 4 to 27 million people are trafficked and/or existing in modern-day slavery around the world. There are an estimated 900,000 persons who are trafficked across borders annually. More than one million children are in the global sex trade. Eighty percent of transnational victims are women and girls. More than 150 countries have been identified as being affected (either sending or receiving) by trafficking. The reason the numbers are so varied speaks to the nature of this issue: the difficulties with victim identification. In 2013, United States Ambassador-at-Large to Monitor and Combat Trafficking, Luis CdeBaca, stated, "We are only seeing a mere fraction of those who are exploited in modern slavery," reiterating the message that modern-day slavery remains one of the most persistent foreign policy priorities (U.S. Department of State, 2013). The need to address this growing epidemic has led to the need to understand the global scope as well as to exchange information and learn from the actions of countries around the world where trafficking is most concentrated. Due to the transnational nature of trafficking, prevention and intervention practices must also be created with an internationalist perspective.

Definition of Trafficking and Modern-Day Slavery

While there has been a recent surge of information, public outcry, and awareness for these issues, the reality is that women and children have long been commoditized, bought, and sold internationally with increasing demand in some form or another since the 15th century (Hatcher & Radpour, 2003). One of the largest efforts in the United States' fight against trafficking has been in defining the phenomenon, particularly when it includes trafficking within their own borders. It was not until 2000 that the United Nations developed a widely accepted definition of trafficking as the recruitment, transportation, transfer, harboring or receipt of persons (United Nations Office on Drug and Crimes, 2006). Though there is an aspect of coercion in the definition, it is a broad one that ranges from physical force (abduction, abuse, assault), deception, and inducement (payment/benefits to achieve consent). This definition encompasses sex trafficking and exploitation, forced labor, and slavery (McGough, 2013).

The term *modern-day slavery* is used to describe more than just sex or labor trafficking. It is a term that is meant to invoke comparisons to chattel slavery of the 18th and 19th centuries (McGough, 2013). This form of slavery, where one person owns another as property they have purchased, is only part of the modern definition of slavery. The definition has been expanded to include debt bondage, indentured servitude, and other forms of control. Modern-day slavery began to be used because the term *human trafficking* assumes that transport must take place across borders. In truth, the phenomenon can and does occur in victims' own neighborhoods (Skinner, 2008).

The Trafficking In Persons Report

The U.S. State Department began to generate the Trafficking in Persons (TIP) report, which monitors efforts to combat modern-day slavery in 2000 (Gozdziak & Collett, 2005). While this report has become a type of "gold standard" for measuring efforts against trafficking, it is important to note that it is composed of government self-reports and information that is sent to a centralized e-mail (providing means for non-governmental organizations, institutions, and individuals to share their input). U.S. Embassies were also utilized to collect information. This information is gathered and used to organize countries into one of three tiers (Tier 1 is the highest ranking; Tier 3 the lowest). Placement on the tiers is dependent of government efforts with the rationale that governments bear the primary responsibility for responding to trafficking. The need to address this growing epidemic

has led to the need to understand the global scope as well as to exchange information and learn from the actions of countries around the world where trafficking is most concentrated. Due to the transnational nature of trafficking, prevention and intervention practices must also be created with an internationalist perspective. As of October 1, 2013, countries that are given the "Tier 3" label countries will be subject to a number of sanctions, including withholding of U.S. government nonhumanitarian, non–trade related foreign assistance. The report is composed annually with the hope that countries will improve and build upon their efforts to combat trafficking (Wyler, 2010).

There are number of controversies around the TIP report because the measurement and evaluation of countries is facilitated exclusively by the U.S. government. This has led to criticisms of favoritism and bias in support of certain countries due to reasons other than their efforts around trafficking (Gallagher, 2001). Also, some critics have stated that the report is not culturally sensitive, resulting in an inability to understand interventions that may not fit into U.S. paradigms of intervention but may be effective in country contexts (Sharma, 2003). Regardless of these issues, the TIP report is the most utilized mechanism for obtaining country by country data. It is widely referenced and used to further intervention and policy. For Tier 3 countries, the U.S. can also oppose support from the international financial institutions (U.S. Department of State, 2013). According to the TIP report, countries in Southeast Asia range from Tier 2, to Tier 2WL (watch list), to Tier 3 due to the prevalence of trafficking in those countries and the noncompliance of their governments to eliminate trafficking. The Philippines has vacillated between these two distinctions of Tier 2 and Tier 2WL.

Types of Trafficking and Modern-Day Slavery

Sex trafficking is the most widely referenced type of trafficking. In most cases, this means coercion into the sex industry through forced prostitution. It also includes instances of sexual slavery when individuals are physically held against their will. Sexual debt bondage, when sex is demanded in exchange to "pay off debts," real or imagined, also falls under the definition of sex trafficking. It is important to note that it does not matter how an individual entered prostitution as he or she may have been psychologically manipulated into providing "consent" (U.S. Department of State, 2013). The most concentrated areas of sex trafficking are in South and Southeast Asia. Bertone (1999) identified these regions as where sex trafficking first developed. For instance, as early as 1986, almost 300,000 Filipina women and 50,000 Thai women were trafficked between their countries and others in Asia. Women and children are trafficked for sexual purposes, which include sex tourism, prostitution, pornography, cybersex and cyberpornography, and militarized sexual services (Bertone, 1999). To date, sex trafficking does not include the phenomenon of mail order brides, even though there is evidence to indicate that many of these women are also trafficked (Constable, 2012).

The incidence of sex trafficking overlaps with the even higher incidence of forced labor, also referred to as modern-day slavery or labor trafficking. This may be due to the fact that women and children who are trafficked for purposes of forced labor are then vulnerable to sexual exploitation. Forced labor may also include a form of debt bondage. Debt bondage grows as workers are charged for various "expenses" or even from debt that is "inherited" or passed down from one generation to another. In order to pay off this debt, they are forced into some type of labor, usually in the labor in what is referred to as "3-D" jobs: those that are dirty, dangerous, or degrading (World Vision, 2013). Forced labor is most prevalent in South Asia, where there are some estimates as high as 20 million persons in India, Pakistan, Bangladesh, and Nepal (Dixon-Mueller, 2011). Worldwide, over 115 million children's labor is exploited in "3-D" jobs (World Vision, 2013). Forced labor is also prevalent in developed countries like the U.S. and some areas of Europe, mainly in the farming industry, sweat shops, and the service industry.

Cyber trafficking occurs over the Internet and includes a range from pornography to sites that feature live sexual acts, voyeurism, and other types of "virtual" transactions. This is a growing area of child exploitation internationally, where online bartering for sex, pornography, molestation, and other types of transactions occur (Burgess, Mahoney, Visk, & Morgenbesser, 2008). Thousands of these types of sites exist, and it is very difficult to prosecute cyber trafficking, as there is an element of "real" harm that has to be proven due to questions of the virtual nature of the exploitation. Further, there is a question of tracking the perpetrators, particularly with technology being able to mask or hide movement and transactions (Office for Victims of Crime, 2001). Cyber trafficking is quite literally not just a new frontier, but an unknown one in terms of the ability to address where and how to target interventions. There have been some studies that have shown that the strong national policies around Internet policies in general have been able to provide some detriment to cyber-trafficking crime (Umali, 2005).

A new designation was added to the trafficking protocols with the passage of the Child Soldiers Prevention Act of 2008, which identifies countries whose governments recruit and use child soldiers in armed conflicts. This act is consistent with the United Nations Convention on the Rights of the Child (U.S. Department of State, 2013) Child soldiers are defined by their age (under 18), forced or compulsory recruitment into armed forces, and any children who are used in national armed hostilities. This also includes children who may not be combatants but are in conflict zones serving in other capacities such as domestics, messengers, cooks, guards, and so on. In its first year, most of the countries identified as perpetrators of child soldiers were in located in Africa and some parts of Asia (Odhiambo, Kassilly, Maito, Onkware, & Oboka, 2012).

COUNTRY CASE STUDY: THE PHILIPPINES

The Philippines is an interesting case study to consider because of its unique and long history with the U.S. This relationship has resulted in the development of Philippines into a country whose practices are highly Westernized and indeed, very American in outlook and design (Constantino, 1975). The colonial and semi-colonial relationship between the U.S. and the Philippines is further apparent when the responses to trafficking at every level—macro, mezzo, and micro—are revealed. Thus, there is much to gain in examining Philippine efforts against trafficking and perhaps being able to apply this experience as a potential resource in shaping the U.S. efforts to abolish sex trafficking and modern-day slavery.

Despite the growing international awareness around trafficking and modern-day slavery as well as the thousands of organizations and government programs created to ameliorate the situation, incidents have actually increased instead of lessening (U.S. Department of State, 2014). However, this is not to imply that there has been a lack of awareness or cover up of trafficking issues. In fact, the Philippines women's movement has been a leader in the international fight against trafficking, beginning at the grassroots levels, even before it was a UN Agenda Item (Enloe, 1989). This chapter will examine three examples of practices from the Philippines that aim to either prevent or intervene, on a macro, mezzo, and micro level. Though these practices are not meant to imply evidence-based studies, they offer a solid base for social workers in the U.S. to begin to compare, evaluate, and create their own programs.

Country Context: History, Culture, and Values in the Philippines

For 400 years, the Philippines was a colony of Spain. This resulted in a country that continues to be 80% Catholic with no separation of Church and State, making it both culturally and spiritually unique from its neighbors in the region.[1] The Spanish Encomienda system created feudal economics where indigenous workers were subjected to the whims of the hacienderos whom owned the land and the means of production. It was no surprise that this system also included the first recorded instances of tenant farmers paying off debts by selling women's domestic services. It was not uncommon to hear of young girls being sent up to the "Don or Dona's home" to serve as a maid, laundress, or other such function (Constantino, 1975). The exchange then, as now, left girls and women vulnerable to sexual abuse. These instances are the first forms of bond labor in the Philippines, forming the backbone of the feudal relationships at first between the landlords and the peasant class and morphing into a continuing power struggle based on class that still exists (Constantino & Constantino, 1978).

In 1896, Filipinos led a successful revolution against the Spanish but did not beat the U.S., who bought the Philippines from the Spanish in the infamous Treaty of Paris, which also include the sale of Puerto Rico, Cuba, and Guam for the amount of $20 million. Thus, the Philippines went from one colonial ruler to another (Agoncillo, 1956). For the U.S., the Philippines was a strategic conquest that they would not formally release until 1946, and only with the requirement that the Philippines sign an agreement allowing for U.S. military bases (Enloe, 1989).

As an archipelago in Southeast Asia, the Philippines has served since 1898 as a strategic position for the U.S. military. Located close to China, Korea, and Muslim strongholds such as Indonesia, the U.S. military has used the Philippines as a key location for its campaigns in Vietnam, Korea, and even the Middle East. The Philippines became a U.S. military stronghold that at one time was the outpost of the U.S. Pacific Fleet. Because of this, the Philippines was a target of the imperial

---

[1] The Philippines is the only Catholic country in the Asia Pacific Region. The lack of separation between church and state affects not only culture but policy in the Philippines, especially around the areas of family law. For instance, the Philippines remains the only country in the world where divorce is illegal and issues like birth control continue to be controversial. This type of conservative political and social structure make issues such as trafficking difficult to discuss and, therefore, combat (Constantino, 1975).

powers during World War II, including Japan (Constantino, 2010). When the Japanese occupied the Philippines between 1942 and 1945, its war atrocities included the mass rape and sexual slavery of thousands of women and girls whom the Japanese called "Comfort Women" (Henson, 1999). Even after the U.S. granted the Philippines its independence after the war (in 1946), the U.S. Bases Agreement of 1947 gave the U.S. exclusive access to over 100,000 acres of Philippine land for which to house its bases for military operations for 99 years (Ferrer, 1992).[2] A residual effect of serving as a strategic military installation was that though the U.S. officially states that there have never been any wars fought in the Philippines, the large "R and R," or Rest and Recreation, industry that has grown around the U.S. bases became and continues to be epicenters of trafficking in the region (Enloe, 1992).

Social workers operate from a strengths-based paradigm, the reference to cultural values is meant to demonstrate the role that cultural values play, especially in terms of program efficacy and replication and not to use culture as a mechanism of blaming (Oyserman & Sakamoto, 1997). Such importance placed on cultural values have at times (more often than not) been cited in the literature and instead of increasing understanding have created the trap of cultural determinism, inciting victim blaming of those trafficked. These values are widely acknowledged to form the core of Filipino "psychology." The influence of these values in Filipino human behavior and motivating factors is so strong that the study of them has become central in the growing indigenization of social work in the Philippines. Values such as *pakikisama* (harmony) and *amor propio* (self-esteem) emphasize the importance of smooth interpersonal relations, striving for harmony and nonconfrontational behavior. These two values often are mediated by the value of *hiya* (shame), wherein a person is cognizant of how his or her actions will reflect on his or her entire family. Therefore, any

controversial or unseemly behavior is avoided so as not to bring shame onto oneself or one's family. Another value, *bahala na* (whatever), has been cited in the literature as responsible for asserting that Filipinos espouse a fatalistic attitude, which does not encourage or allow fighting back. Finally, the value of *utang ng loob* (debt of gratitude) operates to create bonds wherein those involved are morally indebted to one another (Agbayani, 1997). In terms of trafficking, these values may operate together to create situations where people are more likely to be vulnerable to victimization, unable to immediately identify their risk, and/or construct scenarios where they feel they cannot find a way out of a situation.

Trafficking and Modern-Day Slavery in the Philippines

Sex trafficking and modern-day slavery have taken many forms in the Philippines. This is a country that is considered to be both a "sending" and a "receiving" country when it comes to trafficking. This trend of Overseas Contract Workers that began in the 1980's continues to exist with labor migration as one of the premier programs for the current Philippine government, who has come to rely on the more than $20 billion of remittances that are sent to the Philippines from those overseas workers. The remittances keep the national economy afloat, and there is little incentive to end or tightly regulate the program, even though studies have shown that widespread labor migration increases vulnerability to trafficking (De Castro, 2010). A significant amount of the Philippines' economy depends on the migration of labor. As of 2001, approximately 8% of Filipinos lived abroad and 20.3% of the country's earnings consisted of officially recorded remittances (Migration Policy Institute, 2004).

Similar to the persistence of labor trafficking is the persistent problem of sex tourism in the

---

[2] The Military Bases Agreement was approved for a term from 1947 to 2046 but was shortened to run only until 1991 for a number of reasons, namely issues of sovereignty.

Philippines. This issue has continued unabated and, in fact, has only gotten bigger with the advent of new tourism campaigns aimed at making the Philippines a premier destination spot for foreign tourists. Sex tourism can either be foreign or domestic and is exactly what it implies: tourism for the express purpose of sexual activities (Guzder, 2009). It is a multi-billion dollar industry that exacerbates the issue, especially of child trafficking (ECPAT, 2013). While young women are involved, most victims of sex tourism are children. In addition to sexual pedophiles are also trends such as the "virgin cure," wherein it is believed that sex with a virgin will cure medical ills such as HIV/AIDS (Mathipa, Margaret, & Maile, 2014). Most sex tourists in the Philippines come from Northeast Asia, Australia, New Zealand, Europe, and North America.

Widespread poverty, an established sex trade, and a predominantly English-speaking population has made the Philippines a high-demand source country for child trafficking. Child sex tourism remains a serious problem in the Philippines. Another common area of trafficking is the labor trafficking of children, mostly internally (within country borders). Millions of children are exposed to dangerous working conditions in industries such as mining, scavenging, and domestic service (http://www.ilo.org/manila/areasofwork/child-labour/lang--en/index.htm).

MICRO PERSPECTIVE

Assessment

When assessing trafficking victims or survivors, it is imperative that the clinician is able to build rapport and set a client-centered tone. Assessments should occur in a comfortable environment that is safe. This is a priority for clients who may fear retaliation or further harm from their traffickers. Whether the practitioner is speaking in person or over the phone to a client, the most important thing is to establish safety. Physical locations as well as body language can help set the tone of the client assessment. Clinicians should be open and practice reflective listening. They should also respond appropriately by making eye contact and not employing any judgmental stances. Language is also a large consideration and practitioners should take clues from the clients themselves. For instance, if the client refers to her "pimp" or "trafficker" as her "boyfriend," practitioners should not dispute the title. This will come later, during the assessment, it is more important to begin to get the client's story.

Agencies and organizations may have a number of differing assessments used on this population. However, agencies in the United States such as the Department of Justice, Human Trafficking task forces, and other entities may have guidelines that clinicians could use as a resource, or a guide to follow. In general, assessments should include questions related to safety, general trafficking situations (fraud, coercion, force), and a narrative of their story. Do not force details that clients are not able or ready to tell you. Practitioners must be cautious of retraumatization or anything the client may construe as victim blaming. For instance, Alma arrived at the agency in total silence and remained so for weeks. It was apparent that something was wrong, but the workers at the agency did not push Alma or force her to speak. They were all too aware that anything, however inadvertent, could set off her trauma, especially if she were to be asked questions about her "choices" and decision-making processes. Alma was very young, so people will tend not to victim blame; however, any questioning related to her experience was difficult, making any initial discussion one that was often done through other means.

Diversity Considerations

The very nature of trafficking speaks to diversity on numerous levels. The transnational situation that includes cycles of migration within and between countries means that at any given moment, persons are being trafficked. This necessitates cultural competency and sensitivity. Differences in ethnicity, nationality, and even religion create circumstances where language must be a consideration. Often, what adds to exploitation is the inability for victims or survivors to understand what is occurring in the places they are trafficked or to understand what they are "agreeing" to (this is especially true in the case of labor trafficking). Cultural norms and religious customs are also important for practitioners to understand. For instance, understanding the case of Alma from the perspective of Filipino values will help practitioners assess her case and provide effective interventions.

It is not only at an ethnic or national level that diversity must be considered in trafficking situations. The biggest area of diversity is in terms of power. Consistent to almost all trafficking situations are dynamics of power: physical, psychological, and/or economic. For example, in labor trafficking, traffickers hold power over their victims by indenturing them to slave-like conditions where they charge exorbitantly for their "fees" so much so that victims are never able to leave the situation and are afraid to leave (usually due to threats to their family or themselves). However, it would be a mistake to think that all trafficking victims or survivors fit the same profile. Though there are specific identifiers for both victims and perpetrators, nothing is universal. Being keen to this will help practitioners keep an open mind when working with this population.

Intervention

Unequivocally, the most utilized micro-intervention for trafficking victims has been intensive case management (Macy & Johns, 2011). This is due to the fact that victims of trafficking that are able to escape, run away, or who are freed from their traffickers and perpetrators have immediate needs that must be taken care of. This first stage of crisis mode can last for an unspecified amount of time, especially when victims become involved in lengthy legal proceedings. For many service providers, the intensity of case management that occurs leave little room for the development of further interventions. This is the case for agencies in the Philippines. In fact, there are a very few agencies in the Philippines who engage in clinical micro-interventions, much less evidence-based practices (www.humantrafficking.org).

Intensive case management is a critical component in the recovery of those who have been victimized by abuse and trafficking. When individuals suffer from significant traumatic events and often develop mental health symptoms, all dimensions of their life are impacted and they experience serious impairments in the functioning of their daily lives (Dixon, 2000). Intensive case management models have been mostly derived from Assertive Community Treatment (Dixon, 2000). Although ACT was originally developed to treat individuals with serious and persistent mental illnesses, it has been adapted to serve a range of populations in the global community. In the case of Alma, intensive case management would be an essential tool in providing her with the services that she needs. It is apparent from the case that Alma has suffered severely from neglect, emotional abuse, physical abuse, and sexual abuse. All of these are elements that could potentially contribute to complex trauma. Given her history it is evident that a potential medical evaluation, assessment of cognitive and learning capacities in addition to resocialization need to be addressed. The intensive case management team would be able to utilize a multidisciplinary team of doctors, clinicians and child behavioral specialists and housing and resource specialists from the community to help address her needs.

The main goal of intensive case management in the global community is to provide comprehensive community based treatment to rehabilitate and support those who suffer from mental health issues. A signature part of this treatment models is the use of an integrative approach that includes a multidisciplinary team to address a range of life domains that are inextricably impacted by trauma and mental health issues often rooted or exacerbated by trafficking and other forms of exploitation. The main components of almost all intensive case management models include a multidisciplinary team, community-based services, highly individualized services, long-term planning, vocational planning, community integration, and attention to health care needs (Allness & Knoedler, 2003). The multidisciplinary team, community-based services, and the focus on client and service provider relationships are what differentiate intensive case management from traditional case management.

In varying case management models, there is a focus on resource coordination and case manager task completion (Vanderplasschen, Rapp, Wolf, & Broekaert, 2004). In contrast, intensive case management models place much of the focus on the case manager, client, and team relationship. While providing a range of critical services, the multidisciplinary team works to build a trusting relationship with the client. With the foundation of this relationship, services are provided in an emotionally safe environment with the hopes that the safe and trusting relationship will make services more effective and long lasting (Allness & Knoedler, 2003).

Accessibility is one of the major barriers in providing services to marginalized communities. When communities and individuals are affected by trauma, poverty, and marginalization, resistance, fear, and a state of emotional and mental instability often debilitate and affect one's ability to access much-needed services. Intensive case management makes it a point to provide services in the community and more so in the home of the individual seeking services. While tackling issues of accessibility, the multidisciplinary team assesses the strengths and assets of the individual and community, which will be utilized in creating a care plan to achieve client-driven goals (Vanderplasschen et al., 2004).

PREDA, or the People's Recovery, Empowerment, Development, Assistance Foundation, located in Olongapo, Philippines, is one of the first agencies in the Philippines to address the sexual exploitation of children. As PREDA formed, it became obvious that the children were not only victims of incest and other sexual abuse but were being exploited for commercial means and also being trafficked as sex slaves. Fr. Shay's vision was to change the societal injustices that criminalizes and abandons children and leaves them vulnerable to prostitution and exploitation and incarceration (personal communication, June 13, 2013).

Children like Alma were unable to be treated before the formation of this organization.

At the time that PREDA was founded, it was the mid-1970s, only two years after the declaration of Martial Law in the Philippines. The Filipino people struggled in a rebellion against the Dictator Marcos (Aquino, 1982). Coinciding with the development of PREDA was the rising popularity of primal therapy. Developed by Arthur Janov (1974) of the Primal Institute and popularized by celebrities like John Lennon, Yoko Ono, and James Earl Jones, primal therapy became widespread and a highly glamorized form of treatment during this era. With its growing popularity in Western culture blended with the highly impressionable nature of the Filipino culture, the practice of primal therapy was adopted by PREDA.

The ideology behind this therapy is to encourage and even trigger an emotional response from clients while they are in a safe space. Primal therapy is based on Freudian conceptualizations of defense mechanisms, particularly the power of the mind to repress pain and trauma (Janov, 1991). At the time of the trauma, this type of defense mechanism is meant to protect or even shield the victim. However, if it is not dealt with, Freud felt that this repression could lead to invisible injuries and misplaced expression such as mood or anxiety disorders (Black & Mitchell, 1996; Arbiser, 2013).

Primal therapy is structured to address three levels of consciousness. The therapy begins at Level Three and goes down to Level One. Beaulieu (1995) suggests primal feelings begin at the brain stem then move to the limbic system where feelings are processed, then progress to the cognitive mind, thus a reverse approach to traditional therapy. At Level Three, Janov (1991) describes the initial pain of early childhood that surrounds a serious physical injury (i.e., deprivation of oxygen at birth, deprivation of nourishment, etc.) that is repressed and imprinted in the brain stem. According the Beaulieu (1995), this is somatosensory level of pain in which the injury is experienced and relieved viscerally. At this point in therapy the client is called to a cathartic and physical expression of their pain through the facilitation of the therapist. Traditionally this is done in a safe protected room, commonly called a "scream room." After the initial catharsis the client is expected to feel a sense of relief, thereby opening the mind to the next two levels of consciousness.

Level Two addresses pain that has occurred later in childhood and is drawn from memories that are repressed due to the painful feelings associated with them. Primal literature states that these injuries could range from a death of a parent to sexual molestation or abuse (Barash, 2012). The pain associated with this level of consciousness tends to express itself through tears and verbal language. At this point in therapy, the therapist continues to provide a safe space for expression and offers an active and reflective forum to identify and process feelings associated with the identified injuries. An understanding of cognitive processes and the relationship of thought and feelings, both current and repressed are essential tenets of this level. Some therapists utilize individual and group therapy to interpret this level of consciousness.

At the final Third Level, the line suggests that the line of pain is directly related to a person's intellectual interpretation and defenses against their traumatic experiences. These types of injuries tend to occur in adulthood. In treatment, this level calls for the social worker to work with the client to understand their intellectual defenses that shield them from healing from the trauma that has occurred. The foundation of this level is based in the client's developed neocortex brain's ability to challenge feelings and emotions and reframe thoughts and experiences (Beaulieu, 1995).

Through its range of programs, PREDA utilizes Janov's framework to provide treatment to children and adolescents. Employing multiple components of Janov's levels of treatment, PREDA attempts to address the effects of complex trauma and childhood exploitation. With the use of the primal scream room and individual and group therapy, PREDA addresses the range of individualized needs of those they serve (personal communication, June 13, 2012).

Although a formal evaluation has not been conducted, PREDA reports that it has been able to successfully treat and rehabilitate many of their clients (personal communication, June 13, 2012). The effectiveness of PREDA's practice could largely be drawn from their ability to adapt this Westernized practice to the needs of the Filipino people. For instance, because of Filipino values discussed earlier in the chapter, many of the children self-blame, operating from the idea that no one will believe their story or they may feel so ashamed about what happened to them. Some of the children may believe they did something to cause the abuse or that in being abused, their family would now be ashamed of them. These feelings result in the stigma of silence, wherein children do not talk about or even cry about the abuse they faced. Primal therapy, then, is utilized to encourage the children to emote, to yell, scream, cry, and in short, express the pain, sense of injustice, and hurt they are feeling.

In addition to other adaptations of the framework, PREDA has been able to hone in on Filipino values of "togetherness" and redefining a sense of "family." Through their group work, PREDA staff utilizes their working relationships with the clients to model healthy interactions between adults and children. In practicing healthy exchanges, staff are able to model appropriate relationships, provide a safe space for emotionally corrective experiences, while simultaneously providing the familiarity and comfort of the Filipino value of "togetherness" (personal communication, June 13, 2012). Adaptations like this have been helpful in reframing cognitive distortions, redefining roles, and providing healthy modeling for attachment, which according to the National Children's Trauma Stress Network (2013) are essential for rehabilitation and recovery.

Although primal therapy was highly popularized in the United States, there were many critiques on the evidence of its effectiveness on many fronts. In its truest form, primal therapy has not been empirically tested in a global community and at its conception did not take into account the treatment of children in developing countries who have experienced trauma and have been victimized by trafficking (Barash, 2012). PREDA is one of the first organizations to utilize strategies from primal therapy in a global context. Alma's case is one in which primal therapy worked. Her inability to express herself made her become more and more introverted. There were weeks when her silence would stretch. However, she continued to deface her toys and refer to them as symbols of herself. She was referred to the Primal Therapy program where she was encouraged to emote her feelings by screaming, yelling, crying, and hitting padded walls/ground. Her emotions spent, Alma was able to start speaking her story.

Adaptation and Implications to Global Social Work

Interventions drawn from one source and implemented internationally have to be done with a complex contextual lens. Social work ethics dictate that service delivery meet a level of competency and promote the dignity and worth of a person by having a thorough understanding of culture while practicing the capacity to contextualize interventions. With the international nature of trafficking and modern-day slavery, it is even more imperative to be sensitive not just to cultural nuances but how interventions can be applied (or not). In some cases, there may even be better applications when applied in global contexts or when adapted to fit cultural norms. This also underscores the need to develop interventions that have a global reach. At the minimum, interventions should take into account needs of multiple communities since many trafficked victims are foreign nationals, requiring a slightly (or majorly) different skill set than those who are trafficked domestically. Finally, at a mezzo and macro level, social work is challenged to create partnerships and advocacies that cut across borders and are more multidisciplinary in nature.

Transference and Countertransference Issues

Transference and countertransference are processes that occur naturally in therapeutic relational work. Transference is the projection of unwanted feelings onto an external person. In the case of trafficking, the unwanted feelings of the victim are being projected onto the service provider or therapist. In response to transference, countertransference is the process of receiving these projections and thus evoking a response from the service provider that leads to emotional entanglement. Both transference and countertransference are inevitable processes that can manifest and positive and negative ways. For instance, Alma is the child of a Filipina mother and an African American father whom she had never met. When an African American international aid worker volunteered at the agency, it was clear that Alma had both positive and negative feelings toward her because of her ethnicity. Alma would respond to her for comfort, as if making up for her father leaving her, but would also push her away in anger. Similarly, the volunteer, being an African American woman and having experienced racism, could understand (and more than imagine) how difficult it had been for Alma, growing up biracial in a country whose colonial mentality means people literally believe the lighter one's skin is, the better. This fed into Alma's already growing feelings of inadequacy and abandonment. The most notable feature in these complimentary processes is the exchange of intense feelings that are inaccurate or unfitting to the current situation. In working with victims of trafficking, management of the service provider's countertransference is an essential skill that will promote favorable outcomes for the client.

The depth of issues that lead to the victimization of trafficked individuals makes the process of change and healing very difficult. This level of challenge and complexity can often manifest in a client's resistance to treatment. It is important for service providers to be fully aware that resistance often invokes strong countertransference surrounding feelings of conflict, rejection and inadequacy. Contrastingly, with proper attunement, discernment of feelings, and keen clinical intervention, the healing and change process could be facilitated.

Legal and Ethical Concerns

When dealing with complex cases of trafficking, there are significant legal and ethical considerations. In most cases surrounding the provision of services to minors, parental consent is required. However, providers may be unable to obtain this, especially with young children who have been domestically or internationally trafficked and may not be able to find their parents or guardians. It is important that the practitioner assess the necessity and appropriateness of parental and family involvement while being mindful of the potential barriers, assumptions and challenges associated with receiving services for particularly for trafficking. For instance, in some cases, parents or extended relatives may be involved with the trafficking of their children. They may also be actively threatened by the traffickers, or children may be afraid that by "telling" who their parents are, they will be putting their families in danger.

Another important ethical consideration is the self-efficacy of the client. Alma was taken to the agency in a sorry state. Extremely young and totally exploited, Alma had few opportunities when she could have felt positively or mastered enough of the skill set that is needed for some semblance of self-efficacy. In many instances, there is a strong likelihood that the referred maybe involuntary or exhibiting significant resistance to treatment. Ethically, it is essential that the practitioner assess an appropriate way to enter into treatment and build rapport. Engaging mindfully can help decrease resistance and can prevent the practitioner from replicating potentially traumatic themes of power and control through treatment. This type of engagement was necessary for Alma to regain her voice and a feeling of relative safety. Her resistance to treatment was based on a number of assumptions that were made because of how she was found and brought to the agency. It took Alma months to feel that she was safe, and it was only when she felt safe that she began to confide in her therapist.

MEZZO PERSPECTIVE

Before clinical interventions were developed, awareness raising and prevention were measures taken against trafficking. Unlike large, international media campaigns, these types of awareness raising and prevention programs are grassroots and community based. In 2013, the Ople Policy Center and Training Institute was honored by the TIP Report as a "hero" against trafficking for their formation of Skills Up! and Tulay (Bridge) Program, both of which are focused on providing supports to Overseas Contract Workers, helping them understand their rights and making sure they are able to protect themselves from traffickers (U.S. Department of State, 2013).

The Visayan Forum Foundation of the Philippines was formed in 1991 mainly to do work with girls who were domestic workers. One of their programs, the Movement of Anti-Trafficking Advocates (MATA) was established in 2009. More than an acronym, *mata* in Pilipino is the word for "eye." This refers to the goal of their program, which is to develop a youth-led network that encourages youth to have an active voice in the fight against human trafficking through awareness raising. Further, youth in the MATA program are encouraged to be "vigilant eyes" against trafficking and report incidents to the proper authorities. The MATA program is founded on a series of school-based workshops. The workshops are meant to identify students who may be interested in working to end trafficking, and then these student groups are organized into MATA chapters. By using workshops and going into schools, MATA is able to bring information about trafficking to their peers. Their largest event nationwide is "Traffick Jam," an annual concert dedicated to raising trafficking awareness. In order to accomplish their goals and events, MATA partners with various businesses and media outlets, including the MTV network (Visayan Forum, personal communication, n.d.).

Gabriela Philippines, a grassroots women's organization, launched a small-scale media campaign composed of startling images of trafficked women, such as one with hands bound and circling the baggage claim belt at an airport. These images were found in 15- and 30-second public service announcement spots that played on local television stations. Still images were also created and placed on newsprint posters; they were cheap to make and easy to paste up on construction fences and other areas. As such, they proliferated even mainstream areas of the country. The images were accompanied by community-based trainings, which were given to mainly urban poor and peasant women and girls who are not able to access school-based models (Enrile & Levid, 2009).

Although there is a lack of evidence-based literature for these types of anti-trafficking programs, there is literature that indicates youth-led peer groups based on social change, grassroots models are, indeed, effective (Ginwright & James, 2002; Jennings, Parra-Medina, Hilfinger-Messias, & McLoughlin, 2006). Success of these programs are based on the ability for youth to be able to plan and take ownership of their own activities; identify their own explanations and rationale for social issues; innovate solutions; and engage with the community. Research on transformational models further stress the importance of imparting genuine critical thinking skills among youth within a safe environment, such as these organizations (Mezirow, 2000). While peers are important, the types of adults that are also helping structure the programs and provide trainings are also critical. Quinn (1999) found that adults have to be partners in building skills so that youth learn how to goal set and work toward achievement. The crucial factor was that of relationship, similar to the success factors of more traditional mentoring projects. Alma was quite young when she was taken to the agency and given services. Due to her age, she was placed in groups where there was no formal mentorship. Instead, she was put into peer groups that did offer support but through less conventional means, such as playing and pretend. As more of these programs are evaluated, the hope is that quantitative and qualitative data will reveal what is already being practiced on the ground: that empowering youth is integral to a multidisciplinary approach against trafficking, especially when empowerment includes the development of capacity and action of agency (Van Impe, 2000).

MACRO PERSPECTIVE

In 2003, the Philippines passed its first Anti-Trafficking in Persons Act (Republic Act 9208).

Regionally, this law was one of the few in Asia and established the Inter-Agency Council Against Trafficking (IACAT) which was composed of several governmental, nongovernmental, civic, and other organizations aimed at preventing and suppressing trafficking in persons. The IACAT was instrumental in not only setting policy precedence but also in providing temporary shelter for witnesses and victims, operating a regional help line and an operations center witness location program (Wuiling, 2006).

As with the U.S. Trafficking Victims Protection Act (TVPA), the Philippines' law is not without its own challenges. To begin with, the implementation and prosecution aspects of the law are where the most difficulties arise. Within the framework of corruption, it is extremely difficult for the law to be effective. For instance, everyone from the police to judges has been accused of mishandling trafficking cases (at best) to blatantly using the cases to their own advantage, further traumatizing or exploiting the victim (at worst). In order to address this, the Philippine government has taken steps such as prosecuting officials accused of colluding with traffickers, even Philippine diplomatic staff (including Philippine Ambassadors) serving abroad (personal communication, NAME, June 14, 2012).

The presence of The Anti-Trafficking in Persons Act is a message to the country for several things: that trafficking is morally and legally wrong; that citizens have a responsibility to report suspicious behavior; and most important, that victims have legal recourse. This law also comes with strict penalties such as life imprisonment. Finally, the law is representative of the work of grassroots and community efforts to end trafficking. Before its passage, women's organizations, human rights groups, and other entities from educational institutes to private corporations lobbied for its passage (Largoza-Maza, 1995). With regard to children, this law, like so many others across the world, began to shed light on the issue of child trafficking, especially sex trafficking. Through the use of such legislation, Alma and others are not only able to give voice to their stories; they are able to receive justice.

CONCLUSION

Trafficking is a global phenomenon and social work needs to examine, analyze, and create solutions with an international perspective. This chapter has provided an overview to the various forms of trafficking and using a case study model, explored micro, mezzo, and macro perspectives that can be used to inform social work practice in the area of trafficking. While the trafficking and modern-day slavery of people is not a new circumstance, many of the interventions designed to address victims, survivors, and communities are still being proto-typed. As the overall fight to end trafficking and modern-day slavery grows, social workers will have the unique vantage point as both the clinician and the advocate in areas where healing is needed and where a stand for justice has to be made.

INTERNET RESOURCES

- International Labour Organization: http://www.ilo.org/global/lang-en/index.htm
- Polaris Project: http://www.polarisproject.org/resources/resources-by-topic/international
- Coalition Against Trafficking of Women (CAT-W): http://www.catwinternational.org/
- HumanTrafficking.org: http://humantrafficking.org/countries/united_states_of_america/ngos

DISCUSSION QUESTIONS

1. What are the various forms of trafficking? What is the difference between the terms *trafficking* and *modern-day slavery*?

2. What are vulnerabilities that may lead to people being trafficked? To what extent are these vulnerabilities addressed at the micro, mezzo, and macro level?

3. Identify the role of "demand" in trafficking and modern-day slavery. How might social workers address demand?

4. Describe possible barriers for trafficking victims to receive help. How do these barriers differ if a victim is domestic versus international?

Child versus adult? Depending on the type of trafficking they have experienced?

5. What is the role of social workers in the movement to end trafficking and modern-day slavery? Provide examples at the international, national, and local levels.

REFERENCES

Agbayani, P. (1997). The dual world of Filipino Americans. *Journal of Multicultural Social Work, 6*(1–2), 59–76.

Agoncillo, T. A. (1956). *The revolt of the masses: The story of Bonifacio and the Katipunan.* Quezon City: University of the Philippines.

Allness, D. J., & Knoedler, W. H. (2003). *A manual for ACT start-up: Based on the PACT model of community treatment for persons with severe and persistent mental illnesses.* Arlington, VA: National Alliance on Mental Illness.

Aquino, B. (1982). *Cronies and enemies: The current scene.* Honolulu, HI: University of Hawaii.

Arbiser, S. (2013). *On Freud's inhibitions, symptoms, and anxiety.* Honolulu, HI: University of Hawaii.

Barash, D. (2012). Many emotions: Primal therapy and beyond (Doctoral dissertation). Retrieved from ProQuest Database. (UMI 1492872)

Beaulieu, R. (1995). Techniques of primal therapy. *Primal Therapy Support Group.* Retrieved from http://primal-page.com/beau5.htm

Bertone, A. M. (1999). Sexual trafficking in women: International political economy and the politics of sex. *Gender Issues, 18*(1), 4-22.

Burgess, A. W., Mahoney, M., Visk, J., & Morgenbesser, L. (2008). Cyber child sexual exploitation. *Journal of Psychosocial Nursing & Mental Health Services, 46*(9), 38–45.

Constable, N. (2012). International marriage brokers, cross-border marriages and the U.S. anti-trafficking campaign. *Journal of Ethnic and Migration Studies, 38*(7), 1137–1154. doi:10.1080/1369183X.2012.681457

Constantino, R. (1975). *The Philippines: A past revisited.* Quezon City, PH: Tala.

Constantino, R. (2010). A history of the Philippines: From the Spanish colonialization to the Second World War. New York, NY: Monthly Review Press.

Constantino, R., & Constantino, L. R. (1978). *The Philippines: The continuing past.* Quezon City, PH: The Foundation for Nationalist Studies.

De Castro, R. C. (2010). Weakness and gambits in Philippine foreign policy in the twenty-first century. *Pacific Affairs, 83*(4), 657–717.

Dixon, L. (2000). Assertive community treatment: Twenty-five years of gold. *Psychiatric Services, 51*(6), 759–765.

Dixon-Mueller, R. B. (2011). *Rural women at work: Strategies for development in South Asia.* New York, NY: RFF Press.

ECPAT International. (2013). *Child sex tourism.* Retrieved from www.ecpat.net/ei/csec_cst.asp

Enloe, C. (1989). *Bananas, beaches and bases: Making feminist sense of international politics.* Oakland: University of California Press.

Enloe, C. (1992). *It takes two.* In S. Sturdevant & B. Stoltzfus (Eds.), *Let the good times roll* (pp. 22–27). New York. NY: The New Press.

Enrile, A. V., & Levid, J. (2009). GABNet: A case study of transnational sisterhood and organizing. *Amerasia Journal, 35*(1), 92–108.

Ferrer, M. C. (1992). The dynamic of the opposition to the U.S. bases in the Philippines. *Kasarinlan: Philippine Journal of Third World Studies (2012–080X), 7*(4), 62.

Gallagher, A. (2001). Trafficking in persons report (Review). *Human Rights Quarterly, 23*(4), 1135–1141.

Ginwright, S., & James, T. (2002). From assets to agents of change: Social justice, organizing, and youth development. *New Directions for Youth Development, Special Issue: Youth Participation: Improving Institutions and Communities, 96,* 27–46.

Gozdziak, E. M., & Collett, E. A. (2005). Research on human trafficking in North America: A review of literature. *International Migration, 43*(1–2), 99–128.

Guzder, D. (2009). The economics of commercial sexual exploitation. *Pulitzer Center on Crisis Reporting.* Retrieved from http://pulitzercenter.org/blog/untold-stories/economics-commercial-sexual-exploitation

Hatcher, W., & Radpour, M. (2003). Confronting structural violence against women and girls: The principle and practice of gender equity. In M. L. Penn & R. Nardos (Eds.), *Overcoming violence against women and girls: The international campaign to eradicate a worldwide problem* (pp. 23–40). Boulder, CO: Rowman & Littlefield.

Henson, M. (1999). *Comfort woman: A Filipina's story of prostitution and slavery under the Japanese military.* Lanham, MA: Rowman & Littlefield.

Janov, A. (1974). The nature of pain and its relation to levels of consciousness. *Journal of Primal Therapy, 2*(1), 5-50.

Janov, A. (1991). *The new primal scream: Primal therapy twenty years later.* New York, NY: Abacus Books.

Jennings, L. B., Parra-Medina, D. M., Hilfinger-Messias, D. K., & McLoughlin, K. (2006). Toward a critical social theory of youth empowerment. *Journal of Community Practice, 14*(1–2), 31–55.

Largoza-Maza, L. (1995). The medium term Philippine development plan toward the year 2000: Filipino women's issues and perspectives. In J. Peters & A. Wolper (Eds.), *Women's rights human rights: International feminist perspectives* (pp. 62–66). New York, NY: Routledge.

Macy, R. J., & Johns, N. (2011). Aftercare services for international sex trafficking survivors: Informing U.S. service and program development in an emerging practice area. *Trauma, Violence, & Abuse, 12*(2), 87–98.

Mathipa, E. R., Margaret, K. N., & Maile, S. (2014). Factors contributing to the rising HIV/AIDS infection rate among Soshanguve school girls in the FET band. *Journal of Human Ecology, 45*(1), 49–59.

McGough, M. (2013). Ending modern-day slavery: Using research methods to inform U.S. anti-human trafficking efforts. *NIJ Journal, 127,* 26–32.

Mezirow, J. (2000). *Learning as transformation: Critical perspectives on a theory in progress.* San Francisco, CA: Jossey-Bass.

Migration Policy Institute. (2004). *Labor export as government policy: The case of the Philippines.* Retrieved from http://www.migrationinformation.org/feature/display.cfm

National Child Trauma Stress Network. (2013). *Childhood trauma.* Retrieved from http://www.nctsn.org

Odhiambo, E. O. S., Kassilly, J., Maito, L. T., Onkware, K., & Oboka, W. A. (2012). Kenya's constitution and child trafficking as a security threat. *Journal of Defense Resources Management, 3*(2), 75–88.

Retrieved from http://go.galegroup.com.libproxy.usc.edu

Office for Victims of Crime. (2001). *OVC bulletin: Internet crimes against children* (Publication No. NCJ 184931). Retrieved from http://www.ojp.usdoj.gov/ovc/publications/bulletins/internet_2_2001/NCJ184931.pdf

Oyserman, D., & Sakamoto, I. (1997). Being Asian American: Identity, cultural constructs, and stereotype perception. *The Journal of Applied Behavioral Science, 33*(4), 435–453.

PREDA. (2013). *About us.* Retrieved from http://www.preda.org

Quinn, J. (1999). Where need meets opportunity: Youth development programs for early teens. *The Future of Children, 9*(2), 96–116.

Sharma, N. (2003). Travel agency: A critique of anti-trafficking campaigns. *Refuge: Canada's Journal on Refugees, 21*(3), 53–65.

Skinner, B. (2008). *A crime so monstrous.* New York, NY: Free Press.

Umali, V. (2005). The cyber-trafficking of Filipino girl-children: Weaknesses of Philippine policies. *Asian Women, 20*(6), 175–206.

United Nations Office on Drug and Crimes. (2006). *Trafficking of persons: Global patterns.* Retrieved from http://www.unodc.org/pdf/traffickinginpersons_report_2006ver2.pdf

U.S. Department of State. (2013). *Trafficking in persons report.* Retrieved from http://www.state.gov/documents/organization/82902.pdf

U.S. Department of State. (2014). *U.S. bilateral relations fact sheet: Philippines.* Retrieved from http://www.whitehouse.gov/the-press-office/2014/04/28/fact-sheet-united-states-philippines-bilateral-relations

Vanderplasschen, W., Rapp, R. C., Wolf, J. R., & Broekaert, E. (2004). The development and implementation of case management for substance use disorders in North America and Europe. *Psychiatric Services, 55*(8), 913–922.

Van Impe, K. (2000). People for sale: The need for a multidisciplinary approach toward human trafficking *International Migration, 1,* 113–131.

Visayan Forum Foundation Inc. (2005). *Looking from within: A primer on trafficking in persons in the Philippines.* Retrieved from http://www.visayanforum.org/article.php?mode_id=773

World Vision. (2013). *The three d's of child labor.* Retrieved from http://www.worldvision.org/news-stories-videos/video-three-ds-child-labor

Wuiling, C. (2006). Assessing criminal justice and human rights models in the fight against sex trafficking: A case study of the ASEAN region. *Essex Human Rights Review, 3*(1), 46–63.

Wyler, L. S. (2010). *Trafficking in persons: U.S.A. policy and issues for congress* (Vol. 7, No. 5700). Darby, PA: Diane.

CHAPTER 32

Psychosocial Support for Youth Affected by Armed Conflict in Northern Uganda

Eric Awich Ochen

CHAPTER OBJECTIVES

- Engage with issues related to working with children and young people affected by conflict;
- Describe methods of carrying out assessment of children in need of psychosocial care after exposure to a violent or critical event;
- Discuss contextually relevant intervention methods in the lives of children and young people affected by armed conflict;
- Translate adaptations of the Northern Uganda situation to psychosocial interventions globally.

CASE VIGNETTE

Alobo Harriet was abducted at 11 years old while on her way to school. She narrates that when she was on her way to school one morning in her rural village of Lapenga, she reached a particular bend in the road. Suddenly, two soldiers jumped on the road and ordered her to stop and abducted her. She was taken to the bush where initially she was made the babysitter of an older rebel wife who had two children. There were five girls staying at the home of the rebel commander, all being prepared to be his wives. After three years, when she turned 14 years old, the rebel soldier told her she was now a big woman and should become his wife. He then sexually assaulted her. She became pregnant following this first sexual assault and later gave birth to a baby boy.

After a year and half of staying with her then-husband, she got pregnant again and gave birth to another child, a girl. During her captivity she has experienced many difficult situations, balancing motherhood roles in the bush, fighting to protect her life, and also looking for food for herself and her children. Alobo spent a total of seven years in the bush and was later released by the rebels along with several other child mothers (young women). Alobo spent three months at the Gulu Support the Children (GUSCO) organization's rehabilitation and resettlement center and was later resettled/reunited with her family. While Alobo was in the bush, however, both her mother and father passed away, leaving her young siblings in the care of her uncle. By the time she returned, the uncle and his family were living in an internally displaced persons camp. They have since moved back to their original home in Okungedi Parish, Amuru District, but Alobo's uncle's capacity to meet Alobo's and her children's basic needs is much diminished due to his advanced age and ill health.

At 17 years of age, with no father for her children, Alobo has to take full charge of providing for her children economically, socially, and emotionally. Within the community, Alobo joined a group of young women who, although they were not abducted themselves, had also been abandoned by their husbands. They started a Village Savings and Loans Association group (VSLA). They pooled resources and lent each other money to start small businesses.

Since her return to the community, Alobo has only been visited once by a child protection committee member who, apart from asking her questions on whether she was okay and what challenges she was experiencing, could not offer much in terms of psychosocial support or resources to the support group. Alobo still experiences nightmares and sees images of her abduction experience and rape, but she is determined to fight on for her children and dependents.

INTRODUCTION

In this chapter, the social worker will explore and assesses the psychosocial support processes for the formerly abducted young people in Northern Uganda. These are young people who were abducted at the ages of 9 to 14, taken into rebel captivity, but managed to escape or were rescued by government troops and were later rehabilitated and resettled within the community. With a key focus on the post-reinsertion period during the resettlement of the formerly abducted young people in the community, consideration is also made on their adjustments to life in the new context. The chapter highlights the challenges of effective psychosocial support and reintegration of young people affected by the armed conflict. Such evidence is reflected on by analyzing an individual intervention framework, young people's post-resettlement experiences, and how the social, political, cultural and economic environment and structures intersect with the prevailing support network to enhance or constrain their reintegration opportunities. This author argues that the nature of support and dynamics have in most cases not

been considered on an individual basis, thus have not taken into account the unique situational circumstances of each young person affected by the conflict. It should also be noted that the support provided emphasized provision of material goods rather than long-term psychosocial care, with minimal attention to the latter after resettlement in the community. In other words, the depth of support and the structures necessary to provide psycho social care and support were not rigorous, conspicuous or sustainable in addressing the changing psychosocial needs of the young people to ensure adequate and effective reintegration. The question then becomes "how well has the individual's intrapsychic resources, immediate support systems and local government/central government programmatic and policy strategies addressed the needs and rights of the young people?" The chapter argues that a framework that recognizes young people's individual and unique experiences needs to be developed; however this framework should be cost effective enough to operationalize and implement within a given context, in this case, Northern Uganda.

Background

Between 1986 and 2006, Northern Uganda was engulfed in armed conflict that displaced up to two million people and disrupted the sociocultural, political, and economic situation within the region (Norwegian Refugee Council, 2010). The conflict had far-reaching implications on social welfare indicators and development prognosis within the region. Northern Uganda is currently emerging from the prolonged period of conflict in which it has been engulfed since 1986. During this period, an estimated 20,000 people have been killed, and over two million displaced (United States Institute of Peace, 2010). The majority of the displaced persons were relocated to internally displaced persons camps (IDPCs). These camps were established in the mid-1990s following calls from the Ugandan government for their formation as means of protecting the general population from the Lord's Resistance Army (LRA). By 2005, the number of such camps had grown to 250, housing around 1.8 million people. By March 2010, it was suggested that although three-quarters of the Internally Displaced Persons (IDPs) had returned to their homes, an estimated 25% of the population in Northern Uganda (especially Acholi subregion) still languished in IDPCs (Norwegian Refugee Council, 2010).

Over the years, various armed groups have operated in Northern Uganda with the major ones being the Uganda Patriotic Democratic Army (UPDA; 1986–1988), Alice Auma Lakwena group (1986–1988), and the Lord's Resistance Army (LRA; 1988–2006). Of all the fighting forces, the LRA have been the most brutal and long lasting, with varying intensity over the years. There is, however, one agreement among scholars that the Northern conflict is complex and located within the geopolitical forces within the region and the nature of domestic politics within Uganda (Dolan, 2006; Omach, 2010a).

Political commentators have noted that the nature of the domestic politics in Uganda (i.e., weak state) and the overall approach to governance is at the core of the Northern Uganda insurgency (Omach, 2010a; Omara-Otunnu, 1992), however, the brutality of the National Resistance Army (NRA), which captured power through a guerilla war, has generally been regarded as the spark that set off the Northern conflict.

Other commentators have noted that the failure at state building is the result of desires to centralize and monopolize state power (Oloka-Onyango, 2001; Omach, 2010b). If the State was strong, inclusive and accountable, perhaps the conflict in Northern Uganda would not have occurred. However, it is suggested that when states are weak, they often lack "domestic, political and social consensus" (Omach, 2010a, p.289). Such struggles are at the root of armed conflict and the incessant insurgencies over the years.

In early 2002 the government of Uganda got permission from the government of Sudan to pursue the rebels inside the Sudanese territory. The operation was codenamed "Operation Iron Fist" and had far reaching consequences for the direction of the war, especially escalation in the abduction of children. This operation opened a new phase in the Northern conflict and increased the internationalization of the conflict and the generation of greater public interest in the war. The improved relationship between the government of Uganda and the government of the Sudan curtailed the support to the LRA and reduced the areas for their operations.

Since the beginning of the conflict, between 25,000 and 30,000 children are estimated to have been abducted (Human Rights Watch, 2006). Between 2002 (the beginning of Operation Iron Fist) and 2004 when the peace process started, up to 8,500 children were said to have been abducted. McKay and Mazurana (2004) put the proportion of girls abducted at 30% of the total while Annan et al. (2006) indicated a figure of 15%. The disparity could be a result of methods used in the estimation of the number. It should be noted here that data gathering and management in Uganda, especially by local and central government authorities is rather weak. The abducted children (both boys and girls) were subjected to extreme brutality, including walking long distances, being trained to fight, forced to kill fellow children and other community members and made to witness several macabre and violent incidents. While the roles of boys were mainly to fight and work as porters carrying luggage, the abducted young girls found themselves playing a multiplicity of roles within the rebel establishment. For example, most of them were subjected to sexual abuse and forcefully made "wives" to the rebel commanders, or they were sexually abused and made to embrace motherhood at an early age (Mazurana & Carlson, 2006; McKay, 2004). Significantly, the young girls and child mothers in the bush had to fight to defend their positions, procure food, and fend off their enemies. The situation of the girls and their individual experiences and construction of events around them during captivity present a rich (though difficult) experience that is yet to be fully explored in the conflict literature.

To respond to the conflict and its aftermath on the region, several development agencies, including local and central governments, made efforts to respond to the development challenges arising and to enhance and compliment family, community, and individual coping strategies (Allen & Schomerus, 2006; Angucia, 2010; Maina, 2010). While this is appreciated, analysis of studies done within the region (e.g., Abola, Omach, Ochen, Anena, & Barongo, 2009; Ochen-Awich, 2012) seems to suggest that while responses have been significant, expected and preferred changes in the target groups appear to be slow. Moreover, questions have also been raised regarding the specificity of interventions vis-à-vis the intervention outcome, contextual relevance, and influence of institutions, along with the due process of such an outcome. This chapter attempts to utilize data generated from studies in Northern Uganda over a three- to four-year period to analyze how an appropriate social work model can be built to respond more effectively and efficiently to the challenges of reintegration experienced by the formerly abducted young men and women. It is the expectation of the researcher that such an analysis will take into account issues at the individual and family (micro) level, the community (mezzo) level, and the national policy implication (macro) level.

The Continuum of Care and Support for Formerly Abducted Youth

The Pre-Bush Experience

Appreciating the importance of interactions of the formerly abducted youth and assessing their inherent philosophy, strategy, focus, and outcomes necessitates going back to the pre-abduction period to contextualize a young person's experience of conflict. It should be reported that these young people (including Alobo) were already embroiled in the context of conflict by the time they were abducted by the rebels. This is because they could have witnessed the abduction of many of their peers and age-mates and also experienced firsthand some of the difficulties and challenges of living in a conflict-ridden environment. The environment was that of uncertainty, fear, minimal protection, and helplessness. Moreover, the presence of government structures—as exemplified by a protective force, medical services, and school services—was not absolute. In other words, the government protective structures, the community support structures, the family support structures, and mechanisms of support were plummeting. Additionally, systems and modalities to address psychoemotional and mental health as well as provide socioeconomic support were at a tipping point. While I do not intend to objectify and reduce the enormity of the experiences or exposure to different situations in the bush, the children were already accustomed to difficulties and challenges of survival within a precarious context.

Within the context of Northern Uganda, no one situation or characteristic can effectively describe the pre-bush situation of children's experience. In other words, the context was characterized by periods of tranquility amidst trouble and active conflict/engagement between the LRA rebels and the Uganda People's Defense Forces (UPDF). Spates of tranquility occurred when the rebels on their own volition withdrew from Northern Uganda or when they were pursued by the UPDF and went to Sudan and did not have any full military engagement. Indeed, Alobo gave birth to her children in Southern Sudan when the rebels had withdrawn to their bases there.

The children of Northern Uganda grew up in the context of vulnerability bedecked with social, cultural, political, economic, and military challenges. For most of the children, rights known and practiced, such as the right to grow up and develop in a secure environment and the right to protection from harmful situations, were violated. Moreover, the home environment where children's potentials could have been actualized was fundamentally broken down by the conflict. The situation was so hopeless that the children grew up seeing their parents as helpless and unable to support them effectively. The image of parents and adults as providers of basic needs such as food, safety and protection, health care, sanitation, and education among others was compromised, thus children were forced to become independent and meet their own basic needs at young ages. This resulted in some children adopting various detrimental coping strategies. According to key informants from the study, some of the young persons entered into sexual relationships with people who had resources to meet some of their needs. Such people included small scale business men, soldiers, teachers and other people in the community. From a cultural point of view, young girls (such as Alobo at abduction) are not expected to enter into relationships with men where such relations do not lead to marriage. Moreover, only girls above 18 years were culturally defined as old enough to engage in pre-marriage courtship and dating. It is evident, that for most parents, support and management of their children was almost surrendered if not taken away. Moreover, the displacement and congregation of households in makeshift settlements (IDPCs) made it difficult for the parents to keep track of what their children were exposed to. For the children who were living in the uncertainty of the conflict, but were not displaced from their original homes, their situation was slightly different however; they were also affected by the wider geopolitical issues.

The Bush Experience of Young People

Most of the girls in the study had been abducted either from home or on their way to school (as in the case of Alobo), either at night or during broad daylight, as depicted in testimonials. The vulnerability of the girls to abduction was partly explained by the rebels' strategy of abducting young children who would be more amenable to implementing rebel objectives and activities. It was the view of the key informants, especially local government and nongovernmental organizations (NGO) staff, that the decision to abduct young girls was apparently predicated on the presumption that they would be free from HIV/AIDS. These were abducted mainly to provide sexual services to the rebels and mother their children, although many later on took multiple roles. Regarding boy child abduction, a view was presented that these young children are easier to manipulate and control in order to accept the rebel cause (indoctrination). On arrival in rebel camps, the abducted children were made to undergo military training in preparation for being fully absorbed into the rebel army. The abducted children faced significant risks and challenges as soldiers in the bush. Testimonies from the child mothers indicated that many of their peers died in battles, some lost their children and many were severely injured in battles.

The exposure of the young people (including Alobo) to battles and other combat environments in the bush significantly predisposed them to critical events and trauma. It is therefore, plausible that girls and child mothers, who experience such traumatic events or exposure to these events, would have more difficulties and challenges reintegrating within the community compared to those that did not. Consultation with agency staff in the rehabilitation centers also indicated that child mothers who were exposed to a significant amount of trauma through their direct or indirect participation in battle and as fighters, often showed more signs of trauma including depression (of different magnitude), aggressive behaviors, hyperactivity, social withdrawal, and isolation, among others. Comparatively, it was revealed that those with less exposure to battles did not present with much trauma symptoms.

It is important to note that the young people were subjected to a life of hardship and blind obedience. They were forced to comply with decisions made by powerful adults (mainly male) with no opportunity to question the orders of their superiors. The socialization and acclimatization of these children within an environment of fear, brutality, and violence affected their psychosocial and psychoemotional wellness upon return. As indicated earlier, an understanding of the bush experiences is paramount to contextualizing the latter experiences of life of the formerly abducted young persons.

MICRO PERSPECTIVE
Reception Center Support

When the young people returned from rebel captivity, their first points of contact were the local leaders who, in turn, would refer them to the army, where they were kept for a few days with the Child Protection Unit (CPU). Later on, they were transferred to the reception and rehabilitation centers run by psychosocial support agencies. At the reception center, which was utilized as a first rehabilitation point, the focus of support was on the physical, psychological, and emotional health and mental well-being of the returning young people. So all children were assessed along key parameters to gauge their level of exposure to critical events and therefore determine how much time they will spend at the reception center. The support methodology used at these centers presented different outcomes for the many children who passed through the reception centers. It appears that while assessment of readiness for resettlement after support at the reception center was done using certain parameters, the decision to reunite and resettle a child with their families depended on the discretion of the social worker. And yet, levels of training among the social workers varied with some staff better trained and experienced.

Consultation with the social workers and other staff of psychosocial support agencies also suggested that most of the social workers deployed at the reception centers were using only basic counseling methods and approaches. While efforts at post-reception center support existed, the professional orientation and training of the social workers was in many instances inadequate with some taking on roles of social workers without formal training in social work. The argument of some of the psychosocial support agencies was that the emergency nature of the context required fast response and so an in-house training mechanism had been preferred for their social work staff. However, follow-up meetings with the young people and consultations with other stakeholders suggest that many of these agencies were preoccupied with numbers and outputs and little real and sustained interest in the qualitative changes in the lives of the targeted young people. Such revelations necessitate strong follow up support to ensure that the young people resettled within the community are coping effectively. Indeed, a recent study on suicide levels and incidence in Northern Uganda indicated that stress and depression were combined first with alcoholism as a cause of suicide in the region ("What is the major cause of suicide?" 2013).

It is thus doubtful that issues of self-determination and life goals of young people are very well executed within the project period.

Return, Resettlement and Reintegration in the Community

The reception center support was provided for a small number of days to ensure the young people stabilize and then move on to other things in the community. The process of going back to the community has been challenging, but it has also provided a great learning experience to both the children and the social workers.

Different resettlement and reintegration approaches have been applied by psychosocial support agencies and are described in the proceeding section:

- Category 1: Reception center support, resettlement (and no follow up at home).
- Category 2: Reception center support, resettlement, follow up (mainly psycho-social),

but no effort made to provide any educational or training support.

- Category 3: Reception center; resettlement (inbuilt socioeconomic support post-resettlement); provision of basic education, school fees, vocational training, and other income-generation activity support.
- Category 4: Self-resettlement and reintegration (the young person returns from captivity and goes directly to the community with no support from reception center or any psychosocial agency).

It should be noted that for all these categories of support to the returning young people, there was no clear decision on which child/young person will receive what support. There were only general guidelines that have some direction. It is only in the case of the formerly abducted young mothers who were categorized as high risks and thus regarded as in need of more follow-up support in the community. But again many of them were only followed up a couple of times by the psychosocial support agencies staff.

In regard to the first category, the young people are reunited with their families but initially no follow-up effort is made. Questions have arisen on the quality, outcome, sustainability, and longevity of support provided to the former fighters and abductees from the region. Sustainable psychosocial support and mental health pathways for young men and women are not created or sufficiently aligned. In other words, while initially a plan to follow up with the young people on resettlement exists, it is never followed up due to either organizational or logistical challenges.

Similarly, for the second and third categories, while support is provided after reinsertion into the community, the interests and life goals of the young people is only addressed to some extent. The last category (4) represents no formal support at all to the young people, and it is the most problematic. This also raises the importance of strengthening psychosocial intervention at the community level, yet the veracity of the social support institutions and traditional coping methods and arrangements seemed to be overstretched and also inadequate to prepare the young people to cope with adverse effects of trauma and manage the challenges of resettlement within the community.

Moreover, the focus and targeting of interventions seemingly leave out the issues and structures that would significantly enhance the reintegration experience (Maina, 2010; Ochen, 2012). Another key issue which a critical analysis of the integration model reveals is the inability to effectively link the young people in need of support and services (psychosocial, social, and economic) to agencies, institutions, and individuals that can provide for them (Angucia, 2010; Bainomugisha, 2011). In places where certain arrangements exist, they are not systematic nor are they effectively and efficiently coordinated.

Moreover, analysis of the support strategies further suggests that many of the reintegration models leave out the critical roles of assessment and appreciation of unique issues at an individual, family (micro), community (mezzo) and national (macro) levels. While institutions and structures exist at the micro, mezzo and macro levels, the current state of practice does not provide a good framework and coordination strategy within which existing facilities and services effectively benefit formerly abducted young persons (McKay, Veale, Worthen, & Wessels, 2010). There were also little efforts to link long term psychosocial support to socioeconomic interventions that aim at general family and community transformation. Yet more recent consultations with resource persons within the community suggest that it is such unheralded interventions that could provide a good framework for the provision of psychosocial support to resettled young people within the community. During the fieldwork exercise, some key informants reflected on the activities supported by CARE International (a U.S.-funded international development organization) and suggested that the VSLA model of community socioeconomic regeneration (mezzo level) provides an important forum where the psychosocial needs and demands of members are addressed (Abola et al., 2009). Such a forum provides an environment for mutual help and psychosocial support, which can enhance coping. While the VSLA currently responds mainly to the direct needs of older household members, transferring such an approach to mobilize and organize the youth around such economic objectives as savings and to utilize the groupings to also address their psychosocial needs would be in the view of the social worker an appropriate strategy to effectively engage young people. What is important is to ensure that the group members receive relevant training in basic counseling and are provided with information for identifying unique cases and for referral to other structures for support (at the community and district level). Discussion with community members and further analysis of return support indicated that structures (at micro and mezzo level) were created to support the reintegration process. Several psychosocial agencies trained individuals within the community to provide basic counseling and other support to the young people coming from the bush. These structures took different forms and nomenclature. Some were called Community Volunteer Counselors (CVCs), others were called Community Care-Givers (CCGs), and others were known as Child Protection Committees (CPCs), which was more recent and favored by the local and central government institutions. It should be noted however, that these structures reportedly worked only during emergency situations and soon after (except CPCs). However, when funding became minimal, most of them were disbanded, leaving many of the young people unsupported. Several resettled young people indicated that they have not been able to access counseling support from the early created structures and trained individuals in a systematic and sustained manner. Any support that may have been given is due to either proximity, relationship between the young person and another person or simply by chance. With regard to the child protection committees, while they are still active, their training and orientation is not favorable to adequate psychosocial support for young people.

Implications for Developing a New Model of Care and Support for Youth Affected by Armed Conflict

Several interventions have been carried out in Northern Uganda to respond to the different phases of the conflict right from its commencement in 1986. These interventions have been carried out by state agencies comprising various government departments within the social services and social development sectors, along with other state departments. Development partners comprising international humanitarian and development agencies, and local and indigenous development agencies have also been active within the region supporting both temporary relief and remedial support, as well as the more time-factored long-term interventions. While these interventions have targeted the communities within Northern Uganda generally ranging from internally displaced communities uprooted from their homes, and other people affected by the conflict, a significant portion was devoted to support the process of rehabilitation, resettlement and reintegration of children and young people directly affected by the conflict (Allen & Schomerus, 2006). The interventions that have been reflected upon here include reception center-based support to provide remedial short term care for the formerly abducted child mothers (FACM) and other young people. This kind of support is intended to prepare them for a resettlement within the community, as well as preparing the community and the families of the young people to receive them.

A critical analysis of the interventions and support structure indicates that while support has been provided to young people and children affected by the conflict, attention to the process of support, details, and the individuated needs of the young people seem to have been largely ignored. In the opening vignette, we find that Alobo is, indeed, in need of myriad support to enable her to function adequately within the community. She is in need of support of a moral, social, and economic nature. Yet the support base she can rely on for all these kinds of support is weak, uncoordinated, and in some cases even incompetent. While Alobo can call upon her colleagues in the savings group, they are all of similar socioeconomic background and circumstances and can only offer mutual care. Her colleagues cannot offer much psychosocial support that Alobo needs for effective social functioning and for her children. Further analysis of Alobo's story thus suggests the need to rethink psychosocial support in the aftermath of conflict or a major critical event exposure. It suggests the importance of follow up support in long-term psychosocial care and support. Yet structures within the community do not adequately provide that, nor are they sustainable at the current degree of conceptualization. It is imperative to consider an approach where support for the young women, FACM or CBCs are inbuilt within a community's micro and mezzo systems. Such a system could include self-sustaining groups (e.g., the VSLA I talked about earlier). Although in other countries it could be different, structures and social workers can then train and support these groups to reach out to the young people such as Alobo and her children.

As a social worker reflecting upon the support and interventions to aid in the reintegration process, particular attention is directed to the efficacy of the long-term community based psychosocial support. Currently, no effective model of post-reinsertion psychosocial support nor structures and resources are available to support the young people who have been resettled within the community. Yet, anecdotal evidence and community interviews indicate that many young people exhibit the need for psychosocial and psychiatric support. This situation if not fully addressed could increase the incidence of mental illness in the community, increment in depression and attendant inability of young people to cope effectively with lives in their villages. Indeed, studies and consultations have indicated that issues of suicide and mental illness are on the rise within the Acholi subregion. A model of care and support post-reception center that effectively responds to both the emotional, physical and developmental needs of the young person while paying attention to rights' fulfillment should be developed. It should be noted that any attempt to develop an effective model should pay close attention to the life changes of the young persons and also determine the efficacy and applicability of a support mechanism.

The proposed psychosocial support model for young people affected by conflict should thus consider such factors as the situational realities and localities that the young people are resettled in, and linkages to development issues and wider contextual programming of other agencies. It should also include the local government structure and the prevailing opportunities within the community to provide effective psychosocial services. This is to ensure that the young people meet their needs and aspirations in order to actualize their full potentials. The support model should therefore ensure that the young people are accountable and are supported on a continuous basis by certain structures and individuals. Doing so would address their psychosocial, socioeconomic, and psycho-emotional needs as well as other social needs, which will enable them to function adequately within the community.

Interventions for Supporting Young People Affected by Armed Conflict

Children and young people who have been exposed to critical life events, including witnessing killing, rape, sexual abuse, and exploitation, require supportive care (local Ugandan context) or psychotherapy (Western discourse), which allows greater involvement between the social worker and young people in need of support. It is recognized by this social worker, however, that the support referred to in this chapter is the post-reception and rehabilitation center support. So while a series of activities and actions to support the recovery of the young persons are provided at the reception and rehabilitation centers, more support is required in the post-resettlement period to enhance reintegration chances. This study also recognizes that the support in the community would be given by community resource person (trained) working for an intervening psychosocial agency. The support provided could, however, still draw from narrative exposure therapy (NET; Schauer, Neuner, & Elbert, 2011), which specifically allows for reflection on the young person's life experiences and exposure to complex traumatic events; and other relevant social work case support and group therapy approaches. It should be remembered that these young people have in the course of their abductions been exposed to various traumatic events of a repeated nature but also to singular occurrences at different points in time. It is also possible that in the process of their reintegration through sociocultural, individual, family, and other such social circumstances, the young people will have been exposed to more complex challenges (e.g., alcoholism, prostitution, criminal behaviors, and vagrancy) as they negotiate the reintegration process in the community. It is thus crucial that the supportive relationship allows for the verbalization of feelings of the young person on all those issues. NET is a therapy method used to address complex and multiple traumas and is considered important in the case of Alobo or other such young people with similar background. NET provides opportunities for the young person in need of treatment to remember the varied events he or she has been exposed to in the order in which they occurred, when he or she is being listened to in an empathetic way. The social worker /therapist will listen attentively, encourage the client and probe for specific issues as and when deemed necessary (Schauer, Neuner, & Elbert, 2011).

According to Schauer et al. (2011), the therapist will pay special attention to and probe for emotions exhibited, cognitive behavior, and how the individual responds to the situations encountered. In this way, the experiences of the client could be linked to the events and thereby allow for processing and derivations of meanings from the stories and experiences of the client (young person).

So, in the case of Alobo, the support will include a series of meetings with the social worker where she is given an opportunity to purposefully verbalize her feelings about the experiences she has undergone. The treatment and support approach that could be used will still involve a series of actions geared towards restoring and/ or improving social functionality and reintegration outcomes on the part of the individual client (Alobo), and exploring options and avenues through which Alobo could be supported to take charge of her life. The main objective will, however, be to support psychosocial recovery and improve social outlooks and interactions of the concerned individuals.

Support provided will also depend on the situation of the young person, her coping strengths and resources, support accessed earlier before returning to the community and other social and psychosocial assistance received. It is also the view of the social worker that the psychosocial or social support developed should also consider the resources the individual could draw upon in the community such as their relatives, friends and the level of interactions at home, the significant others in the environment of the persons, drawing upon system theory approaches and the eclecticism of social work (Walker, 2012). The churches, mosques and traditional support structures that exist within the community would also be drawn upon to encapsulate the intervention support provided to the young person. Such an approach provides an avenue for ownership, sustainability and continuation of care and support within a situation/environment where the young person is accepted, appreciated and valued. For those in schools and other institutions, the resources within those institutions especially those that are acceptable to the young people should also be explored and utilized.

Support at Family Level for Young People Exposed to Traumatic Critical Events

At family level, the social worker employs an approach that supports the family to understand and appreciate the experiences of the individual who has been exposed to critical events and the kind and nature of emotions and behavioral symptoms they are likely to exhibit. It cannot be assumed that families would understand the situations of the young people. Efforts should be made to make such families aware of the needs and situations of the children and young people and their needs for support. It is the view of this social worker that this can best be done through holding a series of small group meetings revolving around key topical issues in psychosocial care of people exposed to violence and traumatic events such as our case vignette, Alobo. A series of discussions with families in such situations could be organized for the family members and significant people in the lives of the young person (Alobo). While the topics and themes to explore in group therapy sessions could be many and variant, context experience from Northern Uganda suggests that the following key issues and themes should be presented: effects of exposure to critical events in the life of the young person; new normalcy post-resettlement and adjustment to life from captivity; continued psychosocial care and role of the family in that, and signs and symptoms of post-traumatic stress disorders; the significance of high quality relationships in psychosocial adjustments; managing mood swings and behavioral challenges among young people previously exposed to trauma; supporting children and young people experiencing post-traumatic stress disorders; spousal support in post-critical event period; suicide assessment and when to seek help, and managing life transitions for victims of torture/abduction/conflict.

Beyond support to the family, mechanism for engaging with the community to create an environment where the young person (in this case, Alobo) will feel accepted and supported should also be considered. Some sessions could be for only individual (Alobo's) families and others could be joined with other families in similar situations (multi-family groups with children in similar situations as Alobo). In considering the support nature, note should be taken that some of the young people could already be experiencing long term relationships such as marriage and it is imperative that their partners are also involved in the therapy sessions so that all issues and experiences are explored and negotiated. So if, for example, Alobo was married already, her husband would be involved in the group sessions. It is also suggested that this approach be done in a nonprescriptive but facilitative and participatory manner where the issues of respect, self-determination,

nonjudgmentalism, and purposive expression of feelings are given space.

MEZZO PERSPECTIVE
Community-Based Psychosocial Support Model

Resources may consist of a reexamination and identification of opportunities within the young people's immediate environment, their family and harnessing such structures as well as a linkage to policy issues and program dynamics. While the social worker has also examined outcome issues, his main preoccupation here has been with the process of support and how these support processes, structures and arrangements have enabled or disabled the young people targeted in this study from enjoying their lives post-reinsertion (resettlement within the community). The aim, ultimately, is to suggest a response framework and model which recognizes strengths, and appreciates weaknesses and the uniqueness of the personal circumstances, personal experiences and the contextual peculiarities where the young people have resettled. While it is argued that young people resettled within the community require more support at reunion and a long-term monitoring, an assumption of "one-shoe-fits all approach" is rejected and instead a case is made for a framework which protects the individuality, contextual experience and sociocultural positioning and orientation of the young people. This is important if the emotional health and well-being of the young people are to be protected. While it is suggested that these issues be considered, it is also important to recognize the limitations of time-space and situational difficulties and challenges that arise from the governance framework. These include the macro, the prevailing political parties and structures of local government as well as the prevailing factors at the mezzo and community levels, for instance, the poverty and inaccessibility to resources, and certain cultural factors. These limitations constitute both opportunities and barriers for the resettlement and reintegration process in addition to the process of change negotiations by the actors. The young people themselves are a factor on their environment as well as their immediate family, the community, the family, the extended family, the clan systems, and other factors within the local contexts/realities in which they live. These issues and factors need to be taken into consideration to determine their impact on the overall resettlement and reintegration process.

In suggesting a new model to support young people within the community, a number of issues have been considered including the linkages that exist between service actors and the potentials for positive collaborations; spaces that can be exploited and utilized by social workers and other service providers within the service delivery framework as well as opportunities and limitations for linking micro interventions and mezzo issues within the continuum of care support to young people emerging from conflict.

MACRO PERSPECTIVE

It will also be imperative to reflect on the kind of policy and programmatic environment that must prevail for effective support to young people affected by war to be realized (macro analysis). It is important to consider the critical and proactive role that can be played by the state and the implications of all this for crisis response social work in conflict-affected communities. What is clear is that government response in a post conflict context is crucial for maintaining the peace after violent conflict. Alobo will need support from the state institutions in, for example, reclaiming her land rights in a situation where the only place she calls home is her father's land. In Northern Uganda, government responded to the major development issues by launching a recovery plan—the Peace Recovery and Development Plan (PRDP)—which considers both psychosocial and social reintegration issues and the economic and infrastructure rebuilding process in the conflict-affected region. While the PRDP implementation process has not been smooth, it has at least demonstrated the commitment of the

State to redress some of the effects of the conflict on the region.

CONCLUSION

In this chapter, the social worker has attempted to reflect on the experiences and situations of formerly abducted young people in Northern Uganda. The experience in Northern Uganda suggests that there is need to consider long-term follow-up support to children and young people affected by conflict. Such support is important for the functionality and effectiveness of their reintegration after years suffering abuse and exploitations in the hands of their oppressors. Such also applies to critical events exposure that brings a "new normal" into the lives of the children and young people. Our experience suggests that sustainable support can be achieved if it is in-built into existing family (micro) and community (mezzo) structures, while advocating for the development of program and policies which harness such structures and resources/support arrangements. This suggests the need to focus beyond the post-NGOs and actors in spite of their roles in the rehabilitation, resettlement, and reintegration phase.

While effort has been made to paint a complete picture of the experiences of the young person coming back from rebel captivity, the main emphasis has been on their post-resettlement experiences and how their psychosocial and mental health needs have been addressed in the period after their resettlement in the community. The chapter suggests that post-resettlement psychosocial support apparently has not been very well delivered in a strategic and durable way. What is required is a model that takes cognizance of human rights issues, the unique and individuated situations of the young people, contextual issue and changes, advancement in knowledge and scholarships, and other relevant issues that can guarantee more sustainable support systems that are both cost-effective and also developmental. In applying such a model issues of context, specificity, and relevance come into play and should be considered.

INTERNET RESOURCES

- Human Rights Watch: http://www.hrw.org
- Narrative Exposure Therapy: http://www.vivo.org
- Norwegian Refugee Council: http://www.nrc.no
- Refugee Law Project: http://refugeelawproject.org
- Trac FM: https://tracfm.org/p/view/408/e

DISCUSSION QUESTIONS

1. How have children and young people been affected by the conflict in Northern Uganda?

2. How can social workers effectively carry out assessment of children in need of psychosocial care after a violent or critical event exposure?

3. What micro, mezzo, and macro interventions are required for effective post-reinsertion support to children formerly associated with fighting forces?

4. How can we use resources of both a micro and mezzo nature present at community level for sustainable psychosocial support?

5. What lessons for social work practice with children and young people affected by conflict can we generate from Northern Uganda's situation?

REFERENCES

Abola, C., Omach, P., Ochen, E. A., Anena, C., & Barongo, A. (2009). *Evaluation of Norwegian development cooperation through Norwegian non-governmental organizations in Northern Uganda (2003–2008)*. Oslo, Norway: Norwegian Agency for International Development.

Allen, T., & Schomerus, M. (2006). *A hard homecoming: Lessons learnt from the reception center processes in Northern Uganda*. Retrieved from http://pdf.usaid.gov/pdf_docs/pnadi241.pdf

Angucia, M. (2010). *Broken citizenship: Formerly abducted children and their social reintegration in Northern Uganda*. Amsterdam: Rosenberg.

Annan J., Blattman, C., & Horton, R. (2006). *The State of Youth and Youth Protection in Northern Uganda: Findings from the Survey for War Affected Youth; A Report for UNICEF Uganda and AVSI*. Retrieved from http://www.sway-uganda.org/SWAY.Phase1.Final report.PDF

Bainomugisha, A. (2011). *Child soldiers in Northern Uganda: An analysis of the challenges and opportunities for reintegration and rehabilitation* (Unpublished doctoral thesis). University of Bradford, United Kingdom.

Human Rights Watch. (2006). *Abducted and abused: Renewed conflict in Northern Uganda*. New York, NY: Author.

Maina, G. M. (2010). *An analytical study of the reintegration experience of the formerly abducted children in Gulu, Northern Uganda* (Unpublished doctoral dissertation). University of Bradford, United Kingdom.

Mazurana, D., & Carlson, K. (2006). *The girl child and armed conflict: Recognizing and addressing grave violations of girls' human rights*. Paper presented at the UN Division for the Advancement of Women (DAW) in collaboration with UNICEF, Florence, Italy.

Mazurana, D., Carlson, K., Blattman, C., & Annan, J. (2008). *A way forward for assisting women and girls in Northern Uganda: Findings from phase II of the Survey for War Affected Youth*. Retrieved from http://chrisblattman.com/documents/policy/sway/SWAY.Females.RBrief.pdf

McKay, S. (2004). Reconstructing fragile lives: Girls social reintegration in Northern Uganda and Sierra Leone. *Gender and Development, 12*(3), 19–30.

McKay, S., & Mazurana, D. (2004). *Where are the girls? Girls in fighting forces in Northern Uganda, Sierra Leone and Mozambique: Their lives during and after war*. Montreal: Rights and Democracy.

McKay, S., Veale, A., Worthen, M., & Wessels, M. (2010). *Community-based reintegration of war affected young mothers: Participatory action research in Liberia, Sierra Leone and Northern Uganda*. Retrieved from http://www.crin.org/docs/par_report.pdf

Norwegian Refugee Council. (2010). *Peace recovery and development: Challenges in Northern Uganda*. Retrieved from http://www.nrc.no

Ochen, E. A. (2012). Protecting and meeting rights of children during conflict: Reflections on the activities of three indigenous social work agencies in Northern Uganda. *British Journal of Social Work Special Issue: Social Work and Political Context: Engagement and Negotiations, 42,* 1192–1212.

Oloka-Onyango, J. (2001). Constitutionalism in Africa: Yesterday, today and tomorrow. In J. Oloka-Onyango (Ed.), *Constitutionalism in Africa: Creating opportunities, facing challenges.* Kampala: Fountain.

Omach, P. (2010a). Regionalisation of rebel activities: The case of the Lord's Resistance Army. In W. Okumu & A. Ikelegbe (Eds.), *Militias, rebels, and Islamist militants: Human insecurity and state crises in Africa* (pp. 287–312). Pretoria: Institute of Strategic Studies.

Omach, P. (2010b). *Politics, conflict and peace building in Uganda.* Dusseldorf: VDM Verlag Academic.

Omara-Otunnu, A. (1987). *Politics and the military in Uganda, 1890–1985.* Oxford: McMillan Press.

Omara-Otunnu, A. (1992). The struggle for democracy in Uganda. *Journal of Modern African Studies, 30*(3), 443–463.

Refugee Law Project. (2004). *Behind the violence: Causes, consequences and the search for solutions to the war in Northern Uganda* (Working Paper No. 11). Kampala: Refugee Law Project.

Schauer, M., Neuner, F., & Elbert T. (2011). *Narrative exposure therapy: A short-term treatment for traumatic stress disorders* (2nd ed.). Cambridge, MA: Hogrefe.

United States Institute of Peace. (2010). Uganda/Lord's Resistance Army Peace Negotiations. Retrieved from http://www.usip.org/resources/ugandalords-resistance-army-peace-negotiations

Walker, S. (2012). *Effective social work with children, young people and families: Putting systems theory into practice.* Thousand Oaks, CA: Sage.

What is the major cause of suicide in Northern Uganda? (2013). *TRAC.fm.* Retrieved from http://tracfm.org/p/view/408/

CHAPTER 33

From Helplessness to Active Coping in Israel

Psychological First Aid

Shira Hantman & Moshe Farchi

CHAPTER OBJECTIVES

- Explain the development of perceived trauma;
- Describe concepts of interventions;
- Demonstrate intervention skills;
- Formulate first response intervention protocols.

CASE VIGNETTE

It was the third evening of incessant shelling in the southern city of Ofakim, Israel. Most residents were safe in their shelters. I, Shirr a third year social work student, was sitting with my supervisor in the local Psychological First Aid Center (PFAC) when an intensive care ambulance drove up. The doors opened and a young woman, more or less my age, was brought out on a stretcher. She did not speak, nor did she move as the paramedics carried her out. Her eyes were open, but her expression was hollow. She was accompanied by her parents. The paramedics reported no physical injury. As she was carried into the PFAC I felt my own pulse accelerate as the adrenaline surged through my body.

She was placed on a chair, lifeless and soulless like a block of wood, disconnected, catatonic, and totally dissociated. 'Hello, my name is Shirr, what is your name?' No response. I took her hand and asked that she squeeze it each time I squeezed hers. On the fifth attempt she responded by squeezing my hand a number of times and then began to communicate verbally, telling us her name was Michelle. "I am with you and you are not alone," I kept assuring her.

At first she gave monosyllabic answers, disclosing only a few details about herself. Eventually, she responded in more coherent sentences. We challenged her to stand up and take a few steps with us toward a designated point in the room and back. When she returned to her chair, we offered her a choice of soft drinks. She chose water and after the first gulp her face "melted" and her flat affect disappeared. She smiled.

We asked her to describe the events in chronological order. She was in the car with her mother when suddenly the air raid siren sounded; she stopped the car on the side of the road, encouraged her mother to step out quickly, and they both lay on the ground with hands over their heads. She insists that she saw the missile and at that second she knew that there was nothing she could have done. She felt totally helpless. She heard the very loud boom, and all she could remember was the smell of gunpowder and her mother screaming and the silence following the boom. The next thing she remembered was just now, talking to us. Throughout the entire intervention she was dissociative and her progress was very slow. We noted that there were numerous gaps in her story and much displacement and disorder. We questioned her, trying to help her reconstruct the missing content of her story and rearrange it chronologically, while simultaneously reassessing her condition.

She started walking on her own with little support from us. Throughout the entire time, we encouraged her to continue talking and repeat her story, adding new information that created a coherent narrative beginning a few minutes before the event and ending in the present. After 30 minutes, I noticed that her verbal abilities had improved significantly. She laughed when I joked with her and called me by my name. She was back! I asked her what she felt her level of anxiety was at this moment (1 = low, 10 = high); after an interval of nearly 40 minutes, she answered, "Three." I asked what she thought her anxiety level was when she arrived at the center. She answered, "Ten." We explained to her what she should expect during the coming days and encouraged her to return to her normal routine and activities.

INTRODUCTION: WHAT MAKES AN EVENT TRAUMATIC?

Psychosocial responses to traumatic events at the individual and community level have received growing attention in recent years. The role of the mental health practitioner has come to be recognized as an important buffer in the development of post-traumatic stress disorder (PTSD; Rowlands, 2013).

A traumatic event is defined as an experience that causes physical, emotional, or psychological distress or harm. It is an event that is perceived and experienced as a threat to one's personal sense of safety and to the stability of one's world (Van der Kolk et al., 1996). However, individual reactions are diverse. Not all people who experience a potentially traumatic event will perceive the event as traumatic. Perception of such an event is rooted in the individual sense of threat and resulting sense of helplessness (American Psychiatric Association [APA], 2013).

Unlike routine life, traumatic or emergency situations are unexpected, unstructured events—an individual does not know where or when they will occur or who will be in need of help. Such a situation demands among other things, instant mental health interventions and adaptation of these interventions to the particular characteristics of the event (Schreiber et al., 2004). "First response" in these situations is of utmost importance: immediate, focused and efficient interventions are beneficial for the reduction of acute stress reactions and a return to normal functioning as well as decreasing risk for future onset of post-traumatic symptoms (Shapiro, 2012).

It has been estimated by the Israel Home front Command (Colonel A. Bar, personal communication, January 4, 2010) that on the micro and macro levels, the ratio between casualties suffering from physical injuries and mental health injuries is 1:4–1:8. In other words, for every individual incurring a physical injury, four to eight will suffer from acute anxiety and may develop an Acute Stress Reaction (ASR; APA, 2013). These figures emphasize the importance of developing a working model by which social work practitioners are trained to provide psychological first aid (PFA) as early as possible (Cacciatore, Carlson, Klimek, Michaelis, & Steffan, 2011). Accordingly, the Israeli welfare system has designated social workers to be the first responders in time of emergencies. Therefore, providing specific training for first responders is crucial. It is important that social workers be equipped not only with basic intervention techniques but also with extensive knowledge of the biopsychosocial aspects of trauma.

The aim of this chapter is to provide a first response practice model for social workers that equips them with the knowledge base and intervention skills necessary to manage and assist others with traumatic events. This model is based on the broad hands-on experience that social workers in Israel have had over the past two decades intervening in natural disasters and terror attacks. In light of the understanding that while interventions in emergencies are brief, at times lasting only seconds or minutes, their subsequent consequences may reverberate for many years after the event (Herman, 1992).

MICRO PERSPECTIVE: PERCEIVED PSYCHOLOGICAL TRAUMA

Assessment in the context of PFA must be a rapid, concise, and accurate process. Three major symptom clusters are assessed in clients. The first is the acute stress reaction, demonstrated by the existence of fear, threat, and helplessness. The second is the

therapist's functional assessment of the client: dependency, motivation to return home, verbal fluency, controlled motor activity, and nonintrusive memories. The third is assessment of the client's hyperactivity related to the sympathetic system: cold sweat, hyperventilation, hands/legs shaking, increased heart rate, reddish face, and "cold feeling."

When Michelle described the event, she was talking about two major factors that led to her seemingly catatonic reaction: (1) a huge existential threat (she heard and could even see the rocket coming toward her) and (2) a total sense of helplessness (she immediately realized that she could do nothing about it).

The combination of these two factors created a sensation of *perceived trauma* (WHO, 1992) rating 10 on a scale from 1 (low) to 10 (high), as demonstrated in Figure 33.1.

Because threat and the sense of helplessness are both subjective, each person will experience them differently. An event can be very frightening for one person and be perceived as traumatic but can be no more than a challenging event for another person. Whereas Michelle experienced total helplessness, Shirr, not much older than Michelle but in a professional position, when faced with an adverse situation, would react *actively and effectively* rather than helplessly and therefore would not perceive the event as traumatic.

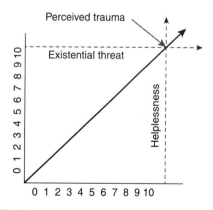

Figure 33.1 The Perceived Trauma: Existential Threat vs. Sense of Helplessness

The Timeline of Perceived Trauma. We know when the trauma begins, but when will it end? As we have just seen, the perceived trauma happens only when helplessness and huge threats join together. Figure 33.2 demonstrates the timeline of the perceived trauma.

The Neuropsychology or Neurobiology of Acute Stress Reaction: The Use of Cognitive Communication. The limbic system controls the autonomous reactions, that is, those not dictated by cognition and will (e.g., hormonal secretion, accelerated heart rate, increased blood pressure and perspiration). The limbic system includes the limbic lobe and the amygdala. These are the brain areas that are implicated in the stress

response. The amygdala is the integrative center for emotions and motivation. The limbic lobe is responsible for automatic physiological reactions (e.g., blood pressure, heart rate) and reactions (defense instincts). The frontal cortex is in charge of our ability to think, choose, prioritize, and make decisions. Yet, hyperactivity of the amygdala leads to hyperactivity of the limbic lobe and for deactivation of the frontal cortex. Deactivation of the frontal cortex results in a significant reduction in our ability to think, make decisions, and prioritize (Bremner, 2006). All these lead to a sense of helplessness, which is one of the major parameters for perceiving the event as traumatic. Figure 33.3 describes this process.

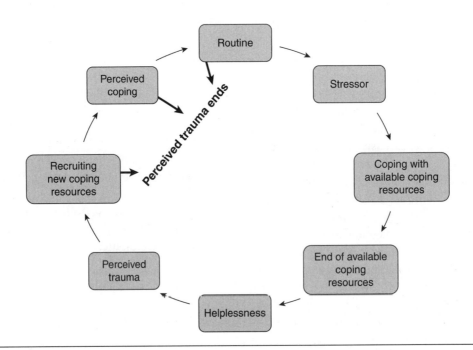

Figure 33.2   Timeline of Perceived Trauma

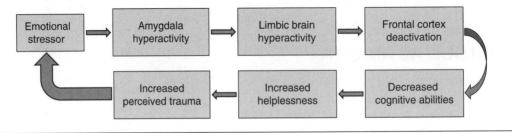

Figure 33.3   The Impact of the Emotional Stressor on Perceived Trauma

The outcome of this process can be surprising for mental health personnel: Using emotional communication channels during the acute phase increases and worsens the perceived trauma and also increases the risk for future PTSD. This is what Shirr was doing with Michelle: Instead of using ventilation with her at an emotional level, she used structured cognitive communication aimed to activate Michelle's prefrontal cortex and help her make sense of the event.

The Traumatic Memory. In the event of a perceived trauma, our sympathetic system become hyper active, sharpening our senses. As a result, every detail of the event becomes highly significant and is stored in our working memory. Our five senses (sight, smell, taste, touch, and hearing) are transmitting an enormous amount of data over a very short period into our working memory. This overload makes it difficult to differentiate between significant and trivial details confusing the chronological continuum of the event. This continuum is extremely important for defining and experiencing a sense of closure of the event. If the event has no clear conclusion, it will continue and continue, creating nagging, intrusive thoughts that refuse to heal. Michelle could not differentiate between the various details of the event; only after she was able to reconstruct her story from beginning to end did she achieve closure.

Reactions to perceived trauma can be divided into a number of stages:

1. Acute Stress Reaction (ASR; 0–48 hours post event): occurs when symptoms develop due to a particularly stressful event that may pose a perceived existential threat to one's life, followed by a total sense of helplessness. Since these two factors are subjective, each person might perceive and react differently to the same event.

2. ASR symptoms: There are a wide range of symptoms occurring during the acute stress stage (Soldatos, Paparrigopoulos, Pappa, & Christodoulou, 2006). The International Classification of Diseases (ICD-10) describes three major elements that create the ASR: fear, threat, and helplessness—all of them must be extreme (World Health Organization [WHO], 1992). These elements cause a chain reaction.

3. Confusion and disorientation: The "flooding" of information pouring in from all five senses that are "photographing" the event from a variety of angles causes difficulty in organizing the event's chronological order, making it impossible for the individual to define its beginning, middle, and end.

4. Loneliness: Helplessness causes the feeling of aloneness.

5. Hysteria: A state of "psychomotoric agitation" is a reaction characterized by extensive ineffective movement and verbal expression. The sympathetic nervous system is in a hyperactivation mode, increasing pulse, blood pressure, and general metabolism.

6. Catatonia: Hypertonus of the muscles (spasm) causes a feeling of "paralysis." The sympathetic system is in a hyperactive mode that increases pulse, blood pressure, and general metabolism, but unlike hysteria, this hyperactivity is trapped in a paralyzed hypertensive body. This state can create hyperventilation, confusion, and frustration, while cognitive functioning continues.

7. Dissociation: may be expressed in *full dissociation*, aimed to detach the person's consciousness from reality, creating a flat affect with no ability to communicate and cooperate with others or *partial dissociation*, a state in which the individual is active but partially dissociated. This is characteristic of first responders (physicians, police, firefighters, and social workers) who are exposed to extreme events that require them to be emotionally detached in order to ensure optimal functionality.

Michelle was brought into the center in a catatonic-dissociative condition that gradually dissipated, revealing her confusion and disorientation.

Acute Stress Disorder

Acute stress disorder (ASD) occurs 48 hours to one month post event and is the second stage of the reaction to perceived trauma. This stage is characterized by a clustering of the previous symptoms into three main groups (APA, 2013).

Intrusion. Various flashbacks from the incidents of the perceived trauma appear both as photographs and as film clips. These flashbacks, known as *intrusive thoughts,* include other memories of the event such as noises, taste, and touch, turning it into a threatening, multidimensional live film.

Avoidance. In an effort to depress the intrusive thought phenomena, the individual makes every possible effort to avoid any situation in which he or she might be reminded of the event.

Arousal. A reaction to the above hyper arousal symptoms that develops in response to stimuli reminiscent of the trauma (e.g., difficulty sleeping, irritability, poor concentration, hyper vigilance, an exaggerated startle response, and motor restlessness).

ASD lasts, in most cases, for approximately one month. While it is not complicated to treat, the afflicted individual feels miserable, primarily because of the various symptoms he or she is experiencing, and the inability to control them. If the ASD has not receded after a month's time, whether spontaneously or through treatment, the individual will likely advance to the next stage of the disorder spectrum to PTSD.

The immediate intervention that Michelle experienced provided her with the opportunity to terminate the deterioration of the ASR she experienced into ASD and eventually prevented her from developing PTSD.

Posttraumatic Stress Disorder

PTSD occurs from one month following the traumatic event until approximately one year or longer, in cases of prolonged and chronic PTSD (APA, 2013). The event is commonly relived by the individual through intrusive, recurrent recollections, flashbacks and nightmares. There is an intense psychological distress reaction whenever the individual encounters situations reminiscent of the trauma or aspects of it (e.g., anniversaries of the trauma). In many cases there will be incidents of psychological amnesia (i.e., the repression and distortion of memories pertaining to the traumatic event).

Among trauma survivors, those suffering from PTSD are in a state of constant agitation, restlessness, nervousness, have a tendency to chain smoke, and have sensitivity to noise (WHO, 1992). Social support is an important component that influences the individual's resilience (Ellis, Nixon, & Williamson, 2009). Love, support and the understanding of those individuals that are close to the survivor will enhance resilient coping patterns whereas feelings of rejection and abandonment will increase vulnerability.

Chronic Post-traumatic Stress Disorder

Chronic post-traumatic stress disorder (CPTSD) occurs from one year after initial exposure to perceived trauma and becomes a chronic condition (APA, 2013). This stage is very similar to PTSD with one clear difference: The individual feels that from now on, the symptoms will be an integral part of his life and, in most cases, he or she is correct. However, less than 5% of the population exposed to an event that was perceived as traumatic will, in fact, reach the syndrome's chronic stage. It is important to note that the symptoms are similar to ASD; however, the prognosis worsens as the stages progress (APA, 2013).

Coping and Resilience. There are many ways of coping with stress. Their effectiveness depends on the type of stressor, the particular individual and the circumstances. Lazarus (1991) and Lazarus and Folkman (1984) suggested two types of coping responses, "emotion focused" and "problem focused": (1) *Emotion-focused coping* involves trying to reduce the negative emotional responses associated with stress, such as embarrassment, fear, anxiety, depression, excitement, and frustration. This may be the only realistic option when the source of stress is outside the person's control. Drug therapy can be seen as emotion-focused coping as it focuses on the arousal caused by stress and not the problem. Emotion-focused strategies include keeping oneself busy, letting off steam, praying, ignoring the situation in the hope that it will go away, distracting oneself, and preparing to expect the worse; (2) *Problem-focused coping* (PFC) targets the causes of stress in practical ways by tackling the problem or stressful situation that is causing stress, consequently directly reducing the stress. Problem-focused strategies aim to remove or reduce the cause of the stressor (McCleod, 2010). Strategies include *taking control* by escaping from the stress or removing it; *information seeking* to understand the situation; and *evaluating the pros and cons* of different options for dealing with the stressor. Michelle was using PFC: During the event she was focusing on activating herself and her mother, encouraging her mother to get out of the car, trying to protect her from the missile with her own body, and covering her head with her hands.

The trauma does not occur solely because of the threat, but rather simultaneously, as a consequence of the perception of existence or lack of resources necessary to cope with the situation. This is the explanation for the subjectivity of the trauma: We all have various resources, adapted to our particular habits and lifestyles. However, not all these resources can be used effectively in response to the threat. During emergencies we tend to use those resources that are available and can contribute effectively to coping with the event reducing the sense of helplessness and increasing resilience. Michelle was using mostly her physical resources, although generally she has a much wider pool of resources.

The term *resilience* matured as a term during the 1970s (Garmezy, 1971) to describe an individual's ongoing efforts to cope in general with daily hardships, and specifically with stress, while at the same time maintaining a stable balance throughout life. Resilience refers to a dynamic process encompassing positive adaptation within the context of significant adversity. Implicit within this notion are two critical conditions: (1) exposure to significant threat or severe adversity, and (2) the achievement of positive adaptation despite major assaults on the developmental process (Luthar et al., 2000; Masten et al.,1990; Rutter, 1990).

Most individuals do, in fact, perceive various situations as traumatic during their lives; yet they continue to live and think in a positive manner, exhibiting only a slight disruption in their normal functioning during the specific period. The extent to which we can live in such a fashion, testifies to the measure of our emotional resilience. This is not to say that resilient individuals do not experience sadness following loss, but rather their general level of functionality is maintained (Harvey, 2007; Mancini & Bonnano, 2006).

One of the leading theories supporting this notion is Hobfoll's Conservation of Resources Theory (Hobfoll, 2001). It is based on the supposition that people strive to retain, protect, and build resources and that what is threatening to them is the potential or actual loss of these valued resources. These resources can come in the form of an object, state of being, personal characteristics and energies and differ from one person to the next; and are culturally diverse. Hobfoll (2001) identifies 74 specific resources classified according to four main categories: (1) material resources (e.g., home, car); (2) personal resources, with an emphasis on social support; (3) resources relating to the individual's living conditions; and (4) resources such as money, knowledge and credit, and so on. The strength and intensity of any one resource is determined by individual, subjective interpretation. It is these resources that provide the individual with the necessary strength and resilience to cope with challenging and potentially traumatic events

This approach states that the effect of stress on an individual depends first and foremost on the perceived and/or tangible loss of one's resources. It is from this idea that the two principles of the Conservation of Resource Theory stem:

1. People who lack resources are more sensitive and vulnerable to resource loss, so that any initial loss predicts an additional future loss of resources.

2. People who conserve their resources over time tend to accumulate additional resources that can be useful in future events (Hobfoll, 2001).

This model suggests that resilience reflects humans' constant and ongoing efforts to cope with adversity, hardships, and crises. These efforts strengthen the individual during times of reduced organizational capacities. Therefore, during crises, the primary objective is to restore to the individual his ability to function, by identifying and developing coping skills that are situation specific (Lahad & Ben-Nesher, 2008). There is, however, an additional possibility that the threat itself encourages the creation of new resiliency resources. These resources are accrued to promote effective coping and resistance of the occurring threat. Forty-eight hours following the intervention at the PFAC, Michelle was back to her normal functioning, fully independent and busy with her applications for her academic studies.

First Responders

One of the conclusions of the above discussion is the importance of immediate, professional intervention following a traumatic event. It is not surprising that the role of the 'first responder' in emergencies is intrinsic to the social work profession. "Understanding of grief counseling, crisis intervention and the trauma process represents the core professional education for social workers" (Rowlands, 2013, p.131). Social work has traditionally defined one of its roles as restoring individuals to normative functioning. The holistic and strength based approaches coupled with the practice values and ethics are at the heart of the profession (Farchi, Cohen & Mosek 2013; Saleebey, 2006). This is why social workers can be seen at the forefront of traumatic interventions.

A Practice Protocol for Emergency and Disaster Response

Acute Stress Reaction

Early intervention in acute trauma situations is based on the assumption that the earlier the intervention, the more likely that the victim will return to normal functioning. There is a brief window of opportunity: The first window opens during the initial 48 hours, when proper and effective intervention can very well prevent further deterioration to the ASD stage and certainly to the PTSD stage. The second window occurs during the first month of post event exposure, when focused intervention can reduce the chances of a subsequent development of PTSD (Campfield & Hills, 2001; Solomon, 1993). It is important to note that the significance of early intervention has yet to be sufficiently researched and therefore remains a matter of contention between researchers and practitioners in the field. Nevertheless, various clinical experiments do in fact report noteworthy improvement among those who received early intervention. In Israel, a concept encouraging intervention at the earliest possible stages has been formulated and adopted for use in hospitals in the military mental health unit of the Israel Defense Forces (IDF; Farchi, 2010) and in civilian networks.

The intervention among stress victims is divided into two main stages:

1. The immediate stage. The ASR stage is treated on scene, in an ER or a Stress Trauma Treatment Center.

2. The acute stage. The ASD stage continues, generally following the immediate stage for the duration of one month following the event. This stage is treated on an ambulatory basis in clinics/aid centers/mental health centers and/or welfare service departments in the community.

Intervention at the ASR Stage

Psychological: The earliest interventions aim to reduce helplessness and increase self-efficacy.

Neurological: Decrease dominance of the limbic lobe and increase levels of prefrontal cortex activity. The principles supporting these interventions, known as PIE, were formulated as early as World War I (Jones, Thomas & Ironside, 2007).

Proximity: The intervention takes place at a location relatively close to the site of the event, by individuals from the nearest mental health services.

Immediacy: The intervention takes place as soon as possible providing victims with fresh air, social and emotional support and initial confirmation of the event.

Expectation: Assure the victim that his or her reactions are normal and temporary and he will soon return to his normal functioning.

This intervention was illustrated in the case described at the beginning of the chapter.

Zone 1: On-Scene Intervention

Zone 1 is the scene of the traumatic event: *Michelle and her mother continue to lie on the ground long after the rocket exploded. They are picked up by the paramedics who happen to drive by.* They are at the acute stage, suffering from a regressive reaction. They feel very small and insignificant in light of their inability to react effectively to the threat. Their instinctive reaction is to sever touch with reality.

The main risks at this stage include (a) "infecting" people close by with similar anxiety reactions, and consequently losing control of the event (especially in the case of a multiple casualty event); (b) reinforcement of helplessness, threat, and fear; (c) progressive reduction in the victim's cooperation; (d) glorification of the rescuer and reduction of the victim's sense of self-efficacy and effectiveness.

Locating the ASRs in Zone 1

Anxiety victims are identified by the following criteria:

1. Ineffective activity, either catatonic or agitated-hysterical

2. "Flat" (facial expression) affect

3. Inability to execute simple tasks and total dependency on responders

4. Inability to assist others

5. Acute anxiety reactions of close family and friends

6. Aggressive and/or use of verbal and physical violence towards responders

The Six-C's Model: First Responders Psychological First Aid

The Need for Nonprofessional Intervention During Emergencies

Disasters have serious consequences for both mental and physical health. Norris (2005), in a review of 220 samples from natural and human-made disasters, found that the overall impairment was very severe in 20.9% and severe in 38.2% of the samples, concluding that the sheer number of affected people demands a public health or collective approach. Dyregrov (2008) studied the challenges involved in early and long-term intervention to reduce distress and prevent chronic mental health problems after disasters. Their main conclusion was that there is no justification for mental health responses to be delayed for weeks after a disaster occurs. Hobfoll et al. (2007) recommended five core principles that should be used to guide intervention efforts in communities following exposure to crises and emergencies: (1) a sense of safety, (2) calming, (3) a sense of self- and community efficacy, (4) connectedness, and (5) hope. These most important recommendations underline again the need for immediate psychological interventions, yet they were aimed originally at professional teams and are focused on the "what to do" and not on the "how to do it."

Volunteers are among the most common nonprofessional group who are involved during crises and emergencies. In the absence of a formal volunteer protocol management system, individuals seek to perform services using only their own judgment which may sometimes cause more chaos than the event itself in the affected community (Fernandez, Barbera, & Van Dorp, 2006). The WHO has developed a comprehensive manual for PFA. Yet, this manual is stated to be applicable only for low- and middle-income countries and is not universal (WHO, 1992). Yet another WHO manual states that the initial on-scene PFA intervention can also be provided by nonprofessional helpers. Lack of standard tools for nonprofessionals can create chaos and improper interventions. Just as in primary physical first aid, in which every person should know how to provide the very basic assistance in order to help physically injured people, the same need exists in the case of PFA. There is a need to provide a common knowledge base for all community levels and provide large-scale but brief interventions that can reduce distress sufficiently so that survivors can benefit from whatever other supports are available in their community. This common knowledge is in the process of being assimilated into the education system in Israel, starting from primary schools. We hope that this will dramatically increase community resilience and decrease the dependency on professional mental health providers to be present in each and every disaster zone.

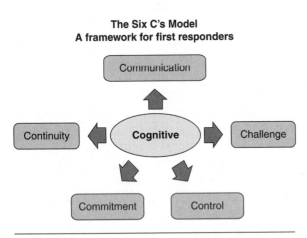

The Six C's Model
A framework for first responders

Figure 33.4 Six C's Intervention Domains

SOURCE: Farchi, M. (2013). The Six-C's Model - Guidelines for the Emergency Mental Health Providers. Paper presented at the XIII ESTSS Conference, Bologna, Italy.

The Six C'S model was created to fill this gap and to provide a simple user-friendly model based on neurobiological and psychosocial aspects.

The Six C's model addresses the need to standardize mental health interventions during ASR and to *shift the person from a helpless victim to a coping survivor*. It is based on four concepts. *Hardiness* (Kobasa, 1979; Maddi, 2006) is composed of commitment, control, and challenge. They provide the needed courage and motivation to turn stressful circumstances from potential disasters into opportunities for personal growth, *Sense of coherence* (Antonovsky, 1979) describes the psychological, social, and cultural resources that people can and do use successfully in resisting illness. It is a way of making sense of the world and is a major factor in determining how well a person manages stress and stays healthy. *Self-efficacy* (Bandura, 1988) is the belief in one's ability to influence events that affect one's life. *Neurobiology* reflects the relation between the limbic system and the prefrontal cortex during stressful events (Gidron et al., 2001). Figure 33.4 presents the Six C's intervention domains.

Cognitive Communication. In extreme stress situations, functioning transfers from the frontal lobe associated with complex activity and thoughts to the limbic lobe that is associated with emotions and motivation. Cognitive communication activates the frontal lobe and weakens the limbic lobe's control in order to restore self-efficacy and perception, and enhance coping. This can be accomplished as follows:

1. The care provider introduces himself and describes the location.

2. Directed personal questioning: "What is your name?" "Where do you live?" "How old are you?" and "Where do you work/study?"

3. Time-based questions: "How long have you been here?" "How did you get here?"

4. Contextual questions: "What did you see?" "What did you do?" "Where did you go?"

Challenge. Activation through physical and cognitive challenges decreases the victim's regressive process and restores a sense of self-efficacy (e.g., walk person around the room and ask questions regarding past and present activities; rearrange objects in the room).

Control. Activation with encouragement to choose from different options. This provides the victim with a sense of control over his situation while empowering him. Initially, the options are simple and slowly progress to more complex choices (e.g., allow person to select between alternatives, "Do you want to call now or later?" "Do you want to wait a few minutes before going back or should we stop now?"). *Michelle was asked where she wanted to sit.*

Commitment. Verbal commitment to one's safety alleviates the feeling of loneliness that is characteristic of the initial stages of ASR. Responder's commitment provides the person with a support system (e.g., responder to Michelle: "From now on I am here and not going anywhere until you feel better").

Continuity. Restructuring one's memory into a logical chronological sequence in order to prevent disorientation on both the chronological level and the perception of the event's occurrences. Reorganization of the event will alleviate anxiety and stress (e.g., responder to Michelle: "Tell me what happened . . . and what happened after that").

In summary, Zone 1 interventions must be efficient and focused and cognitive behavioral therapy (CBT) based, while emphasizing activation of the victim and enhancing self-efficacy in the first few minutes after the event.

Shirr's story is now clearer. Shirr was functioning according to the Six C's model. First she tried to establish verbal *cognitive communication* with Michelle. Not having succeeded to establish verbal communication, Shirr tried to bypass the lack of verbal communication with the hand squeezing protocol. This protocol plus continuous cognitive communication created the initial cooperation with Michelle. Shirr created the *commitment* by stating to Michelle that she was with her. The next step was *challenging* Michelle to stand and start walking. In order to establish a *sense of control*, Shirr encouraged her to choose between different options (where to sit, what to drink, where to go in the room). When cognitive communication was established more properly, Shirr encouraged Michelle to talk about the event and helped her to put the events into the right chronological order. That was done to establish the sense of *continuity* and to underline that the threatening event was already over.

MEZZO PERSPECTIVE: GROUP INTERVENTIONS

Group intervention principles are fairly similar to individual interventions. However, group intervention has both organizational and therapeutic advantages. It saves professional manpower. This is particularly important in case of mass casualty events in which there generally is a shortage of professional first responders. While individual intervention requires one care provider per casualty, group interventions can be implemented with two care providers for up to 12 participants per hour (Somer & Bleich, 2005). The therapeutic advantage is that the group enables participants to conduct a more detailed examination of the event as each one adds missing details.

The objective of group intervention is to restore the victims' sense of familiarity and control and reduce disorientation through group dynamics (Somer & Bleich, 2005). The group consists of individuals who have recently undergone a similar experience. This shared environment reduces loneliness and provides mutual support. The ability of each member to give or receive support contributes to creating a safe environment and facilitating a feeling of control and autonomy. The group members assist each other in reconstructing their narrative of the event's occurrences while filling in missing details. Reconstruction improves understanding of the difficult event being in the past and not in the present. Survivors, who often express negative interpretations related to their functioning during the event, receive an opportunity to reframe their narrative, thereby presenting their actions in a more positive light. Initiated and controlled repetition of the event's details serve to reduce disorderly and overpowering intrusive thoughts. It also facilitates desensitization—a central objective in any CBT.

A Recommended Protocol for Immediate Group Interventions Following Exposure to an Emergency or Disaster

Previous attempts at treating the ASR and in prevention of PTSD have often included various types of debriefing, which mostly have failed to prevent the ASD and PTSD (Arendt & Elklit, 2001; Mansdorf, 2008; Rose, Bisson, Churchill, & Wessely, 2002). Furthermore, reviews of the effectiveness of early interventions in preventing PTSD have concluded either that there is no evidence for their effectiveness (Roberts et al., 2009) or that only CBT may prevent PTSD (Roberts et al., 2010). Similarly, a recent review of 19 intervention trials found no evidence for debriefing and some evidence for the effectiveness of early trauma-focused CBT (Forneris et al., 2013). Neuroscientific studies have revealed that perceived trauma is processed in fragmented and implicit memory processes (Van der Kolk & Fisler, 1995; Foa, Rothbaum, Riggs, & Murdock, 1991; Hendler et al., 2003) and pathological conditions are associated with trauma processing in brain regions reflecting little prefrontal and enhanced limbic activation (Shin et al., 2004). Such findings call for an attempt to shift the processing of traumatic memories from fragmented and limbic manners to more organized and prefrontal manners. It is possible that our focus may need to shift from relatively simplistic trauma narrative-based and emotional ventilation based interventions to interventions based on a neuroscientific rationale and/or on intervention strategies from stress models, to reduce the ASR and, ultimately, to prevent PTSD and enhance recovery.

Based on the Six C's Activation Model, the objective is to return participants to routine functioning by taking the following steps:

1. Explain the session's objective;

2. Summarize the event from the moderator's point of view;

3. Emphasize the challenges, both individual and collective;

4. Ask group members to add information/facts;

5. Have participants share their coping strategies in each stage of the event;

6. Have group members suggest points for improvement;

7. Have a moderator to improve strategies (i.e., what should be conserved and what should be improved, building on strengths);

8. Define a detailed and concrete timeline, beginning with the session and concluding with a return to normal routine;

9. Group members summarize the session;

10. Moderator summarizes the session.

Helping the Helpers

Working with traumatized clients can have profound, long-lasting, and harmful effects on the helpers. Various terms to describe the phenomenon have been suggested. Herman (1992) used the term *traumatic countertransference* to describe the reactions that are experienced when the therapist's traumatic past experiences are triggered during therapeutic intervention with traumatized clients. Figley (1995) offered the term *compassion fatigue* to describe the stress resulting from helping or wanting to help traumatized or suffering clients. Eth and Pynoos (1985), and Mollica (1988) suggested that therapists become "infected" by contagious PTSD symptoms. Likewise, McCann and Pearlman (1990) proposed the concept of vicarious traumatization (VT) to portray the cumulative negative effects of engaging in a therapeutic relationship with trauma victims. This concept is based on a constructivist self-development theory (McCann & Pearlman, 1990; Pearlman & Saakvitne, 1995) and is assumed to affect the same general aspects of self as those affected by traumatic life events: self-capacities (e.g., management of affect, sense of self-worth), frames of reference (e.g., identity, worldview), basic beliefs and psychological needs (e.g., safety, esteem, control), and realms of perception and memory (e.g., verbal, somatic, visual imagery).

Stressors Associated With First Responder Work

- Exposure to unpredictable physical danger;
- Encounter with violent death and human remains;
- Encounter with suffering of others;
- Negative perceptions of disaster and assistance being offered;
- Long hours, erratic work schedules, extreme fatigue;
- Cross-cultural differences between workers and community;
- Lack of adequate housing;
- Communication breakdowns;
- Low funding/allocation of resources;
- Overidentification with victims;
- Injury of self or close associate;
- Pre-existing stress or traumatization;
- Low level of training or preparedness;
- Self-expectations;
- Low level of social support.

Helping the Helper Protocol

- Self-preparation before the event;
- Before arriving to the disaster zone:
  - *Cognitive*: Go over all the main protocols that are the most common and most expected;
  - *Communication*: Consult with colleagues;
  - *Challenge* yourself with more unexpected scenarios;
  - *Control*: Try to choose between different intervention options for the expected scenario;
  - *Continuity*: Go over (imaginary) different stages of the most expected protocol from beginning to end.

MACRO PERSPECTIVE: SOCIAL WORK INTERVENTIONS IN TRAUMA AND EMERGENCIES: THE ISRAELI EXPERIENCE

The Israeli reality requires social workers in general, and particularly those employed in Social Service agencies and hospitals, to have emergency response skills. Unfortunately, Israeli social workers have had too much hands-on experience. The ongoing terror attacks, suicide bombers, Scud missiles, and sniper killings on the borders, in addition to natural disasters, have demanded immediate and efficient professional response on the part of our practitioners. The common denominator of all these interventions is the need for immediate and first-hand response addressing multiple needs.

Until 2006, each organization and agency implemented its own protocol. In 2006, with the outbreak of the Second Lebanon War, and following a growing understanding of the importance of developing a standardized policy for first response intervention, a number of Stress & Trauma Treatment Centers were opened. The rationale of these centers was the understanding that the best location for these centers was not within the confines of the ER or local hospitals, but rather in specially designated areas, unrelated to any specific "illness."

The Centers' objectives are to (1) provide initial care to anxiety and trauma casualties in the acute stage that occurs from the moment of injury to two days following (ASR); (2) create a neutral setting in the community in conjunction with local social services that would not have the stigma of physical or mental illness; and (3) create a location to which stress casualties can be quickly evacuated.

The number of identified anxiety casualties during the Second Lebanon War was nearly 2,700 individuals. Only 500 of those injured were treated at seven Stress and Trauma Treatment Centers set up in Northern Israel (from Tiberius to Nahariya). A number of years later, in 2008, during Operation Cast Lead, of the approximately 1,800 individuals who were identified as suffering from anxiety symptoms, 1,300 were treated in the various Stress and Trauma Treatment Centers. By the time Operation "Pillar of Defense" took place in 2012, the overwhelming majority of anxiety casualties received treatment in Stress and Trauma Treatment Centers and not in hospital emergency rooms. This, obviously, has an important effect on the quality of treatment that is provided by both hospitals, who can offer better care for the physically injured and the Centers who can provide better care for those in need of psychological first aid. Furthermore, Israel's National Insurance Institute, responsible for compensation related to civilian war injuries, has recognized for the very first time, the forms issued by the Stress and Trauma Treatment Centers as an official medical document for all stress related compensation claims.

A Community Intervention Case Study: The Town of Ofakim

The vignette described at the opening of the chapter depicts one story of one person out of many residents in the Ofakim community.

Ofakim is a small town in the south of Israel recently targeted by the Hammas rockets. Our interventions were based on the Six C's protocol as an "umbrella" model (see Figure 33.5).

In addition, a more focused intervention covered three areas:

1. 24/7 hotline available to those individuals who were too frightened to leave their home bomb shelters and reach the PFA center. Most calls were from parents asking for advice regarding their children's anxieties and stress caused by the massive rocket and missile attacks.

2. Face-to-face individual or small group treatment for those who came to the centers.

3. Community outreach: Initiated day and night patrols throughout the various neighborhoods and shelters were conducted by students wearing orange glowing vests so that they could be identified by the residents. People identified as suffering from ASR were treated in place.

Results of the Interventions

Over a period of eight days, 250 individuals were treated for various stress reactions in the towns of Ofakim and Kiryat Malachi. None of the patients required hospitalization or even referral to a hospital. Even the most acute cases of stress showed significant recovery after no more than 45 minutes of treatment. The use of the Six C's model proved its effectiveness as a basic model for stress interventions (see Figure 33.6).

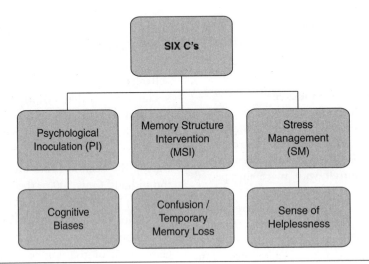

Figure 33.5 Advanced Interventions for Zone 2

SOURCES: Farchi and Gidron (2014).

Changes in Anxiety Level Before and After Six C's Orientation (using MSI + VB, PI, SM)				
Anxiety symptoms	Mean before	Mean after	t-test	Significance
Anxiety level (autonomic reactions, emotional balance)	4.9	2.12	6.90	P<.000
Anxiety level–patient report	8.24	4.23	10.03	P<.000
Anxiety level–therapist estimation	4.00	2.32	3.3	P<.001

Figure 33.6   Results of the Intervention

SOURCES: Farchi (2013).

The combined working model of treatment at the Center, telephone hotline, and initiated patrols in the community proved most effective in providing the local residents with a sense of safety and increased community resilience (see Figure 33.7).

CONCLUSION

The aim of this chapter was to identify the mental health needs of civilians exposed to emergency and disaster events and delineate the role of the social worker as a first responder. Traditionally seen as an agent of social change, social workers are expected to provide immediate, precise and effective interventions, aimed at restoring normative functioning to the community, the group and the individual. They work as part of a team of emergency workers (e.g., medical, EMT, firefighters, Search and Rescue (SR) units, forensic teams, K-9 search units, and other forces).

Specifically, in the event of an emergency situation this means alleviating stress symptoms and enhancing self-efficacy and resilience in those individuals impacted by potentially traumatic events. This is implemented by (1) opening and managing information centers; (2) transmitting relevant information to those calling in for assistance; (3) providing assistance and emotional support to individuals suffering from ASR and their families; and (4) accompanying family members to the morgue/forensic center in the event of a death.

While this concept focuses on the many needs that arise during emergencies, and the relevant effective interventions, it also emphasizes the need to provide appropriate training to enable these functions. This type of training is rarely offered in the basic Bachelor of Social Work curriculum and only partially implemented in a number of graduate programs. This is what makes the Tel Hai College study track of Stress and Trauma Studies an important program. The current overview has provided a theoretical knowledge base for social work interventions in emergencies and disasters. It also provides a hands-on manual for mental health first aid interventions on the individual,

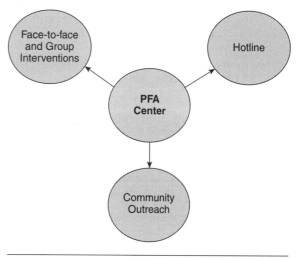

Figure 33.7   A Systemic Aid Model

SOURCES: Farchi (2013).

group and community level. Being able to provide professional assistance immediately following an emergency situation, thus reducing the chance of PTSD onset, has long-range psychosocial and economic effects. The combination of professional PFA training models on the one hand and the Six C's model to be used by nonprofessionals on the other dramatically increases community ability to provide PFA during any kind of emergency, thus enhancing community resilience.

INTERNET RESOURCES

- IDF Homefront Command: http://www.oref.org.il
- Eran telephone mental health first aid: http://www.eran.org.il
- Magen David Adom: http://www.mdais.com
- Stress, Trauma, & Resilience Studies Program, Tel-Hai College: http://english.telhai.ac.il/content/stress-trauma-and-resilience-studies-program
- *The Times of Israel:* http://www.timesofisrael.com
- *Haaretz:* http://www.haaretz.com/

DISCUSSION QUESTIONS

1. What are the advantages of immediate intervention at times of disaster?

2. What is the rational of the six elements of basic interventions during emergencies? Explain.

3. How can we identify a traumatized person? What are his or her basic needs?

4. What is the difference between "perceived trauma" and a "traumatic event"?

5. From a macro perspective, how can we apply the Six C's model to encourage community resiliency?

REFERENCES

American Psychiatric Association. (2013). *Diagnostic and statistical manual of mental disorders* (5th ed.). Washington, DC: Author.

Antonovsky, A. (1979). *Health, stress and coping.* San Francisco, CA: Jossey-Bass.

Arendt, M., & Elklit, A. (2001) Effectiveness of psychological debriefing. *Acta Psychiatrica Scandinavia, 104,* 423–437.

Bandura, A. (1988). Self-efficacy conception of anxiety. *Anxiety Research, 1,* 77–98.

Bremner, J. D. (2006). Traumatic stress, effects on the brain. *Dialogues Clinical Neuroscience, 8*(4), 445–461.

Cacciatore, J., Carlson, B., Klimek, B., Michaelis, E., & Steffan, S. (2011). Crisis intervention by social workers in fire departments: An innovative role for social workers. *Social Work, 56*(I), 81–88.

Campfield, K. M., & Hills, A. M. (2001). Effect of timing of critical incident stress debriefing (CISD) on posttraumatic symptoms. *Journal of Traumatic Stress, 14,* 327–340.

Dyregrov, A. (2008). *Grief in children: A handbook for adults.* London, UK: Jessica Kingsley.

Ellis, A., Nixon, R., & Williamson, P. (2009). The effects of social support and negative appraisals on acute stress symptoms and depression in children and adolescents. *British Journal of Clinical Psychology, 48,* 347–361.

Eth, S., & Pynoos, R. S. (Eds.). (1985). *Post-traumatic stress disorder in children* (pp. 171–83). Washington, DC: American Psychiatric Press.

Farchi, M. (2010). *A training curriculum for homefront command units for stress trauma situations.* Tel Aviv: IDF Homefront Command, Mental Health Division.

Farchi, M. (2012). From helpless victim to a coping survivor: Innovative mental health intervention methods during crises and emergencies. Paper presented at the conference Trauma Through the Life Cycle From a Strengths-Based Perspective. Hebrew University, School of Social Work.

Farchi, M. (2013). *The Six-C's model – Guidelines for the emergency mental health providers.* Paper presented at the XIII ESTSS Conference, Bologna, Italy.

Farchi, M., Cohen, A., & Mosek, A. (2013). Developing specific self-efficacy and resilience for first response among students of social work and stress and trauma studies. *Journal of Teaching in Social Work, 34*(2), 129–146.

Farchi, M., & Gidron, Y. (2014). *Reduction of acute stress reactions (ASR) in emergency room patients via stress management or memory structure.* Paper presented at the IPEDIII conference held by the IDF Home Front Command & Israeli Ministry of Health, Tel-Aviv, Israel.

Fernandez, L., Barbera, J., & Van Dorp, J. (2006, October). Strategies for managing volunteers during incident response: A systems approach. *Homeland Security Affairs, 2*(3). Retrieved from http://www.hsaj.org/?article=2.3.9.

Figley, C. R. (1995). Compassion fatigue: Secondary traumatic stress disorders from treating the traumatized. New York, NY: Brunner/Mazel.

Foa, E. B., Rothbaum, B. O., Riggs, D. S., & Murdock, T. B. (1991). Treatment of posttraumatic stress disorder in rape victims: A comparison between cognitive-behavioral procedures and counseling. *Journal of Consulting and Clinical Psychology, 59*(5), 715.

Forneris, C. A., Gartlehner, G., Brownley, K. A., Gaynes, B. N., Sonis, J., Coker- Schwimmer, E., ... & Lohr, K. N. (2013). Interventions to prevent post-traumatic stress disorder: a systematic review. *American journal of preventive medicine, 44(6),* 635-650.

Garmezy, N. (1971). Vulnerability research and the issue of primary prevention. *American Journal of Orthopsychiatry, 41,* 101–116.

Gidron, Y., & Farchi, M. (2013). *Scientifically-based early interventions for reducing the ASR and preventing PTSD.* Symposium presented at the XIII ESTSS Conference, Bologna, Italy.

Gidron, Y., Gal, R., Freedman, S., Twiser, I., Lauden, A., Snir, Y., & Benjamin, J. (2001). Translating research findings to PTSD prevention: Results of a randomized controlled pilot study. *Journal of Traumatic Stress, 14*(4), 773–780.

Harvey, M. R. (2007). Towards an ecological understanding of resilience in trauma survivors: Implications for theory, research and practice. *Journal of Aggression, Maltreatment and Trauma, 14*(1–2), 9–32. doi: 10.1300/J146v14n01_02

Hendler, T., Goshen, E., Zwas, S. T., Sasson, Y., Gal, G., & Zohar, J. (2003). Brain reactivity to specific symptom provocation indicates prospective therapeutic outcome in OCD. *Psychiatry Research: Neuroimaging, 124*(2), 87–103.

Herman, J. L. (1992). *Trauma and recovery.* New York, NY: Basic Books.

Hobfoll, S. E. (2001). The influence of culture, community, and the nested-self in the stress process: Advancing conservation of resources theory. *Applied Psychology: An International Review, 50*(3), 337–421. doi: 10.1111/1464-0597.00062

Hobfoll, S. E., Hall, B. J., Canetti-Nisim, D., Galea, S., Johnson, R. J., & Palmieri, P. A. (2007). Refining our understanding of traumatic growth in the face of terrorism: Moving from meaning cognitions to doing what is meaningful. *Applied Psychology, 56*(3), 345–366. doi: 10.1111/j.1464-0597.2007.00292.x

Jones, E., Thomas, A., & Ironside, S. (2007). Shell shock: An outcome study of a First World War "PIE" unit. *Psychological Medicine, 37,* 215–223. doi:10.1017/S0033291706009329

Kobasa, S. C. (1979). Stressful life events, personality, and health: An inquiry into hardiness. *Journal of Personality and Social Psychology, 37,* 1–11.

Lahad, M., & Ben-Nesher, U. (2008). Community coping: Resilience models for preparation, intervention and rehabilitation in manmade and natural disasters. *Phoenix of Natural Disasters: Community Resilience,* 195–208.

Lazarus, R. S. (1991). Progress on a cognitive-motivational-relational theory of emotion. *American Psychologist, 46*(8), 819–834. doi: 10.1037/0003-066X.46.8.819

Lazarus, R. S., & Folkman, S. (1984). *Stress, appraisal and coping.* New York, NY: Springer.

Luthar, S. S., Cicchetti, D., & Becker, B. (2000). The construct of resilience: A critical evaluation and guidelines for future work. *Child Development, 71*(3), 543–562.

Maddi, S. R. (2006). Hardiness: The courage to grow from stresses. *The Journal of Positive Psychology, 1*(3), 160–168. doi:10.1080/17439760600619609

Mancini, A. D., & Bonanno, G. A. (2006). Resilience in the face of potential trauma: Clinical practices and illustrations. *Journal of Clinical Psychology, 62*(8), 971–985. doi: 10.1002/jclp.20283

Mansdorf, I. J. (2008) Psychological interventions following terrorist attacks. *British Medical Bulletin, 88,* 7–22.

Masten, A., Best, K., & Garmezy, N. (1990). Resilience and development: Contributions from the study of children who overcome adversity. *Development and Psychopathology, 2,* 425–444.

McCann, I. L., & Pearlman, L. A. (1990). Vicarious traumatization: A framework for understanding the psychological effects of working with victims. *Journal of Traumatic Stress, 3*(1), 131–149.

McLeod, S. A. (2010). Problem focused coping: Managing stress. *Simply Psychology.* Retrieved from http://www.simplypsychology.org/stress-management.html#prob

Mollica, R. F. (1988). The trauma story: The psychiatric care of refugee survivors of violence and torture. *Post-Traumatic Therapy and Victims of Violence,* 295–314.

Norris, F. H. (2005). Range, magnitude, and duration of the effects of disasters on mental health: review update 2005. *Research education disaster mental health,* 1-23.

Norris, F. H., Stevens, S. P., Pfefferbaum, B., Wyche, K. F., & Pfefferbaum, R. L. (2008). Community resilience as a metaphor, theory, set of capacities, and strategy for disaster readiness. *American Journal of Community Psychology, 41*(1–2), 127–150. doi: 10.1007/s10464-007-9156-6

Pearlman, L. A., & Saakvitne, K. W. (1995). Treating therapists with vicarious traumatization and secondary traumatic stress disorders. In C. R. Figley (Ed.), *Compassion fatigue: Coping with secondary traumatic stress disorder in those who treat the traumatized* (pp. 150–177). New York, NY: Brunner/Mazel.

Roberts, N. P., Kitchiner, N. J., Kenardy, J., & Bisson, J. I. (2010). Early psychological interventions to treat acute traumatic stress symptoms. *Cochrane Database System Review, 3.*

Rose, S. C., Bisson, J., Churchill, R., & Wessely, S. (2002). Psychological debriefing for preventing post-traumatic stress disorder (PTSD). *Cochrane Database of Systematic Reviews, 2.* doi: 10.1002/14651858.CD000560.

Rowlands, A. (2013). Social work training curriculum in disaster management. *Journal of Social Work in Disability & Rehabilitation, 12,* 130–144.

Rutter, M. (1990). Psychosocial resilience and protective mechanisms. In J. Rolf, A. S. Masten, D. Cicchetti, K. H. Nuechterlein, & S. Weintraub, (Eds.), *Risk and protective factors in the development of psychopathology* (pp. 181–214). New York, NY: Cambridge.

Saleebey, D. (Ed.). (2006). *The strengths perspective in social work practice.* Boston, MA: Pearson.

Schreiber, S., Yoeli, N., Paz, G., Barabash, G., Varssano, D., Fertel, N., . . . Halpern, P. (2004). Hospital preparedness for possible nonconventional casualties: An Israeli experience. *General Hospital Psychiatry, 26*(5), 359–366. doi: 10.1016/j.genhosppsych.2004.05.003

Shapiro, F. (2012). EMDR therapy: An overview of current and future research. *Revue Européenne de Psychologie Appliquée/European Review of Applied Psychology, 62*(4), 193-195.

Shin, L. M., Shin, P. S., Heckers, S., Krangel, T. S., Macklin, M. L., Orr, S. P., . . . Rauch, S. L. (2004). Regional cerebral blood flow in the amygdala and medial prefrontal cortex during traumatic imagery in male and female Vietnam veterans with PTSD. *Archives of General Psychiatry, 61,* 168–176.

Soldatos, C., Paparrigopoulos, T., Pappa, D., & Christodoulou, G. (2006). Early post-traumatic stress disorder in relation to acute stress reaction: An ICD-10 study among help seekers following an earthquake. *Psychiatry Research, 143,* 245–253.

Solomon, Z. (1993). *Combat stress reaction: The enduring toll of war.* New York, NY: Plenum.

Somer, E., & Bleich, A. (2005). *Mental health in terror's shadow: The Israeli experience.* Tel Aviv: Ramot, University of Tel Aviv.

Van der Kolk, B. A., & Fisler, R. (1995). Dissociation and the fragmentary nature of traumatic memories: Overview and exploratory study. *Journal of Traumatic Stress, 8*(4), 505–525.

Van der Kolk, B. A., Pelcovitz, D., Roth, S., Mandel, F. S., McFarlane, A., & Herman, J. L. (1996). Dissociation, somatization, and affect dysregulation: The complexity of adaptation to trauma. *American Journal of Psychiatry, 153*(7), 83-93.

World Health Organization. (1992). *The ICD-10 classification of mental and behavioral disorders: Clinical descriptions and diagnostic guidelines.* Geneva: Author.

CHAPTER 34

The Development and Current Status of the Social Work Profession in China

Xiaoyan Han, Juan Guo, & Wen-Jui Han

CHAPTER OBJECTIVES

- Examine the recent evolution of social work practice in China using the example of youth positive development;
- Describe the growth and advancement of social work practice on micro, mezzo, and macro levels through the lens of a school-based youth positive development program;
- Identify the resources available and the advantages and limitations to implementing social work practice in contemporary China;
- Understand social work development and trends in China to stimulate and exchange conversations within China and with other societies (e.g., United States).

CASE VIGNETTE

Jun, a teenage boy, once was a stellar student in his teachers' eyes, but he dropped out of high school after his father died at a young age. Growing up in a single-parent family and lacking parental warmth and supervision, Jun still dreamed of becoming a basketball player. Although Jun's mother provides care for him, she is addicted to playing mahjong with neighbors, which often involves long hours out of the home including evening and night hours. Jun's mother often left him home alone to heat up meals and take care of himself. Occasional part-time, poorly paid work and playing basketball at a neighborhood park became

Jun's daily life after he dropped out of school. As a result, his neighborhood perceives him to be a youth at high risk of delinquent behavior.

A social worker with a close working relationship with Jun's old school reached out to him after he dropped out, but with no success. After talking with Jun's teachers about his academic and socioemotional well-being and observing his daily life, the social worker realized that perhaps connecting Jun with a local basketball team will revive his motivation to pursue his dream once again.

INTRODUCTION

Jun's story was portrayed in the 2013 Chinese film *I Have Sunshine* (see the Internet Resources section of this chapter), which brought public awareness to the role of social workers in China. Importantly, the film about a teenage boy from a single-mother family whose life prospects changed through the help of social workers provides an accurate representation of the current status of the social work profession in China. The boy was able to join a municipal-level basketball team, restore his interpersonal network, and make his mother proud. The social worker's engagement with this teenage boy and the resources she was able to mobilize to help him attain his dream provides the public with insight into the social work profession.

This chapter will examine social work practice in contemporary China through the lens of programs addressing adolescent issues. Social work education programs and social work professional training got off to a slow start in China, but as the country has transitioned to a market-based economy, the need for and awareness of the importance of having properly trained social work professionals to deliver social services has picked up speed. Social issues related to the economic reforms have emerged since the early 1980s, and today approximately half a million people are involved in delivering social work practice and social services at the governmental level (Li, Han, & Huang, 2012). The overwhelming majority of them, however, have not received any formal social work professional training. Consequently, the scope of social work practice has been limited compared to the wide array of services provided by social work practitioners in the United States. To date, most social work practice in China has involved delivering programs and services to clients in group and community settings (e.g., classes on skill building for the elderly, in recreational facilities, and activities for the elderly and for youths). Face-to-face individual counseling is not widely practiced by social workers in China and is mainly delivered by trained psychologists or psychiatrists (Zhang, 2008).

This chapter also discusses a youth intervention program that has been introduced in a small number of middle schools in Shanghai since 2005, the Positive Adolescent Training through Holistic Social Programmes (PATHS). This intervention was adapted from Hong Kong's PATHS program by the first author of this chapter (see Shek & Sun, 2009 for details of this program implemented in Hong Kong). The program uses professionally trained social workers to deliver services to youths using a group work approach in a school setting. PATHS in Shanghai, which adopts a sensitive approach in a culture that may not perceive mental health (or mental illness) in a positive light, is a youth mental health program that is in line with current school curriculum in China.

Before describing the Shanghai PATHS program, the next section provides background information on the development and status of to social work profession in China in order to place this youth mental health program in context.

Social Work Profession in China

In recent decades, the social work profession in China has gone through many transformations, and education in the field has also evolved (Li et al., 2012). These various changes reflect the many challenges brought on by the country's swift economic growth since the late 1970s. In the *National Medium and Long-Term Talent Development Outline* (2010–2020), released on June 6, 2010, the Central Government of China identified the "Social Work Talent Troop" as one of the top six priorities for cultivating much-needed professionals. The outline called for a total of 2 million trained social workers by 2015, increasing to 3 million by 2020. New government policies are attempting to meet this demand by allowing colleges and universities to freely establish social work programs and by eliminating undergraduate and graduate quotas in social work programs (All educational programs in China are assigned quotas by the central government for the number of students each department, school, and university may accept every year).

Despite this recent push, the profession lacks much of the infrastructure necessary to fulfill the central government's goals. For example, in 2012, the Shanghai municipal government declared that every hospital must have at least one social worker for every 200 beds. While this is a laudable start, many other settings such as schools, criminal justice institutions, and nursing homes also need social workers in place. Even in Shanghai, which is one of the few metropolitan areas in China with a well-established social work system, this type of infrastructure, such as including social work professionals in their human resources system, has yet to be realized.

Furthermore, because the central government's primary goal behind promoting the profession is to maintain and establish a "harmonious society" (Li et al., 2012), social workers typically do not provide clinical one-on-one counseling services in China. Such services have traditionally been delivered by professionals trained in psychology-related disciplines. Hence, none of the established social work programs and services to date have been designed to provide clinical practice; rather, community organizing and services has been the dominant form of social work provision in China (Zhang, 2008). A small number of social work–trained professionals do deliver mental health services in some locales, notably in the Shanghai area (authors' personal observation and conversation with mental health professionals).

Current Issues Facing Chinese Adolescents and the Corresponding Interventions

The economic reform or so-called Open Door Policy of the late 1970s and early 1980s led to tremendous changes in China, including a rise in social problems. As the country moved from a controlled, planned economy to a free-market economy, new, unavoidable social issues emerged such as labor disputes and injuries, misplaced laborers, migration from rural to urban areas, and abandoned children (Li et al., 2012). These issues have led to a rise in juvenile delinquency. Since 2000, the number of crimes committed in China by adolescents aged 14 to 17 has increased dramatically by 120%, from 30,000 to 67,000 youths between 1997 and 2011, and the ages of the adolescents who commit crimes is decreasing (Shi, 2014).

Several interconnected issues have led to this increase in juvenile crime. A large body of research shows that stability and security are the most important protective factors to promote positive development of the child (Eccles & Gootman, 2002). However, the economic reforms in China also brought changes to the workforce that have affected children: many families now have two working parents, and parents are seeking job opportunities in other communities and cities, sometimes leaving their children with relatives. Such shifts in the workforce have brought turbulence to children's lives that can affect adolescent behavior and well-being. Additionally, school systems (particularly vocational schools) in China have typically assisted youths transitioning from school to the labor market. However, these transition programs have not kept up with the demands of the rapidly transforming labor market, leaving youths without a means of navigating entry into the workforce or the skill sets needed in the current labor market. Lack of family cohesion and poor parent-child relationships also contribute to increases in school drop-out rates, mental health issues, and youths engaging in risky behaviors such as violence, prostitution, drug use, and overmedication (Wong, 1994). The Community Youth Center of Shanghai City, as an example, was founded to acknowledge and address the increasing issues of juvenile delinquency and youth idleness (i.e., unemployed individuals aged 16–25 who are not enrolled in schools).

China is not alone in facing a rise in juvenile delinquency issues. The United States, Japan, and Hong Kong are also dealing with youth issues, particularly violence and poor mental health (Shek & Sun, 2009). Scholars in China have begun looking at the strategies, policies, and programs implemented in other countries as possible means of combatting China's juvenile delinquency problem. For example, Liu and Han (2007) examined programs designed to improve parent-child relationships and encourage family cohesion as well as policies that promote safety. However, such policies and programs tend to be introduced in isolation, creating a fragmented system for addressing youth well-being. Most important, most of the policies and programs currently being considered in China are problem oriented, focused on intervention rather than prevention (Liu & Han, 2007).

Instead of viewing adolescent issues as problem focused or as deficiency oriented, a strengths-based perspective can be more useful in understanding and addressing the current issues adolescents in China face. Successful youth development programs with a strengths-based perspective have been widely adopted around the world, particularly in the United States (Catalano, Berglund, Ryan, Lonczak, & Hawkins, 2004). Such a perspective allows professionals and policy makers to design policies and programs that take advantage of adolescents' strengths and are more sensitive to their needs (Liu & Han, 2007).

MICRO AND MEZZO PERSPECTIVES OF JUN'S CASE

Growing up in a single-mother family without sufficient family socioeconomic resources and without maternal warmth and proper parental supervision, Jun felt isolated and sometimes abandoned by his mother. Jun's teachers were not trained to address the youth mental health issues he faced. His declining academic performance was particularly problematic in a society that emphasizes academic achievement. Consequently, Jun was labeled "problematic and delinquent." He worked occasionally in the local community, but the meager hourly wage was unsatisfactory, engendering a hostile relationship with his employer. Jun often spent his days at neighborhood parks shooting hoops. Children in the neighborhood were scared of him because they perceived him to be a delinquent youth. This label, however, did not stop Jun from helping younger children who were being bullied.

Jun's challenges were noticed by the social worker who was assigned to the community where Jun's school was located and whose tasks were to address issues faced by adolescents in schools in Jun's neighborhood. After months of observations of Jun's daily routines and extensive conversation with Jun's school teachers, the social worker provided the following assessment and intervention.

Assessment

Given Jun's developmental age, the family and school issues he faced are particularly troublesome. The early teen years are a time of rapid cognitive, physical, and emotional development. Jun's failing academic performance could be a manifestation of his feelings of isolation and abandonment by his mother, teachers, and the community. However, he also shows hope and promise, with dreams of becoming a basketball player. His positive side is evident as he helps younger children. Jun seems to need a mechanism to help him feel connected, cared for, and loved. Note that Jun, his mother, and the community were not aware of the positive role that the social work profession could play in such cases, making the social worker's initial efforts challenging and often misunderstood.

Intervention

Social workers in China are typically trained in and offer community-based services to address issues such as those faced by Jun. The community social worker who had close ties with Jun's school explored ways to mobilize community resources to help the boy reconnect with the community and society. After talking with Jun's teachers and observing his daily life, the social worker realized that connecting him with a local basketball team might provide the teen with the resources he needed to get back on track.

The sections that follow examine a positive youth development initiatives implemented in Chinese schools that are similar in spirit to the community resources provided to Jun to help with his mental health issues. A new model for the practice of social work in China is then presented using a strengths-based perspective.

POSITIVE YOUTH DEVELOPMENT IN CHINA

This section first discusses prevention theory and then introduces the strengths-based perspective as background information to understand the PATHS intervention. Finally, other social work programs focused on adolescents in China that have adopted concepts from both the prevention and strengths-based development literature are examined.

Prevention Science and Its Strategies

Prevention science employs two primary categories of preventive strategies (National Research Council Institute of Medicine, 2002; Weissberg & Greenberg, 1997). The first, considered the "traditional" preventive strategy, includes three dimensions: *tertiary prevention,* preventing the deterioration of the problem; *secondary prevention,* identifying the high-risk profiles of adolescents as soon as possible; and *primary prevention,* reducing or eliminating the possibility of the occurrence of the problem. Secondary prevention, perceived to be an "operative" preventive strategy, includes *indicated prevention* (e.g., helping adolescents with problem

behaviors), *selective prevention* (e.g., helping adolescents with high-risk profiles), and *universal prevention* (e.g., applying the preventive interventions to all adolescents). Primary and universal prevention strategies are often used to address adolescent problem behaviors such as drug use and mental health issues.

Prevention Science and Positive Youth Development

The field of prevention science initially was problem oriented, focusing on supporting youth before problem behaviors occurred; thus, risk factors are emphasized in this body of research (Catalano et al., 2004). The field evolved as researchers and practitioners became aware that adolescent problem behaviors could be effectively addressed by focusing on positive rather than adverse outcomes (e.g., You finished your homework today vs. You have not been doing your homework every day). More recent scholarship on prevention and positive youth development has underscored the importance of focusing on the strengths and potential of adolescents, rather than on problems and treatments (Catalano et al., 2004).

Based on this line of research, Catalano and colleagues (2004) reviewed the literature on prevention science and positive youth development. They identified four characteristics associated with prevention science that are in line with the perspectives focusing on adolescents' strengths and potential: identifying risk and protective factors, attending to adolescent developmental needs, examining the common contributors to adolescent positive well-being, and putting less emphasis on risk factors and more on protective factors to address issues related to adolescent well-being. The authors also concluded that positive youth development should be targeted at adolescent well-being as a whole instead of one aspect at a time and that a lack of observable problem behaviors does not necessarily mean that adequate preparation and prevention have been in place to avoid future problem behaviors (Berglund et al., 2002; Catalano, Hawkins, Berglund, Pollard, & Arthur, 2002). Finally, Catalano et al. (2002)

found that human behavior is closely connected with the surrounding environment and thus the focal perspectives as well as the corresponding solutions should consider environmental influences.

In China, the concept of primary and universal prevention, together with selective prevention, has been adopted to nurture positive adolescent development (Liu & Han, 2007). Specifically, prevention programs that target all middle school and high school students have used a primary and universal prevention model. The PATHS curriculum, which incorporates positive youth development, are taught to all adolescents in the selected schools. Additionally, in line with the idea of secondary or selective prevention, in the work with positive youth programs implemented in Shanghai middle schools, school social workers have provided additional support to adolescents who may have more challenges than others in order to overcome their difficulties and problems.

Shek and Yu (2011) recently reviewed positive youth programs in Asia. Despite a long history of such programs in the region, the authors identified fewer than 50 in Asia and fewer than 10 well-regarded positive youth development programs in China, Taiwan, and Macau. This review suggests that China is in the beginning stages of implementing programs built upon positive youth development in contrast to the widespread application of this perspective in the United States.

The Introduction of Positive Youth Development Programs in China

In 2005, the Hong Kong Jockey Club Charities Trust invited five Hong Kong universities to establish a research team to create an intervention with a positive youth development focus, and it then donated 400 million Hong Kong dollars to implement the program. The initiative is ongoing and is currently in its third phase of funding, which covers both Hong Kong and Shanghai locations (PATHS I was funded from 2005 to 2012, PATHS II was funded from 2009 to 2016, and PATHS III was funded from 2013 to 2016). The research team designed a curriculum driven by positive youth development for all Hong Kong middle school students and provided training on curriculum delivery to teachers. Social workers evaluated the programs with follow ups after a year of implementation. In the same year, Han expanded this positive youth development curriculum to mainland China (Shek, Han, & Lee, 2006). This program was initially implemented in a publicly funded middle school (serving youths aged 13–15) in the Minhang district in Shanghai. Since 2010, with private foundation support, the program has expanded to three additional privately funded middle schools run by the Tin Ka Ping Foundation in the Jiangsu Province of China. The program is currently expanding to schools similarly funded by the Tin Ka Pin Foundation in western areas of China such as Lanzhou. The goal is to implement this curriculum in 167 middle schools currently run by the Tin Ka Ping Foundation across China.

Approximately 10% of middle schools in Shanghai are privately funded. The push to implement the program in privately instead of publicly funded schools is based on many considerations. The public school system overseen by the government has several constraints that make implementation in public schools difficult. Privately funded school systems are flexible enough to allow for PATHS to be implemented as part of the general middle school character education curriculum (i.e., curriculum to promote morals and norms among students such as respect, gratefulness, generosity, etc.). Importantly, funding for the program comes from both a government contract-for-service grant that aims to bring social services to vulnerable populations (i.e., youths) and from research funds from governmental and nongovernmental sources to enhance social science research. The hope is to expand the PATHS program to more schools, including public schools, in the years to come after demonstrating to the government its positive effects on youth mental health and character-building capacity. The next section describes the PATHS curriculum (see Appendix).

INTERVENTION: THE POSITIVE YOUTH DEVELOPMENT PROGRAM

The concept of positive youth development is likely to vary across cultures. The scope and meaning of this subjective positive experience are conceptualized and prescribed by a particular set of values, norms, and morals within society. Building upon the seminal review by Catalano and colleagues (2004), several factors were considered when determining how best to apply prevention science and strategies to adolescent issues in contemporary China. First, separate prevention strategies seem to be more realistic and feasible in addressing individual issues such as violence, drug addiction, or gambling addiction. Schools are the best setting for delivering positive youth development materials, but schools face time and resource constraints. Consequently, it was determined that implementing multiple kinds of prevention strategies might not be feasible.

Second, given that prevention science at times still emphasizes problem behaviors, the corresponding strategies could be overly problem-focused rather than strengths-focused. Third, Chinese parents do not tend to recognize their children's behaviors as problematic. Interventions that address adolescent problem behaviors could deter parents from allowing their children to participate. Finally, it was determined that a holistic prevention strategy that attends to the developmental needs of adolescents was likely to be the most appropriate framework for applying the strengths-based perspective to ensure adolescents are seen as resources with great potential to develop (Liu & Han, 2007).

The Curriculum

Curriculum Design

The core principles of positive youth development are to identify and cultivate adolescents' strengths, enhance the relationships between the youth and others, and establish positive attitudes and concrete goals for adolescents to promote positive development (Liu & Han, 2007).

Although Western societies have implemented many programs designed to promote positive youth development, not all have met with success. Catalano and colleagues (2004) reviewed 77 studies of programs promoting positive youth development and found that only 25 were deemed successful in terms of observable positive youth well-being outcomes. According to Catalano et al., the successful programs had at least one of the following constructs as their program objective, and programs that cover as many of these constructs as possible have a higher likelihood of success: promoting bonding, fostering resilience, promoting social competence, promoting emotional competence, promoting cognitive competence, promoting behavioral competence, promoting moral competence, fostering self-determination, fostering spirituality, fostering self-efficacy, fostering clear and positive identity, fostering belief in the future, providing recognition for positive behavior, providing opportunities for prosocial involvement, and fostering prosocial norms. For example, under the category "promoting bonding" was a group of workshops in which youth role-played about developing the knowledge and capacity to build bonds between youths and their parents, peers, teachers, and the larger community. In the role-play, for example, students will be instructed with a scenario such as, "Your good friend laughs at your tripping in a track race, and you decided not to race anymore." Role-playing students are asked to practice what they would and would not do under such circumstances. Through these exercises, the youth not only built self-efficacy but also benefited from these improved relationships, which become a resource youths can mobilize when they need support.

In Jun's case, the community social worker used a combination of constructs such as fostering clear and positive identity, fostering belief in the future, providing recognition for positive behavior, and providing opportunities for prosocial involvement to mobilize teachers and community resources (e.g., local basketball team) to facilitate Jun's belief in the future and his own identity with basketball. Becoming involved in the local basketball team gave Jun the opportunity for prosocial involvement and hence fostered prosocial behaviors.

In line with previous studies on Chinese adolescents in Hong Kong (Shek, Siu, & Lee, 2007), Han and colleagues adapted the Hong Kong PATHS curriculum (Liu & Han, 2007; PATHS, please see Shek & Sun, 2009 for details on Hong Kong's curriculum) for Shanghai into seven chapters/sessions to introduce topics such as competence, emotion, interpersonal relationships, family cohesion, and morality (see Appendix). These seven chapters/sessions incorporate the following eight core constructs demonstrated to be important for successful positive youth development programs (Shek et al., 2007; see Appendix for these eight core constructs).

The ultimate goal of this curriculum is for students to achieve seven C's (Liu & Han, 2007):

1. Self-identity and self-esteem (*Character*)

2. Self-determination, self-efficacy, resilience, and positive future orientation (*Confidence*)

3. Healthy relationships with others (*Connection*)

4. Social competence, emotional regulation, cognition capability, proactive behavior, and the ability to distinguish right from wrong (*Competence*)

5. *Compassion* for others

6. Participation and competence in caring for the community (*Caring*)

7. Responsibility to contribute to the society (*Contribution*)

Strengths-Based Perspective

Scholarship emphasizing the importance of a strengths-based perspective (Saleebey, 1992) has endorsed four key constructs in carrying out positive youth development programs: (1) *empowerment*—seeing the client as an active person who has much potential to be cultivated through collaboration with family, others, and the environment; (2) *membership*—acknowledging that the people we serve are similar to us and thus they share the characteristics of having self-esteem, dignity, and responsibility; (3) *resilience*—recognizing that human beings tend to possess this competence when facing challenges and difficulties; and (4) *dialogue* and *cooperation*—through dialogue, appreciation for each other's importance is gained, which helps bridge the gaps in understanding among individuals and between individuals and systems. The PATHS curriculum embraces these perspectives.

Practicing the Strengths-Based Perspective

Built upon the presumption that adolescents possess potential that needs to be cultivated, the PATHS curriculum endorses the following ideas: (1) every individual, group, and community has its strengths; (2) trauma, abuse, and disease are all unfortunate circumstances that could also be transformed into challenges and opportunities; (3) social workers can best serve clients when working together with the client; (4) the environment contains important resources; and (5) every individual has strengths, and these strengths can be recaptured (Tian & Hou, 2012).

Specifically, strengths-based theory stresses when working with clients to look for, explore, and utilize the resources that they already have as well as helping clients retain and gain hope from and through the difficulties and traumas they experience. At the same time, this curriculum underscores the belief that people have many strengths such as good character and morality that motivate them to have a good life. In addition, people can always find ways to utilize and mobilize the resources in their environment, no matter how bad they think their situation is. This is particularly important in Chinese culture: Negative behaviors are undesired and considered shameful, and people who engage in such behaviors are considered "bad" and without any strengths. Thus, a focus on strengths allows people to refocus attention and transform negative into positive behaviors. Jun was perceived to be a delinquent youth by the community and thus to be a "bad person with no strengths." The community social worker was able to highlight Jun's strengths by connecting him with a local basketball team. Doing so transformed his view of himself as well as that of his mother, his peers, his teachers, and the community: he became a productive member of society whose strengths were apparent to all.

Using a similar perspective, social workers who deliver PATHS in Shanghai are trained to focus on their clients' strengths and competences and to emphasize these strengths among individuals, groups, families, and their communities. PATHS training advocates equality of the social worker and the client, which creates a mutually cooperative relationship (Tian & Hou, 2012).

Implementing Positive Youth Development Programs in Shanghai

To date, the government has established very little infrastructure to assist social workers in providing services needed to help vulnerable populations such as youths. Two primary mechanisms are used currently in Shanghai to implement positive youth programs within schools: (1) nonprofit social service organizations contract with the Chinese government to provide social work services to the schools, and (2) nonprofit social service organizations apply for research funds from either the Chinese government or from nongovernmental foundations to implement school-based prevention and intervention programs.

Because the positive youth development program is considered a prevention service, it is particularly well-suited to implementation in middle schools by school social workers. However, to date the Ministry of Education has not taken school social workers into consideration when designing curriculum or allocating resources. Thus, the PATHS program has relied on contracted services and research funding for service deliver in the middle schools.

In China, every middle school curriculum must include a character education course. Because one goal of positive youth development programs is to establish and nurture youths' characters, it is a natural starting place for implementing a strengths-based positive youth development program in participating middle schools. Before being placed in the schools to deliver the PATHS program, social workers are trained on the curriculum content and the skill set needed to implement it, such as problem solving and how to listen. In addition, regular on-the-job training such as monthly small-group meetings is provided. Twice a year, large-scale conferences are held that allow social workers to share and exchange ideas and challenges. They also meet professionals from Hong Kong to learn updated knowledge and skills for delivering positive youth development programs.

Promoting Positive Youth Development Programs to Individuals, Communities, and to the Broader Society

In line with Bronfenbrenner's (1979) ecological perspective, the success of positive youth development programs depends on the individuals, families, friends, schools, and the larger society working together to promote desirable character ideals. Thus, the implementation of the PATHS curriculum began with a strengths-based perspective and emphasizes the important roles played by not just individuals but also friends, families, schools, and the larger society.

Social workers work with families to stress the strengths possessed by the individual adolescents and how they and their family members can help nurture these strengths. Similarly, PATHS social workers emphasize students' strengths—rather than looking at weaknesses that need fixing—and what they can contribute to the school environment and/or to the community.

Below, the intervention is broken down into three levels—individuals, communities, and society. The following section describes how intervention activities use the strengths-based perspective to build upon the interrelations among different systems.

Micro: On the Individual Level

Cognitive Intervention for Individuals in the School Settings

The positive youth development curriculum was designed to teach middle school students three primary cognitive capacities. First, in daily interactions with peers, the students are taught to be confident and to accept who they are as individuals. Second, in interactions with teachers and school administrators, students are taught to learn how to share their own perspectives and be confident. Finally, in regard to interactions with family members, students are taught to have regular communication with parents about anything they would like to talk about and to look at the positive side of issues. For example, instead of saying, "I cannot do …," they were encouraged to say, "What I can do.…"

Mezzo: On the School Level

Behavioral Intervention via School Social Workers

In addition to coaching students to approach issues and relationships from a strengths-based perspective, school social workers reinforce positive thinking and behaviors. Specifically, social service workers in the schools are taught by the PATHS team with rigorous ongoing training to use three approaches in delivering the positive youth development perspective. First, these service workers are encouraged to use positive reinforcement when handling issues. For example, they frequently encourage and compliment the positive changes made by adolescents instead of focusing on the problematic behaviors that students have not made progress on. Second, from the "person-in-environment" perspective, the social workers are encouraged to put the adolescents' issues into a useful context, such as teachers, peers, and parents, to see who and how these contexts might help or hinder the positive development of each individual adolescent. Third, through role-play, adolescents learn to assess responses and behaviors, and choose appropriate reactions that could promote their positive well-being.

Mezzo/Macro: On the Community Level

Involving only individual adolescents, their peers and families, and their schools would not be sufficient to ensure the intervention's success. Community involvement is also stressed. To promote the skills training in cognitive and socioemotional well-being in the schools, community resources are essential. The program cannot succeed without complementary local government education policy, the support of nonprofit organizations, scholarly expertise from the universities, and manpower from social service agencies. Funding and manpower support from the community agencies in Shanghai have contributed to the success of the program in middle schools. For example, the local education authority approved the curriculum; nonprofit and government agencies provided financial support for the program, and a community fair promoted public awareness about positive youth development.

PATHS has been implemented in several middle schools in Shanghai, and it has acquired many government supporters, including the local China Communist Youth League Committee, the education department, and the civil affairs department. In addition, grants from philanthropic organizations have been widely reported in the media. The schools that have implemented this curriculum have established long-term collaborative relationships with departments of social work in local universities such as East China Normal University. This public and private support ensures the long-term sustainability of the programs in Shanghai.

Macro: On the Societal Level

Since the implementation of the positive youth development curriculum in select middle schools in Shanghai, many social services and programs related to improving adolescent well-being have gotten under way.

Establishing School Social Workers

School social workers play an essential role in implementing PATHS. Since the program's pilot year in 2005, several middle schools in the program have received funding from the government to hire a full-time school social worker to continue the positive youth development curriculum and to handle day-to-day issues related to adolescent socioemotional well-being. In addition, the Shanghai government has mandated that every hospital needs to have at least one social worker for every 200 beds in the facility. It is the hope that the Shanghai government will soon implement a similar policy for schools in the city.

The Development of Social Work Programs by Nonprofit Agencies

Since 2011, some nonprofit organizations in China have begun implementing positive youth development curriculum in elementary and middle schools in the Shanghai area. One such example is the Green Fantasy program launched by the Shanghai Haixing Service Agency, a program that closely simulates the core concepts and curriculum of PATHS.

The Green Fantasy program includes additional components designed to encourage interactions between schools and communities. The program's aim is for adolescents to learn at school and then use that knowledge in the community. Youths are encouraged to be more actively involved in community activities, such as volunteering at community senior centers. Through these interactions, youths have begun to take the initiative to design community events or small activities such as weekend fairs for seniors. The benefits are two-fold: The community is helped by the youth, and the youth grows through interaction with the community.

Activities Organized by College Students

Using a strengths-based approach, the Big Sisters and Big Brothers of Shanghai is a prevention program that focuses on the well-being of migrant children to promote positive youth development. What is unique about this program is the proactive role-played by college students. College students recruit other volunteers to be a big brother or sister for a matched migrant child (i.e., children who migrated with parents looking for jobs from rural villages to urban cities). These college students provide ongoing training and supervision for the volunteers. Every year, universities recruit approximately 150 volunteers, and the program has been expanding to more schools in Shanghai and to another university in western China.

Advocating for School Social Workers

The success of in-school positive youth development programs in Shanghai has provided a strong foundation for professionals and practitioners to advocate for the implementation of full-time social workers in every school in China. This advocacy effort, which began in early 2013, is expected to be ongoing until the central government considers and implements such a policy throughout the nation.

The Effects of the Positive Youth Development Program

To gauge the effectiveness of the curriculum in establishing the seven "Cs," questionnaires were administered with 15 scales and a total of 90 questions to students from participating middle schools before and after participating in PATHS (see Shek et al., 2007 for detailed questions using these 15 scales). A total of 2,200 students (half of them in the treatment groups and the other half in the control group) from five schools from different provinces responded to the survey between 2007 and 2008. The results indicate that compared to students who did not take part in PATHS within the same school, those who did participate had established more friendships and had significantly improved their social competence (e.g., "I can actively talk to strangers"), emotional competence (e.g., "I am a pleasant person"), clear and positive identity (e.g., "Compared with my peers, I am satisfied with my school performance"), and cognitive competence (e.g., "I believe there is a solution for any problem"; Wang, 2013).

CONCLUSION: THE PRESENT AND FUTURE DIRECTION OF SOCIAL WORK PRACTICE IN CHINA

The social work profession in China evolved sporadically before the 1980s due to the country's turbulent social history. Since then, the profession in China has gone through many transformations. Among China's provinces and cities, Shanghai has been a pioneer for social work professional development due to its economic advantages and its close geographic proximity to Hong Kong, an area with a well-developed social work profession based on the British system. The social work profession in Shanghai has mainly centered on services related to youth. Thus, in this chapter youth issues were focused on to illustrate the development and prospect of social services and profession development in Shanghai in the hopes of providing a model for other cities and areas in China to follow. This overview of youth social work services in Shanghai sheds light on the direction that the Chinese social work profession may take in the years to come—a strong reliance on theories and practice that promote strengths and positive development, infused with a heavy dose of native knowledge about the best ways of working with the population.

Despite strong support from the central government, much work is still needed to establish an infrastructure to sustain a well-rounded social work practice in China at every level of government and in the private sector (Li et al., 2012).

One feature of social work development in China that is unique from other countries is the strong top-down approach. Every level of government, as well as the private sector, follows the policy direction issued by the central government. This, of course, has both advantages and disadvantages. One obvious disadvantage is that political involvement could compromise many of the central tenets of the social work profession, such as human rights

and the concept of grassroots initiatives that are based on the needs of the people.

The advantage of centralized authority is the resources that flow from the policy issued by the central government. Local governments and the private sector will pour resources into programs that follow and carry out the "orders" of the central government. Borrowing from its own positive development perspective, social work practice in China perhaps should take advantage of strong support from the central government and thus the strong flow of resources to establish and strengthen the infrastructure to effectively address issues such as adolescent well-being.

Another advantage of the top-down approach is the strong reliance of the government and private sector on scholarly expertise. The central government depends on advice from people who are knowledgeable about social issues and solutions. Therefore, social work education and research at the university level has been essential to promoting change. For example, many faculty members associated with the social work profession have initiated the establishment of social work agencies that later have become the model for professional social work practice. Through these practices, undergraduate and graduate students gain firsthand experience in the field. In turn, field experience in community settings has informed many university social work faculty members' research. Ultimately, social work educators and practitioners may be able to make systemic changes through their work with individuals and communities. This, in turn, translates into grassroots efforts to advocate for policies and programs from the bottom up when working with the government.

The 2013 film *I Have Sunshine,* which examines a joint social work endeavor by the Shanghai Committee of the China Communist Youth League and the Shanghai Community Juvenile Affairs Office, exemplifies the government's efforts to promote public awareness of the many challenges faced by youths in China. The film also shows how an important resource—the social work profession—plays a pivotal role in addressing such issues. The film illustrates that mobilizing available resources from teachers, social service agencies, and community organizations can support a teenage boy's basketball skills, thereby cultivating his healthy development. The film implies that the social work profession in China is becoming an important force for enhancing individual well-being through the use of a strengths-based perspective.

INTERNET RESOURCES

- Administration for Children and Families: http://www.acf.hhs.gov/program-topics
- NYU-ECNU Institute for Social Development at NYU Shanghai: https://shanghai.nyu.edu/research/social
- PATHS program in Hong Kong: http://www.edb.gov.hk/en/edu-system/special/resources/serc/paths/index.html
- Positive Youth Development: http://youth.gov/youth-topics/positive-youth-development
- Trailer for the film *I Have Sunshine:* http://www.iqiyi.com/v_19rrhayfmo.html

DISCUSSION QUESTIONS

1. Given that the Chinese government is focused on using the social work profession as a tool to create a "harmonious society," is a community-based social work delivery system likely to be the dominant form for China in the coming years? In China, how might the development of the social work profession incorporate clinical practice?

2. Given the lack of social work infrastructure in China (e.g., no formal system for placing social workers into the school system), what role might nongovernmental organizations play in fostering the development of social work professionals?

3. Given that the central Chinese government guides most of the country's policies and programs, is there space for a grassroots effort to nurture and reinforce the social work profession that has formed through such a top-down approach?

4. The concepts and practice of the social work profession are rooted in Western society. How, then, can China learn from the experiences of Western societies and apply the knowledge and skills appropriately to Chinese society?

5. Thus far, social work professionals in China are conforming to the government's requests by using a treatment approach to address issues. How can the social work profession broaden its scope to prevention, in order to truly address the well-being of the larger society?

REFERENCES

Bronfenbrenner, U. (1979). *The ecology of human development: Experiments by nature and design.* Cambridge, MA: Harvard University Press.

Catalano, R. F., Berglund, M. L., Ryan, J. A. M., Lonczak, H. S., & Hawkins, J. D. (2002). Positive youth development in the United States: Research findings on evaluations of positive youth development programs. *Prevention & Treatment, 5*(15), 1–111.

Catalano, R. F., Berglund, M. L., Ryan, J. A. M., Lonczak, H. S., & Hawkins, J. D. (2004). Positive youth development in the United States: Research findings on evaluations of positive youth development programs. *The ANNALS of the American Academy of Political and Social Science, 591,* 98–124.

Catalano, R. F., Hawkins, J. D., Berglund, M. L., Pollard, J. A., & Arthur, M. W. (2002). Prevention science and positive youth development: competitive or cooperative frameworks?. *Journal of Adolescent Health, 31*(6), 230-239.

Eccles, J., & Gootman, J. A. (Eds.). (2002). *Community programs to promote youth development.* Washington, DC: National Academies Press.

Li, Y., Han, W-J., & Huang, C-C. (2012). Development of social work education in China: Background, current status and prospects. *Journal of Social Work Education, 48*(4), 635–653.

Liu, S. Y. P., & Han, X. (2007). *Theories and applications for positive youth development curriculum.* Shanghai, China: Academia Press. [in Chinese]

National Research Council Institute of Medicine. (2002). *Community programs to promote youth development.* Washington, DC: National Academies Press.

Saleebey, D. (1992). *The strengths perspective in social work practice.* White Plains, NY: Longmans.

Shek, D. T. L., Han, X. Y., & Lee, B. M. (2006). Perceived parenting patterns and parent-child relational qualities in adolescents in Hong Kong and Shanghai. *Chinese Journal of Sociology, 26,* 137–157.

Shek, D. T. L., Siu, A. M. H., & Lee, T. Y. (2007). The Chinese positive youth development scale: A validation study. *Research on Social Work Practice, 17*(3), 380–391.

Shek, D. T. L., & Sun, R. C. F. (2009). Development, implementation and evaluation of a holistic positive youth development program: Project P.A.T.H.S. in Hong Kong. *International Journal on Disability and Human Development, 8*(2), 107–117.

Shek, D. T. L., & Yu, L. (2011). A review of validated youth prevention and positive youth development programs in Asia. *International Journal of Adolescent Medicine and Health, 23*(4), 317–324.

Shi, Y-F. (2014). Why the increase in juvenile delinquency? New examinations of the contributing factors in China. *Juvenile Delinquency Problems, 1,* 41–46. [in Chinese]

Tian, G., & Hou, T. (2012). Examining school social work from the strength-based perspectives. *Journal of China Youth University for Political Science, 1,* 138–142. [in Chinese]

Wang, L. (2013). *Examining school social work in preventing youth problem behaviors with curriculum on building characters: A case study of strength-based perspective positive youth development program* (Master's thesis). East China Normal University, Shanghai, China. [in Chinese]

Weissberg, R. P., & Greenberg, M. T. (1997). School and community competence-enhancement and prevention programs. In W. Damon (Ed.), *Handbook of child psychology* (pp. 877–954). New York, NY: John Wiley.

Wong, S. (1994). Prevalence and causes of juvenile delinquency: Dialogue between scholars. *Sociological Studies, 2,* 118–121.

Zhang, Y. (2008). The rationales and reflections of China's native social work practice. *Journal of Social Sciences, 5,* 81–84. [in Chinese]

Chapter	Topics		
	Sixth Grade	Seventh Grade	Eighth Grade
Introduction			
Capacity Building	My Brain (CC) My Talent (SE) I Can Do It (SE) I Control My Own Destiny (SE)	The Secrets of Personalities (CC) Being an Inventor (CC) Secrets of Efficient Learning (SE) My Appearance (SE) Truth About Losing Weight (PI) Balancing Scale (PI)	What Is Real, Cognitively Speaking? (SC) See Through Advertisements (CC) Who Is a Millionaire? (SE) Unbreakable? (PI)
Emotional Regulation/ Competence	Dictionary of Emotions (EC) Expressing Your True Feelings (EC)	Being Reasonable (EC)	Finding the Truth (EC) Escaping Unhappiness/Depression (EC)
Social Competence	Having Mentors (BO) The Power of Temperament (BO) Intersections of Making Friends (BO) Companionship (BO) On-Line Friendship (CC) For My Own Good? (BC) How to Initiate a Conversation (BC)	Be Sensitive/Empathetic (EC) All by Yourself (EC) Ideal Friends? (EC) Constructive Criticism (BC) How to Apologize (BC) Family Relationship (PI)	Less Miscommunication, More True Friendship (BO) Guide to Healthy Relationships (BO) Keeping a Daily Journal (SC) Key to Happiness (BC) Forgiveness and Revenge (BC) Am I Strong? (MC) Passwords to Friendships (MC)
Family Cohesion	I Am Worthwhile (SE) Society Norms, Family Rules (PI)	Sibling Rivalry (BO) Parenting and Authority (BO)	Who Is Right? (SC)
Cultural Identity	China and Me (SC) Together to Make Huangpu River Proud (SC) Do as the Romans Do (PI)	We Are All Chinese (SC) Fantasy of Career Paths (SC) Responsibility (PI)	"She" Is From China (SC) Shanghai versus the World (SC) Idealism (SE)
Moral Competence	Who Can Get on the Bus First? (MC) On the Same Train (MC)	Manners in the Public Space (MC) The Legend in Offering Seats to Others (MC)	Reality versus Ideal (MC) How to Decipher? (MC) Who Can Decide? (PI)

NOTES: CC = Cognitive Competence; BO = Bonding; SC = Social Competence; EC = Emotional Competence; BC = Behavioral Competence; MC = Moral Competence; SE = Self-Efficacy; PI = Prosocial Involvement.

CHAPTER 35

Drug Abuse in Iran

A Psychosocial Perspective

Saeed Momtazi

CHAPTER OBJECTIVES

- Understand drug abuse in Iran;
- Learn about the psychosocial aspects of drug abuse;
- Describe harm reduction programs and policy changes in drug abuse;
- Understand the role of Iranian social workers in drug abuse treatment.

CASE VIGNETTE

Azar is a 27-year-old woman who lives with her mother in Tehran. Recently she went to an outpatient addiction treatment center to stop using crystal meth. She is from a middle class family; her parents divorced when she was 14, and after that she and her 20-year-old brother, Ali, lived with their mother. She started her master's at the age of 24 and quit after two years. Her parents divorced mainly because of her father's drug abuse, which led to neglecting the family. Her father has used opium for as long as Azar can remember. At the age of 10, Azar decided not to touch any drugs and never use alcohol or any other substances as she figured out that all her family's problems were due to her father's drug abuse. Later, in her early 20s, she experienced a depression episode, and because she thought methamphetamine was not an addictive drug and might help to relieve her depression, she used meth with her boyfriend from the university and soon found herself dependent on the drug.

She is now depressed and feels hopelessness about the future. She has not returned to university, and her brother has set limits on any social activity she wants to have outside of the family. Her mother is having a power struggle with Ali, who traditionally wants to control his sister and even his mother. None of them realize Azar's need for treatment or any other psychosocial intervention. She is isolated most of the time in her room.

INTRODUCTION

In contemporary Iran, alcohol use is illicit but it is the most common drug used throughout the country. Opium is another drug commonly used in the country. Actually, in the past few decades, opium use has become one of the major health problems in the country as Iran has one of the largest number of opium addicts per capita (United Nations Office on Drugs and Crime [UNODC], 2009). Drug abuse in Iran is not only a major health problem; it also affects cultural, social, religious, and even political aspects of Iranians' lives. Following the overcriminalization and harsh punishment policy in the first decade after the Islamic Revolution of 1979, in the last two decades Iran has reformed its drug policy and has built a widespread harm reduction system and policy, which is not usual for the region, and has planned and administered drug abuse prevention projects. One of the latest reports on Iran's drug policy, published in "*Foreign Affairs*" magazine, describes Iran's drug policy as a winning policy (Afkhami, 2013).

Historical Overview

Since the dawn of civilization, like any other part of the world, in ancient Iran (Persia), mankind found ways to relieve life's tensions. Agriculture started to flourish in ancient Mesopotamia (in the heart of the Middle East). With the cultivation of wheat and barley came another product: beer. Wine was another drink that, according to an old legend, was invented in Iran. According to that legend, mythical King Jamshid fermented grape juice for the first time.

Although this is just a mythical story, archeological excavations have shown that wine may have originated in Iran in 5400 B.C. (McGovern, 2003). Drinking wine was a usual habit for upper class people for decades. During the Sassanid Empire (224–651 A.D.) in ancient Iran, there was a ceremony for rich people, called "*Bazm*" in Persian, which was a combination of live music and drinking wine. Drinking wine diminished temporarily after the introduction of Islam in the 7th century, but after a short period of time people started drinking wine, and its use continued to be popular, but hidden (Matthee, 2005). Although alcohol is strictly forbidden in Islam, in ancient Iran, even during the Islamic period, "*Mei*" (the Persian word for wine) was a central theme of poetry for more than a thousand years. This word was used to mean actual wine and as a mystic metaphor interchangeably. Shiraz, an ancient city in Iran (located near Persepolis), continued to be a center of wine production in the Islamic era, and today its name is on a very famous dry red table wine (Robinson, 1996).

After the Islamic Revolution, alcohol use became illicit in Iran, but it continued to be popular, this time hidden. Islamic law clearly forbids alcohol use, but it is silent regarding other drugs, including tobacco, cannabis, and opium. There is a sociocultural factor for the changing drug use tradition in the religious society of Iran during the past centuries. Recently, after many years of denial and moral/political approach, high-ranking health officials acknowledged problem drinking in Iran and prepared a road map to control the problem (Mostaghimi, 2012).

Tobacco smoking, mainly in the form water pipe smoking as well as traditional pipes (*Chopogh*), started during the Safavid dynasty. It rapidly spread throughout the country during the 20th century. In 1937, the first cigarette factory opened, with the capacity of producing 600 million cigarettes per year. Currently, Iranian Tobacco Company, a governmental organization, includes more than 10 factories throughout the country and produces about 12 billion cigarettes annually. Almost the same amount is imported each year (Meysamie, Ghaletaki, Zhand, & Abbasi, 2012).

Opium, which is currently the most prevalent drug in Iran, has been a popular drug since the Safavid dynasty, and it became more popular during the Qajar period (1785–1925). Dr. Jacob Eduard Polak (1818–1891), an Austrian Jewish physician, was working in Iran between 1851 and 1860 as a teacher of the first Iranian medical school. After going back to Austria, he published a book about the land and people of Iran, *Persien, Das Land und Seine Bewohner*. He writes that opium use is a very popular habit and it has no negative social stigma or shame for users. It is not forbidden, and every Iranian who can afford its cost uses it daily. Most people take up the habit only in old age and stick to the same amount, so that effects tend to be minimal.

Iranians began to develop a noticeable addiction to opium in the mid-19th century. Although opium has existed in Iran in some form or another for centuries, widespread addiction was not known in the country until about 1860 (McLaughlin, 1976).

Before 1956, "to the casual observer, the most obvious indication of the importance of opium in Iran was the large amount of precious agricultural land devoted to the opium poppy" (Rosa, 1960, p. 353). Effective legislation in 1956 made opium poppy cultivation illegal in the country, and strict law enforcement eliminated completely its cultivation. Iran accomplished a great deal through supply reduction by its own activities, together with international cooperation to combat addiction (Rosa, 1960). During the next few years, the cost of opium increased to 40 times its 1956 price, out of reach of most users, and the number of users was reduced by at least two-thirds. In 1969, the government decided to give opium tokens to those people older than 55 years who were not successful in withdrawing their dependence. This was a basic substitution therapy and a good step at that time (Iran's Drug Control Headquarters [DCHQ], 2005). The introduction of heroin during the early 1970's changed the face of drug abuse and addiction in Iran; this was a grave milestone in the history of drug abuse in Iran.

Geographical Situation

During the 1990s, global opium production shifted from Southeast Asia to Afghanistan, Iran's eastern neighbor. This increase in opium production even exceeded the world demand. This impacted Iran more than any other country (UNODC, 2009). Afghanistan is the producer of more than 90% of the world's opium, which generates an annual income of about $65 billion, mostly for criminals outside of the area. Iran has a 936-kilometer shared border with Afghanistan and a 909-kilometer border shared with Pakistan. Although longstanding conflicts and security threats over there have diminished or even completely disappeared, Iran's biggest challenges include the battle against drug smuggling in the eastern provinces along the border with Afghanistan and Pakistan (Bertelsmann Stiftung's Transformation Index [BTI], 2014). Despite major efforts against drug trafficking, Iran is swamped by Afghan opium: With its estimated 1.2 million opiate users, Iran faces one of the world's most serious opiate addiction problems. Although the highest rate of seizure—83% of global opium seizures and 20% of the total opiate seizure—takes place in Iran, every year tons of opium flow from Afghanistan to the rest of the world, and the biggest share—40%—flows through Iran. The world's consumption of raw opium is estimated at 1,100 tons per year, used by 4 million users; more than 42% is estimated to be used in Iran (UNODC, 2009).

Afghan opium even affects overseas countries, including the United States and Canada. A total of 22 tons of heroin is estimated to be consumed in the U.S. and Canada, and until recent years, the accepted assumption was that the majority of this heroin originated from Mexico and other Latin American countries. But with the amount of opium thought to be produced there, not more than 10 tons of heroin can be produced annually. About 50% of this amount is being trafficked to the U.S. and Canada. The logical conclusion is that either the remaining 17–20 tons of heroin are being trafficked from Afghanistan, or Colombia and/or

Mexico are producing more opium than previously reported (UNODC, 2009).

The lion's share of Afghan opiates continues to pass through Iran along the Balkan Route as well as southward toward the Persian Gulf. The UNODC estimates that 60% of the heroin and morphine from Afghanistan moves through Iran to the external market, principally to Europe. The Iranian passageway is attractive to drug traffickers because of the simple reason that they must cross just two borders to get to the European market (Calabrese, 2007 p.2).

BIOPSYCHOSOCIAL ASPECTS OF DRUG ABUSE
Demographic Features of Iranian Drug Users

The typical Iranian addict is usually using opium, very likely to be male, married, and employed. Data from national surveys and research from various provinces and among different groups have shown that more than 90% of the drug-abusing population is male. In fact, the RSA studies claimed that, on average, 93% of drug abusers in the nation are male, whether imprisoned, in treatment, or on the streets. The lowest preponderance of males belonged to Tehran, at 87%. Around two-thirds of the addict population is married. This figure is lowest in Tehran, where only half seem to be married. Even in the incarcerated group, the majority (51%) was married (Mokri, 2002). In fact, less than 10% of the addicts live alone; a spouse, parent, or sibling is usually present. Employment is also the rule in this group. Unemployed drug abusers comprise only one-fifth of the population. About a quarter of Iranian narcotic abusers have a history of intravenous injection of opioids, mainly heroin. Among MMT patients, a clear majority of the patients are male (96%), and nearly two-thirds are between 25 and 44 years of age and employed (>70%). The most common drug of abuse prior to MMT entry was opium (69%).

Because the majority of drug users in Iran are male, there are a limited number of studies of women entering MMT. A recent study on female MMT patients has shown that within a few months of entering MMT, improvements occurred in heroin use, levels of dependence, social functioning, and HIV risk behavior (Dolan et al., 2012).

Social and Cultural Issues

In Iranian culture, there are myths about the health benefits of opium. Even after researchers have shown opium has many adverse health effects, many Iranians assume it is beneficial and propose its use to friends. Actually, heroin has a negative stigma, but many people consider opium a harmless recreational substance, and there are huge numbers of people who use it recreationally. In a nationwide study, there were 1.5 million opium addicts and 5 million irregular and nondependent opium users (Naghavi et al., 2009). This is an important social determinant of health concerning drug use in Iran. Studies have shown that negative stigma impede health care seeking among those who are already abusing drugs. Even among mental health care providers, including social workers, such a negative attitude affects their willingness to provide services and even their attitude toward clients. On the other hand, negative stigma about drugs and drug use among the youth can be a preventive social factor for those who are not using drugs yet. We can assume drug use stigma as a double-edged sword, with positive preventive abilities and negative effects on treatment seeking and treatment provision (Latkin, Davey-Rothwell, Yang, & Crawford, 2013). Positive attitudes in concordance with lack of negative stigma toward opium can facilitate opium use in Iran. It is shown that increasing social unacceptability of tobacco smoking has decreased significantly its use in the U.S. (Stuber, Galea, & Link, 2008).

Research among drug users showed that some face daily life difficulties such as homelessness, lack of regular employment, poverty, and fragile relationships. Social instability including "chronic sense of uncertainty" and feeling "out of control" is associated with perpetuation of life problems such as unemployment, poverty, and fragile interpersonal relationships among drug users (German & Latkin, 2012a).

Family Issues

Family issues have a mutual relationship with drug abuse, and it is more important, as we know, for many adolescents; the age of drug use onset is under 18 in Iran (Momtazi & Rawson, 2010). There is a relationship between parental substance abuse and subsequent alcohol and/or drug abuse among their children. Even mothers and daughters share similar patterns of drug abuse (mostly prescription drug abuse), and fathers and sons have similar drugs of choice, mostly alcohol and tobacco (Johnson & Leff, 1999).

In Iranian traditional culture, the emotional relationship between parents and children is still strong and long lasting; parents usually retain their presence, responsibility, and support even after children reach adulthood. Consequently, the drug addiction of Iranian youth has caused families to ask the government to control drugs and combat drug traffickers (Rais & Nakhjavani, 2002).

Neglecting parental duties is one of the issues that can ruin intrafamilial relationships. On the other hand, drug abusers' family members can be effective in encouraging them to initiate and continue their treatment. As many Iranian drug abusers are married men who have children, this kind of poor relationship can affect the behavior of their children, although there are controversial findings in this regard (Garrusi, Amirkafi, & Garrusi, 2011). Many drug abusers in Iran experienced traumatic events during childhood and came from dysfunctional families (Mirlashari, Demirkol, Salsali, Rafiey, & Jahanbani, 2012).

Among adolescents, boys were more likely to report lifetime illicit drug use than girls. Also among boys but not girls, history of drug abuse in family members, higher score of attachment, and employment of the mother were predictors of substance use (Khushabi, Moradi, & Habibi, 2012).

Another study among Iranian adolescents has shown that lack of knowledge, positive attitude and interpretation of addiction as a social value, family members' or friends' drug use, economic status, psychiatric problems, and availability of drugs were the most frequent reasons for their drug use (Mohammadpoorasl et al., 2012).

Psychosocial Consequences

Consumption of drugs can originate from psychosocial factors such as poverty, discrimination, unemployment, shortage of recreational facilities and welfare, and social conflicts. In limited cases, it can be related to the high income among higher socioeconomic classes or as a kind of energy-enhancing instrument for some professions that are highly physically or mentally stressful (Rais & Nakhjavani, 2001).

A recently published paper has shown significant positive relationship between unemployment and low family income and crime, including drug smuggling (Musai & Mehrara, 2014). Another study on social heath factors also has shown that reduction of poverty, violence, and unemployment rates can be the main intervention strategies to improve social health status in Iran (Amini, Rafiye, Esmaeil, & Morasae, 2013). Studies have shown that social instability is associated with HIV-related high risk behavior, including illicit drug use (German & Latkin, 2012b).

A study among university students revealed that drug user students had significantly lower mental health and hopefulness and showed more aggression compared to non-user students (Zivari-Rahman, Lesani, & Shokouhi-Moqaddam, 2011).

THE POLICY ROLLER COASTER

In Iran, the earliest measures and services for drug abusing people started in the late 1960's and early 1970's. The first addiction treatment center and first outpatient methadone program in Iran were initiated in the early 1970s in Tehran and Shiraz. These programs consisted of using opioid agonists for assisted detoxification of dependent patients and methadone for inpatient medically supervised assisted withdrawal. There was a limited number of patients in these programs who received methadone as a maintenance treatment.

These efforts were stopped prematurely by the Islamic Revolution in early 1979, and the new government changed all programs to criminalization and moralization as well as supply reduction. The situation continued in the same way until the 1990s. By that time, health officials as well as the country's policy makers found out realistically that supply reduction and overcriminalization was not working, or at least was not enough for drug abuse control.

The following realities were important in this policy change:

1. Drug offenders—including users and drug-related criminals—made up more than 50% of the country's prisoners. Many families were affected by addiction; more than half of reported divorces directly or indirectly resulted from drug abuse.

2. Continuing conflicts in Afghanistan, the eastern neighbor of Iran, made it the main producer of opium, which produced more than 90% of global opium, and opium became cheaper and more easily accessible. The main target of Afghanistan's opium and heroin trade was Europe, and its main transit route was through Iran.

3. A number of HIV outbreaks occurred inside several Iranian prisons in the mid-1990s, and

4. The Iranian Welfare Organization, in collaboration with the United Nation's' International Drug Control Program (UNDCP) office, performed a rapid situation assessment (RSA) as a national study from 1998 to 1999. This study showed that between 1,200,000 and 2,000,000 people in Iran would have a diagnosis of substance-related and addictive disorders, according to the DSM-5 criteria (American Psychiatric Association, 2013).

It is shown in many countries that drug abuse and drug dealing is associated with violence (Latkin, Yang, Tobin, & German, 2013). Iran's drug problem has also contributed to violent criminality and corruption. More than 3,500 Iranian law enforcement personnel have been killed in operations against heavily armed drug traffickers over the last decades. The drug problem is a major burden on Iran's criminal justice system as Iran's prisoner population has swelled.

Drug-related crimes are the most common in most of Iran's provinces. According to the 2007 U.S. *International Narcotics Control Strategy Report,*

> More than 60 percent of the inmates in Iranian prisons are incarcerated for drug offenses, ranging from use to trafficking. Narcotics-related arrests in Iran during the first nine months of 2006 were running at an annual rate of almost 400,000, which is a typical level for the last several years. (Calabrese, 2007, p. 7)

Also in 2012, the majority (63%) of death penalties in Iran were drug-related (BTI, 2014).

In recent years, some prescription drugs, including opiate medication as well as stimulants, are being abused among higher sociocultural groups. Research findings have shown that nonmedical abuse of benzodiazepines is prevalent among participants of methadone maintenance treatment (Babakhanian, Sadeghi, Nader, Mehrjerdi, & Tabatabai, 2012). Among the prescription drugs that are commonly abused is Tramadol, an opioid analgesic (Zabihi et al., 2011).

Amphetamine-Type Stimulants

In the last decade, methamphetamine use added a new health problem to Iran's drug use situation. Its street name in Iran is *Shisheh* (glass), and it is the most commonly available amphetamine-type stimulant (ATS) in the region. Although use and seizure data for the region still remains scarce and levels of methamphetamine use in the region are low, a surge in methamphetamine seizures in the Islamic Republic of Iran points to a possible increasing domestic market. Iran is also the origin of methamphetamine smuggled to Turkey as well as to Southeast Asian countries.

> In Iran, methamphetamine seizures have rapidly increased since 2007 and in 2011 almost tripled reaching up to 4 tons. In spite of a slight drop in 2012, methamphetamine seizures in the Iran remained at high levels totaling around 3.4 tons. (UNODC, 2014)

Harm Reduction Policy

Harm reduction policy is not usual in Middle Eastern countries, but as there are successes in Iran's harm reduction programs, the growth of such programs in Iran could serve as a model for other countries in the region. Although there is governmental support for this kind of policy, it is Iranian NGOs and Iranian civil society who are paving the way for the Middle Eastern harm reduction network (Calabrese, 2007).

In 2000, the Ministry of Health, Treatment, and Medical Education began to train private physicians in the field of scientific methods of addiction treatment. In 2002, the country's first methadone maintenance treatment (MMT) clinic was set up. That same year, the Ministry of Health established the National Committee of Harm Reduction, charged with developing approaches to reduce the damage resulting from drug use, especially in injection form. This change in drug policy attracted international positive attention (MacFarquhar, 2001). By 2003, the Ministry of Health declared methadone treatment programs to be one of its core priorities. In 2005, the parliament voted to allow any doctor in Iran to dispense methadone, but under strict guidelines and monitoring. At the same time, more than 60 "Triangular Clinics" have been established, which are devoted to responding to the health needs of high-risk drug abusers, including sex workers, injection drug users, and those with HIV/AIDS. Now there are more than 300,000 people receiving MMT from more than 1,000 agonist-providing centers. More than two-thirds of these centers are run by NGOs and the private sector. Also, there are increasing numbers of agonist treatment centers that provide buprenorphine and opium tincture as other kinds of agonist therapy. There are studies on a limited needle exchange program, which have shown its effectiveness on high-risk injection behavior (Vazirian et al., 2005).

SOCIAL WORKERS' ROLE IN INTERVENTION

In the United States and many other developed countries, social workers comprise a significant portion of the drug abuse service providers' workforce and are usually the first care providers to come into contact with drug abusers who are seeking treatment and counseling service. In Iran, although the presence of a social worker is mandatory in any addiction treatment center and methadone maintenance unit, there are not enough social workers to cover all centers, and their role is not completely clear. Usually the social worker should contact family members of the client and provide them a better view of the addiction problem. As many drug users are married, the social worker can work on the spousal role and probable situation of co-dependency. For adolescents and even single adult drug users who traditionally live with their parents, a social worker consults with the parents in order to bring their support into the comprehensive management plan. Another family problem that has to be addressed by the social worker is the children of drug user parents. A social worker assesses the children's situation and works with related government and nongovernment organizations, in order to make the children's situations in their parents' home better or move them to foster care homes. Another duty of a social worker in a drug abuse treatment center is the assessment of financial resources for the client. For instance, if the client cannot afford the treatment program costs, a social worker would contact related support institutions, especially the Welfare Organization, to subsidize the clients' costs. Lack of enough specially trained social workers is considered a weak point in Iran's addiction and harm reduction system.

After pilots of prison-based needle exchange programs and methadone maintenance prison-based harm reduction programs, MMT is now provided to opioid-dependent prisoners in most of the country's 230 prisons (Zamani et al., 2010). In 2011, there were 38,256 inmates on MMT in prisons. In 2004, the World Health Organization (WHO) awarded a "best practice certification" to the HIV and AIDS programs of Iran (Behrouzan, 2009).

Since the outbreak, the Ministry of Health has acknowledged prisoners as one of the groups at high risk for HIV; frequent surveys and on-site harm reduction services led to a downward trend of

HIV prevalence after 2005. This trend suggests the effectiveness of such interventions, which need to be continued (Zamani et al., 2010). The coordinator for the United Nations AIDS office in Tehran once said,

> Iran now has one of the best prison programs for HIV in not just the region, but in the world . . . they're passing out condoms and syringes in prisons. This is unbelievable. In the whole world, there aren't more than six or seven countries doing that. (Allam, 2006, para. 10)

The government devotes an estimated $30 million annually to the program. The country's program, which melds deep-rooted religious values with cutting-edge research, is being exported to Afghanistan, Lebanon, Iraq, Syria, Sudan, Pakistan, and other Muslim nations (Allam, 2006).

MICRO, MEZZO, AND MACRO ASPECTS OF SOCIAL WORK INTERVENTION

Micro Perspective

For a complete social work assessment, a social worker should assess both the drug user client and the family. In order to have a comprehensive knowledge about the client's life situation, a biopsychosocial-spiritual assessment is necessary.

Social Worker Biopsychosocial-Spiritual Assessment of the Case Vignette

1. Health factors: Azar is in rather good physical health, but as we know, ATS use usually leads to poor physical health; her condition should be assessed thoroughly. Also, she suffers from clinical depression, which is both a frequent co-occurring disorder with drug abuse and a usual consequence of quitting stimulant drugs.

2. Familial factors: Her parents are divorced and she has no relationship with her father. There is a power struggle between her mother and her brother, Ali. None of them realizes the necessity of treatment.

3. Azar is in Erikson's stage of intimacy versus isolation at the age of 27. She has cut ties with her ex-boyfriend and is completely isolated. She does not feel productive as she is unemployed now and gave up her education.

4. Diversity factors: Azar is a young single girl who lives in a traditional society that usually does not accept independent living for a single woman. As a nonbeliever in an over-religious society, she has to hide her faith-related attitudes.

5. Support system: Azar has emotional support from her mother, but her brother not only does not give her support, he sets unnecessary limits in her personal life.

6. Socioeconomic status: Azar is from a middle class family and has limited financial resources from the family. She is unemployed and has no special skills to get a job. She lives in a society with a high rate of unemployment and a limited job market. From a social perspective, she has to fight with traditional barriers of a traditional Islamic society for women.

7. Grief and loss history: She has had no complicated grief or loss during her life.

8. Current psychosocial functioning: Azar's cognitive functioning is considered good and she is a young intelligent person. Her mood is totally depressed and she feels anxious regarding her future. She has poor coping capacity and seems hopeless. She has recurrent thoughts about suicide, but she does not have a suicidal idea or plan.

9. Specific circumstances: She lives with her single mother and a nonsupportive brother.

10. Interdisciplinary team cooperation: Social worker would communicate and share Azar's needs with other members of the treatment team.

Social Work Intervention

Social workers would use the biopsychosocial-spiritual assessment to build a treatment plan, with the cooperation of the client and the other treatment team members, in order to have an understanding of both addiction and depression as chronic recurrent mental disorders for Azar as the main client as well as for her family. Social workers can help her to break the isolation and improve her self-esteem and self-confidence. This can be accomplished through individual and family counseling as well as social skills training. These are shared responsibilities for the social worker and a clinical psychologist. Also social workers can facilitate the reconstruction of the family system and help Azar to be ready for the treatment of depression. These steps not only are effective for relapse prevention of drug abuse but also to help her with a new start for a productive life. The social worker would help Azar to go back to her education or start a job.

Mezzo Perspective

Social workers will attempt to benefit the client by gaining family members' help and seeking other professionals related to the client's management and treatment. A social worker may help Azar to go back to her education by contacting the university officials, introducing her to work training institutions, and helping her to get on the list of job finding offices. There are specific funds and loans for people in recovery, and a social worker provides information on these programs and contacts the related institutions in order to facilitate Azar's access to these services. A social worker also helps Azar in finding peer support groups such as 12-step programs.

There are studies that have shown that community prevention programs can be effective, and these are opportunities for social workers to intervene (Hawkins, Shapiro, & Fagan, 2010). For example, a long-term community-based lifestyle intervention program can be effective in a developing country like Iran. This program has shown significant change from baseline in mean lifestyle scores, including smoking and high-risk health behaviors (Sarrafzadegan et al., 2009). Thus, the therapeutic community has been shown to be an effective intervention in Iran (Babaie & Razaghi, 2013).

Macro Perspective

There are many laws and facilities in Iran that can be used by social workers for supporting clients such as Azar. These include free training courses for job-seeking women, financial support resources, and so on. In Iran, the state welfare organization is the most important organization; it provides services for drug abuse rehabilitation, finding employment, financial support, family consultation and support, and generally for women needing any social as well as health-related supports.

Social workers are one of the most important professionals for taking a part in policy making, especially regarding lobbying and advocacy for social support laws for drug abusers in treatment and/or recovery. Advocacy can be done at the national level with the state welfare organization and Ministry of Health as well as local support and advocacy through city councils.

The Iranian government is trying to control drugs because the formal political ideology views the high drug use and addiction rates as a conspiracy of the enemy to weaken the Islamic republic. Therefore, the huge annual human losses and economic damage of drug consumption and trafficking have caused the government to give priority to controlling the drug supply (Rais & Nakhjavani, 2002).

CONCLUSION

It seems that Iran's drug policy to admit drug abuse and addiction are major health problems and implement harm reduction programs is becoming a success in the region. Attention to social determinants of this health issue, such as cultural, familial, and economic factors, can improve the prevention and treatment program's effectiveness.

INTERNET RESOURCES

- National Institute on Drug Abuse: http://www .drugabuse.gov
- National Institute on Mental Health: http:// www.nimh.nih.gov

- National Institute on Alcohol Abuse and Alcoholism: http://www.niaaa.nih.gov
- Drug Abuse Prevention: http://www.preventionweb.net
- Iran's Drug Control Headquarters: http://www.dchq.ir/en
- United Nations Office on Drugs and Crime: http://www.unodc.org

DISCUSSION QUESTIONS

1. What are important sociocultural issues in drug abuse?

2. What treatment and social services are available for drug abusing clients in recovery?

3. What effective harm reduction policies are currently available in Iran?

4. What is the drug abuse and addiction situation in Iran?

5. How does opium production in Afghanistan affect Iran and the global community?

6. How can a social worker help a drug abusing client with the recovery process?

REFERENCES

Afkhami, A. A. (2013). How Iran won the war on drugs. *Foreign Affairs*. Retrieved from http://www.foreignaffairs.com/articles/139095/amir-a-afkhami/how-iran-won-the-war-on-drugs

Allam, H. (2006). Iran's AIDS-prevention program among world's most progressive. *Knight Ridder*, April 14, 2006. Retrieved from http://www.mcclatchydc.com/incoming/article24454495.html

American Psychiatric Association. (2013). *Diagnostic and statistical manual of mental disorders* (5th ed.). Washington, DC: Author.

Amini, R. M., Rafiye, H., Esmaeil, K., & Morasae, E. (2013). Social health status in Iran: An empirical study. *Iranian Journal of Public Health, 42*(2), 206–214.

Babaie, E., & Razaghi, N. (2013). Comparing the effects of methadone maintenance treatment, therapeutic community, and residential rehabilitation on quality of life and mental health of drug addicts. *Addiction & Health, 5*(1–2), 16–20.

Babakhanian, M., Sadeghi, M., Nader, M. N., Mehrjerdi, Z. A., & Tabatabai, M. (2012). Nonmedical abuse of benzodiazepines in opiate-dependent patients in Tehran, Iran. *Iran Journal of Psychiatry and Behavioral Sciences, 6*(1), 62–67.

Behrouzan, O. (2009). An epidemic of meanings: HIV and AIDS in Iran and the significance of history, language and gender. In J. F. Klot & V. K. Nguyen (Eds.), *The fourth wave: Violence, gender, culture & HIV in the 21st century* (pp. 319–346).

Bertelsmann Stiftung's Transformation Index. (2014). *Iran country report.* Gütersloh: Author. Retrieved from http://www.bti-project.org

Calabrese J. (2007). Iran's war on drugs: Holding the line? *Middle East Institute Policy Briefs, 3*, 1–20.

Dolan, K., Salimi, S., Nassirimanesh, B., Mohsenifar, S., Allsop, D., & Mokri, A. (2012). Six-month follow-up of Iranian women in methadone treatment: Drug use, social functioning, crime, and HIV and HCV seroincidence. *Substance Abuse Rehabilitation, 3*(1), 37–43.

Garrusi, S., Amirkafi, A., & Garrusi, B. (2011). Experiences of drug dependent fathers in relation with their children: A qualitative study. *Addiction & Health, 3*(1–2), 29–38.

German, D., & Latkin, C. A. (2012a). Social stability and health: Exploring multidimensional social disadvantage. *Journal of Urban Health, 89*(1), 19–35.

German, D., & Latkin, C. A. (2012b). Social stability and HIV risk behavior: Evaluating the role of accumulated vulnerability. *AIDS Behavior, 16*(1), 168–178.

Hawkins, J. D., Shapiro, V. B., & Fagan, A. A. (2010). Disseminating effective community prevention practices: Opportunities for social work education. *Research & Social Work Practice, 20*(5), 518–527.

Iran's Drug Control Headquarters. (2005). *Mavademokhadder be rravayte Asnade SAVAK* [Illicit drugs according to SAVAK documents]. Tehran: Author.

Johnson, J. L., & Leff, M. (1999). Children of substance abusers: Overview of research findings. *Pediatrics, 103*(2), 1085–1099. Retrieved from http://

pediatrics.aappublications.org/content/103/Supplement_2/1085.full.htm

Khushabi, K., Moradi, S., & Habibi, M. (2012). Risk and protective factors of drug abuse in high school students. *Iranian Journal of Psychiatry & Psychology, 17*(4), 313–323.

Latkin, C. A., Davey-Rothwell, M., Yang, J. Y., & Crawford, N. (2013). The relationship between drug user stigma and depression among inner-city drug users in Baltimore, MD. *Journal of Urban Health, 90*(1), 147–156. doi:10.1007/s11524-012-9753-z

Latkin, C. A., Yang, C., Tobin, K. E., & German, D. (2013). Injection drug users' and their risk networks' experiences of and attitudes toward drug dealer violence. *International Journal of Drug Policy, 24*(2), 135–141.

MacFarquhar, N. (2001, August 18). Iran shifts war against drugs, admitting it has huge problem. *New York Times*, p. A6.

Matthee, R. (2005). *The pursuit of pleasure: Drugs and stimulants in Iranian history*. Princeton, NJ: Princeton University Press.

McGovern, P. E. (2003). *Ancient wine: The search for the origins of viniculture*. Princeton, NJ: Princeton University Press.

McLaughlin, G. T. (1976). The poppy is not an ordinary flower: A survey of drug policy in Iran. *Fordham Law Review, 44*(4), 702–772. Retrieved from http://ir.lawnet.fordham.edu/flr/vol44/iss4/1

Meysamie, A., Ghaletaki, R., Zhand, N., & Abbasi, M. (2012). Cigarette smoking in Iran. *Iranian Journal of Public Health, 41*(2), 1.

Mirlashari, J., Demirkol, A., Salsali, M., Rafiey, H., & Jahanbani, J. (2012). Early childhood experiences, parenting and the process of drug dependency among young people in Tehran, Iran. *Drug Alcohol Review, 31*, 461–468.

Mohammadpoorasl, A., Nedjat, S., Fakhari, A., Yazdani, K., Rahimi, F. A., & Fotouhi, A. (2012). Substance abuse in high school students in association with socio-demographic variables in northwest of Iran. *Iranian Journal of Public Health, 41*(12), 40–46.

Mokri, A. (2002). Brief overview of the status of drug abuse in Iran. *Archives of Iranian Medicine, 5*, 184–190.

Momtazi, S., & Rawson, R. (2010). Substance abuse among Iranian high school students. *Current Opinion in Psychiatry, 23*, 221–226.

Mostaghimi, R. (2012, July 7). Iran is confronting its drinking problem. *Los Angeles Times*, p. A1.

Musai, M., & Mehrara, M. (2014). The relationship between drug smuggling and unemployment (Case study: Iran). *International Journal of Academic Research in Economics and Management Sciences, 3*(1). doi: 10.6007/IJAREMS/v3-i1/600

Naghavi, M., Abolhassani, F., Pourmalek, F., Lakeh, M., Jafari, N., Vaseghi, S., . . . Kazemeini, H. (2009). The burden of disease and injury in Iran 2003. *Popular Health Meter, 7*, 9.

Rais, D. F., & Nakhjavani, A. G. (2001). Consumer market of drugs in Iran. *Social Welfare, 1*(1), 67–87.

Rais, D. F., & Nakhjavani, A. G. (2002). The drug market in Iran. *The ANNALS of the American Academy of Political and Social Science, 582*(1), 149–166.

Robinson, J. (1996). *Guide to wine grapes*. Oxford University Press.

Rosa, F. W. (1960). Malaria and opium control in Iran. *Public Health Report, 75*(4), 352–354.

Sarrafzadegan, N., Kelishadi, R., Esmaillzadeh, A., Mohammadifard, N., Katayoun, R. K., Roohafza, H., . . . Malekafzali, H. (2009). Do lifestyle interventions work in developing countries? Findings from the Isfahan healthy heart program in the Islamic Republic of Iran. *Bull World Health Organization, 87*(1), 39–50.

Stuber, J., Galea, S., & Link, B. G. (2008). Smoking and the emergence of a stigmatized social status. *Social Science Medicine, 67*(3), 420–430.

United Nations Office on Drugs and Crime. (2009). *Addiction, crime and insurgency: The transnational threat of Afghan opium*. Retrieved from http://www.unodc.org/documents/data-and analysis/Afghanistan/Afghan_Opium_Trade_2009

United Nations Office on Drugs and Crime. (2014). *Global synthetic drugs assessment: Amphetamine-type stimulants and new psychoactive substances*. Retrieved from http://www.unodc.org/unodc/en/data-and-analysis/addiction-crime-and-insurgency.html

Vazirian, M., Nassirimanesh, B., Zamani, S., Ono-Kihara, M., Kihara, M., Mortazavi, R. S., & Gouya, M. M. (2005). Needle and syringe sharing practices of injecting drug users participating in an outreach HIV prevention program in Tehran, Iran: A cross-sectional study. *Harm Reduction Journal, 2*(19). doi:10.1186/1477-7517-2-19

Zabihi, E., Hoseinzaadeh, A., Emami, M., Mardani, M., Mahmoud, B., & Akbar, M. A. (2011). Potential for tramadol abuse by patients visiting pharmacies in nothern Iran. *Substance Abuse: Research and Treatment, 5,* 11.

Zamani, S., Farnia, M., Torknejad, A., Abbasi, A. B., Gholizadeh, M., Kasraee, F., . . . Kihara, M. (2010). Patterns of drug use and HIV-related risk behaviors among incarcerated people in a prison in Iran. *Journal of Urban Health, 87*(4), 603–616. doi: 10.1007/s11524-010-9450-8

Zivari-Rahman, M., Lesani, M., & Shokouhi-Moqaddam, S. (2011). Comparison of mental health, aggression and hopefulness between student drug-users and healthy students (A study in Iran). *Addiction & Health, 4*(1–2), 36–42.

CHAPTER 36

Australia's Indigenous People

Glenda Bawden

CHAPTER OBJECTIVES

- Develop an understanding of cultural issues and their impact on clients and social work practice;
- Describe and learn to utilize social work interventions that will fine tune interventions within a particular cultural context;
- Assess the organizational setting and evaluate how it assists or restricts social work interventions when there is cultural complexity;
- Learn to search out and identify the broader policy context and its influence on practice.

CASE VIGNETTE

A young Aboriginal couple, Tom and Margaret, are about to have a baby, an exciting and momentous event. The couple is very much in love and this baby is wanted very much. However, both have had difficult lives to date. Neither is confident and both are very wary in unfamiliar situations. Each comes from a different geographical and clan (tribal) area and is new to this district. Tom has lived in a remote area with his extended family in the traditional way, including the spiritual and sacred aspects of the local tribal culture. Margaret has lived a more urban life and spent time in the care of the state, from ages 5 to 15, following some family difficulties that resulted in homelessness, poverty, and depression.

Neither Tom nor Margaret has finished school, and they both have difficulty reading health information and completing forms. They have not had regular employment, though both have had some short-term employment in unskilled jobs. They have pressing financial difficulties. They are currently living with some people whom they met. They have their own room and share the kitchen and bathroom. They hope to obtain accommodation through Aboriginal Housing prior to the birth of their baby.

They have very few family, friends, or community to support them. They have linked with the local Aboriginal Co-operative, which offers a range of services including primary health care, a midwife, family support, social support, and practical assistance. For them, the birthing process is full of uncertainties. They feel unsure about what to expect from a hospital, a big, strange, impersonal building full of strangers. Margaret is not keen to attend prenatal clinic, which involves a lot of waiting around to see a midwife or obstetrician. She is also worried about the staff finding out about her past mental health difficulties. Her partner is unhappy about a male doctor examining his partner, and he wants to arrange for only female staff to be involved, as in his culture giving birth is "women's business." The couple knows that there are medical risks associated with birth, and they have fears about coming to hospital. Many Aboriginal people associate hospitals with death, as most Aboriginal people only attend when very ill and sometimes "'never come home'." They also know that, in the past, babies were sometimes removed from their parents in hospital and given to white families to bring up, as part of a government policy to assimilate the Aboriginal population.

However, given Margaret's particular medical history (i.e., cardiac and mental health risks), she will need to give birth in a facility where a high level support is available (e.g., large tertiary hospital that can support both mother and baby). So for this couple, the arrival of their first baby, a seemingly normal event, has become one of the biggest challenges of their life.

INTRODUCTION AND BACKGROUND

This chapter is organized into micro, mezzo and macro sections to cover three different perspectives on the material. A range of interventions will be discussed. Relevant points of understanding will be identified at each level as part of the person in context viewpoint.

The Victorian Department of Health requires all health services to ask, "Are you of Aboriginal or Torres Strait Islander descent?" Aboriginal people cannot be identified by appearance. Many Aboriginal people do not fit the stereotype of dark skin and dark eyes and may be quite fair and not "look Aboriginal." Most Aboriginal people live on the mainland of Australia and in Tasmania; Torres Strait Islanders are Indigenous people who mostly live on islands between Australia and New Guinea. Some Indigenous people may choose not to identify as Aboriginal or Islander, and some staff feel uncomfortable asking patients this question about identity. Cultural education assists staff to

understand why it is important to record accurate data about Aboriginality, in order to understand and help meet the health issues of Indigenous people. This cultural education can also help staff learn ways to ask this question sensitively and respectfully.

Aboriginal people have a strong relationship with "country," the land of their family and clan. This is more than just a relationship to physical land; it is more of a spiritual relationship with the whole ecological system, involving reciprocal responsibilities to take care of the environment, animals, plants and people. Respect for ancestral beings and care of sacred sites and rituals is part of this undertaking. The dreaming stories, communicating the traditional lore, are also associated with country. While in their own country, Aboriginal people feel most comfortable, whereas when away from country, they may feel more anxious and unsettled (Hunt, 2012). This dislocation from country and the destruction of Aboriginal culture during colonization has been traumatizing for generations of Aboriginal people.

Aboriginal families are much more "extended" (Stewart & Allan, 2013) than the Western nuclear family. As well as having support from their parents, and other family members, children relate closely to elders, leaders and peers in their wider community, all of whom share reciprocal responsibility for those within the clan. It is usual to refer to elders as "Uncle" or "Auntie" as a term of respect, even though they are not biological relatives. Children are seen as very important as they represent the future of the community and the culture.

Globally, indigenous peoples face similar issues worldwide. The social determinants of health (Marmot & Wilkinson, 2006) such as social disadvantage, early life, social exclusion, unemployment, social support, addiction, food and transport reduce health outcomes. This chapter describes a project which engaged clinicians to be more culturally responsive in order to improve indigenous health. Documenting it here will mean that others working in similar fields may exchange ideas.

MICRO PERSPECTIVE: CULTURALLY SENSITIVE ENGAGEMENT

The young couple in the opening vignette, Margaret and Tom, are having a baby and face unexpected issues seeking healthcare. They are anxious and concerned, so it is important to begin by joining with them, and very slowly developing an understanding of their situation, as *they* see it. This cannot be achieved by asking a series of questions based on a structured format enquiring about presenting problem, personal situation, family context, or practical issues. Until trust is established, this is pointless (Herring, Spangaro, Lauw, & McNamara, 2013). A much more indirect approach is needed so the Aboriginal person is able to develop a relationship with the worker in order to decide what information they may be prepared to entrust to him or her.

Yarning is an indirect process used by Aboriginal people. Bessarab and Ng'andu (2010) describe yarning as a cultural form of conversation that is culturally friendly and safe and builds the relationship. They use it in research but they explore social, collaborative, and therapeutic yarning as well. Yarning builds on Aboriginal people's historical role of storytelling in the oral tradition and includes both teaching and handing down information. It is similar to "shooting the breeze." It is sometimes long and time consuming but is a safe way to convey and hear information and communicate the issues that are important. It works like a metaphor where, although there may be one apparent meaning there may also be another meaning, often a more powerful one. So for our family, the yarning would be the exchange of indirect conversation aiming to establish rapport by discussing everyday matters, rather than questioning about current problems or difficulties.

Assessment

After some yarning, a very careful enquiry about straightforward topics such as asking the couple about their day so far, or the journey to the health facility, could follow (e.g., Did you come by car, on public transport, or with a friend? Did you get here easily?). Interactions must be conducted in a respectful way. The clients will make an assessment of the practitioner from such exchanges to determine if he/she is compassionate and empathic, non-judgmental, not racist, and whether he or she is likely to be able to help. This exchange will also provide information for the practitioner about the couple's material resources as many Aboriginal people would not be able to afford a car. Access to transport may be a barrier. Attending scheduled appointments is difficult for many Aboriginal families. The worker may be able to offer something— transport to attend an appointment, a ticket for a train or bus, a taxi voucher, someone to collect them to bring them in. The patient can accept or refuse these practical supports, depending on their situation and preferences. They may entrust other pertinent information to the worker during such an exchange.

The practitioner will need to establish an interaction that moves very carefully and allows the Aboriginal person to begin to trust. It is unlikely that any practitioner would be able to complete a full assessment at the first meeting (Dudgeon, Garvey, & Pickett, 2000; Fejo-King, 2013; Herring et al., 2013). This assessment is much more likely to develop gradually and tentatively over several careful meetings, sometimes going forward and then back. Herring et al. (2013) discuss the need for practitioners to become informed about Aboriginal cultural issues and to take a stance (i.e., to redress disadvantage) and to reach out. Harms et al. (2011) conducted focus groups with urban Aboriginal people to explore what they thought social workers needed to know to work with the Aboriginal community and they urged respect for the client and honesty in the relationship. They wanted the social worker to listen, to understand family and community structures, to provide practical assistance and to involve the client. Families reported the offer of practical assistance to be important (Harms et al., 2011).

The practitioner will gradually become aware of any additional barriers to health care whether they are practical, or from the clients' understanding or fears about their personal health situation. The social worker needs to actively undertake their own cultural education to help develop their cultural awareness, understanding and skills, and to actively listen in order to be able to provide culturally competent, safe and sensitive practice. The worker achieves most by starting with exploring the clients' current concerns and issues and only once trust is established, explores further the background, personal situation or family situation.

Aboriginal clients should be encouraged to remain empowered and in charge of themselves (Whiteside, Tsey, & Earles, 2011.) This approach is also useful with other social groups who are wary of authority, whether from historical treatment or personal experience, or both.

Intervention: Cultural Care Plan

For this young couple, a key social work intervention is to develop an understanding of their concerns and to set up a cultural care plan to guide staff. Aboriginal people bring very different histories, but many are traumatized and saddened by issues affecting their culture, tribe, their family or themselves. It is important to get to know each individual person, reassure them that they can share their concerns, and work together to develop a plan which spells out their wishes. Discussing and planning in advance allows time to explore issues and find acceptable solutions before there is a crisis. Identifying some key people with a cultural understanding who can "interpret" or advocate for Aboriginal clients may also help. This could be their mother, a friend, the midwife from the Aboriginal health service or an Aboriginal hospital liaison officer/cultural support person from within the hospital or community.

For instance, birthing is "women's business," so, where possible, female staff should be involved. If male staff must be involved, then this needs to be negotiated respectfully and the reasons explained and permission sought. Without this understanding Aboriginal people may become anxious, distressed and angry, and then not keep appointments, may leave hospital early, or not complete their treatment. They also may behave threateningly because the professionals have committed a cultural breach, of which the professionals are unaware. Establishing a cultural care plan can make plain the family's wishes and provide guidance to all the professionals who are involved (Stewart & Allan, 2013).

So for our couple, the cultural care plan that would guide the rest of the treating team might be as follows:

1. Anything new should be explained in terms of what, why, and how. Permission to proceed should be sought from each person. Staff need to ensure the couple understand and are in agreement.

2. A cultural care worker such as an Aboriginal Hospital Liaison Officer should be actively involved in order to "interpret," reassure the couple, and advise the staff.

3. Staff caring for Margaret should be female, whenever possible.

4. Margaret needs her medication and respectful and especially reassuring care, in view of her past history of trauma and mental health difficulties.

5. Tom needs to be treated with particular respect as he is an initiated traditional man. (He has undertaken tribal cultural rituals as he entered puberty and beyond.) He takes his responsibilities to protect "his woman" very seriously.

So this is an example of a cultural care plan in this situation. Each Aboriginal patient would need a different cultural care plan, depending on their health issues, their cultural background and their current social and cultural support network.

Ethical Interventions

The Australian Association of Social Workers (AASW) has developed a code of ethics that AASW members are required to follow (AASW, 2013a). The frontispiece of the AASW's *Code of Ethics* depicts an Aboriginal family by a campfire and tells this associated story:

> A traditional Aboriginal family is sitting around a burning campfire. Through the flames of the campfire, the smoke forms a spiralling upward pathway, travelling through the AASW logo and linking the family with the environments of education, housing and health. The goal for social work is to ethically engage and interact with Aboriginal and Torres Strait Islander Australians to promote, achieve and maintain their overall wellbeing. The three core values that members of the social work profession are committed to—Respect for persons, Social justice and Professional integrity—are symbolised as being cyclical and never ending. (p. 2)

The *Code of Ethics* further specifies culturally competent, safe and sensitive practice, acknowledging culture and the worker's own biases. It suggests obtaining a working knowledge of a client's values, customs, spiritual world views, needs and differences and providing accessible, safe, respectful and collaborative relationships. It also suggests

that workers seek guidance from community elders, and actively work to challenge racism and oppression. The *Code* is applicable to all social workers working in Australia including those in direct practice, education and policy.

Legal Interventions

Many Aboriginal people have benefited from legal advice, guidance and advocacy in relation to access to health services, children at risk, social security benefits, land rights and criminal charges. For the couple in the vignette, one potential legal issue is their capacity to care for their newborn. Services will want both parents to be educated and competent in terms of baby care. If the parents are not coping well, additional help may be found from family or community, or from community based Aboriginal family support services, or mainstream services. In addition, Margaret's mental health will need to be reviewed and services arranged and available if she needs extra help. If she is very unwell and refusing help there is the capacity in law to refer her for assessment and care if she or others are at serious risk. Recent new legislation (Mental Health Act, 2014) in this area has strengthened patient rights and set up several new requirements to protect the patient.

In this state, nurses and doctors are required to make a report to child protection if they have "formed a belief on reasonable grounds that the child is in need of protection from physical injury or sexual abuse" (Children, Youth and Families Act, 2005). This law overrides the patient's right to privacy and confidentiality when a child is believed to be in danger (At present these mandatory reporting requirements do not apply to social workers, but social workers may feel ethically obliged to report if the child is seen as "at risk"). The authorized child protection agency will assess and if concerned about risk, will establish supports to make a child safe. Currently in Victoria, the Victorian Aboriginal Child Care Agency (www.vacca.org) offers Aboriginal-controlled and culturally safe child care services to provide support, which helps keep Aboriginal families together and avoid removal of children. Sometimes the extended family or a community member will become involved to assist the family at this difficult time, as the child is seen as a child of the community, not just the nuclear family. If the situation became very dangerous and volatile and there was imminent risk, it may be necessary to call security and possibly, the police. If there were legal consequences, the Victorian Aboriginal Legal Service can provide advice, advocacy and representation in court for Aboriginal people. Social workers can refer clients for assistance or they can self-refer.

However, the value of a cultural care plan is to prepare, plan and ideally prevent issues including legal issues arising by developing shared understandings and an agreed process to resolve any difficulties.

Rights-Based Interventions

Many Aboriginal people do not experience the same human rights as other Australians (Calma & Priday, 2011). Social workers who are aware of this can work toward active empowerment using rights-based practice. Some discrimination is overt and explicit, but often systemic discrimination is more hidden and has a disproportionate impact on vulnerable groups. Social workers can be active in terms of seeking to realize the special rights proposed by the United Nations Declaration on the Rights of Indigenous Peoples (2007); the key principles in this declaration include equality, nondiscrimination, partnership, consultation and cooperation. Briskman (2014) discusses this approach further, challenging social workers to pursue a human rights approach to recognize the strengths of Indigenous communities and to center Indigenous rights and Indigenous voice.

Strengths-Based Interventions

A strengths-based approach recognizes the importance of people's environments and focuses on their potentials, strengths, interests, abilities, knowledge and capacities rather than their deficits.

Client self-determination, collaboration and outreach are important and the principle that all people have the capacity to learn, grow and change is also important (Scerra, 2011). Scerra's research paper reviews evidence for this strengths approach. She found that a strengths-based approach is effective in client engagement. She quotes Price-Robertson (2010), "young parents have the opportunity to identify their own strengths and work toward achieving positive personal and interpersonal outcomes." Some improvement of child health and family well-being has been identified in the use of strengths practice with Aboriginal families by Walker and Shepherd (2008) and Jalaris Aboriginal Corporation. The positive emphasis is valuable with Aboriginal people, many of who have managed to cope in very difficult circumstances and where building on demonstrated resilience can be empowering. She also discusses the Strengths-Based Practices Inventory (SBPI; Green, McAllister, & Tarte, 2004), which is a tool to evaluate programs and measures the following:

- empowerment approach: build on family strengths and skills;
- cultural competency: sensitive and responsive to cultural background and beliefs;
- staff sensitivity-knowledge: knowledgeable and sensitive to family needs;
- relationship-supportive: facilitate relationships with other parents and community members.

These are clearly dimensions of great importance when working with Aboriginal families.

This strength-based approach can also be useful at discharge to support people to be in charge of their own situation. Aboriginal people may require particular support and may have better health outcomes if referred to services provided by National Aboriginal-Controlled Community Health Organizations (NACCHOs). Another option is to refer to professionals who are culturally trained and experienced, such as certain accredited general practitioners, health services or community services who are more likely to understand their cultural context.

In summary, for Aboriginal clients culturally sensitive engagement becomes the starting point for further interventions of assessment, practical assistance, cultural care planning, ethical considerations, legal interventions, rights based and strengths-based practice.

MEZZO PERSPECTIVE: DEVELOPING ORGANIZATIONAL CULTURAL COMPETENCE

When a practitioner is attempting to establish long-lasting change for his or her clients, it is also necessary to work toward changing the workplace or organization. Organizations can become more culturally aware and safe by implementing staff education, leadership and partnerships with the local Aboriginal Services. The New South Wales Hunter New England Health Authority (Hunter New England Health, 2012) challenged this directly using the MacPherson Report's definition of institutional racism:

> the collective failure of an organization to provide an appropriate and professional service to people because of their color, culture or ethnic origin. It can be seen or detected in processes, attitudes and behavior which amount to discrimination through unwitting prejudice, ignorance, thoughtlessness, and racist stereotyping which disadvantage minority ethnic people. (MacPherson, 1999, p. 64)

In metropolitan Melbourne, Australia, less than 0.5% of patients seen are Aboriginal yet Aboriginal women make up 7.2% of all hospital births (Victorian Government Department of Health, 2013c). The racially mixed staff, many of whom are born overseas, have a very limited understanding of indigenous cultures and the issues faced by Aboriginal people who come to hospital.

A range of staff education programs were established and implemented at the health service to broaden the depth of cultural knowledge within the organization and improve cultural safety. Close relationships were established with local Aboriginal agencies and local elders, seeking guidance to foster a more responsive service and make healthcare more accessible to the Indigenous community. Easily accessible internal information, policies, procedures, and guidelines were developed to guide staff toward more culturally sensitive work.

An agreement was reached by the Boards of the Health Service and the Board of the local Aborigines Co-operative to meet together twice a year, and for the Chief Executive Officer of the Aborigines Co-operative to become an ongoing member of the organization's Population Health Committee, thus formally connecting the people and the organizations.

A welcoming environment, with Aboriginal Flags and Aboriginal art, and documented acknowledgement of the traditional owners of the land, enabled Aboriginal people to feel culturally welcomed and to symbolically demonstrate a commitment to respectful practice. Working with the organization in differing ways and at multiple levels, allows the practitioner to influence and enlist a wide range of different people toward achieving an agreed common goal.

MACRO PERSPECTIVE: THE SOCIAL DETERMINANTS OF HEALTH AND GOVERNMENTAL POLICIES

Social and economic factors are known to be the most powerful determinants of population health in society (Carson, Dunbar, Chenhall, & Bailie, 2007; Marmot & Wilkinson, 2006; Raphael, 2002). This is very relevant to Aboriginal people who, like those in our vignette, are socially, economically, and culturally disadvantaged. This disadvantage was formally legislated in a range of Aboriginal Protection Acts in various Australian states, starting in 1869. The Aborigines Protection Act of 1869 was the first Australian legislation for "the protection and management of the Aboriginal natives." The Act prescribed where "any Aboriginal or any tribe of Aborigines shall reside" and set out restrictions on contracts, earnings and employment, the care, custody and education of children: bedding and clothing was "on loan only and shall remain the property of Her Majesty." Any interactions with non-Aboriginal people regarding administering of alcohol (unless as medicine), harboring (unless ill or injured), taking or selling of chattels were governed by the Act. The State Library of Victoria has the archive of this legislation and demonstrates the harshness of these policies. It includes protectorate reports that note that the reductions in numbers are due to "vices acquired by contact with a civilized race." The Aboriginal population diminished from 60,000 to 2,000 across Australia due to massacres, smallpox and other introduced illness, and disadvantage (Department of Health Victoria, Video, 2012). The population is now 47,333 in Victoria (Victorian Government Department of Health, 2013a).

In particular, it is worth noting that in 1951, there were assimilation policies in Australia that aimed to integrate "half caste" children, in particular by removing them from their parents and placing them with white families, resulting in the stolen generations of dispossessed and distressed people (Murphy, 2011). This is the policy which resulted in Aboriginal people's fears of giving birth in hospital, because of the stories passed on by those whose babies had been removed (National Sorry Day Committee, 2014). More than 47% of Aboriginal people have at least one relative who has been forcibly removed (Victorian Government Department of Health, 2013a). For families such as in those in the vignette, these fears will be palpable.

The legislative structures have changed in the late 20th century. The Australian Electoral Commission (2014) notes that the referendum in 1967 changed the constitution to allow the Commonwealth to make laws for Aborigines and to count them in the census. In 1987, a Royal Commission was formed to investigate Aboriginal deaths in custody (Nagel & Summerrell, 1996; National Archives of Australia, 2015) and recommended changes to procedures, liaison with Aboriginal groups and

education for the police in order to reduce these deaths (www.sbs.com.au/shows/thetallman).

The law has also been used to gain some land rights: The case of *Mabo v. Queensland* successfully challenged the notion that the land was no one's (*terra nullius*) before settlement by whites. In this case, an Indigenous man, Eddie Mabo, was granted native title to his land. Symbolically, this granting of land rights also acknowledged in law the primary place of Indigenous people in Australia.

The Council of Australian Governments has recently worked to develop a National Partnership Agreement on Closing the Gap in Indigenous Health Outcomes (2013), which aims to address the life expectancy gap by focusing on smoking, delivering effective primary health care, better coordinating the patient journey, providing a healthy transition to adulthood, and making Indigenous health everyone's business.

Koolin Balit, the Victorian state government's strategic directions for Aboriginal health, has three key dimensions: improving data and evidence, strong Aboriginal organizations, and cultural responsiveness (Victorian Government Department of Health, 2013b). At last there is consistency between local, state, federal, and Aboriginal-controlled organizations in terms of health policy goals.

Reconciliation between Aboriginal and Torres Strait Islander people and the broader Australian community has become a priority and aims to improve understanding by raising awareness and knowledge of Aboriginal and Torres Strait Islander histories and culture (Reconciliation Australia, 2014). This includes social work practitioners needing to familiarize themselves with these current legislative and policy developments and use them as leverage to improve their capacity to meet client needs. The Australian Association of Social Workers has also now developed a Reconciliation Action Plan (2013b), which sets out goals including cultural competence.

CONCLUSION

This chapter outlines micro, mezzo, and macro perspectives, demonstrating ways of understanding and intervening with an Aboriginal family who are having their first baby. Looking from a micro perspective, the social worker will spend time developing rapport and completing an assessment, later organizing significant cultural and social support from within the health system and the community. Looking from the mezzo perspective of the organization in which this couple found themselves, we see that many staff will benefit from developing their cultural knowledge and understanding regarding issues facing Aboriginal people. Furthermore, hospital structures make health care challenging for Aboriginal people, and the organization's implementation of cultural safety processes aim to address this. When the macro is examined, particularly the legislative context, it is easy to see the historical and current reasons for Aboriginal disadvantage. Fortunately, in this example, the young couple successfully established relationships with health providers; negotiated and received culturally safe, personalized health care; and delivered a healthy baby. They have continued to have contact with health providers and have now returned to this same health service for the birth of their second baby.

This work was part of a clinical engagement project that was very successful in terms of improving access, quality and outcomes of care, achieving treatment completion, and improving relationships between families and health services. Senior organizational leadership encouraging more cultural responsiveness has helped. Legislative changes establishing Indigenous rights have also pushed change. Local, state, and federal government have collaborated to develop common goals and developed integrated policies and incentives to promote and support this change and to link with Aboriginal-controlled services.

The health and social inequalities of Australia's Aboriginal people are decreasing. The Australian Bureau of Statistics (2013) states that the life expectancy for Aboriginal men is 69.1 years and women 73.7 years. The gap between Aboriginal and non-Aboriginal people decreased by 0.8 years for men and 0.1 years for women over the period 2010–2012. Perinatal mortality

for Aboriginal babies decreased by 62% between 1991–2010, an average yearly decline of 0.9 deaths per 1000 births. Fetal deaths declined by 27% and neonatal deaths by 22% (Australian Government Department of Health, 2012). However, life expectancy for Aboriginal people is still approximately 11 years less than non-Indigenous Australians, and perinatal mortality is still twice that of other Australians (Australian Institute of Health and Welfare, 2011). This work is a good example of what can be achieved when practitioners broaden their perspective to take a micro, mezzo, and macro multi-level focus in their work, which enables them to achieve effective and sustained change at individual, organizational, and systemic levels for the benefit of individual clients and groups. Extending this broader perspective across health, education, employment, and the justice system will make it possible to further address the health inequalities experienced by Aboriginal people.

INTERNET RESOURCES

- Aboriginal Health Branch, Department of Health: http://www.health.vic.gov.au/aboriginalhealth/
- Australian Institute of Health and Welfare (AIHW): Information about indigenous health: http://www.aihw.gov.au/indigenous-australians/
- Australian Indigenous HealthInfoNet: http://www.healthinfonet.ecu.edu.au/
- Koolin Balit: Victorian Government strategic directions for Aboriginal health 2012–2022: http://www.health.vic.gov.au/aboriginalhealth/koolinbalit
- Aboriginal and Torres Strait Islander Patient Quality Improvement Toolkit for Hospital Staff: http://www.svhm.org.au/aboutus/community/ICHPtoolkit/Pages/toolkit.aspx
- Making Two Worlds Work: http://www.whealth.com.au/mtww
- National Aboriginal Controlled Health Organisation (NACCHO): http://www.naccho.org.au
- Reconciliation Australia: http://www.reconciliation.org.au

DISCUSSION QUESTIONS

1. How would you prepare for your first meeting with the family described in the opening vignette?

2. How would you go about completing a comprehensive assessment and developing a cultural care plan for a culturally complex family seeking health care?

3. What resources would best provide assistance to this family?

4. In what ways do organizational and societal attitudes, processes, and policies make it easier or harder for culturally diverse client groups?

5. Can the utilization of legislation and social work advocacy improve outcomes for vulnerable groups? If yes, how so?

REFERENCES

Aborigines Protection Act of 1869 (33 Vic No. 349).

Australian Association of Social Workers. (2013a). *Code of ethics.* Retrieved from http://www.aasw.asn.au/document/item/1201

Australian Association of Social Workers. (2013b). *Reconciliation action plan.* Retrieved from http://www.aasw.asn.au/social-policy-advocacy/reconciliation-action-plan

Australian Bureau of Statistics. (2013). *Census: For a brighter future.* Retrieved from http://www.abs.gov.au/census

Australian Electoral Commission. (2014). *Indigenous Australians and the vote.* Retrieved from http://www.aec.gov.au/Indigenous/

Australian Government Department of Health. (2012). *Aboriginal and Torres Strait Islander health performance framework, 2012.* Retrieved from http://www.health.gov.au/internet/main/publishing.nsf/Content/oatsih_heath-performanceframework

Australian Institute of Health and Welfare. (2011). *The health and welfare of Australia's Aboriginal and Torres Strait Islander people: An overview.* Retrieved from http://www.aihw.gov.au

Bessarab, D., & Ng'andu, B. (2010). Yarning about yarning as a legitimate method in Indigenous research. *International Journal of Critical Indigenous Studies, 3*(1), 38–40.

Briskman, L. (2014). *Social work with indigenous communities: A human rights approach.* Annandale, NSW: The Federation Press.

Carson, B., Dunbar, T., Chenhall, R., & Bailie, R. (2007). *Social determinants of indigenous health.* Crow's Nest, NSW: Allen & Unwin.

Calma, T., & Priday, E. (2011). Putting indigenous human rights into social work practice. *Australian Social Work, 64*(2), 147–155. doi: 10.1080/0312407X2011.575920

Children, Youth, and Families Act, Act 96. (2005). Retrieved from http://www.legislation.vic.gov.au/Domino/Web_Notes/LDMS/PubStatbook.nsf/edfb620cf7503d1aca256da4001b08af/15A4CD9FB84C7196CA2570D00022769A/$FILE/05-096a.pdf

Council of Australian Governments. (2013). *National partnership agreement on closing the gap in indigenous health outcomes.* Retrieved from http://www.coag.gov.au/node/361

Department of Health Victoria, Video. (2012). Victorian aboriginal population: A snapshot. Retrieved from http://www.health.vic.gov.au/aboriginalhealth/publications/snapshot.htm

Dudgeon, P., Pickett, H., & Garvey, D. (2000). *Working with Indigenous Australians: A handbook for psychologists.* Perth, Western Australia: Gunada Press.

Fejo-King, C. (2013). *Let's talk kinship.* Torrens, ACT: Fejo-King Consulting.

Green, B. L., McAllister, C. L., & Tarte, J. M. (2004). The strengths-based practices inventory: A tool for measuring strengths-based service delivery in early childhood and family support programs. *Families in Society, 85*(3), 27–334.

Harms, L., Middleton, J., Whyte, J., Anderson, I., Clarke, A., Sloan, J. . . . Smith, M. (2011). Social work with aboriginal clients: Perspectives on educational preparation and practice. *Australian Social Work, 64*(2), 156–168. doi:10.1080/0312407x.2011.577184

Herring, S., Spangaro, J., Lauw, M., & McNamara, L. (2013). The intersection of trauma, racism, and cultural competence in effective work with aboriginal people: Waiting for trust. *Australian Social Work, 66*(1), 104–117. doi: 10.1080/0312407X.2012.697566

Hunt, J. (2012). Caring for country: A review of Aboriginal engagement in environmental management in New South Wales. *Australasian Journal of Environmental Management, 19*(4), 213–226.

Hunter New England Health and Aboriginal Torres Strait Islander Strategic Leadership Committee. (2012). Closing the gap in a regional health service in NSW: A multistrategic approach to addressing individual and institutional racism. *NSW Public Health Bulletin, 23*(3–4), 63–67.

Mabo v. Queensland (No 2), (1992) 175 CLR 1.

Marmot, M., & Wilkinson, R. (Eds.). (2006). *Social determinants of health* (2nd ed.). Oxford, UK: Oxford University Press.

MacPherson, W. (1999). *The Stephen Lawrence inquiry: Report.* London, UK: Home Office.

Mental Health Act, Act 26. (2014). Retrieved from http://www.legislation.vic.gov.au/domino/web_notes/ldms/pubstatbook.nsf/f932b66241ecf1b7ca256e92000e23be/0001F48EE2422A10CA257CB4001D32FB/$FILE/14-026aa%20authorised.pdf

Murphy, F. (2011). Archives of sorrow: An exploration of Australia's stolen generations and their journey into the past. *History and Anthropology, 22*(4), 481–495.

Nagel, P., & Summerrell, R. (1996). *Aboriginal deaths in custody: The royal commission and its records, 1987–91.* Canberra: National Archives of Australia.

National Archives of Australia. (2015). *Royal commission into aboriginal deaths in custody—Fact sheet 112.* Retrieved from http://www.naa.gov.au/collection/fact-sheets/fs112.aspx

National Sorry Day Committee. (2014). *Stolen generations.* Retrieved from http://www.nsdc.org.au

Price-Robertson, R. (2010). Supporting young parents. *Australian Institute of Family Studies,* CAFCA Practice Sheet.

Raphael, D. (2002). Addressing health inequalities in Canada. *Leadership in Health Services, 15*(2), 1–8. doi: 10/1108/13660750210427240

Reconciliation Australia. (2014). Retrieved from http://www.reconciliation.org.au

Scerra, N. (2011). *Strengths-based practice: The evidence.* Social Justice Unit Research Paper. Parramatta, NSW: UnitingCare Children, Young People and Families.

Stewart, J., & Allan, J. (2013). Building relationships with Aboriginal people: A cultural mapping toolbox. *Australian Social Work, 86*(1), 118–129.

United Nations Declaration on the Rights of Indigenous Peoples, GA Res 61/295, UNGAOR, 61st Sess., Supp. No. 53, UN Doc A/61/53 (2007).

Victorian Government Department of Health. (2013a). *Aboriginal health population infographic tool: Koolin Balit.* Retrieved from http://docs2.health.vic.gov.au/docs/doc/Aboriginal-Health-population-Infographic-tool-Koolin-Balit

Victorian Government Department of Health. (2013b). *Koolin Balit: Victorian government strategic directions for Aboriginal health 2012–2022.* Retrieved from http://www.health.vic.gov.au/aboriginalhealth/koolinbalit.htm

Victorian Government Department of Health. (2013c). *Koori health counts! 2011–2012.* Retrieved from http://docs2.health.vic.gov.au/docs/doc/Koori-Health-Counts-2012-13

Walker, R., & Shepherd, C. (2008). *Strengthening Aboriginal family functioning: What works and why?* AFRC Briefing No. 7. Melbourne: Australian Institute of Family Studies.

Whiteside, M., Tsey, K., & Earles, W. (2011). Locating empowerment in the context of Indigenous Australia. *Australian Social Work, 64*(1), 113–129.

Index

Figures, tables and notes are indicated by f, t or n following the page number.

DiClemente, C., 87
Diego Vigil, James, 286
Disabilities, 203, 301, 304. *See also* Developmental disabilities (DD); Diversity issues
Disaster relief, 432
Disasters
    overview, 224–225
    assessment, 228, 233
    diversity considerations, 226
    Internet resources, 235
    interventions, 226–229, 227t, 233
    macro level perspective, 232–233
    mezzo level perspective, 231–232
    transference and countertransference issues, 230–231
    See also Psychological first aid (PFA)
Disclosure mandate. *See* Mandated reporting
Discrimination
    in Australia, 518
    employment discrimination, 65
    microaggressions, 61, 189–190, 402
    sexual minorities, 392
Dissociation, 471
Distal stressors, 387
Diversion programs for gambling disorders, 116
Diversity issues
    Australian indigenous people, 521
    autism spectrum disorder, 261–262
    bullying, 301, 303–304
    child maltreatment and neglect, 188–190
    chronic illness and, 43–44
    defined, 4, 60
    depression and, 60–61
    developmental disabilities, 207–208
    disasters, 226, 230
    equine-assisted counseling, 137–138
    gambling disorders, 110–112
    gang-involved/affiliated youth, 289
    HIV/AIDS and, 28–34, 37
    hypersexual behavior and, 101–102
    intimate partner violence, 275
    juvenile detention, 329, 331–332
    Mindfulness-based practices (MBP) and therapies (MBT), 72–73
    NASW on, 245
    palliative and hospice care settings, 17–18
    in school settings, 169, 390
    sexual assault (adolescent), 320
    skilled nursing homes, 155
    substance abuse, 86

suicidal military clients, 419
trafficking/slavery, 443–444
transition in pediatric oncology, 245–246
web-based practice and, 127–128
See also HIV/AIDS
Diversity rooms in schools, 390
Divorce, suicide and, 415
Dix, Dorothea, 343
Domestic Abuse Response Teams (DART), 279
Domestic violence. *See* Intimate partner violence (IPV)
Don't Ask, Don't Tell policy, 127
Dopamine agonists, 110
Dran, D. S., 3
Dropout prevention programs, 174
Drug abuse. *See* Substance abuse
Drug Policy Alliance, 91
Drugs, defined, 85
DSM-5
    autism spectrum disorder, 259–260
    depression, 55–56
    gambling disorders, 109–110
    hypersexual behavior, 103–104
    PTSD and, 274
    substance abuse, 86
DSM-IV-TR, 55, 259
Dual diagnosis, 85, 207, 209, 262–263
Duluth Model, 272
Dunlap, Shannon L., 379
Dunn, Peter, 319

Early intervention programs, 208–209
Eastlund, Elizabeth, 83, 271
Ecological systems theory, 63. *See also specific conditions and issues*
Eco-maps, 270f, 405
Educational Policy and Accreditation Standards (EPAS), 2
Education for All Handicapped Children Act of 1975, 213
Egan, S. K., 384
Ego mastery, 146
Elder abuse, 152
Embeddedness in gangs, 291
Emotion-focused coping, 472–473
Employment discrimination, 65
Endangerment Standard (NIS-2 through 4), 185
Engineering of social work, 353–358
Enrile, Annalisa, 437
Epilepsy, autism spectrum disorder and, 262–263
Equal Employment Opportunity Commission, 65

Equine-assisted counseling (EAC)
  overview, 134–135
  assessment, 137
  background on, 135–136
  benefits of, 136–137, 140
  diversity considerations, 137–138
  Internet resources, 141
  interventions, 138–139, 144–148
  legal and ethical concerns, 139–140
  macro level perspective, 141
  mezzo level perspective, 140–141
  transference and countertransference issues, 139
Erikson, Erik, 146, 147, 287, 316
Esquilin, M., 189–190
E-therapy. *See* Web-based practice
Ethical issues
  bullying, 307–308
  child maltreatment and neglect, 193–194
  chronic illness, 47
  depression, 64
  developmental disabilities, 211–212
  disasters, 231
  equine-assisted counseling, 139–140
  gambling disorders, 115
  HIV/AIDS, 36
  hypersexual behavior, 102–103
  intergenerational trauma of indigenous people, 408
  intimate partner violence, 279
  juvenile detention, 334
  palliative and hospice care settings, 21
  in school settings, 170–171
  in skilled nursing homes, 157
  substance abuse, 90
  suicidal military clients, 420
  trafficking/slavery, 447–448
  transition in pediatric oncology, 250
  web-based practice, 128
Euthanasia, Buddhism and, 20
Evidence-based practice (EBP)
  bullying, 302, 304
  child maltreatment and neglect, 186, 190–192
  as cyclical process, 2
  defined, 155
  designing, 34–36
  gang-involved/affiliated youth, 289–290
  intimate partner violence and, 276–278
  juvenile detention, 332–335
  modifications of, 45–46
  psychoeducation, 62

  requirements of, 3
  in skilled nursing homes, 155–156
  suicidal military clients, 421–422
  time frame for, 167
  trafficking/slavery, 449
Experiential learning, defined, 136
Eye Movement Desensitization and Reprocessing
    (EMDR), 100–101

Faimon, M. B., 406
Fair Sentencing Act of 2010, 91
Fair Sentencing for Youth (Senate Bill 9), 335
Families. *See* Mezzo level; *specific conditions and issues*
Familismo, 29
Family assessment, 205
Family-centered care for people with developmental
    disabilities, 204
Family-centered practice, 186–187
Family Check Up (FCU), 174
Family Resource Centers (FRCs), 174
Family reunification, 195–196
Farchi, Moshe, 467
Fatalism, 230
Fathers, HIV/AIDS and, 31–32
Federal Children's Bureau, 343
Federal Partners in Bullying Prevention Summit, 302
Feuerborn, William, 95
Fight, flight, freeze response, 318
Fight or flight response, 145
Finney, Kimberly, 53
First response, 468–469, 474–477
5-hydroxytryptamine, 56
Flor. *See* Gambling disorders
Fluchel, M., 251
Folkman, S., 225
Fong, Timothy, 107
Food deserts, 344
Forced labor. *See* Trafficking/slavery
Forensic interviews, 192
Franklin, Cynthia, 163
FRCs (Family Resource Centers), 174
Freud, S., 381, 445
Friend, Colleen, 183
Frontal cortex, 56, 470–471, 471f
Full dissociation, 471
Functional Behavioral Assessments, 167

Gabriela Philippines, 448–449
Gambler's Anonymous (GA), 113

Individualized Education Plans (IEP), 166–167, 251, 261

Individualized Family Service Plan (IFSP), 208

Individual with Disabilities in Education Act (IDEA), 175, 208, 267

Information and communication technologies (ICTs), 356

Initiation into gangs, 285

Injection drug users (IDU). *See* Substance abuse

Institutes of Mental Disease, 151

Institutional racism, 519

Insurance, 77, 103

Integrative Treatment for Complex Trauma (ITCT), 191

Intensive case management, 444–445

Inter-Agency Council Against Trafficking (IACAT), 449

Interdisciplinary teams, members of, 15

Intergenerational trauma of indigenous people
    overview, 400–402
    assessment, 405–406
    ethical issues, 408
    experiences of, 402–404
    impact of, 404–405
    Internet resources, 410
    interventions, 406–407
    macro level perspective, 409
    mezzo level perspective, 408–409
    transference and countertransference issues, 407–408

Internally displaced persons camps (IDPCs), 455

International Classification of Diseases (ICD), 22, 86

International Federation of Social Workers (IFSW), 428

International Narcotics Control Strategy Report, 506

International organizations, 431

International volunteering programs, 430

Internet, 98, 116, 440. *See also* Web-based practice

Internet resources
    armed conflict in Northern Uganda, youth affected by, 465
    Australian indigenous people, 521
    autism spectrum disorder, 268
    bullying, 310, 311
    child maltreatment and neglect, 196–197
    China, social work in, 497
    chronic illness, 49–50
    depression and, 66
    developmental disabilities, 215–216
    disasters, 235
    drug abuse in Iran, 509–510

engineering of social work, 358

equine-assisted counseling, 141

gambling disorders, 116–117

gang-involved/affiliated youth, 296

global social work, 433–434

HIV/AIDS, 38

hypersexual behavior, 104

intergenerational trauma of indigenous people, 410

intimate partner violence, 281

juvenile detention, 336

mental health promotion for African Americans, 373

Mindfulness-based practices (MBP) and therapies (MBT), 78

palliative and hospice care settings, 23

psychiatry.org, 62

psychological first aid, 482

public health social work, 350

school settings, 176

sexual assault (adolescent), 324–325

sexual minorities, 393

skilled nursing homes, 159

substance abuse, 92

suicidal military clients, 422

trafficking/slavery, 450

transition in pediatric oncology, 248, 252–253

web-based practice, 130

Intersectional model of assessment, 261

Intersexed people. *See* Sexual minorities

Interventions
    armed conflict in Northern Uganda, youth affected by, 458–463
    Australian indigenous people, 516–519
    autism spectrum disorder, 260–261, 263–264
    bullying, 304–306
    child maltreatment and neglect, 190–192
    in China, 488–489
    chronic illness, 45–46
    crisis intervention, 320–321, 417–418
    depression, 61–63
    developmental disabilities, 208–211
    diversity considerations, 275
    equine-assisted counseling, 138–139
    gambling disorders, 113–115
    gang-involved/affiliated youth, 289–294, 292–293f
    HIV/AIDS, 34–36
    intergenerational trauma of indigenous people, 406–407
    intimate partner violence, 275–278
    Iran, drug abuse in, 507–509

sexual assault (adolescent), 321
Six-C's Model, 475–477, 476f
transference and countertransference issues, 478–479
Psychological First Aid Field Operations Guide (Brymer et al.), 226–229, 227t, 231
Psychopharmacology, 56–59, 57f, 63, 114
Psychosocial crisis, 316
Psychosocial moratorium, 287
Psychotherapy
depression and, 61
gambling disorders, 113
HIV/AIDS, 35–36
hypersexual behavior and, 101
mindfulness and, 70
See also specific techniques
Psychotic symptoms, mindfulness and, 72
Public health social work
overview, 342
ACA and, 347–348
defined, 342
education for, 349–350
history of, 342–343
Internet resources, 350
interventions, 344–346
macro level perspective, 345–346
mezzo level perspective, 345
micro level, 345
prevention focus, 347–348
program planning and evaluation, 346–347, 347f
status of, 343
Pynoos, R., 226

Quality of life, importance of considering, 19
Queer. *See* Sexual minorities

Rabb, L., 32
Racial inequities. *See* Diversity issues
Racial microaggressions, 61, 189–190, 402
Racism, 519. *See also* Diversity issues
Ramble, Missouri. *See* Public health social work
RAND report, 421–422
Rapport building
Australian indigenous people, 515
autism spectrum disorder and, 263, 264–265
gang-involved/affiliated youth, 291–292
substance abuse, 86
web-based practice, 124–125
See also Therapeutic alliance

Recidivism
gang-involved/affiliated youth, 288, 295
intimate partner violence, 274
juvenile detention, 332, 335
Recovery, 87
Recreational gamblers, 109
Red Cross, 231
Reflective supervision (RS), 278–279
Regional Centers in California, 266
Rehabilitation Act Section 504, 213
Rehabilitation services, 151, 328–329
Reid, Rory, 107
Reidents' Bill of Rights, 158
Relaxation techniques, 138
Releases of information, 64
Religion
African Americans, 369–370, 371
biopsychosocial assessments, 154
disasters and, 233–234
HIV/AIDS and, 33
Native Americans, 403
suicide and, 419
travel abroad programs and, 432
Remember the Removal, 409
Renzenbrink, I., 21, 47
Repetitive behavior patterns, 259–260
Resilience, 224, 473–474
Resistance, change talk compared, 88
Resource coordination, 19, 46
Resource utilization, 427
Respect, Hispanics/Latinos and, 29
Response to Intervention (RTI), 172–173
Responsibility for people with developmental disabilities, 203–204
Revolving door for addicts, 91
Reynoso, Alberto, 183
Richards, Gilbert, 121
Riina, E., 323
Risk factors, 224–225
Risk taking, 318, 323
Robbie. *See* Sexual assault (adolescent)
Robert. *See* Mindfulness-based practices (MBP) and therapies (MBT)
Rohsenow, D. J., 89
Role overload, HIV/AIDS and, 27–29, 33
Rollnick, S., 246
Romantic beliefs, 381
Rosa. *See* Intimate partner violence (IPV)
Rosa, F. W., 503